SHAKESPEARE AND TEXTUAL STUDIES

Shakespeare and Textual Studies gathers contributions from leading specialists in the fields of manuscript and textual studies, book history, editing and digital humanities to provide a comprehensive reassessment of how manuscript, print and digital practices have shaped the body of works that we now call 'Shakespeare'. This cutting-edge collection identifies the legacies of previous theories, and places special emphasis on the most recent developments in the editing of Shakespeare since the 'turn to materialism' in the late twentieth century. Providing a wide-ranging overview of current approaches and debates, the book explores Shakespeare's poems and plays in light of new evidence, engaging scholars, editors and book historians in conversations about the recovery of early composition and publication, and the ongoing appropriation and transmission of Shakespeare's works through new technologies.

MARGARET JANE KIDNIE is Professor of English at the University of Western Ontario. She is the author of *Shakespeare and the Problem of Adaptation* and her edition of *Philip Stubbes: The Anatomie of Abuses* won Honorable Mention from the MLA's Committee on Scholarly Editions. She has also edited Jonson for Oxford University Press and her edition of Thomas Heywood's *A Woman Killed with Kindness* is forthcoming. *Textual Performances: The Modern Reproduction of Shakespeare's Drama*, which she co-edited with Lukas Erne, was nominated Book of the Year in the *Times Literary Supplement*.

SONIA MASSAI is Professor of Shakespeare Studies at King's College London. She has published widely in the fields of Shakespeare textual studies and the editing of Shakespeare, including *Shakespeare and the Rise of the Editor* (Cambridge, 2007), an Arden Early Modern Drama edition of John Ford's *'Tis Pity She's a Whore* (2011) and an edition of *Paratexts in English Printed Drama to 1642* (Cambridge, 2014). She has also contributed to refereed journals, such as *Shakespeare Survey* and *Studies in English Literature*, and to collections of essays on the textual transmission of Shakespeare.

SHAKESPEARE AND TEXTUAL STUDIES

EDITED BY
MARGARET JANE KIDNIE
and
SONIA MASSAI

CAMBRIDGE
UNIVERSITY PRESS

University Printing House, Cambridge CB2 8BS, United Kingdom

One Liberty Plaza, 20th Floor, New York, NY 10006, USA

477 Williamstown Road, Port Melbourne, VIC 3207, Australia

314-321, 3rd Floor, Plot 3, Splendor Forum, Jasola District Centre, New Delhi - 110025, India

79 Anson Road, #06-04/06, Singapore 079906

Cambridge University Press is part of the University of Cambridge.

It furthers the University's mission by disseminating knowledge in the pursuit of education, learning and research at the highest international levels of excellence.

www.cambridge.org
Information on this title: www.cambridge.org/9781009045490

© Cambridge University Press 2015

This publication is in copyright. Subject to statutory exception and to the provisions of relevant collective licensing agreements, no reproduction of any part may take place without the written permission of Cambridge University Press.

First published 2015
First paperback edition 2021

A catalogue record for this publication is available from the British Library

Library of Congress Cataloging in Publication data
Shakespeare and textual studies / edited by Margaret Jane Kidnie and Sonia Massai.
pages cm
Includes bibliographical references and index.
ISBN 978-1-107-02374-1 (hardback)
1. Shakespeare, William, 1564–1616 – Criticism, Textual. I. Kidnie, Margaret Jane, editor. II. Massai, Sonia, editor.
PR3071.S458 2015
822.3′3–dc23
2015008861

ISBN 978-1-107-02374-1 Hardback
ISBN 978-1-009-04549-0 Paperback

Cambridge University Press has no responsibility for the persistence or accuracy of URLs for external or third-party internet websites referred to in this publication, and does not guarantee that any content on such websites is, or will remain, accurate or appropriate.

Contents

List of figures	*page* viii
List of tables	xi
List of contributors	xii
Acknowledgements	xiv

	Introduction *Margaret Jane Kidnie and Sonia Massai*	1
	PART I SCRIPTS AND MANUSCRIPTS	11
1	Playwriting in Shakespeare's time: authorship, collaboration, and attribution *Heather Hirschfeld*	13
2	Ralph Crane and Edward Knight: professional scribe and King's Men's bookkeeper *Paul Werstine*	27
3	Shakespeare's 'strayng' manuscripts *James Purkis*	39
	PART II MAKING BOOKS; BUILDING REPUTATIONS	55
4	The mixed fortunes of Shakespeare in print *Sonia Massai*	57
5	'To London all'? mapping Shakespeare in print, 1593–1598 *Helen Smith*	69
6	Shakespeare as leading playwright in print, 1598–1608/09 *Alan B. Farmer*	87

7	Shakespeare between pamphlet and book, 1608–1619 *Zachary Lesser and Peter Stallybrass*	105
8	The canonization of Shakespeare in print, 1623 *Emma Smith*	134

PART III FROM PRINT TO MANUSCRIPT   147

9	Commonplacing readers *Laura Estill*	149
10	Annotating and transcribing for the theatre: Shakespeare's early modern reader–revisers at work *Jean-Christophe Mayer*	163
11	Shakespeare and the collection: reading beyond readers' marks *Jeffrey Todd Knight*	177
12	Encoding as editing as reading *Alan Galey*	196
13	Shax the app *W. B. Worthen*	212

PART IV EDITORIAL LEGACIES   231

14	Theatre editions *Peter Holland*	233
15	Editing Shakespeare by pictures: illustrated editions *Keir Elam*	249
16	Format and readerships *Andrew Murphy*	269
17	A man who needs no introduction *Leah S. Marcus*	285
18	Emendation and the editorial reconfiguration of Shakespeare *Lukas Erne*	300

PART V EDITORIAL PRACTICES   315

19	Full pricks and great p's: spellings, punctuation, accidentals *John Jowett*	317

20	Divided Shakespeare: configuring acts and scenes *Alan C. Dessen*	332
21	Shakespeare's strange tongues: editors and the 'foreign' voice in Shakespearean drama *Matthew Dimmock*	342
22	Before the beginning; after the end: when did plays start and stop? *Tiffany Stern*	358

PART VI APPARATUS AND THE FASHIONING OF KNOWLEDGE 375

23	Framing Shakespeare: introductions and commentary in critical editions of the plays *Jill L. Levenson*	377
24	Editorial memory: the origin and evolution of collation notes *Eric Rasmussen*	391
25	Shakespeare as network *David Weinberger*	398

Works cited 415
Index 452

Figures

4.1	Stage plays published between 1600 and 1616 (first editions)	59
4.2	Stage plays published between 1604 and 1616 (second-plus editions)	67
6.1	The probable second edition of *Love's Labour's Lost* (1598) Huntington Library, San Marino, California	92
6.2	The third edition of *Henry IV, Part 1* (1599) Huntington Library, San Marino, California	93
6.3	The third edition of *Richard III* (1602) Huntington Library, San Marino, California	94
7.1	Title page of *King Lear* (1608) By permission of the Houghton Library, Harvard University. Shelf mark Hyde STC 22292	106
7.2	Title page of *King Leir* (1605) By permission of the Folger Shakespeare Library. Shelf mark STC 22292	107
7.3	Title page of *Volpone* (1607) By permission of the Folger Shakespeare Library. Shelf mark STC 14783 copy 1	108
7.4	Title page of *The Case is Altered* (1609) By permission of the Harry Ransom Center, the University of Texas at Austin. Shelf mark Wrenn Wh J738 609 c WRE	110
7.5	Reissued title page of *The Case is Altered* (1609) By permission of the Huntington Library, San Marino, California. Shelf mark 62109	111
7.6	Title page of *Pericles* (1609) By permission of the Folger Shakespeare Library. Shelf mark 22334	114
7.7	Title page of *Romeo and Juliet* (1599) By permission of the Folger Shakespeare Library. Shelf mark 22323	116
7.8	Title page of *Romeo and Juliet* (1609) By permission of the Folger Shakespeare Library. Shelf mark 22324	117
7.9	Title page of *Sonnets* (1609) By permission of the Folger Shakespeare Library. Shelf mark 22353a	118

7.10	Title page of *Venus and Adonis* (1593)	
	By permission of the Bodleian Library, University of Oxford. Shelf mark Arch.G e.31(2)	120
7.11	Title page of *Venus and Adonis* (1675)	
	By permission of the Folger Shakespeare Library. Shelf mark S2957A copy 2	121
7.12	Manuscript list of plays on verso of front flyleaf of Thomas Percy's copy of the 'Pavier Quartos'	
	By permission of the Folger Shakespeare Library. Shelf mark STC 26101 copy 2	124
7.13	*Westward Hoe* (1607) in its original stab-stitched condition	
	By permission of the Huntington Library, San Marino, California. Shelf mark 59043	128
9.1	William Salt MS 308-40 ff. 96v–97	
	By permission of the Trustees of the William Salt Library	155
11.1	Folger Shakespeare Library shelf mark Prompt Wint.T.27	
	By permission of the Folger Shakespeare Library	187
11.2	Huntington Library shelf mark 69304	
	Reproduced by permission of the Huntington Library, San Marino, California	189
11.3	Huntington Library shelf mark 69305, a 1604 copy of *Hamlet* owned by John Kemble	
	Reproduced by permission of the Huntington Library, San Marino, California	191
11.4	Huntington Library shelf mark 69343, showing cleaned and cropped readers' marks	
	Reproduced by permission of the Huntington Library, San Marino, California	192
12.1	*Mr. William Shakespeares Comedies, Histories, & Tragedies* (London, 1623), sig. O1v; TLN 1725–8	
	By permission of the Folger Shakespeare Library	200
13.1	Gregory Moss, *Play Viewed from a Distance*. Postcard	214
13.2	Robert Quillen Camp, *The Secret Bear*. Postcard	215
15.1	Frontispiece to *The Tempest*, drawing by François Boitard, copperplate engraving by Elisha Kirkall (Nicholas Rowe, 'Some Account of the Life of Mr. William Shakespear', *The Works of Mr. William Shakespear*, 1709)	253
15.2	Frontispiece to *The Tempest*, designed by Francis Hayman, engraved by Hubert Gravelot (*The Works of Shakespear*, ed. Thomas Hanmer and Francis Hayman, 1744)	256
15.3	Note to Charles Knight's *Pictorial Shakespeare*	262

15.4	Note to *The Tempest* 3.2 from Charles Knight's *Pictorial Shakespeare* (1838–43)	263
15.5	Illustration to *The Tempest*, 2.2, designed by John Gilbert and engraved by the Dalziel brothers, from *Plays*, ed. Howard Staunton (1858–62)	265
15.6	The Cartoon illustrated *Tempest*, 1.1, designed by Simon Greaves (2006d)	267
16.1	Bryce 64mo edition of *Cymbeline* (1904)	270
16.2	Final page of Richard Appignanesi/Paul Duffield manga *Tempest* Courtesy of SelfMadeHero (2007)	282
17.1	Introductory Image in Dicks's 'People's Edition' of *The Tempest*	286
22.1	Aernout van Buchel after Johannes de Witt, *The Swan Playhouse*, c.1596 University Library, Utrecht, MS 32, f. 1r	360
22.2	Aernout van Buchel after Johannes de Witt, close-up of trumpeter from *The Swan Playhouse*, c.1596 University Library, Utrecht, MS 32, f. 1r	361

Tables

5.1 Printed Shakespeare texts, 1593–1598   70
5.2 Books published and entered in the Stationers' Company Registers by Thomas Millington   82

Contributors

ALAN C. DESSEN, University of North Carolina at Chapel Hill
MATTHEW DIMMOCK, University of Sussex
KEIR ELAM, Università di Bologna
LUKAS ERNE, Université de Genève
LAURA ESTILL, Texas A&M University
ALAN B. FARMER, Ohio State University
ALAN GALEY, University of Toronto
HEATHER HIRSCHFIELD, University of Tennessee, Knoxville
PETER HOLLAND, University of Notre Dame
JOHN JOWETT, University of Birmingham
MARGARET JANE KIDNIE, University of Western Ontario
JEFFREY TODD KNIGHT, University of Washington
ZACHARY LESSER, University of Pennsylvania
JILL L. LEVENSON, University of Toronto
LEAH S. MARCUS, Vanderbilt University
SONIA MASSAI, King's College London
JEAN-CHRISTOPHE MAYER, CNRS and Université Paul Valéry, Montpellier
ANDREW MURPHY, University of St Andrews
JAMES PURKIS, University of Western Ontario
ERIC RASMUSSEN, University of Nevada

List of contributors

EMMA SMITH, University of Oxford

HELEN SMITH, University of York

PETER STALLYBRASS, University of Pennsylvania

TIFFANY STERN, University of Oxford

DAVID WEINBERGER, independent scholar

PAUL WERSTINE, University of Western Ontario

W. B. WORTHEN, Barnard College, Columbia University

Acknowledgements

We are indebted for funding support for the book's illustrations from King's College London, from Graham and Gale Wright, who generously sponsor the Graham and Gale Wright Distinguished Scholar Award at Western University, and from the J. B. Smallman Research Fund, also at Western University. We are also grateful to Fleur Jones and Beata Mako, who patiently and efficiently saw the collection through production, and to Paul Smith, who read the collection at the copy-editing stage and made a number of very helpful suggestions. Lauren Abrams provided enormous research support, helping us to standardize citations and check references. Emily Sugerman was instrumental in preparing the index, and we appreciate her willingness to devote herself to this project on relatively short notice. Our greatest thanks, as ever, are owed to Sarah Stanton, who supported this project and provided invaluable suggestions on the collection's structure and shape in its early stages.

Introduction

Margaret Jane Kidnie and Sonia Massai

Editing and textual studies achieved an unprecedented visibility in the 1980s and 1990s alongside the advent of a certain type of historically oriented scholarship. Critical analysis extended from the interpretation of Shakespeare's texts to include widespread discussion of early modern print culture and rationales underpinning modern editorial methods. This interest was further intensified by the launching of such projects as the *Arden Shakespeare* third series (Arden 3) and *The Oxford Collected Middleton*, long-term efforts that draw on the expertise of scholars who may not have previously thought of themselves as editors and who brought with them new perspectives on materials and process. The debates generated through these years and in the decade that followed not only redefined editorial practices but also prompted new directions in textual scholarship.

This collection gathers a wide range of contributions from leading Shakespearean scholars in the fields of editing, textual studies, book history and digital humanities. Their contributions give a comprehensive overview of the current state of play in these fields and their development since the so-called materialist turn that marks an important point of departure from earlier New Bibliographical methods of textual and bibliographical analysis. Building on the lessons learned from their predecessors, textual scholars and editors committed to the study of the transmission of Shakespeare's works have queried received notions of authenticity, originality and textual stability, carrying out a major re-examination of archival evidence. These efforts are supported by the vast number of textual artefacts from the period now made available, and more easily searchable, by digitization projects such as *Early English Books Online* (*EEBO*) and the *English Short-Title Catalogue* (*ESTC*). Contributors to this collection have been at the forefront of this important movement, often referred to as 'New Textualism', and collectively offer an unprecedented insight into the magnitude of the paradigmatic changes that have affected textual scholarship and the editing of Shakespeare and early modern drama in recent years. More specifically, they propose a different understanding of, or altogether new alternatives to, central categories that may otherwise continue to shape editorial theory and practice, including problematic distinctions between 'foul papers' and 'prompt-books', 'editions' and 'reprints', or 'substantive' and 'accidental' variants in the texts of the early editions of Shakespeare's works.

In this respect, this collection fulfils an important dual purpose: it takes stock of recent developments in Shakespeare textual studies and begins to chart how evolving conceptions of the conditions of textual production in the early modern period will impact on editorial approaches to the reproduction of Shakespeare for the modern reader. This collection takes as its special focus key issues in the history of the textual production and readership of Shakespeare's plays and poems from the publication of the earliest editions to the present day. Essays progress through authorship and manuscript studies (Part I), to book history and reading studies (Parts II and III), to the legacies and practices of Shakespeare's editorial tradition (Parts IV and V), to the fashioning of knowledge by means of editorial apparatuses (Part VI). In an effort to address the textual particularity of specific moments of this history, contributors illustrate the issues under discussion through reference to individual plays and/or poems. They also draw on the textual complexities associated with the transmission of non-Shakespearean drama whenever it can lend fresh insights or reveal blind spots in the way in which Shakespeare's texts have been edited over time.

Mapping new territory: the whole and its (augmented) parts

The six parts into which this collection is arranged – 'Scripts and manuscripts', 'Making books; building reputations', 'From print to manuscript', 'Editorial legacies', 'Editorial practices' and 'Apparatus and the fashioning of knowledge' – cover areas of research interest within which recent scholarship has made the greatest impact on the study of Shakespeare and the text. The contributions in each part consider specific topics that have come to the forefront of scholarly debates in the field as a result of the momentous transition from a predominantly receptive deployment of New Bibliographical principles and rationales, which characterized the editing of Shakespeare from the mid- to the late twentieth century, to the production of a new body of textual knowledge, which affects the way in which Shakespeare is now being re-presented to readers.

The publication of Walter Greg's influential study *Dramatic Documents from the Elizabethan Playhouses* (1931) led earlier textual scholars to classify early modern dramatic manuscripts according to categories ('foul papers', 'fair copies', and 'prompt-books'), which under-represent the variety and the complexity of the 'precious few' extant specimen from the period. Part I, 'Scripts and manuscripts', tests post-Gregian accounts of manuscripts produced and used by early modern playwrights and the theatres for which they wrote against a selection of representative documentary evidence. It begins with a preliminary account of playwrights and authorship. Heather Hirschfeld weighs the intrinsically collaborative conditions of theatrical production in Shakespeare's theatre against emergent models of proprietary authorship, moving then to consider the challenges confronted by attributionists. Tackling the theoretically and empirically difficult notion of 'style', Hirschfeld comments on how modern attribution studies are conducted within, and are in part shaped by, the funding exigencies of a modern humanities academy for whom computational stylistics and big-data analysis carry a certain institutional appeal.

Paul Werstine takes up considerations of textual agency with a discussion of the contributions made by Ralph Crane and Edward Knight, the two scribes associated with Shakespeare whose names we know. Werstine sets out each scribe's different characteristic practices and their relative textual accuracy, and challenges arguments for attribution to Crane, rather than to 'Anonymous', Folio plays such as *Othello, Henry IV, Part 2* and *The Comedy of Errors*. James Purkis rounds out this part with a reconsideration of the manuscript of *Sir Thomas More*, drawing connections between this manuscript and *The Second Maiden's Tragedy* and *The Captives*. Close examination of 'the traces left by the agents on the surfaces of the manuscripts' in light of recent developments in textual studies leads Purkis to develop a more complex model of collaborative writing than one that either privileges, or effaces, the author.

Part II, 'Making books; building reputations', focuses on early modern stationers as a key category of agents, who, by investing time, money and their professional expertise in printing and publishing the first editions of Shakespeare's works, transformed Shakespeare from popular poet and playwright into a best-selling author. This part therefore marks an important point of departure from earlier approaches to the study of the transmission of Shakespeare's works into print, according to which the process of publication diluted or distorted their meaning as intended by their author. Eighteenth-century editors, for example, notoriously described the transmission of Shakespeare's works from manuscript to print during his lifetime and throughout the seventeenth century as a process of increasing deterioration of his language and of his original intentions. The advent of sociological approaches to the study of early modern print cultures has led Shakespeare scholars to regard the process of textual transmission and publication as formative rather than de-formative. A competitive and antagonistic model of theatrical and textual production, which tended to regard publication as separate from, or even detrimental to, performance, has given way to revisionary accounts of early modern stationers as non-authorial and non-theatrical collaborators, who nevertheless were entrusted by Shakespeare and his company with the realization of his works on the page. This part is therefore devoted to a close analysis of the making of Shakespeare's early printed playbooks in different formats and for different types of readers and to a re-evaluation of the impact of early modern printing house practices and publishing strategies on the rise of Shakespeare in print.

Chapters 4 to 8 explore the networks of collaborators who contributed to the publication of Shakespeare in the late sixteenth and early seventeenth centuries, and consider how focusing on this group of agents makes us think differently about Shakespeare's works (as texts *and* as books). Sonia Massai, for example, argues that the sudden drop in the number of first editions of Shakespeare's plays in the early seventeenth century was due to the rise in print popularity of playbooks which originated with the newly re-established children's companies, thus showing that Shakespeare was not uniformly popular with early readers during his lifetime. Similarly, Helen Smith qualifies the recent theory about Shakespeare's popularity in print (see, for example, Erne 2013) by considering the Elizabethan editions of Shakespeare's plays and poems within the wider context of their publishers' overall outputs. Collaborations among members of the book trade and specific publishing strategies and trends seem to have played as significant a role in determining the rise of Shakespeare in print as any plan that Shakespeare and his company may have had regarding the publication of his works.

Alan Farmer, on the other hand, building on recent scholarship on the preparation of dramatic copy for press (see, for example, Massai 2007), reinforces the idea that Shakespeare's transmission into print already marked him out as exceptionally admired by his contemporaries as a 'literary dramatist', because of the frequency with which the title pages of his playbooks refer to the correction, revision and augmentation of the texts they reproduce. Zachary Lesser and Peter Stallybrass, lending resonance to the narrative of Shakespeare's 'mixed fortunes' in print put forward by Massai and Smith, argue that the Jacobean editions of Shakespeare's playbooks show no straightforward trajectory towards the establishment of Shakespeare's reputation as 'literary dramatist', by considering the marketing strategies deployed by his publishers on a selection of title pages. They conclude by advancing a new theory about the genesis of the so-called 'Pavier Quartos'. The last chapter in this part by Emma Smith strikes another sobering note in its re-assessment of the literary qualities usually ascribed to the First Folio by scholars who concentrate their attention on the preliminaries, which are indeed aimed at fashioning Shakespeare as a literary author (see, for example, Marcus 1996 or de Grazia 1991b). By focusing on character lists instead, Smith highlights both the ingenuity and the half-hearted effort that must have gone into their preparation: these lists display a degree of the literary connotations associated with this paratextual feature in the period, but they are only sporadically prefaced to individual plays in the Folio and they are often marred by local inaccuracies and oversights.

'From print to manuscript' highlights the idiosyncratic reading practices brought to Shakespeare's text from the seventeenth century to our own day. Recent developments in the history of reading and the consumption of vernacular literature in early modern England have led to a re-assessment of how Shakespeare was experienced not only on the stage but on the pages of the earliest editions of his works. Seminal studies into literacy and attempts to fashion readers' taste and reading habits, along with growing numbers of case studies devoted to early modern private libraries, have created a renewed interest in how Shakespeare was read, annotated, collected and curated. This consideration of 'active' readers is then extended forward to the present day, to embrace strategies of reading by actors and others that are enabled by digital technologies. Laura Estill broadens our sense of who read Shakespeare during the early modern period and how reading practices may have differed from our own. The commonplaces discussed by Estill show that Shakespeare was indeed enjoyed by a 'great variety of readers', as anticipated by the famous address prefaced to the Folio, and that writing, or the re-inscription, contextualization and (often radical) adaptation of printed lines into commonplacing books, was integral to this thoroughly interactive mode of reading. Jean-Christophe Mayer considers a different category of more specialized readers, who annotated printed editions or manuscript transcriptions of Shakespeare's plays for performance. Amidst a wide range of annotating practices, Mayer identifies two of the most recurring types of interventions – cuts and corrections – which aimed to adapt Shakespeare's plays to the very specific needs of different kinds of theatrical events.

A different kind of interpretive performance is the topic of Jeffrey Todd Knight's chapter, which examines the practice, widespread among early modern book collectors, of 'collective binding'. Knight argues that the selection and juxtaposition of printed texts within a bound collection shapes the way in which individual texts, including Shakespeare's plays, were read by their original owners, producing meaning in a bibliographical context that is provisional and unfixed. The fourth chapter in this part, Alan Galey's 'Encoding as editing as reading', shows how a process of transfer and recontextualization continues to have interpretive implications in our modern digital moment. Challenging the view that, from an encoding perspective, 'all texts are simply content to be copied and pasted from one form into another', Galey illustrates some of the ways in which choices about how to translate from one medium to another provoke literary discovery. W. B. Worthen approaches digital textuality by thinking about do-it-yourself postcard plays that allow reader–performers to reflect not only on '(post) dramatic performance, but on the performance of writing in postprint media'. The performance of professional scholarship, Worthen notes, is likewise already an intermedial experience – dependent on materials and methods of dissemination as varied as books, manuscripts, libraries, databases and blogs – and apps for Shakespeare should be understood within this broader textual and performative context. Worthen explores apps such as *Explore Shakespeare*, *The Tempest for iPad*, and *Actsophia*, noting that apps aimed at actors seem more permissive than those aimed at students of forms of readerly intervention that transform/deform the text into personalized events.

The collection's fourth part, 'Editorial legacies', takes the long historical view on current editorial practice, revealing its sometimes surprising genealogies. The five chapters in this part reflect from various perspectives on how the book trade, theatrical traditions and literary markets have shaped, and continue to shape, both the canon and individual plays and poems within it. The first two chapters, by Peter Holland and Keir Elam, tackle from different perspectives issues of performance and editing. Holland, in a chapter that connects in certain respects to Mayer's work in the previous part on theatrical adaptation, considers the 'versions of Shakespeare in print that theatre generates'. The textual ambiguities of theatrical adaptations such as Davenant's 1676 edition of *Hamlet*, ostensibly as acted at the Duke of York's Theatre, and Michael Grandage's edition of the same play as performed at the Donmar Warehouse in 2009, mark for Holland the 'messy' worlds of theatre and theatre research. This leads into an analysis of modern performance editions, which Holland identifies as the 'progeny' of eighteenth-century acting versions such as those by Bell and Gentleman. Elam's 'Editing Shakespeare by pictures' offers a semiotic analysis of illustrated editions, up to and including modern graphic novels, in order to argue that images are typically more interpretively integral to the editorial work than scholars have previously recognized, playing within the covers of a book 'a number of "editorial" and paratextual roles'. Where early scholars have seen illustrations freezing a theatrical moment – an effort they consider counter-intuitive to the experience of performance – Elam sees the desire to illustrate Shakespeare as generically consistent with theatrical representation, which balances (or even privileges) images and sounds against text.

Andrew Murphy likewise ranges across a 400-year publishing history, and one of his many insights in a chapter which details the 'intimate relationship between formats and readerships' is the intertwining of theatrical performance and small-format publication. Murphy shows how publishers' desires to open new markets for Shakespeare – beginning with Pavier, but extending through the nineteenth century and into modern-day forms of digital packaging – generate innovation in terms of format, pricing models and, latterly, platform that have continued to redefine the publishing industry. John Bell's eighteenth-century theatre editions feature in four of the chapters in this part. Leah Marcus picks up the tradition of the introduction with Bell to show that the long, formal editorial introduction with which we are now so accustomed is a relatively recent phenomenon, the origins of which can be traced back to the British Empire, and specifically to the teaching of Shakespeare in India. In our own vastly different cultural, political and technological moment – one characterized by the brevity and polyvocality of contributions to debates on the World Wide Web – Marcus speculates that we may have arrived at a point in the history of Shakespeare publishing when the tide is about to turn, at least in terms of editorial introductions, in a quite different direction.

The topic of the last chapter in this part, 'Emendation and the editorial reconfiguration of Shakespeare', by Lukas Erne, provides a strong transition into the next part, 'Editorial practices'. For Erne, Shakespeare editing is characterized by 'two opposed trends' that are particularly evident in attitudes towards emendation. Where some scholars advocate a hands-off approach to the text in order to arrive at a richer understanding of its meanings, other scholars insist that those meanings are only revealed by means of editorial intervention. Erne provocatively labels these trends 'Protestant editing' and 'Catholic editing', arguing that editorial leanings one way or the other not only shape the editions we read, but grow out of attitudes towards textual mediation, authority and the value of tradition that first came into sharp focus within Reformist and Counter-Reformist movements in the sixteenth century.

'Editorial practices' centres on the basic principle that the presentation of Shakespeare's text on the page has a significant impact on how it is read and received. All of the contributors to this part address a particular aspect of the editorial process in order to explore its broader methodological and, where relevant, theoretical implications; in some cases such reflection points to future possible directions, while in others it sharpens our perception of the costs and benefits of current practices. John Jowett opens this part by revisiting procedures for the editing of early modern pointing. This methodologically groundbreaking chapter argues that Greg's famous distinction between accidentals and substantives is misguided: Greg himself recognized that there was little likelihood that authorial manuscript punctuation would survive transmission into print. To preserve copy-text punctuation in old-spelling editions then, when pointing so powerfully shapes sense, is 'a kind of faux-conservatism'. Jowett proposes abandoning Greg's distinction in order to deal simply with emendations, which one would record without regard to Gregian differences between 'substantive' words or 'accidental' (or 'semi-substantive') punctuation.

Matthew Dimmock takes up an edited play's verbal texture in 'Shakespeare's Strange Tongues'. Dimmock's interest is in those voices that are conspicuously different – along with the particular ways in which a voice can register on Shakespeare's stage as ethnically different – in order to reflect further on how such lines are transmitted (or even translated) editorially. Drawing on examples that illustrate the signifying potential of features of the text even as seemingly small as irregular punctuation, Dimmock illustrates how modernization potentially risks effacing early modern fictional encounters with strangeness. Alan Dessen and Tiffany Stern explore act and scene breaks, and how they are managed in modern editions. In keeping with Dimmock, Dessen alerts us to the interpretive losses potentially associated with modernization. He considers, in particular, the fourth act of *Henry IV, Part 2* (specifically, the lack of any break in either quarto or folio between what are conventionally understood as the fourth and fifth scenes) in order to think about a possible ironic patterning of this sequence in performance. Taking as her starting point Arden Early Modern Drama's policy of marking act breaks with a treble clef, Stern asks why some of the earliest performative moments in a play are marked and not others. This question prompts a detailed exploration of what might have happened on the earliest stages before and after the actors delivered their lines, an analysis of performance that in turn begs the question of what a 'play' is, theatrically and editorially.

The final part examines how features of the modern edition such as commentary and collation organize and so create forms of knowledge. The kinds of information that an edition 'remembers' for its readers and the means it uses to disseminate that knowledge is a major focus of all three of these contributions. Jill Levenson, in a chapter that speaks to Marcus's examination of the rise of the long introduction as a response to the pressures of Empire, documents the evolution of critical introductions, especially from the mid-nineteenth century to the present day. Her emphasis rests on the way innovation tends to be accommodated and tradition perpetuated through a combination of pedagogy (especially editorial training in the graduate classroom), series guidelines and personal mentorship. She concludes with a consideration of three major recent types of project – the Cambridge Jonson, the Middleton *Collected Works* and two internet editions (the *Internet Shakespeare Editions* and *Digital Renaissance Editions*) – as standing 'at different points on a spectrum of possibilities' in relation to apparatus. Eric Rasmussen describes how the much-maligned collation line serves as a volume's 'editorial memory', and he takes account of new developments in formatting (especially in terms of digital visualization) that allow readers to attribute emendations more easily than print editions (and some electronic editions) have previously made possible.

David Weinberger wraps up this part, and the collection, with a chapter on networked knowledges in our internet age. He begins with an extended consideration of the challenges *Hamlet* – which exists as quartos, folios, performances, editions, recordings and films – presents to library cataloguers. Rather than attempt to adjudicate these generic boundaries, Weinberger proposes managing them, and ultimately benefiting from their ontological variety and confusion, through an imaginative shift to the model of a network without centre or edges. In a move that is consistent with current Open Access initiatives such as those with which the Folger Shakespeare Library, for example, is experimenting, Weinberger envisions how networked scholarship is likely to alter existing publishing models, both economically and in terms of what scholars traditionally consider publication-worthy (or publication-ready). For Weinberger, this model of knowledge dissemination is in keeping with our understanding of Shakespeare the man and his works, since both exist as 'messy links, always in contention'.

Collectively, the chapters in this collection present, and reflect on, the new bodies of textual knowledge that inform the editing of Shakespeare in the early twenty-first century. They provide students and scholars new to the field with a wide-ranging introduction to current approaches and debates, especially in relation to the study of early modern drama. These research-led contributions will also give established textual scholars, editors and book historians much with which to engage in ongoing conversations about the recovery of an early period of composition and publication, and the subsequent appropriation and transmission of Shakespeare's plays and poems by means of manuscript, print and digital technologies.

Shakespeare textual scholars and Shakespeare editors have learned important lessons from the momentous advent of poststructuralism and digital technologies in the late twentieth century but they have also achieved a more complicated perspective on the most immediate response to these two major events, namely the dictum that editors should now edit without the 'author' and without the 'work' as their guiding principles. Even editors who have championed the cause of 'unediting' Shakespeare in order to show their readers what Shakespeare in print would have looked like before the rise of the editorial tradition would agree that any form of textual (re)production is a form of textual mediation, and therefore a form of editorial (re)presentation of an earlier textual artefact. Restarting from the assumption that editing is unavoidable and that 'rather than expect an infinite array of textual and dramatic possibilities to be unfolded within a given edition, we should expect and encourage a greater range of editions than presently available' (Marcus, in Murphy 2007: 142), the scholars gathered in this collection provide a critical re-evaluation of what we think we know about textual (re)production in Shakespeare's time and since (Parts I–III), and how this knowledge is shaping or might continue to shape editorial practice (Parts III–VI).

PART I

Scripts and manuscripts

CHAPTER 1

Playwriting in Shakespeare's time: authorship, collaboration, and attribution

Heather Hirschfeld

In his epistle to *The Repentance of Robert Greene* (1592), the printer Cuthbert Burby acknowledges a special place secured in the hearts of his readers by the tract's remorseful writer – courtesy of his quill. Burby lauds Greene, 'whose pen in his lifetime pleased you as well on the Stage, as in the Stationers shops' (A2r). Today this pen is best recognized for rebuking Shakespeare as an 'upstart crow' in *Greene's Groatsworth of Wit* (1592). Here I suggest that Burby's reference to Greene's pen – a favored early modern trope for conceptualizing writers and their work – can help us to organize and analyze the complex issues of dramatic authorship central to the study of Shakespeare and text. Burby's conflation of pen, writer, and work; his supposition that Greene's audience of viewers and readers sees the dramatist, as a pen, in the plays he crafts; and his expectation that this audience carries such an identification into their experience of both performance and print: all these assumptions offer avenues into our understanding of the cultural meaning and significance of writing plays in Shakespeare's time.

Following Burby's intimations, then, I start by sketching central concepts in authorship studies, particularly the critical challenge to the definition of the 'author' as the origin and determinant of the meaning of a text. I then discuss more fully the place of the professional playwright in the sixteenth and seventeenth centuries, including the kinds of writing activities in which he was engaged, the perceived role and value of these activities, and today's scholarly strategies for addressing them and their significance. Because the world of the playwright was a fundamentally collaborative, performative environment which simultaneously privileged personal expression and was deeply engaged with the published book, I pay special attention to the influences – and consequences – of joint work and print culture on notions of theatrical authorship, particularly Shakespearean authorship. I return along the way to

Burby's evocative image as a means of enlivening our own understanding of the relation between playwright and text, the permutations and implications of which are the subject of this book's other chapters.[1]

The author and the dramatist

Today's readers and viewers of Shakespeare inherit a view of the 'Bard' conditioned by Romantic notions (now grown commonplace) of the poet and playwright as a respected, solitary artist whose conscious intentions and personality govern the meaning of a literary work. This view, although tenacious, has been under attack for several decades from distinct critical camps (see Bennett 2005: 1–28). New Critics of the post World War periods played down the role of the author in favor of the text as a self-sufficient artifact in which language was the only determinant of value and meaning. In the late 1960s and 1970s, Roland Barthes and Michel Foucault each offered more sustained, theoretical challenges, which – like the New Critics' – privileged language and discourse over the subjectivity of the author but reached radically different interpretive conclusions from them. Barthes, arguing for the destruction or death of the author at the moment of composition, refused for the text a 'single "theological" meaning' (1977: 146). Foucault, working from the position of a historian, offered a catalogue – in his terms, an 'archaeology' – of the social and historical imperatives that led to the construction of the sovereign author-as-agent in its earliest forms.

As Andrew Bennett has written, 'Roland Barthes and Michel Foucault laid the foundations for later literary-critical and theoretical thinking about authors', and – however ironically – the strategies linked with their names continue to influence thinking about the work of Shakespeare and his contemporaries (2005: 28). But alternative approaches to Renaissance dramatic authorship were flourishing during these theorists' primes and have persisted in their wake. These methods were and remain deeply informed by the material and ideological conditions of theatrical production for the early modern stage, and thus deeply aware of the various shapes a writing life could take and of the way these shapes were a consistent concern of the playwrights themselves. As we shall see, some continue to assert a principled skepticism about the individual agency of playwrights at

---

[1] Our understanding is only further enriched by the possibility that Greene did not write (and that his audience knew he did not write) *The Repentance of Robert Greene* (see Greene 1994: 6). The possibility suggests a cultural climate in which the imaginative need to identify a work with a given writer is more important than historical or biographical facticity.

this time, while others advocate a qualified but nevertheless robust 'return' or 'rebirth' of the author which argues for Shakespeare's self-conscious literary aspirations or for his – and his fellows' – deliberate manipulation of their interests in the production of plays for the stage and for the page.

The title of G. E. Bentley's important *Profession of Dramatist in Shakespeare's Time, 1590–1642* (1971) names the key condition shaping the place of the early modern playwright: he (and in this case the exclusivity of the masculine pronoun is warranted) was writing for a new, burgeoning commercial operation based in London. Dramatists were part of an emerging urban entertainment industry, one that trafficked in specifically literary enterprises: stories, plots, dialogue, characters. Their role was thus governed by the 'inescapable realities of the theater' such as the demand to keep the repertory novel or the threat of unemployment during plague time (1971: 9). But it was also influenced by more abstract, though equally pressing, exigencies, including 'laureate' ambitions nourished by secondary school and university curricula oriented around exemplary classical writers: Homer, Vergil, Horace, Cicero, Seneca.[2] Across his oeuvre Shakespeare gives us glimpses, in his surrogate 'playwright' figures, of these realities and ambitions. Hamlet sets down 'a speech of some dozen or sixteen lines' for the traveling players (2.2.541), Duke Vincentio attempts to arrange the rescue of Claudio and the marriage of Angelo and Marianna (and his own to Isabella), and Prospero magically orchestrates a shipwreck and its aftermath. Nowhere are the complexities more explicit, though, than in the epilogue of *Henry V*, when the Chorus laments: 'Thus far with rough and all-unable pen / Our bending author hath pursued the story; / In little room confining mighty men, / Mangling by starts the full course of their glory' (Epilogue 1–4).

We are now familiar with the range of conditions – the 'set of imaginative, material, and institutional possibilities' (Kastan 1999: 5) – that influenced dramatists and their production of texts: the building of permanent playhouses in the English capital in the middle of the 1570s that made playing a fixed feature of the city landscape; the organization of commercial acting companies around sharers and hired men and for which actors were or became writers; the 'legal fiction' of aristocratic and royal patronage that both protected the theatre from the animosity of civic and religious leaders and offered opportunities for remunerative court performance; a repertory system which demanded multiple plays in

---

[2] I take the term 'laureate' from Richard Helgerson's seminal study of the authorial aspirations fueled by an early modern 'literary system' distinct from but related to the Renaissance theatre.

rotation at any given time, putting extraordinary pressure on dramatists and actors alike; an arrangement of textual ownership according to which play scripts, once purchased by an acting company, became its property; and a rehearsal structure based on the dissemination to actors of their 'parts' (their lines and cues culled from the play) rather than entire scripts. These conditions have been seen by various scholars as paradoxically 'enabling': they tempered what we often assume to be the dramatist's unfettered control and propriety over his work even as they fueled his creativity and imagination (3). Bentley, referring primarily to the dramatist's reliance on the actors to embody his script, reminds us that 'in the world of the theatre ... the impact of the author's creation is in good part determined by the playwright's cooperation with his colleagues' (1971: 8). Nora Johnson's more recent, trenchant analysis suggests that dramatic authorship itself must be recognized as a 'relational form, a contest, a negotiation' within the broad contours of the theatrical scene (2003: 4).

As an actor and sharer in the Chamberlain's/King's Men and as a part owner of the company's theatres, Shakespeare's unique experience of these circumstances undoubtedly informed his investments in his scripts, his sense of ownership of them and their language, and his sense of their 'cultural capital' in a community that alternately reviled and praised the drama. Scholars have used these contexts to justify views of Shakespeare as an 'author,' as more or less artistically self-conscious and more or less concerned with the printing of his texts. Lukas Erne, for instance, offers forceful claims for a 'literary' Shakespeare who 'was keenly aware of what is and is not his property, concerned about his reputation, proud of his name and unwilling to have it associated with lines that did not flow from his pen', and who was interested in quarto publication as a way to 'present what the dramatist William Shakespeare ha[d] originally written' (2003: 2, 77). Gary Taylor, in contrast, argues for a 'theatrical' Shakespeare who 'intended his words to be acted' and whose intentions are best represented by texts that offer Shakespeare's works 'as performed' (1997: 3, 16). Despite their distinct approaches, however, both Erne and Taylor equate 'literariness' with print publication, so that what establishes Shakespeare's special relation to his text is either his commitment to or his disregard for seeing it in print. But there is no reason for us to assume that what counts most in assessing the nature and significance of dramatic authorship is the Shakespearean text's ultimate destination for either stage or page. (Indeed, both are forms of publication, of making public.) What seems more productive to me, then, is to return to Burby's image and to suggest that Shakespeare, like his fellow dramatists (though with uniquely inflected personal and professional motivations), was compelled by a model of dramatist-as-pen, a model that stresses the playwright's identity with his writing instrument and the language it inscribes for both playhouse and printing house.

Robert Weimann has explored at length the idea of the 'author's pen', discussing it, as the title of his book suggests, in relation to the 'actor's voice'. His approach, consonant with a career-long emphasis on acting conventions and their meaning, emphasizes the place of 'both writing and playing in the Elizabethan theatre as different modes of cultural production marked by intense mutual engagements, by both disparity and concurrence' (2000: 8). Thus, while he does not 'underrate, let alone downplay the power and the poetry' of Elizabethan play texts, he does advocate a view of staged performance as neither 'reducible to' nor 'derivative of' a script, and thus ultimately 'something that is neither fully contained nor anticipated in the written representation itself' (6, 7, 17). And Shakespeare, he suggests, as a 'writer for performance', avoided 'any facile bias in favor of writing' (9).

In emphasizing the 'author's pen' here, then, I do not wish to reinstate that bias or to discount the prospect of the acted, embodied play in the process of Shakespeare's dramatic composition. But I do want to examine the 'author's pen' – or, more precisely, the 'playwright's pen' – as a figure of speech that named for its audience a connection between the early modern dramatist and the instrument of his script. Of course, as Margaret Jane Kidnie and Lukas Erne warn us, we must not adopt a naive assumption that this script is 'the play as one might assume the author, in an ideal world, would have wished to see it presented' (Erne and Kidnie 2004: 7). Nor can we forget that 'the acting text of a play always was different from the written text. This means not simply that it was different from the printed text, though it certainly means that, but that it was different from the *script*, what the author wrote' (Orgel 2002: 238). But the construct of writer as pen bears further scrutiny in our understanding of Shakespearean texts precisely because it was a Renaissance commonplace, one that announced the relation between the playwright and his texts in terms of the invention and cultivation of an idiosyncratic style meant to be recognized, as the dramatist's, on the stage.

Style and collaboration

'Style' is a vexed term, referring to a distinctive mode of expression manifested in both specific linguistic features as well as in broad effects of tone and genre. Scholars such as Jonathan Goldberg and Richard Halpern, stressing the ways in which early modern pedagogical practices worked towards the paradoxical 'social reproduction of individuality', have taught us to be especially cautious of the ideological assumptions that prop up our faith in the verbal uniqueness of a given writer (Goldberg 1991: 9). From a more practical vantage point, the nature of the drama, which depends upon different characters speaking in different ways, cautions us against assuming an uncomplicated association between dramatist and rhetorical style (Dogberry, for instance, cannot sound like Leonato or Benedick). Nevertheless, theatrical and other documentary evidence suggests that audiences connected certain 'habits of the pen' – from diction and rhetoric to writing speed – with certain writers. The possibility of this kind of stylistic identification inhabits the trope of the 'author's pen' and relies upon the 'viewer's eye and ear' as well as the 'actor's voice'.

Francis Meres's 'Comparative Discourse of Our English Poets' in his 1598 *Palladis Tamia* (best known now for helping us to date a number of Shakespeare's poems and plays but at the time conceived as a sweeping effort to create a national canon with reference to the classics) catalogues writers specifically in terms of style. 'As *Sophocles* was called a Bee for the sweetnes of his tongue', Meres tells us at one point, 'so ... *Drayton* is termed *Golden-mouth'd*, for the purity and pretiousnesse of his stile and phrase' (Meres 1598: 281r). He goes on to speak of Shakespeare and other dramatists in terms of their generic affiliations:

> As *Plautus* and *Seneca* are accounted the best for Comedy and Tragedy among the Latines: so *Shakespeare* among ye English is the most excellent in both kinds for the stage; for Comedy, witnes his *Gentlemen of Verona*, his *Errors,* his *Loue labors lost,* his *Loue labours wonne,* his *Midsummers night dreame,* & his *Merchant of Venice*: for Tragedy his *Richard the 2. Richard the 3. Henry the 4. King John, Titus Andronicus* and his *Romeo and Iuliet*. (Meres 1598: 282r)

Finally, he compares the dramatic compositions of Shakespeare and Plautus specifically in terms of 'tongues' and 'phrases': 'As *Epius Stolo* said, that the Muses would speake with *Plautus* tongue, if they would speake Latin: so I say that the Muses would speake with *Shakespeares* fine filed phrase, if they would speake English' (282). So although Peter Stallybrass and Roger Chartier have suggested that Meres 'detach[es] Shakespeare's scripts from the theatre and, indeed, from dramatic action altogether', it seems more accurate to see Meres's commonplace book as nurturing the stylistic idiosyncrasy of playwrights as it was realized on the stage (2007: 44). Indeed, Meres has not 'detached' Shakespeare from 'dramatic action': he connects the two in so far as the Muses speak the language of Plautus or Shakespeare precisely because their languages were spoken by actors-as-characters and because those languages were both distinct and inspiring.

But no theatrical phenomenon better makes the case for the relevance of dramatic style, and the audience's awareness of the dramatist's quill as part of the performance, than the set of turn-of-the-century plays called by Thomas Dekker the 'Poetomachia' or Poets' War. As various scholars have pointed out, these plays, in which dramatists such as Shakespeare, Dekker, Ben Jonson, and John Marston presented caricatures of one another on stage, represent a moment of dramatic self-reflexivity and self-critique, when playwrights 'used their plays to master each other's language and drama' (Bednarz 2001: 8) and came to be 'identified with particular voices or styles' (Bruster 2000: 67).

The irruption of the Poets' War on the public and private stages of late Elizabethan London was richly indicated by the theatrical milieu. Greene's attack on Shakespeare in *Groatsworth* registered the competitive energies generated by the commercial stage, as the university-trained Greene criticized the common man of Stratford for supposing that 'he is as well able to bombast out a blanke verse as the best of you: and beeing an absolute *Johannes fac totum*, is in his owne conceit the onely Shake-scene in a countrey' (1994: 82–3). James Shapiro has traced this kind of jockeying, particularly as it took shape later between Marlowe, Shakespeare, and Jonson, as the effect of an imitative rivalry exacerbated by the close connections among theatre personnel; more recently, Edward Gieskes has suggested that the Poets' War was enabled by the professionalization of the theatre and its development as an autonomous 'cultural field' in which 'internal pressures and conflicts generated' distinctions among writers and players (2006: 15–16). Both scholars, then, though in different ways, highlight the material and ideological conditions that made individual, recognizable linguistic style so important to the dramatist and to notions of the profession of playwright. Style – which could be possessed, altered, parodied – was the material and conceptual notion lurking in the image of the dramatist's pen and therefore the ground of early modern dramatic authorship. The dynamics of the Poetomachia indicate that Shakespeare and his fellows expected style to be identified, by general audiences as well as a coterie of fellow playwrights, on the boards as well as read on the page.

This notion is given a complex twist, however, by a central feature of the early modern theatre: the collaborative composition of its plays. The drama, as we noted above, is a fundamentally social medium, requiring the participation of writers, actors, stage- and bookkeepers, costumers, censors, and audience members in the making of meaning. But many of the plays performed on popular stages between 1576 and 1642 – roughly half, according to Bentley – were written by two or more writers (1971: 199). The account book of the theatre owner Philip Henslowe, which chronicles expenditures for different acting companies in the late sixteenth and early seventeenth centuries, records payments to dramatists such as Henry Chettle, Michael Drayton, Thomas Dekker, Ben Jonson, Thomas Middleton, Anthony Munday, and John Webster for their work in partnerships of two or in syndicates of up to five dramatists at a time.

Theatre historians have long been aware of the existence of this kind of collaborative writing during Shakespeare's period; it is documented not only in *Henslowe's Diary* but also on various title pages (perhaps most ostentatiously, if not entirely accurately, in the 1647 Beaumont and Fletcher *Comedies and Tragedies*) and in early literary biographies like those of Gerard Langbaine and John Aubrey. In the nineteenth and early twentieth centuries, scholars began systematic attempts, using various linguistic measures, to assign 'shares' of collaborative plays to individual authors. Cyrus Hoy's mid-twentieth-century effort to divvy up the Beaumont and Fletcher canon was in many ways the apogee of this kind of work, matched in the next decades by David Lake and MacDonald P. Jackson's studies of Middleton. In the 1970s, Bentley gave the phenomenon its most expansive discussion to that date in a full chapter in *The Profession of Dramatist*, exploring its evidence (including a wonderful anecdote about Beaumont and Fletcher being overhead discussing the killing of a king) and explaining its sociology, particularly the distinction between the kinds of joint writing done by large groups in the 1590s and the more intimate pairs of Beaumont and Fletcher or Middleton and Rowley in the early seventeenth century. But it was Jeffrey Masten's *Textual Intercourse: Collaboration, Authorship, and Sexualities in Renaissance Drama* (1997) that plumbed the implications of the practice for the idea of dramatic authorship itself. Informed by the methodologies of Barthes and Foucault as well as other postmodern theorists, Masten studied the phenomenon of joint writing to launch a full critique of both entrenched convictions about the dramatist's agency, prerogative, and singularity as well as of the brand of 'disintegrationist' textual study that sought to determine who wrote which act, scene, or line.[3] Masten's complex argument situated joint writing within early modern sex/gender systems – particularly the 'socially sanctioned bonds among men within the institutions of the theatre and ... the more widespread bonds in this culture among those who were, or desired to be, English gentlemen' – to place the dramatist 'within a paradigm that insistently figured writing as mutual imitation, collaboration, and homoerotic exchange' (1997b: 9). In so doing Masten took aim at the assumption – adopted by even the shrewdest analysts of the conditions of early modern playwriting – that collaboration was simply a 'doubling' of the work of a single author. As Masten writes, 'collaboration is ... a dispersal of author/ity, rather than a simple doubling of it; to revise the aphorism, two heads are different than one' (19). Masten's goal was not only to challenge this reigning approach to collaborative work; rather, he argued that the protocols of shared playwriting prove the idea of the singular, proprietary dramatic author in early modern England to be an anachronism. For Masten, early modern dramatic texts, whether by one or more playwrights at a time, represent 'material ... that largely resists categories of singular authorship, intellectual property, and the individual' (1997a: 361–2). Thus he claims that Shakespeare, even though he wrote the bulk of his plays alone, favors in his plays models of the author that are both collaborative and non-proprietary. Masten then sets this collaborative Shakespeare against the team of Beaumont and Fletcher, dramatists who were widely known to work together but whose plays (and later whose treatment by critics) preserve a sense of authorial agency or exclusivity. One of the most serious casualties of Masten's treatment of collaborative writing is individual style. Joint writing, he suggests, like the theatrical context more generally, 'implicitly resists the notion of monolithic personal style' (373). Thus he is particularly hostile to scholarship that slices plays into sections based on authorial 'fingerprints'.

For multiple reasons – its theoretical range, its polemical orientation, its implications for editing – Masten's book has been extremely influential; it is cited in almost every discussion of collaboration as well as of early modern authorship more generally. In fact, its intellectual force may be measured best by the way it has provoked challenges to its own argument, most notably Brian Vickers's twelve pages in his *Shakespeare, Co-Author* (2004). Although these challenges come in multiple forms, they all tackle from historicist perspectives Masten's diminishment of the playwright as

---

[3] For an important earlier critique of disintegrationism, see Schoenbaum 1966.

author, his reduction of the dramatist's agency as a result of his interpellation in broader discourses of sexuality and reproduction. They thus assert both the playwright's self-conscious agency in the creation of plays for the stage as well as his manipulation of ideas of authorship; the playwrights, they argue, 'set out how they wished to be valued by their audiences and, more importantly, how they valued themselves' (Ioppolo 2006: 60). Gieskes and Bednarz, for instance, provide accounts of the material and philosophical conditions that would justify the dramatists' investment in singular styles and their participation in a 'debate on the social function of drama and the standard of poetic authority' (Bednarz 2001: 7). My own *Joint Enterprises: Collaborative Drama and the Institutionalization of the English Renaissance Theater* (Hirschfeld 2004) addresses the issue of collaborative writing even more explicitly, demonstrating that joint work could have models and purposes far more varied than Masten's options of non-proprietary versus possessive authorship. These models were dependent upon a variety of theatrical contexts: whether the collaboration was done for the private or public theatres, whether it was done between older and younger playwrights, or whether it was done by writers associated with different companies.

But the most polemical reconsiderations of Masten's work have come from scholars who wish to wrest Shakespeare in particular from Masten's paradigm, either to claim him as an authorial personality or to establish more instances of collaboration in Shakespeare's canon while simultaneously identifying his own and others' hands in a range of play texts. Jeffrey Knapp's *Shakespeare Only* occupies the first camp: in it he refutes a range of scholars, including Masten, who have promoted a 'vision of a theatre where authors figured only marginally or not at all', and he argues for an 'institutional analysis of Renaissance drama [that] keep[s] authors squarely in the picture' (2009: 3). For Knapp this translates into an affirmation of Shakespeare's 'singularity' precisely as the result of his immersion in his theatrical environment, which allowed the Bard to 'experiment with various styles and theories of authorship throughout his career' (29, 30). Such an approach echoes, though with more emphasis on Shakespeare's (counter) laureate intentions and commitment to literary fame, in Patrick Cheney's *Shakespeare's Literary Authorship* (2008).

A longer list occupies the second camp. These scholars are deeply familiar with the working conditions of the early modern playhouse which Masten associates with the author's 'dispersal', but they view these contexts as prompts rather than as hindrances to identifying individual hands in play texts and to maintaining notions of the author as a consistent, developing 'self' or personality. Their studies look back to the custodians of the Library of Alexandria and find Renaissance roots in Lorenzo Valla's and Erasmus' investigations of the Donation of Constantine and the writings of St. Jerome (Vickers 2004: 510–15; Love 2002: 18–23). But they have been energized by the resources of twenty-first-century computing and computational stylistics. The advent of machine-readable databases of early modern texts and the ability to compare and assess the linguistic characteristics of large samples of printed plays have enabled a kind of 'renaissance' in attribution studies in the last several decades. The results of such studies reinforce the notion of individual fingerprints in jointly written plays; as Hugh Craig and Arthur Kinney have written, 'computational stylistics offers abundant evidence that writers leave subtle and persistent traces of a distinctive style through all levels of their syntax and lexis' even as they 'share the words they use in a given language. They could not communicate otherwise. Yet from that common set speakers and writers make individual selections that persist across all their uses of the language'. And computer technology allows us to track these personalized selections in order to 'establish the identifiable, distinguishing use of language of individual Renaissance English playwrights, William Shakespeare foremost among them' (Craig and Kinney 2009: xvi, 5). Although their methodology and techniques differ, the principle of this manifesto is shared by Jackson and Vickers, whose work offers comprehensive as well as innovative linguistic analyses of Shakespeare's lexical, metrical, and syntactical patterns against those of his fellow dramatists.[4] The latter two have thus established on quantitative as well as qualitative grounds the Shakespearean authorship of parts of *Pericles*, which was not included in the 1623 Folio, George Peele's contributions to *Titus Andronicus*, and Middleton's contributions to *Timon of Athens* (which are confirmed by the editors of *Thomas Middleton: The Collected Works*) (Taylor and Lavagnino 2007b).

Of course, the stylometric discovery of Shakespeare's and other dramatists' signatures is as much the *assumption* of computer analysis as it is the *conclusion*, a hazard of circularity as well as presentist thinking. And stylometrics, which almost always relies on early printed editions rather than plays in manuscript, also underestimates the collaborative process of textual reproduction, potentially assigning to a playwright linguistic

---

[4] For Vickers' critique of Craig and Kinney, see Vickers 2011: 106–42.

characteristics that could be traced to scribe or compositor. But the greater danger, as Vickers notes, is that stylometrics might become an end in itself. It would thus be used simply to substantiate or deny a writer's presence rather than advance or complicate our understanding of joint playwriting in Shakespeare's time, and it would thus miss or neglect what Ton Hoenselaars calls the real interest of joint writing, the 'supra-individual fallout of collaborative crossover or fusion' (2012: 113). As Hoenselaars queries, 'in the process of identifying individual shares and the relations between them, are current attributionists not concentrating their efforts on what is perhaps the most predictable and prosaic, and certainly the least poetic aspect of collaboration?' (113). For Hoenselaars, the poetic aspects of collaboration are the rhetorical and dramatic achievements enabled by joint work, but an equally valid concern for textual scholarship should be the 'poetic' – because material – encounters between the writers. What circumstances led them to write together on a particular play? What kind of cultural or political statement did their collaboration aim to make? How best to present this relationship in a contemporary edition?

Current attributionists surely have various reasons for their interests in things 'predictable and prosaic', but we should not be blind to their reinforcement by the institutional appeal of computational stylistics and big-data analysis within the academy. In a period in which the relevance and status of the humanities are often perceived to be in decline, digital projects on literary topics make serious claims on the attentions of scholars as well as administrators and funding organizations. It is an irony worth noting that the explicitly 'humanist' convictions of the scholars who seek to identify individual authors – scholars opposed to Masten's theoretically postmodern approach – are enabled now by what can seem like the de-humanizing, mechanizing, and economizing work of computerized number-crunching that turns style into machine-readable coordinates.

The trick will be to insist that mathematized and mechanized approaches to style accommodate the contours of Shakespeare's theatrical milieu, that they not only, as Vickers demands, observe a 'more accurate theory of language' but that they remain alert to the institutional as well as personal contexts of dramatic writing in this time (2011: 135). We can see a version of and a prompt to such an approach – done specifically in terms of Shakespeare's pen – in recent work by Douglas Bruster on the additional passages in the 1602 quarto of *The Spanish Tragedy*. For several decades scholars have entertained the possibility that Shakespeare was behind additions to Thomas Kyd's influential revenge play (first published in

1592); recent stylistic analyses (Craig and Kinney 2009: 162–80 and Vickers 2012) have made the claim increasingly persuasive. Bruster confirms and buttresses the claim by going to the archive as well as to the computer, to the pages in the manuscript copy of the play *Sir Thomas More* believed to be in Shakespeare's hand. He suggests the additions to the 1602 *Spanish Tragedy* 'replicate characteristic spellings found in the three pages of *Sir Thomas More* attributed to Shakespeare as well as elsewhere in the canon' and that a number of awkward spelling 'mistakes' in the quarto could be the result of Shakespeare's 'bad penmanship' as it was interpreted by the compositors (Bruster 2013b: 421, 424). Bruster, then, returns to the style of the *stylus* to make his case for Shakespeare's authorship of additions to another playwright's play.

Such a case sparked enough popular interest for the *New York Times* to run a front-page article about it with the headline 'Much Ado about Who'. Generalist curiosity usually stops here, at the attribution of more lines to Shakespeare. But this 'here' is where the kinds of textual and historical scholarship represented in this volume actually begin, with assessments not only of the veracity of the claim but also of the meaning and consequences of a 300-line contribution by Shakespeare to an older play. Among those assessments should be a consideration of why Shakespeare might have agreed or volunteered to pick up his pen on behalf of another dramatist's play. Of course, there are many possible answers, including the potential for extra payment or the intrigue of contributing to a powerful revenge plot. And, of course, as James Marino has explained for other Shakespearean revisions, Shakespeare might not have phrased or framed his additions in such a proprietary way, as work for someone else, as opposed to himself or his company.

But I want briefly to suggest that the play's own representation of authorship might have motivated Shakespeare's participation. For *The Spanish Tragedy* calls special attention to – and offers complex representations of – the playwright and his pen. Hieronimo, the protagonist compelled to seek a violent revenge for the murder of his son, serves not only as the Spanish court's knight marshal but also as its resident master of revels. In the first act he orchestrates an elaborate dumb show that displays the triumphs of England over Spain and Portugal. In the final act he becomes a full-fledged dramatist, crafting for a marriage feast a multilingual play in which the actors – two of whom are his enemies – are actually slain. Scholars have long noted the fantastic way in which the inset play crystallizes the drama's interrogation of the relationship between acting and being, between illusion and reality. At the same time, it also crystallizes the drama's fascination with the meaning and role of the early modern playwright. As he goes about constructing the stage and set for his performance, Hieronimo explains that he labours on behalf of 'the author's credit / To look that all things may go well' (4.3.3–4); later, as he explains to the Iberian royalty how their children came to be killed, he tells them to 'behold Hieronimo, / Author and actor in this tragedy' (4.4.146–7). Immediately after, threatened by the royals, he bites out his tongue and kills himself with a knife – a *penknife*. I would suggest, then, that Shakespeare's – or any other dramatist's – appetite in adding to this play might have been whetted by the play's insights about playwriting and its instruments, including their power to captivate and horrify, to bring to life and to destroy.

CHAPTER 2

Ralph Crane and Edward Knight: professional scribe and King's Men's bookkeeper

Paul Werstine

As the only two scribes associated with Shakespeare whose names we know, Ralph Crane and Edward Knight are often linked. In 1942, W. W. Greg called 'Knight, Crane, and the anonymous third scribe [who copied *The Second Maiden's Tragedy*] ... the great playhouse scriveners connected with the King's company in the first half of the seventeenth century' (Greg 1954 [1942]: 31). To Greg's credit, in 1955 he no longer called Knight great (Greg 1955: 78–9). In the interim Greg had edited Knight's transcript of John Fletcher's *Bonduca* and called attention to the scribe's many errors (Greg 1951, *passim*). By a number of measures, Crane is by far a greater scribe than Knight. Much more of Crane's work survives, and his lost work has been conjectured, with more or less probability, to have been used as printer's copy for more printed plays, especially Shakespeare plays. (The merits for thinking particular plays reproduce Crane's copy are weighed below.) While Knight produced one transcript (*Bonduca*) as beautiful as Crane's usual work, Knight could not match this beauty with Crane-like accuracy. In contrast to Crane, Knight, though employed by an acting company constantly delivering verse drama on stage, apparently remained ignorant of the nature of verse, as evidenced by his frequent mislining. Crane, who sometimes worked for the King's Men, although he never was a member of the company, wrote his own (undistinguished) verse and therefore could be depended on usually to transcribe others' properly, even though his refusal sometimes to distinguish verse from prose must have tested the skill of the compositors who set type from his transcripts. For quality and quantity of extant work, Crane trumps Knight, and the differences between the two caution scholars against generalizing about scribal practice in the early modern period.

Crane flourished between 1589 and 1632. His association with drama appears confined to the years 1618 to 1625. He references his work for the

King's company in 'the autobiographical preface to his only known published poetry', his 1621 *The Works of Mercy, both Corporal and Spiritual*: 'some imployment hath my usefull Pen / Had 'mongst those civill, well-deserving men, / That grace the Stage with honour and delight/ ... Under the Kingly Service they doe hold' (Howard-Hill 2004). As far as surviving documents can inform us, his connection with the company (rather than just with individual dramatists who wrote for it) began in 1619 and was over no later than 1624 – provided, as is doubtful, his transcripts, annotated by a company bookkeeper and dating from 1622 and 1623, later served as printer's copy for some of the plays attributed to Beaumont and Fletcher in the seventeenth century, the so-called 'Beaumont and Fletcher canon'.

He made most of his dramatic transcripts for individual dramatists. These include the Chatsworth manuscript of Ben Jonson's *Pleasure reconcild to Vertue* (performed 6 January 1618), the Archdall (Folger MS 7043, dated 13 August 1624), Lansdowne (British Library MS Lansdowne 690), and Malone (Bodleian MS Malone 25) manuscripts of Thomas Middleton's *A Game at Chesse*, and the undated manuscript of Middleton's *The Witch* (Bodleian MS Malone 12; recently dated, according to watermark evidence, to 1625 (O'Connor 2007: 995)). Crane is also judged responsible for the lost printer's copy for the 1625 Third Quarto of *Game* and for several other lost manuscripts of the play that textual critics posit in their stemmata (Howard-Hill 1995: 153–91; Taylor and Lavagnino 2007: 712–848). Crane's copy of John Fletcher and Philip Massinger's *The Tragedy of Sr Iohn Van Olden Barnauelt* (British Library MS Add. 18653; a play licensed in August 1619), though, was apparently made for the King's company, for whom Crane helped ready it for use in performance; it also contains production notes in the hand of a theatrical bookkeeper. The Crane transcript of John Fletcher's *Demetrius and Enanthe* (National Library of Wales, Brogyntyn MS 42; dated 27 November 1625) belongs to a third category; it is a presentation copy dedicated by the scribe himself to the prospective patron Sir Kenelm Digby. (In addition, there survives much non-dramatic work in Crane's hand (Howard-Hill 2002: 154–5).)

Crane's dramatic transcripts contain an array of distinguishing features. However, 'no single manuscript shows all the characteristics which are now called Crane's' (Howard-Hill 1974: 9), and the more plays he copies, the more punctuation he appears to add. He consistently divides plays into acts and scenes. Sometimes he heads scenes with massed entries in which he collects all roles appearing in the scene, even though some clearly do not enter until after the scene begins. Some of the entries in the 1623 Shakespeare First Folio *The Winter's Tale* are massed: 2.2 begins '*Enter Paulina, a Gentleman, Gaoler, Emilia*' when only Paulina and the Gentleman come on stage initially, the Jailer and Emilia appearing successively later, their mid-scene entrances left unnoted. Such massed entries seem to be Crane's flawed adaptation of the convention in neoclassical drama of opening a new scene every time there is a change in the major characters on stage and listing them all together at the head of the scene, a convention used by Jonson in his 1616 Folio (Greg 1910: xvi–xvii; Greg 1942: 137). Copying dialogue, Crane is lavish with italics, capitals, and punctuation of all kinds, including parentheses, apostrophes, and hyphens. He uses apostrophes not only for such commonplace elisions as 'i'th'' (for 'in the') and 'o'th'' (for 'of the' or 'on the') but also for the omission of common words ("has' for 'he has' and ''at' lower end' for 'at the lower end') and for the omission of notional letters ('has't' for 'hast'). His transcripts contain distinctive Jonsonian elisions, such as 'I'am', a Jonsonian elision being defined as 'the use of an apostrophe between two unelided but lightly sounded syllables to indicate that they are metrically equivalent to one syllable' (Herford, Simpson and Simpson 1925–52: 9.50). And Crane hyphenates the verb with a following pronoun ('come-it'), the indefinite article with a noun ('a-devill'), the possessive with the following noun ('vertue's-sake', 'heaven-sake', with loss or assimilation of the inflexional *s*), the adverb with a relative pronoun ('some-what'), the adjective with a pronoun ('brave-ones'). Some of his hyphenated compounds are elaborate ('bemockt-at-Stabs' and 'make-a-de-sot'), and T. H. Howard-Hill reasonably infers that the 'less common kinds of hyphenation give more reliable evidence of [Crane's] influence on a [printed] text' (1974: 42).

Scholars begin to study Crane's transcripts in the 1920s. After Thornton S. Graves first notices Crane's work, F. P. Wilson studies it in detail; however, by focusing on the possible manifestation in the First Folio of only two features of Crane's style of copying – division into acts and scenes, and massed entries – he denies himself the opportunity to identify those plays that are likely to bear Crane's influence. Greg, who studies Crane's transcript of *The Witch* in great detail (Greg 1942; Greg and Wilson 1950), is more judicious. Adding to Wilson's features Crane's fondness for parentheses, exotic compounding hyphenation, and Jonsonian elisions, Greg, following to some extent J. Dover Wilson (Dover Wilson 1931: 114), judges that the first four of the Folio's comedies, together with the last of its comedies (*The Tempest, The Two Gentlemen of Verona, The Merry Wives of Windsor, Measure for Measure,* and *The Winter's Tale*), may all have been set from Crane transcripts (Greg 1942: 141, 151). Whether these scribal copies were among the texts that Heminges and Condell say they collected for the volume or, instead, transcriptions made for the purpose of providing printer's copy cannot be known. Only *Two Gentlemen, Merry Wives,* and *Winter's Tale* contain massed entries, although *Measure* may have occasional vestigial forms of them, but then only the Malone *Game,* among Crane's extant transcripts, has massed entries. As Howard-Hill writes, 'Because no Crane transcript survives between the 1619 *Barnauelt* and the 1624 *Game* [Archdall, Lansdowne] there is no direct evidence of his habits during the period which is most interesting. Accordingly, the absence of a particular characteristic of Crane's from a particular text need not necessarily tell against his influence on the preparation of copy for the Folio' (Howard-Hill 1974: 73–4).

In 1974, in one of the earliest investigations in digital humanities, Howard-Hill sets out to test the hypothesis that the five comedies identified by Dover Wilson and Greg were printed from Crane's work. Howard-Hill enjoys greatest success in this investigation when he compares the density of punctuation and capitalization in Crane's surviving manuscripts to that of the five comedies. He programs his computer to count words, capitals, and punctuation marks (including parentheses, apostrophes, and hyphens) in the extant Crane transcripts, in the five comedies thought to be printed from his copies, and, for the purpose of establishing a control group for comparison to these five, in another five Folio comedies – *The Comedy of Errors, Much Ado About Nothing, Love's Labour's Lost, The Taming of the Shrew,* and *All's Well That Ends Well.* (Of course, before he can program the computer, he has to make judgements or trust others' published judgements about just what punctuation Crane employed in particular transcripts. As Greg and F. P. Wilson write of Crane's transcript of *The Witch,* which is peculiar in this respect, 'much [punctuation] is vague and undetermined and very faint, so that we may wonder whether he intends a period or a comma, a colon or a semicolon, or whether, indeed, a mark is merely accidental' [Greg and Wilson 1950: xiii].) Adding the total for punctuation marks to that for capitals and then dividing the sum by the number of words in each extant Crane transcript, Howard-Hill discovers that the density of punctuation and capitalization increases from the earliest transcripts to the later ones, with *Barnauelt* (1619), for example, having a punctuation mark or a capital for every 3.9 words, but Malone *Game* (?1625) for every 2.3 words (1974: 32).

When Howard-Hill turns to the Folio comedies, he can demonstrate that punctuation and capitalization in the five thought based on Crane's work are more dense (3.1 in *Merry Wives* to 3.7 in *Measure*) than they are in the five other comedies set into type by the same three compositors (3.8 in *Shrew* to 4.5 in *Much Ado*), thereby establishing that the increase in density must arise from printer's copy and not from the typesetters themselves. (The proximity of *Measure*, at 3.7, to the control group makes it the most doubtful to be Crane copy.) What is more, the density in the five comedies previously associated with Crane is precisely comparable to that in the early Crane transcripts, *Pleasure* and *Barnavelt*, rather than to the later ones, the *Game* manuscripts, *Demetrius*, and *Witch*. Howard-Hill also stresses that the 'overall frequency' of parentheses in what now may be called the Crane-copy Folio comedies resembles that of *Pleasure* and *Barnavelt*, as does the great preponderance of non-vocative parentheses to vocative; vocative parentheses are of the form '(my lord)' (1974: 34, 86). Only in *Merry Wives* do vocative parentheses predominate (87). The evidence of massed entries, act-and-scene division, elaborate hyphenation, and Jonsonian elisions adduced by earlier scholars buttresses Howard-Hill's case. Spelling evidence, on which Howard-Hill expends great effort, proves disappointing in providing grounds for identifying Crane copy behind the comedies (92–103). Nonetheless, Howard-Hill's attention to the peculiar uses of hyphens and apostrophes and their frequency in the 1623 quarto of John Webster's *The Duchess of Malfi* secures the longstanding suspicion (Bald 1931: 244–7; Brown 1954: 134; and Brown 1964: lxv–lxvi) that it too was printed from a Crane manuscript (Howard-Hill 1974: 136–7).

However, for a good number of scholars who have produced other fine work, Crane proves an 'ignis fatuus, or a ball of wildfire' leading them onto uncertain ground from which they issue claims to discover the writing of the scribe behind printed plays by Shakespeare and by others. These claims are doubtful generally because there are so few points of comparison between the extant Crane transcripts and the printed texts in question. Exclusively on the evidence of parentheses, for example, R. C. Bald declares early printed texts of four plays in the 'Beaumont and Fletcher canon' (*The Spanish Curate, The False One, The Maid in the Mill,* and *The Prophetesse*) to be printed from Crane copies (1938: 113). M. A. Shaaber makes the same claim for Folio *Henry IV, Part 2*, based only on a vague and questionable impression of the appearance in it of Crane's style: 'the habit of expanding contractions [an inaccurate representation of Jonsonian elision], the free use of italics, the capitalization of nouns, and a rather heavy system of punctuation' (1940: 513). Against this attribution is the demonstrable bibliographical influence of the 1600 quarto printing on the Folio text (Reid 2007), as well as a fussy tidying of colloquial language, in marked contrast to Crane's transmission of colloquial speech in other Folio plays. In *The Merry Wives of Windsor*, for example, Mistress Page's style is informal – 'Thou'rt a good boy' (TLN 1378) – but in the Folio's *Henry IV, Part 2*, Doll Tearsheet's is ever so proper: 'Thou wilt [Quarto 'thou't'] set me a weeping ... well, hearken the [Quarto: a'th] end' (TLN 1304–6). As Howard-Hill notes, 'In 1953 ... Albert Feuillerat roundly proclaimed that ... Crane prepared the copy for the first quartos of *Richard II* [187], *Richard III* [232], and *Romeo and Juliet* [283], over twenty years before the date of Crane's first known transcript ... solely on the evidence of parentheses' (Howard-Hill 1965: 335). H. J. Oliver's theory that copy for Folio *Timon of Athens* was in part a Crane manuscript rests only on the text's elisions and on its alleged 'fondness for hyphens, colons and parentheses' (1959: xix). Actually, though, there are only half as many parentheses in *Timon* as there are in *Measure*, the Crane comedy with the fewest. 'Furthermore, in the 34 pages set by Compositor B in the Crane-copy comedies, there are only four pages in which the number of parentheses is lower than the *greatest* number per page (4) of the supposedly Crane share of the *Timon* copy' (Howard-Hill 1965: 339).

Cyrus Hoy follows Bald in attributing to Crane printer's copy for the four 'Beaumont and Fletcher' plays listed above, but on the slender grounds that they are divided into acts and scenes and contain vocative parentheses (which, as Howard-Hill demonstrates, become evidence for Crane only if his work can be dated in 1624–25, and in this case it can be dated, if at all, to 1622 and 1623) (Hoy 1957: 149–50; Hoy 1960: 97). Hoy adds from the same canon *Four Plays in One* and *The Knight of Malta* (Hoy 1959: 97–8), even though the former is not divided into acts and scenes (as are all the Crane transcripts) and the latter does not contain appreciably more parentheses than does another play printed by the same printer in the same year from non-Crane copy (Howard-Hill 1965: 336; see also Howard-Hill 1991: 126 n. 46). J. R. Mulryne claims Middleton's *Women Beware Women* was first printed from a Crane MS on the basis of 'mere hints' of the scribe's hand – parentheses, 'spellings ... more like Crane's idiosyncrasies than Middleton's', and dashes associated with stage directions (Mulryne 1975: xxvi), which are actually common in playhouse manuscripts and not peculiar to Crane (Werstine 2012: 240). In re-editing the play, John Jowett silently sets aside this attribution to Crane, noting only that the parentheses that Mulryne would assign to Crane 'seem . . . localized in the copy', rather than distributed throughout as would be expected in a Crane manuscript (2007b: 1140). According to Elizabeth Story Donno, a Crane manuscript also served as copy for *Twelfth Night* because of 'the heavy use of colons and semi-colons', commonplace elisions, and allegedly 'heavy use of parentheses for parenthetical remarks and single words of address; and, lastly, hyphenated forms' (1985: 155). However, there are very few semi-colons and parentheses in *Twelfth Night* in comparison to the Crane-copy Folio plays, and the 'parentheses for . . . single words of address' or vocative parentheses are not evidence for Crane because printer's copy must have been transcribed before 1624–25. (For parentheses and hyphenation, see Howard-Hill 1991: 128 n. 51.)

E. A. J. Honigmann favours a Crane transcript behind the First Folio *Othello*, primarily because of what he calls 'swibs (single words in brackets [i.e., parentheses])' (1996: 60) in this text and, in great numbers, in Crane's transcripts of *The Witch* and *Demetrius and Enanthe*, written in 1625 and, as Howard-Hill shows, differing significantly from Crane's earlier copies. To these 'swibs' Honigmann adds as evidence of Crane's work about a dozen and a half spellings and expurgation of profanity. Howard-Hill's apparently generous acceptance of this 'entirely convincing' case (2002: 151) is undone by his own subsequent dismissal of the bulk of Honigmann's evidence – the 'swibs' because over 80 percent of these are vocatives (Honigmann 1996: 61; Howard-Hill 2002: 156–7 n. 17), but, as Howard-Hill observes concerning these as evidence of Crane, 'the point about swibs seems to be that they are *not* vocative' (2002: 156–7 n. 17). Honigmann's spelling evidence is no better. Without being able to access today's databases, Honigmann judges as characteristic of Crane spellings that occur hundreds of times in print and manuscript before 1623, such as 'worsse', 'quight', and 'trym', and spellings that, while much rarer, are not unique to Crane, like 'For-sooth' (hyphenated also by Joseph Hall, George Chapman, Samuel Daniel, and others) (1996: 64–6). There is also no need for Honigmann to invoke Crane in particular to account for the expurgation of profanity from Folio *Othello*, for, as Barbara A. Mowat shows (2005), intolerance of profanity increases across the whole culture as the seventeenth century advances. Finally, the pattern of punctuation in Folio *Othello* is against Crane: there are only about half the semi-colons of the Crane-copy plays. Honigmann's revival of Shaaber's attribution to Crane of Folio *Henry IV, Part 2*'s printer's copy closely resembles this *Othello* argument both in its grounds and their inadequacy (165–8). In his

2007 *Shakespeare and Text*, John Jowett twice assigns to Crane printer's copy for *The Comedy of Errors* (2007a: 82, 187), without providing any evidence for the claim and in spite of Howard-Hill's having used this Folio play as part of his control group of comedies to exhibit the difference between the control and the Crane-copy texts. In view of the army of scribes occupying early modern London, scribal printer's copy for this or any particular play is probably not Knight's or Crane's but Anonymous's. Crane-spotting is hard to do.

Standing apart from the questionable Crane attributions just reviewed is J. C. Maxwell's tentative suggestion that *Cymbeline* may have been printed from a Crane copy. While Maxwell notes the absence from the play of such common hyphenations as verb-pronoun and verb-preposition, he points to the elaborate 'not-fearing-Britaine' (TLN 1164), 'rich-left-heyres' (TLN 2536), and 'scarse-cold-Battaile' (TLN 3801) (1960: 126). Gary Taylor rightly indicates that 'the overall proportions of parentheses, hyphens, and apostrophes are consistent with Crane's practice' (Taylor and Wells 1997: 604). As Martin Butler establishes, the same is true for question marks, colons, semi-colons, and commas (2005: 259). It is also the case that only about one-fifth of the parentheses enclose vocatives, a proportion in line with Crane's work before 1624. (See also Jowett 1983: 113–14; Howard-Hill 1991: 128 n. 51; Warren 2004: 68–74; Butler 2005: 257–62.) All in all there is good reason to regard *Cymbeline* as a Crane-copy text. Such an identification would put Crane at the alpha and the omega of the Folio. Still it would hardly substantiate the claim first advanced by Feuillerat (1953: 332) and then revived by Howard-Hill (1991) that Crane served as editor of the First Folio. In the nature of the case (*pace* Honigmann 1996, e.g., 177 n. 25 and Hirsch 2011), there can be no good evidence for any such assertion.

For editors of Crane-copy plays, the question of greatest importance is Crane's accuracy. Stage directions call for separate consideration because Crane, to some extent resembling Knight (Werstine 2012: 94–7), allows himself greater license to revise directions than dialogue. The strongest testimony comes from Malone *Game* where he employs his massed entries when Middleton in his own manuscripts, of course, does not. However, again from comparison of Middleton's *Game* directions to those transcribed by Crane, the scribe can be shown to alter and embellish other stage directions (Roberts 1980: 216). Jowett attempts a precise discrimination of Crane's possible elaboration of directions in *Tempest* by comparing their vocabulary to that of stage directions in other Shakespeare texts (1983: 111–13). For example, in '*Enter seuerall strange shapes, bringing in a Banket;*

and dance about it with gentle actions of salutations, and inuiting the King, &c. to eate, they depart' (TLN 1536–8), the exceptional vocabulary is '*seuerall strange shapes*' and '*with gentle actions of salutations*'. In '*with a quaint deuice the Banquet vanishes*' (TLN 1583–4), it is '*with a quaint deuice*'. Jowett terms such elaboration 'non-theatrical' (1983: 107); it is of no practical use in the playhouse. As Greg points out, such phrasing as '*with a quaint deuice*' resembles 'descriptions of many masques at court ... [I]t is descriptive of the thing seen, a compliment to the machinist' (1942: 150–1) and may be inspired by Crane's association with the masque-writer Jonson or, as Jowett suggests, by directions in the Jonson Folio (Jowett 1983: 120). Therefore, however 'non-theatrical', such phrasing nonetheless may be a flattering 'account of [the experience of seeing] what happened onstage' (Roberts 1980: 214). Finding '*no* Shakespeare directions closely comparable with some of those for *The Tempest*' (Jowett 1983: 109, emphasis his), Jowett flirts with the notion that part-authorship for the latter is Crane's (107).

In transcribing dialogue, Crane's exhibition of his own orthography means that his exemplars' elisions, punctuation, and spelling will disappear. He introduces his own elisions and 'other improvements' without regard to metre (Howard-Hill 1974: 55). Crane is far less careless with the substantives of his copy than his contemporary Knight, making, for example, only a half-dozen obviously careless errors in his Malone transcript of *Game* (Bawcutt 1993: 683, 851, 1052, 1060, 1184, 1268). Howard-Hill records the following numbers of substantive errors in Crane's transcripts: *Pleasure* 2, Lansdowne *Game* 13, Malone *Game* 27, *Witch* 24, *Demetrius* 27 (1974: 56–9). Like Knight, Crane may sometimes prefer the beauty of his work to its accuracy; editing *Demetrius*, Philip Oxley notes the omission by Crane of 'eighteen short passages, mostly only a single line'. He traces these lacunae perhaps to Crane's 'unwillingness to blot a line by correcting his own error' (1987: 14). While Crane has been cited frequently for his refusal to distinguish between verse and prose by leaving verse lines without capitals (as they are generally left in early modern manuscripts) and by not driving prose lines out to the right margin (Howard-Hill 1974: 36–7, 109–10; Orgel 1993: 280; Gurr 2006: 92, 99), nonetheless he can be depended on usually to divide verse lines correctly. I find only ten errors in verse division in *Demetrius* (Werstine 1984: 77) and only four in a sample of nearly a thousand lines from *Witch*. Just how much influence finally Crane will be thought capable of exerting on a text will depend on whether one thinks, with Howard-Hill (e.g., 1991: 123–4) that the abridgement of *Game* extant in Crane's

Malone transcript is the work of the scribe or, with Taylor, that it is Middleton's (Taylor and Lavagnino 2007: e.g., 843–4). 'The general level of Crane's accuracy was high, but he was not reluctant to interfere with his text, consciously or unconsciously, when its meaning was obscure to him' (Howard-Hill 1974: 133).

While reliable evidence of Crane's work for the King's Men is limited to *Barnauelt*, the extent of his involvement in this case is so great that it might persuade us that he already in 1619 had some experience of working in the playhouse. Crane behaves

> as a 'playhouse scribe' in serving the interests of the King's players by trying to negotiate [the state censor Sir George] Buc's objections so that the play can be staged. Crane reinforces marks for deletion of passages to which Buc objected and, whether on his own authority or at the direction of the playwrights [Fletcher and Massinger] or of others, fills in gaps left in lines by the censor's excisions. Yet Crane goes beyond the single function of handling Buc's requirements and also assists the company by (sometimes tentatively) subsuming some characters' roles under others', by cutting some roles from scenes ... and by calling for a prop ... The possibility that he sometimes acts independently persists when he can be observed censoring and cutting dialogue to which Buc has registered no objection. (Werstine 2012: 286)

Unlike Crane, whose relations with the King's Men were occasional, Knight is recorded to have been employed by the troupe. When he was first employed by them, though, is impossible precisely to determine. While it is often said that he joins the company by 1616 (Howard-Hill 1966: 139; Bowers 1974: 136; Ioppolo 2012: xvii), then he just signs as a witness 'Articles of Agreement between Edward Alleyn and Jacob Meade and certain players' (Gerritsen 1952: xxi–xxii). While the signature establishes his association with the London acting community, nothing indicates his place within it. This is specified only by the appearance of his name in a list of 'Musitions and other necessary attendantes' of the King's Men dated 20 December 1624 (Bentley 1941–68: 1.15). His employment may not begin until after 1619. Although his role is bookkeeper (so called by Sir Henry Herbert, Master of the Revels in 1633 [Gerritsen 1952: xxiv]), his writing does not appear in the production notes to *Barnauelt* in 1619; however, the company may have had more than a single bookkeeper at a time since the 1625 transcription of *The Honest mans Fortune* by Knight also contains a few production notes in another hand. Knight's name fails to appear in a list of the King's Men of 27 March 1619, but this is a list only of the company's most prominent members, among whom Knight cannot necessarily be presumed to belong (Bentley 1941–68: 1.5). Nonetheless, it is safest to say that Knight joins the King's Men between 1619 and 1624. The last record of his association is dated October 1633 (Gerritsen 1952: xxiv).

Only two of Knight's transcripts survive: *The Honest mans Fortune* by Nathan Field, John Fletcher, and Philip Massinger (Victoria and Albert Museum MS Dyce 25. F.9) dated 8 February 1624/25 by Herbert in his license to this playhouse manuscript and *Bonduca* by Fletcher (British Library MS Additional 36758), undated. His hand can also be found copiously annotating for production the 1631 autograph manuscript of Philip Massinger's *Beleeue as You List* (British Library MS Egerton 2828) and adding a very few notes to the scribal transcript of John Cavell's *The Sodderd Cittizen* (Wiltshire and Swindon Record Office MS 865/ 502/ 2, conjecturally dated to 1628–30). These documents indicate no distinctive style of transcription like Crane's. Knight divides plays into acts but not scenes; separates names in stage directions with colons (Bald 1938: 63), as does Crane; prefers *you* to Fletcher's *ye* in *Bonduca*; tolerates the putatively Fletcherian *um* for *them*; often writes *her* as *hir*; and, as bookkeeper, adds production notes, as, for example, to *Honest mans Fortune*. (It is often impossible even in his beautiful *Bonduca* transcript to tell his commas from his periods, his semi-colons from his colons [Greg 1951: vii], and his 'spelling is consistent with the orthography of the period' [Ioppolo 2012: xv].) On the basis of one or more of these features alone, he has been identified as having prepared the MS that served as exemplar for the Folger's Lambarde manuscript of Fletcher's *Beggars Bush* (Bald 1938: 64; Bowers 1974: 114), the manuscript printer's copy for Massinger and Field's *Fatall Dowry* (printed 1632) and Massinger's *Unnatural Combat* (1639) (Bald 1938: 63 n. 1) and for the following in the 'Beaumont and Fletcher canon': *The Womans Prize* (Hoy 1956: 141), *Wife for a Month* (printed 1640; 141), *Rule a Wife* (142), *Custom of the Country* (Hoy 1957: 146), and *The Two Noble Kinsmen* (printed 1634; Hoy 1962: 75). Shakespeare collaborates only on the last, and the scribal provenance of its copy is also attested by mislineation that can be traced neither to the collaborative dramatists nor the compositors (Werstine 1989: 27); Knight elsewhere frequently misdivides verse lines (see below). These attributions of copy to Knight can be usefully contrasted with those to Crane already scrutinized and, in such a context, cannot but be judged doubtful, grounded as they are on scant evidence.

Knight's accuracy varies greatly between *Honest mans Fortune*, a playhouse manuscript, and *Bonduca*, evidently from its nearly Crane-like beauty as presentation copy. In the first case, appearance did not matter, and, as I wrote in 2012,

> Knight fixed about ninety of his mistakes; and, not counting his acts of possible self-censorship, he left standing only about forty errors that are obvious from their violation of either sense or metre. If he had achieved the same standard of accuracy in *Bonduca*, a text approximately 83% as long as *HMF*, there would be about 75 corrections, with 33 obvious errors remaining. Instead in *Bonduca* we find only 31 erasures of errors, and 104 obvious errors left unrepaired. (Werstine 2012: 78)

The great majority of these are careless scribal errors (literals, omissions, contextual repetitions, and dittography) that Knight evidently chose not to fix lest he mar the beauty of his work. What he accidentally omitted he often restored to another place in his text (83–9, 91–4). He also showed himself capable of substituting his own words for those of his copy when he either did not understand or did not like what he read (80–1).

Finally, in a sample of 500 lines of *Honest mans Fortune* Knight made dozens of errors in verse line division as if it was of no value to transcribe verse correctly in a playhouse manuscript for use in prompting. A few of his errors may shed light on some peculiar mislineation in Folio *Coriolanus*. While the Folio's Compositor A can be shown to have substituted irregular for regular verse at the beginning or in the middle of speeches because he frequently ended verse lines at the ends of clauses, confusing metre with syntax (Werstine 1984: 97–8), it has been impossible to account for occasional instances of the same error in pages set by Compositor B (109, 125), who cannot be shown to share his fellow compositor's failing. Thus these errors in Compositor B's pages of *Coriolanus* seem to come from copy. In *Honest mans Fortune*, Knight can be observed sometimes making Compositor A's mistake (Ioppolo 2012, e.g., lines 25, 428, 1129, 1511). This coincidence is no proof that *Coriolanus* was set from a Knight manuscript, but it does show that an employee of the King's Men was capable of the kind of error we find in the verse of the play, and, if one employee could commit this fault, so could another.

Given the great difference between Crane and Knight, the term *scribal copy* in textual studies of early modern drama needs to be understood to embrace considerable diversity. While both named scribes might choose to alter texts, especially in stage directions, Crane, for all his transformation of his exemplars' orthography, can be counted on for the greater accuracy.

CHAPTER 3

Shakespeare's 'strayng' manuscripts

James Purkis

Eighteen manuscripts are known to have survived from use in the early-modern playhouse. Of these, it is likely that six found employment in the professional theatre at some point during Shakespeare's career. Manuscript evidence of theatrical practice in Shakespeare's time is therefore meagre. This documentary evidence is complicated by another factor. Surveying the extant playhouse manuscripts with which he was acquainted in 1931, W. W. Greg notes that '[d]iversity is the characteristic that strikes the reader most and is most bewildering to the student' (1931: 1.208). Some manuscripts show extensive revision, with new scenes or substantial passages added, and others are little marked by their passage into production. The 'fierce particularities' of these documents resist formulation of hard and fast rules for how playwrights first composed, and for how playwrights, bookkeepers, and other theatrical personnel revised, the texts that were used to manage performance (Werstine 1997: 492). However, studies by William B. Long and Paul Werstine have made clear how *occasional* (in the dual sense of infrequent and responsive to a particular problem) was the revision of manuscripts in the theatre of Shakespeare's time (Long 1989; Werstine 2012). 'Playbooks', to adopt Long's favoured term, were functional documents that were employed in conjunction with the professional conventions of the players and a backstage plot that listed entrances and gave details of casting (1999: 415). In such circumstances, and with production details likely to change depending on venue and the availability of playing personnel, there was evidently no will on the part of the company to produce a text containing the sort of thorough and consistent performance details that are associated (perhaps sometimes erroneously) with a modern 'prompt-book'. This chapter is founded on such an understanding of playhouse manuscripts, and by tracing the inscription of dramatic character in some of the documents closest to Shakespeare, it seeks to convey a sense of how dramatic manuscripts were written and revised for use in the theatre. It also attempts to make another intervention in critical practice that at present shapes the reception of Shakespeare's texts. As Heather Hirschfeld explains in her contribution to this volume, the traditional centrality of the author to textual study has been subject to profound critique. W. W. Greg's perception of playhouse revision as the source of corruption that 'wrested the text from the true intention of the author' (1942: 156) has been challenged by work on the collaborative nature of dramatic textual production, with the result that the senses in which the individual contributions of authors, revisers, and bookkeepers may be differentiated are open to reappraisal. The intermingled traces of different agents' work legible on the surface of playhouse manuscripts may prompt further ways of thinking about the relationship between dramatic authors and the playhouse personnel for and with whom they made plays.

Out of character

If any of Shakespeare's dramatic writing exists among the extant playhouse manuscripts, it does so in *The Booke of Sir Thomas Moore* (British Library MS Harley 7368). The original text of the manuscript is written in Anthony Munday's hand. Subsequent revision, to which at least five agents contributed, saw the removal of at least two leaves from Munday's text and the addition of seven new leaves and two slips. Of this added matter, three pages, which present More quelling an uprising of native Londoners enraged by injuries inflicted on them by exiled foreign 'strangers', are thought by many scholars to be in Shakespeare's hand. When John Dover Wilson advanced new arguments for the Shakespearean attribution of the three pages in the second decade of the twentieth century, he predicted that by revealing Shakespeare's spelling, handwriting, and punctuation, the supposed Shakespearean addition would become 'the indispensable key to his text' with which scholars would 'be able to solve most of the textual cruxes which have puzzled editors for two centuries' (Dover Wilson 1919: 251). It is fair to say that the three pages of *More* have not lived up to Dover Wilson's expectations. Indeed, after more than four decades of familiarity with the manuscript, Greg wrote that it is so untypical of the sort of revision that Shakespeare's plays would customarily undergo in the playhouse that it should be regarded as 'an unfortunate red herring in Shakespearian textual criticism' (1955: 102–3).

Nevertheless, from time to time, editors do turn to the three pages for evidence of how Shakespeare wrote, and if they do indeed contain Shakespearean matter they must represent some sort of material evidence of Shakespeare's practice, as well as of the forms of revision that his plays – untypically or not – could undergo. In fact, I shall argue that, while it is exceptional, the addition attributed to Shakespeare is also in some ways exemplary of how practical theatrical concerns shaped the composition and revision of playhouse manuscripts. I begin this short reflection on how *More* may redirect thinking about Shakespeare's writing and its fate in the playhouse with an instance of the document's use by an editor.

In 4.3 of his Arden 3 edition of *Othello*, E. A. J. Honigmann reassigns a sentence to Emilia that the first Folio text gives to Desdemona. After Desdemona recalls how her mother's maid Barbarie died singing 'a Song of Willough', the Folio text reads:

Æmi. Shall I go fetch your Night-gowne?
Des. No, vn-pin me here,

This *Lodouico* is a proper man.

Æmil. A very handsome man.
Des. He speakes well. (vv3)

Honigmann's version of the exchange reads:

EMILIA.   Shall I go fetch your night-gown?
DESDEMONA. No, unpin me here.
EMILIA.   This Lodovico is a proper man. A very handsome man.
DESDEMONA. He speaks well. (4.3.32–6)

Honigmann explains the emendation by remarking that '[f]or Desdemona to praise Lodovico at this point seems out of character' (1997: 291). With the change, as Michael Neill puts it, Desdemona's following line of praise for Lodovico – 'He speaks well' – becomes 'a polite deflection, like Cassio's replies to Iago's nudging remarks about Desdemona in 2.3' (2006: 358).

Honigmann's emendation follows a conjecture made on similar grounds by his Arden predecessor, M. R. Ridley, in 1958. Ridley explains the change in his introduction's discussion of character, where he comments that Emilia 'has the same matter-of-fact materialism' as Juliet's nurse, 'and the sentiment of "Romeo's a dish-clout to him" might have been hers, though she would have phrased it more elegantly' (1958: lxvii). A footnote, referring to the phrase reassigned by both Arden editors to Emilia, adds: '[i]ndeed, if one could venture on a shifted speech-heading at iv. iii. 35 this is exactly what she does' (lxvii). Honigmann finds justification for Ridley's explanation, and avoids any straying on Desdemona's part from the character that he sees elsewhere in the play, through reference to *More*. He adds to his note on Desdemona's character that 'Shakespeare sometimes omitted SPs [i.e. speech prefixes] or added them later (cf. his pages in STM [i.e. *Sir Thomas More*]), so misplaced SPs are understandable' (1997: 291). Ridley's 'venture' is given apparent authority through the documentary evidence of the *More* manuscript.

The evidence to which Honigmann appeals is not unequivocal. Like many other writers of dramatic manuscripts, the person who penned the three Hand-D pages (to adopt the designation used by Greg for the writer of the supposed Shakespearean addition) does appear to have written the speech prefixes after writing the dialogue. D, though, does not omit any speech headings and on the occasions that they are not perfectly aligned with the first lines of speeches – on folio 9a, for instance, D's heading for 'all' is a full line too high (Add. II, ll. 263–4) – at no point does his tendency to allow speech headings to roam upwards on the page leave a speaker unclear.[1] But consideration of character and its erring in the *More* manuscript may provide an altogether more interesting insight into how Shakespeare wrote his drama and speak to how critics detect and explain textual corruption. To recognize what the *More* manuscript reveals of Shakespeare's writing, it is necessary to think about it rather differently from how the great majority of scholars have done over the last century.

More's straying characters

Initial consideration of *More* cannot stray far from the matter of character because it has been at the heart of the manuscript's reception since 1911. When Greg set in motion a tradition of reception that regards the Hand-D addition as the work of an author 'who has no respect for, perhaps no knowledge of, the play on which he is working', his analysis was underpinned by his judgement that D's 'characters are unrecognizable' (1911: xiii). As further evidence of D's lack of regard for the rest of the play, Greg pointed to a further detail of D's writing of character: D's leaving open of four speech headings by writing 'other' (or 'oth' or 'o'), requiring the bookkeeper 'to assign the speech to whom he pleases' (xiii). Greg's arguments remain central to interpretation of Shakespeare's supposed contribution. Giorgio Melchiori, the most prolific student of the

---

[1] D's use of unusually long speech rules, the lines written horizontally on the page to separate speeches, further helps to distinguish speakers. However, surprisingly unremarked by Honigmann, at one point D fails to inscribe a speech rule. The full complement of speech headings on the same page nevertheless leaves the text unambiguous. All citations from *More* are taken from Greg's Malone Society Reprint (1911).

manuscript in the last decades of the twentieth century, writes of the Hand-D addition:

> from the indignant, dignified and purposeful character presented by Munday in the rest of the play, including the scene of his execution, John Lincoln is turned into an exact copy of the malicious and foolish Jack Cade ... D in his addition ignores the characterization undertaken by Munday of the other rebels: he remembers the names of Doll, Betts and Sherwin, while ignoring Williamson (Doll's husband) and prefixing several speeches with the heading 'other', leaving to somebody else the task of identifying the speaker. (Melchiori 1989: 84–5)

Eric Rasmussen writes similarly and more recently of Shakespeare's participation in the revision that 'it seems that he did not even know the names of the characters in the play, for he uses the place-holder speech heading "other" in several places, and the individual characters' names were subsequently inserted by a theatrical scribe' (Bate and Rasmussen 2007: 2464). Even John Jowett, who argues that two other passages in the manuscript are the transcribed or revised work of a Shakespeare who participates actively and imaginatively in the revision of the middle sections of the play, describes the writer of the Hand-D addition as 'perhaps uncertain as to how the scene would fit into the play' (2011: 20).[2] His evidence again refers to character designation. The addition's writer, states Jowett, 'was unsure or even confused when he supplied two speeches for "Sher"' that 'must be spoken by different roles' within a few lines (20).

The revising bookkeeper, C in Greg's edition and subsequent scholarship, certainly performs a lot of work to fit the Hand-D addition into the manuscript. C provides speakers for the four speeches that D leaves to 'other' and its shorter forms, and alters five further speech prefixes. So doing, C assigns lines for the clown introduced into the revised text by the writer labeled by Greg as B. C also cuts a role by reassigning to the Lord Mayor the line evidently assigned to a Sheriff, denoted by one of the supposedly troublesome instances of 'Sher'. (C further changes the other 'Sher' speech heading by reallocating to Williamson the line initially given to Sherwin.) C also adds two entrance directions, in the process introducing a double entrance, and twice edits D's dialogue. Such extensive revision, however, does not mean that the addition penned by D is

---

[2] The passages, both in Hand C, that Jowett attributes to Shakespeare are More's soliloquy on folio 11*b, which is commonly thought to be by Shakespeare, and More's report of Erasmus' departure on folio 13*a, which Jowett suggests was revised by Heywood before its transcription (2011: 457).

inadequate for its purpose due to its author's indifference towards the work of the other writers. Continuities in the treatment of character between D's work and that of the manuscript's other revisers argue against the customary perception of D's aloofness.

As Melchiori, following a succession of scholars, observes, there are echoes of the Cade scenes from *Henry VI, Part 2* in early parts of the Hand-D addition. Objecting to the 'straing rootes' (Add. II, l. 130) brought by the foreigners and expressing 'false economics based on the *halfpenny loaf*', the rebels initially diverge markedly from their first appearances in the play as decent citizens suffering what Cholmeley describes in scene three as 'base abuse, / and dayly wrongs' at the hands of the 'strangers' (Chambers 1939: 218; ll. 382–3). However, the native Londoners' erring in D's early speeches from their first representation may be better understood as a part of the revisers' collective project of toning down the danger of the rebellion, both to make More's intervention more agreeable to the audience and not to run foul of the censor. Tilney had rejected the original text of the play on the grounds of its representation of the rebellion. Across the revised pages of the rebellion scenes, written by B, C and D, the rebels become increasingly figured in terms of their 'simplicitie' as they add 'rage to [their] Ressolutione' (l. 474; Add. II, l. 15) – a straying from their initial appearance that appears to illustrate Alan Sinfield's contention that in dramatic writing character is 'a strategy, and very likely one that will be abandoned when it interferes with other desiderata' (1992: 78).

Yet, despite the shifting representation of the rebels, the writing of character is apparently not insignificant to D. After the initial exchanges, D's characters are strikingly conformable with their appearances elsewhere in the play. As Lincoln and the Betts brothers in the opening scene watch the strangers, Caveler and de Barde, 'helping themselves to the citizens' property and wives', Lincoln restrains George Betts from 'beat[ing] downe' the foreigners, telling him 'we may not Betts, be pacient and heare more' (Levine 2007: 48; ll. 26, 27). Once More and the nobles enter in the Hand-D addition, Lincoln calls for peace and, with his fellow rebels, submits to More's rhetoric of order and hospitality as the drama, if not accurate history, requires. Each of Lincoln's speeches after the rebels are addressed by the nobles in D's addition see him attempting to restrain and quiet the rebels in a manner coincident with his first appearance (Add. II, ll. 157–8), calling on them, in effect, to 'heare more' from More and the nobles (Add. II, ll. 154, 164), or lamenting the rebels' unruliness (Add. II, ll. 176–7). The difference between the conduct of D's Lincoln and Cade's bullying behaviour, with the latter's spurious claims to authority and dominance in verbal exchanges, could hardly be more pronounced.

After he has called for peace and expressed embarrassment that 'the deule Cannot rule' the rebels, Lincoln has no further individual lines in the Hand-D addition (Add. II, l. 177). The rebels' responses to More come twice from George Betts, twice from Doll and four times from 'all'. C reassigns two of these speeches (one from Betts and one from 'all') to Lincoln (Add. II, ll. 212, 265–6). C's intervention may give the impression that D does not understand Lincoln's importance as a character. But, while C's changes are purposeful and dramatically sensitive, D's version is more consistent with the original text in terms of character. Despite Lincoln's attempts at restraint, in the opening scene the impetuous George Betts steps forward to 'reuendge' the injuries inflicted by Caveler and de Barde (l. 31). Lincoln remains silent once Betts challenges the foreigners and it is not clear whether he is involved in the confrontation in any way. It is thus appropriate that it is Betts who responds to the nobles in D's addition to deliver the only speech from this point in the action that expresses their grievances, while Lincoln does not speak (Add. II, ll. 193–4). Notably, Lincoln is similarly quiet in Munday's dramatization of the rebels' surrender that follows the Hand-D pages, as the manuscript reverts to the original text. Lincoln has only one (differentiated) speech in Munday's text (l. 501), delivered once the confrontation is over and the rebels are sent off to prison, compared to the two that are given to 'All' and the one assigned to D's other favoured designation, Doll (ll. 476, 480, 498). Lincoln is (through the combined work of Munday and D) ready to deliver his penitent and (as Melchiori puts it) 'dignified' speech, recognizing the importance of obedience, on his next appearance on stage in the Munday-penned execution scene.

There is nothing in D's treatment of the other named characters that tells of his ignorance or indifference. Jowett's identification of D's confusion in supplying two speeches for 'Sher' that must be spoken by different characters probably creates rather than identifies a problem. Munday uses the abbreviation 'Sher' for Sherwin and '1. Sher' and '2. Sher' for sheriffs (although when Sherwin is on stage they are never so shortened) (ll. 1863, 1865). Vittorio Gabrieli and Melchiori simply give the first of D's lines prefixed by 'Sher' to a Sheriff and the other to Sherwin in their edition (2.3, 29, 33). Other extant playbooks carry similarly ambiguous speech prefixes and Melchiori even comments that the speech that D gives to the 'recalcitrant' Sherwin, calling for the rebels to listen to the Earl of Shrewsbury, is more consistent in terms of character with the other scenes than is C's reassignment of the line to 'the resentful Williamson' (1985, 109).[3] Williamson's silence in the Hand-D addition is probably not telling. He does not speak in the half-page continuation of the scene of the rebels' surrender in Munday's text on folio 10a and he has only one short speech in the course of the scene that depicts the rebels facing execution in Munday's hand (ll. 679–80). Williamson is also silent in B's added scene on folio 7a until C intervenes.

Moreover, throughout the Hand-D addition, the crowd as a whole also remains closer to the affronted native Londoners that populate the opening scene than to Cade's followers. The anger of *More*'s rebels remains focused on the 'strangers' throughout (even if it expands to a more general xenophobia), against whom they have profound grievances, unlike the shifting and occasional targets of the Kentish rebels. When Cade's rebels finally submit they show themselves as 'lightly blown to and fro' as a feather as they change sides simplemindedly again and again (4.7. 209). Contrastingly, Lincoln and his followers comprehend More's rhetoric that calls on them to consider the strangers' plights by casting the rebels as exiles in a foreign land, summarizing his argument for hospitality by agreeing 'letts vs [*sic*] do as we may be doon by' (Add. II, l. 264). And in responding to More's description of the horrors that come with the loss of order, Lincoln's followers reject the premise of Cade's call that '[a]ll the realm shall be in common' and rediscover the deep sense of obedience and place that they articulate earlier (4.2, 70). In the opening scene, Sherwin cites the 'strict obedience that we a<re> bound too' as the reason he is 'brau'de and abusde' without retort, while even the impulsive Betts acknowledges that he is 'cur<bd> by dutie and obedience' (ll. 58–9, 57, 41–2). D's More provides a necessary reminder of this duty, describing the rebellion as 'a sinn / which oft thappostle did forwarne vs of vrging obedienc to aucthory<ty' (Add. II, ll. 216–17). As Jowett notes, '[o]bedience to the magistrate is one of the play's most conspicuous themes. It is elaborated at length in the passage added by Shakespeare, but it lurks everywhere' (2011: 81). The play's interest in obedience 'lurks' conspicuously in D's addition in the characterization of Lincoln and his fellow rebels.

This section answers one aesthetic interpretation of the Hand-D addition with another. It cannot therefore claim to offer definitive evidence of D's engaged participation in the revision. I hope that it does, though, place in doubt the prevalent assumption that if the Hand-D addition is

---

[3] Werstine gives a list of ambiguous character designations that appear in playhouse manuscripts (2012: 365–71).

Shakespeare's work it reveals him to be an aloof author, indifferent to, or ignorant of, the work of the other modest 'hacks' involved in the revision. Of course, like the positions of Honigmann, Ridley and the scholars of the *More* manuscript cited above, this new interpretation invokes a sense of character as an interpretative principle. But, if contiguity of character is not irrelevant to D, character in the addition is also fragile, uneven or occasionally dispensable. In the rebels' fall into 'simplicitie', character is revealed as something like 'a mere function of the script', prone to erring when required (Orgel 1995: 108). The writing of character is also something that is evidently open to and dependent on collaborative revision. And if the addition's writing of character cannot be explained by D's singularity, then the openness of some of his character designations, and the generally precarious nature of character in the Hand-D addition, may be more representative of dramatic writing and revision than supposed. Looking beyond the Hand-D addition, at the work of the *More* manuscript's other agents, as well as the other extant theatrical documents closest to Shakespeare, goes some way towards confirming this.

More straying characters

One need not look far from the Hand-D addition to find further evidence of a similar openness towards character designation. Munday uses a similarly, although not identically, indefinite 'Another' for a speech heading in the original text of *More*, in assigning a line to one of the 'other Iustices' that appear in his entrance direction (ll. 272, 105). At the end of folio 16, his addition to a later section of the *More* manuscript, B writes a draft of a short speech that is transcribed by C elsewhere in the manuscript and assigned to a messenger. B's draft does not identify a speaker nor offer any indication of where it is to fit. It is more open than anything written in Hand D. Most notably, C's entrance direction for the Hand-D passage demonstrates an almost identical openness to that evident in D's speech-prefixes. C writes at the foot of folio 7b: '*Enter Lincoln. Doll. Clown. Georg betts williamson others. And A sergaunt at armes*' (Add. II, ll. 121–2). Clearly, 'other' is not just a term used by indifferent or ignorant authors, and C here uses the term to leave open the details of who is to appear on stage in the play's most populous scene for determination in the plot and through the provision of roles as occasion demands.

The extant manuscript that may be considered most proximate to Shakespeare after *More* – the scribal copy of *The Second Maiden's Tragedy* (British Library MS Lansdowne 807, fols. 29–56), which was prepared for performance by Shakespeare's company, the King's Men, in 1611 – offers an instance of revision suggestively similar in its treatment of character to those described above. The original script of the play, probably written by Shakespeare's occasional collaborator and reviser Thomas Middleton and inscribed by a professional copyist, underwent significant revision before its first performance. Some small 'literary' changes to the text are made in at least one hand that is not Middleton's and the bookkeeper has added some inscriptions to facilitate performance. Sir George Buc, the Master of the Revels, also marks some words for excision or replacement and makes some changes to the text himself. Six additional passages of dialogue, transcribed on five different addition slips by the scribe who wrote out the original text, are also pasted into the document. One such addition is a speech of eleven lines that remedies a breach of the law of re-entry and accounts for the later appearance at court of a character who, according to the original text, should still be in prison. The scribe's text of the added speech gives no speaker. The bookkeeper determines who is to deliver the lines and the required playhouse action in a single inscription, writing in the left-hand margin next to the addition slip '*Enter m^r Goughe*' (ll. 1723–4).[4] It may only be conjectured which character Mr Goughe played as he spoke the lines. If the slip is indefinite as to who in the dramatic world of the play is to deliver the line, the addition is signally productive in its development of the Tyrant's character. As Mr Goughe reports the 'straunge fitts' that 'growe vpon' the despairing Tyrant, a sense of interiority on the part of the character emerges that is absent in the original text (l. 1724^1).

The other added slips introduce other elements: a topical allusion to the incarceration by James I of Arbella Stuart and William Seymour; an explanation of why another formerly incarcerated character appears at liberty; and a 'small but unforgettable peripeteia' in which a jealous character, who dies in the original text believing that his wife has remained chaste, stirs at the report of her infidelity to denounce her and die in a burst of misogynist sentiment (Briggs 1998: 114). The addition of the slips further contributes to a deepening of the Tyrant's character. He becomes more cruel and less certain as he determines that the deposed ruler Govianus and his 'Lady' will be imprisoned separately. His homosocial anxiety is also heightened as he determines to exhume the Lady's body. At the moment at which he orders Govianus's release, he expresses on one slip the hope that

---

[4] All citations from *The Second Maiden's Tragedy* are taken from Greg's Malone Society Reprints (1909).

his rival 'will flie the kingdome / & neuer know [his] purpose' (ll. 1700$^{3-4}$). The authorship of these additions is uncertain. The play's most recent editor accepts them as Middleton's work (Briggs 2007: 834), but their short length and transcription by the scribe leave the matter 'intractable' (Werstine 2012: 280).[5] If they are not the work of Middleton, then the additions see Middleton's conception of the Tyrant diverge considerably through another writer's intervention. If Middleton is the revising author, the additional passages are unlikely to be his work alone. Anne Lancashire proposes that concern with re-entry was the 'primary reason' for Goughe's speech, with the writer of the addition 'not caring who spoke the lines, and leaving the matter to the prompter to work out ..., or perhaps even providing the lines on specific instructions from the prompter' (1978: 206). The 'theatrical' nature of some of the revisions strongly suggests that at least the initial impulse for their writing derived from the company, and there is no reason to suppose that other aspects of the revision cannot also have originated with the players. If Middleton is the writer of the additional passages, 'Thomas Middleton' appears an insufficient locus of explanatory agency, as his work apparently strayed from its original conception through the intervention of other agents.

If, as many scholars suppose, B of the *More* manuscript is Thomas Heywood, then his other work in an extant playhouse manuscript offers further evidence of characters straying at another's hand. Two characters are cut by the bookkeeper from the final scene of Heywood's autograph manuscript of *The Captiues* (British Library MS Egerton 1994, fols. 52–73). The loss of one character leaves an initial conversation of seventeen verse lines reduced to a ten-line soliloquy for his interlocutor. The other cut character, Isabel, is the mother of the family whose reunion forms an important part of the climax of the play. Her absence thus represents a not insignificant intervention in the drama, even if Heywood's original conception of the ending gave her only two lines. That one of Isabel's lines is simply reassigned to her spouse (the other is cut), enabled by an alteration in the following dialogue that sees Thomas Ashburne's address to his 'sister' delivered to his 'brother', shows how this utterance is not unalterably fixed to an individual character (ll. 3024, 3073).[6] The playbook also shows sufficient indeterminacy in its designation of character that it is impossible to determine whether the character that strays from

---

[5] The fullest argument for Middleton's authorship is given by MacDonald P. Jackson (1990).
[6] All citations from *The Captiues* are taken from Arthur Brown's Malone Society Reprints (1953).

'ffisher' (and 'ffisherm' and 'ffish') to 'Grip' or 'gripus' and back again in speech headings and stage directions (e.g. ll. 2919, 3102, 2850) is 'I ffisher' or '2 ffisher' in the scene of his earliest appearance (ll. 905, 911).

Another King's Men play – which is written in part by Shakespeare's collaborator John Fletcher, and transcribed by Ralph Crane, who was involved in the transmission of several plays in the first Shakespeare folio – exhibits a more extensive rearranging of characters. In transcribing and revising *Sr Iohn Van Olden Barnauelt* (British Library MS Add. 18653), Crane cuts the part of Grave Henry by cancelling his name in entrances and reassigning all of his lines to his cousin William. As Werstine notes, while Henry disappears from the drama, both Crane and the bookkeeper leave a number of the prefixes for his speeches unaltered as their transfer to William was evidently established sufficiently by the alterations to the entrances, some changed speech headings, and, presumably, the distribution of parts (2012: 168–9). Two unnamed lords are cut and their lines are given to the named supporters of the Prince of Orange, Bredero and Vandort, while the bookkeeper also removes from the play Orange's '*Collonells*', whose speeches must be taken by the Prince's other military supporters (l. 334).[7] Two Arminian 'divines', Taurinus and Utenbogart, are cut and their speeches given to 'the Pensionary of Rotterdam,' Hogerbeets (Howard-Hill 1979: xv). Moreover, as Werstine details, 'the role of Barnavelt's son-in-law Vandermitten … subsumes the part of a burgher … Then, in turn, Vandermitten's part is taken up into that of Grotius, a scholar and poet' (Werstine 2012: 171). As with the movement of Henry's speeches to William, the designation of the speech headings involved in the revision's transfers lags behind the revision of stage directions. The unrevised speech headings offer a graphic reminder of how lines may shift between characters and that playhouse collaborations are not always matched by thorough textual revision.

'Strayng' manuscripts

While the unfixed characters of the Hand-D addition may in some ways be exceptional, they appear to exhibit a far from unusual concern. The alterations to the *Captiues* and *Barnauelt* manuscripts are readily explained by demands of casting. Among the other theatrical and aesthetic concerns that lie behind the revision of the *Second Maiden's Tragedy* manuscript, a clear concern with playhouse personnel is apparent in the incorporation of

---

[7] All citations from *Barnauelt* are taken from T. H. Howard-Hill's Malone Society Reprints (1979).

the speech for Mr Goughe. Scott McMillin, more thoroughly and persuasively than any other scholar, has shown that some of the revisions to the *More* manuscript are similarly introduced in order to reduce 'the ambitions of the original text to the proportions of manageable casting' (1987: 44). Three passages – one soliloquy and two conversations between just two characters – are added between heavily populated scenes in order to allow for costume changes. These passages include the two other additions that Jowett attributes at least in part to Shakespeare. Casting demands are also lightened in parts of the manuscript close to the Hand-D addition. A scene in which Sir John Munday and '<t>hree or foure Prentices' appear is cut from the original text (l. 453), as is Munday's later appearance in the scene immediately preceding the personnel-heavy Hand-D addition, where he reports that he has been attacked by apprentices whom, he fears, 'are gon to Ioine / wth Lincolne Sherwine and ther dangerous traine' (Add. II, ll. 74–5). The presence of the term '*others*' in C's entrance direction for the following scene leaves open whether an apprentice presence will appear on stage, as well as the size of Lincoln's 'traine'. In using the term 'other', D, like C, is writing to accommodate the practical needs of this instance of playhouse writing.

The Hand-D addition's dependence on subsequent theatrical revision contradicts an image of theatrical textual production that would, in Greg's words, present 'merely theatrical considerations of casting, censorship, and the like' as factors that 'wrested the text from the true intention of the author' (1942: 156). The absence of a final, or at least determinate or definite, authorial 'intention' for some of D's (and B's) writing shows the notion of non-authorial interventions as corruptions that stand in the way of the author's text to be inappropriate for consideration of at least some dramatic writing. Middleton's possible role as his own reviser of *The Second Maiden's Tragedy*, perhaps performing the role under the guidance of one or more players, offers a different but related complication of the distinction between the author's text and non-authorial corruptions. Indeed, the revisions that I have described suggest that a sense of openness pertains to all dramatic writing. It was not, after all, only the speech headings left open by D that C found occasion to revise. In an extremely influential essay, Stephen Orgel addresses the openness of the playwright's manuscript, which he describes as a 'working model' (1981: 3). Orgel insists that as 'the text belonged to the company', 'the authority represented by the text – I am talking now about the *performing* text – is that of the company, the owners, not that of the playwright, the author' (3). In the spirit of Orgel's argument, many recent editors have sought where possible to present 'the more theatrical versions of each play' and have been less concerned with identifying and excising playhouse interventions (Wells *et al.* 2005: xxxix). Jeffrey Masten has pursued this line to one possible end to argue against the appropriateness of the author as a category for interpreting and establishing early-modern drama. To identify and edit out playhouse interpolations and other non-authorial material from a text, for Masten, 'is to deploy authorship as a constraint on interpretation that is at odds with the manner in which the texts were originally composed and circulated' (1997b: 19).

Neither Greg's privileging nor Masten's effacement of the author sits comfortably alongside the materiality of the extant manuscripts. Orgel's insistence that, under the circumstances of early-modern drama's production, 'the very notion of "the author's original manuscript" ... is a figment' (1981: 3) must feel exaggerated when consulting the manuscript copy of *Captiues* that is in Heywood's hand, even if the 110 or so marks made by the bookkeeper attest to the fact that the material document was once very much the property of the Lady Elizabeth's Men to do with as they pleased. The most striking material feature of the extant dramatic manuscripts – *More, The Second Maiden's Tragedy, Captiues* and *Barnauelt* among them – is the manner in which each document cannot be reduced to either the 'original' text (the proximity of which to the author's writing may not always be established) or the theatrical revision. The processes of the texts' straying, diverting and resolution is graphically displayed in the revisers' additions and overwritings and the continued presence of the earlier inscriptions under the marks of cancellation. These textual circumstances, in which drama was written with the understanding that it would almost unavoidably be diverted or supplemented by the intervention of a reviser, pose a challenge for how dramatic texts have been established by editors, as I have implied, and for considering the agents involved in its production.

The history of the *More* manuscript's reception presents a term that may provide a productive starting-point for rethinking manuscript writing and revision. One of the textual errors best known to students of *More* crops up in early printings of *Love's Labour's Lost*. In the first extant quarto text, Biron explains that love, like the eye, is '[f]ull of straying shapes', presumably instead of the intended 'strange shapes' (I4). As Dover Wilson proposes, the assumed misprint 'can be neatly explained by the presence of "straing" or "strayng" (with the n perhaps written in three minims) in the copy' (1923: 128). *Strayng/straing*, an arrangement of graphic characters that, at least when one considers the actions of one conjectured compositor, incorporates both *straying* and the *strange*, may provide an interpretative model that neither disintegrates the collaboratively produced dramatic text nor effaces all differences among the text's contributors.

A part-line of dialogue from the *Second Maiden's Tragedy* manuscript effectively captures the sense of *strayng*ness for which I am arguing, although the same model of reading would equally apply to the Hand-D addition of *More*. As she contemplates committing suicide rather than submit to capture from the Tyrant's men, the Lady in the original text in the scribe's hand explains that she 'scornes death / as much as great men feare it' (ll. 1353–4). The word 'some' is interlined before the word 'great' in a hand and ink identifiable as that of the censor, George Buc. Judging by the ink, another, unidentified playhouse agent has struck out the offending 'great', restoring the metre of the line and avoiding any residual offence. Both interventions gain meaning through the identification (if partial) of the agents responsible: Buc's qualification shows the subversive text being contained (to use some old-fashioned terms), while the unknown playhouse agent provides an aesthetic and practical response to the document's brush with authority. The text's strangeness and strayingness is materially insistent and meaningful as the line errs from its initial iteration through the legible interaction of identifiably different textual agents. However, given the deeply imbricated nature of the inscriptions, which gain meaning and purpose through their textual interaction, the limitations of an attribution of agency also become insistent. The signifier by which we label each contributor is itself a locus for *strayng*ness, revealed as meaningful and insufficient as each agent potentially diverts another's work, bends to another's demands, or finds his work the subject of an alien, strange, intervention. Rather like the dramatic characters with which much of this chapter has been concerned, the designations that we give to different agents are the *loci* of meaningful, contiguous identity and at the same time precarious things, threatened by the practical textual interactions of the playhouse.

PART II

Making books; building reputations

CHAPTER 4

The mixed fortunes of Shakespeare in print

Sonia Massai

The rise of Shakespeare in print has attracted a considerable amount of attention over the last ten years. Building on the pioneering work of earlier textual scholars,[1] Lukas Erne galvanized debate on this topic by positing that Shakespeare wrote his plays with both the stage and the page in mind and that the Chamberlain's Men 'had a coherent strategy to try to get [his] plays into print' (2003: 26). Since then other scholars have reinforced the current understanding of early modern stationers as skilled craftsmen, shrewd businessmen and subtle readers who turned dramatic manuscripts into reading texts and actively shaped readers' demand for specific types of printed playbooks.[2] However, there are lingering, unresolved questions regarding the rise of Shakespeare in print, which seem as impervious to plausible explanation now as they did before the latest 'bibliographical turn' in the fields of Shakespeare and Early Modern Drama Studies.

I am particularly interested in the vexing question as to what caused a vertiginous drop in the number of first editions of Shakespeare's plays in the early seventeenth century and its far-reaching implications for our grasp of the commercial, theatrical and literary trends that affected the production and consumption of printed playbooks at the time. Undoubtedly, as Alan Farmer and Zachary Lesser have argued, 'not only was Shakespeare England's first best-selling playwright, but the success of the printed editions of his plays also helped to establish the playbook market itself' (2005: 11). In his new book, *Shakespeare and the Book Trade*, Erne provides a wealth of quantitative data to reinforce this view and to amplify Adam Hooks's claim that 'Shakespeare's works were not great books; they were good business' (2013: 127). It seems all the more surprising, then, that only four first editions of Shakespeare's plays reached the press between 1603 and his death in 1616.

---

[1] Cf., for example, de Grazia and Stallybrass 1993, Blayney 1997 and Kastan 2001.
[2] Recent studies include Lesser 2004, Massai 2007, Hooks 2012 and Straznicky 2013.

Accounting for this sharp decline in the publication of first editions of Shakespeare's playbooks has proved difficult both among earlier scholars who believed Shakespeare's stationers to be on the whole careless and often unscrupulous[3] and among recent scholars who regard them as discerning collaborators, mostly because there are no straightforward reasons to assume either that stationers suddenly became less successful at stealing Shakespeare's plays or that Shakespeare suddenly started to resist, or even postpone, publication in the face of his unchanging popularity in print.[4] Similarly, theories focusing on 'local' circumstances that may have affected the rate at which first editions of Shakespeare's plays were published in the early seventeenth century[5] fail to explain why, when the number of first editions of plays by Shakespeare's contemporaries picked up again after a significant contraction in 1603–04, Shakespeare's did not.

My contention is that this puzzling change in the fortunes of Shakespeare in print starts to seem understandable, if not inevitable, when viewed in the context of the publication of *all* professional drama in the period, in terms of the different types of plays that were printed and reprinted during the first two decades of the seventeenth century and how different types of playbooks were presented to their first readers. The most

---

[3] The theory of textual piracy in relation to the publication of Shakespeare's plays in quarto format during his lifetime goes as far back as the eighteenth century. Cf., for example, Samuel Johnson's indictment of Shakespeare's early stationers, who, he believed, 'printed [his plays] ... without the concurrence of the author, without the consent of the proprietor, from compilations made by chance or by stealth out of the separate parts written for the theatre' (1923 [1756]: 3). This theory was qualified by Alfred Pollard, who introduced the influential notion that only some early quartos, the so-called 'bad quartos' (1909), had been set up from unauthorized and textually defective manuscript copies of Shakespeare's plays. In turn, late twentieth-century studies, such as Maguire 1996 and Werstine 1999, questioned Pollard's distinction between 'good' and 'bad' quartos, by arguing that, while the former were not unmediated reproductions of authorial manuscript, textual variation in the latter could not be entirely accounted for by narratives of textual piracy.

[4] By querying a possible lack of supply of new plays staged by adult companies as the most likely explanation for a drop in the number of first editions of Shakespeare's plays in the early Jacobean period, I therefore depart from Farmer and Lesser, who posit a decline in supply without accounting for what may have caused it, at a time when, as they themselves point out, 'consumer demand for playbooks held steady' (2005: 12). Cf. also Erne's theory that Shakespeare and the King's Men were already planning a collected edition of his works (2003: 110–12). However, there seems to have been no expectation for a collected edition to include only, or even mainly, plays never printed before. All the stage plays included in Jonson's first Folio, for example, had been printed in quarto editions before 1616, and some of them, such as *The Alchemist* and *Epicene*, as recently as 1612.

[5] Cf., for example, Blayney's theory according to which a glut in the market was created by the exceptionally high number of new plays entered for publication in the Stationers' Register between May 1600 and October 1601 (1997: 385) or Leeds Barroll's view that a drop in supply of play texts was caused by the closures of the theatre due to protracted bouts of plague between 1603 and 1610 (1991: esp. 173).

The mixed fortunes of Shakespeare in print 59

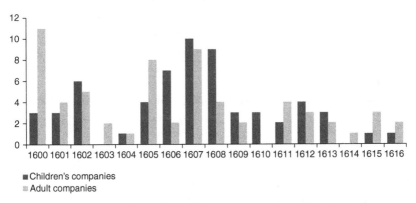

Figure 4.1 Stage plays published between 1600 and 1616 (first editions)

striking realization, when the rise of Shakespeare in print is reconsidered within the context of dramatic publication in the period more generally, is that the rate at which first editions of different types of stage plays reached the press varied considerably during the Jacobean period of Shakespeare's career. As Figure 4.1 shows, soon after the turn of the century the recently established market for commercial playbooks began to be increasingly dominated by plays written for the children's companies, which had been reconstituted at St Paul's in 1599 and Blackfriars in 1600. After a relatively slow start, first editions of plays staged by the children outnumbered first editions of plays staged by the adult companies for the first time in 1602. After a contraction in the number of both types of plays published in 1603 and 1604, first editions of playbooks linked with the children's companies grew in popularity until they exceeded the number of first editions of plays originally staged by the adult companies in four consecutive years, from 1606 to 1609. In 1610, all first editions were plays written for the children. Between 1611 and 1613, plays staged by the children continued to account for at least half of all first editions published then. After the longest-surviving boy company, the Children of the Revels, merged with the Lady Elizabeth's Men in 1613, the number of first editions of stage plays (both children's and adult) published up to Shakespeare's death in 1616 reached an all-time low, with an average of just under three first editions a year. Crucially, none of the plays printed in these years had been staged by the King's Men. In short, what these figures show is that demand for new plays by Shakespeare may have fallen dramatically after 1605, not because Shakespeare's plays had become less popular *per se*, but because the general demand for plays originally staged by the adult companies shrank in comparison to plays originally staged by the children.[6]

The theatrical impact of the children's companies has been thoroughly investigated. According to Andrew Gurr, Shakespeare and his company responded creatively and proactively to their success on stage by veering towards a new, socially neutral repertory, which positioned the company somewhere between the elitism of the boys and the broader appeal of the 'citizens' plays' staged at the northern amphitheatres (2004a: 156). Other scholars, such as Roslyn Knutson and Lucy Munro, have similarly shown how repertories of adult and children companies were far less polarized then previously assumed. Also crucial in this respect was the King's Men's acquisition of the Blackfriars in 1609, which gave Shakespeare's company unique ownership of both an indoor and an outdoor venue, where they performed all year round to audiences from a wide range of social backgrounds. However, the impact of the children's companies on the publication of stage plays at the turn of the seventeenth century has so far been largely overlooked.[7]

A comprehensive overview of the number and the bibliographical make-up of playbooks printed from the turn of the century to 1616 shows that the children's companies not only secured a significant share of the market for new playbooks but also presented stage plays to their first readers as different, more self-consciously literary texts.[8] While plays staged by adult companies had either no paratext at all or theatrical paratexts primarily aimed at evoking the experience of watching a play on stage, plays staged by the children often included theatrical paratexts, eliciting a detached, critical mode of spectatorship and sprawling readerly paratexts,

---

[6] Earlier scholars have commented on the increased number of first editions of plays written for the children's companies at a time when 'the number of other printed plays, including Shakespeare, dwindled' (Erne 2003: 102) but have ascribed this increase solely to the popularity of the children's plays on the stage and not to related but distinctive trends in the market of playbooks, as this chapter will go on to show. Others have linked this increase to the disbanding of the children's companies (Farmer, in conversation). However, availability of playbooks does not necessarily result in publication, as suggested by the fact that the popularity of children plays in print pre-dates 1606, when the Children of Paul's were suppressed, and did not extend beyond the merger of the Children of the Revels with the Lady Elizabeth's Men in 1613.

[7] Lesser and Farmer 2000 is one of the most helpful exceptions. Considering the frequency of attributions of playing spaces, as well as authorial attributions (and authorial status) and the use of Latin on the title pages of early modern playbooks, Lesser and Farmer conclude that, 'whatever the actual conditions of playgoing' or the similarities between children and adult repertories identified by recent scholars, 'publishers ... seem to have felt that ... an "indoor attribution" would sell more than an outdoor [one]' (91, 95).

[8] For annotated transcriptions of all paratextual materials included in printed playbooks at the time, see Berger and Massai 2014.

including dedications, addresses to the readers and dedicatory poems, informed by a sustained metadiscourse about the purpose of playing, playwriting, playgoing and playreading in the period. In fact, most of the insights that have shaped and continue to shape critical thinking about Jacobean drama originated in the paratextual apparatus prefaced to plays originally staged by the children.

Plays staged by adult companies generally acquired no readerly paratext at all when they were first committed to print and the theatrical paratext retained in some of them invariably contributed to recreate for readers a specific type of experience aptly described by Neil Carson as 'theatre of enchantment' (quoted in Gurr 2004a: 158). The most popular theatrical paratext in this type of plays is the chorus or chorus-like character, who encourages audiences (and, later on, readers) to use their imagination to overcome the material limits of theatrical (and textual) representation. The most famous example, the Chorus in Shakespeare's *Henry V*, was not published until the play was printed in the First Folio in 1623, but its famous appeal – '*And let vs, Cyphers to this great Accompt, / On your imaginarie Forces worke*' (TLN 19–20) – resounds in the lines spoken by other Chorus characters throughout the period. In Thomas Dekker's *Old Fortunatus* (Admiral's, 1599; publ. 1600), for example, the Prologue announces: 'our muse intreats, / Your thoughts to helpe poore Art, and to allow, / That I may serue as Chorus to her scences' (A2v). Similarly, the Chorus in the anonymous *Captain Thomas Stukeley* (Admiral's, 1596; publ. 1605) acknowledges that 'Thus farre through patience of your gentle ears / hath Stukleys life . . . / But new reuiude' (I4v), while the 'Prologue attired like fame' in John Day, George Wilkins and William Rowley's *The Travels of Three English Brothers* (Queen Anne's, 1607; publ. 1607) warns his audience (and his readers) that 'Our Sceane lies speechlesse, actiue, but yet dumbe: / Till your expressing thoughts giue it a tongue' (A2). Other examples range from the better-known lines spoken by Gower in *Pericles* (King's Men, 1608; publ. 1609) – 'what by me is told, / In your imagination hold' (E1v) – to the more obscure lines spoken by Homer in Thomas Heywood's *The Golden Age* (Queen's Men, 1610; publ. 1611) – 'We grow now towards our port and wished bay, / Gentles your loue, and *Homer* cannot stray' (I3v).

The children's plays offered an entirely different theatrical *and* readerly experience. Even the theatrical paratexts reproduced in the first printed editions of this type of plays focus on matters of style: they critique older models of playwriting and encourage audiences and readers alike to adopt a detached, critical stance towards the children's plays both as stage performance and as dramatic literature. In John Marston's *Jack Drum's Entertainment* (Paul's, 1600; publ. 1601), one of the children addresses the audience, prologue-like, to reassure them that the author 'vowes not to torment your listning eares / With mouldy fopperies of stale Poetry' and 'Vnpossible drie mustie Fictions' (A2v). In characteristically Jonsonian fashion, one of the three children in the 'Preludium' prefaced to *Cynthia's Revels* (Chapel, 1600; publ. 1601) promises to exorcize the ghost of 'Playes, *departed a dozen yeares since,* [which] *haue been seene walking on* [the] *Stage*' and announces that the author's muse '*shuns the print of any beaten path; / And prooues new wayes to come to learned eares*' (A4v, B1), thus stressing the experimental quality of Jonson's writing. Aligning his work with the new style of comedy staged by the children, Edward Sharpham has his Prologue in *Cupid's Whirligig* (Revels, 1607; publ. 1607) denigrate the types of plays staged by the adult companies: 'OVr Authors Pen, loues not to swim in blood, / He dips no Inke, from out blacke *Acheron*: . . . / He taxes no Goddesses for foulest lust, . . . / Nor doth he touch the falles of mightie Kings, . . . / He onely striues with mirth to please each one, / Since laughter is peculiar vnto man' (A2v). Playwrights who wrote for the children's companies did experiment with a variety of genres, including tragedy, but what Sharpham critiques here is primarily sensationalism as the trademark of the plays staged by the adult companies, especially in the northern amphitheatres.

As well as distancing themselves from older styles of playwriting, the theatrical paratexts included in the first editions of plays staged by the boys also invited their auditors and readers to engage their *critical*, rather than their *imaginary*, powers. While wary of the short-sighted, capricious scorn that fashionable gallants often bestowed on plays to prove the sophistication of their taste and understanding,[9] playwrights who wrote for the children's companies often encouraged their audience and readers to judge their work, thus assuming a shared interest in the literary and artistic qualities of their writing. John Marston repeatedly encouraged critical judgement whilst condemning affected denigration: the prologue in *The Dutch Courtesan* (Revels, 1605; publ. 1605) pleads 'you'le not taxe, vntill you iudge our Play' (A2); similarly 'Prologus' in *Parasitaster* (Revels, 1604; publ. 1606) flatters the 'Atick *iudgements*' who filled the hall playhouses and praises them for being 'ablest spirits', 'exact', 'full' and 'strong', and yet crucially 'benigne in censuring' (A3).

---

[9] See, for example, 'Prologus' in George Chapman's *All Fools* (Revels, 1601; publ. 1605): '*if our other audience see / You on the stage depart before we end, / Our wits goe with you all, and we are fooles*' (A3v).

Readerly paratexts, that is dedications, addresses to the reader and commendatory poems, were almost exclusively included in playbooks linked with the children's companies. These types of paratexts brimmed with critical thinking about dramatic literature, and they were, once again, clearly aimed at a discerning readership. Most memorable is John Fletcher's definition of tragicomedy in his address to the reader in the first edition of *The Faithful Shepherdess* (Revels, 1608; publ. 1610): 'A tragic-comedie', as Fletcher famously put it, 'is not so called in / respect of mirth and killing but in respect it wants deaths, / which is inough to make it no tragedie, yet brings some neere / it, which is inough to make it no comedie' (A2v). What is less well known is that this type of metadiscourse about new, experimental writing for the theatre is essentially ubiquitous in readerly paratexts which framed the printed editions of plays staged by the children. Marston, for example, discusses the 'freedome of poesie' (A4) in his address to the reader in *The Malcontent* (Revels, then King's Men, 1604; publ. 1604) and '*the scope of... Comedie*' according to Juvenal in his address 'To my equall Reader' in *Parasitaster* (A2), while Chapman defines the 'limits of an autenticall Tragedie' (A3v) in the dedication prefaced to *The Revenge of Bussy D'Ambois* (Paul's, 1604; publ. 1613).

The literary quality of these paratexts and the discerning readers of these playbooks contrast starkly with the target readership of plays written for the adult companies, if the address 'to the Comicke, Play-readers, Venery, *and Laughter*' signed by Thomas Middleton and prefaced to *The Roaring Girl* (Prince Henry's Men, 1611; publ. 1611; co-authored by Thomas Dekker) is at all representative. This address offers a memorable and vivid profile of the type of reader who would be drawn to *The Roaring Girl*: 'you shall finde this published Comedy', the address goes, 'good to keepe you in an afternoone from dice, at home in your chambers; and for venery you shall finde enough, for sixepence'. The comedy itself, ostensibly a substitute for gambling or a visit to the brothel, is described as 'light-colour Summer stuffe' (A3) and has no literary pretensions, at least no overt ones.

Recent scholars, including Heidi Brayman Hackel and William Sherman, have shown that the target readership (or ideal reader) implied in paratextual materials did not always reflect the buying habits or reading practices of *actual* early modern readers. However, the strategic positioning of plays originally staged by the children's companies within a select reading market is so widespread that it must have functioned as a distinctive trademark of playbooks which generated and met a large share of the demand for printed plays in the period. Telling in this respect is Jonson's attempt not only to remove all traces of theatrical provenance from plays originally written for Shakespeare's company but also his commitment to furnish them with the sort of readerly paratexts routinely added to the plays belonging to the children's companies.

As early as 1600, Jonson's *Every Man out of his Humor* was advertised on its title page as a '*Comicall Satire . . . Containing more than hath been publickely Spoken or Acted*' (A1). It is safe to assume that the Globe audiences were not treated to the full version of the exceedingly long induction which restarts, chorus-like, at key moments during the play. In the opening section, two of the characters in it discuss in great detail the rules informing the generic model from which Jonson's play sprang, namely '*Vetus Comœdia*' according to the 'Terentian manner'. They also wonder whether playwrights should follow such rules unconditionally, given that the classical authors who devised them also adapted them from even earlier models, as shown in the following extract:

> 'tis extant, that that which we call *Comœdia,* was at first nothing but a simple and continued Satyre, sung by one only person, till *Susario* inuented a second, after him *Epicharmus* a third, *Phormus,* and *Chionides* deuised to haue foure actors, with a *Prologue* and *Chorus;* to which *Cratinus* (long after) added a fift and sixt; *Eupolis* more, *Aristophanes* more than they: euery man in the dignity of his spirit and iudgement, supplied something: and (though that in him this kind of Poeme appeared absolute, and fully perfected) yet how is the face of it chang'd since, in *Menander, Philemon, Cecilius, Plautus,* and the rest; who haue vtterly excluded the *Chorus,* altered the property of the persons, their names, and natures, and augmented it with all libertie, according to the elegancie and disposition of those times wherein they wrote? I see not then but wee should enjoy the same *Licentia* or free power, to illustrate and heighten our inuention as they did; and not bee tied to those strict and regular formes, which the nicenesse of a fewe (who are nothing but Forme) would thrust vpon vs. (B4v)

The register of this extract suggests that it was not written with the Globe audience in mind, even allowing for the wider social spectrum of theatre-goers which historians like Gurr believe the Globe attracted, especially when compared to the northern amphitheatres. The readerly paratext prefaced to *Volpone* (King's Men, 1606; publ. 1607), which had also been staged at the Globe in 1605–06, is equally suggestive of the extent to which Jonson was determined to remove any trace of the play's affiliation with Shakespeare's company. Jonson dedicated *Volpone* to

'THE MOST NOBLE AND MOST AEQVALL SISTERS THE TWO FAMOVS VNIVERSITIES' and in this dedication he discussed his decision to adapt the *'Comick* Law[s]' to suit his 'special aime', viz. 'to put the snafle in their mouths, that crie out, we neuer punish vice in our *Enterludes*' (¶3v). Although a play like *Volpone* may reflect, as Gurr points out, 'Jonson's awareness of the neutral position of the Globe repertory' (2004a: 166), its transmission into print gave Jonson the opportunity to re-present it to its reader as an ultra-literary playbook which looked more like the printed versions of plays originally staged by the children than those of plays staged by adult companies.

Jonson was not the only playwright who used dramatic publication in order to elevate plays staged by adult companies to the status of readerly texts, thus making them more appealing to the readers who had created such a significant demand for printed versions of plays originally staged by the children. Thomas Dekker, like Jonson, wrote for adult companies and for at least one of the main boy companies, the Children of Paul's, whose repertory was less ambitious and less experimental than that of the Children of the Revels, but nevertheless aligned with new modes of playwriting. When his Prince Henry's Men play *The Whore of Babylon* (1606) reached the press in 1607, Dekker headed his address to the reader with the Latin tag 'Lectori', referred to his play as a '*Drammatical Poem*', and attacked the actors for mangling his work on stage: having stressed that he was nowhere near that theatre when his play was performed – '*mine eare stood not within reach of their Larums*' – he then explains that, though '*the Poet set the note of his Nombers, euen to* Apolloes *owne Lyre, the Player will ... sing false notes, in dispite of all the rules of Musick*'. '*The labours therfore of Writers*', he concludes, '*are as vnhappie as the children of a bewtifull woman, being spoyld by ill nurses, within a month after they come into the world*' (A2v). The textual patronage Dekker sought to secure for himself by furnishing *The Whore of Babylon* with the sort of readerly paratext that had become associated with playbooks linked to the children's companies may have proved elusive or ultimately unrewarding, judging from the fact that, later the same year, two plays he co-authored with John Webster for the Children of Paul's, *Northward Ho!* (1605) and *Westward Ho!* (1604), were published with no paratext at all. Even more suggestive is Dekker's decision to dedicate *If it be not Good the Devil is in it* to the Queen's Men, who had staged it shortly before it was printed in 1612. In this dedication, Dekker launches into a self-conscious attack against 'bad *Benefactor*[s]' who let '*Merit* [go] a *Begging & Learning* staru[e]' and pledges his renewed allegiance with the actors, who saved the play from oblivion, when '*Fortune* (in her blinde pride) set her foote vpon' it (A3).

Shakespeare, on the other hand, never penned a readerly paratext and never contributed, at least overtly, to the contemporary metadiscourse about the purpose of playing, playwriting, playgoing and playreading that flourished in the playbooks linked with the children's companies. Shakespeare's contemporaries praised his plays and poems for their literary qualities: passages from Shakespeare had been included in the first anthologies of selected poetical extracts published at the turn of the seventeenth century to showcase English as a literary language on a level with other vernacular or classical languages (Stallybrass and Chartier 2007: esp. 43–52). However, Shakespeare never wrote about his art, the laws of comedy or the limits of tragedy.[10] Besides, his Jacobean plays may have contributed to the theatrical success of the new repertory, which made the Globe distinctive for its broad appeal to audiences from different social backgrounds, but they may not have appealed either to those readers who were drawn to the new, literary self-conscious style of the children's playbooks nor to those who preferred an older style of plays and playbooks.

Interestingly, as Gurr has pointed out, two of the four first editions of Shakespeare to reach the press in the Jacobean period, *Hamlet* and *King Lear*, 'harked back to the amphitheatre plays of the previous decade ... [being] rewritings of old Queen's Company plays from 1590 or earlier' (2004a: 162). Similarly, *Pericles* may reflect Shakespeare's own experimentation with the generic conventions of tragicomedy, but Gower's role as chorus is, as explained above, more immediately in keeping with the theatrical paratexts included in playbooks linked to the adult companies. *Troilus and Cressida*, on the other hand, with its classical subject-matter and its reliance on acerbic satire, may have struck its stationers, Richard Bonian and Henry Walley, as the closest Shakespeare ever came to writing the type

---

[10] In this respect, I agree with Patrick Cheney's notion of Shakespeare's 'self-effacing' model of authorship. However, unlike Cheney I believe that Shakespeare's failure to write about his art is not due to a personal inclination but rather to the fact that distinctively readerly and literary paratextual materials, the most common context within which early modern playwrights discussed the principles informing playwriting, playgoing and playreading in the period, were only routinely added to plays originally written for the children's companies or to plays which their authors tried to distance from their origins in outdoor theatres, as mentioned earlier in this chapter. I therefore no longer regard the absence of any readerly paratexts by Shakespeare as a 'glaring anomaly' in its own right, as I did in 'Paratext' (Massai 2009: 4), but as a distinctive feature of playbooks which, like Shakespeare's, had originated with adult companies. I still think, though, *pace* Erne (2013: 128), that Shakespeare might have been tempted, at the very least, to repackage his plays for publication, if not as aggressively as Jonson, at least as often as Thomas Heywood did from 1607–08 onwards (cf. Massai 2007: 166–7), had he really felt that there was an unchanged appetite for his plays in print during the Jacobean period of his career.

of play that had become the trademark of the children's companies. Their marketing strategy certainly seems to have been aimed both at those who saw it on stage – the title page of the first issue of the first edition of 1609 advertises the play as '*acted by the Kings Maiesties seruants at the Globe*' – and at those who would appreciate its literary qualities – the title page of the second issue of the same edition removes theatrical provenance and is followed by the only readerly paratext in a Shakespeare play published during his lifetime. The peculiar title of this address to the reader, 'A neuer writer, to an euer reader' (¶2), confirms that Shakespeare didn't write it. This address, where Shakespeare is compared to Terence and Plautus for his talent as a writer of witty comedies, was most probably written or commissioned by Bonian and Walley to make the second issue of the 1609 edition resemble the bibliographical make-up of the playbooks associated with the children.

Having offered an alternative account as to why Shakespeare lost his foothold on the market for first editions of stage plays during the Jacobean period of his career, I should stress that reprints of his Elizabethan plays remained very popular within the buoyant market for second-plus editions within which the children's companies had little impact. As Figure 4.2 shows, the large majority of plays reprinted between 1604 and 1616 (52 out of 63) had been staged by adult companies. Shakespeare alone outnumbered the children with 13 reprints over the same time period.

Shakespeare's mixed fortunes in print in the early seventeenth century have far-reaching implications. Farmer and Lesser have identified a similar split from 1629 to 1640 between an increased demand for new editions of

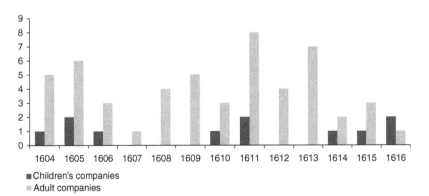

Figure 4.2 Stage plays published between 1604 and 1616 (second-plus editions)

new plays which seldom reached a second edition and a steady demand for reprints of older plays. What Farmer and Lesser describe as the 'Caroline paradox' would seem to apply quite neatly to the turn of the seventeenth century, in both numerical and qualitative terms. As they explain, 'while there had always been old plays, in the Caroline period what had earlier been a mere fact of chronology had now become an important division among two kinds of playbooks' (2006: 30). Although the reprints of older plays in the Jacobean period, unlike Caroline reprints, were not as yet explicitly presented to their readers as rediscovered classics, playbooks linked to the children's companies and to the adult companies looked different and must have sold differently. Besides, Jacobean stationers gravitated towards either type of playbook, though possibly not to the same extent as their Caroline successors. It is nevertheless suggestive, for example, that all the first editions of stage plays published by Nathaniel Butter, including the first edition of *King Lear*, had belonged to the adult companies. Conversely, Bonian and Walley, who had clearly gone out of their way to present *Troilus and Cressida* as a satirical comedy, had never ventured and would never venture into the market for plays written for adult companies, the rest of their dramatic output including children's plays and a courtly masque.

To conclude, I believe that the rapid growth in the number of first editions of plays belonging to the children's repertories from 1605 to 1613 and the concurrent contraction in the demand for new plays staged by the adult companies, alongside the steady publication of reprints of plays belonging to the adult companies, can most usefully be described, borrowing Farmer and Lesser's suggestive phrase, as the 'Jacobean paradox'. The 'Jacobean paradox' offers a new set of answers to the question of why demand for first editions of Shakespeare's plays may have dropped shortly after the turn of the seventeenth century. It also explains why the publication of the apocrypha would seem to suggest otherwise. Why would the title pages of plays such as *Thomas Lord Cromwell*, *The London Prodigal* and *The Yorkshire Tragedy* include Shakespeare's name or his initials, if Shakespeare was no longer popular? Shakespeare *was* still popular but he was primarily sold in print as the author of plays, which, like the apocrypha, harked back to an older style of playwriting and which, like older plays, were still being reprinted. The 'Jacobean paradox', in other words, seems the most economical and logical way to understand Shakespeare's mixed fortunes in print in the early years of the seventeenth century.

CHAPTER 5

'To London all'? mapping Shakespeare in print, 1593–1598

Helen Smith

It was in 1593 that Shakespeare's writings entered print. The first recorded Shakespearean book-purchase followed quickly: on 12 June, Richard Stonley, Teller of the Exchequer, paid sixpence 'For the Survay of Fraunce, with the Venus and Athonay p^r Shakspere'.[1] Over the next five years, another poem, *Lucrece*, and ten plays followed, in eighteen editions (see Table 5.1), alongside a handful of works at some point associated with Shakespeare.[2] These publications involved the labour and capital of eight identifiable members of the London book trade, alongside numerous compositors, correctors, printers, warehouse-men and bookbinders. Since the eighteenth century, much of the scholarship on early modern English printing and bookselling has been driven by the search for Shakespeare's 'original' texts. This perspective has influenced our sense of book making and use, privileging the study of drama, and focusing attention on particular stationers at specific moments in their careers.

It would be impossible to offer here a full account of printing in the mid-1590s: an account in which Shakespeare would appear only fleetingly. Instead, this chapter treats each Shakespeare text published between 1593 and 1598 as a means to explore the textual and social communities manifested in, and shaped by, his books. I thus seek to extend Julie Sanders's insight that 'play-texts not only represent but alter, foster, and enable practices of space, place and landscape' (2011: 235), demonstrating that the spaces (both linguistic and literal) of play-*books* equally both reproduce and contribute to literary and social meaning. I begin with the narrative poems, arguing that *Venus and Adonis* and *Lucrece* were much more

[1] Folger MS V.a.460, f. 9.
[2] These are *[The] troublesome raigne of Iohn King of England* and *The second part of the troublesome raigne of King Iohn*, which survive in a single volume, though with separate title pages and registers; *A pleasant conceited historie, called the taming of a shrew*; *The lamentable tragedie of Locrine*; *The raigne of King Edward the third*. See also *Love's labours won* (see below, p. 85).

69

Table 5.1 *Printed Shakespeare texts, 1593–1598*

STC	Title page	Size	Stationers' Company Register
22354	VENVS	AND ADONIS ‖ *Vilia miretur vulgus: mihi flauus Apollo*	*Pocula Castalia plena ministret aqua.* ‖ LONDON	Imprinted by Richard Field, and are to be sold [by John Harrison] at	the signe of the white Greyhound in	Paules Church-yard.	1593.	4°	Entered to Field as 'Venus and Adonis', 18 April 1593. Assigned to Harrison 25 June 1594.
26099	[*2HVI*] THE	First part of the Con=‖ tention betwixt the two famous Houses of Yorke	and Lancaster, with the death of the good	Duke Humphrey: ‖ And the banishment and death of the Duke of	*Suffolke*, and the Tragicall end of the proud Cardinall	of *VVinchester*, vvith the notable Rebellion	of *Iacke Cade*: ‖ *And the Duke of Yorkes first claime unto the*	*Crowne.* ‖ LONDON	Printed by Thomas Creed, for Thomas Millington,	and are to be sold at his shop vnder Saint Peters	Church in Cornwall.| 1594.	4°	Entered to Millington as 'the firse parte of the Contention of the two famous houses of York and Lancaster with the deathe of the good Duke Humfrey and the banishement and Deathe of the Duke of Suffolk and the tragicall ende of the prowd Cardinall of Winchester with the notable rebellion of Jack Cade and the Duke of Yorkes ffirste clayme unto the Crowne', 12 March 1594.
22345	LVCRECE. ‖ LONDON.	Printed by Richard Field, for Iohn Harrison, and are	to be sold at the signe of the white Greyhound	in Paules Churh-yard. 1594.	4°	Entered to Harrison as 'the Ravyshement of Lucrece', 9 May 1594.
22328	THE	MOST LA-	mentable Romaine	Tragedie of Titus Andronicus: ‖ As it was Plaide by the Right Ho-	nourable the Earle of *Darbie*, Earle of *Pembrooke*,	and Earle of *Sussex* their Seruants. ‖ LONDON,	Printed by Iohn	4°	Entered to Danter as 'a Noble Roman Historye of Titus Andronicus', 6 February 1594.

70 HELEN SMITH

Table 5.1 (*cont.*)

STC	Title page	Size	Stationers' Company Register
	Danter, and are | to be sold by *Edward White* & *Thomas Millington,* | at the little North doore of Paules at the | signe of the Gunne. | 1594.		
22355	VENVS | AND ADONIS || *Vilia miretur vulgus: mihi flauus Apollo* | *Pocula Castalia plena ministret aqua.* || LONDON. | Imprinted by Richard Field, and are to be sold [by John Harrison] at | the signe of the white Greyhound in | Paules Church-yard. | 1594.	4°	
21006	[*3HVI*] The true Tragedie of Richard | *Duke of Yorke, and the death of* | good King Henrie the Sixt, || *with the whole contention betweene* | the two Houses Lancaster | and Yorke, as it was sundrie times | acted by the Right Honoura- | ble the Earle of Pem- | brooke his seruants. || Printed at London by P. S. [Peter Short] for Thomas Milling- | *ton, and are to be sold at his shoppe vnder* | *Saint Peters Church in* | *Cornwal.* 1595.	8°	
22356	[VENUS AND ADONIS] [London: Richard Field for John Harrison? 1595?]	8°	
22357	VENVS | AND ADONIS. | *Vilia miretur vulgus: mihi flauus Apollo* | *Pocula Castalia plena ministret aqua.* || Imprinted at London by R. F. for | Iohn Harison. | 1596.	16°	
22307	T H E | Tragedie of King Ri- | chard the se- | cond. || *As it hath beene publikely acted* | *by the right Honourable the* | *Lorde*	4°	Entered to Wise as 'The Tragedye of Richard the Second', 29 August 1597.

Table 5.1 (cont.)

STC	Title page	Size	Stationers' Company Register
	*Chamberlaine his Ser-	uants.*		LONDON	Printed by Valentine Simmes for Androw Wise, and	are to be solde at his shop in Paules churchyard at	the signe of the Angel.	1597.		
22314	THE TRAGEDY OF	King Richard the third. || Containing,	His treacherous Plots against his brother Clarence:	the pittiefull murther of his iunocent nephewes:	his tyrannicall vsurpation: with the whole course	of his detested life, and most deserued death. || As it hath beene lately Acted by the	Right honourable the Lord Chamber-	laine his seruants. || AT LONDON	¶ Printed by Valentine Sims, for Andrew Wise,	dwelling in Paules Church-yard, at the	Signe of the Angell.	1597. [From sig. H onwards probably printed by Peter Short]	4°	Entered to Wise as 'The tragedie of kinge Richard the Third with the death of the Duke of Clarence', 20 October 1597.
22322	AN	EXCELLENT	conceited Tragedie	OF	Romeo and Iuliet.	As it hath been often (with great applause)	plaid publiquely, by the right Ho-	nourable the L. of *Hunsdon*	his Seruants. || LONDON,	Printed by Iohn Danter.	1 5 9 7 [From sig. E onwards printed by Edward Allde]	4°	
22279a	[*King Henry IV, Part 1*] [London? Peter Short for Andrew Wise, 1598?]	4°	

Table 5.1 (cont.)

STC	Title page	Size	Stationers' Company Register
22280	[*1HIV*] THE | HISTORY OF | HENRIE THE | FOVRTH; || With the battell at Shrewsburie, | *betweene the King and Lord* | Henry Percy, surnamed | Henrie Hotspur of | the North. || *With the humourous conceits of Sir* | Iohn Falstalffe. || AT LONDON, | Printed by P. S. [Peter Short] for *Andrew Wise*, dwelling | in Paules Churchyard, at the signe of | the Angell. 1598.	4°	Entered to Wise as 'The historye of Henry the IIIJth with his battaile of Shrewsburye against Henry Hottspurre of the Northe with the conceipted mirthe of Sir John Falstoff, 25 February 1598.
22294	*A* | PLEASANT | Conceited Comedie | CALLED, | Loues labors lost. || As it vvas presented before her Highnes | this last Christmas. || Nevvly corrected and augmented | *By W. Shakespere.* | Imprinted at London by *W.W.* | for *Cutbert Burby.* | 1598.	4°	
22346	LVCRECE. || AT LONDON, | Printed by P.S. [Peter Short] for Iohn | *Harrison.* 1598.	8°	
22308	T H E | Tragedie of King Ri- | chard the second. || As it hath beene publikely acted by the Right Ho- | nourable the Lord Chamberlaine his | seruants. || *By William Shake-speare.* || LONDON | Printed by Valentine Simmes for Andrew Wise, and | are to be sold at his shop in Paules churchyard at | the signe of the Angel. | 1 5 9 8.	4°	
22309	T H E | Tragedie of King Ri- | chard the second. || As it hath beene publikely acted by the Right Ho- | nourable the Lord Chamberlaine his | seruants. ||	4°	

Table 5.1 (*cont.*)

STC	Title page	Size	Stationers' Company Register
	By William Shake-speare. || LONDON | Printed by Valentine Simmes, for Andrew Wise, and | are to be sold at his shop in Paules churchyard, at | the signe of the Angel. | 1 5 9 8.		
22315	THE | TRAGEDIE | of King Richard | the third. || Conteining his treacherous Plots against his | brother *Clarence*:the pitiful murther of his innocent | Nephewes: his tyrannicall vsurpation: with | the whole course of his detested life, and most | *deserued death.* || *As it hath beene lately Acted by the Right honourable* | *the Lord Chamberlaine his seruants.* || *By William Shake-speare.* || LONDON | Printed by Thomas Creede, for Andrew Wise | dwelling in Paules Church-yard, at the signe | of the Angell. 1598.	4°	

products of print than critics routinely claim, and move chronologically through the plays, investigating the textual cultures from which printed Shakespeare emerged and to which he contributed.

A plague and two houses: *Venus and Adonis* and *The Rape of Lucrece*

The theatres were closed due to plague between 23 June and 29 December 1592 and for the whole of 1593. Whilst the impact of the disease upon players and playwrights has been widely noted, its influence on the London book trades is less often discussed. In 1596, Thomas Nashe recalled 'the ragingest furie of the last Plague' when, he claimed, his rival, Gabriel

Harvey, was imprisoned in the Paul's churchyard premises of his printer, John Wolfe,

> not beeing able almost to step out of dores, he was so barricadoed vp with graues ... nor to open his window euening or morning, but a dampe (like the smoake of a Cannon) from the fat manured earth with contagion (being the buriall place of fiue parishes), in thick rouling clowds would strugglingly funnell vp, & with a full blast puffe in at his casements. (1596, N4v)

The landscape of *Venus and Adonis* is shadowed by the urban context in which it was produced, haunted by 'infection', 'the plague' and the fears of 'one sore sick that hears the passing-bell' (508, 510, 702). On bookstalls, the poem sat alongside the work of 'star-gazers' who had 'writ on death' (509), like William Cupper's *Certaine sermons concerning Gods late visitation in the citie of London*, produced by the same printer, Richard Field, in 1592, or *Present remedies against the plague*, printed by John Danter, Nashe's printer, and the first publisher of *Romeo and Juliet* (a play in which the spectre of plague hastens on the tragedy), in 1592 and 1594.

While some scholars view *Venus and Adonis* and *Lucrece* (first published 1594) as symptoms of a forced interruption in Shakespeare's theatrical career, Patrick Cheney interprets them as a 'career announcement for the famed man of the theatre's turn from stage to page' (2004: 92). The poems are regularly agreed to be different from the plays: for Douglas Bruster, 'there is no doubt that Shakespeare personally arranged for *Venus and Adonis* and *Lucrece* to be printed' (2013a: 113). *Venus and Adonis* is distinguished by a title page Latin epigraph from Ovid's *Amores*: '*Vilia miretur vulgus: mihi faluus Apollo Poxula Castalis plena ministret aqua*' ('Let the crowd wonder at cheap things; for me / let yellow-haired Apollo give cups full / of water of Castalia'), whilst *Lucrece* marks its literary status by the inclusion of marginal printed quotation marks, anticipating, and helping to shape, its fragmentary inclusion in manuscript and print commonplace books. Both feature dedications to the earl of Southampton, subscribed 'William Shakespeare'.

Field entered *Venus and Adonis* in the Stationers' Company Registers on 18 April 1593, establishing his right to publish the poem. He did not specialize in poetry; it may have been Richard Stonley's interest in France, manifested in his purchase of John Eliot's *Suruay ... of France* (1592), that first led him to Field, who was married to a French printer's widow, and whose earliest publications were centrally concerned with French politics. It has often been noted that Field and Shakespeare were Stratford acquaintances. We might ask whether Field's Stratford history also played a material role in the composition of his books: his father, Henry, was a tanner, producing leather that might be used both in the printing house (for tools) and for bookbinding. Further research would reveal connections between the commercial knowledge and physical paraphernalia of the London book trades, and the trade and material insights possessed by the sons and daughters of tanners, mercers and husbandmen.

Field's edition was sold in Harrison's shop, suggesting the two shared the financial risk of *Venus and Adonis*, but also the profits. He assigned his rights in the poem to Harrison on 25 June 1594, shortly after Harrison had registered his own rights in *Lucrece*. Ovid, the man 'for the elegancy, facility, and golden cadence of poesy' (*Love's labour's lost*, 4.2.122–3), was a familiar figure for both men. In 1589, Field had printed for Harrison a Latin edition of Ovid's *Metamorphoses*, the text through which Lavinia pages frantically in *Titus Andronicus*. They would go on to publish the *Heroides* and *Amores* in 1594. As Adam Hooks notes, 'Shakespeare would not have had to look any further than Harrison's shop or Field's printing house' to discover his Ovidian motto (2011: 269). The emergence of Shakespeare's most self-consciously Ovidian books within this milieu reminds us that Shakespeare's writings circulated on the bookstalls alongside the texts they drew upon. Thus, in 1595, around the moment Shakespeare was composing *The comedy of errors*, Thomas Creede published Plautus' *Menaechmi*, whilst Harrison (with four fellow stationers) invested in the 1587 edition of Holinshed's *Chronicles*, and Field printed another key Shakespearean source, Thomas North's translation of Plutarch's *Lives*, in 1595.

The decision to preface poems with a Latin motto was scarcely innovative. Both Field and Harrison had previously published books distinguished by Latin tags: Field, for example, printed Sir John Harington's elegantly produced translation of Ariosto's *Orlando Furioso*, which prominently displays a line from Horace on the title page, and Robert Greene's *Pandosto*, distinguished by not one but two Latin phrases. In 1593, Latin epigrams graced the title pages of roughly half of all poetry publications: T.W.'s *The tears of fancie*, Thomas Lodge's *Phillis*, Michael Drayton's *Idea*, Giles Fletcher's *Licia* and the mingled prose and verse of *Bacchus bountie* by 'Philip Foulface of Ale-foord, student in good felloship'.[3] *Lucrece*'s commonplace markers also had a print history. Marginal quotation marks

---

[3] Latin epigrams were not unique to poetry; among the other 1593 books to feature them were *Resurgendum. A notable sermon concerning the resurrection* and a language textbook, Claudius Hollyband's *The French Littelton* (both printed by Field), as well as Nashe's *The apologie of Pierce Pennilesse* and Gervase Markham's popular equestrian guide, *A discource of horsmanshippe*. Karen Raber reads Markham's text alongside *Venus and Adonis* to explore the attitudes of both texts to the pleasures of equestrianism, suggesting a conceptual as well as a paratextual link (Raber 2013: ch. 2).

highlighted extractable passages in texts ranging from the 1570 second edition of *Gorboduc* to Sidney's *Arcadia*. Field printed George Puttenham's *Arte of English poesie* in 1590, a text whose passages of verse are distinguished by commonplace markers. *Lucrece*'s margins are shaped by emerging conventions of print that both reflected and encouraged readerly practices of use and appropriation (Lesser and Stallybrass 2008).

Venus and Adonis was a hit. The second of sixteen editions before 1636 was printed by Field for Harrison in 1594, and a third almost certainly in 1595, though the surviving copy lacks the first quire, including the title page carrying the date of publication. For this edition, Field and Harrison reduced the poem from quarto to octavo. An early purchaser bound it together with Spenser's *Amoretti*, Daniel's *Delia and Rosamond augmented*, Barnfield's *Cynthia*, Mary (Sidney) Herbert's translation of Garnier's *Antonie* and Constable's *Diana*.[4] *Delia and Rosamond augmented* (1594 and 1595) added Daniel's *Cleopatra* to his 1592 complaint, forging a connection between the sonnet sequences and Herbert's closet drama. *Diana* was another 'augmented' text, first published in 1592. *Amoretti*, *Antonie* and *Cynthia* were each published for the first time in 1595. Each edition of *Delia* featured a title page Latin motto, as did *Cynthia* and the 1595 *Diana*, further evidence of the commonplace poetic use of the classical epigraph.

The collection prompts us to read Shakespeare's poems not as discrete units but as malleable and flexible objects in conversation with a range of texts.[5] Early modern readers 'physically aggregated, resituated, and customized' their books, creating new contexts of meaning and interpretation (Knight 2013: 8; see also Knight's discussion of composite collections as 'embodied frameworks for reading, canons in miniature, or models for composition', in this volume). Some imaginative combinations went beyond the book: the recent Arden editors of the poems note that 'Lucretia' could be encountered in a wide range of visual and material locations: 'in shop signs, printers' devices, illustrated initials and seal rings [including Olivia's in *Twelfth Night*], as well as in paintings and tapestries' (Duncan-Jones and Woudhuysen 2007: 35). The early reader who gathered these texts was influenced by their generic continuities, but also, perhaps, by their proximity on the London bookstalls, since the stationers who sold these books (Richard Smith, William Ponsonby, Humphrey Lownes and Simon Waterson) all had premises in Paul's churchyard.

---

[4] This copy is now Folger Shakespeare Library PR2749.Y4 n.d.
[5] The Bodleian copy of 1596 *Venus and Adonis* contains a note from Edmond Malone recording that it was part of a 'small volume of rare old poetry', sold in 1698. Arch. G.d.44 (1).

When compared with these companions, rather than contrasted with the plays, Shakespeare's poems look less determinedly authorial. Neither features Shakespeare's name on the title page.[6] Barnfield's *Cynthia* and 1592 *Delia* similarly possess no title page attributions, but signed dedications. 1594 *Delia*, however, announces that it is 'By *Samuel Daniel*'; *Diana* that it is 'By H. C.'; the *Amoretti* that it was '*Written not long since* by Edmonde *Spenser*'; and *Antonie* that it has been '*Doone into English by the* Countesse of *Pembroke*'. Shakespeare's verse publications are less insistent about authorial identity than, for example, Spenser's or Daniel's. This pattern is anticipated in the Stationers' Company Registers. Though, in 1609, Thomas Thorpe would enter 'a book called Shakespeares sonnettes', the narrative poems were identified simply as 'Venus and Adonis' and 'the ravyshement of Lucrece' (Arber 1875–94: 2.630, 648). None of Shakespeare's early printers named the author when they registered his works. In contrast, the entries for *Amoretti and Epithalamion* and *Antonie* pre-empt their title pages, recording that *Amoretti* was 'written not longe since by Edmund Spenser' and *Antonie* was written by Garnier and 'donne into Englishe by the Countesse of Pembroke'.

The collection discussed above is mirrored in William Covell's celebration of English poets, *Polimanteia* (1595). Among many others, Covell commends Mary Herbert, 'the pure flowing streame of Chrystallin Spenser' and 'thy courte-deare-verse happie *Daniell*' (R3r, Q2v, R2v). Written by a Cambridge graduate in praise of the universities, and published by the University Printer, *Polimanteia* attests to the popularity of Shakespeare's poems in student circles, and the circulation of his books in a self-consciously poetic, provincial milieu. Next to the description of Daniel's 'dearly beloued *Delia*, and fortunatelie fortunate *Cleopatra*', a marginal note proclaims:

All praise
worthy.
Lucrecia
Sweet Shak-
speare.
Eloquent
Gaueston.
Wanton
Adonis.
Watsons
heyre.

---

[6] *Lucrece* would first do so in 1616; *Venus and Adonis* saw both title and author appropriated on the title page of the third edition of *The passionate pilgrim* (1612), which promises *Certaine amorous sonnets, betweene Venus and Adonis, newly corrected and augmented. By W. Shakespere.*

Drayton's *Piers Gaveston* pre-empts *Venus and Adonis* in many aspects of its presentation: a Latin tag, no author name on the title page and a dedication with the author's name. Thomas Watson's works, however, make much of their authorship. The title page to *The hekatompathia or passionate centurie of loue* (1582) explains that its contents have been 'Composed by *Thomas Watson* Gentleman', whilst *The first sett, of Italian madrigalls englished* (1590) proclaims it is '*By Thomas Watson Gentleman*' and *Amintæ gaudia* (1592) states 'Authore Thoma VVAtsono'. In contrast, *Venus* and *Lucrece* make no strong statement about Shakespeare's authorship. They present themselves as fashionable poetry publications – a decision almost certainly influenced more by Field and Harrison than by the poet. Viewed from the perspective of print, not only are the poems less thematically distinct from the early plays than their critical history suggests, their differing presentation is also much less significant than is routinely claimed: the plays look like printed drama of the 1590s, whilst the poems follow the conventions of printed poetry at the same moment.

Even the dedications may have been a product of print convention, increasingly a staple of the well-made book. This is not to suggest that Shakespeare did not use the dedication to advance his own ends, though the relationship between manuscript and printed text remains obscure. The dedication to *Venus and Adonis* suggests that the poem functioned as a bid for patronage, tentatively (and conventionally) claiming 'I know not how I shall offend in dedicating my vnpolisht lines to your Lordship' (¶1r). Southampton was just beginning to emerge as a patron: in 1593, Barnabe Barnes included a verse epistle celebrating the Earl in *Parthenophil and Parthenope*, whilst in 1594, Thomas Nashe's *The unfortunate traveller* recommended itself to Southampton. The dedication to *Lucrece* suggests Shakespeare's bid was successful, testifying to 'the warrant I haue of your Honourable disposition' (A2r).

'What company is this?' Shakespeare's early plays in print

Many scholars align Shakespeare's turn to narrative verse with a turn to noble patronage, arguing that Shakespeare used his poetry to bid for 'the help of a fashionable patron' in the absence of a theatrical income (*Oxford Dictionary of National Biography*). Yet the theatrical companies too depended on the support and advocacy of influential patrons. The shifting landscape of noble favour is mapped on the title pages of the dramatic quartos, from *Titus Andronicus*, 'Plaide by the Right Honourable the Earle of *Darbie*, Earle of *Pembrooke*, and Earle of *Sussex* their Seruants', in 1594, to *Richard II*, 'publikely acted by the Right Honourable the Lord Chamberlaine his seruants', in 1598. Shakespeare's early quarto title pages identify not where the play was performed, but by whose players, with the emphasis upon the patron, identified by name or title.[7]

The reopening of the theatres was accompanied with a marked increase in dramatic printing, with twenty-seven plays entered into the Stationers' Company Registers in 1593–94, fourteen of which – alongside a number of unregistered plays – had been printed by 1595. The year 1594 saw the performance of the three *Henry VI* plays at Edward Alleyn's Rose theatre and the publication of *The first part of the contention*, printed by Creede for Thomas Millington. Its title page imprint reveals the place of publication, the name of the printer and bookseller and the main site at which the book was sold. This short, conventional text had its own social and geographical effects, reinforcing Londoners' mental maps of their changing city. For readers further from the capital, imprints might offer a space to imagine the metropolis, especially in *The first part of the contention*, where, to fill blank space after the play's concluding lines, Creede repeated the bottom half of his title page. The text ends with England on the brink of civil war, Henry VI 'fled to London', and York and Warwick determined to pursue him there, with a rousing cry of 'to London all' (H4r). Creede's pragmatic decision to reproduce his imprint relocates the national geopolitics of Shakespeare's history play to a contemporary urban landscape, reminding metropolitan readers that the history the text tells is, at least in part, the history of the city they inhabit.[8]

The most lamentable romaine tragedie of Titus Andronicus was registered and printed in 1594 by Danter, but sold by Millington and Edward White.[9] When he registered *Titus Andronicus* on 6 February 1594, Danter entered 'the ballad thereof' for the same price of sixpence.[10] Shakespeare's name is not recorded, in contrast to Ling and Busby's registration, a few lines above, of 'a booke called Cornelia / Thomas Kydd being the Authour'.

---

[7] The exceptions are *Henry VI, Part 2* and *Henry IV, Part 2*, which offer details of plot, action, and character, and *Love's labours lost*, printed 'As it vvas presented before her Highnes this last Christmas'.

[8] Creede's topography is notably more precise than the play's references to London, which are reworked in the Folio *Henry VI, Part 2*. I thank Richard Rowland for drawing this to my attention.

[9] Erne notes that *Titus* has the distinction of being the first playbook to be printed with an initial blank leaf (2013: 117–18), suggesting the increasing status of plays. It was not, however, the first book Danter had printed with a blank leaf; stationers simply followed many of their usual practices when preparing plays for print, rather than singling them out either as especially valuable, or as especially ephemeral.

[10] Arber 1875–94: 2.644.

More than half the texts Danter registered were ballads, quick to print and easy to sell; his co-entry of book and ballad reminds us of the mutuality of public theatre and itinerant popular song. Millington launched his bookselling career in 1594 with *Titus Andronicus, The first part of the contention*, and a pamphlet recounting *Newes from Brest*. Sonia Massai notes that *Titus* and the two *Henry VI* plays were published soon after the dissolution of Pembroke's Men in 1593, and Millington and his collaborators may have profited as the players disposed of their stock (2007: 98).

Shakespeare's writings made up a significant proportion of the seventeen extant texts Millington published, but his record of publication remains too sparse to suggest his output 'was strongly focused on the plays of Shakespeare' (Erne 2013: 164; see Table 5.2). In 1595, Millington published four texts, including *The true tragedie of Richard Duke of York*. Shakespeare re-emerges in 1600, with *The chronicle history of Henry the fift*, and new editions of *1 Contention* and *Richard Duke of York*. If any connecting thread can be found between the books in which Millington had an interest, it is the interrelationship of foreign and national politics, and the revelation of God's providential designs, rather than a specific interest in Shakespeare. The rights to *Titus Andronicus* passed to Millington from Danter, as did those to the robber Luke Hutton's scaffold speech in 1598, indicating an ongoing association between the two men, which involved the transfer of rights in texts.

In contrast, Edward White's investment in *Titus Andronicus* in the same year he published Greene's *The honorable historie of frier Bacon, and frier Bongay*, Marlowe's *The massacre at Paris* and the second edition of Thomas Kyd's *The Spanish tragedie*, in partnership with Abel Jeffes, whose rights in the play he had infringed two years earlier, brought Shakespeare's play into a distinctly dramatic milieu. The connection between *Titus* and *The Spanish tragedie* is reinforced by their long titles' insistence upon the plays' 'lamentable' trajectories. 'Lamentable' had been a term predominantly attached to accounts of miraculous omens, current affairs and religious polemic. Between 1592 and 1600, however, the word appeared on twenty-five title pages, only eight of which were not play texts. The 'lamentable' events of Shakespeare's first 'Romaine' play might, in 1594, have chimed with a readerly hunger for portents and providential news, but by the second quarto in 1600 the term was a dramatic marker, tying the printed text to its theatrical effects.

The year 1594 also saw the publication of *A pleasant conceited historie, called the taming of a shrew*, a play whose relationship to Shakespeare's *The taming of the shrew* is debated by scholars (see, most

Table 5.2 *Books published and entered in the Stationers' Company Registers by Thomas Millington*

Year	Publications and entries
1594	Shakespeare, *Titus Andronicus*. Shakespeare, *The first part of the contention*. *Newes from Brest* (London: Peter Short for Thomas Millington). STC 18654. Entered (with Ling) Christopher Marlowe, *The Jew of Malta*, published as *The famous tragedy of the rich Iew of Malta* (London: John Beale for Nicholas Vavasour, 1633). STC 17412.
1595	Shakespeare, *The true tragedie of Richard Duke of York*. *A most certaine report of a monster borne at Oteringham in Holdernesse* (London: Peter Short, sold by Thomas Millington). STC 18895.5. *The copie of a letter sent by the French king* (London: Peter Short for Thomas Millington). STC 13119. *The decree of the court of Parliament against Iohn Chastel* (London: Peter Short for Thomas Millington). STC 5066. Entered *The Norfolke gentleman his last will and testament* (London: John Wright, 1635?). STC 18644.
1596	Entered *A worthy example of a vertuous wife* (London, c. 1625). STC 10611.7.
1597	Geneviève, Petau de Maulette, *Deuoreux. Vertues teares for the losse of the most christian King Henry* (London: James Roberts for Thomas Millington). STC 19793. Entered Thomas Deloney, *The pleasant historie of Iohn Winchcomb, in his yonguer* [sic] *yeares called Iack of Newbery* (London: Humphrey Lownes, sold by Cuthbert Wright, 1626). STC 6560.
1598	Luke Hutton, *Luke Huttons lamentation* (London: for Thomas Millington). STC 14032. *The true lamentable discourse of the burning of Teuerton* (London: Thomas Purfoot for Thomas Millington). STC 24093. Entered *The householders new-yeeres gift* (London: [Elizabeth Purslowe] for Francis Coules, c. 1640). STC 13852.
1600	Shakespeare, *The cronicle history of Henry the fift* (London: Thomas Creede for Thomas Millington and John Busby). STC 22289. Shakespeare, *The first part of the contention* (London: Valentine Simmes for Thomas Millington). STC 26100. Shakespeare, *The true tragedie of Richarde Duke of Yorke* (London: William White for Thomas Millington). STC 21006a. *The wonderfull example of God shewed upon Jasper Coningham* (London: for Thomas Millington). STC 5631.3.
1603	Henry Chettle, *Englands mourning garment* (London: [Edward Short?] for Thomas Millington). STC 5121 and 5122 (5122 'sold by Walter Burre'). *The true narration of the entertainment of his Royall Maiestie* (London: Thomas Creede for Thomas Millington). STC 17153.

recently, Marino 2011: ch. 2). The play made no claims to a Shakespearean heritage, locating its authority in having been 'sundry times acted by the *Right honorable the Earle of* Pembrook his seruants'. Alongside *Henry VI, Part 3*, Shakespeare's drama was represented on the page in 1595, at least for unwary readers, by *The lamentable tragedie of Locrine*, published by Creede. After a lengthy, descriptive title, this play declares it has been 'Newly set foorth, overseene and corrected, By *VV. S*'. It was also Creede who, in 1605, suggested that *The London prodigal* was 'By VVilliam Shakespeare'. *Locrine*'s title page is laid out in Creede's usual, though not ubiquitous, house style. A title in Roman type is followed by an advertisement of the contents, an italic addition (more content for the plays, the translator's name or a Latin tag for other genres), Creede's memorable device – a naked woman clutching a book whilst being scourged by a hand emerging from the clouds, framed by the motto 'Viressit [*sic*] vulnere veritas' ('Truth flourishes through being wounded') – and an imprint. *Locrine* is, on first impression, visually aligned not only with *Henry VI, Part 2*, but the anonymous *The true tragedie of Richard the third* (1594), Thomas Lodge and Robert Greene's *A looking glasse for London and England* (1594) and William Warner's 1595 *Menaecmi*, as well as non-dramatic texts ranging from a celebration of the military exploits of Drake and Hawkins to 'Greene's' deathbed confession.

The connection to *Menaecmi* is the most tenuous: different capitals mark the Latin title, and, where other plays detail the action, this states that it has been 'chosen purposely from out the rest, as least harmefulle, and yet most delightfull'. Nonetheless, Creede's house style sets in conversation a series of dramatic and prose works. The 'Creede effect' troubles the recent critical distinction between the mechanical or jobbing printer and the discriminating bookseller, specializing in particular authors or genres.[11] Alongside the evidence of copy entered by printers (Field, Danter, Short) and published in 'a shared-risk, shared-reward arrangement' (Syme 2013: 31) with booksellers, the shaping influence of Creede's printshop suggests the artificiality of any firm division between roles in the geographically, socially and economically close-knit world of the London stationers.

In 1596, Thomas Scarlet printed *The raigne of King Edward the third* for Burby, and Field printed a further edition of *Venus and Adonis* for Harrison. Burby's commitment to Shakespeare publishing should not be overstated: he published second editions of *Romeo and Juliet* (1599) and *Love's labour's lost* (1598) and two editions of *Edward III* (the second in

---

[11] For an influential example, see Lesser 2004: 28.

1599), a play which no evidence suggests that contemporary readers attributed to Shakespeare. The play's insecure authorial status is mirrored in its title page's lack of specificity: it claims only to be 'Printed for Cuthbert Burby. 1596' and to have been *sundrie times plaied about the Citie of London*', a formula which Burby repeated on the successful contemporaneous *A knacke to know an honest man*. Burby's publications of the 1590s place Shakespeare firmly in the context of London print authorship, next to popular writers including Greene, Nashe and Lyly. Most of Burby's ventures subsequent to 1602, however, were sermons or works of practical divinity written by some of the most popular preachers of the day: Arthur Dent, John Dove, John Downham, Henry Smith and Christopher Sutton. Whilst they may reflect Burby's mainstream Protestantism, these texts were also sought after by readers. Given their length, it makes sense that Burby published them only once he had built up capital. The move to religious printing represents a change in Burby's published output, but scarcely 'a sudden and astonishing conversion' (Erne 2013: 166).

Alongside Q1 *Richard II* and *Richard III*, 1597 welcomed *An excellent conceited tragedie of Romeo and Iuliet*, a play which would lose its witty 'conceited' status to become '*excellent and lamentable*' in Burby's second quarto. Whilst *Romeo and Juliet*'s title page attributes the printing to Danter, material evidence reveals that Danter printed only the first four quires. The rest was done by Edward Allde, who printed over 700 items during a long career. Similarly, whilst the first quire of *Richard III* was set in the house of Valentine Simmes, the remaining text was printed in Short's workshop. Allde's smaller typeface means he fits thirty-six, rather than Danter's thirty-two, lines on a page. The Friar's demand, in response to Romeo's transfer of his love, 'Holy *S. Francis*, what a change is here?', occupies the left-hand side of the opening in which the change of printers is visible, functioning as much as a comment on the changing face of the book as on Romeo's mutable affections.

Allde's portion of *Romeo and Juliet* is visually distinct from any other Shakespeare play, yet it materializes the playwright's concerns in an unexpected fashion. Woodcut devices are used liberally from G2v onwards, where Allde's compositor realized he had overestimated the number of sheets of paper required, and needed to fill space. In other quartos, printers instead squeezed the play to fit, as in Q2 *Richard II*, which shifts from stage directions elegantly centred between lines to directions which, from quire G onwards, sit in the margin. Allde's devices recall the use of decorations in sonnet sequences, where individual poems were often enclosed in floral frames. Repeated patterns forged links between books 'according to a visual code that overrides, and may take no account of, their contents' (Fleming 2011: 54). Whilst Q1 *Romeo and Juliet* famously omits elements of the play that refer to the sonnet tradition (Folio Mercutio mocks 'the numbers that Petrarch flowed in'; in both Q2 and the Folio the verse prologue is amended to form a sonnet), its physical form invokes precisely that tradition.[12]

It was in 1598 that '*William Shake-speare*' finally appeared on a printed title page. Two editions of *The tragedie of King Richard the second*, printed by Simmes for Andrew Wise, and *The tragedie of King Richard the third*, printed by Creede for Wise, featured Shakespeare's name; *The history of Henrie the fourth*, printed for Wise by Short, did not. *A pleasant conceited comedie called, loues labours lost*, printed by William White for Burby, suggests the existence of an earlier edition (now lost), claiming to be 'Newly corrected and augmented | By W. Shakespere'; the line break imposes an uneasy division between the work of revision and a claim for authorship.[13] Wise is perhaps the first stationer who can be described as specializing in Shakespeare, whose plays make up eleven of the twenty-one items he published between 1593 and 1602.

Shakespeare's name appeared in print twice more in 1598. Celebrating English poetry, Richard Barnfield commemorated Shakespeare's 'hony-flowing Vaine', citing his '*Venus*' and '*Lucrece* (sweete, and chaste)' (E2r). Where Barnfield invokes Shakespeare the poet, Francis Meres's *Palladis tamia* offers an 'intermedial and transgeneric' Shakespeare (Halasz 2013: 20) in whom 'the sweete wittie soule of *Ouid*' is reincarnated (Oo1v–Oo2r), a critical response that reflects the physical presentation of the poems, as well as the self-consciously Ovidian content of plays like *A midsummer night's dream*. Alongside *Love's labour's lost*, *Richard II*, *Richard III*, *Henry IV*, *Titus Andronicus*, and *Romeo and Juliet*, Meres catalogues two plays – *The Dream* and *The merchant of Venice* – that would not appear in quarto until 1600, three – *The two gentlemen of Verona*, *The comedy of errors*, and *King John* – not printed until the First Folio of 1623, and the mysterious *Love's labours won*, perhaps a lost play, perhaps an alternative title for one of the extant comedies. Meres does not mention the *Henry VI* plays, despite their

---

[12] Lesser reaches a similar conclusion in his forthcoming Luminary Shakespeare *Romeo and Juliet* app.
[13] 'Only twenty-four out of 836 single editions, and seven out of forty-five collections' listed in Greg's *Bibliography of the English Printed Drama to the Restoration* 'inform their readers about the quality, provenance, and reliability of the printer's copy' (Massai 2011: 91). Between 1594 and 1598, eighteen out of forty-three playbook editions carried an author attribution on their title pages, just over 40 per cent (Erne 2013: 95).

recent presence both in print and on stage. He does, however, celebrate the narrative poems and the circulation of Shakespeare's 'sugred Sonnets' among his 'priuate friends', testifying to the vibrancy of early modern manuscript publication.

Like Covell and Barnfield, Meres situates Shakespeare in relation to his contemporaries, and to the greats of Latin and vernacular Italian literature, imaginatively recombining Shakespeare's texts just as purchasers and publishers brought them into new and changing physical contexts. Produced by two stationers, Burby and Short, both of whom had previously had a hand in composing Shakespeare's drama upon the page, *Palladis tamia* highlights not only how the decisions of book trade agents contributed to the emergence of a literary canon, but the need to restore Shakespeare's early texts to the contexts of the bookstalls on which they first appeared, and the readers who first encountered them. Shakespeare's writings were physically and conceptually close to ballads, prose pamphlets and plague tracts, as well as to dramatic texts, sermons and fashionable poetry collections. Making visible the overlapping networks of theatrical performance, patronage and print publication, the material forms of early printed Shakespeare situate the national, classical and literary landscapes of their contents within an equally rich and vibrant landscape of performance and publication, re-creating and transforming those spaces for readers and buyers in the layout and content of the printed page.

CHAPTER 6

Shakespeare as leading playwright in print, 1598–1608/09

Alan B. Farmer

The emergence of Shakespeare as a leading playwright in print can be dated quite precisely, to the year 1598, when for the first time he was named as the author of a printed play. Four editions of three different plays were published that year with Shakespeare's name on the title page: *Love's Labour's Lost*, *Richard III*, and two editions of *Richard II*. Not only was this burst of editions and authorship attributions unprecedented – no other playwright had ever been advertised as an author of four playbooks in a single year – but it was also a harbinger of even greater success for Shakespeare's plays in print. In the ensuing decade, from 1598 to 1609, Shakespeare would become England's best-selling dramatist and, indeed, one of the top-selling authors in the entire English book trade.[1] Twice as many editions of Shakespeare's plays were published in these years as of any other playwright, and Shakespeare was named as an author on twice as many play title pages as any other dramatist.[2] Already successful on stage, Shakespeare's plays were clearly proving to be popular with publishers and

---

[1] Three types of Shakespearean playbooks were published from 1598 to 1609: plays now ascribed to Shakespeare and sold with his name on the title page (twenty-one editions); plays now ascribed to Shakespeare but published without naming an author (nine editions, excluding *Taming of A Shrew*, which is sometimes attributed to Shakespeare); and plays now ascribed to another author but with Shakespeare's name on the title page (two editions, *The London Prodigal* (1605) and *The Yorkshire Tragedy* (1608)). In addition, *Thomas Lord Cromwell* (1602) and *The Puritan* (1607) were issued with the author attribution 'W.S.', which may have been intended to suggest Shakespeare was their author since he was the only professional playwright with those initials to appear in print before 1615. In total, twenty-three editions of playbooks were published in this period with Shakespeare identified as the author, plus two more naming W.S. All my publication figures are derived from *DEEP: Database of Early English Playbooks* 2007 and Pollard and Redgrave 1976–91 (*A Short-Title Catalogue of Books Printed in England, Scotland, & Ireland and of English Books Printed Abroad, 1475–1640: STC*).

[2] Fourteen editions of plays by John Marston and fourteen by Thomas Heywood were published from 1598 to 1609, compared to thirty editions of plays by Shakespeare. Eleven playbooks were published with John Marston's name on the title page (and two others with 'I.M.'), whereas twenty-three playbooks were published with Shakespeare's name (and two others with 'W.S.'). Only three playbooks named Heywood as an author.

readers. The same was true of his poetry, too. Multiple editions of Shakespeare's poems made him one of the best-selling poets in this period.[3] No other English author writing fiction – as drama, verse, or prose – exceeded the thirty-five editions of playbooks and poetry books published under Shakespeare's name. Beginning in 1598, Shakespeare was unquestionably England's top-selling dramatic poet.

The popularity of Shakespeare in print has recently been examined by Lukas Erne in *Shakespeare and the Book Trade* (2013), in which he convincingly demonstrates that Shakespeare's 'arrival in the book trade was sudden and massive' and that he 'had a commanding bibliographic presence among the dramatists of his time' (2, 18). The publication history of Shakespeare's plays and poems, Erne proposes, suggests that Shakespeare wanted to be read and was acutely aware of the success of his works in print (2013: 23; see also Erne 2003). Erne's project grew out of the increased scholarly attention during the past couple of decades given to the printing of Shakespeare's plays in early modern England, scholarship that has often, unlike Erne, endorsed the view that Shakespeare was indifferent to their appearance in print (2013: 2). Although Shakespeare has come to be recognized as a hugely successful author in the early modern book trade, critics have nevertheless continued to argue that he was uninterested in, and perhaps even opposed to, the printing of his plays.

This long-established view of Shakespeare's indifference to print appears repeatedly in biographies (Schoenbaum 1991: 30; Honan 1998: 115; Greenblatt 2004: 194; Shapiro 2010: 225), in introductions to standard editions of his plays (Taylor 1997: 2; Mowat and Werstine 1993: lii), and in studies of authorship and the early modern book trade (Bentley 1971: 280; Brooks 1998: 55; Loewenstein 2002: 100; Murphy 2003: 16; Grafton 2011: 148). To quote one prominent example, G. Blakemore Evans writes in *The Riverside Shakespeare* (1974a) that 'there is essentially no evidence that Shakespeare was himself at all concerned with preserving an authoritative text of his plays for future readers' (28). Frequently underlying this idea is

---

[3] From 1598 to 1609, twelve editions of poetry books were published under Shakespeare's name: *Venus and Adonis* (five editions) and *Lucrece* (four editions), each with an epistle by Shakespeare dedicated to the Earl of Southampton; *The Passionate Pilgrim* (two editions around 1599) and *Sonnets* (one edition in 1609), each with Shakespeare's name on the title page. The first edition of *The Passionate Pilgrim* is incomplete and lacks its title page, but it is dated to [1599?] in the *STC*. The second edition was published in 1599 with Shakespeare's name on the title page, so it is certainly possible that the first edition also included it. Not all of the poems in this collection were actually written by Shakespeare. The only poets with more editions of their verse published in this period with their names on the title pages or in the preliminaries were Samuel Rowlands (twenty-two editions), Michael Drayton (sixteen editions), and Nicholas Breton (thirteen editions).

the belief that the printed texts of Shakespeare's plays are too corrupt and contain too many 'gross errors' for Shakespeare to have been involved in their printing (Schoenbaum 1991: 30; Wells 1997: 270). According to this line of thinking, Shakespeare's plays were printed too often in texts with egregious typographical mistakes and stylistic faults, suggesting a lack of authorial concern about their publication in accurate texts. Further, Shakespeare's playbooks lack any paratextual material, such as dedications or addresses to the reader, which would indicate the author's involvement in their printing. The presence of so many gross errors and the absence of any authorizing paratextual material have helped solidify the perception that Shakespeare wrote his plays with only theatrical performance in mind, not for publication in print.

In this chapter I want to extend Erne's skeptical examination of this critical orthodoxy by considering the unusual ways in which Shakespeare's plays were sold to readers in the dramatist's own lifetime, evidence that has too often been dismissed or overlooked. As this chapter will show, Shakespeare was not merely England's best-selling playwright from 1598 to 1609, but one of the top-selling authors in the entire book trade. This recontextualization leads to a second argument about the advertisement of Shakespeare's authorship by the publishers of his plays, particularly Cuthbert Burby, Andrew Wise, Nicholas Ling, and Matthew Law. Beginning in 1598, these publishers started identifying Shakespeare as an author conspicuously concerned with the printing of his plays in 'corrected' and 'augmented' texts. These editions provide suggestive evidence that Shakespeare may have taken more of an interest in the publication of his plays – in corrected and revised texts – than any other dramatic author through the Restoration, and arguably more than any author active in the English book trade during the late sixteenth and early seventeenth centuries. Although Ben Jonson is usually held up as the playwright most committed to print, Shakespeare was being sold as a dramatic author dedicated to the printing of his plays in correct texts before even Jonson was. Ultimately, I want to suggest that the publication history of Shakespeare's plays should cause us to rethink our narratives of the popularity of Shakespeare in the early modern book trade, of the textual transmission of his plays and poems, and ultimately of the history of Shakespeare's authorship.

Selling Shakespeare: 'corrected' and 'augmented'

While it is increasingly understood that Shakespeare was a best-selling playwright, the popularity of Shakespeare in the larger early modern book trade has still not yet been widely recognized. Instead, what often happens is that popular authors writing in other genres are invoked in order to diminish the impressive number of early modern editions of Shakespeare that were printed.[4] Within the context of the entire book trade, however, Shakespeare was one of the top selling authors *in any genre* from 1598 to 1609, when thirty-five editions (twenty-three editions of fifteen plays and twelve editions of four works of poetry) were sold with his name on the title page or in the preliminaries (thirty-seven if the 'W.S.' on *Thomas Lord Cromwell* [1602] and *The Puritan* [1607] are considered attributions to Shakespeare). This total makes Shakespeare the author with the fourth highest number of editions published under his name in this period. The only authors with more named editions are Thomas Sternhold and Samuel Hopkins (seventy-two editions of four different versions of their translation of the Psalms); William Perkins (sixty editions of thirty-three works); and King James I (thirty-eight editions of twenty works).[5] Shakespeare was therefore both the leading playwright in print from 1598 to 1609 and a best-selling author more generally, who was outsold only by the most popular title in the entire early modern period (Sternhold and Hopkins's *Whole Book of Psalms*), by the newly installed King of England, and by an influential theologian whose death in 1602 led to a surge of posthumous publications.[6]

The significance of Shakespeare in the book trade during these years has led Erne and others to conjecture that Shakespeare must have been cognizant of the printing and selling of his own works.[7] Supporting this theory – and the central concern of this chapter – is the distinctive way in which Shakespeare's authorship was advertised by publishers: as a revising author attentive to the accuracy of the printed texts of his plays. Few other

---

[4] See, for instance, Andrew Murphy's comparison of Shakespeare and Henry Smith (2003: 416 n. 54); and Kari Konkola's comparison of Shakespeare and William Perkins (2000: 25–6).

[5] Only a few writers had even as many as twenty-five editions published in this period in which they were identified as the author: Hugh Broughton (thirty-five editions, three of which advertise 'H.B.'); Joseph Hall (thirty-two editions, five of which advertise 'I. H.'); Nicholas Breton (thirty-two editions, five of which advertise 'N.B.'); Arthur Dent (twenty-six editions); Thomas Dekker (twenty-five editions, one of which advertises 'T.D.'); and Henry Smith (twenty-five editions). In order to compute these figures, I examined every entry in the *STC* for books printed from 1598 to 1609, and most often using *Early English Books Online* (*EEBO*) and the *English Short Title Catalogue* (*ESTC*), sought to determine whether each edition includes an author attribution on its title page or somewhere within the volume itself.

[6] All the editions of King James I's works that name him as the author were published from 1603 to 1609; *The Trew Law of Free Monarchies* (Edinburgh, 1598) was published under a pseudonym and *Basilikon Doron* (Edinburgh, 1599) with no author attribution. Seventeen editions of Perkins's works were published from 1598 to 1602 (3.4 per year), but forty-three from 1603 to 1609 (6.1 per year).

[7] See also Bruster 2013a.

authors writing in any genre were being sold as so committed to the correctness of their printed works.

Six Shakespeare plays were reprinted from 1598 to 1609 with claims that their texts had been revised in some fashion. These can be divided into two groups. The first comprises three plays with title pages that directly state Shakespeare revised the plays himself but whose texts are very similar to earlier editions: the probable second edition of *Love's Labour's Lost* (1598), 'Newly corrected and augmented | By W. Shakespere'; the third edition of *Henry IV, Part 1* (1599), 'Newly corrected by W. Shake-speare'; and the third edition of *Richard III* (1602), 'Newly augmented, | By William Shakespeare' (Figures 6.1–6.3).[8] The second group includes three Shakespeare plays published with texts that substantially differ from earlier editions but that do not explicitly state it was Shakespeare who altered them: the anonymous second edition of *Romeo and Juliet* (1599), 'Newly corrected, augmented, and | amended';[9] the second edition of *Hamlet* (1604), 'Newly imprinted and enlarged to almost as much | again as it was, according to the true and perfect | Coppie', which is preceded by the authorship attribution, 'By William Shakespeare'; and the second issue of the fourth edition of *Richard II* (1608), 'With new additions of the Parlia- | ment Sceane, and the deposing | of King Richard', which is followed by information about the play's performance by the King's Men at the Globe Theater, and then '*By William Shakespeare*'. In total, from 1598 to 1609, publishers brought out ten editions of these six Shakespeare plays with advertisements of corrected or enlarged texts. And publishers continued to print 'editorial pledges' on subsequent editions so that by the time of Shakespeare's death, in 1616, fourteen editions of these plays had been published with advertisements of revision.[10]

If these title pages are true, they would suggest that Shakespeare revised his printed plays and was committed to the accuracy of their printing. Scholars, however, routinely caution that these pledges are best considered deceptive exaggerations, not statements of fact. W. W. Greg, for instance, noted in 1942 that the title pages of *Love's Labour's Lost*, *Henry IV, Part 1*, and *Richard III* all announce the plays were revised by Shakespeare.

---

[8] On the relationship between the probable lost first edition of *Love's Labour's Lost* and the 1598 edition, see Woudhuysen 1998: 298–327.
[9] The year before this edition was printed, Francis Meres identified Shakespeare as the author of *Romeo and Juliet* (sig. 2O2r).
[10] The phrase 'editorial pledges' is from Massai 2007: 11. Editorial pledges were typically repeated from one reprint edition to another, which had a sound logic underlying it. Even if the third edition of *Romeo and Juliet* (1609) uses the same the editorial pledge as the second edition and had not itself been 'newly' altered, the pledge still serves to distinguish the text of the third edition from that of the uncorrected, unaugmented, and unamended first edition.

A

PLEASANT

Conceited Comedie
CALLED,

Loues labors loſt.

As it vvas preſented before her Highnes
this laſt Chriſtmas.

Newly corrected and augmented
By W. Shakeſpere.

Imprinted at London by W.W.
for *Cutbert Burby.*
1598.

Figure 6.1 The probable second edition of *Love's Labour's Lost* (1598)

THE
HISTORY OF
HENRIE THE
FOVRTH;

With the battell at Shrewsburie,
betweene the King and Lord Henry
Percy, *surnamed* Henry Hotspur of the North.

VVith the humorous conceits of Sir
Iohn Falstalffe.

Newly corrected by *W. Shake-speare.*

AT LONDON,
Printed by *S. S.* for *Andrew VVise*, dwelling
in Paules Churchyard, at the signe of
the Angell. 1599.

Figure 6.2 The third edition of *Henry IV, Part 1* (1599)

Figure 6.3 The third edition of *Richard III* (1602)

He went on to reason, though, that the punctuation on these title pages must be 'misleading' because *Love's Labour's Lost* was probably 'not a reprint at all' and because in the cases of '*1 Henry IV* and *Richard III* there was no ground whatever for the assertion that the text had been corrected or augmented'. What each title page *should* have publicized was 'that Shakespeare was the author of the play, and that the text had been revised', i.e., by someone else, an interpretation, Greg acknowledges, that requires denying what the title pages themselves actually say (1954: xlii n.1). This type of rejection of the claims of authorial revision on Shakespeare's playbooks has commonly been repeated by later editors and critics. As Stanley Wells writes in his overview of the first extant edition of *Love's Labour's Lost*, the play 'abounds in gross errors', leading him to conclude 'that the title-page claim is a publisher's exaggeration' (1997: 270). Or, as David Scott Kastan comments in his Arden edition of *Henry IV, Part 1*, the title page claim on the play's third edition is 'a marketing ploy rather than a bibliographic fact' (2002b: 111). The revisions made to *Romeo and Juliet, Hamlet,* and *Richard II* meanwhile are typically credited to members of Shakespeare's company, to annotating readers, to publishers, to anyone other than Shakespeare.[11] What these title pages do not provide, according to most scholars, is evidence that Shakespeare himself participated in the correction or augmentation of the printed texts of his plays.

These playbooks thus raise the question of whether these editorial pledges should be considered credible statements of authorial revision or whether they are better seen as disingenuous blurbs added by unscrupulous stationers. Are the title pages of *Love's Labour's Lost, Henry IV, Part 1,* and *Richard III* deceptive marketing ploys, or did the publishers believe the claims about authorial revision they included in their editions? Should we likewise think Shakespeare was uninvolved in the publication of two other revised plays that carry his name (*Hamlet* and *Richard II*) and of one that does not (*Romeo and Juliet*)? In considering such questions, scholars have yet to situate their claims about authorial revision in an analysis of the larger market of printed plays in early modern England, of the larger market of the entire English book trade during this period (1598–1609), or of the other books brought out by

---

[11] As Joseph Loewenstein has suggested, the 'editorial or revising Shakespeare' on play title pages 'was a useful figure, a printer's ornament' (2002: 101). Loewenstein curiously reasons that Shakespeare became a revising author by noticing editorial pledges others had added to the title pages of his plays, rather than from his own authorial efforts: 'having seen the title pages of the most recent editions of *Love's Labours Lost, Romeo and Juliet,* and *1 Henry IV,* Shakespeare would be confirmed in understanding himself as an author who both revises and rectifies' (102).

the four publishers who first added these editorial pledges. Doing so indicates how unusual these types of pledges were, which can help us begin to reevaluate these statements and whether they should continue to be seen as exaggerated and misleading.

Editorial pledges: categories of revision

Editorial pledges on title pages, although easy in theory to identify, can be tricky to differentiate in practice. Pledges vary in what they claim about the accuracy of a book's text, about the kinds of revision that have taken place, and about the persons responsible for the revision. Most broadly, editorial pledges can be grouped into three categories. The first includes claims that a work has been reliably printed based on an accurate source text.[12] The second consists of title pages that note specific additions to a reprinted book but that do not identify the additions as 'new'.[13] The last kind comprises advertisements of revision to a previously printed work, including 'new' additions. Of these three broad categories, relatively few title pages highlight fidelity to an accurate source text (3.6 percent of first editions from 1598 to 1609; 4.7 percent of second-plus editions) or mention new additions that are not specifically identified as 'new' (4 percent of second-plus editions).[14]

---

[12] These statements cover fidelity to a variety of different kinds of source texts: to a manuscript source, to a text previously printed in a different country, or to the text of a performance, such as a play, sermon, or speech. These statements also include works that have been revised after their performance but prior to their first printing and works that were printed earlier but have been freshly edited for a new collection. Three plays were sold with advertisements of reliable source texts that were revised between their performance and first printing: *Locrine* by W.S. (1595), *Every Man out of his Humor* by Ben Jonson (three editions in 1600), and *The Devil's Charter* by Barnabe Barnes (1607).

[13] Many title pages announce that more than one text is included in a book, usually with such phrases as 'with the addition of', 'together with', 'augmented with', 'annexed to', etc. When a phrase like 'augmented with' is used without clarifying whether the additions are 'new,' the only way to determine their newness is to compare that volume to a previous edition, something early modern readers would typically have been unable to do. These phrases, in fact, usually do *not* indicate new material was added, serving instead to call attention to ancillary texts in a volume. There are no editions of professional plays that advertise additions but do not identify them as 'new'.

[14] To compute the following figures, I examined the title page of every speculative publication in the *STC* from 1598 to 1609, usually through *EEBO*, though sometimes using the less reliable transcriptions in *ESTC*. Given the number of editions involved – 2,317 first editions and 1,349 second-plus (or reprint) editions – any small errors in these sources are unlikely to affect my claims. The statistics for first editions and second-plus editions have been adjusted in the following ways. For works for which the first extant edition seems to have been preceded by an earlier lost edition (as probably happened with *Love's Labour's Lost* and *The Spanish Tragedy*), I have counted the first extant edition as a second-plus edition. I have also counted the second issue of a first edition as a second-plus edition when revisions of some sort are advertised on the title page of the reissue. For instance, the second issue of the first edition of Thomas Middleton and William Rowley's *A Fair Quarrel* is advertised with 'new additions' and is thus counted as a second-plus edition. These alterations lead to adjusted totals of 2,306 first editions and 1,375 second-plus editions, which are the figures upon

The most prevalent type of editorial pledge is a claim about the revision of a text (29.5 percent of second-plus editions). These pledges usually describe three kinds of revision: texts that have been corrected ('reviewed', 'amended', 'emended', 'perused', 'reviewed', 'checked', 'reformed', 'perfected', etc.); texts that have been enlarged ('augmented', 'amplified', etc.), including with specific 'new' additions; or texts that have been 'revised' (a word that could be used to describe correction, enlargement, or both). Publishers often note some combination of these three kinds of revision on title pages, as on the second edition of Andrew Willet's *Hexapla in Genesis, That Is, a Sixfold Commentary Vpon Genesis* (1608): '*Now the second time reuised, corrected, and with diuers additions enlarged*'.

Beyond advertising the kind of revision that had taken place, title pages many times, though not always, identified an agent of revision. This was often the author, but it could also be an editor (of another writer's work), a translator, or a stationer. Or the individual could be left unspecified, which regularly occurs in books that are anonymous, such as Q2 *Romeo and Juliet* (1599). In cases like Q4 *Richard II* (1608), which advertises 'new additions' and afterward names an author, the author attribution seems to have been intended to cover both the original text and the new additions to it. Greg's hair-splitting interpretation of this title page, in which he contends the authorship of the play is 'not connected with the revisions' made to it (1954: xlii n.1), denies what such attributions are plainly meant to communicate. There can be little doubt, for instance, that Andrew Willet is supposed to be seen as the author who wrote and who 'revised, corrected, and . . . enlarged' the second edition of his *Hexapla*, even though in the case of both Shakespeare and Willet neither edition spells out the author's precise involvement in each step of preparing the revised text, getting it to the printer, and having it printed.[15]

Shakespearean revision in context

These categories of revision can be used to analyze the editorial pledges added to Shakespeare's plays from 1598 to 1609, and they can thereby help determine what these statements would have likely communicated to early modern readers. It turns out that publishers rarely advertised plays from the professional London theater as revised. Nor did they sell other

which my ensuing claims are based. For the definition of 'second-plus editions' and 'speculative publications', see Farmer and Lesser 2005: 6–7, 13–14.
[15] See Massai's discussion of the process of preparing a revised text for printing (2007: 3–6).

dramatists as 'revising' playwrights in the way they did Shakespeare. The selling of Shakespeare as a revising dramatist was truly unusual in the early modern book trade. Up to his death in 1616, most reprints of Shakespeare's plays include an editorial pledge of revision, whereas relatively few non-Shakespearean plays do (56 percent compared to 19.8 percent).[16] The difference between Shakespeare and other playwrights is even more striking for playbooks printed with an author attribution. From 1576 to 1616, reprint editions of playbooks with Shakespeare's name were overwhelmingly more likely to be advertised as revised compared to playbooks with another author's name (66.7 percent versus 7.1 percent).[17] The same is true if only playbooks that advertise revision specifically carried out by an author are considered: 55.6 percent of reprint editions with Shakespeare's name highlight authorial revision compared to 7.1 percent of reprint editions with the name of a different author.[18]

Regardless of whether editors believe Shakespeare himself 'corrected' or 'augmented' his plays, these types of editorial pledges were rarely used on the title pages of plays not written by Shakespeare, and almost no other dramatists were advertised as having revised their printed plays. Prior to Shakespeare's death, only two other professional playbooks named authors as revisers: John Marston and John Webster on the third edition of *The Malcontent* (1604), and John Marston on the second edition of *Parasitaster* (1606). During this same period, up to 1616, Shakespeare was named as a revising author on at least ten editions of four plays (*Love's Labour's Lost, Henry IV, Part 1, Richard III*, and *Richard II*).[19] After Shakespeare's death, only Thomas Middleton and William Rowley were named as revising authors on a reissue of the first edition and on the second edition of *A Fair Quarrel* (1617; 1622), and then Thomas Heywood on the second editions of *The Four Prentices*

---

[16] This figure includes only plays now ascribed to Shakespeare, regardless of whether Shakespeare's name appears in the playbook, and excludes plays mistakenly attributed to Shakespeare on their title pages. The same contrast holds if the entire early modern period is considered. From 1576 to 1642, 52 percent of Shakespeare's plays have editorial pledges of revision compared to 23.5 percent of non-Shakespearean plays.

[17] The equivalent figures for 1576 to 1642 tell the same story: 54.6 percent of second-plus editions of playbooks with Shakespeare's name advertise revisions compared to 20 percent of second-plus editions with the names of other dramatists.

[18] Again, the same is true for the period 1576–1642: 36.4 percent of reprint editions of playbooks with Shakespeare's name advertise revisions made by the author, compared to 6.7 percent of reprints with the names of other dramatists. The comparisons in the above paragraph of different rates for Shakespearean and non-Shakespearean playbooks are all statistically significant, with p-values under 0.01.

[19] I am including the second issue of the fourth edition of *Richard II* among the plays that name Shakespeare as a revising author. If the second edition of *Hamlet* were included too, as it justifiably could be, then twelve editions of five plays named Shakespeare as a revising author before his death.

of London (1632) and *Love's Mistress* (1640). Other playwrights simply were not sold as revisers of plays with anywhere near the frequency that Shakespeare was. If these editorial pledges were misleading exaggerations by publishers, they were exaggerations used almost exclusively for Shakespeare and his plays.

What is true for printed playbooks is likewise true for other publications in the English book trade from 1598 to 1609, from the year Shakespeare was first named on a title page to the year the last new play by him was published in his lifetime (*Pericles* (1609)). As with plays, it was unusual for authors to be identified as revisers of reprinted editions of their work. Publishers included editorial pledges of revision on just under one-third (29.1 percent) of reprint editions of books intended for retail sale, but less than half of these pledges claim the work was revised by an author: 13 percent of reprint editions advertise revisions by an author; 8.2 percent by an editor; 1.2 percent by a translator; 0.5 percent by a printer; and 6.3 percent by (an) unspecified agent(s) (these figures all exclude editions of Shakespeare's plays). Some types of books – especially law books (51.2 percent), school and language books (51 percent), and science books (44.7 percent) – were regularly published as having been corrected or enlarged in some manner, but these revisions were rarely attributed to an author (15 percent of reprints of law books, 5.7 percent of school and language books, and 21.4 percent of science books). In this same period (1598–1609), reprints of Shakespeare's plays were vastly more likely to be advertised as revised (52.6 percent of reprints of Shakespeare's plays advertise revision, while 36.8 percent highlight revision by the author).[20]

In addition to being named as a revising author about three times as often as other authors were, Shakespeare was identified as a revising author on a greater number of individual titles. Seven editions of four different plays printed from 1598 to 1609 state the play was revised by Shakespeare himself (*Love's Labour's Lost, Henry IV, Part 1, Richard III*, and *Richard II*; if *Hamlet* is included, then eight editions of five plays). No other author was identified as a reviser of so many different works. The two who come closest are William Perkins, who died in 1602 and the majority of whose

---

[20] For reprint editions with author attributions, and therefore excluding anonymous publications, the same trends are apparent: 31.3 percent of reprint editions were sold with editorial pledges of revision: 16.2 percent by an author, 9.6 percent by an editor, 1 percent by a translator, 0.5 percent by a printer, and 4 percent by (an) unspecified agent(s). Among plays with title-page attributions to Shakespeare in this period (1598–1609), 66.7 percent of reprint editions were sold with pledges of revision and 58.3 percent with pledges of revision by the author.

works (nineteen editions of eleven works) were advertised as having been edited by his posthumous literary executors (William Crashaw and Thomas Pierson); and Samuel Daniel, who was named as the reviser of three different works, one edition of his *Civil Wars*, two of his *Panegyric Congratulatory*, and three of the various iterations of his collected *Works*.[21] Within the larger context of the English book trade from 1598 to 1609, therefore, Shakespeare was being sold to readers as an author unusually scrupulous about the printing of his plays in corrected, enlarged, and revised texts. He was arguably portrayed as the author most concerned about the printing of his works in accurate texts.

One final issue that might affect these figures is if Shakespeare was published by stationers who routinely made exaggerated claims about authorial revision. Maybe, as has repeatedly been implied, the image of Shakespeare the revising author was actually the creation of stationers who used deceptive editorial pledges to sell their books, most notably Cuthburt Burby, Andrew Wise, Nicholas Ling, and Matthew Law. Once again, the facts do not support this theory. In the case of two of these publishers, Wise and Law, it is easy to describe their typical practices. Andrew Wise, who brought out *Henry IV, Part 1* and *Richard III*, never advertised any of his other twenty publications as revised, although the dedication to two editions of a sermon by Thomas Playfere, *The Meane in Mourning* (1596; 1597), do indicate that it had been revised by its author.[22] Matthew Law, who issued *Richard II* with 'new additions' in 1608, and who continued to reprint *Henry IV, Part 1* and *Richard III* as revised after acquiring the rights to them from Wise in 1603, otherwise rarely advertised corrections. Among the twenty-four reprint editions he published from 1595 to 1629 (excluding Shakespeare's plays), the only book with an editorial pledge of revision was the second edition of a sermon by Thomas Sutton in 1616.[23] Wise and Law appear to have used advertisements of authorial revision almost exclusively for Shakespeare's plays.

Shakespeare's two other publishers, Nicholas Ling, who brought out *Hamlet* in 1604, and Cuthburt Burby, who issued *Love's Labour's Lost* and

---

[21] Other authors frequently named as revisers in this period include Arthur Dent (seven editions of a religious treatise); John Stow (six editions and a reissue of three works, one of which is from after his death in 1605); Michael Drayton (five editions of two poetry books); John Dod and Robert Cleaver (five editions of a religious treatise); and John Hayward (five editions of a prayer book).

[22] On the publishing career of Wise, see also Hooks 2013.

[23] Sutton 1616 was sold as 'The second Impression, Perused and Corrected by the Authour'. In addition, Law published three editions of Playfere's *The Meane in Mourning* with the same dedication describing the sermon's revision. For an overview of Law's career, see also Erne 2013: 167–8.

Romeo and Juliet, were comparatively more likely to advertise revisions. Ling brought out thirty-five reprint editions in his career from 1580 to 1607; these contain editorial pledges of revision at about the same rate as the overall market (25.7 percent for Ling versus 29.5 percent for the market). More important, though, is that the pledges on these revised texts – including four editions of Drayton's *Englands Heroicall Epistles*; three editions of *Politeuphuia*, the poetical commonplace book that Ling himself edited and helped compile; one Henry Smith sermon; and Shakespeare's *Hamlet* (1604–05) – do not appear to be erroneous (scholars do not doubt that Drayton and Ling carried out the revisions advertised on their title pages). The editorial pledge on *Hamlet* – 'Newly imprinted and enlarged to almost as much | again as it was, according to the true and perfect | Coppie', which appears below an author attribution to Shakespeare – does not unambiguously indicate who supplied the 'true and perfect Coppie'. But in the context of Ling's other publications, especially Drayton's poetry books, it would not be unreasonable to infer that Ling meant to suggest Shakespeare was behind the enlarged version of this play.[24]

Cuthburt Burby was the publisher most likely to advertise revisions. During his career, from 1592 to 1607, he occasionally advertised first editions as having been printed from an accurate source (four editions), and he twice noted that translations corrected or enlarged the original texts upon which they were based. He also published or wholesaled thirty-nine reprint editions in his career. Among these, he included editorial pledges of revision on just over half of his non-dramatic publications (51.5 percent) as well as on *Love's Labour's Lost* and *Romeo and Juliet*, though not on any of the other four reprinted playbooks he published or sold. Burby evidently embraced the advertising of accurate and revised texts, but this tendency does not seem to have resulted in a rash of spurious pledges or deceptive claims of authorial revision.[25] And what was true of Burby is equally true of the three other publishers who added editorial pledges to Shakespeare's plays. These were not stationers regularly misleading readers with false claims of authorial revision.

---

[24] Ling published both the second (1598) and third editions (1599) of Drayton's *Englands Heroicall Epistles* as 'enlarged'. In the second edition, Ling identified Drayton as the agent of revision ('Newly enlarged, | By *Michaell Drayton.*'), but in the third edition, Ling separated the book's revision from its authorship by inserting a period at the end of the editorial pledge of enlargement ('NEWLY ENLARGED. With *Idea.*') and then adding a fleuron before the author's name ('❧ By *Michaell Drayton*').

[25] Burby often repeated editorial pledges from one edition to another, which, as noted above, was a standard trade practice. For four of the reprinted works he published or wholesaled as revised, the pledge was originally added to an earlier edition by another publisher. For more on Burby's career, see Erne 2013: 166.

'Gross errors' and ad hoc authorial revision

Far from there being 'essentially no evidence that Shakespeare was himself at all concerned with preserving an authoritative text of his plays for future readers', as the *Riverside Shakespeare* contends, there is indeed ample evidence that Shakespeare was committed to the printing of his plays in corrected and enlarged texts. The editorial pledges of authorial revision that were added again and again to the title pages of his plays were not standard marketing ploys, nor mere 'printer's ornaments'. They were a rare way of selling professional plays, an uncommon way of selling books from 1598 to 1609, and a relatively unusual way for Shakespeare's stationers to advertise the books they published.

This way of selling Shakespeare is worth taking seriously even in light of the 'gross errors' that editors have pointed to as proof that Shakespeare did not 'correct' his plays. How printers tried to rectify such errors has been studied most thoroughly by Sonia Massai, who shrewdly calls into doubt what many scholars have assumed about the changes made to reprinted plays. As she points out, for instance, the editorial pledge on the third edition of *Henry IV, Part 1* ('Newly corrected') is not in fact erroneous, as editors have long asserted. Rather, there are several changes to stage directions and speech prefixes, alterations that point more to an 'annotating reader' than to a press corrector employed by the printing house. An annotating reader was also probably responsible for the changes made to the third edition of *Richard III*, which was sold as 'Newly augmented' and in which five new stage directions were added and two others modified (two lines had also been added to the second edition of this play) (2007: 102–5). Changes like these, Massai explains, depend 'on having a working knowledge of the fictive world of the play'. Most printshop compositors and press correctors did not concern themselves with such matters, focusing instead on the physical and formal properties of the printed text (Massai 2011: 99)

The evidence of annotating readers assembled by Massai reveals that the changes they made closely resemble the alterations thought to have been made by dramatists to their plays, such as those carried out by John Marston to the second edition of *Parasitaster* (1606). Marston's play was published as 'now corrected of many faults, which by reason of the Au- | thors absence, were let slip in the first edition'. As in Shakespeare's quartos, the changes introduced by Marston are local, minor, and far from rigorous (Blostein 1978: 42–52). And what was true of Marston was true of other playwrights as well. The types of changes dramatists made to plays were rarely thorough and systematic; their revisions were instead usually ad hoc and erratic. In her overview of all the professional plays sold with editorial pledges, Massai concludes that, 'even when authors were personally involved, the annotation of copy was sporadic and superficial at best', adding that even when 'the number of corrections may be more extensive, their quality is hardly distinctive enough for the majority of them to be firmly attributed to the author'. Authors, in other words, typically corrected plays in the same haphazard way that other annotating readers did. The difference between changes made by an author and by an annotating reader is therefore usually impossible to distinguish: 'no category of corrections and no specific level of intervention can be firmly ascribed to authorial, as opposed to non-authorial, agents' (2011: 102, 103). Despite the understandable caution of this conclusion, it also helps make the contrasting point about Shakespearean revision.

The types of 'gross errors' taken by editors to be evidence of Shakespeare's indifference to the printing of his plays are routinely found in other printed plays overseen and corrected by early modern dramatists. Annotating readers and playwrights alike were, by modern standards, idiosyncratic, unsystematic, and careless proofreaders and copyeditors. The irregular corrections made by Marston to his plays closely resemble those made to Shakespeare's plays. Although this similarity cannot prove that Shakespeare himself oversaw the reprinting of his plays, the editorial pledges on Shakespeare's playbooks should not be dismissed simply because the printed texts do not demonstrate the level of accuracy that scholars believe an author would have or should have achieved. The ad hoc revision of Shakespeare's plays is exactly what one would expect of an early modern playwright correcting his plays.

If the editorial pledges on Shakespeare's plays are credible, then these playbooks suggest that Shakespeare sometimes pursued large-scale revisions of his plays, as happened with *Romeo and Juliet* and *Hamlet*, and at other times made smaller, more local corrections to their printed texts, tinkering with minor details such as speech prefixes and stage directions.[26] These pledges thus present modern scholars with a couple of choices. Critics might continue to maintain that Wise, Law, Ling, and Burby sought to deceive early modern readers, perhaps intentionally, about Shakespeare's involvement in correcting and augmenting his plays; that point of view, however, can now be qualified by the recognition that this

---

[26] Implicit in my argument here is that the later, longer versions of Shakespeare's plays were the products of later moments of revision. On this question, see also Marino 2011; Dutton 2011.

was a highly unusual way of advertising printed plays and a relatively uncommon practice within the larger early modern book trade. Scholars might thus decide to go further and begin to credit what these publishers claim happened, that Shakespeare revised his plays for print publication. In light of the typical practices of the early modern book trade, this latter option strikes me as the more likely. The image of Shakespeare as a revising author was first sold to readers in 1598, continued to appear through 1609, and would persist until well after his death.[27] Far from being uninterested in the printing of his plays, these editions suggest that Shakespeare, the period's leading playwright in print, was not only one of the writers whom publishers were most eager to publicize as a revising author, but also one of the authors in the early modern book trade most concerned about the printing of his works in corrected and augmented texts.

---

[27] Following Shakespeare's death, publishers continued to sell *Richard III* (1622; 1629), *Henry IV, Part 1* (1622; 1632; 1639), and *Richard II* (1634) with advertisements of authorial revision. Other works were also reprinted after 1616 with claims that someone else had revised them. The sixth edition of *The Rape of Lucrece* (1616) was first sold as 'Newly Reuised', *The Whole Contention* (1619) as 'newly corrected and enlarged', and *The Merry Wives of Windsor* (1630) as '*Newly corrected*'. In each of these later editions, the editorial pledge of revision is separated from the authorship attribution to Shakespeare, suggesting these revisions were 'newly' carried out by someone other than the author.

CHAPTER 7

Shakespeare between pamphlet and book, 1608–1619

Zachary Lesser and Peter Stallybrass

1608: 'his'

The year 1608 was a particularly significant date in the history of Shakespeare as a published playwright. For the first time, Shakespeare's name was printed prominently on the title page of one of his plays as the major marketing appeal. Shakespeare's name was already well established by 1600, but the title page of *King Lear* marks a real change (Figure 7.1). Never before had Shakespeare's name appeared at the top of the title page of a play, prior to the genre or title, and never before had it appeared in so large a typeface as to fill the whole width of the page. Why this radical departure from earlier formats? One possible explanation is that Shakespeare was rewriting an anonymous 1590s version of *Lear* that had been published only three years earlier. If one takes away the authorial ascription of the 1608 play to Shakespeare, the two title pages are remarkably similar (Figure 7.2). Like the 1605 *Leir*, Shakespeare's *Lear* is a 'True Chronicle Historie' and has the same three daughters. Given these striking similarities, it was clearly necessary for the publisher Nathaniel Butter to differentiate his playbook from the earlier one, and Shakespeare's authorship was a primary way of doing so.

But that is not the whole story. From 1607 to 1609, some publishers began to experiment with marketing plays by emphasizing the importance of their writers, above all Ben Jonson and William Shakespeare. While the names of dramatists had been appearing with increasing regularity on title pages from the late 1590s, they had never been such a dominant visual feature. In 1607, Thomas Thorpe published Jonson's *Volpone*, which radically departed from the way any previous professional play had been printed (Figure 7.3). Not only is the visual primacy of the dramatist a major innovation; so too is the grammatical priority of the author and the assertion that the play is 'his'. The 1608 *Lear* quarto can thus be read as

M. William Shak-speare:

HIS
True Chronicle Historie of the life and death of King LEAR and his three Daughters.

With the vnfortunate life of Edgar, *sonne* and heire to the Earle of Gloster, and his sullen and assumed humor of TOM of Bedlam:

As it was played before the Kings Maiestie at Whitehall vpon S. Stephans *night in Christmas Hollidayes.*

By his Maiesties seruants playing vsually at the Gloabe on the Bancke-side.

LONDON,
Printed for *Nathaniel Butter*, and are to be sold at his shop in *Pauls* Church-yard at the signe of the Pide Bull neere St. *Austins* Gate. 1608.

Figure 7.1 Title page of *King Lear* (1608)

THE
True Chronicle Hi-
ſtory of King LEIR, and his three
daughters, *Gonorill,* *Ragan,*
and *Cordella.*

As it hath bene diuers and ſundry
times lately acted.

LONDON,

Printed by Simon Stafford for Iohn
Wright, and are to bee ſold at his ſhop at
Chriſtes Church dore, next Newgate-
Market. 1605.

Figure 7.2 Title page of *King Leir* (1605)

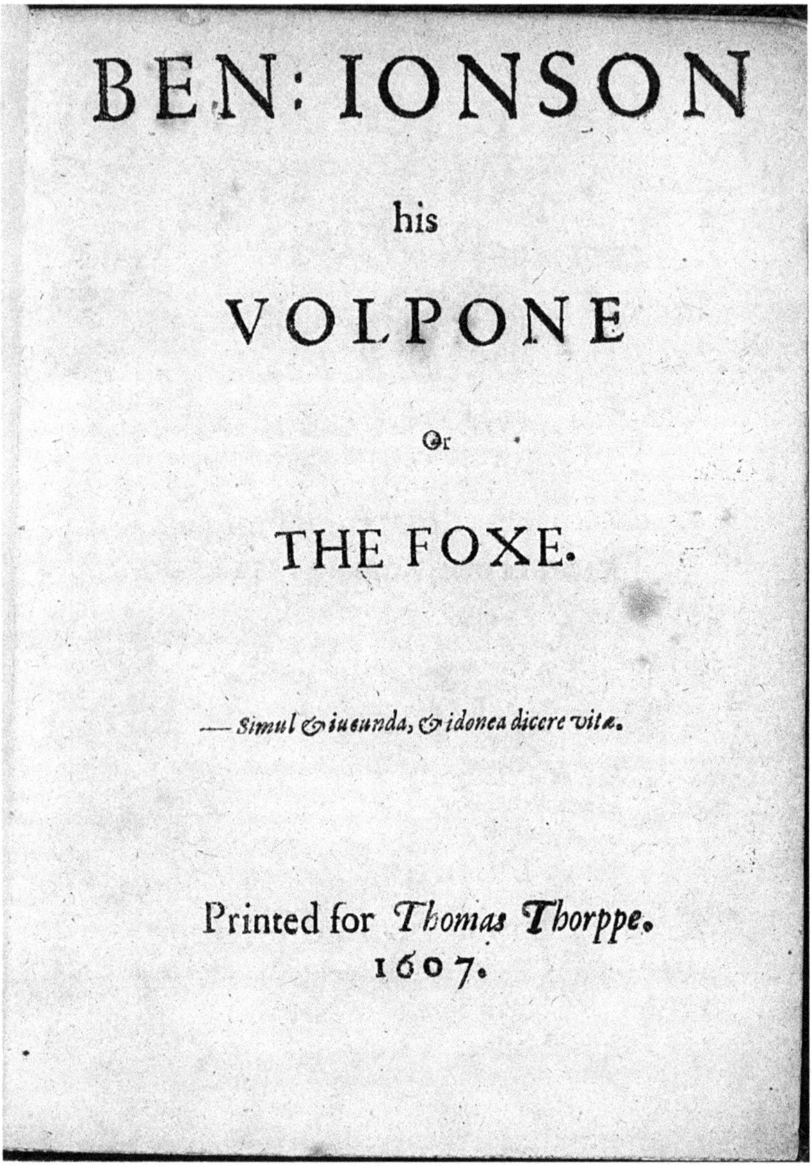

BEN: IONSON

his

VOLPONE

Or

THE FOXE.

—— *Simul & iucunda, & idonea dicere vitæ.*

Printed for *Thomas Thorppe.*
1607.

Figure 7.3 Title page of *Volpone* (1607)

an imitation of the 1607 *Volpone*. On both, the word 'his' exists in splendid isolation, a whole line devoted to these three letters; and, in *Lear*, the letters have also been capitalized and italicized. It is difficult to imagine a more theatrical staging of proprietary authorship.

A further piece of evidence to suggest the new significance of Shakespeare's name in 1608 can be found in Thomas Pavier's publication of *Yorkshire Tragedy*. Here, the author's name appears in the usual position, low on the page and in a small font: but the name is that of 'W. Shakespeare', as if that name were already useful in selling any play, whether or not written by him. In the same year, then, London stationers published the Shakespearean tragedy that would go on to become paradigmatic of his mature art, and an abbreviated domestic tragedy that would be largely discarded from the canon by the eighteenth century. As Lukas Erne has argued, both playbooks testify to the importance of Shakespeare as a dramatic author in 1608, despite the vastly different literary value accorded them today (2013: 77–9).

Yet it is worth pausing to note as well the differences between the title pages of *Volpone* and *Lear*. What is striking about Thorpe's publication is not merely the prominence of Jonson's name but also the lack of any competing claims: there is no mention of a theatrical company or the play's genre or any elements of the plot. The title page of Jonson's play has the uncluttered simplicity that was increasingly associated with the authority of classical antiquity. *Lear*, on the other hand, tries to crowd as much information onto the title page as possible, fully staging the multiple agencies and authorities that go into the performance of a play: from the author, to the 'True Chronicle Historie' from which the tale was taken, the characters for which it was known, the patron, the acting company, and the performance venues. By contrast, Jonson's title page erases all evidence that the text that follows is a *play*. It could be anything. But what is not in doubt is that it is 'his'.

The playbook of *Volpone* thus goes considerably further than *Lear* in establishing the playwright as the most important agent responsible for its production. And this marketing strategy continued for Jonson the following year, when Bartholomew Sutton published an edition of *The Case is Altered* that again highlighted the proprietary author (Figure 7.4). While Jonson is still the prime mover here, the Latin quotation that established Jonson's classical precedents on the title page of *Volpone* has been replaced by the more conventional recognition of the collaborative nature of the theatre. Still, a pattern is beginning to be established: 1607: *Ben: Ionson his Volpone*; 1608: *M. William Shak-speare: His . . . King Lear*; 1609: *Ben: Ionson, His Case Is Alterd*.

BEN: IONSON,

HIS

CASE IS ALTERD.

As it hath beene sundry times Acted by the
Children of the Blacke-friers.

AT LONDON
Printed for *Bartholomew Sutton*, dwelling in Paules
Church-yard neere the great north doore of S.
Paules Church.   1609.

Figure 7.4 Title page of *The Case is Altered* (1609)

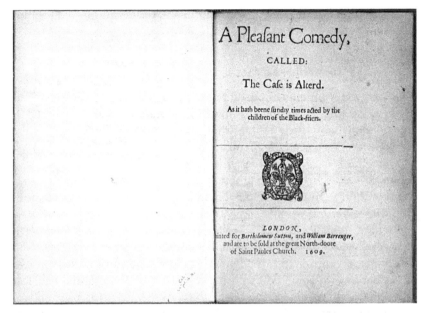

Figure 7.5 Reissued title page of *The Case is Altered* (1609)

But the pattern ends there. No publisher continued to market individual plays for the professional theatre in this way. Indeed, this strategy collapsed even during the publication of *The Case is Altered* (Figure 7.5). Long before Jonson's play had sold out, Bartholomew Sutton joined forces with another bookseller, William Barrenger, printing a new title page to announce the merger. And on this cancel title page, the name of the author has not just been demoted; it has been erased altogether. This second title page makes clear that authorial ascription is the work of the publisher, not of the writer. Even if the omission of Jonson's name seems to have been accidental, and was corrected in a later state of the title page with the more typical attribution that the play was 'Written by BEN. IONSON', it was Thorpe, Butter, Sutton, and Barrenger who decided how to market the plays that they chose to publish. In these years, they briefly attempted to market the plays of Jonson and Shakespeare by giving striking visual prominence to the name of the dramatist as proprietary author. But they rapidly gave up on this strategy. Until the First Folio announced its contents with the authorial possessive – *Mr. William Shakespeares Comedies, Histories & Tragedies* – no publisher attempted to link Shakespeare as a dramatic author to one of his plays in this way.[1]

1609: Shakespeare as author and anonymous

The year 1609 presents another important confluence of the ways that Shakespeare the playwright was imagined, marketed, and transformed in the London book trade. While this period did ultimately lead to the monumental construction of Shakespeare as a literary author 'for all time' in the First Folio of 1623, there was no easy progress toward that moment. Publishers continued to experiment with Shakespeare as a dramatic author, both named and anonymous, and to negotiate his relationship with other playwrights and with the theater for which he wrote.

Richard Bonian and Henry Walley's edition of *Troilus and Cressida* in that year betrays an uncertainty about how best to market the play and Shakespeare's authorship to potential readers. The edition exists in two issues because, at some point during the printing, the original title leaf was replaced by a folded half-sheet, containing a new title page and an address to readers. Initially, the publishers followed a traditional design for their title page, pairing an author attribution with a somewhat larger-sized performance attribution that included both a troupe and a theatre. This combination, which figures the playwright as an author working within the professional institutions of the London theatre, had become fairly standard since author attributions and theatre attributions began to proliferate on the title pages of professional plays around the turn of the century.[2] In their reissue of the play, however, Bonian and Walley followed a different model of dramatic authorship. They retained the author attribution but removed all mention of performance from the title page, replacing it with a plot summary ('*Excellently expressing the beginning* of their loues, with the conceited wooing of *Pandarus* Prince of *Litia*'). And their added preface to the reader stressed that the play was '*neuer stal'd with the Stage, neuer clapper-clawd with the palmes of the vulger*'. Now the play's worth was attested precisely by its *lack* of connection with the professional theatre. Instead, Shakespeare is linked with

---

[1] When *Lear* was reprinted in 1619 and 1655, the attribution of proprietary authorship was retained. As we discuss below, however, this has more to do with how books were reprinted in the period than with trends in the marketing of Shakespeare. For the most thorough and impressive account of this period in the publication of Shakespeare's plays, see Erne 2013: 90–129, 186–232.

[2] Attributions to the playing company had been common even earlier. On title page design, see Farmer and Lesser 2000.

the classical playwrights who had already become canonical authors: the play should be valued '*as well as the best Commedy in* Terence *or* Plautus'. And when Shakespeare '*is gone, and his Commedies out of sale*', he too shall become a prized author: '*you will scramble for them, and set vp a new English Inquisition*' (*Troylus*, sigs. ¶2ʳ⁻ᵛ; on Bonian and Walley, see also Massai's chapter, in this volume).

But just as Bonian and Walley were pursuing this antitheatrical strategy, another play of Shakespeare's, far more popular on stage and in print than *Troilus and Cressida*, was entering the bookstalls. The title page of Henry Gosson's first edition of *Pericles* (1609) advertises its author's name, but it stresses equally, if not more, the play's success on stage: not only is the play presented 'As it hath been diuers and sundry times acted by his Maiesties Seruants, at the Globe on the Banck-side', but it is also 'The Late, And much admired Play' (Figure 7.6). Much admired the play had indeed been. In the same year that the play was published, an anonymous author compared the crowd at an inn to a theatre at the performance of a hit play: 'all the Roomes / Did swarme with *Gentiles* mix'd with *Groomes*. / So that I truly thought, all These / Came to see *Shore*, or *Pericles*' (*Pimlyco*, sig. C1ʳ, roman typeface substituted for black letter and italic for roman).

And, within the play itself, *Pericles* appeals to a different kind of 'ancient' authority than Bonian and Walley's second issue of *Troilus and Cressida*. Rather than the classical antiquity of Terence and Plautus, Shakespeare's play is here positioned as authentically English, a novel source of literary authority in the early seventeenth century.[3] In the prologue, Gower tells us that the story is 'a Song that old was sung' at the kind of village celebrations that brought together all ranks and statuses: 'It hath been sung at Feastiuals, / On Ember eues, and Holydayes; / And Lords and Ladyes in their liues / Haue red it for restoratiues' (Shakespeare and Wilkins sig. A2ʳ). It was this combination of the 'ancient' English source and the nostalgic, ballad-like invocation of festival singing that Jonson would ridicule when he complained about the popularity of 'some mouldy tale, / Like *Pericles*', while his own drama incurred only '*vulgar censure*' (Jonson, '*Iust*', sig. H2ʳ).

This appeal to a 'popular' national past is mirrored in Nathaniel Butter's publication of *The Painfull Aduentures of Pericles Prince of Tyre* the year before. This 'novelization' of the stage play – the only one of its kind that we have from the period – appears to have been written by George Wilkins,

---

[3] On this development, see Cook 2011.

THE LATE,
And much admired Play,
Called
Pericles, Prince of Tyre.

With the true Relation of the whole Historie, aduentures, and fortunes of the said Prince:

As also,

The no lesse strange, and worthy accidents, in the Birth and Life, of his Daughter *MARIANA*.

As it hath been diuers aad sundry times acted by his Maiesties Seruants, at the Globe on the Banck-side.

By William Shakespeare.

Imprinted at London for *Henry Gosson*, and are to be sold at the signe of the Sunne in Pater-noster row, &c.
1609.

Figure 7.6 Title page of *Pericles* (1609)

Shakespeare's collaborator on the stage play, since one of the two extant copies includes a dedication signed by him.[4] Wilkins's narrative claims to be the 'true History of the Play of *Pericles*, as it was lately presented by the worthy and ancient Poet *Iohn Gower*'. The allusion to the typical title page performance attribution ('as it was lately presented'), merely substituting Gower's name for the theatrical company, is a striking testimony to the remarkable popularity of *Pericles*, as is the mere existence of this unique novelization. But, in Butter's publication, Shakespeare's name nowhere appears, only Wilkins's, just as in Gosson's publication Wilkins's role in the writing of the play is erased in favor of Shakespeare's.

In the two issues of *Troilus and Cressida* and in the first edition of *Pericles*, published less than a year apart, we can thus see three models of dramatic authorship, none of them quite the same as the possessive authorship of the *Lear* quarto. First, the by-then conventional title page assertion that *Troilus and Cressida* was 'Written by' Shakespeare, paired with a performance attribution; second, the antitheatrical erasure of the King's Men and the Globe from that title page and the location of authority instead in classical antiquity; and, finally, the enthusiastic embrace of the popularity of *Pericles* in performance, combined with an appeal to an 'ancient' English poetic tradition.

During this period a *fourth* model for marketing Shakespeare's plays co-existed alongside these three, one driven more by the exigencies of the book trade than by the rise of dramatic authorship. In 1609, John Smethwick brought out the third quarto of *Romeo and Juliet*, which indicated that it was 'Newly corrected, augmented, and amended'. But there is no mention of who was correcting, augmenting, and amending, nor of who had written the play in the first place. In this Smethwick was not charting any new ground, however; he was merely following the previous two quartos, neither of which had provided an author attribution (Figures 7.7 and 7.8). Since it was always easier in the production of any book to follow a previous edition than to make changes, and since the first quarto of the play appeared in 1597 before it became common to include a playwright's name on the title page, we can see here the routines of the book trade overriding the growing authorial reputation of Shakespeare. We can trace the effects of such an anonymous title page even in the case of someone as knowledgeable as Sir William Drummond of Hawthornden. When he donated his books to the

---

[4] The copy at the Zentralbibliothek in Zurich contains the dedication; the British Library copy does not.

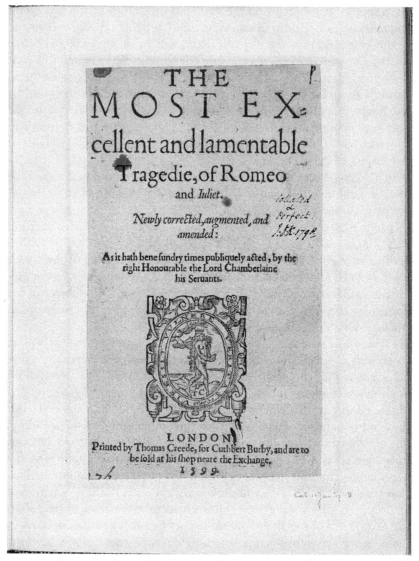

Figure 7.7 Title page of *Romeo and Juliet* (1599)

University of Edinburgh in 1627, his copy of *Love's Labour's Lost* (1598), which had Shakespeare's name on the title page, was catalogued under 'S' for the author's name. But the anonymous 1599 *Romeo and Juliet* was catalogued under 'R' for the play's title (Erne 2013: 196–7).

THE
MOST EX-
CELLENT AND
Lamentable Tragedie, of
Romeo and Juliet.

As it hath beene sundrie times publiquely Acted,
by the KINGS Maiesties Seruants
at the Globe.

Newly corrected, augmented, and
amended:

LONDON
Printed for IOHN SMETHVVICK, and are to be sold
at his Shop in Saint *Dunstanes* Church-yard,
in Fleetestreete vnder the Dyall.
1609.

Figure 7.8 Title page of *Romeo and Juliet* (1609)

Figure 7.9 Title page of *Sonnets* (1609)

The most striking staging of Shakespeare's name prior to 1623, however, was not for any of his plays but for his poems. In 1609, for the first time, Shakespeare's name appeared not only at the top of the page but also in all capitals (Figure 7.9). The publisher of 'SHAKE-SPEARES SONNETS' was Thomas Thorpe, who, as noted above, had published 'BEN: IONSON / his / VOLPONE' two years earlier. Thorpe, in other words, seems to have seriously thought about promoting Jonson and Shakespeare through their names – although, more conventionally in the case of Shakespeare, through his poetry rather than his plays. The *Sonnets*, however, was not a success and the authorial publicity that Thorpe adopted was at the furthest remove from the Shakespearean poem that was most reprinted between 1590 and 1650: *Venus and Adonis*. From this period, we have thirteen surviving editions with title pages (and others without). Without exception, every title page reprints the title, 'Venus and Adonis'; without exception, each reprints the Latin quotation from Ovid; and without exception, no title page mentions Shakespeare, despite this being the most popular of all his works. Our point is not that buyers did not know that Shakespeare was the author: that, in any case, was made clear by the dedicatory epistle signed with his name. But no publisher thought it worthwhile to sell the book by displaying that name prominently on the title page. Edition copied edition, changing only the visual layout, the decorative woodblocks and printer's lace, and the publishing information (including printer's and publisher's devices). In 1675, the last seventeenth-century edition of the poem included the same information that had appeared in 1593, more than eighty years earlier (Figures 7.10 and 7.11).

In the bookstalls of London in this period, alongside the anonymous *Venus and Adonis* and *Romeo and Juliet*, customers could find *Titus Andronicus* (Q3, 1611) and *Henry V* (Q3, 1619) likewise reprinted with no author attribution on the title page, dutifully following their earlier editions even as such attributions had become common for new plays. The anonymity of the third quarto of *Henry V* is perhaps even more striking than that of Q4 *Romeo and Juliet*, still anonymous when reprinted in 1623, for *Henry V* not only appeared in the same year as a Shakespeare collection but as a *part* of that collection: the 'Pavier Quartos' published in 1619 and including ten plays by Shakespeare.[5] Among these, only *Henry V* is anonymous on its title page.

1619: The Pavier/Jaggard/Shakespeare/Heywood Quartos

What were the so-called 'Pavier Quartos'? Since W. W. Greg's modestly titled essay 'On Certain False Dates in Shakespearian Quartos' (1908) first announced their bibliographic discovery, the general scholarly consensus has been that these playbooks, all printed in 1619, represent an early and

---

[5] For the dating of Q4 *Romeo and Juliet*, which has no date in the imprint, see Hailey 2007.

VENVS
AND ADONIS

Vilia miretur vulgus : mihi flauus Apollo
Pocula Castalia plena ministret aqua.

LONDON

Imprinted by Richard Field, and are to be sold at
the signe of the white Greyhound in
Paules Church-yard.
1593.

Figure 7.10 Title page of *Venus and Adonis* (1593)

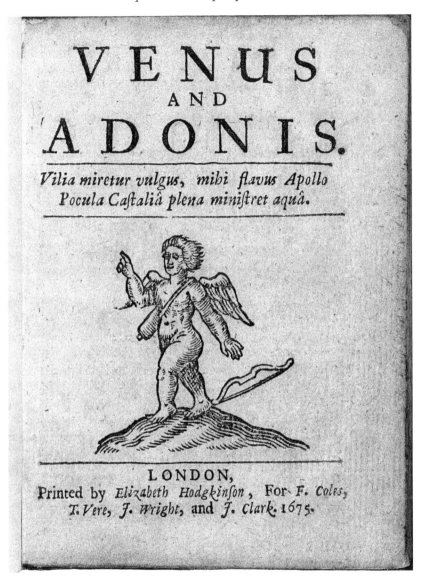

Figure 7.11 Title page of *Venus and Adonis* (1675)

interrupted attempt to create a collection of Shakespeare's plays. Several of the plays have false dates or no date at all in the imprint, which was why Greg's discovery that they were indeed a collection, all published in the same year, was a major piece of New Bibliographic detective work. Scholars have generally followed Greg in asserting that the 'Pavier Quartos' consisted of ten plays (in nine playbooks), with *The Whole Contention* (which combines *Henry VI, Parts 2 and 3*), *Pericles*, and *Yorkshire Tragedy* printed first, and then (in the most commonly cited order) *The Merchant of Venice, The Merry Wives of Windsor, King Lear, Henry V, Sir John Oldcastle,* and *A Midsummer Night's Dream*.[6] The two plays that are now not attributed to Shakespeare, *Yorkshire Tragedy* and *Oldcastle*, both have Shakespeare's name on their title pages, although *Henry V*, as noted above, follows the earlier quartos of the play in being anonymous. That the plays were at first intended as a collection is suggested by the fact that *The Whole Contention* and *Pericles* have continuous signatures, although that leaves the problem of why all the other plays do not. They have been called the 'Pavier' quartos because Thomas Pavier's initials appear in the imprint of five of the nine playbooks.[7]

A series of questions have been the focus of scholarly inquiry into the 'Pavier Quartos' since Greg's discovery. Why were false imprints placed on several of the title pages? What was the connection between these false imprints and the Lord Chamberlain's order in May 1619 that attempted to prevent the publication of the King's Men's plays? Who was the main agent behind the publication of these plays? What was the relation of this collection to the First Folio, published four years later? But one assumption has almost always been taken for granted: namely, that these ten plays either by Shakespeare or attributed to him were an attempt to create the first 'collected Shakespeare'.[8] There is, indeed, some evidence for this. The Folger Shakespeare Library has a copy of the ten plays in an early seventeenth-century binding with Edward Gwynne's name on it. And another collection of these same plays survives at Texas Christian University in a seventeenth-century binding.

Greg was undoubtedly right to say that several plays by or attributed to Shakespeare were being sold bound together as a book in 1619. Moreover, we now have a fairly clear idea of the order in which the plays were printed, which has in turn led to an ideal version of the order in which the plays should be bound – above all with *The Whole Contention* and *Pericles* beginning the collection, since they have continuous signatures. Indeed, the bibliographical code that Greg established has been so powerful that it

---

[6] On the order of printing, see Neidig 1910, who is followed by many later scholars, for example, Massai 2007: 107.
[7] Important recent studies of the 'Pavier Quartos' include: Johnson 1992; Kastan 2001: 57–61; Murphy 2003: 36–56; Massai 2007: 106–35; Knight 2009; Halasz 2013; Erne 2013: 75–9, 174–9, 222–3.
[8] For an important recent exception, see Lyons's excellent essay (2011) on alternative principles of collection underlying Pavier's work.

has often overridden the physical evidence of the books themselves.[9] The catalogue record for Gwynne's volume is a perfect example of how modern bibliography has erased the material reality of the seventeenth-century book: 'STC 26101 copy 3: Folger Copy: Contains *The whole contention pts. 1–2* and *Pericles*. MS table of contents. Bound with seven other 1619 Shakespeare quartos.' The implication of the Folger's record is clear: we should expect to find the continuous signatures of *The Whole Contention* and *Pericles* bound first in Gwynne's volume, followed by seven other Shakespeare plays. But that is not the case. Not only does the Gwynne volume 'fail' to bind *The Whole Contention* and *Pericles* consecutively; it matter-of-factly records this 'failure' (with no concern for its being a 'failure') in an early list of the volume's contents bound in at the beginning, where *The Whole Contention* appears first but *Pericles* seventh. This ordering is noted in the Folger catalogue – but only as an error: 'This work is mis-bound after leaf Q4', meaning that five plays have been bound *between* the continuous signatures of *The Whole Contention* and *Pericles*.

The modern bibliographical invention of the 'Pavier Quartos' can also be seen in the case of a volume owned by Thomas Percy in the eighteenth century, the remains of which are also at the Folger. As Jeffrey Todd Knight has shown, when Percy owned this book (which has now been rebound in multiple volumes), it contained *eleven* not ten plays. And the eleventh play was manifestly not a Shakespearean drama, as demonstrated by a seventeenth-century list of the contents on the verso of the front flyleaf (Figure 7.12). Leading off this list is Thomas Heywood's *A Woman Killed with Kindness*, clearly attributed to Heywood on the title page of every extant early edition. And, again, 'The contention of the Houses of York and Lancaster' and *Pericles* are not consecutive.

So how does Percy's copy of *The Whole Contention* come to be bound with *Pericles* today to make a 'perfect' volume of the beginning of the 'Pavier Quartos'? Percy himself disbound the collection in 1763 to give away three of the plays (*Woman Killed*, *Lear*, and *Yorkshire Tragedy*) to friends. But when Folger bought the copy, the remaining eight plays were

---

[9] For one thing, like many libraries, the Folger catalogues *Pericles* under the heading of *The Whole Contention*, since *Pericles* is, from the perspective of the New Bibliography, a continuation of the same 'book'. But this has some bizarre consequences: the Folger claims to have sixteen copies of *The Whole Contention*, but classifies only three of these as 'complete', not because anything is missing in *Henry VI, Parts 2* or *3* in these other thirteen copies but rather because they do not contain all three elements that the Folger considers 'the' book, namely both parts of *The Whole Contention* and *Pericles*.

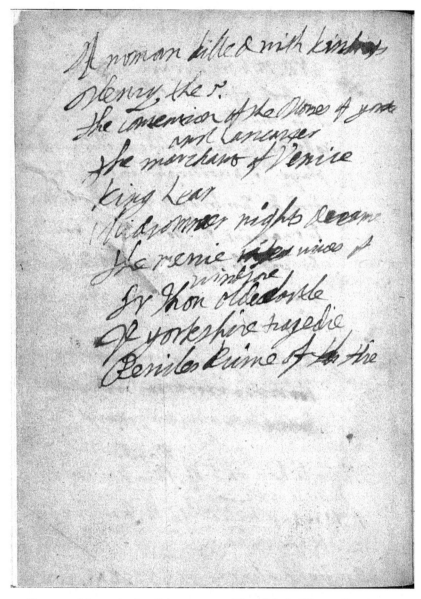

Figure 7.12 Manuscript list of plays on verso of front flyleaf of Thomas Percy's copy of the 'Pavier Quartos'

in a Victorian binding. In 1963, however, the Curator of Books and Manuscripts at the Folger, Giles Dawson, disbound the collection, rebinding five plays as individual volumes and *The Whole Contention* and *Pericles* together as the 'correct' beginning of the 'Pavier Quartos' according to Greg's reconstruction. Now, for the first time, these copies of *The Whole Contention* and *Pericles* were 'perfected'. (To his credit, Dawson carefully recorded exactly what he had done in a note on a flyleaf at the end of the rebound volume, enabling us to reconstruct this history.)

The 'Pavier Quartos' thus turn out to be an impressive modern hypothesis that has been materialized by modern cataloguing and rebinding practices. This is confirmed by another of the Folger's copies of *The Whole Contention* and *Pericles* (Copy 1). This 'perfect' copy was sold to Folger by the famous London bookseller Quaritch, a year before the publication of Greg's discovery of the 'Pavier Quartos'. But the bibliographer at Quaritch's who collated the volume before the firm had it bound was Frederic Sutherland Ferguson, a close friend of Alfred Pollard, who, in 1906, had first drawn attention to the 'Pavier Quartos' as the earliest attempt to produce a 'collected' Shakespeare – not as a 1619 printing but as a collection of remaindered copies. Pollard fully acknowledged his debt to Ferguson for the latter's outstanding contribution to the *STC*.[10] In other words, the Folger's Copy 1 of *The Whole Contention* and *Pericles* may well have been bound up *so as to create the material artifact* that Pollard and Greg's brilliant bibliographic work presupposed.

The copy of the 'Pavier Quartos' now at Texas Christian University gives us yet another ordering of the plays. So does the copy that once belonged to Edward Capell and is now in Trinity College, Cambridge (rebound in two volumes). And so does a fifth example (once owned by E. W. Hussey) that was disbound in 1906. The striking fact is that none of the bound collections that exists or that we can now reconstruct follows the same order of plays.[11] And not one of them even binds *Pericles* immediately after *The Whole Contention*. In other words, seventeenth-century booksellers and collectors do not seem to have read and understood the

---

[10] Tomlin 2006. Pollard and Redgrave noted that Ferguson was 'largely responsible for any bibliographical polish which the catalogue possesses' (1926: ix).

[11] The copy at Texas Christian University is bound in the following order: *Whole Contention, Yorkshire Tragedy, Pericles, Henry V, Oldcastle, Lear, Dream, Merry Wives,* and *Merchant*. See www.library.tcu.edu/spcoll/web-exhibits/Shakespeare/ShakespeareWeb/PavierBinding.htm; and, on the significance of the ordering, see Knight 2013. Greg gives the order of Capell's copy as: *Yorkshire Tragedy, Merry Wives, Dream, Lear, Merchant, Oldcastle, Henry V, Pericles,* and *Whole Contention* (Greg 1908: 116). The Hussey volume was bound as follows: *Whole Contention, Yorkshire Tragedy, Henry V, Pericles, Lear, Dream, Merchant, Merry Wives,* and *Oldcastle* (see Pollard 1906).

New Bibliography, or indeed to have had any conception of the 'Pavier Quartos'.

The fact that *no* existing books correspond in detail to Greg's hypothesis is profoundly problematic. Just how problematic has been demonstrated by Knight, who in 2010 discovered another instance in which a bound book of 'Pavier Quartos' had originally included the very same non-Shakespearean play that was once included in Thomas Percy's volume: the 1617 'third edition' of Heywood's *Woman Killed*, published by Isaac Jaggard.[12] On the blank final verso of the Huntington Library's copy of *Henry V*, there appears a faint 'ghost image' of the title page of *Woman Killed*. As Knight writes, that trace is not an offset, or an image 'transferred from page to page while the ink was still curing in the printing house'. Instead, it derives from the two plays being bound consecutively: the 'almost imperceptible darkening of the paper ... comes from the oil in ink or its acidity relative to a facing leaf'. The Huntington *Henry V* cannot be the one formerly bound in Percy's volume, since that copy is at the Folger, and furthermore in the booklist at the front of Percy's copy, Heywood's play precedes *Henry V*, whereas Knight's 'ghost image' reveals that in that volume *Woman Killed* came immediately after *Henry V*.

The variability of the 'Pavier Quartos' thus extends beyond the *ordering* of its plays to the actual plays it included. As Knight argues, this 'ghost image', together with the Percy book list, suggests that 'the series was not necessarily Shakespearean – that readers and booksellers were free to compile the works with non-Shakespearean material'. But, while he acknowledges that the inclusion of Heywood's play could have been 'possibly the work of publishers', he concludes that the 'textual combination is likely the work of readers'.[13] Tara Lyons suspects, however, that 'this *Sammelband* may have been formed in [the Jaggards'] shop, either the product of the stationers marketing bundles of books from their press or perhaps the result of displaying or storing together similar kinds of recently printed material' (2011: 203).

---

[12] See Knight 2010. We cite here the revised and elaborated discussion in Knight 2013: 151. Only two quartos of *Woman Killed* are extant, but the 1617 edition includes 'the third edition' on its title page, suggesting that a second edition has been lost. Sturgess claimed that the lost edition was published between 1607 and 1617, but, in her textual introduction, Kidnie (forthcoming) argues persuasively that it preceded 1607.

[13] Knight 2013: 154–515, 235 n. 15. See also Erne: 'the composition of such bound volumes was typically determined not by the playbooks' publishers or booksellers but by their owners' (2013: 222).

Here we present new evidence that confirms Lyons's suspicion, and indeed can allow us to go even further: despite the high variability of the order, and to a lesser extent the contents, of the 'Pavier Quartos', Heywood's *Woman Killed* was not bound with Shakespeare by readers but by a stationer; it was not added to the series later but often formed part of it from the start, offered for sale with all or some of the 1619 Shakespeare quartos, and possibly with other plays altogether. In other words, we need to rethink at the most basic level exactly what the 'Pavier Quartos' were.

The evidence that leads us to conclude that *Woman Killed* was part of a stationer's collection offered for sale in bookshops, rather than a reader's idiosyncratic binding up of plays that he or she had previously bought as pamphlets, concerns a minute material feature of early modern pamphlets: stab-stitch holes. In sixteenth- and seventeenth-century English bookshops, playbooks and other short items were sold 'stab-stitched' without a binding. These pamphlets were simply punctured with an awl three or four times, slightly in from the fold, and then stitched with thread to hold the gatherings together (Figure 7.13). Sometimes a blank wrapper would be used as a rough cover to protect the first and last leaves, although this almost never survives. The slits made for stab-stitched pamphlets can usually still be detected, even when, as is almost invariably the case in surviving playbooks, they have later been bound or rebound as expensive antiquarian relics.

But longer books were generally bound up at the time of initial sale, not, as has usually been claimed, by the purchaser after sale.[14] As with pamphlets, booksellers would warehouse these longer texts in sheets. They would then bind a few copies as needed, since binding them all at once offered no reduction in cost. Ten copies cost ten times as much to bind as one, and it made more economic sense to have only a few copies ready for immediate purchase and then, if they sold, to bind up more. While pamphlets could be stitched by just about anyone, including family members and apprentices, bound volumes were the work of skilled professionals, however much booksellers might cut corners to reduce cost.[15] Binding, as opposed to stab-stitching, required the sewing of each individual gathering, the attachment

---

[14] On stationers selling books (as opposed to pamphlets) pre-bound, see Bennett 2004. We are also indebted to conversations with Bennett, Robert Darnton, James N. Green, Aaron T. Pratt, Goran Proot, and Thierry Rigogne. For an example of the sale of pre-bound books, see Downes 1620?. For a counter-view, see Pickwoad 2005. Our work on the 'Pavier Quartos' was both enabled by Bennett's arguments and, we believe, helps to confirm them.
[15] On such cost-cutting, see Pickwoad 1995.

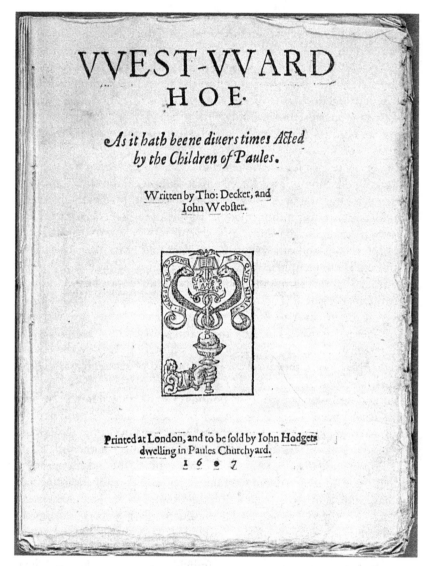

Figure 7.13 *Westward Hoe* (1607) in its original stab-stitched condition

of the gatherings together, sewn onto bands, the securing of the bands in boards, and the covering of the boards in leather. More cheaply (although still professionally), the binder could attach the sewn text-block to a limp vellum cover. In the sewing of a bound book, the needle passes directly through the fold and so it does not leave the same kind of holes or slits in the paper that stab-stitching does, since the holes are hidden deep in the binding.

There were thus two fundamentally different ways of getting books ready for sale, two types of books that readers purchased at stationers' shops, and – importantly – two different kinds of material traces left in the books. If a book has stab-stitch holes, it was probably sold originally as a pamphlet, a single unbound item, although it is possible that it was initially stab-stitched but then bound together with other pamphlets as a book for retail sale. If a book lacks these stab-stitch holes, however, we can be sure that it was originally sold as a bound volume.

The crucial point to note is that, other than in the most exceptional of circumstances, individual playbooks were *unbound pamphlets*.[16] It was highly unusual to bind up fewer than twenty-four sheets (or 192 pages) in quarto as a book.[17] While longer collections of plays such as Seneca's *Tenne Tragedies* (1581) or John Lyly's *Six Court Comedies* (1632) were sold sewn and bound, it is exceedingly rare to find an individual professional play that does not have stab-stitch holes. The main exception to this rule is not surprising: numerous copies of the plays traditionally considered part of the 'Pavier Quartos' survive *without* these stab-stitch holes.[18] This evidence confirms what scholars have long argued: several of the 'Pavier Quartos' (*without* stab-stitch holes) were bound together to sell as a single volume, while others were sold individually (*with* stab-stitch holes).

We have not seen a single other individual professional play from the Shakespearean period without stab-stitch holes – except for the 1617 edition of Heywood's *Woman Killed*. Strikingly, of the seventeen copies of this edition that we have examined or that others have examined for us, six do not have stab-stitch holes.[19] This does not mean that the same

---

[16] On pamphlets, see Raymond 2003: esp. 81–2; and Robinson 1980.
[17] For discussions of the lengths of books typically sold stab-stitched, see Foxon 1975: 111–12; Dane 2012: 171–2; Knight 2013: 4; Pratt (in progress), 'Stab-Stitching and the Status of Playbooks as Literature'; Farmer n.d. Joad Raymond suggests twelve sheets as the usual maximum in quarto (2003), but this seems to be an error.
[18] Of the Folger's nine copies or part-copies of *The Whole Contention*, only three have stab-stitch holes, while six do not (and were therefore sold not as pamphlets but as parts of bound books); of their six copies of *King Lear*, four have stab-stitch holes and two do not. Of the Huntington's nine 'Pavier Quartos', only two have stab-stitch holes.
[19] The copies without stab-stitch holes include one at the Bodleian (Mal. 182[2]); one at the Victoria and Albert (Dyce 26 Box 20/1); two at the Folger (STC 13372 Copy 1 and Copy 2); one at the University of Texas (Pforz 488 PFZ); and one at Yale (Ih H519 607wc). Thanks to Douglas Bruster, Michael Winship, and Olivia Primanis for looking at the copies at Texas; and to Aaron T. Pratt for the copies at Yale.

proportion (about a third) of the original press run of Q3 *Woman Killed* was sold in bound volumes; we cannot extrapolate in any simple way from the surviving examples, nor have we been able to examine each of the (at least) twenty-four surviving copies of the edition. More importantly, the copies *without* stab-stitch holes are likely to survive in disproportionate quantities, since they originally formed part of sturdier, bound books.[20]

Nonetheless, the crucial fact is that a significant number of the copies of Q3 *Woman Killed* originally formed part of the 'Pavier Quartos'. This must surely be the case for the simple reason that, apart from the 'Pavier Quartos', there was no other bound volume of playbooks from the professional theatres that was on sale during these years of which they could have been a part. It was, of course, relatively common for collectors to buy play-pamphlets and then to have half a dozen or more of them bound up afterwards. In the latter case, each of the individual playbooks would have stab-stitch holes, showing that they were originally purchased as pamphlets. But the 'Pavier Quartos', even if they were not a resolutely 'Shakespearean' collection, were nevertheless the first attempt by a publisher to sell a bound book composed exclusively of plays from the professional theatre. In this sense, and this alone, the 'Pavier Quartos' are indeed a precursor of the First Folio, but *not* in terms of a single-authored collection.

But why would an edition of a play by Thomas Heywood, published two years earlier, have been bound up with the Shakespeare quartos of 1619? The answer may be that the 'Pavier' quartos are not as much Pavier's as we have thought. Sonia Massai has already argued that the printer-publishers William and Isaac Jaggard played a more important role in the project than previously imagined (Massai 2007: 108). In fact, we believe the Jaggards were the central figures in the publication. Pavier's name or initials appear on five of the Shakespearean title pages. But Nathaniel

---

[20] The staggering difference between the survival rate of the 'Pavier Quartos' (excluding the apocryphal plays) and of previous Shakespeare quartos can be calculated from Erne's research: on average, just over eight copies of each of the earlier editions survive compared with thirty-five for the 'Pavier Quartos' (Erne 2013: 188–9). The relation between the quarto format and literary value is an important point of contest at the moment. See Dane and Gillespie 2010. In a major new piece of research, Aaron T. Pratt has rightly emphasized that the primary reason for selling plays as pamphlets was to keep the cost down – and that the cost is not directly related to literary value, since collectors often waited until they had collected from about six to fifteen plays (depending on length) before having them bound together (we are deeply indebted to Pratt for sharing his work with us). But few of the early collectors' volumes bind up plays by *author* and that does indeed relate to literary value. For the relation between format and literary value in the *formation* (as opposed to the dissemination) of a literary canon, see Chartier and Stallybrass 2013.

Butter is listed as the publisher of *King Lear*, and Arthur Johnson as the publisher of *Merry Wives*, and there is no reason to doubt their involvement in the project. The only stationer who we know for certain was involved in all of the playbooks was the printer William Jaggard. And Jaggard's is the only name that never appears on any of the title pages, suggesting that he more than Pavier may have been behind the false imprints in an attempt to hide his involvement.

Exactly who Jaggard may have been trying to deceive – other stationers? the King's Men? the Lord Chamberlain? book-buyers? – and why remains obscure. But the fact that he *was* trying to deceive is suggested not only by the false imprints and the abandoning of the continuous signatures that began with *The Whole Contention* and *Pericles* but also by the fact that in all of the seventeenth-century bound volumes that we know of *Pericles* was separated from *The Whole Contention*. Moreover, the inclusion of Heywood's *Woman Killed*, together with the variety of publishers and publication dates, does indeed make these unstandardized volumes of playbooks look like *Sammelbände*, collections put together by early readers after their sale. That this was *not* the case is shown by the lack of stab-stitch holes in so many copies: the individual plays in such readers' collections inevitably contain the stab-stitch holes that reveal how these pamphlets were originally purchased.

Jaggard's centrality to the project also explains the presence of Heywood's *Woman Killed* in these bound volumes. Before 1619, William and Isaac Jaggard had been involved in ten professional playbooks, but almost always as the printers of the book for a bookseller-publisher (including Pavier on four occasions). But William had co-published the first edition of *Woman Killed* (1607) with the bookseller John Hodgets.[21] And the 1617 edition was published solely by the Jaggards, the only professional play that either William or Isaac had solely published to date.

What seems to have happened, then, is that the Jaggards bound up their own edition of Heywood's play with the Shakespearean dramas that William Jaggard was publishing with the help of Pavier, Butter, and

---

[21] The imprint reads, typically for this kind of co-publishing arrangement, 'Printed by William Iaggard dwelling in Barbican, and are to be sold in Paules Church-yard by Iohn Hodgets.' Jaggard may have also helped to finance the 1607 edition of *Westward Ho*, but that imprint does not include his name – 'Printed at London, and to be sold by Iohn Hodgets dwelling in Paules Churchyard' – and, since the play was entered in 1605 by Henry Rocket, the publishing arrangements behind this edition remain murky. We are grateful to Adam Hooks for discussions about Jaggard's printing and publishing around 1619.

Johnson (and possibly Lawrence Hayes, who entered his rights to the copy of *The Merchant of Venice* in 1619). Jaggard may well have had copies of *Woman Killed* on his hands in 1619, two years after publication, since sales of this third edition never justified a fourth. It seems unlikely that he was trying to smuggle this poorly selling edition into the Shakespearean collection without customers noticing, since the play appears first in Bishop Percy's booklist. Rather, Jaggard appears to be going to great lengths to convince someone (who?) that what might appear to be a 'Shakespeare collection' is actually highly variable – and therefore unlikely to be the work of a bookseller.[22] For all we know, some volumes might have included only certain of the Shakespeare plays but not others; they might even have included other plays altogether, ones not yet discovered.

Knight has shown that readers frequently bound items together into volumes in ways that now seem eclectic to us. But the kind of malleability that we have demonstrated here, in a dramatic collection offered for sale by stationers, was highly unusual. We do not, for instance, find copies of the First Folio with plays bound in varying orders (although *Troilus and Cressida* is included in some copies but not others); nor do we find such extremely variable ordering in any other publisher-issued dramatic collection in the period. Most importantly, the 'Pavier Quartos', traditionally seen as the earliest attempt to create a collection of Shakespeare's plays, turns out to be the only publisher's collection of professional drama in the period to bind together the plays of one playwright (or playwrighting partnership) with a play explicitly advertised as by someone else entirely.[23] While readers often created *Sammelbände* of plays by multiple authors, the principle of collection for publisher-created volumes of professional plays was always authorial, with this one exception. By including *Woman Killed* in some proportion of his bound volumes of plays in 1619, Jaggard did something unprecedented.

Greg brilliantly revealed that there was a 'Shakespeare' collection being planned in 1619, but he failed to note that if Jaggard (rather than Pavier) was indeed attempting to establish Shakespearean authorship he was simultaneously making his collection look *non*-Shakespearean: the three

---

[22] Our argument bears some similarity, therefore, to Massai's argument that Pavier was attempting to make the collection look like a 'nonce collection' of previously published plays (2007: 115–16).

[23] The Beaumont and Fletcher folio of 1647, of course, includes plays that Fletcher wrote with Philip Massinger and perhaps others as well. And the Shakespeare folios likely include work by Middleton and others. But these collections only advertise the authorship of Beaumont and Fletcher and of Shakespeare.

'apocryphal' plays; *Pericles*, which would be excluded from the First Folio; and the regular inclusion of *Woman Killed*. What we might now call the 'Jaggard Quartos' show that there was no inevitable trajectory from the early Shakespeare pamphlet-playbooks to the 1623 single-authored collected plays.[24] To the contrary, most of the marketing strategies that we have explored in the case of the individual plays of 1608–09 were still being practiced by Jaggard in 1619: a play might have no named author (*Henry V*); it might simply reproduce the printer's copy from earlier editions (hence Shakespeare's name prominently at the top of *Lear*); it might be falsely attributed (*Yorkshire Tragedy* and *Oldcastle*). If the 'Jaggard Quartos' also crucially diverge from these earlier practices, it is because they marketed plays that could equally well be sold as individual pamphlets or as bound collections. But these bound volumes were never fully 'Shakespearean', and they thus offer a radically different notion of a dramatic collection from the more famous one that Jaggard printed in 1623.

---

[24] Marino (2011: 111) makes the same point, referring to the group as the 'Jaggard Quartos'. See also Adam Hooks's excellent discussion of the relationship of the 'Jaggard Quartos' to the First Folio in his forthcoming book, *Vendible Shakespeare*.

CHAPTER 8

The canonization of Shakespeare in print, 1623
Emma Smith

It has become standard procedure to begin an investigation of the 1623 First Folio with its preliminaries: its title page, engraving, dedication to patrons, prefatory epistle to readers, dedicatory poems and catalogue.[1] These elements of the book designed to attract early bookbuyers have proved irresistible to recent scholars, and what Margreta de Grazia has influentially anatomized as their 'arrogational rhetoric' has tended entirely to dominate discussions of the First Folio (1991b: 42). Clearly this material, specifically generated for the edition, was actively designed to record and perform its multiple allegiances to stationers, aristocratic patrons, actors, a literary community and to its readers. This makes it important. But our exclusive focus on these carefully prepared prefatory pages has made it more difficult for us to perceive the Folio's textual contradictions beyond this opening pose. In this chapter I want to focus on a different aspect of the text, which, since it has no proven provenance in the theatre and does not appear in previous quarto publications, can also be said to be a Folio-specific commission, albeit an incomplete one, and one which tells a different story from the narrative of economic and cultural control convincingly read into the prefatory material. Lists of dramatic characters appear at the end of seven Folio plays. My argument suggests that the ambivalences and inconsistencies in these lists offer a challenge to readings of the Folio's aspirations to turn Shakespeare into a literary dramatist.

At the end of seven of the Folio's thirty-six plays, a list of the characters is added. These carry different but related headings: 'Names of the Actors' (for *The Tempest, The Winter's Tale* and *Othello*), 'The names of all the Actors' (*Two Gentlemen of Verona* and *Measure for Measure*) and 'The Actors names' (*Henry IV, Part 2* and *Timon of Athens*). Some of the lists are

---
[1] See, for example, Marcus 1988; Donaldson 2008; Taylor 2006; de Grazia 1991b; Scragg 1997; Bergeron 2002.

simply reasonably accurate accounts of speaking parts: most modern editions of *Two Gentlemen of Verona*, for instance, copy the Folio, only adding supernumerary attendants and musicians. By contrast, *The Winter's Tale* list omits the speaking parts of Mopsa, Dorcas and Time, and *Timon of Athens* omits Timon's steward Flavius as well as a number of minor characters. On occasion these lists give us evidence that we would not otherwise have – the clarity that Bianca in *Othello* is 'a Curtezan', for instance, or that *The Tempest*'s Caliban is 'a salvage and deformed slave'. At others they give us a simple map of the play, dividing the characters between the two kingdoms of Sicilia and Bohemia in *The Winter's Tale*, or deploying an extensive system of brackets on the full-page list after *Henry IV, Part 2* which enacts the play's rivalries by dividing its groups of characters: 'Opposites against King Henrie the Fourth', 'of the Kings Partie' and 'Irregular Humorists'. The hierarchy and information of these lists, that is to say, are often preliminary forms of interpretation of their plays with readers in mind, and that interpretation implies, but does not identify or locate, agency.

Since most plays in the Folio do not have such a list, why do these? What can they tell us about the provenance of the play texts, and the process of their preparation for print? Surprisingly little attention has been paid to these character lists, but they raise questions about purpose and effect which can epitomize or reframe the more extended debates about agency and authority in the Folio as a whole. And since character lists, as we shall see, are a feature of play texts designed explicitly for readers – theatrical texts do not include them and they have no practical place in the processes of performance organized around actors rather than roles – these Folio examples are fundamentally concerned with the question of Shakespeare's canonization in print and the marketing of his plays as literary dramas.

The extant Folio character lists are all appended after the end of plays. One simple explanation of their presence is proposed by W. W. Greg: that character lists were generated in the printing shop as a contingent solution to problems in casting off manuscript copy – a textual equivalent to Jaggard's large triangular satyr-ornament – or, in the case of *Timon*, the added difficulties created by the substitution of that play in the space that had been allocated for the longer *Troilus*. The Folio is set in formes, as Charlton Hinman so painstakingly discovered, and begins each new play on a new page. Greg suggests character lists are positioned so as to fill up otherwise blank space on the play's final page. Only that following *The Tempest* was, according to Greg, 'certainly printed because it was in the copy and not specially supplied to fill up space', but he does not supply any evidence for this assumption (1955: 418). Perhaps he was influenced by the fact that this list is the only one to occupy a single-column, rather than double-column, space: it is set as the right-hand column adjacent to the Epilogue in the left.

But were this the whole story we might expect more character lists than the Folio includes. The final pages of a number of plays, including *The Comedy of Errors, All's Well that Ends Well, Hamlet* and *Anthony and Cleopatra*, have an excess of white space at their conclusion but no character list. Twenty-four plays have room for the satyr-ornament after their final lines. Greg suggests that someone 'drew up the list of personae to fill up a blank page at the end' of *Timon of Athens* (411), but does not comment on the completely blank page after *Troilus and Cressida* which did not prompt similar attention, or the ten other blank pages in the Folio that remain unadorned. If the extant character lists were to fill up space, space which opened up during the processes of typesetting and printing, they did so only inconsistently. Furthermore, the material they provide is unnecessarily, and problematically, descriptive, including information such as the name of the Duke in *Measure for Measure*, which is nowhere to be found in the play text. There is no evidence that Jaggard's printshop had any experience in interpolating this kind of material. Their theatrical experience was largely connected with playbill printing, and the only public stage plays they printed prior to the Folio were the 1607 edition of Heywood's *A Woman Killed with Kindness* and the so-called 'Pavier Quartos' in 1619, none of which has any paratextual material. Indeed, the only character list in any printed playbook that shows specific signs that it might have derived from the printshop is in Nicholas Okes's 1635 edition of *The Knight of the Burning Pestle*. Whereas the first edition of this play in 1613, also printed by Okes, has no character list, this 1635 text carries a list in the order of characters' appearance linked with the narrative 'then' (this does not appear in any other play text list), which may suggest a list quickly derived from serial reading through the text's entry stage directions. The Folio character lists do not share these features, and a printshop assessment of space requirements, therefore, cannot fully explain their distribution or content.

The absence of one putative list could, however, be connected with available page space. Of the initial four plays in the Folio's first section of plays, 'Comedies', only one, *The Merry Wives of Windsor*, does not have a list of characters. It is generally thought that these four plays were based on manuscripts made by the scribe Ralph Crane (for an extended discussion of Crane's dramatic transcripts, see Paul Werstine's contribution to this volume). The case has further been made that *Othello* and *Henry IV, Part 2* also derive from Crane transcripts, leaving only *Timon* as a Folio play not associated with Crane's scribal practices but carrying a list of roles. Perhaps there was a list in the original manuscript copy for *Merry Wives* that could not be fitted into the space available (unusually, that play text finishes near to the foot of its final page). Crane's own orthographic and organizational priorities have been extensively studied. Trevor Howard-Hill summarizes that Crane's

> transcripts probably contained clear and correct act and scene markings, and in some of them the entrances might be massed at the beginning of each scene, with consequent though not complete loss of later entrances and most other stage-directions. His stage-directions had features which might be characterized as 'literary' and attributed to his copy, but his interference with the text of stage directions makes them doubtful evidence for the kind of copy he transcribed. (Howard-Hill 1974: 71)

It is hard to be clear about Crane's habitual practice on the matter of character lists. If his manuscript provided the copy for the 1623 edition of Webster's *The Duchess of Malfi*, there the character list is headed, like those for *Henry IV, Part 2* and *Timon*, 'The Actors Names'. Of his extant dramatic manuscripts, *Barnauelt* (a theatre playbook) and *A Game at Chesse* (probably a presentation copy) do not have any list. His presentation copy of Middleton's *The Witch* (c.1619–27) shows a number of practices which are not echoed in the lists in the Folio (Wilson 1950: vii–viii). *The Witch* character list opens with a double-column list headed 'The Persons' (perhaps influenced by Jonson's apparent preference for this formula), organized by sex and hierarchy: the left-hand column begins with 'Duke' and ends with the clown Firestone; the right-hand column mirrors this by beginning with the Duchess and ending with mute roles of 'other witches and servants'. The Folio lists are generally organized by social hierarchy, and so Alonso, King of Naples, heads the character list after *The Tempest*, rather than its main character Prospero. This is not always the case: in *Othello* the list is headed by 'Othello, the Moore', with the play's socially dominant figure, the Duke, only fifth in the list, thus inscribing a dramatic rather than a social hierarchy. Elsewhere the lists are organized by gender, so, for instance, the women of *Henry IV, Part 2* form a cohort separate from any of the other groupings. Arrangement by either social hierarchy or gender is common but by no means standard in play printing at this date. No Folio character list makes use of the two columns, in the manner of *The Witch*, meaningfully to organize the information in the list: the nearest is *The Winter's Tale*, but, rather than being headed by the two royal 'twinned lambs', 'Emilia, a lady' has strayed into the right-hand column, pushing Polixenes into second place. None of the Folio lists includes mutes or supernumeraries: these are part of Crane's complete list for *The Witch*. Further, there is no evidence that Crane's manuscripts ever placed any character list at the end of the play, so the possible scribal provenance does not help with the question of their position.

Crane is thus connected to the appearance of character lists in the Folio but cannot have been their sole author, as a more extensive case study reveals. The 'Names of all the Actors' appended to *Measure for Measure* has a number of anomalies and thus raises important issues about the provenance of that text and its list. Honigmann notes that it 'in particular deserves pondering, for its incompleteness as well as over-completeness discredits the notions of a scribal or printer's compilation' (1965: 46). It includes the otherwise unknown name Vincentio for the Duke. It distinguishes, even as it brackets together, '2. Friers', Thomas and Peter, whom editors since Johnson have felt were intended as, or should be collapsed into, a single character. It omits three minor roles: the non-speaking part of Varrius who is indicated in a stage direction at the beginning of Act 5 and addressed in Act 4, the boy who sings at the beginning of Act 4 and the small role of the Justice. Modern editions reinstate them along with supernumerary characters 'Lords, Attendants, Officers, Servants, Citizens'.[2] The Folio list denotes Pompey only as 'Clowne', his speech prefix designation, whereas Mistress Overdone, called 'Bawd' in stage directions and speech prefixes, is given both her proper name and a function in the character list. Writing in 1922, John Dover Wilson suggested that, taken collectively, these features indicate that the list, 'whencesoever derived, relates to a form of the play different from that which has come down to us' (1922: 115).

Dover Wilson's observation – although not his elaborate schema of putative revision to amplify it – is helpful in that it stresses the disconnect between the play text and its Folio apparatus. The explanatory apparatus that should clarify the play is here misaligned. Greg suggested that the list's specific features were scribal: 'unless the scribe omitted [Vincentio] from

---

[2] This example is from *Measure for Measure* (Bawcutt 1991: 85).

the direction at I.i.1 he apparently invented it for the list. If he did, he may also have invented the names of Thomas and Francisca in the directions', but this does not correspond with Crane's known working practices elsewhere (1955: 355). (Indeed, giving specific names, sometimes unnecessarily, to individual characters is often seen to be a distinctively Shakespearean practice.) The genetic edition of *Measure for Measure* included in *Thomas Middleton: The Collected Works* (Taylor and Lavagnino 2007b) can throw some light on the inconsistencies of the character list. John Jowett (2007a) suggests that as part of a relocating of the revised play to the topical location of Vienna, Italian names were deleted to make the change less obvious, including that of Vincentio (although Francisca the nun's Italianate name is retained in both text and character list). His reconstructed text 'reinstates' the name Vincentio as part of the original opening scene (1.1.2). Jowett also suggests that the exchange between Escalus and the Justice at the end of 2.1 is a later addition bringing on an additional character who does not find his way into the character list. The stage direction which opens 2.1 certainly makes the entrance of the Justice look like an afterthought: 'Enter Angelo, Escalus, and servants, Iustice'. Both these proposals about the text's revision construct the character list as a remnant of an *earlier* version of the play, which still calls the Duke by his Italianate name and does not include a Justice. But other suggestions about the provenance of the text contradict this idea that the character list is a residual marker of the erased original. Jowett proposes that the Middletonian name 'Overdone' was added to the generic 'Bawd' as part of the later revisions, here suggesting that the character list represents the *later* revision of the text. He also points out that the format of the phrase 'Two other like Gentlemen' is unique in pre-1640 drama except for Middleton's *Nice Valour* (1543–47); the relational term 'like' links the gentlemen to Lucio as a 'fantastique', an association not otherwise indicated in the text. These factors suggest that the character list is derived from and relates to the revised version of the play. The cumulative force of the suggestions about the revision of *Measure for Measure*, therefore, does not help us resolve the provenance of the character list. The list offers some of the evidence for Middleton's revision of the text, but does not appear to represent this revised state entirely: it is a palimpsest of different stages of the text's incarnation bearing the impress of different agents of composition and transmission. It is a document of textual flux rather than the authorizing apparatus of paratext. Interestingly, these contradictions turn the character list into an ongoing accompaniment to a changing text, and undermine any assumption that it might stand as a post-hoc supplement to the printed play.

Would those readers 'from the most able, to him that can but spell' have expected lists of characters as part of this substantial book? It was not yet the norm for single-play quartos to carry a list of characters. Of ninety-two play quartos published between 1616 and 1625, only twenty-eight, or 30 percent, had such lists, and those lists were most commonly found on the verso of the title page. No printed play by Shakespeare before the Folio had included a character list (Marmaduke Parsons's 1637 edition of *The Merchant of Venice* is the first Shakespeare quarto to do so, and it is not until Rowe's edition in 1709 that all the plays were provided with such a list). The placement of the Folio's seven character lists, following rather than preceding their play, is almost unprecedented. No other printed play of the period, printed singly or in a collection, places its character list after the play, except for Marston's *Jack Drum's Entertainment* (1601, 1616 and 1618). The opening of *Henry V* in the Folio illustrates the peculiarity: the standard layout increasingly familiar from quarto playbooks would place the character list on the verso page opposite the play's opening scene. Here the page opening mimics this convention, but the character list is a textual curtain-call belonging to the previous, rather than forthcoming, play. It is hard to imagine readers becoming accustomed to the emerging protocols of printed drama being able to make use of these belated character lists as aids to their reading.

If character lists were an emerging trend in the publication of commercial stage plays, they were firmly established in the print presentation of play collections and of closet (i.e., unacted) drama. Published collections of play texts, or of plays published alongside works in other genres, were very much more likely than standard play quartos to contain character lists. Jasper Heywood's *Seneca His Tenne Tragedies* (1581), for instance, provides 'the speaker's names' before each play. Samuel Daniel's plays, included in various editions with other poems, are always preceded by a character list. In the 1601 folio edition of his *Works*, for example, the opening speech of the Egyptian queen in *Cleopatra* faces a list of 'The Actors'. Ben Jonson's 1616 *Workes*, so often cited as the precedent for the Shakespeare volume, was organized with a character list on the verso page facing the beginning of each play, ruled into two columns and usually adopting the heading 'The Persons of the Play'. While in 1623 character lists were not yet an indispensable part of a printed quarto play, habitual readers of collected, higher status or closet drama would be justified in having the expectation that a list of the characters would be included. Indeed, it might even be said that having a character list was one significant marker of the literary status of closet drama (150 of 185 closet plays in the period carried a character list).[3]

It has often been noted that Edward Blount, described as the first folio's 'chief publisher' or 'principal investor',[4] was not previously involved with the printing of commercial stage plays (Hinman and Blayney 1996: xxviii). Indeed, Blount's only attested professional interest in the texts of the public theatre was his registering of the rights to a handful of plays including Jonson's *Sejanus* in 1604, Daniel's *Philotas* the following year and Fletcher's *A King and No King* in 1611. Blayney observes caustically that 'it is a striking testimony to the nature of Edward Blount's interest in Shakespeare's plays that although he had himself registered *Antony and Cleopatra* in 1608, by 1623 he had apparently forgotten that he owned it' (21). But this obscures the fact that Blount, particularly early in his career, had an active list of high-status closet drama. These texts were routinely presented with character lists as part of their self-consciously literary and classical forms of address. Blount's edition of Matthew Gwinne's Latin *Nero Tragaedia Nova* (1603), for example, carried a prominent page opening listing 'Actorum nomina', and the equivalent list in his *Vertumnus siue Annus recurrens Oxonii*, published by Blount in 1607, is headed 'Personae'. Blount's edition of Daniel's *Certaine small poems lately printed with the tragedie of Philotas* (1605) and its second edition in 1607 both include a list of 'The Actors'. William Alexander's collection of Senecan closet dramas *The Monarchick Tragedies* (1604) names a list of 'Actors' or, sometimes, 'The persons names that speakes' before each play. Alexander's collection, dedicated to 'his sacred Majestie' the king, was published by Blount in two volumes in 1604 (it had been printed in Edinburgh the previous year) as part of a suite of pro-James publications, including Daniel's *Panegyrike Congratulatorie* (1603), William Cornwallis's *The Miraculous and happie union of England and Scotland* (1604) and Jonson's *Magnificent Entertainment* (1604). Blount published a second edition of Alexander, 'Newly enlarged' into four volumes, and noting its author as 'Gentleman of the Princes privie chamber' in 1607. Alexander's character lists, like his own social status and the broader aspirations of his publisher, marked out his texts as distinctly literary.

---

[3] Numbers derived from DEEP (Database of Early English Playbooks), http://deep.sas.upenn.edu/.
[4] 'Blount, Edward (*bap.* 1562, *d.* in or before 1632)', Gary Taylor, *Oxford Dictionary of National Biography*. Online edition. www.oxforddnb.com/index/2/101002686/ (accessed 29 May 2013).

We can begin to see the development of character lists, therefore, as a kind of imperfect synecdoche for the development of literary printed drama in the period. Learned Senecan-inspired dramas that disavowed performance in favour of reading routinely bore lists of their characters, and, increasingly, plays from the public and private London theatres mimicked this paratextual form. From the mid-1620s onwards, stationers began to refurbish previously printed plays with character lists when reprinting.[5] This corresponds with other scattered markers that the drama was developing a literary identity: the excerpting of plays alongside poetry in anthologies such as *England's Parnassus* (1600), the increasing presence of playbooks in gentry libraries discussed by Heidi Brayman Hackel and Lukas Erne's argument that 'a close "readerly" attention to the play's text is not a modern aberration' (Erne 2003: 24). Erne claims that the gradual process of 'legitimation of dramatic publications leading to their establishment as a genre of printed texts in its own right rather than as a pale reflection of what properly belongs to the stage' began during Shakespeare's writing career (33). For many critics, the move into the Folio format is decisive in establishing both Shakespeare as a literary author and vernacular stage plays as literary works. Gary Taylor has written that the Folio 'attempted to move Shakespeare into an entirely different market' from previous quarto publications, and that the physical format of the book 'asserts its cultural legitimacy: the double-column folio format was strongly associated with serious and significant works'. He spots that contemporary dramatists such as Fletcher or Middleton would have been obvious candidates to write prefatory verses for the Folio, but that they are left out in favour of 'cosmopolitan intellectuals' such as the Oxford Hispanist James Mabbe and the poet and translator Leonard Digges: the material form of the book thus combines with the cultural capital paraded in its prefatory documentation to produce Shakespeare as an 'elite commodity' (Taylor 2006: 64–6). Given this narrative of cultural and economic aspiration, it is striking that the Shakespeare Folio, directed by the 'upmarket literary stationer' Edward Blount (Massai 2013: 133), himself so thoroughly conversant with the presentation of high-status drama, takes so little interest in presenting itself according to these paratextual status markers.

---

[5] See Taylor, Daileader and Bennett 2007: Table 1, 'Tables Added in Reprints, 1515–1664'. There are, however, some counter-examples, such as the second edition of *Philaster* (1622), which drops the character list that was present in the 1620 edition.

Part of the Folio cartel's reconstruction of public theatre plays as an elite cultural commodity involved a complex negotiation between the plays' past on the stage and their future in the hands of its readers. It is clear that the Folio's opening address is to readers. Ben Jonson's poem 'To the Reader' is placed before the title page so that it forms the first printed words in the book, stressing the address to 'Reader' in the final injunction: 'looke/ Not on his Picture, but his Booke'. Leah Marcus suggests that Heminge and Condell 'tie the idea of recovering the "Originall" Shakespeare to the reading audience's *amour-propre*', and that the Folio constructs a 'nascent world of timeless communication between the Author and his Readers' (1988: 43–4). But the prefatory material cannot forget the theatre. The Herbert brothers are invited to 'descend to the reading of these trifles' but reminded of their 'likings of the severall parts, when they were acted, as before they were published'.[6] The epistle 'To the great Variety of Readers' reminds the book-buying public that 'these Plays have had their triall alreadie' before theatre audiences. Dedicatory poems continue to toggle between the stage and the page. One intervening piece of prefatory material is headed with a new Jonsonian title – 'The Workes of William Shakespeare, containing all his Comedies, Histories, and Tragedies: Truely set forth, according to their first originall'. The stress here is on the literary quality of the 'workes' and the authority of the texts 'truely set forth', but the heading is over another list of actors' names: 'The Names of the Principall Actors in all these Playes'.

Here, of course, at the beginning of the book, the names of the actors are not, as they are after *Othello* or *Two Gentlemen of Verona*, the names of the characters. Bernard Beckerman has traced how the word 'player' in sixteenth-century character lists is replaced in the seventeenth century by the preferred term 'actor', and allows that there was some ambiguity in the usage of the term 'actor' meaning either role or performer (1980). This ambiguity is illustrated in another playbook publication of 1623. The 1623 quarto edition of *The Duchess of Malfi* (Nicholas Okes for John Waterson) was the first printed play with a character list headed 'The Actors Names' which included both character and player names. 'Actor' here signals both role (Bosola) and performer (J. Lowin), and the *Malfi* list also disrupts the idea of a one-to-one correspondence between actor and role, indicating doubled characters and the substitution of other actors in the same role. Some of these same ambiguities are evident in the Folio, where the first list

---

[6] On the use of the Herbert dedication to implicate the Folio in a network of Sidneian literary associations, see Massai 2013: 132–46.

of 'Actors' means, as we would now use the term, the real names of the professional performers of the King's Men, although the company is, as Marcus points out, curiously absent from the Folio (1988: 106). The list of twenty-six actors, however, is a company roll call from its earliest days in 1594, apparently organized historically (the first names are the original sharers, the last names are those company members still acting at the time the Folio was published), and thus it memorializes the ongoing company rather than the specific cast of any single play.[7] One early reader annotated this list with memories of his own theatre-going, writing 'by report' next to Burbage's name and, proudly, 'know', next to Benfield and Taylor and 'by eyewitnesse' next to Lowin.[8] Jonson's example in his folio *Workes* is an instructive contrast. Jonson's plays are each preceded with a list of characters usually headed 'the Persons of the Play'. After the end of each play, a separate page details its original performance conditions. The page after the first play, *Every Man in his Humour*, reports that

> This Comoedie was first Acted, in the yeare 1598. By the then L Chamberlayne his Servants. The principall Comoedians were, Will Shakespeare. Aug. Philips. Hen. Condel. Will. Slye. Will.Kempe. Ric. Burbadge. Ioh. Hemings. Tho. Pope. Chr. Beeston. Ioh. Duke. With the allowance of the Master of the Revells.

Jonson places the names of the actors after the play; the Shakespeare Folio places the names of the characters in this position. Jonson distinguishes between 'persons' or roles and 'comedians/tragedians' or actors; the Shakespeare Folio conflates these two categories and interposes the professional actors as the plays' most prominent agents.

The list of actors is on its own recto page, demonstrating the preliminaries' lavish use of space. Steven K. Galbraith has usefully distinguished folios of 'necessity', 'luxury' and 'economy' among late sixteenth-century literary folio texts (2010: 48–9), arguing that the folio format does not always have the connotations of elegance and significance that are traditionally ascribed to Shakespeare's collected plays. Galbraith argues that the Shakespeare folio was one of 'necessity', given the large amount of text that needed to be printed, and shows that the amount of paper needed to print the double-column pica pages of the Folio was more efficient than quarto publication (for the eighteen plays previously printed in 176 sheets in quarto, the Folio took only 115 sheets). What is more striking is that the

---

[7] On the members of the King's Men, see Gurr 2004b: Appendix 1.
[8] Manuscript annotations in Glsasgow University Library, Sp Coll BD8-b.1.

book is a folio of necessity, even economy, masquerading in its opening pages as a luxury item. The prefatory material, particularly aimed at readers, is set in single column and heavily decorated with Jaggard's ornamental blocks, and is closely modelled on the layout and typography of the Jonson folio. As the Shakespeare Folio – unlike Jonson's – changes from its luxurious preliminaries into the crowded double-column pages of the plays, it turns away, too, from its initial stress on readers. As the absence of character lists indicates, most of the plays are, at best, only lightly prepared with conventions of reading in mind.

Although it has been customary to call Heminge and Condell editors, their own description of their labours, in the dedication to the Herberts, is that of collection:

> We have but collected them, and done an office to the dead, to procure his Orphanes, Guardians, without ambition either of selfe-profit, or fame: onely to keepe the memory of so worthy a Friend, & Fellow alive, as was our SHAKESPEARE, by humble offer of his playes, to your most noble patronage.

In their epistle 'To the great Variety of Readers' they again figure themselves as gatherers: we 'onely gather his works, and give them to you'. Perhaps Heminge and Condell's modesty here should be taken seriously. The provenance of the Folio texts is an ongoing critical question, which tugs in two directions. The Folio has been claimed both as the text that packaged Shakespeare for upmarket reading – a playbook that could break through Thomas Bodley's oft-quoted prohibition on riffraff books and find its way into the Oxford University Library – *and* the book which bears the closest marks of King's Men performance. The second may be more true than the first. The deployment of the character lists at the end of a handful of plays is an index to the lack of attention to readerly apparatus and priorities in the Folio as a whole, perhaps confirming that collection, rather than more substantial editing, was how Heminge and Condell perceived their obligation to their colleague. Proofing and correction seem to have been minimal, particularly compared with the other Jaggard volumes in press at the same time. There are any number of examples of obscurities and difficulties for readers arising from texts which do not routinely regularize entrance or exit directions, provide descriptive stage directions, or clarify the names of the speakers. Confusions over the names of the twin Antipholuses in the Folio *Comedy of Errors* (both are called 'E Antiph.' at different points in the text) or the speech prefix 'Rich.' (disconcertingly shared between hunchback king and

Tudor avenger at the end of Folio *Richard III*) are just two small examples of functional problems with Folio texts as reading texts.

Despite being printed in a format to encourage the serious study of the plays, therefore, the Folio makes few concessions to its readers and shows little sign of having been prepared with their experience in mind. Later studies of the way the book positions itself have focused on the richness of the prefatory material, and therefore may have been misled by the preliminaries' presentational and direct address to its readers. After its first pages, the Folio ignores the developments in playbook presentation that are specifically targeted at reading, and steps away from the Jonsonian precedent that has so often been cited as its model. 'Reade him, therefore; and againe and again': the Folio makes it less easy than it might have been to fulfil Heminge and Condell's exhortation.

PART III

From print to manuscript

CHAPTER 9

Commonplacing readers

Laura Estill

By and large, early modern readers were commonplacing readers: that is, interactive readers. In Tudor schools, students were taught the value of extracting selections from religious and classical works into their notebooks (Crane 1997: 53–92; Donker 1992: 7–112). Commonplaces (also called *sententiae*) are rhetorically well-phrased sayings that express a pearl of wisdom. Commonplacing readers treated Shakespeare's texts, like other works, as sources of advice and wit that could be used in daily life, and commonplace books and miscellanies, both in print and manuscript, reveal that readers approached Shakespeare's texts not as complete units but rather as repositories of phrases and ideas to be excerpted and appropriated. In this examination, I show how extracts from Shakespeare's work could be commonplace in two senses: both sententious (edifying) and ubiquitous. I demonstrate that commonplaces from Shakespeare's works were part of quotidian seventeenth-century life, found in schools, churches, and conversations.

The wide variety of Shakespearean commonplaces and other extracts from his work reflects the range of readers and modes of interaction with his text. Manuscript commonplace books and miscellanies enable us to consider Shakespeare's readers as individuals rather than as an abstract, imagined, unified group, just as the commonplaces themselves reveal that those individual readers did not always consider Shakespeare's plays as cohesive wholes. This analysis focuses on witty or sententious extracts found in seventeenth-century commonplace books or miscellanies rather than on those instances where a song or numerous extensive passages appear. The commonplaces from Shakespeare's work discussed here can be placed on multiple continua: from attributed to anonymous;

I am grateful to the Social Sciences and Humanities Research Council of Canada and the Banting Postdoctoral Fellowship programme for funding this research. I would also like to thank J. Matthew Huculak, Kailin Wright, and Joel Swann for their insightful suggestions.

from high-minded literary quatrains to bawdy one-liners; from personally chosen excerpts to pre-selected snippets.

Manuscript compilers chose to copy many parts of Shakespeare's works, but not all extracts from his plays were commonplaces. While the readers discussed in this chapter copied commonplaces for their own use and to share with others, some readers turned to pre-selected material that appeared in print commonplace books. As is well known, commonplaces from Shakespeare began to appear around 1600 in printed commonplace books such as Robert Allott's *Englands Parnassus: or The Choysest Flowers of our Moderne Poets* (STC 379) and John Bodenham's *Bel-vedére: or The Garden of the Muses* (STC 3189) (Stallybrass and Chartier 2007: 43–52). In his introduction, Bodenham emphasizes that he has undertaken the 'labour' of collecting commonplaces; the opening commendatory poem echoes the 'paines' Bodenham has taken 'in laborious care' (sigs. A3, A7).[1] With the prefatory material in their print commonplace books, Allott and Bodenham position commonplacing readers as active readers, working to find knowledge. Print commonplace books had their detractors precisely because they allowed readers access to wise phrases without committing to the labour of commonplacing: that is, read complete texts, copy out extracts, and arrange them by commonplace heading. Despite their differences, both those who read print commonplace books and those who commonplaced from complete plays demonstrate that, in the early modern period, Shakespeare was valued for his articulate wit and insight, which could be captured in commonplaces, adapted by interactive readers, and repurposed for use in conversation or writing.

Before turning to the Shakespearean commonplaces circulating around the universities, churches, and in conversation, it is important to recognize the printing conventions that urged readers to commonplace from Shakespeare's works. Early modern plays often contained gnomic pointing, those typographical indicators that signaled the sententious passages for readers to copy or memorize. These passages could be marked by a change in typeface or commonplace markers, those familiar single or double quotation marks.[2] Commonplace markers appear, for instance, in the three earliest *Lucrece* printings (1594, 1598, 1600), in the first *Hamlet* quarto (1603), and throughout the first folio. Commonplacing readers did not always copy the passages marked – indeed, according to Beal's

---

[1] In this chapter, common manuscript abbreviations have been silently expanded and i/j, u/v, and long s normalized. Intralinear insertions are marked with carets unless otherwise noted.

[2] For more on commonplace markers in early modern plays, see Hunter 1951; de Grazia 1991a; and Lesser and Stallybrass 2008.

Catalogue of English Literary Manuscripts, there are no known instances of readers copying the passages highlighted by the many commonplace markers in *Lucrece* – but the very presence of commonplace markers indicated to readers that the work should be read for the well-phrased words of wisdom. Readers' engagement can be seen from the marks they left in their texts, such as underlines, marginal crosses, braces, or manicules; some even added their own commonplace markers, as in the 1594 *Venus and Adonis* copy at the Huntington Library (call number 69260). This chapter, however, focuses on those commonplaces that readers copied into manuscripts.

A wealth of commonplace books and miscellanies can be traced to Cambridge and Oxford, particularly from the 1620s and 1630s. Just as early modern grammar-school students were taught to fill commonplace books with edifying and moralizing lines from classical and religious texts, university students kept commonplace books with notes from their readings.

Just because commonplaces from Shakespeare's work appear in manuscripts from the universities does not imply that Shakespeare was being treated as a great humanist writer. On the contrary: it is often bawdy couplets from *Venus and Adonis* that can be found in university miscellanies. These selections were often chosen because of their erotic turns, such as this combination of two couplets from Shakespeare's Ovidian poem found in multiple university manuscripts:

> **Kissing: a song**
> Come sweet sit heere where never serpent hisses,
> And being sate Ile smoother thee with kisses,
> Let me graze on thy lips, if those hills are too dry
> Then Ile stray lower where the fountaines lye.[3]

This titillating quatrain, remixed from Shakespeare's longer lurid poem, was not unusual in university manuscripts: as Ian Moulton points out, 'the overwhelming majority of surviving manuscripts containing erotic verse can be linked either to the Inns of Court or to the universities' (2000: 41). Furthermore, in manuscript culture, it was not unusual for verse to be abridged, expanded, revised, or combined into new poems (Marotti 1993: 135–46).

Robert Bishop's miscellany, one that also includes this adapted 'Kissing' poem, highlights that commonplace readers did not always commonplace from full works. Bishop's sources for his Shakespearean commonplaces are unclear. As the 'Kissing' song is found in multiple university manuscripts,

---

[3] Rosenbach MS 1083/16, f. 279; adapted from *Venus and Adonis* ll. 17–18 and 233–4. For a facsimile of this page, see Roberts 2003: 88.

Bishop could have copied from one of them and never read Shakespeare's complete poem.[4] In his miscellany, Bishop also copied sonnets 2 and 106 as well as a stanza from *Venus and Adonis*, 'Now the worlds Comforter with weary gate / ... / Doe summon us to part, & bid good night' (ll. 529–34) titled 'Goodnight to you'.[5] Sonnet 2 was the most popular in early modern manuscript culture and so offers no proof that Bishop ever saw a complete version of Shakespeare's sonnets. Likewise, sonnet 106, given in Bishop's manuscript with an additional fourteen lines, can be found in another extant miscellany and as such we cannot guarantee that Bishop turned to the printed text.[6] The *Venus and Adonis* stanza, as published alone in *Englands Parnassus*, is a potential intermediary print source. Commonplacing readers at the universities and beyond would have had much fodder from which to select Shakespearean extracts (both ascribed and not), including Shakespeare's published works, manuscripts that were passed from person to person, and printed commonplace books.

Legal students at the Inns of Court, like their counterparts at the universities, commonplaced from Shakespeare – some, also with the intention of finding phrases to use with women. One manuscript, collectively written at the Inns of Court, includes Romeo's admiration of Juliet that culminates in 'I'll watch her place of stand / And touching hers, make blessed my rude hand'.[7] The compiler has added a brief note, 'taking her by the hand', before continuing with Romeo's direct address to Juliet,

> If I profane with my unworthiest hand
> This holy shrine, the gentle sin is this,
> My lips, two blushing pilgrims, ready stand
> To smooth that rough touch with a tender kiss.   (1.5.93–6)

Beal identifies 'taking her by the hand' as a stage direction, though it is not one that appears in the printed play. This direction could apply to more

---

[4] As Roberts points out (2003: 86–9), this poem also appears in Daniel Leare's miscellany (British Library MS Add. 30982, f. 22). The poem can also be found in Folger MS V.a.262, a Christ Church compilation (f. 155). British Library MS Egerton 923, another Christ Church manuscript, contains a different adaptation that begins with Shakespeare's couplet and segues into selections from Thomas Randolph's 'A Pastoral Courtship', including the thematically apt 'and why soe coy with it, you feare / no speckled serpent lurketh heere' (ff. 65v–6).

[5] Transcriptions from Bishop's manuscript are taken from Redding's edition (1960).

[6] Morgan Library, MA 1057, p. 96.

[7] Meisei University, MR 0799, p. 56; *Romeo and Juliet*, 1.5.44–51. As I was unable to consult this manuscript, I follow the description in Beal's Catalogue (ShW 86.8) and use modernized spelling. This manuscript is also known as the Monckton-Milnes manuscript or the Crewe manuscript. The line numbers for this reference are Beal's.

than Shakespeare's Romeo wooing Juliet in a fictional or staged world; it also serves as an instruction by the compiler to take a woman's hand before launching into these lines in an actual conversation. Romeo's words would not make sense unless spoken by a man holding his love interest's hand. As the following example will also demonstrate, it was not just students who had ambitions to appropriate Shakespeare's words into amorous conversations.

Clergy, like students, were interactive readers – indeed, many clergymen likely took up the practice of commonplacing while at school. James Whitehall, Rector of Checkley, was an Oxford graduate who kept a small miscellany with notes about university life and the parish of Ipstones, and literary extracts (William Salt Library MS 308-40). Whitehall copied pages of commonplaces from Sir Philip Sidney's *Arcadia*, followed by selections from Marston's *The Dutch Courtesan* and Shakespeare's *Richard II* and *The Merchant of Venice*, which have, to date, gone unnoticed by scholars.[8] While the Shakespearean extracts are not themselves dated, some appear on an opening with anonymous poetry dated 'Aug: 19: 1609' (ff. 97v–98). In July 1609, Whitehall earned his MA from Oxford and was ordained.[9] Whitehall's miscellany, which he likely eventually took with him to Checkley in 1620, shows how commonplacing readers moved beyond the universities.

Whitehall was drawn to sententious passages from the final act of *Richard II* about two of the play's main themes: reputation and pardon. Rather than focusing on the play's main action, Bullingbrook's rise and Richard's fall, Whitehall was interested in the familial drama between York, his wife, and Aumerle. When York discovers his son has plotted against the new king, Henry, he immediately reveals his son's treason, despite his wife's pleas. Whitehall began this section of commonplaces with York's words to the new king undermining his son's apology, 'feare & not love begets his penitence', adding the explanatory note '(quod old Yorke / to the kinge against his sonne Aumerle)' (f. 97, 5.3.55). Whitehall's presentation of the extract allows readers to see both the general, commonplace application and the particular, moving moment in Shakespeare's play where a father demands the harshest judgment for his son. The extracts from *Richard II* that follow are all couplets on the same theme that juxtapose York's unflinching desire for justice with his wife's entreaties for lenience:

---

[8] I am grateful to Joel Swann for pointing me to this manuscript and sharing his transcriptions.
[9] See the *Clergy of the Church of England Database* (http://theclergydatabase.org.uk/), person ID 16113.

> If thou doe pardon because you they pray
> more faultes for this forgivenes prosper may }
> This festred joynt cut of the rest are sound } quod Yorke
> this let alone will all the rest confound
>
> ....
>
> I never longed to heare a word till nowe
> Say pardon kinge let pitty tell thee howe
> the word is short but not so short as sweet
> no word like pardon for kings mouths so meete.
>
> (f. 97r–v; 5.3.82–5, 114–17)[10]

By contrasting two opposing voices, Whitehall captured the onstage clash of wills and engaged with the rhetorical practice of incorporating dialogic texts into one miscellany.[11]

Whitehall's Shakespearean commonplaces are, on the one hand, decontextualized from their places in the play and made common by being removed from the plot and characters. On the other hand, Whitehall sometimes added notes referring back to the play and attaching words to particular speakers, such as 'quod old Yorke'. These references to the play would serve to jog his memory about the scene or speaker in which they originally occurred, which would help Whitehall apply them appropriately to new situations. Paradoxically, reference to their original context prepares Shakespearean commonplaces to be thoughtfully recontextualized.

As well as copying selections about the clash of family loyalty and a subject's duty, Whitehall altered and personalized some of *Richard II*'s romantic passages. He copied Richard's touching farewell with his queen: 'Come, come, in woeing sorrowe lets be breiff / since wending it there is such length of greif' (f. 97, 5.1.93–4). Whitehall presented Richard's words and his Queen's response surrounding their final kiss:

> One kisse shall stop our mouthes, and dumbly part
> Thus give I mine, & thus I take thy heart
>
> queene. Give mee mine owne againe twer no good part
>
> to take on mee to keepe & kill thy heart[12]

Whitehall's interlinear additions offered an alternate version of Richard's lines that the reverend himself could use if the situation arose: 'One kisse

---

[10] The first 'thou' is unclear, possible written over 'I'.
[11] For more on 'dialogic literary practice', see Roberts 2007.
[12] William Salt Library MS 308-40, f. 97, interlinear additions omitted; *Richard II* 5.1.95–8.

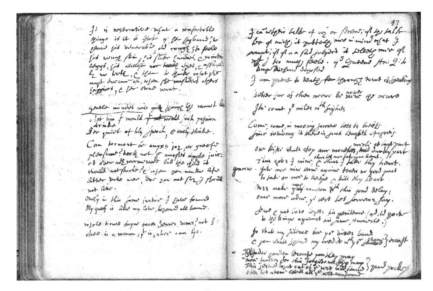

Figure 9.1 William Salt MS 308-40 ff. 96v–97

shall stop our mouthes, **weele at last part** / Thus give I mine, **thus let mee take your heart**' (see Figure 9.1).[13] Whitehall's manipulation of Shakespeare's words gives the interlocutor, a love interest, the chance to speak (she is no longer 'dumb') and accept a kiss ('let me' rather than 'I take').

In another case, Whitehall offered an alternative interlinear reading that changes one of the Duchess of York's heartfelt exhortations for the king to forgive her son into potential material for courtship; he changed an unromantic plea into words with romantic potential. In Shakespeare's play, the Duchess imagines an alternate past as a way she could change the present situation. In the Duchess's imagined past, she was the king's nurse and raised him properly so he would, in the actual present, save her son: 'If now I were thy nurse thy tonge to teach, / Pardon should bee the first word of thy speach'.[14] Whitehall's interlinear optional emendation suggests not a maternal speaker but a wooing subject who problematically infantilizes the interlocutor/love object: 'If now I were thy nurse thy tonge to teach, / **I love thee** should bee

[13] William Salt Library MS 308-40, f. 97; Whitehall's interlinear revised text emphasized in bold; *Richard II* 5.1.95–6.
[14] William Salt Library MS 308-40, f. 97v; interlinear addition omitted; *Richard II* 5.3.112–13.

the first word of thy speech'.[15] While the Duchess boldly imagines herself instructing the king, Whitehall imagined himself teaching his romantic interest. Unlike his modification of Richard's words that supposes the love interest can be a speaking agent, this adaptation imagines a mute, tractable *tabula rasa*. In both cases, however, Whitehall amended Shakespeare's text so it could be spoken not only by characters in a play but also by hypothetical real-life speakers. Whitehall's manuscript indicates that he commonplaced with a view to apply Shakespeare's *bon mots* in conversation. By changing only a few phrases, Whitehall shows that a play is, truly, what the reader makes of it; and *Richard II* can be a primer for both the responsibilities at court and the language of courtship.

Even though commonplacing readers were selective readers, in that they chose the ideas to copy, Whitehall's miscellany reminds us that they were not always discriminating arbiters of taste. From *The Merchant of Venice*, Whitehall collected further lines of courtship such as

> you have devided mee
> one halfe is yours: the other halfe yours,
> mine own I would say; but if mine then yours
> and so all is yours. O these naughty times
> put barrs between the owners & their rights

and 'You have bereft mee of all words / because onely my bloud speakes to you in my vaines' (f. 98 r–v, 3.2.15–19, 175–6).[16] This section of Whitehall's miscellany clamours with lovers, from Sidney's Pamela, 'My hart, my word, my word hath giv'ne my hart / the giver giv'n from gift shall never part', to an anonymous poet-speaker whose trite doggerel begins, 'In other loves no joy or comfort is / The love of you is all my earthly blisse'.[17] Whitehall does not mention the author of these assorted verses, but, occasionally, the speaking lover: 'quod Pamela', 'quod Portia to Bassanio' (f. 98). Like other miscellanies, Whitehall's manuscript underscores that readers who commonplaced from Shakespeare were generally not interested in centralizing Shakespeare in the canon, but rather, in treating Shakespeare's plays like other texts: as sources to be mined for potentially useful phrases.

---

[15] William Salt Library MS 308-40, f. 97v, Whitehall's interlinear changes emphasized in bold; *Richard II* 5.3.112–13.
[16] 'Because' appears in shorthand.
[17] William Salt MS 308-40, ff. 98, 97v; anonymous poem, Sidney's *Arcadia* (1593), sig. Gg5v. This poem is not listed in the Folger *Union First Line Index* or found in ProQuest *Literature Online*.

Unlike Whitehall, whose Shakespearean commonplaces are scattered amidst other material, Abraham Wright, an Oxford-educated clergyman and one of the better-known Shakespearean readers, methodically arranged his selections by play, noting the authorship of each.[18] Wright copied selections from *Othello* and *Hamlet*, as well as plays by Jonson, Webster, and others in his mid-seventeenth-century miscellany, British Library MS Add. 22608. Wright deemed *Othello* 'A very good play both for lines and plot, but especially the plot. Iago for a rogue and Othello for a jealous husband 2 parts well pen[ne]d' (f. 84v), but criticized *Hamlet* as 'But an indifferent play, the lines but meane' (f. 85v). Wright judged most early modern plays in terms of 'lines' and 'plot';[19] he copied dozens of extracts from both plays seriatim, that is, in the order they appeared in the plays, but a reader approaching his selections without having read the plays would not have been able to gather the plots of either.

Wright commonplaced from Shakespeare and contemporary dramatists for his own edification, with his son in mind and perhaps even thinking of the useful turns of phrase for his sermons (Kirsch 1969: 260). Wright left marginal notes (added later), presumably for his son James, including some that highlight the importance of commonplacing: 'Marke Sydenham for penning epistles and imitate him. Take out of these some expressions … and make common use of them upon their severall occasions' (f. 69).[20] 'Silver-tongued Sydenham', as he was known, was Humphrey Sydenham, a preacher (Fuller [1662]: sig. DDD3; Wood 1691/2: sig. F3v). Wright wanted his son to read, imitate, and use plays as he used other texts. This commonplacing father positioned his son to read the commonplace book, seek out new texts, and become a commonplacing reader as well. Wright passed down not only his commonplaces from plays, but also a love of pre-1642 theatre. In his 1694 *Country Conversations*, James Wright's imagined conversants, 'who omitted no occasion to Magnifie the Wit of the Dramatick Poets of the last Age' (1694: 54), agree that 'there is hardly a Scene in *Shakspeare* (tho' he Writ near 100 years since) but we have it still in Admiration, for the Vivacity of the Wit, the Justness of the Character and the True, Natural and Proper Expression' (4). James Wright's inherited appreciation of Renaissance drama included the ability to see Shakespeare's

---

[18] For more on Wright, Sancroft, and the widespread practice of copying selections from plays, see Estill 2015.
[19] For a transcription of Wright's commentary on early modern plays, see Kirsch 1969. In 'Excerpta', McManaway transcribes some of the Shakespearean extracts (McManaway 1967).
[20] Wright used a simple substitution code for his notes to his son. Here, Wright's words have been decoded and abbreviations expanded. See also McManaway 1967: 120–1; Kirsch 1969: 260.

plays on two levels: both the macro level of scenes and characters and the micro level of wit and expression.

Abraham Wright valued his Shakespearean commonplaces not just for his son's education but also for their potential usefulness in conversation. Wright included explanations for some of his selections, which would make them easier to understand, both for his son and if he were himself turning back to his manuscript for ideas. For instance, Wright explicated Hamlet's 'Too much water hast thou poore Ophelia, and therefore I forbid my ^teares^' by adding the parenthetical note that he was '(speaking of one ^drownde^)' (f. 85v, 4.7.185–6). Wright also jotted explanations for unfamiliar words: 'A puny, a Quat, a Whipster. all the same for a feeble weake fellow'.[21] Wright's glosses and explanatory notes, like Whitehall's, make Shakespearean commonplaces easier to reuse.

Unlike Whitehall, Wright rarely mentioned the speaker's name, though he did copy some brief exchanges for their wit. Rather than giving character names, when Wright recorded an exchange between two speakers, he used 'A.' and 'B.' to show that the second line responds to the first, as in 'A. would you doe such a thing for all the world. B. the world's a huge thing, it is a great price for a smal vice'.[22] Even though Wright eschewed speech prefixes or character names, he did not always abstract the speakers' words, as in Othello's confrontation with Emilia: 'A. my husband. B. woman I say thy husband: dost understand the word? my freind thy husband, honest, honest Iago. A. If hee say soe may his pernicious soule / rot halfe a graine a day' (f. 84, 4.3.65–7).[23] Othello and Emilia's exchange seems inextricably tied to the play's action (Iago's duplicity, Emilia's initial consternation), yet Wright extricates it nonetheless. Wright's miscellany highlights how a wide variety of Shakespearean text could be commonplaced, even material that was not aphoristic in its original contexts.

Whitehall and Wright are just two examples of commonplacing clergymen who interacted with Shakespeare's text differently. While some of Whitehall's commonplaces could have been used in courtship, some of Wright's selections from plays could have found their way into his sermons. Acclaimed as 'a good Orator' and 'elegant preacher' himself (Wood 1691/2: sigs. Ss4v–Tt1), Wright urged his fellow Church of English clergy to 'change the *Theater* into a *Church*; having a greater power over the passions of their *Auditorie*, then the *Actor* hath upon the

---

[21] British Library MS Add. 22608, f. 84v; referencing *Othello* 5.2.242.
[22] British Library MS Add. 22608, f. 84; *Othello* 4.3.65–7.
[23] Virgules in transcriptions of British Library MS Add. 22608 appear in the manuscript.

Stage' (sig. A3v); incorporating commonplaces from drama would be one way to channel the actor's power. While many of the extracts might not be on appropriately religious topics, their rhetorical flourishes could well be adapted for the pulpit.

In one of his sermons, Wright noted, "Tis a clear Sun-set that commends the day and the chief grace of the Theater is a good com off' (sig. C5v). Wright's commonplaces from Shakespeare range widely in topic and style, but much of his interest in *Othello* lies in its 'com off' or conclusion. Unlike the majority of his extracts, which are brief phrases, Wright's longest selections from *Othello* are the Moor's final speeches. Wright copied Othello's 'Behold, I have a weapon' speech in its entirety (though not verbatim). Rather than copy Shakespeare's text as poetry, Wright wrote margin-to-margin, marking line breaks with virgules. In this visually unrelenting block of text, Othello's 'dead, O, O, O,' draws the reader's eye (f. 84v, 5.2.279). Ignoring Lodovico's, Cassio's, and Iago's lines, Wright continued with Othello's next speech, beginning, 'I have done the state some service', and running directly to 'I tooke by'th'throat the circumcised dog, / and smote him thus. (stabs himselfe.) I kissd thee ere I killd thee, noe way but this, / killing my selfe to die upon a kiss' (f. 84v, 5.2.335–52, 354–5). These final speeches include some of the most poignant lines in the play, 'then you must speake, / of one that loved not wisely, but too well: / of one not easily jealous, but beeing wrought, / perplext in the extreames' (f. 84v, 5.2.339–42). Similarly, from *Hamlet*, Wright gave the eponymous hero the last word, with Hamlet's 'Wast Hamlet wrongd Laertes?' and, perhaps fittingly, ending with 'His madness is poore Hamlets enemie' (f. 85v, 5.2.205, 211). As an interactive reader, Wright both commented and commonplaced, ultimately shaping the text as his own.

Decades later than Wright, the Archbishop of Canterbury himself, William Sancroft, also actively copied commonplaces from Shakespeare's text (Bodleian MS Sancroft 29). Sancroft, who, like Wright, extracted widely from many early modern dramatists, often chose short, pithy phrases and glossed unfamiliar words. Some of Sancroft's selections are clearly sententious, such as 'There's small choice in rotten apples' (p. 83, *The Taming of the Shrew* 1.1.134–5) or 'Falser than vows made in Wine' (p. 84, *As You Like It* 3.5.73) or chosen for their vivid imagery, such as 'Who is abroad without Lang[uage] his tongue is of no more use to him than unstrung Harp or Viol' from *Richard II* (p. 77, 1.3.161–2). Sancroft was also drawn to some of the more vicious Shakespearean insults, such as this string of insults from *Troilus and Cressida*:

> Thou Bitchwolfe Son. beefwitted, soddenwitted Lord,
> that hath no more braine, than I have in my Elbow: an
> Asinego may Tutor thee. thou wear'st thy Wit in thy
> Belly, & thy guts in thy Head. – Hast not so much Wit
> as would stop the Ey of a needle. Thy pia mater is not
> worth the 9th part of a farthing.[24]

While one can hardly imagine the Archbishop of Canterbury, who is often characterized as retiring and bookish, using these vitriolic invectives, his selections show that he revelled in Shakespeare's plays at least in part for the language (Collinson 2006: 173–200).

Though Sancroft might not have ever used some of Shakespeare's more colorful insults, his brief explanations suggest that he intended to reuse at least some of the extracts he selected. For clarity's sake, Sancroft explained his selections from the descriptions of Portia's potential suitors: 'The German. I like him in the morning (sober) very vildly; most vildly in the afternoon (drunk.)' (p. 85, *The Merchant of Venice* 1.2.70–1). He similarly glossed the description of Hermione-as-statue, 'A statuary. | Could he but breath into his Work, He'd beguil N[atu]re of her ~~Work~~ Custom; so perfectly he is her Ape' (p. 80, *The Winter's Tale* 5.2.84–5). Sancroft's additions, like Wright's, would help him customize and aptly apply Shakespeare's turns of phrase for new uses, possibly in conversation, letter-writing, or sermons.

Though this chapter has established that commonplacing readers were, well, commonplace, they were not limited to commoners. Alnwick Castle Northumberland MS 525, a manuscript that can be linked to the court, includes a generally overlooked line from *The Rape of Lucrece* – 'revealing day through every Crany peepes' – squeezed into a messy page that includes letter-form practice, a table of contents, and doodles.[25] One reader jotted a couplet from *Venus and Adonis*, 'Fayer flowers that are not gathered in there prime / Rot and consume themselves in littill Tyme', into a medieval miscellany with sections that date back to the fourth century that is now part of the British Library's Royal manuscripts collection.[26] The early modern additions are perhaps in keeping with the miscellany's other contents, which include both verses and commonplaces. These two manuscripts show that Shakespearean commonplaces could be copied at court or make their way to courtly circles. The Alnwick and Royal

---

[24] Bodleian MS Sancroft 29, p. 77; adapted from *Troilus and Cressida* 2.1.8, 9, 38–9, 65, 70, 72, 63–4. Sancroft was similarly drawn to insults in *Timon of Athens*.
[25] See Burgoyne 1904 and Loomis 2002: 68–9.
[26] British Library MS Royal 8 A XXI, f. 153b; *Venus and Adonis* ll. 131–2. See also Roberts 2003: 90.

manuscripts, moreover, remind us that while some readers copied Shakespearean commonplaces neatly organized, attributed, and arranged by heading, others scribbled lines on any available paper: there was no single way of interacting with Shakespeare's text.

Very few unbound Shakespearean commonplaces survive, though this does not suggest it was unusual to copy extracts from Shakespeare onto loose manuscript pages. Many commonplaces copied into manuscript, especially those jotted on single pages or manuscript separates, like their oral counterparts, may not have survived.[27] We do, however, have at least one example: one practical reader copied sententious selections from Shakespeare's plays onto a slip of paper that was later used as a bookmark.[28] Like many bookmarks tucked away on today's bookshelves, the slip of paper is dark and crumpled at the top but crisp where it rested safe in the book – except this one lay untouched for hundreds of years. This bookmark exemplifies Shakespeare not as hallowed author, but as part of daily life. The remarkable fact that this single piece of paper survived suggests that there were others like it, single pages with a few 'notes / drawn out of playbooks' that we no longer have (Jonson, *Volpone*, 5.4.41–2). This bookmark reveals one reader's interaction with plays and suggests new ways of thinking about intertextuality by considering the commonplaces both in relation to their sources and their destinations: in this case, Shakespeare's words were placed in a now unidentified early seventeenth-century German publication.[29]

Both the physical object of the bookmark and the text written on it remind us of the quotidian uses of early modern dramatic texts. The bookmark copyist chose sententious passages, such as the moralizing warning to speak no evil: 'Curses never passe the ~~mouths~~ ^lipps^ of them that breath / them in the aire'.[30] Richard III's 'small herbs have grace great weeds grow apace', reported by his nephew, was meant as an insult to the growing boy, but on this slip of paper is offered without comment surrounded by other Shakespearean adages, such as Richard's ominous adage, 'Soe wise soe young, they say never live long'.[31]

From the universities to the inns of courts, from churches to the royal court; in print, manuscript, and spoken word – commonplacing readers

---

[27] May and Wolfe suggest that the survival rate of small, unbound manuscripts could be comparable to that of broadside ballads at around one in 1,000 (May and Wolfe 2010: 133).
[28] British Library MS Add. 41063, f. 87.
[29] British Library MS Add. 41063, f. 88 (letter from J. N. Collie about the bookmark).
[30] British Library MS Add. 41063, f. 87; *Richard III* 1.3.285–6.
[31] British Library MS Add. 41063, f. 87; *Richard III* 3.1.79.

were paradigmatic of an active mode of reading in the early modern period. Commonplacing readers demand that we consider Shakespeare's works as mutable and, above all, modular. Many seventeenth-century readers would not have approached Shakespeare's plays the way we do in our classrooms and our research, that is, as unified artistic texts that cannot be disassociated from Shakespeare's name and canonical position. Shakespearean commonplaces circulated (both attributed and anonymously) in early modern times like the ubiquitous Shakespearean quotations that can now be found on coffee mugs, magnets, bumper stickers, and greeting cards. Perhaps the Archbishop of Canterbury's seventeenth-century commonplace book holds the seeds of today's Shakespearean insult generator. While much Shakespeareana can be considered novelties, the short selections of text they often bear are not novel or new: early modern commonplacing readers knew how to do things with Shakespeare, too.

CHAPTER 10

Annotating and transcribing for the theatre: Shakespeare's early modern reader–revisers at work

Jean-Christophe Mayer

Theatrical annotations vary considerably in type and frequency from one early modern play text to another. This chapter will nevertheless try to highlight a number of common practices. First, I will concentrate on early printed editions annotated for the theatre in or around the Restoration and will then move on to consider manuscript books based on printed editions of Shakespeare's plays. In the pre-Restoration non-Shakespearean manuscript play texts examined by Paul Werstine in his recent study (2012), the most frequent theatrical annotations are, in descending order: passages cut; notation of sounds; addition of stage directions; corrections, changes, or additions of speech prefixes; corrections or change of dialogue; partial repetition of existing stage directions; and censorship by a bookkeeper or some other agent.[1] This list concurs for the most part, but to varying degrees, of course, with the Restoration printed editions of Shakespeare which were annotated for the stage. Indeed, I hope to show the *continuity* as well as the diversity of many annotating practices among theatrical revisers throughout the seventeenth century. As few Shakespearean texts used for performance before the Restoration are extant, the majority of the examples in this chapter will inevitably be taken from the period after 1660.[2] Often idealized by editors or scholars, these texts offer a window on the way Shakespeare's works were transformed for the stage almost continuously for a multiplicity of purposes: aesthetic, pragmatic, but also private or political. The story of why Shakespeare was kept alive on stage is also the story of books, but it is necessarily as well a story of cultural

---

[1] I am citing only the most frequent in Werstine's list. For further details, see Werstine 2012: 243–4.
[2] For an account of some early Shakespearean editions probably used in the theatre before the Restoration, see Sisson 1942.

practices and historical processes, as literary texts remain alive only by the will and desire of those who want to *engage* with them.

Early printed editions of Shakespeare annotated for the theatre

Most of the annotated play texts under consideration are part of large format Shakespearean editions (First Folios and a Third Folio). These bulky volumes might seem ill adapted to the theatre, and yet, with their text printed in double columns on large pages, they allowed the bookkeeper to visualize more of the play at a glance than was the case with smaller volumes. Notations of sounds, props, as well as prompt-warnings and advance character-calls are fairly common in these books. But the most recurrent and most instructive practice for our purposes are the numerous cuts and also the equally frequent manuscript corrections, alterations, and in some cases rewritings that these annotated editions display. The cutting of printed Shakespearean text is a frequent, but not systematic, phenomenon. Some theatricalized texts are very lightly cut, if at all, and although passages could be crossed out or hashed in ink, sometimes they were simply circled to allow the unwanted text to remain visible, in case the cut was reinserted at a later stage or used in another production. Thus, some annotators created in fact a more flexible text where options could be kept open. Annotations pertaining to Restoration theatrical practices, such as descriptions of stage settings, also appear.[3]

A first category of cut affects parts and thus characters in the play. In a First Folio currently held by the University of Padua and annotated for the theatre after 1640, a reviser has endeavoured to reduce the length of Macbeth's part in a number of ways, including the deletion of the first interview between Macbeth and the murderers (Act 3.1).[4] If lengthy parts are often trimmed, another way of cutting consists in reducing secondary characters' lines. Titania's part in Act 3.1 of *A Midsummer Night's Dream* is cut so much in a First Folio connected with the Hatton Garden Nursery in London, *c.*1672, that she almost entirely disappears from the play: the quarrel with Oberon over the little Indian boy is omitted, as is the consequent Bottom-enchantment episode (Evans 1960–96: vol. 3). Likewise, the actress playing Adriana, Antipholus of

---

[3] Blayney also surmises that First Folios' decline in price at the Restoration made them more readily available to theatre companies (1991: 34).
[4] See Evans 1960–96. The online edition of these volumes will be cited throughout.

Ephesus's wife in *The Comedy of Errors*, has far fewer lines to speak in a Third Folio belonging to the Smock Alley Theatre in Dublin, c.1676–85 (Evans 1960–96: vol. 8).

Another cutting technique consists in reassigning omitted characters' lines to other parts. In the same annotated edition of *The Comedy of Errors*, the character of Balthazar has disappeared but some of his lines are spoken by Angelo. In the Smock Alley *Macbeth*, Macduff is substituted for Ross (as in William D'Avenant's version of the play), while in the Padua *Macbeth* the reviser appears simply to have wanted to reduce the number of extras: in Act 3.1 and 3.4, 'Angus' replaces the Folio 'Lords' and in Act 5.6 'Angus Rosse, Y [i.e., Young] Seyward' are substituted for 'their Army' (Evans 1960–96: vols. 5 and 1). A more ambiguous case is the complete omission of the Bawd's part in Act 3.2 of the Padua *Measure for Measure*, which may have been done for moral reasons (D'Avenant also cuts this material) (vol. 2).

This brings us now to examine some of the reasons why passages of Shakespeare's texts were rejected by his early modern theatrical readers and revisers. Passages considered over-long, or digressive, are often cut by revisers who wish to tighten up the action of the play. Thus, in the Padua *Measure for Measure*, several passages are clearly considered inessential and are marked out to be omitted: the conversation between Lucio and the two Gentlemen (1.2), the dialogue between Escalus and Pompey (2.1), part of the Duke's speech on death, the conversation in which Pompey tries to persuade Lucio to get bail for him (3.2), the Duke's rhymed moralizing in Act 3.2 and Pompey's list of Mistress Overdone's customers (4.3). Short parenthetical comments also disappear under the pen of the reviser.

Similarly, but perhaps less drastically, one of the revisers of the Padua *Macbeth* has omitted the Porter Scene in Act 2.3 (also cut in the Smock Alley *Macbeth* and frequently omitted in modern productions), the first interview with the two murderers (3.1), the scene of comment on Banquo's murder (3.6) and part of the Malcolm–Macduff interview (4.3). Polonius – an often long-winded orator – does not speak his protracted instructions to Ophelia (1.3) in the Smock Alley *Hamlet* (vol. 4). In the same way, the ghost's lines are not left untouched – parts of the speech in which he describes his murder in Act 1.4 were probably considered too 'wordy' and are cut. Portions of a digressive passage between Rosencrantz and Guildenstern and Hamlet, which includes Hamlet's now famous '*Denmark*'s a prison', disappear.

Rife with rumours and side-comments, Shakespeare's *Henry VIII* has also been cut to a considerable degree in the Smock Alley Third Folio (vol. 8). Conversations deemed unnecessary are excised – the discussion between Buckingham and Norfolk on the state of the kingdom and its relation to Cardinal Wolsey (1.1); the chitchat preceding Wolsey's entry in 1.4; the conversation between *'two Gentlemen'* about Buckingham's sentence and Wolsey's responsibility in it (2.1); another comment from the *'two Gentlemen'* (2.1); the conversation between Anne Bullen and the *'Old Lady'* in 2.3; the side-comments of the *'Gentlemen'* before the 'show' of 'The Order of the Coronation' (4.1); the discussion between Gardiner and Sir Thomas Lovell about the plot against Cranmer and Cromwell (5.1).

However, the type of passage considered to impede performance varied from one reviser to another. Often, they reveal the personal tastes of the revisers and their idea of what would work on stage at a specific time and for a particular audience. While some retained poetic or gnomic passages, others cut them out, thus going against the grain of the commonplacing practices of a good many of their contemporaries. In the Padua *Measure for Measure*, nearly all of the most poetic speeches in the play are affected by omissions, including Isabella's elevated speech in Act 2.2, which begins with 'Could great men thunder / As *Ioue* himselfe do's, *Ioue* would neuer be quiet'. Likewise, all six lines of Othello's impassioned speech in the Smock Alley annotated Third Folio, 'Farewell the neighing Steed, and the shrill Trump' (3.3), are excised (vol. 6). Sententious passages in the Padua *Measure for Measure* also tend to vanish. They were probably considered untheatrical by the reviser and their compact and self-contained nature made it all the easier to cut them. For instance, Escalus's aphoristic side-comment, '*Some rise by sinne, and some by vertue fall:* / *Some run from brakes of Ice, and answere none,* / *And some condemned for a fault alone*' (2.1), is done away with, together with the Duke's series of proverbial and moral conclusions beginning with 'Hence hath offence his quicke celeritie, / When it is borne in high Authority' in Act 4.2.

While modern editors would seek to resolve textual cruxes, or clarify difficult passages in footnotes or introductions, early modern revisers simply tended to dispose of them. No doubt considered too cryptic and thus unnecessary, Macbeth's lines about 'this Banke and Schoole of time' in Act 1.7 of the Padua First Folio are omitted. The same goes for Lady Macbeth's lines, which begin 'And to be more then what you were, you would / Be so much more the man. [. . .]' (1.7). In the Padua *Measure for*

Measure, the reviser took a dislike to Angelo's admittedly arduous lines in Act 2.4 of the First Folio, 'As these blacke Masques / Proclaime an en-shield beauty ten times louder / Then beauty could displaied [...]'. Somewhat cerebral passages, such as Laertes's reply to Ophelia in Act 1.3 of the Smock Alley *Hamlet*, 'For nature cressant does not grow alone, / In thews and Bulk: but as his Temple waxes', could be literally crossed out.

At times, revisers acted as censors. However, in the annotated play texts which I have examined, such instances are fairly rare and reveal that religious, rather than sexual issues were avoided most. Malcolm's 'but God aboue Deale betweene thee and mee' in Act 4.3 of the Padua *Macbeth* is crossed out and badly smeared, and Angelo's reply to the Duke in the Padua *Measure for Measure* (5.1) is equally censored, no doubt for its attribution of divine powers to the Duke: 'When I perceiue your grace, like powre diuine, / Hath look'd vpon my passes'.

As we have seen, there were numerous reasons for cutting Shakespeare's text, and while, generally speaking, these cuts were designed to tighten the performance text, in some cases they were necessary in order to introduce *other material*, such as songs and dances. Annotators thus broke the barriers of the printed book to introduce circumstantial material. This is where the activities of cutting and rewriting overlap. In the Hatton Garden Nursery First Folio, two distinct revisers have divested *The Comedy of Errors* of many parts of its arguably overlong speeches and light comic passages so as to be able to insert a number of songs and dances.[5]

This brings us now to consider another widespread annotation practice, that of making corrections and changes to the text. The purpose of these changes is often to summarize or gloss a passage that the reviser has previously cut. In the Smock Alley *Hamlet*, the passage following Claudius's instructions, which are aimed at ensuring that Hamlet sets off to England (4.3), and in which the King addresses England in menacing terms, is cut and replaced by the manuscript line 'And England if our present love thou holdst at ought let it be testify'd by Hamlets death'.[6] The first six lines of the murderers' dialogue in the Smock Alley *Macbeth* (3.3) are crossed out and replaced by the more portentous 'It is about ye howre'.

---

[5] Between scenes 1 and 2 of Act 1; between Acts 3 and 4 (Evans 1960–96: vol. 3). See also Act 2.4 of *Macbeth* (Evans 1960–96: vol. 5).
[6] Evans suggests that this line may have been lifted from either of two *Hamlet* prompt-books prepared by the actor John Ward probably around 1745, which would date this particular revision much later than the Restoration. See n. 3 of Evans's introduction (Evans 1960–96: vol. 4).

Nor were Shakespeare's sometimes wild flights of fancy and poetry to every reviser's taste either. When considered too ornate, his text was often simplified. Adriana's six-line passage, which begins, 'The time was once, when thou vn-vrg'd wouldst vow, / That neuer words were musicke to thine eare' (2.2), is reduced to the more laconic, 'The time was once, when you lov'd mee' in the Hatton Garden Nursery version of *The Comedy of Errors*. In the Smock Alley *Hamlet*, the main character promises to remember injunctions within 'the table of my memory' – a manuscript addition that simplifies the crossed-out Third Folio text: 'Within the book and Volume of my brain, / Unmixt with baser matter; yes, yes, by heaven' (1.4). In the same way, one of the theatrical annotators of the Smock Alley *Macbeth* changed Banquo's famous lines about Macbeth 'New honors come upon him / Like our strange Garments, cleave not to their mould, / But with the aid of use' (1.3) into 'Like strange Garments which weare not easy but wth help of use'.

The extent to which Shakespeare's text should be modernized can be a contentious issue among scholars today and yet, of course, such processes were already at work in the four successive Shakespearean folio editions and in his early modern single-play editions.[7] Moreover, there is ample evidence that his late seventeenth-century theatrical revisers were similarly keen to modernize. Many theatrical practitioners deemed the books' silent editorial modernizations insufficient. One of the annotators of the Smock Alley *Midsummer Night's Dream* has a particular knack for spotting and changing outmoded words and difficult phrasing (vol. 7). In the Smock Alley *Hamlet*, the ghost's parting words are no longer 'Adieu, adieu, Hamlet:', but 'Farewell, Farewell' (1.4) and Claudius's line about Hamlet, 'Yet must not we put the strong Law on him' (4.3) is modernized and turned into 'yet must we not lay our strict justice on him'.[8]

In some cases, the alterations are close to rewritings and the reviser can be seen to accomplish work similar to that of an adaptor. There are several modes of rewriting and in the case of perhaps one of the most talented of these revisers – an anonymous annotating hand in the Smock Alley *Midsummer Night's Dream* – these modes range from condensing and

---

[7] See, in particular, Massai 2007: 180–95 *et passim*.
[8] Evans 1960–96: vol. 4. Modernization can sometimes take the shape of a silent cut, as in the Smock Alley *Macbeth* where two of the revising hands delete all references to Macbeth's armour (5.3) and shield (5.8). The intention was probably to dress the actor playing Macbeth in some more modern costume (Evans 1960–96: vol. 5).

paraphrasing to almost complete rewriting. Let us examine three passages, among the many, which illustrate the changes introduced by this particularly thorough reviser.[9] Where the Third Folio has Hermia speak the following:

> Before the time I did *Lysander* see,
> Seem'd *Athens* like a Paradise to me.
> O then, what graces in my Love do dwell,
> That he hath turn'd a heaven into Hell? (1.1)

this reviser condenses the passage, preserving a similarly sounding couplet rhyme, but cutting the last two lines:

> for since I cannot wth Lysander be,
> at Athens, tis a perfect hell to me[.]

Another spectacular example of rewriting appears in part of a dialogue between Lysander and Helena in Act 2.2, which reads as follows in the original Third Folio text:

> Where *Demetrius*? oh how fit a word
> Is that vile name, to perish on my sword?
> *Hel.* Do not say so *Lysander*, say not so:
> What though he love your *Hermia*? Lord, what though?
> Yet *Hermia* still loves you, then be content.

The changes made to the passage are clearly akin to paraphrasing and the reviser has been especially careful to retain as many of the original rhyming words as possible:

> Where is *Demetrius*? y^t disdainful L^d
> tis iust y^t he shoud perish by my sword?
> *Hel.* Now you're unkind *Lysander*, say not so:
> What though he love your *Hermia*? what though?
> while *Hermia* still is yours, be you content[.]

A final example will serve to show the range of the annotator's techniques. Lines spoken again by Lysander, in Act 3.2:

> Why should you think that I should wooe in scorn?
> Scorn and derision never comes in teares:
> Look when I vow I weep, and vowes so born,
> In their nativity all truth appears

---

[9] Evans highlights these three passages in his introduction to the play in the facsimile edition of the folio (Evans 1960–96: vol. 7).

are paraphrased and rewritten in a fashion that is much closer to a form of adaptation, as we are here quite a step removed from the Third Folio text:

> Why do you think I follow you in scorn?
> Scorn cannot well be masqud in sighs & teares:
> See while I vow I weep, and vowes so born,
> like truth her selfe in her first dresse appeares[.]

Even when they worked within the bounds of the so-called 'authentic' book, these examples show how revisers shifted the borders of the text by opening it up to new aesthetic possibilities and reinvented its performability.

Among the various corrections and changes to the text which we have studied, there is one final category which we have not yet mentioned – textual emendations. Although arguably of great importance to modern editors, they did not appear to preoccupy theatrical annotators to any great extent. With a few exceptions, textual cruxes would be left as they were by early revisers. As we have seen, the solution for theatre people was to cut difficult passages or to rephrase them – thus efforts were made to reshape the text, rather than to try to establish a 'correct' meaning. What was 'correct' was what worked on stage and spoke to the moment.[10]

This does not mean, however, that early printed play texts are devoid of textual emendations. Like many texts which have travelled through time, printed plays are *communal* texts. They often display several levels of annotation and it is not rare to find editorial emendations which tend characteristically to be the work of non-theatrical eighteenth-century readers. Thus, a number of plays we examined for their theatrical notes in the Smock Alley Third Folio have become hybrid annotated texts in that they also contain editorial emendations. Indeed, an eighteenth-century hand was at work in the Smock Alley *Hamlet, King Lear, Merry Wives of Windsor* and *Midsummer Night's Dream*, as the Third Folio text is corrected 'by inserting emendations proposed by editors from Rowe (1709) through Hanmer (1743)' (Evans 1960–96: vol. 8). Other types of hybridity are possible – as early texts annotated for the theatre can also contain passages marked up by their commonplacing readers. This is the case of a First Folio currently held by the Shakespeare Birthplace Trust in Stratford-upon-Avon (Shakespeare 1623), which contains numerous manicules pointing

---

[10] See Orgel 1988: 12.

to passages of literary beauty, as well as indications of possible theatrical cuts ('stop' and 'go on') on several pages of *Richard III* (q5^v onwards). While printed books may appear bounded and locked into the deceptive fixity of print, the annotations they contain are often a reflection of the myriad professional, artistic, editorial and personal purposes they were made to play across the generations.

Early Shakespearean manuscript play texts

If early printed plays annotated for the theatre are not common, early Shakespearean manuscript play texts are extremely rare. Very few survive and only a handful can be directly related to some kind of theatrical use.

The Douai Municipal Library in northern France holds transcripts of *Twelfth Night, As You Like It, The Comedy of Errors, Romeo and Juliet, Julius Caesar* and *Macbeth* (cited in the order of their binding), which were probably used to stage amateur performances (MS 787).[11] All of these bear the date 1694, apart from *As You Like It* (dated '1694/5 9° Martij'). Scholars agree that all of these texts were probably prepared at the English College of Douai in the late seventeenth century and that the transcripts were at least partly based on a copy of Shakespeare's Second Folio (1632).[12] Strictly speaking these manuscripts are not annotated texts like the ones studied previously. Yet none of them is a word-by-word transcript of the Second Folio. All have been adapted to various extents for stage use and thus allow us to catch a glimpse of how late seventeenth-century readers and amateur performers escaped from the constraints of print by moving back to a manuscript medium, which enabled them to give free rein to their creativity and shape Shakespeare's texts to their personal idea of how they should be performed.[13]

Overall, the technique used in cutting the plays and in modernizing them is not far removed from the practices we have highlighted in annotated printed editions of Shakespeare. The plays most affected by cuts are *Romeo and Juliet* (some 971 lines) and *As You Like It* (477). Those least affected are *The Comedy of Errors* (18) and *Julius Caesar* (25), which are both

---

[11] Their binding is near-contemporary to their transcription and the manuscript also contains transcripts of Lee's *Mithridates* (1678), Dryden's *Indian Emperor* (1667) and D'Avenant's *Siege of Rhodes* (1663). For details, see Evans 1962 and Hedbäck 1979.
[12] For evidence of theatrical activity at the Douai College, see Dusinberre's edition of *As You Like It*, which cites and translates extracts of the College's diaries (Dusinberre 2006: 380–2).
[13] What follows is partly based on Dusinberre's and Evans's detailed examinations of the manuscripts (Dusinberre 2006 and Evans 1962).

short plays. Many of the cuts in *Romeo and Juliet* are meant to tighten up the play by reducing what could be considered as chatter, quibbling, or elements less directly serving the action and plot of the play.

The cuts in *As You Like It* also strive to create a faster-moving narrative, and to achieve their ends the revisers had no qualms about omitting three entire scenes, among other more minor cuts: Act 2.5, a scene between Amiens and Jaques, disappears completely, together with a scene between Touchstone, Audrey and William (5.1) and Act 5.8, a scene between Touchstone, Audrey and two Pages. Another feature of the revision is that potentially lewd jokes and allusions have vanished in the manuscript, especially those originally spoken by Rosalind and Celia. The fact that the play may have been performed in a Catholic religious institution could explain the censorship. A noteworthy feature of this manuscript is that the texts of the songs in Act 2.7 (Amiens's 'Blow, blow, thou winter wind') and Act 4.2 ('What shall he have that killed the deer?' and 'Take thou no scorn to wear the horn') are replaced by a stage direction for 'Musicke and Song' (ff. 45v and 57r). One may imagine that they were copied separately so that they could be rehearsed independently from the play, or that other songs were introduced, as was the case in other theatrical texts.

Another early Shakespearean manuscript related to the stage deserves our attention. It is Sir Edward Dering's (1598–1644) copy of *The History of King Henry the Fourth* (c.1623; Folger MS V.b.34). Whereas the Douai manuscripts offers examples of how plays could be prepared for the theatre in an institutional and probably educational setting, Dering's *Henry IV* is, as we shall see, the largely *personal* work of a wealthy early amateur adaptor of Shakespeare's works, who was a keen theatregoer, amateur theatre director and playbook collector in his spare time.

Dering was admitted to the Middle Temple in 1617 and appears to have frequented the theatres fairly assiduously in the ensuing years. His 'Booke of expenses' records that he made twenty-six payments for 'seeing a play' in London between 1619 and 1626 (Lennam 1995: 146–7). He was also an avid book collector with a passion for playbooks, of which he owned over 200 (purchased between 1619 and 1624 (149–51)). He sometimes bought multiple copies of the same play, perhaps to be able to use some copies as scripts for his amateur productions. He also probably owned two copies of Shakespeare's First Folio, bought in December 1623.[14] Clearly, this was a

---

[14] The fact that he paid two pounds suggests that he purchased two bound copies (Krivatsy and Yeandle 1992: 256–7).

man who had a passion for drama. That Dering was interested in staging private amateur performances in his own home at Surrenden in Kent is made apparent by the presence in the manuscript of *Henry IV* of a scrap of paper which bears on one side a deleted cast list for Fletcher's *The Spanish Curate* (licensed to be played in 1622). The list gives names of Dering's family members and neighbours and includes his own name twice, which implies that Dering acted in at least some of his own productions.[15]

The manuscript is a small folio volume of fifty-five leaves in which two hands are apparent: Dering's and his scribe's – most certainly a 'Mr Carington', whom Sir Edward paid for copying the manuscript, as an entry in his 'Booke of expences' for 27 February 1623 testifies: 'P[ai]d mr Carington for writing oute ye play of K: Henry ye fourth'.[16] Carington was responsible for copying out all but the first page of the manuscript, which is in Dering's hand. The play text itself is a conflation of the two parts of *Henry IV* based on a copy of Q5 of *Henry IV, Part 1* (1613) and on the second issue of the 1600 quarto of *Henry IV, Part 2*. However, the play text which Dering commissioned Carington to copy had a specific design – it is a five-act play which abridges an estimated 11 per cent of *Part 1* (347 lines out of 2,968) but eliminates about 75 per cent of *Part 2* (2,374 out of 3,180).[17] Only Act 2.1 and Act 4.4 of *Part 1* disappear completely, no doubt to reduce the number of minor characters (2.1) and to eliminate a short inessential passage (4.4). However, *Part 2* is bereft of most of its text and is basically reduced to a few scenes staging the response of Northumberland to the death of Hotspur, the King's final illness, the rejection of Falstaff and only one comic scene with Falstaff and Mistress Quickly.

The play text, which Dering imagined, began to transcribe and then undoubtedly handed over to the scribe to write out, shows signs of having been edited and reworked by Dering at a later stage. Indeed, Sir Edward's hand can be seen correcting the text, adding missing words, short phrases and stage directions (marking mainly exits and entrances), all in different inks. Like the professional revisers we examined previously, this playbook reader and collector, amateur actor-director and adaptor would also change his mind at times and decide to drop a passage transcribed by his scribe. On f. 14v, for instance (Act 2.2 of Dering's

---

[15] For this list and a complete facsimile of the manuscript, see Evans and Williams 1974: viii and 2–3. A colour digital facsimile is also made available on the Folger's Luna website at http://luna.folger.edu/luna/servlet/FOLGERCM1-6-6.
[16] Cited in Yeandle 1986: 224. Carington was paid a penny halfpenny per sheet.
[17] These figures are based on Evans and Williams 1974: ix.

conflated play), five lines of dialogue between the Vintner and the Prince are crossed out.

Thus, the text which Dering and his scribe have left us is one where the comic and subversive world of Falstaff and his associates has almost totally disappeared, the emphasis being rather on the defeat of the rebels and the death of the monarch. The overall tonality of the two plays is effected, as the new conflated play is more serious and at times more political or nationalistic – especially if we consider the contents of Dering's two major additions, revealingly situated at the beginning and at the end of the play and thus acting like the prologues and epilogues often supplied by professional theatrical companies for the revival of a play (Jowett 2013: 6). These are often crucial moments when paratexts readapt plays to the circumstances of their performance.

The first of these additions is written on a scrap of paper attached to the first page of the manuscript (on the reverse of the scrap of paper is Dering's cast list for Fletcher's play). In Dering's hand, this addition makes King Henry sound more outspoken about his will to chase the infidels. A marginal cross and a horizontal line after the manuscript's 'To chase these Pagans from those holy feildes' indicate where the following should be inserted:

> And force proude Mahomett from Palestine.
> The high aspiring Cresant of the turke,
>   Wee'll plucke into a lower orbe. and then
>   Humbling her borrowed Pride to th' English lyon,
>   With labour and with honour wee'le fetch there
>   A sweating laurell from the glorius East
>   And plant new jemms on Englands crowne.
>   Wee'll pitch our honores att the sonnes uprise
>   And sell our selves or winn a glorious prize.   (f. 1r)

Writing in a vein which was perhaps closer to Marlowe's *Tamburlaine* than to Shakespeare's *Henry IV* plays, Dering rounds off the speech with a rhyming couplet to drive his point home. Whatever their literary quality, and well before Restoration theatrical adaptations of Shakespeare, these lines, and the conflated play as a whole, demonstrate how a reader–reviser like Dering would take great pains to adapt Shakespeare's text to his time and preoccupations, some seven years only after the playwright's death and at a time of European war. Not content to cut *Henry IV, Part 2* drastically, Dering was also clearly determined to add his personal touch by changing the play's ending. The final speech is spoken by Shakespeare's newly crowned King Henry V (who is reformed and rejects his low life companions), but the very last words of the play are mostly Dering's own invention and no doubt his parting thoughts and words to his private audience of family and friends and possibly his household servants. Their ring is nationalistic and somewhat threatening and the inspiration behind them stemmed arguably in part from the war-torn European world of the 1620s. Three lines in the speech also echo a passage in Shakespeare's *Henry V*,[18] thus demonstrating that Dering had read the so-called sequel and had a fair knowledge of what Shakespearean scholars now call the Henriad (*Henry IV, Parts 1 and 2* and *Henry V*):

> Now change our thoughtes for honour and renowne.
> And since the royalty and crowne of Fraunce,
> Is due to us wee'll bring itt to our awe,
> Or breake itt all to peeces. Vanities farewell
> Wee'll now act deedes for Chronicles to tell.   (f. 55v)

That Dering altered two plays where royal power appears weak and incapable of chasing the infidel may reflect this resolutely anti-Catholic man's interventionist wishful thinking or his frustration about the way national and international politics were conducted. As John Jowett points out, these plays express 'an ambiguity of outlook towards public life that would have made the ambiguous act of privately staging a play about political history congenial to Dering' (2013: 8). From a book history point of view, it is noteworthy that Dering's *Henry IV* escapes the constraints both of the print medium and the public theatre (where plays had to be licensed) to 'recrystalise in manuscript in a new cultural milieu' (8), but also in a private setting where a new and perhaps more politically incisive performability could be sought for Shakespeare's two plays.

Conclusion

Dering's *Henry IV* reminds us of the extent to which theatrical texts are circumstantial documents. The words of Jerome McGann, 'that textuality cannot be understood except as a phenomenal event', apply particularly well to play texts (1991: 4–5). As we have seen, annotations made for the theatre can be dictated not only by theatrical convention but also by circumstances, necessity, the immediacy of stage concerns or the will to engage with the text for personal or ideological issues. The increasing

---

[18] 'France being ours, we'll bend it to our awe, / Or break it all to pieces [...]' (Act 1.2.224–5).

circulation of playbooks, as well as the occasional return of Shakespeare's text to manuscript, were factors that could lead to remarkably inventive and varied reinventions of his texts. While the increasing circulation of manuscript extracts of Shakespeare was to give the playwright and poet a central role in eighteenth-century commonplace culture, professional and amateur theatrical revisers and adaptors explored the limits of his text. In doing so, they constantly demonstrated theatre's incredible 'ability to comprehend the widest variety of versions of a dramatic text within the concept of a single play' (Orgel 1988: 14) – and some, like Edward Dering, even challenged the unit of the single play.

New Bibliography's idealized 'prompt-book' – a theatrical version of the play which was supposed to be much tidier than the author's so-called 'foul papers' – is nowhere to be found in the early texts which we have surveyed. Well before the current questioning of this category in editorial studies, those who examined theatricalized texts closely had underlined their suggestive and sometimes bewildering protean nature. Thus, in his wide-ranging study, *The Shakespeare Promptbooks: A Descriptive Catalogue*, published in 1965, Charles H. Shattuck had warned that theatricalized texts 'are tricky, secretive, stubborn informants' and that 'the word "prompt-book" in the title of this catalogue is to be interpreted rather loosely', as the term was mostly a convenient way of bringing together under one caption a wealth of different texts, whose common point was that they had been used for dramatic productions (1965a: 3, 5). Likewise, Edward A. Langhans, in his *Restoration Promptbooks*, remarked that some theatrical texts could be especially 'chaotic' (1981: xv). What is paramount in all the texts we have surveyed is the (partial) view they give us on the cultural processes at work when Shakespeare was revived for the stage in the course of the seventeenth century. They remind us in particular that the reason why Shakespeare is still performed today worldwide is because, from the very beginning, there were people who changed the parameters of the printed text by rescripting his works, making them as flexible as was necessary to serve their aesthetic, personal or ideological needs, as well as those of their audiences.[19]

---

[19] See Kidnie 2009: 30.

CHAPTER 11

Shakespeare and the collection: reading beyond readers' marks

Jeffrey Todd Knight

In a 19th-century English gold tooled red grained sheep binding. The flat spine is divided into three gold tooled decorative compartments. Author, title and date of publication are lettered in gold up the second spine compartment. The turn-ins are gold tooled with the date '1623' tooled in gold at the top of the turn-in of the lower cover. With plain paper endleaves with a crown tooled in gold on the pastedowns of both covers.

Binding signed by Macdonald. Last leaf in facsimile from British Library copy; inlaid; trimmed at head.

These epigraphs are taken from catalogue entries for the two known first-edition copies of *Hamlet* (1603), now at the British Library and the Huntington Library, respectively.[1] The entries describe more-or-less identical books: Shakespeare's play is complete, bound in leather, decorated (copiously) with gold, lettered with the author, title, and date, flanked with protective endpapers, and given a class mark reflecting the order of acquisition in an institutional collection.[2] The uniformity is unremarkable, indeed expected by a modern reader of *Hamlet*, trained to see copies in predetermined material configurations that are consistent with the literary value and distinction of the work. But this uniformity is at variance with the material histories of the copies themselves.

The British Library copy, according to the earliest accounts, was part of a 'bundle of old pamphlets' found in a gentleman's library in the Midlands and was sold to a Dublin bookseller in 1856 (Rooney 1856: 11). The 'pamphlet' containing the 1603 *Hamlet* had been 'interleaved, with MS. notes and

---

[1] British Library shelf mark C.34.k.1 and Huntington Library shelf mark 69304; STC 22275.
[2] Digital reproductions of the books can be found online at the Shakespeare Quartos Archive (www.quartos.org).

177

printed extracts from subsequent editions of the play'.[3] Also among the manuscript insertions – in multiple hands dating from c.1726 to 1761 or later – were miscellaneous writings: drafts of a letter requesting 'the years Intrest Due Last Jan^y' and verses on the subject of King George III.[4] The book, now 'a very dirty looking little 4to. in a brown paper cover',[5] passed to the antiquarian and scholar James Orchard Halliwell-Phillipps (1820–1889), and then to the British Museum in 1858. Sometime in the twentieth century, it was sent to the British Museum bindery, where the text – minus the insertions – was repackaged as we find it today.[6]

Likewise, the Huntington Library copy was discovered in 1823 in a Suffolk country house in a 'little volume ... barbarously cropped, and very ill bound' (Bunbury 1838: 80 n.), containing no fewer than twelve playbooks.[7] This *Sammelband*, or 'collective binding', was sold to book dealers and then to William Cavendish, the sixth Duke of Devonshire (1790–1858), in whose custody it seems to have been taken apart, as the catalogue entry from his library for the 1603 *Hamlet* reads, 'the text is intact and in good clean state, unbound'.[8] The *Hamlet* copy resurfaces – bound in a different 'collective' configuration – in the library of Henry Huntington, who bought Devonshire's plays and playbills in 1914. The Huntington *Sammelband*, apparently containing five plays, was broken up between 1916 and the early 1920s, its constituent units rebound individually as indicated now in the catalogue note.[9] *Hamlet*, long missing its final page, was completed with a facsimile leaf from the British Library copy.

The permutations of the two extant copies of the first *Hamlet* reveal the essential involvement of collectors, curators, conservators, and consumers

---

[3] Quotation from the British Library catalogue copy-specific note. The note continues, 'This interleaving is now bound separately and placed at C.34.k.1.*'.

[4] On the dates and contents of the interleaved material, see Freeman and Freeman 2001, esp. 362–3.

[5] From the account of an early witness, Frederic Madden, as quoted in Freeman and Freeman 2001: 350 n.

[6] This according to the British Library provenance record: 'Bound by the British Museum Bindery'. See the bibliographic descriptions in the British Library's online *Shakespeare in Quarto* database, Hamlet, First Quarto, 1603, British Library Copy: 'Binding'. www.bl.uk/treasures/shakespeare/playhamletbibs.html#second.

[7] Bunbury, who discovered the volume, gives a list of its contents in the same note (1838).

[8] See Devonshire n.d. The catalogue was taken sometime between 1820 and 1858; the printed edition was issued by Sotheby in the early twentieth century (year unknown).

[9] The *Sammelband* at the Huntington was shelf mark K-D 342. There is still some question as to the composition of this volume. The *ESTC* records five playbooks with former K-D 342 shelf marks, all with Devonshire provenances from the twelve-item volume. The assumption is that the other items were sold off as duplicates (a common occurrence at the library from 1916 into the 1920s). My thanks to Stephen Tabor for this information.

Reading beyond readers' marks 179

in the materiality of these texts. The permutations are also, in an important sense, *readings* of the play. *Hamlet* did not arrive in 1603 in a decorated binding with author, short title, and publication date emblazoned on the cover (Shakespeare's name, in fact, had only recently begun to be associated with plays on title pages).[10] The perception of uniformity – that two works, if printed, will be configured and used the same way – is a function of the desires of the texts' modern owners. Specifically in the case of *Hamlet*, the sense of timelessness, literariness, or artistic origin is extrinsic to the work, an interpretation advanced by means of fine leather, gold leaf, acid-free paper, and prescriptive cataloguing over and against earlier instantiations of the same pages in different contexts. What kind of reading, in this sense, was expressed in the 'bundle of pamphlets' or the 'barbarously cropped' *Sammelbände* in Dublin, Suffolk, and San Marino? How was *Hamlet* read by owners who were free within the norms of their time to interleave a playbook with printed clippings, personal accounting, and verse? What surplus meaning might have inhered in the play's 'brown paper' covers or unbound sheets?

Readers and collectors

Research on early modern reading unfolded in three stages in twentieth-century literary scholarship in English. The first – which never went away but merely lost primacy in Anglo-American (particularly American) criticism – centred on bibliographical tools and methods: inventories of historical library catalogues and book-lists, source study and the reconstruction of authors' libraries through allusions in their works, provenance research, and philological modes of analysis.[11] The second stage arrived with continental literary theory in the 1970s and the associated reader-response criticism, whose most influential contribution was the idea that an 'implied reader' exists in constitutive relation to the structure of any work, silently limiting the work's meaning to a range of possible interpretations through genre conventions, paratexts, and other embedded codes.[12] Recently, a new materialist criticism focused on empirical traces

---

[10] See Erne 2003: esp. 92–3.
[11] For summary account of traditional bibliographical-philological questions and findings in Shakespeare and the history of reading, see Nelson 2005. The best example of the continuity of such approaches is the *Private Libraries in Renaissance England* project, which has both print versions (Fehrenbach and Leedham-Green 1992) and an expanding online database (http://plre.folger.edu/), and which has roots in a 1956 print resource (Jayne 1956).
[12] For an overview of reader-response criticism in the broadest sense, see Tompkins 1980. On the 'implied reader', see Iser 1978.

of reading, most often marginalia, has called both of these methodologies into question for being overly idealizing.[13] On the one hand, reader-response critics are said to 'ignore actual readers in favor of theoretical constructs', which do not reflect historically specific practices (Brayman Hackel 2005: 6). On the other, philological and bibliographical approaches are said to privilege major historical figures – wealthy book owners, canonical authors, the figures most visible in libraries and archives – over the 'great Variety of Readers', famously hailed by the editors of the 1623 first folio.[14]

Studies of marginalia and 'book use' (now the preferred term for early modern reading)[15] have been fruitful in capturing the range of active, instrumental models of reception in Shakespeare's era. But there is a serious obstacle when it comes to works by Shakespeare himself: few copies that survive actually show evidence of use. The 1603 *Hamlet* quartos are instructive on this point. Both texts passed through the hands of multiple owners or dealers, each with varying ideas about preservation, before being assimilated into prominent twentieth-century libraries, where they were rebound to look like clean, modern books. As Stephen Orgel and William Sherman have shown, the drive to clean and modernize texts regularly extended to the pages themselves in this period: not only did nineteenth- and early twentieth-century collectors tend to take apart *Sammelbände* and interleaved or 'hybrid' texts to form individual, leather-bound books, they also erased marginal annotations, excised ownership marks on title pages, or discarded what they saw as soiled endpapers.[16] The more valuable a text was, the more likely it would be submitted to these routines of conservation. *Hamlet* may have had any number of early annotators or active readers, but we wouldn't know it from the artifacts available to us.

The turn to the empirical, in other words, founders, when the evidence is so singularly selective – when a series of de-historicizing 'readers' (nineteenth-century book dealers, early twentieth-century librarians and binders), stand between us and the historical readers we seek to recover. This is a helpful reminder of the limits of marginalia study, and the

---

[13] See especially Brayman Hackel 2005 and Sherman 2008. For foundational works on marginalia in early modern reading, see Grafton 1997; Grafton and Jardine 1990; Orgel 2000; and Zwicker 1998.
[14] See Kastan 2002a and also Brayman Hackel 2005: esp. 17–18. Andersen and Sauer (2002) provide a useful summary and cross-section of the field in its high materialist moment.
[15] See Cormack and Mazzio 2005 and also Sherman 2008: esp. xiii.
[16] Orgel 2000 and Sherman 2008: ch. 8. On *Sammelbände* and nineteenth- and twentieth-century rebinding practices, see Knight 2013.

immensity of the history of reading as an intellectual project by comparison. The emphasis placed on readers' marks and other empirical traces in the most recent wave of work on early modern literary reception carries a similar bias and risk of reductionism as its predecessor methodologies, reader-response criticism and source study. In the first place, markings in Shakespearean and other early modern literary texts are sparse relative to those in less valuable, and therefore less treated, texts from the period. Where markings do survive, and reading becomes recognizable to scholars only or primarily in forms of marginal response, the history of reception can be unhelpfully restricted to a sequence of particularizing case studies. The more abstract forces of reading and interpretation – markets, norms of ownership, classification systems – that shape literary texts across multiple temporal planes are made to seem natural or objective in turn. We may gain a rich and vital knowledge of how individual early readers used almanacs, prayer books, or other works likely to have escaped conservation in the modern era, but Shakespearean works will remain unduly bound to nineteenth- and early twentieth-century notions of textuality and canonicity, with few real opportunities for critical reflection on that framework as a framework for reading.

A more dialectical approach is needed – one that gives renewed attention to the 'theoretical constructs' that define and obscure early modern reading without sacrificing the historical specificity of empirically minded material-text analysis. Such an approach might begin with the idea that early Shakespearean texts have 'implied collectors' and 'implied collections', which inform a work's meaning by virtue of its situation in a larger network (a binding or library, for example; often several of them over time). The idea brings two key advantages. First, it lends historical specificity to the well-worn poststructuralist insight that no text is generated or read in isolation.[17] In the early period of print, before books were sold ready-bound in whole editions,[18] the choice of physical format for a work was also the choice among different collection-networks. As many have observed, an early modern literary work printed in folio was either a rare display of ambition in a long-form genre such as epic or it was one among multiple texts in a collected volume such as a 'collected works', or both.[19]

---

[17] On the poststructuralist notion of 'intertextuality' as it was formulated vis-à-vis traditional source study, see Kristeva 1980.

[18] Books were for the most part issued unbound in the early part of the period, leaving the binding arrangements to the buyer and sometimes the retailer. See Foot 2006: esp. 15–22.

[19] See Robinson 2002 on the prestige of collected editions. On folio and quarto formats and their connotations, see Kastan 2001: 50–78.

More important, a work in folio would become part of an imagined 'collection' of highly esteemed or popular works – the Bible, the Book of Martyrs, chronicles, classics – which could ordinarily command their own bindings on library shelves. For Shakespeare's quartos and other small formats, a book would most often have been bound only when multiple works were brought together, the sheets of one having neither the status nor the bulk normally required for an individual binding.[20] The implied collection, in such cases, was the *Sammelband*.

Second, and conversely, the 'implied-ness' of this concept lends portability to historically specific types of collection, allowing scholars of early modern reading to develop broad insights from particular case studies. Medievalist literary scholars have been quick to take up miscellanies, anthologies, and other collections not just as material artifacts but as culturally resonant *ideas*: among them, frameworks for reading and canon-formation, and templates for literary production, including Chaucer's.[21] Alexandra Gillespie has shown that in the first half-century of print in England the *Sammelband* was the default context for publishing Chaucer, Lydgate, and other medieval writers, as their works circulated in small, linkable quartos that could be bound with each other (to form collections of poetry) or with other quarto-sized texts, literary or non-literary ('texts that suggest the wide-ranging interests of an early compiler' (2004: 206)). Scholars of Shakespeare have been largely unable to make similar moves from particular historical artifacts to big ideas about reception because – again, as suggested by the 1603 *Hamlet* – the implied collector of most extant Shakespearean texts is the nineteenth-century gentleman, not the seventeenth-century reader. *Hamlet*'s leather bindings imply, in this sense, a context (literally, a 'text-with' or 'in combination')[22] in which Shakespeare's books are near-contemporary with ours. But, as Peter Stallybrass and Roger Chartier have explained, 'The texts that Shakespeare wrote were published as pamphlets, not bound books' (2007: 41) – their units of organization were less uniform, more contingent and 'collective' than a nineteenth-century standard

---

[20] According to Dane (2012: 172), an early printed book needed around fifty pages or more for a typical leather binding to be financially and technologically feasible. In terms of Shakespearean book history, that amounts to more than one play. On Shakespeare's works in *Sammelband*, see Knight 2013: ch. 2.

[21] See, in particular, Hanna 1996: esp. 7–34, 247–57 and Lerer 2003.

[22] From the prefix in 'con-text': 'The sense is "together, together with, in combination or union"' (*Oxford English Dictionary Online*, 'con-, prefix').

of curatorship can indicate.[23] We know relatively little about Shakespeare's works in these earlier contexts. The fact that most of the surviving pamphlets are now bound individually means that research on Shakespeare's readers must account for, and draw its insights from, both the imagined collection(s) of early modern book culture and that of the modern library.

What actual collections might have embodied frameworks for reading, canons in miniature, or models for composition in Shakespeare's era? As the modern book and library are taken less and less for granted as literature's natural state (a transition hurried along, perhaps, by our own contemporary permutations of the book), scholars have begun to attend to the works outside the paradigm of the gold-tooled, leather binding. In recent studies of early modern print, publishing, and even performance, the group context for works – the collection, broadly construed – is revealed to be a prime mediator of reception. Stallybrass, Chartier, and others have done preliminary work on Shakespearean *Sammelbände*, taking up the few surviving examples to speculate on links between (to us) disparate-seeming texts: *Lucrece* and *Venus and Adonis* bound with works by Thomas Middleton and others, for example; or *Pericles* stitched in paper with Samuel Daniel's play, *The Queen's Arcadia*.[24] Where collections themselves do not survive but records of them do, scholars have been able to take a fresh look at early library catalogues and shelf lists, less as sources for *what* texts were read (for catalogues in this period are notoriously unreliable in registering collected and vernacular literary titles),[25] but rather *how* texts were read – their criteria of order and coherence for consumers. In one example cited by Stallybrass and Chartier, a well-known early reader of Shakespeare and his contemporaries 'amassed a collection of 135 printed plays ... bound up into 11 volumes, each volume containing between 9 and 13 plays' that were not linked by author, the category that organizes the same material for readers today (41).

Similarly, in the domain of early publishing, Adam Hooks has examined the organization of plays in booksellers' catalogues, which, more so than the extant texts themselves, 'allow us to see how booksellers and their

---

[23] The *Oxford English Dictionary* defines 'pamphlet' explicitly as a kind of sub-book that cannot stand on its own: 'having fewer pages than would constitute a book' (n., 1b).
[24] See Stallybrass and Chartier 2007: 40–2; Knight 2013: ch. 2; and Lyons 2011.
[25] See Leedham-Green 1986 on book lists in probate inventories from the period: 'Usually, where two or more items were bound together, only the first title was entered' (xii), and 'we may suppose that such entries as "item all his other bookes" conceal, among other things, a quantity of current vernacular literature not deemed worth the binding' (xiii).

customers represented and identified their objects . . . as a viable conceptual category' (2008: 445–6). Zachary Lesser, investigating publishers' lists from the period, has called for a turn away from 'the text' traditionally defined and toward the text-in-context of a given shop's specialization – the implied collection, in other words, that limits and shapes the text's meaning for early book buyers. In establishing specialties reflected in their lists, Lesser demonstrates, 'the publisher does not merely bring a commodity to market but also imagines, and helps to construct, the purchasers of that commodity and their interpretations of it' (2004: 17). Tara Lyons has shown that, on the Shakespearean stage, group contexts for plays in the form of 'serials and spinoffs' became templates for collective publication, particularly for histories. 'Works that were performed in historical series in the theatres were readily acquired by London stationers who could capitalize on their narrative or character relationships', Lyons writes. 'By highlighting and prescribing organizational frameworks for readers, booksellers could hawk their books in a variety of pairs, sets, and sequences' (2013: 186).

Taken together, these recent and emerging approaches have emphasized the collective, the proximate, the implied or imagined order of Shakespearean books, and have expanded early modernists' sense of reading itself in turn. Marginal annotation stands as one empirical subset of a larger enterprise of active response, one that includes theoretical constructs of organization and assemblage, each with the potential to create meaning beyond the confines of the individual text. Such a perspective offers a useful elaboration on an argument that Jennifer Summit has made regarding the early English library, the arch-collection of early modern literary culture. No mere repositories for written records, libraries were seen in Shakespeare's time 'as creative, rather than static, entities, the products of selection rather than simple retention' (2008: 4). For this generation of readers, Summit explains, 'libraries . . . do not simply store but rather select and arrange their contents to make them meaningful' (5). To see acts of storage, selection, and arrangement as creative and productive of meaning – especially where such acts were not yet prescribed in universal catalogues and commercial book-binding, but also where they were, much later, in modern literary culture – is the challenge of a post-materialist history of reading.

From the book to the collection

I have argued, in sum, that research on how Shakespeare was read demands balance between the empirical and the theoretical, facility with more than one period of literary history (for example, early modernity and the nineteenth century, when much early modern literature was reshaped), and attentiveness to forms of textual organization *as reading*, as meaning-making. In this light, 'collection' has a lot in common with 'performance' in the current scholarly idiom. A performance is never merely an iteration of a text, but rather a reading or interpretation with its own material grounds; its temporality is multilayered and unfixed; it is both abstract and embodied, determined and improvisational. To illustrate the ways in which collections mediate – and, in the sense of performance, interpret and create – Shakespearean texts, I want to close by returning briefly to the British Library and the Huntington Library for two examples. Both are collectors (and not incidentally, performers) whose readings, manifest in their books, have shaped the source materials for Shakespearean textual studies without becoming objects of textual study themselves. I offer these brief examples as notes toward a better integration of the collection, implied and real, in the field.

Garrick

David Garrick, the eighteenth-century actor and director, was one of two main sources of the playbooks in the foundation collections at the British Museum, now the British Library.[26] Garrick's collection was known in his time to have been 'formed, with great assiduity, during the course of his theatrical life' (Saunders 1823: introductory note). It arrived at the library a year after his death in 1780, numbering over 1,200 items bound into *Sammelbände*, with titles ranging from the early sixteenth century to Garrick's own era, gathered from numerous sales and historical libraries in London and beyond.[27] As an actor, Garrick was famous for his versatility, and a certain openness to adaptation and contingency is present in his books. Though the *Sammelbände* were all custom-bound and personalized, the material in their covers caused vexation in readers from the nineteenth century onwards with their 'varied contents and lack of recognizable order', leading to several reorganization campaigns at the library (Anderson 1980: 3–6). Garrick, for his part, made good use of the collection in the seeming disorder and muddled categories. In his letters, he vacillated between devaluing the books – referring to them at one point as 'more

---

[26] The other was King George III. See De Ricci 1930: 60–1.
[27] See De Ricci 1930: 61. Kahrl and Anderson (1982) list Garrick's sources in their historical introduction.

matters of curiosity than of merit' (Little and Kahrl 1963: 732) – and ennobling them – singling them out in his will, for example, to be preserved 'for the Use of the Publick' (1365) – suggesting a readiness to re-categorize his library. Most visibly, Garrick seems not to have had his books cleaned as a matter of routine but left them to retain signs of use, so much so that a librarian writing in 1980 could remark that 'the evidence of their earlier history, of previous owners and readers, is apparent in the books themselves: the marks of owners, signatures, scribbles, mysterious symbols, and prices; and of users: corrected letters, inserted notes, exclamatory crosses, and marginal marking' (Anderson 1980: 1). Garrick was long championed for opening his collection to friends and colleagues who wanted to produce editions or new plays (1). The marks of users in Garrick's own theatrical community mingle with those of the books' earlier owners, reflecting a deep, layered history in the circulation of literary work.

The creative link between Garrick's books and his theater – between the literary artifacts and the literary ideas issuing from Garrick's theatrical milieu – can be glimpsed in a pair of well-known episodes in the history of English drama. In his early biography, Thomas Davies tells of how Garrick, around 1760, called for the proscenium doors at Drury Lane to be closed off, paving the way for a major innovation in stage architecture. The norm at the time, Davies notes, was for there to be 'two audiences, one on the stage, and another before the curtain; more especially at the actors benefits', leading to 'incoherence' in the play (1780: 269). Garrick had heard that Thomas Sheridan in Dublin had 'conquered the refractory tempers of the Irish gentlemen, by shutting his stage door against them' (270), so he sought a permanent measure along these lines in London. According to Davies, Garrick held in his memory a 'ridiculous circumstance' from years before when he was playing King Lear: 'When the old king was recovering from his delirium, and sleeping with his head on Cordelia's lap, a gentleman stepped at that instant from behind the scenes, upon the stage, and threw his arms round Mrs. Woffington, who acted that character' (270). After Garrick, the doors of entrance – the portals to the stage – would be replaced with spectator boxes.[28]

Flash forward to 1777 and to one of Garrick's playbooks: *Florizel and Perdita*, his adaptation of Shakespeare's *The Winter's Tale*. Figure 11.1 shows a page from Garrick's copy of the play, printed in 1758 and then turned into a prompt-book for a 1762 performance before being passed to

---

[28] My thanks to Odai Johnson for calling my attention to this anecdote.

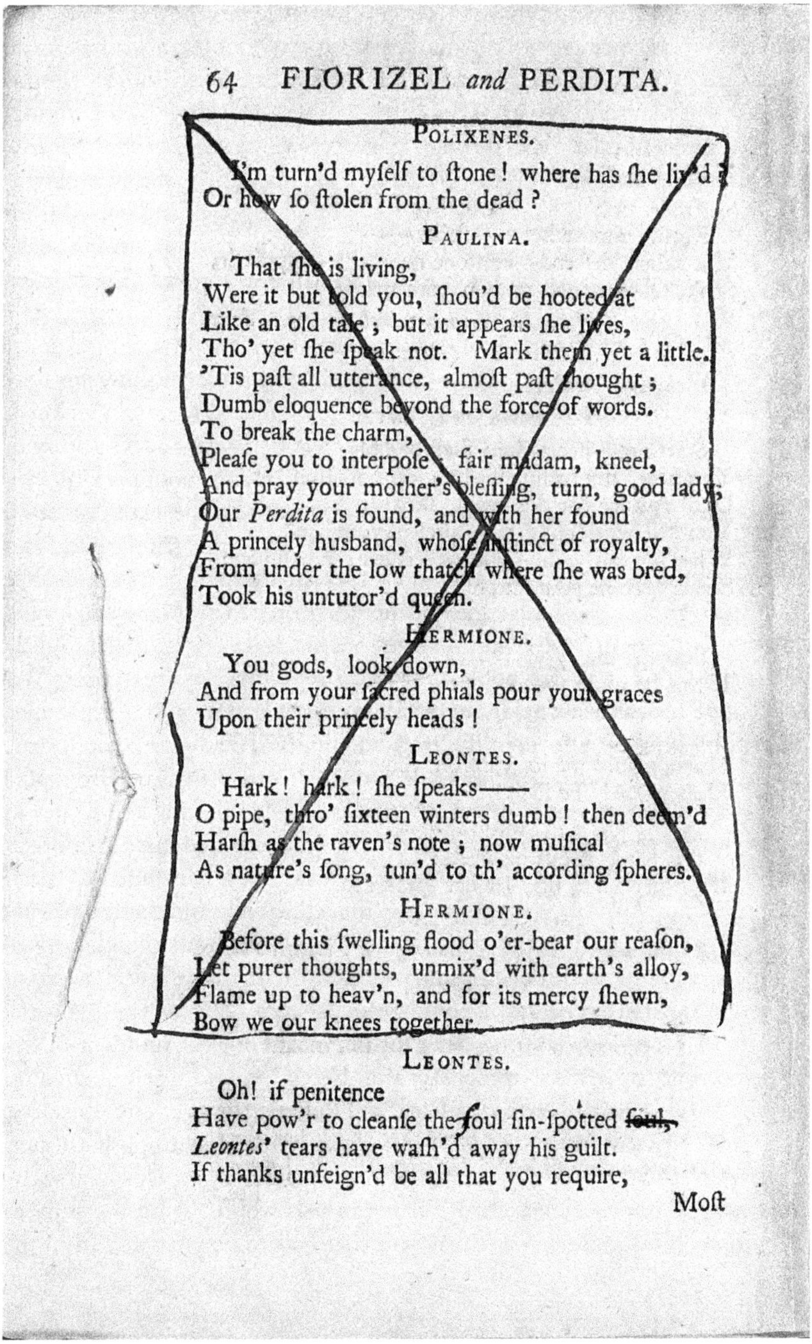

64   FLORIZEL *and* PERDITA.

POLIXENES.

I'm turn'd myself to stone! where has she liv'd?
Or how so stolen from the dead?

PAULINA.

That she is living,
Were it but told you, shou'd be hooted at
Like an old tale; but it appears she lives,
Tho' yet she speak not. Mark them yet a little.
'Tis past all utterance, almost past thought;
Dumb eloquence beyond the force of words.
To break the charm,
Please you to interpose, fair madam, kneel,
And pray your mother's blessing, turn, good lady;
Our *Perdita* is found, and with her found
A princely husband, whose instinct of royalty,
From under the low thatch where she was bred,
Took his untutor'd queen.

HERMIONE.

You gods, look down,
And from your sacred phials pour your graces
Upon their princely heads!

LEONTES.

Hark! hark! she speaks——
O pipe, thro' sixteen winters dumb! then deem'd
Harsh as the raven's note; now musical
As nature's song, tun'd to th' according spheres.

HERMIONE.

Before this swelling flood o'er-bear our reason,
Let purer thoughts, unmix'd with earth's alloy,
Flame up to heav'n, and for its mercy shewn,
Bow we our knees together.

LEONTES.

Oh! if penitence
Have pow'r to cleanse the foul sin-spotted soul,
Leontes' tears have wash'd away his guilt.
If thanks unfeign'd be all that you require,

Most

Figure 11.1 Folger Shakespeare Library shelf mark Prompt Wint.T.27

his friend and fellow dramatist George Colman, who used it in his own adaptation, performed at Haymarket in 1777.[29] Colman's adaptation, published as *Sheep Shearing* later that year, was a drastically shorter version of Garrick's play, and as part of the cutting process, Colman (it is assumed) drove a needle and thread through pages 57–64 of *Florizel and Perdita*, making the stitch that you can see in the left margin in the photograph (Pedicord 1981: 189). The text that is now bound together and barred from view – also, apparently, from performance – is the famous closing scene from Shakespeare in which the statue of Hermione comes to life to greet the unbelieving Leontes.

There is a suggestive symmetry between Garrick's proscenium doors blocked off and these pages of his *Florizel and Perdita* sewn shut, not only in the material sense of something that once opened now forcibly closed, but also in the literary-interpretive work of the two gestures. The story of the proscenium doors communicates a shift in thinking about performance long considered Garrick's lasting contribution to Shakespearean drama – a reduction of artifice through tighter control over theatrical space and audience interaction. No longer could actors enter downstage, at a distance from the scene, or mix with audience members on benefit nights; no longer could zealous gentlemen leap on stage to console Lear's Cordelia. Subtly and persistently, the playbook of *Florizel and Perdita* also reflects this celebrated creative agenda, here set in motion over time and in the hands of multiple reader-performers. Garrick's adaptation is advertised on its title page as 'altered from ... Shakespeare', and altered it was, cut from *The Winter's Tale*'s 3,084 lines down to 1,370 (189), eliminating the scenes in Sicily and the problematic passage of time to enforce a neoclassical unity on the play. Colman's adaptation, built out of Garrick's, continued to 'alter' the text in the spirit of Garrick's theater, first editorially and then physically (Figure 11.1). In addition to cutting 524 more lines from the play (189), Colman fashions a crude binding mechanism in the physical book to prevent the final scene from being read. In this copy of the play, the miracle of Hermione coming back to life, or the logical problem of her being spirited away for sixteen years after being interred, is eliminated, as an inexplicably joyous Leontes is left to close the action. The objective, here again, is to reduce artifice for a post-Restoration English theater. Colman's stitch preserves the imaginative plan of Garrick's drama by removing an implausible exchange between two worlds. With the story of the proscenium doors, it was the action that had to be separated from the

---

[29] In the chronology and other details of FSL Prompt Wint.T.27, I follow Pedicord (1981)

audience; in this altered playbook, it is the living that have to be separated from the reportedly dead.

Kemble

Garrick's *Florizel and Perdita*, to be sure, was converted into a prompt copy – a special kind of playbook – and is separate from his main collection at the British Library, with only a bookplate to indicate its provenance. I turn now to a less exceptional case in the library of Garrick's successor on the London stage, John Philip Kemble, whose books were sold in 1914 to Henry Huntington, then an emerging American collector. If a reader calls up an early English play at the Huntington Library today, the chance is good that something like the book pictured in Figure 11.2 will arrive at her desk. This is, of course, the most famous item in what is now called the Kemble–Devonshire collection at the library; it is the first quarto of *Hamlet* from my epigraph, the text 'inlaid', or, as its earliest catalogue entry from Chatsworth elaborates, 'cut down and inlaid on large white paper' (Devonshire n.d.: 8). This copy of *Hamlet* was never owned by Kemble. It was bought along with Kemble's library by William Cavendish, Duke of Devonshire,

Figure 11.2 Huntington Library shelf mark 69304

who had the pages cut and mounted individually, as you see here, forming a kind of prosthetic margin or frame around the text.[30] In the frame, we see the persistence of Kemble's curatorial example, an example that is as eccentric as it is widespread in the drama holdings at the Huntington (Figure 11.3). According to early assessments, Kemble collected close to 4,000 plays including fifty-seven Shakespearean quartos (Sherburn 42–3). The first issue of the Huntington *Bulletin*, from 1931, reports that 'The plays collected by Kemble were all dismembered, and the leaves, each inlaid in a leaf of quarto size, were rebound, usually in volumes containing a half-dozen plays' (Sherburn 2008: 42–3). As Garrick's treatment of the literary text seems to have carried through to Colman, so too did Kemble's 'inlaid' Shakespeare become a template for conservation under Devonshire.[31]

Kemble's unusual practice of collection, observes the *Bulletin*, 'insures the perfect preservation of the text, but has impaired the bibliographical value of the editions' (42–3). Otherwise stated, Kemble held and continually reproduced a notion of 'perfect' textuality at a time when 'bibliographical value' was not yet keyed to the ideal of the self-enclosed book, as it would be for modern collectors. On each individual title page in his roughly six- to eight-item *Sammelbände*, Kemble wrote 'collated and perfect', his initials, and the date (see Figure 11.3, right); notoriously, this mark of ownership is present even where it is clear that a given play is not perfect and therefore likely not collated, a fact that has complicated the work of modern bibliographers. For modern readers, Kemble's cut-and-inlaid pages give the play collection the look and feel of a guard book or specimen book, an album of preserved documents. Each leaf is cleaned and cut down to the very inner margins, eliminating earlier readers' marks and other copy-specific information (Figure 11.4). The play's abstraction from its history as a circulated or working text is finally assured by the artificial quiring that Kemble introduces; with each page mounted separately, it is no longer possible to count leaves in gatherings and to produce a collation formula – that is, to trace the printing and binding of the work by anyone other than Kemble himself.

---

[30] On the conservation method of mounting and inlaying the pages of a book, see Schweidler 2006: 123–6.

[31] When Devonshire acquired Kemble's books, he assimilated them into his existing shelving system, which is still mostly intact at the Huntington. The current state of the collection suggests that Devonshire began having books inlaid after acquiring Kemble's library; he continued this practice with some inconsistency in subsequent acquisitions.

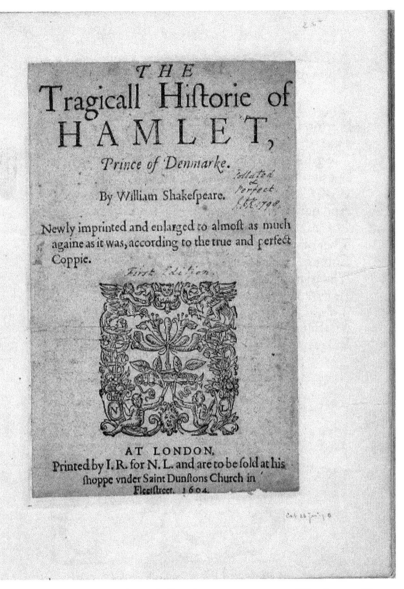

Figure 11.3 Huntington Library shelf mark 69305, a 1604 copy of *Hamlet* owned by John Kemble

King Richard the second.
A deed of slaunder with thy fatall hand,
Vpon my head and all this famous Land.
  Exton. From your owne mouth my Lo. did I this deed.
  King. They loue not poison that do poison neede,
Nor do I thee; though I did wish him dead,
I hate the murtherer, loue him murthered:
The guilt of conscience take thou for thy labor,
But neither my good word, nor Princely fauour;
With Cayne go wander through shades of night,
And neuer shew thy head by day nor light.
Lordes, I protest my soule is full of wo,
That bloud should sprincle me to make me grow:
Come mourne with me, for what I do lament,
And put on sulleyn blacke incontinent,
Ile make a voiage to the holly lande,
To wash this bloud off from my guiltie hand:
March sadly after, grace my mournings heere,
In weeping after this vntimely Beere.

FINIS.

Figure 11.4 Huntington Library shelf mark 69343, showing cleaned and cropped readers' marks

In collecting and preserving these plays, then, Kemble too was creating something, something that goes beyond the particular case study. But if his books are bound up with a creative project as Garrick's were, it is one that seems – on the textual surface – to stand in sharp opposition to that of his predecessor, whose playbooks had a deep, visible, and malleable history. Indeed, a critical opposition suggested itself in performance. When Garrick took to the stage, according to contemporary accounts, he 'gave [his characters] every embellishment that was calculated to strike the eye, engage the ear, and charm the imagination'; his naturalistic style was protean and unorthodox, 'wholly repugnant to the elaborate doctrine of the schools' (*London Chronicle* 1769: 222). Kemble, on the other hand, was studied and exact. He saw the play as a 'vehicle in which to communicate universal truths' (Quinn 1972: 87), and Shakespeare in particular as a 'heavenly-inspired bard' (Kemble 1817: 5), one of a chosen few in the arts to possess 'an excellence that soars above the control of its ordinary laws' (5). In contrast to Garrick's versatility, Kemble was depicted as cold and steadfast by his contemporaries. His theory of performance, articulated in several exchanges in print in his time, attested to a fundamental belief in constancy (Thomson 2004). Because he thought that 'all human behaviour is explicable' (Thomson), Kemble took as his objective in every role he played to find a single ruling passion in his character – a defining, stable trait that could be isolated, named, and thus commanded. 'Once that discovery had been made, he reshaped the text to show that passion in conflict with circumstance' (Thomson).

This imagined relationship between character and circumstance, figure and ground, evokes, I suggest, both Kemble's Shakespeare, who soars above ordinary laws, and Kemble's *Shakespearean page*, set off from history in an immaculate paper frame. Kemble's fight against contingency carried over from the book collection into theater and back such that the two spaces could be common points of origin in a broader program of creative interpretation. One of the many familiar legends surrounding Kemble's career is that he studied *Hamlet* by copying the text (presumably the one pictured in Figure 11.4) forty times by hand (Devonshire n.d.: iii), a story that conjures a theatrical world that is never far from age-old routines of book preservation and reproduction, however obliquely they may have been present in Kemble's frame of mind. In the 1825 commentary to his memoirs, James Boaden seems to observe this slippage between antiquarianism and performance in Kemble's arrangements for putting on a play:

Mr. Kemble's notion of the business, was, not to order the prompter to write out the parts from some old mutilated prompt-copy lingering on his shelves; but himself to consider it attentively in the author's genuine book ... The stage arrangements throughout the play were all distinctly marked by him in his own clear, exact penmanship, and when he had done his work his theatre received, in that perfected copy, a principle of exactness. (quoted in Child 1935: 6)

Here we perhaps hear echoes of the old, marked-up copy of Garrick's *Florizel and Perdita* in the 'mutilated' prompt-book against which Kemble sets himself and his theatrical-textual world. In the end, Garrick's innovations in stage space and acting style may have been the more lasting of the two in the English theater, but Kemble's desire to return to a purer, cleaner point of origin – an 'author's genuine book', a 'principle of exactness' in reproduction – would define succeeding generations of book collectors whose work forms the basis for theater *history*.

Conclusion

David Garrick and John Kemble are responsible for much of what scholars can know about early English drama, their collections forming a major part of the relevant holdings at the British Library and the Huntington respectively. The crucial idea to take away from this, I have argued, is that the materials of literary history, and particularly Shakespearean literary history, are shaped by the interests of collectors *as readers*. And I mean 'interests' not merely in the sense of taste or selection, which have occupied scholars in the past, but in the creative investments brought to bear on primary texts, investments that persist over time, across periods, and in the hands of many readers. The curatorial histories of texts are a vital, underexplored part of what James Simpson has recently called the *préjugés* upon which any hermeneutic act depends: 'An artifact implies its history, and is illegible without habituated understanding of that history' (2013: 30). It would not be far-fetched to imagine that the processes of distillation and purification set in motion by John Kemble have habituated part of our understanding of Shakespeare: first at the level of the page in his own collection; later at the level of the text in the collections of Devonshire and Huntington, who separated individual works of exceptional value, such as the 1603 *Hamlet* with which I began.

Garrick and Kemble are two highly prominent examples of something that permeates the early library and ours: that is, the imaginative work of collection and preservation in the history of reading, the fact that the organization and interpretation of literary books can and do issue from the same space. As William St. Clair has recently observed, 'Although there has always been much interest in the meaning of certain texts, how they came to be written, and in the lives of their authors, little attention has been paid to the processes by which the texts reached the hands, and therefore potentially the minds, of different constituencies of readers' (2007: 1). For a long time, the meanings generated or shaped by those processes have been submerged in seemingly objective or scientific routines of publishing and knowledge organization. It is perhaps the right moment now to return to the previous generation's bibliographical and philological resources – the catalogues and book lists, compendia of sources, and provenance notes, many of which are reborn online – as not just records of reading but theories of reading, waiting to be discovered.

CHAPTER 12

Encoding as editing as reading

Alan Galey

One of the great things about digital textual scholarship is that its difficulty makes us all students again. I was reminded of this recently when I happened upon an account of the creation of one of the earliest digital databases for early modern theatre history, thanks to Ben Ross Schneider Jr.'s 1974 book *Travels in Computerland; or, Incompatabilities and Interfaces: A Full and True Account of the Implementation of the London Stage Information Bank*. Schneider, a professor of English at Lawrence University, undertook in 1970 to digitize – or to computerize, in the parlance of the time – the eleven-volume reference work *The London Stage, 1660–1880* and from it to build a database to support queries by actor, role, theatre, performance, and other parameters. This would be no small enterprise even today, and Schneider's account offers a glimpse of the experience of humanities computing in the days before email, the Web, social media, Skype, cell phones, and even inexpensive long-distance telephone calls. Yet Schneider's book also speaks to the future by triangulating with the past in the form of his playful adoption of the eighteenth-century novel's picaresque form, as in the argument for one of the opening chapters, titled 'Of Feasibility':

> *The author becomes entangled in the* London Stage *Information Bank & conceives of a Pilot Project. He questions Administrators & Computer Scientists, visits Widener Library & the Association for Computing Machinery, where he encounters a Living Advertisement. He considers the scarcity of Funds, and draws to an Inside Straight.* (Schneider 1974: 7)

I am grateful to Alan Stanbridge for his advice on musical transcription, to Ashley Bodiguel for her advice on acting exercises, and to Rebecca Niles for the many conversations about Shakespeare encoding that inspired this chapter. I am also grateful to the participants, organizers, and funders of the NEH-supported 'Early Modern Digital Agendas' summer institute at the Folger Shakespeare Library in July 2013, and especially to Julia Flanders and Heather Wolfe for the opportunity to teach text encoding and transcription with them. Any errors are my own.

Encoding as editing as reading

Those who have undertaken a large humanities computing project – and the fewer still who have completed one – may have trodden some of the same roads, and thus will have no difficulty imagining the travails of such work in the form of a novel (if not an eighteenth-century satire such as Schneider's possible model, *Tristram Shandy*, then perhaps *Bleak House* or *Ulysses*). Schneider's appropriation of literary form to narrativize a digital project says something about his experience as an early modernist venturing into an unfamiliar world. His fascinating account also reads like a message in a bottle sent from the distant shore of an earlier era of humanities computing – one that helps us see our present with new eyes.

The most striking difference between Schneider's experience as a computing humanist in the early seventies and my own today (beginning in the late nineties), was that computing in his time required much greater amounts of time and energy for the task of data entry. Indeed, *Travels in Computerland* reads not as an early seventies reflection on the whole lifecycle of a digital project, but specifically as an adventure in humanities text encoding. This adventure includes truly heroic feats of data entry: at one point, Schneider mechanically modifies an IBM type 'golfball' to prevent the capital letter O from scanning as the numeral zero (149–57). Reading as someone who grew up amid the luxuries of personal computing, I was reminded that computing in 1970 was not something one did at home on a sunny back porch with a dog at one's feet, on a relatively inexpensive machine that an individual might own, glutted with enough surplus processing power to permit inefficient programming and memory-management, and with barely seconds (not hours or days) intervening between the act of writing a bit of code and testing its success or failure. Even screens were a luxury, prompting Schneider to record his delight upon seeing a Cathode-Ray Tube monitor for the first time (104–5). Computing in 1970, like printing throughout its history, was a mechanical art. For Schneider in the episode of the IBM type golfball, computing even became something one did with a sliding saw-mount, vicegrip, and grinding wheel (pictured in Schneider's book), all for the sake of altering a tiny bit of metal that skewed his data model.

What can all this teach us about encoding, editing, and reading Shakespeare today? All three of the terms in my title have scholarly lineages and literatures which deserve a fuller treatment than I can give in this short chapter, and which cannot be conflated merely by stringing them together with the word 'as'. *Reading* and *editing*, for example, are terms that Eric Rasmussen and W. B. Worthen productively complicate in their chapters on apparatus and post-print performance, respectively. *Encoding*, likewise, takes on different connotations in the context of the highly networked scholarship that David Weinberger advocates in his chapter. The present chapter should not be mistaken as an introduction to text encoding, though I hope it will introduce new and established digital Shakespeareans to alternatives to project-centric best practices in the digital humanities, in which the imperatives of a funded project (and the acquisition of more funding) can often foreclose the broader processes of intellectual inquiry that distinguish scholarship from business.[1]

Shortly before the mainstream humanities suddenly began to embrace digital humanities around 2009, Willard McCarty published his foundational book, *Humanities Computing*, in which he warned against thinking of computers as mere 'knowledge jukeboxes' (2005: 27). Although he was well aware of the value and potential of digitization projects – and had won that knowledge the hard way, as a coder and scholar long before humanists showed that combination much respect – McCarty nonetheless felt compelled to warn that 'the torrent rushing out of computers into the various disciplinary heartlands pull[s] attention away from the difference between cultural artifacts and the data derived from them – away from the analytic concerns of earlier work . . . to a great stocking of the shelves' (5). That was 2005, but today any digital Shakespeare project that seeks to investigate that very difference between artifacts and data could find itself strongly at variance with funding models. The result is that the shelf-stocking instinct has been internalized by many digital humanists, and project management often overshadows the other forms that digital scholarship can take. Might there be a middle ground between the extremes of business-model projectism, on the one hand, and ungrounded speculation about digital technologies, on the other?

My approach seeks that middle ground at the intersection between method, theory, and pedagogy – including the reflexive pedagogy of scholars willing to become students again within their own projects. Specifically, I take *Travels in Computerland*'s historical alterity as a spur to consider the idea of *thinking through making* in relation to some of its specific implementations in Shakespearean textual scholarship, namely editing and digital text encoding. Schneider would almost certainly have understood his project as a form of thinking through making, and his book is full of reflections on the nature of information, computing,

---

[1] The literature on text encoding is very large, but two complementary starting points I recommend are Deegan and Sutherland 2009: 59–88 and the TEI By Example Project.

history, the London stage, and the conditions of research in the humanities and the sciences. However, in his account, moments of critical engagement with digitized materials happen under pressure – even the literal pressure of vicegrips – and emerge in tension with the project's size, complexity, and need to produce results. The luxuries of twenty-first-century computing afford us greater opportunities to slow down and explore the moments of critical understanding that pass by so fleetingly in Schneider's account. This chapter considers what Schneider called data entry – or, as I prefer to call it, encoding – as a crucial moment when we can understand our materials anew through the act of making digital representations of them. Close reading is often dismissed if not maligned in big-data approaches to digital humanities, but I would like to consider how digital text encoding, like the more traditional activities of textual criticism and editing, lead back to granular engagements with texts that resist, challenge, and instruct us.

***

Many disciplined forms of reading begin with acts of writing in the form of transcription. Textual scholarship and its subfields have long depended on various kinds of transcription – paleography cannot be taught without it – but what can textual scholars learn from transcription as a practice that spans domains? The multiple meanings of *transcription* in music, for example, mirrors encoding in humanities computing, in the sense that transcription can refer to the practice of writing out pieces of music in standard notation for the sake of documentation, or as a process by which students learn the music itself. As in many digital Shakespeare projects, the one rationale for transcription may blur into the other. For example, one of the great exemplars of transcription in rock music is the guitarist Steve Vai, who as a student in 1979 sent Frank Zappa a transcription of a particularly difficult Zappa drum instrumental along with a sample of his playing, which prompted Zappa to hire Vai to create transcriptions of several of Zappa's labyrinthine guitar solos, most of which had never been written out in musical notation. Vai's now-legendary transcription feats led to *The Frank Zappa Guitar Book* in 1982 and, more significantly, to Vai developing such a deep understanding of the music that he joined Zappa's band (Watson 1993: 390). The lesson in this example is not only the link between discipline and art, but also the value of transcription in coming to understand complex materials. Here transcription serves as an intermediate stage between the music and the musician, and exploits the imperfections of the medium of writing to slow down the act of listening, forcing the transcriber to notice the details and patterns that otherwise go unperceived, though not unheard. Vai listened by writing.

I learned how to read by encoding while an undergraduate research assistant with the Internet Shakespeare Editions (ISE) in the late nineteen-nineties, which involved long hours of proofing transcriptions of the Folio and quarto play texts that had been marked up in SGML and needed conversion to XML. It was not exactly the same as musical transcription, but it called forth similar forms of attention. One formative experience came in the form of a problem in the 1623 Folio text of *A Midsummer Night's Dream*, when the four lovers lost in the forest awaken and may or may not share the stage with an awakening Bottom (around 4.1.195 in most modern editions). Figure 12.1, below, shows how this moment is represented in the First Folio.

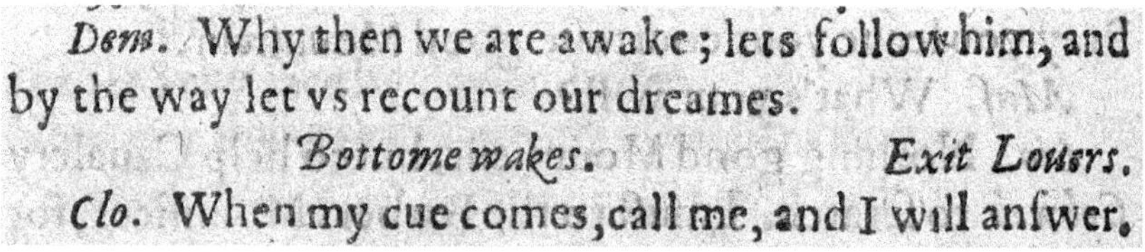

> *Dem.* Why then we are awake; lets follow him, and by the way let vs recount our dreames.
> *Bottome wakes.* *Exit Louers.*
> *Clo.* When my cue comes, call me, and I will anfwer.

Figure 12.1 *Mr. William Shakespeares Comedies, Histories, & Tragedies* (London, 1623), sig. O1v; TLN 1725–8

Modern editions tend to move Bottom's stage direction to the line below, fixing it in temporal sequence after the lovers leave the stage. I realized that XML, which requires that tagged entities not only be named explicitly but also *ordered* in non-overlapping hierarchies, would impose a logical structure in which Bottom and the lovers might share a fascinating dramatic moment of mutual awareness on stage. Any query of the sequence of stage directions in the scene (tagged as separate <sd> elements in the ISE's encoding scheme) would return '*Bottome wakes*' in order before '*Exit Louers*'. Furthermore, any digital model or visualization of the play's entrances and exits based on this digital transcription would incorporate this intriguing overlap, but digital models based on most modern editions, including the ubiquitous Globe text, would not.

As an undergraduate just discovering the performance criticism of W. B. Worthen and Alan Dessen along with the unediting sorties of Randall McLeod and Leah Marcus, my reading had primed me to notice a textual ambiguity that permitted the worlds of Bottom and the lovers to intersect as they awoke. The placement of the Folio's stage directions may simply be an effect of a compositor trying to save space – perhaps with an eye to the long prose passage that follows these lines – or it may be an artifact of the simultaneity of action available to the stage, wrenched into sequentiality by modern editions and XML structure alike. My experience as an editorially minded encoder in this case was borne out many years later in Stephen Ramsay's description of the value of thinking through making in code: 'Encoding texts in XML . . . places one in a simultaneously cooperative and antagonistic relationship with the codes that already subsist in written works. . . . Rather than hindering the process of critical engagement, this relentless exactitude produces a critical self-consciousness that is difficult to achieve otherwise' (2011: 34). I could not have arrived at the instance of 'critical self-consciousness' Ramsay describes had it not come in the course of transcription as sustained labour. However, it was equally important that the ISE's coordinating editor, Michael Best, and I afforded ourselves the opportunity to pause and learn from the problem, as opposed simply to putting it aside it as an inconvenience that slowed down the project.[2] For textual scholars, like scientists, the discovery of illuminating problems is a form of success that outweighs project milestones; indeed, the rewards of curiosity are the reason many of us undertake digital projects, and why they are worth funding.

For digital Shakespeareans and aspiring musicians alike, there is also a lesson here in the value of the constraints that apply in translating a text from one medium to another, and from one notation system to another. Those constraints, and the transcriber's response to them, make the difference between intellectual inquiry and the unreflective rule-following demanded by assembly lines. For example, Vai's transcriptions, like Zappa's original compositions, dealt creatively with the shortcomings of traditional musical notation in representing the rhythmic nuances of jazz, blues, and other musical forms that reached beyond the European tradition (Watson 1993: 415–18). Similarly, Friedrich Kittler describes a creative solution to the problem of non-Western music's supposed unintelligibility to European ears in 1904, in the form of a musicologist's proposal to use the phonograph to slow down recordings, thus making strange melodies and

---

[2] Michael offers his own reflections on this encoding crux in Best 2009: 34–5. His article alludes to a simple Javascript animation I created at the time for this and similar variants, which I am developing through my Visualizing Variation project: www.visualizingvariation.ca.

rhythms discernable through deformation (2006: 3–4). Both examples use an intermediate stage of representation to tease out complexity through constraint. Both also blend *technology* – the gramophone and writing itself – with *technique*, reminding us that both words share the same Greek root: *techne*. This productive tension between technology and technique has long been exploited by musicians, as the jazz saxophonist Dave Liebman describes in his introduction to a transcription exercise:

> This mode of thought holds especially true in jazz because outside of the specific notes and rhythms, the intangible essence of this music cannot be noted exactly. This includes but is not limited to the subtleties of rhythmic feel and how the artist interprets the beat as well as the use of expressive nuance in one's sound, aspects of which are usually lumped under the word 'phrasing.' In transcribing, a musician is forced to hear and duplicate everything – even the intangibles. (Liebman n.d.)

Liebman's rationale in this last sentence comes remarkably close to Fredson Bowers's rationale for the value of transcriptional thinking in the very different domain of descriptive bibliography, specifically the practice of title page transcription of printed books. In describing the intellectual value of title page transcription over photographic reproduction, Bowers points out that imperfections such as flyspecks may appear as punctuation in photographic facsimiles, but the act of transcription 'forces one to determine what every letter and punctuation mark is' whereas photographic facsimile reproduction 'tempts one to ignore uncertainties' (1962: 136).

Early modern print, like jazz and its musical relatives, productively challenges the rules of the intermediate notational systems we use to transcribe it. W. W. Greg offers the example of the early modern half-italic colon as a transcriber's *bête noir*. As Greg puts it in his contribution to a 1926 round table article (in what could be the title of a Frank Zappa song), 'There is a peculiar terror lurking in the colon' due to the deliberate visual and typographic ambiguity built into this piece of type, which was a solution to the nuisance of needing separate roman and italic sorts for punctuation in typographically hybrid early modern books (Pollard, et al. 1926: 326). According to Greg, 'it apparently struck some bright spirit to cast a colon that would do for either [roman or italic], being intermediate between the two. It is not quite upright like the roman one, but much less sloped than in italic'. This example of a printed intangible also offers a window into an encoding insight of an early modern type-founder, who was thinking digitally by exploiting contextuality and ambiguity to save resources. However, as Greg also points out, 'the result was not quite what was intended, for in a roman passage of course it looked like italic, and in an italic passage like roman! What is the unhappy facsimile printer [or transcriber] to do?'

Greg asks a good question. As anyone who has worked with Optical Character Recognition (OCR) methods in digitization can attest, teaching a machine to transcribe a text can become an exercise in frustration and illumination alike.[3] A primitive version of OCR existed at the time of Schneider's project, and his *Travels in Computerland* relates a moment of insight that arose out of the problem of the OCR scanner's difficulty in interpreting white spaces in the source. At certain points their text used two consecutive white spaces as a field delimiter to indicate that a title followed immediately afterward, yet the scanner registered these two spaces as a single space, such that these two-space units became semantically indistinguishable from spaces between words. As Schneider puts it, the scanner 'was aware of space but did not measure it. So all space had to be one space' (1974: 111). This problem, however, triggers a passing reflection upon the nature of writing and human-machine interfaces: 'this machine's failure to register meaningful space probably resulted from the designer's overlooking one of our unconscious assumptions about writing – that space is a delimiting character. It was one of those cases in which computer logic forced into my consciousness an assumption about the nature of things that I wasn't aware of making' (111). Part of the answer to Greg's question, then, is that an encoder can pause to recognize encoding cruxes as teachable moments.

One imagines the lessons to be learned from transcribing texts that make even more complex use of inline white spaces, such as postmodern poetry. A related Shakespearean example can be found in the New Variorum Shakespeare (NVS) editions' policy of not including the white spaces that editors since George Steevens have added to the play texts to indicate – or impose – metrical part-lines shared among speakers.[4] This form of legacy markup from the eighteenth century has become so embedded in Shakespeare's editing infrastructure that it determines modern line numbering, as in this example from the 2007 Cambridge edition of *The Winter's Tale* that numbers two typographical lines as a single pentameter line:

POLIXINES ...
      The art itself is nature.
PERDITA   So it is.
                                 (4.4.97)

---

[3] See, for example, the Early Modern OCR project: http://emop.tamu.edu/.
[4] On this editorial policy, see Knowles 2003: 12–13. On the handling of metrical part-lines in Shakespeare editing, see Werstine 1985 and Bertram 1981.

The effect of the added white space is to imply an underlying formal unity to argumentative, even hostile exchanges between characters who nonetheless complete each other's pentameters. In this example, the dialectic between art and nature enacted by Polixenes and Perdita is played out within an overriding metrical order shared by all – or at least by characters entitled to speak in verse. The NVS edition, by contrast, presents the play text of *The Winter's Tale* as a lightly corrected transcription of the 1623 First Folio text, and does not add the structuring space that would normally precede Perdita's 'So it is' in a modern edition (Turner, Haas, Jones, et al. 2005). Maurice Hunt connects this editorial policy to postmodernism's 'purposeful creation of irregular aesthetics' out of 'white spaces ... and related concepts of absent presences / present absences' (1999: 64). In that light, the NVS policy presents alert readers with a Shakespeare text that raises questions about its own nature. Is any given short line actually part of an adjacent line or just a loose fragment? Is aesthetic cohesion the product of innate linguistic patterns or of imposed editorial desires? Do metrical forms, like numbers and harmonies, have an ideal existence that precedes writing, or does inscription call them into being?

These kinds of questions are pedagogical opportunities, which is why many textual scholars have constructed transcription and editing exercises that ask students to engage with editorial challenges. Anne Hawkins's valuable collection *Teaching Bibliography, Textual Criticism and Book History* offers several examples, some specific to Shakespeare. Tatjana Chorney's chapter, for example, describes an exercise based on the multiple-text plays *Romeo and Juliet* and *King Lear*, in which students collate authoritative versions, and then, like good editors, consider the interpretive possibilities that each version opens up and forecloses. As Chorney describes, the exercise prompts students to consider the consequences of granular details such as word choices, and to notice gaps and omissions of longer passages that might not otherwise be apparent (Hawkins 2006: 168–9). Another contributor, Erick Kelemen, has his students work even more closely within the editorial tradition in an assignment he calls a 'collaborative edition', in which students work as a group on the apocryphal play *The London Prodigal*, carrying out stages in the editorial process: 'transcribing, proofing, preparing the text, preparing the textual notes, preparing the content notes, and preparing the editor's preface' (163–4). Although Kelemen's students don't face a transcriptional challenge on a par with Vai's notation of Zappa, the transcription stage forces them to begin their process by encountering the strangeness of early modern typography and orthography, including the dual forms of the letters *s, i/j,* and *u/v*. A key element in this stage of Kelemen's assignment is that the students then proofread each other's transcriptions, which elevates transcriptional errors into teachable moments. That debate continues in later stages, as students must decide which conventions of capitalization and italicization to preserve in the edited text (164). The point in these exercises, as Matthew Kirschenbaum describes with regard to his own digitization exercises elsewhere in the volume, is that 'the students constantly [make] decisions about what counts as information' (158). The act of making something – a transcription, an edition, a digital archive – shapes the forms of attention that we pay to our materials.

***

My own counterparts to the editing exercises described above attempt to close the ouroboros implied in my title by linking *reading* back to *encoding*. The two exercises I describe below owe a debt to Jerome McGann's game-like deformation experiments with poetry in *Radiant Textuality* (2001a: 106–35, 139–46, 150–1), and to Rob Pope's playful exercises in literary production as described in his book *Textual Intervention* (1995) – with the difference that mine is not primarily a literature classroom, but an information studies classroom in the University of Toronto's iSchool. As such, we begin with the history of digital markup and its roots in electronic typesetting, and then consider the emergence of descriptive markup as implemented in the metalanguages SGML and then in XML. One of the key concepts here is the distinction between *procedural markup* and *descriptive markup* (TEI Consortium n.d.: part v.1). Procedural markup consists of embedded imperatives for the interface or information system; for example, I might mark up the end of my preceding sentence procedurally as

> the distinction between <italic>procedural markup</italic> and <italic>descriptive markup</italic>.

The <italic> tag tells an information system not what an element is, only what to do with it (i.e., to render it in italics). However, procedural markup cannot distinguish between the different contextual meanings of italics, which may indicate emphasis, book titles, foreign words, quotations, subheadings, references to a word or letter as such, or (as in my example) the highlighting of an introduced term. Descriptive markup, by contrast, seeks to describe what the marked-up elements mean, not how they appear:

the distinction between <term>procedural markup</term> and <term>descriptive markup</term>.[5]

This distinction is fundamental to markup theory and practice, as is the idea that descriptive tagging constitutes interpretation.

Descriptive markup thus raises even more opportunities for interpretive ambiguity and debate than musical transcription. Supposedly a C♯ is a C♯ for everyone, though the aural nuances of a note or chord may change when played in different locations on a stringed instrument, the same chord may be voiced in different ways, and rhythmic patterns may be expressed differently in notation.[6] Descriptively tagging a Shakespeare text can be just as subjective and intellectually rigorous as writing a critical essay, yet even prior to tagging there is the question of distinguishing markup from text. Sperberg-McQueen defines *markup* as 'all the information in a document other than the "contents" of the document itself, viewed as a stream of characters' (1991: 35). However, he then goes on to show the inadequacy of the scare-quoted notion of 'contents' by demonstrating that the presence of markup in all texts makes the notion of pure content chimerical: 'word boundaries are interpretive if the source is in *scriptio continua*. Vowels are interpretive if the source is unpointed Hebrew or Arabic. Verse boundaries are interpretive in all editions of *Beowulf*, since the manuscript does not mark them' (35). What would be the equivalents in Shakespeare's texts? We have considered some already and will return to others before the end, but what matters here is the process of finding them.

My first exercise tests the notion of pure content by attempting to replicate the process by which James Coombs, Allen Renear, and Steven DeRose arrive at an example of supposedly unmarked text, one of a set of examples of the same Milton quotation represented in four different states of markup: descriptive, procedural, presentational (i.e., using indentation rather than explicit tagging to indicate a block quotation), and, finally, 'no markup' in the form of Sperberg-McQueen's 'stream of characters':

> miltonexpressesthisideamostclearlylaterinthetracticannotpraiseafugitiveandcloisteredvirtue (936)

Coombs and his co-authors present this 'no markup' example at the beginning of their continuum, with descriptive markup at the other pole

---

[5] On the TEI <term> element, see www.tei-c.org/release/doc/tei-p5-doc/en/html/ref-term.html.
[6] Traditional notation as a musicological tool has been criticized for its reductiveness and formalist bias; for critiques relevant to Shakespearean page/stage/code debates, see Randel 1992: 11–13 and Citron 1993: 37–9.

as the most overtly interpretive and therefore the most powerful for humanities computing. My first exercise with the students, however, interrogates the continuum itself by presenting the classroom with a copy of Gerard Manley Hopkins's sonnet 'As Kingfishers Catch Fire' and asking students to subtract everything that could be considered markup, metadata, bibliographic codes, or elements otherwise extraneous to the pure scare-quotable 'content' of the poem. Students usually identify the stress marks on the vowels first, then move on to the italics in the final lines of the octet, which gives us an opportunity to consider the procedural/descriptive markup distinction described above. The dismantling of the poem carries on with the removal of the assumed title and author's name (as editorial metadata), indentations to indicate line groupings, the space between octet and sestet, capitalization, punctuation, and finally spaces between words (often suggested by a student mindful of Sperberg-McQueen's point about *scriptio continua*). The resulting text looks as disconcerting as the unspaced Milton example above, but the process of getting there helps us all to notice the textual equivalents of Liebman's musical intangibles.

One of the virtues of using literary texts to teach digital encoding is that the interpretive richness of certain texts, coupled with the material strangeness of their early forms, can combine to subvert the notion that all texts are simply content to be copied and pasted from one form into another. One could perform the same exercise with just about any literary text, including Shakespeare's, but this Hopkins sonnet offers two particular advantages. One is that it also appears in an excellent companion reading for this exercise, Jerome McGann's 'Visible and Invisible Books in N-Dimensional Space', in which he uses this sonnet to illustrate the idea that 'because works of imagination are built as complex nets of repetition and variation, they are rich in what informational models of textuality label "noise",' which challenges all text encoders to question 'the informational content and expository structure' of texts that digital tools tend to assume (2001a, 175). Assigning this companion piece also gives us the opportunity to perform some textual criticism on one of our own readings, thanks to the anomaly of McGann's article having been published in at least five places in print and online, but with no two versions reprinting the Hopkins sonnet exactly the same in terms of layout and accidentals (2001a: 176; 2001b: 290; 2002: 68; 2004: 150–1).[7] A related advantage of using Hopkins is

---

[7] See also the undated HTML version on McGann's personal website: www2.iath.virginia.edu/jjm2f/old/nlh2000web.html.

that students can view Hopkins's manuscript thanks to Norman MacKenzie's facsimile edition, which shows the elaborate diacritical marks that Hopkins (anticipating Zappa) used to indicate his sprung rhythms (1991: 106–7).

The second exercise – likely a familiar one to many Shakespeareans – asks students to restore the punctuation and capitalization to a sonnet, using their own judgment to make decisions that best suit the text. The exercise is similar to those of Shakespearean actors and dramaturges, for whom de-punctuating verse can help actors to find their breathing patterns (Donnellan 2002: 255–8). In my classrooms, we use this exercise in a similar manner to explore the TEI Guidelines' premise that 'encoding a text for computer processing is, in principle, like transcribing a manuscript from *scriptio continua*; it is a process of making explicit what is conjectural or implicit, a process of directing the user as to how the content of the text should be (or has been) interpreted' (TEI, part v). The perilous gap between 'should be' and 'has been' is where encoders, editors, and readers alike do their best work. To illustrate this idea I present students with paper copies of a stripped-down original-spelling transcription of Shakespeare's Sonnet 129:

```
     th expence of spirit in a waste of shame
  2  is lust in action and till action lust
     is periurd murdrous bloudy full of blame
  4  sauage extreame rude cruell not to trust
     injoyd no sooner but dispised straight
  6  past reason hunted and no sooner had
     past reason hated as a swollowed bayt
  8  on purpose layd to make the taker mad
     made in pursut and in posession so
 10  had hauing and in quest to haue extreame
     a blisse in proofe and proud and very wo
 12  before a ioy proposd behind a dreame
     all this the world well knowes yet none knowes well
 14  to shun the heauen that leads men to this hell
```

Students work in groups for ten to fifteen minutes to punctuate and capitalize the text, during which time they weigh the interpretive consequences of each other's choices. Stephen Booth's helpful extended commentary in his edition/facsimile of *Shakespeare's Sonnets* (1977), along with Randall McLeod's provocative unediting of the poem (247–53) (1991: 247–53), both elucidate some interesting challenges for encoders, including the unmetrical trainwreck of adjectives that pile up in lines 3–4, the orthographical and typographical dilemma of 'mad' and 'made' in lines 8–9 (the same word spelled differently? different words yet homonyms to early modern ears?), and the McLeodian visual homonym (typonym?) in line 11 between the quarto's 'proud' and the word we would pronounce as *proved*, which modern editors often emend to *prov'd*.[8] Showing the students the poem as it appeared in the 1609 quarto helps to settle some questions, raise others, and establish that our real objective isn't the right answer but the right frame of mind.

All encoding involves choice, but the *proud/prov'd* case in particular challenges encoders with a provocative dilemma when they consider McLeod's point that the particular sequence of typographic marks in the 1609 quarto represents two words at once in early modern typography, which Shakespeare, his compositors, and his readers would have known. Digital humanists could learn a thing or two from early modern readers' willingness to accommodate ambiguity and hybridity.

***

Presented with this chapter's examples of typographic homonyms, overlapping stage directions, half-italic colons, Zappa-esque rhythms, and other encoding cruxes, a sober, professional, results-oriented encoder might call such detailism a distraction from the needs of a digitization project – an indulgence in special cases at the neglect of the world's overwhelming normality. After all, Schneider's businesslike mantra for the London Stage Information Bank, impressed upon him by a well-meaning colleague, was 'get results' (1974: 17). However, moments of thinking through making afford encoders an experiential lesson in how to avoid the ossifying mistake, as McLeod describes it, of providing 'an answer to the question, while hiding the fact that there *is* a question: at which point *an* answer becomes *the* answer becomes the *Truth*' (1991: 253; emphasis in original). For textual scholars – including students, who are scholars in the most fundamental sense – the understandings that arise in these moments *are* results.

The mistake McLeod points out happens all too often in digital projects today, especially those that simply ingest literary texts as normalized data.[9] The problem is worsened by many digital humanists' narrow conception of their field as fundamentally large project-based, which, wittingly or not,

---

[8] For another worthwhile companion reading for this exercise, see Sherman 2008.
[9] I critique the misapplication of the term *data* to Shakespeare texts in the final chapter of *The Shakespearean Archive* (see Galey 2014: 248–57).

plays into the neoliberalization of the academy on a business model. I suggest that a well-conceived digital project should afford, even demand, reflection upon materials and tools alike, such that one emerges with new insights into both, and which would not be possible without the hands-on activity of making. The size, shape, and computing resources of the London Stage Information Bank forced Schneider and his team into a relentlessly progress-driven program of data entry, with many false starts and Herculean efforts required to render the text of *The London Stage* machine-readable and computationally tractable. Those pressures are amplified today, but it is always worth asserting the choice to approach encoding as an intellectual exercise that rewards the interdisciplinarity that happens not just between individuals, but within them.

Those two kinds of interdisciplinarity have been named, respectively, 'normal' and 'deviant' by the sociologist Steve Fuller. As he puts it, 'Normal interdisciplinarity is designed for teamwork, as each disciplinary expertise is presumed to make a well-defined contribution to the final project, whereas deviant interdisciplinarity assumes that the differences in disciplinary expertise themselves pose an obstacle to the completion of the project' (2013: 1901). Deviant interdisciplinarity, which I am championing along with Fuller, therefore runs counter to capitalist divisions of labour and specialization, and hews closer to what I would identify as traditional humanistic values – even specifically Shakespearean values – of eclecticism, curiosity, and lifelong education. We are all encoding, editing, and reading subjects, whatever role we might play in a project, and to be a humanist is to appreciate the potency of literary works in shaping our subjectivity, for better and for worse. Deviant interdisciplinarity calls us to listen to our texts, even if it takes our attention away from the project manager at the head of the conference table. The challenge facing the digital humanities, and digital Shakespeare studies in particular, is to evolve new forms of scholarship – and models of education – that do not force this unnecessary dilemma upon us.

McLeod's point about the disambiguation of *proud/prov'd* also shows the value of slowing down and of welcoming high-friction texts into digital scholarship: as he says, 'the older forms of texts remain questionable for us: at moments like this they posit knowledge in a ratio with uncertainty' (1991: 253). Preserving that ratio allows encoding to progress reciprocally with reading, leading to the realization, as McGann puts it, that 'there is no such thing as an unmarked text, and [that] the markup system laid upon documents to facilitate computerized analyses are marking orders laid upon already marked up material. (Thus all texts implicitly record a cultural history of their artifactuality)' (2001a: 138). In other words, every act of transcription requires us to read the prior acts of encoding (typographical, scribal, digital, graphical, or otherwise) that persist in documents, and to play the role of editor in a controlled collision between information systems that may be centuries apart in origin. To these ends, I usually conclude my sequence of exercises by taking a page from Peter Stallybrass and unpacking the myriad forms of markup in the opening page of Genesis from the 1611 King James Bible (2011: 91–4; cf. Norton 2005: 47–51). Its typographic encodings of interpolations, glosses, and cross-references – as well as the political agendas of the book's makers – remind us that for early modern readers, decoding complex markup was not only a matter of reading competence, but also part of the textual machinery of salvation. New media and digital tools have apparently become the latest machinery of salvation for the humanities in the early twenty-first century, and their associated truisms deserve critical scrutiny all the more. To see the artifactuality of texts is to apprehend the same quality in our tools: we use artifacts to understand other artifacts. There is no standing outside that circle, but it makes for an expansive horizon.

CHAPTER 13

Shax the app

W. B. Worthen

> What I prefer, about post cards, is that one does not know what is in front or what is in back, here or there, near or far, the Plato or the Socrates, recto or verso. Nor what is the most important, the picture or the text, and in the text, the message or the caption, or the address.
>
> Jacques Derrida, *The Post Card* (1987), 13

Consider the postcard: a homely object, vestige of residual technologies, capturing a nexus of communications at the apogee of print culture, the moment of its incipient transformation by photography, the mid-nineteenth century. Postcards were patented in the USA in 1861, and the first penny postcards, preprinted with postage by the US Post Office in 1873, depicted scenes from the Interstate Industrial Exposition. Postcards have, of course, taken a wide range of forms since: plain and illustrated, artistic, kitschy, pornographic. They are used for advertising plays (both mailed and distributed by hand) and tourism; inexpensive prepaid postcards facilitated popular communications in late nineteenth-century India; they were printed with heroic illustrations for soldiers on all sides to send home during the Second World War.[1] Postcards are an emblem of the complexity of technological succession: a mass-produced object in which print continues to guarantee the identity of the material document, which will nonetheless gain its poetry, so to speak, from manual inscription.

But not all postcards are just postcards: some are 'Postcard Plays: Stage them. Trade them. Collect them all!'; published by Paper Theatre, the first six in the series were staged in Seattle in 2006 (Moss 2006). On the verso (or, following Derrida, perhaps we should say the 'postage' side), Paper Theatre asks, 'What happens when a playwright has only 4" × 6" on which to capture a theatrical event?' These plays help to seize a specific problem,

[1] Delitologists now refer to pre-stamped cards as 'postal cards'.

interrogating the place of writing and print in the *post* field of performance – and Shakespeare – studies today. While the postcard plays evidently inhabit the technology and rhetoric of print they do so with a difference, deploying print precisely to contest the tendentious legacy of 'dramatic theatre': that quaintly residual, rather inert genre of performance, the theatre of textual reproducibility, the theatre of the declamation and illustration of an authorial fiction, arguably displaced by the postdramatic *event*, an event that may use texts but is not limited in its signification to what the text might say (see Lehmann 2006: 21, 61). More suggestively, the postcard plays illustrate the mobility of technological change, and provide a moment of *restance*, a moment for reflection not only on (post) dramatic performance, but on the performance of writing in postprint media (Derrida 1987: 27).

Gregory Moss's *Play Viewed from a Distance* (Figure 13.1) reminds us of Hans-Thies Lehmann's concerns about the aesthetic and ultimately political limitations of 'dramatic theatre' now, in the postdramatic era, where 'What is experienced and/or stylized as "drama" is nothing but the hopelessly deceptive "perspectivation" of occurrences as action', fictive action that occludes, displaces, avoids the *real* (2006: 181). Troubling this apparently constitutive dichotomy of dramatic theatre, Moss's play enforces an oscillation between the unmarked and the marked, the real and the aesthetic; it also enforces an exchange between spectator and performer as well, recalling Jacques Rancière's critique of the 'oppositions – viewing/knowing, appearance/reality, activity/passivity' – constructing the spectator as passive across a range of social institutions, institutions which 'specifically define a distribution of the sensible, an *a priori* distribution of the positions and capacities and incapacities attached to these positions' (2009: 12). If 'Emancipation begins when we challenge the opposition between viewing and acting', we might take *Play Viewed from a Distance* to refuse a sense of dramatic theatre as one of the 'embodied allegories of inequality' (12–13).

Imagining dramatic performance as the reciprocal implication of performer and spectator, of the aesthetic and the real, *Play Viewed from a Distance* displaces a sense of dramatic theatre as the delivery of narrative fictions from the stage. Robert Quillen Camp's *The Secret Bear* (2006) provocatively situates dramatic writing on the horizon of genre and technology. The card has a white border framing a narrow blue border, and within the blue border is a brown-toned photograph of fur, bear fur (Figure 13.2). Superimposed on the fur photo is a narrative text, printed in white. Every so often a phrase is 'highlighted' – framed by a white box, *a*

1. Gently bend the play, so point *a* (above) touches point *b* (below). Fix the two points with a small length of scotch tape. *NOTE*: You will need to *fully memorize* these instructions prior to bending.

2. The play should now resemble a tube, with a perfect circle at either end.

3. Choose one of these two perfect circles (whichever one you like more, at either end of the play), and *gently* lift the play to your eye (whichever one you like, either side of your face). DO NOT PRESS.

4. Through the far end of the play, the performance has already begun. Don't worry: you haven't missed very much.

5. Unlike other plays, you may talk, eat, and move about during this performance. In fact, you can do *whatever you want*.

6. To call for an intermission, *gently* remove the end of the play from your eye. The actors, stage manager, stagehands and other audience members will happily wait until you are ready to begin again.

7. When intermission is over, simply begin again at step 3.

8. NOTE TO CRITICS: Please, if the dialogue seems to you diseased with cliché, if the lovers' caresses look cold and forced, if the sets show their armature and the policeman's costume looks a bit threadbare and shabby, *please*: don't judge them too harshly. They are, after all, amateurs.

b

Figure 13.1 Gregory Moss, *Play Viewed from a Distance*. Postcard

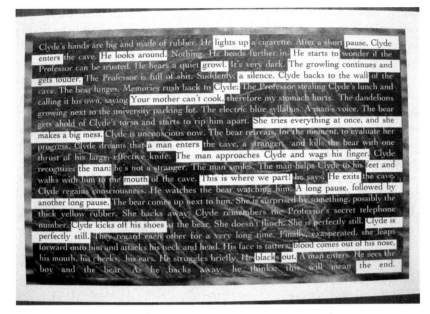

Figure 13.2 Robert Quillen Camp, *The Secret Bear*. Postcard

punctuating the brown background, and transforming the white text to black. In the narrative, a boy, Clyde, enters a cave, apparently on the advice of 'The Professor'. He meets a bear, who springs on him and begins to rip him apart: 'She tries everything at once, and she makes a big mess' of him. He falls unconscious, dreaming that 'a man enters the cave' and kills the bear; he awakens briefly, 'kicks off his shoes at the bear', and then 'blacks out' under the bear's assault. 'A man enters. He sees the boy and the bear. As he backs away, he thinks: this will mean the end.' That's the end of the story.

The highlighted passages, however, read as follows:

> lights up pause, Clyde enters He looks around. He starts to growl. The growling continues and gets louder. a silence. Clyde backs to the wall Clyde: Your mother can't cook, She tries everything at once, and she makes a big mess. a man enters The man approaches Clyde and wags his finger. the man: feet and mouth This is where we part! He exits A long pause, followed by another long pause. Clyde kicks off his shoes Clyde is perfectly still. blood comes out of his nose black out. the end.

Camp's play interrogates the dialectic of epic and drama: the narrative information that might be used to constitute the 'story' exceeds the drama in ways that are apparently irrelevant to performance, much as details mentioned in Homer are omitted from Greek tragedies. The performance script – signaled by the conventional textual apparatus, 'lights up' and 'black out' – involves the application of a specifically theatrical mode of production to the text, from which the words gain a different, newly instrumental leverage; it transforms grammar and syntax ('lights up' from third-person-singular indicative to second-person-plural imperative); recasts narrative description both as stage direction and as dialogue; emends specific words ('blacks' becomes 'black'). Here, Clyde addresses the man, impugning his mother's cooking; the man 'wags his finger' and departs. Clyde kicks off his shoes and blood runs out of his nose. A chilling tale of mystery becomes a brief performance, something like a play by Maria Irene Fornes: the dream world is recast as actual; the narrative cause becomes irrelevant (the Professor); and, perhaps most intriguing, the bear never enters, cannot exit, and so pursues no one.

The postcard plays enact a reluctance to locate dramatic theatre as a parasite of writing, print, literature. But *The Secret Bear* also represents the interplay of print and digital technologies, both in its evidently photoshopped design and more engagingly in the boxes of *selected* text, which emulate the interface conventions of the 'Edit' feature of digital wordprocessing. *Selecting* the narrative into theatre emphasizes that what identifies the script as dramatic, performable, is not intrinsic to its inscribed, literary design, but arises as an effect of its use, its absorption and re-presentation in an external logic of practice. *The Secret Bear* articulates a critical analogy between digital and theatrical technologies, and their relation to print. While the cultural rhetoric associated with print technology (and the modern institutions of literature predicated on it) insists that its standardization, repeatability, durability, and linearity reproduce the identity of the inscribed work across a range of different material forms, this rhetoric is counter both to digital and to theatrical technologies, which enact a practice of performance and so a logic of transformation.

As Jerome McGann memorably noted at the dawn of the digital humanities, 'We no longer have to use books to analyze and study other books or texts. That simple fact carries immense, even catastrophic, significance', altering the understanding of textuality on all fronts, including those where the use of texts is not limited to reading them but is more akin to 'processing' them, using them as one input in a multiplex armature of creation (2001a: 168).[2] Of course the *post* in postcard is not the same as the *post* in postmodern, postdramatic, posthuman, *postprint*. Yet, as avatars of a repositioned medium of social exchange and representation, the postcard plays urgently foreground the intermediality of dramatic performance, staged at the confluence of technological change. Produced by digital instruments to instigate a possibly residual form of performance (writing postcards, making plays), the postcard plays mark a decisive moment of rhetorical failure: the inability of our dominant categories of critique – stage versus page, live versus mediated, performance versus writing, repertoire versus archive – to capture the work of dramatic performance. The persistence of these terms is surprising – the 'specific communal nature of an event which will never be repeated stands in direct contrast to digital technology which confuses the issues of location, time and perhaps most dramatically of "liveness"' – especially since the performance of professional scholarship is a fully intermedial experience (Carson 2008: 283). Where would we be without the Royal Shakespeare Company and The Wooster Group, libraries and archives, printed books and manuscript notes, YouTube, JSTOR, *Global Shakespeares, Internet Shakespeare Editions, EEBO*, the sites for various theatre companies, to say nothing of Apple and Dell and Google and Microsoft, and blogs like Sarah Werner's *Wynken de Worde*? We'd be partying like it's 1999, connected, but without the kind of access to textual, visual, and performance materials we now have come to expect, and without the digital means for making and disseminating – performing – contemporary scholarship.

Perhaps the most concentrated image of the multiplex mobile interface of writing and performance is, for now at least, not the postcard but the mobile *app*: a self-contained software application typically designed to run on the operating systems of mobile devices like smartphones and tablet computers. Apps are synonymous with mobile communications and visual interface design, and so mark one dimension of the participation of digital media in the material and conceptual making of drama – text and performance – today. Apps are instruments for doing something and there are a variety specifically created toward doing something with dramatic writing, often with Shakespeare. Some, for instance, provide backstage information on productions and festivals (*Stratford Shakespearean Festival*); others clearly address pedagogical performance, gathering play texts, video,

---

[2] N. Katherine Hayles dates the term 'digital humanities' to the late 1990s at the University of Virginia (2012: 24).

commentary, and other instructional materials in one 'place'; still others situate Shakespeare's plays among the material professional actors might need to learn and rehearse. Apps provide a target – a momentary target, to be sure, perhaps already vanished by the time you read this – for assessing the conception of dramatic performance emerging as digital means intervene in the historical dialectic of page and stage.

As Anne Burdick and her collaborators note, 'A digital project is always an expression of assumptions about knowledge: usually domain-specific knowledge given an explicit form by the model in which it is designed' (2012: 18–19). Two apps evoke the intervention of digital media in the pedagogical culture of stage-and-page Shakespeare: Luminary's *The Tempest for iPad* and Cambridge University Press's *Explore Shakespeare* series. Priced in the range of an inexpensive paperback edition of the play, both apps are clearly designed for classroom use, as well as to provide a study supplement for students. Though hardly identical, these apps represent dramatic writing and dramatic performance within a decisive modeling of Shakespeare knowledge, in part by structuring the kind of '*thinking through making*' that, as Alan Galey shows in his chapter in this collection, is essential both to the practice and to the epistemological process advocated by digital humanities today.[3]

Although the teaching apps use performance, their descent from book-based Shakespeare is dramatized in part by their design: conceived to enable a variety of approaches to Shakespeare, the apps largely sidestep using the app as an instrument for making performance, for *acting, theatre*. Design represents and constitutes epistemology: while each app has a variety of ancillary structures, the text of the play has been constituted as the central 'home' location. In the tiles on the homepage of *The Tempest for iPad*, 'the tempest' occupies the central square, flanked on the left by 'resources' and 'experts', on the right by 'preferences' and 'bookshelf', and above and below by 'workshop' and 'about'. In the *Explore Shakespeare* app, the home page has three major options centered on 'the play': EXPERIENCE: 'Experience the play, with photos, notes, activities and audio'; EXPLORE: 'Explore the play's characters, themes and use of language'; and EXAMINE: 'Examine the play, diving deeper into meaning and context'. But beyond locating the text as the central coordinating

---

[3] As Alan Liu notes, 'design theory and practice', alongside 'science and technology studies', understands 'design as a principle of knowledge discovery and generation rather than (more typical in the digital humanities) as an after-the-fact rendering of data in scatter plots, social-network graphs, and other stale visualizations or, equally tired, book-like or blog-like publication interfaces' (2013: 416).

site for other materials and processes, the two apps stake out somewhat different representations of Shakespeare and dramatic performance in digital culture.

In *Explore Shakespeare: Romeo and Juliet*, the EXPERIENCE link opens the play. The play text scrolls vertically, and a range of commands appear across the menu bar at the top of the screen: the text can be vocalized by activating the speaker icon and touching the text. The Prologue is delivered in a British accent (one nod to the proprieties of performance), with various sound effects of a Veronese market, including what seems to be an alto recorder in the background (another nod to propriety: performance = realistic mimesis of the narrative). The text can be set to scroll forward automatically, and a marker in the right margin identifies which line is being spoken. A question-mark-in-a-circle icon enables three levels of glossaries to appear in the text: 'Standard glossaries', 'Academic glossaries', and 'Academic notes'. A third icon opens activities liberally strewn through the text: Solo activities, Pair activities, and Group activities. Some of these activities are writing/criticism-oriented ('Identify the opposition in line 14, and look out for other oppositions as you read through the play'), but many are more performance/criticism-oriented: 'Prepare a short scene to show what long-ago incident sparked off the age-old hatred ("ancient grudge") between two of Verona's leading families. Present your scene to the group.' The right margin of the text has a series of circles, which when activated show a relationship diagram of the characters in the scene; photos can be loaded to appear at the beginning of most scenes.

Performance – preparing a short scene, miming the Prologue's described action, writing a sonnet – is clearly conceived as a mode of pedagogy, a way to 'explore the play', an exploration largely designed to evoke a familiar, mimetic understanding of the proper work of performance on and with writing. Many of the exercises and activities, for example, involve engaging characters through a kind of performance invention. Under the EXPLORE commands, for instance, users can 'Read' a character's 'story', which in effect summons all the scenes of a single character to the screen, repressing scenes in which that character does not appear. While this feature coordinates with the notion of a dramatic role, it provides much more than a side: the entire scene in which the relevant character appears is loaded, not just the role's cues and lines. There are three pages of links, fifteen in all, under the EXAMINE page; the first page of six are directed toward a secondary audience – 'Why did Romeo and Juliet die? Who's to blame? For hundreds of years people have argued over the reason for the deaths of the young lovers' (EXAMINE>WHY DID THEY DIE?). But the menu links on the second and third pages are considerably more advanced, fully in keeping with university-level instruction: 'How *Romeo and Juliet* was presented on the Elizabethan stage can only be conjectured from what we know generally of the earlier theatres (the Theatre, the Curtain, the Swan) and contemporary stage conventions and, more specifically, from the text and stage directions of Q1 (1597) and Q2 (1599)' (EXAMINE>IN THE THEATRE OVER TIME).

On *The Tempest for iPad*, *The Tempest* is also formally located at the center of the app, and from the text page one can activate the audio feature, a NAVIGATION feature (taking the reader to any scene), a COMMENTARY feature which loads the Experts' commentaries alongside the text, and various commands: a copy and paste feature, highlighting, search, bookmark, and 'MyPath', which allows the reader to cut and paste passages to a separate file, 'MyPath' through the play. The ROLES feature, rather than cutting the text, highlights all the speeches of a given role and the preceding speech as well. *The Tempest for iPad* has a rich and richly illustrated chapter on 'Watching Shakespeare' by Peter Holland and Katherine Rowe, and a complete audio recording of the play (again, British accented), which can be activated from the text and causes it to scroll forward; there are also 'Alternative Takes' (all British accent) on some speeches, as well as a set of podcasts (notably by Michael Witmore, 'Data-Mining Shakespeare'), and two 'Duets' in which famous American scholars – Joe Roach and Marjorie Garber – read two different takes on Prospero and Ariel in 5.1 (the accent of scholarly reading is American, but onstage Shakespeare is the property of the theatah?). The Cambridge app has a rich bibliography, while *The Tempest for iPad* has a list of twenty-two 'Experts' – scholars and performers – whose comments can be loaded to appear in a window alongside key lines called out in the text (the 'Bookshelf' feature is a listing of their books).[4] The most striking difference between the two apps, though, is that *The Tempest for iPad* is significantly more suggestive of the socialization of knowledge representation championed in the contemporary Digital Humanities: both Facebook and private networks can be enabled to facilitate discussion, share notes, and generate queries while reading and during class. As the blog on the

---

[4] On 29 May 2013 Luminary announced that it would partner with Simon & Schuster and with the Folger Shakespeare Library to produce versions of all of Shakespeare's plays along the model of *The Tempest for iPad*. See the blog at https://luminarydigitalmedia.com/.

Luminary website notes, 'Much more than a digital book, *The Tempest for iPad* is designed for social reading, authoring, and sharing, for all readers from students to professional scholars'. The iPad itself assumes some of the functions of a course website, enabling digitally mediated interaction between students, or indeed between anyone who has Facebook, and *The Tempest for iPad* also provides a short set of useful links accessible from the site, though, as David Weinberger rightly observes in this volume, apps are 'almost always self-contained environments'. In this regard, digital interaction replaces the live interaction prompted – but not contained – by the Cambridge app. As in most social media sites, Luminary retains the right to collect information, including 'Personal Information collected through the App', which may be shared with third-party vendors, or with 'third parties for their own marketing purposes' (ABOUT>PRIVACY POLICY): 'You hold the copyright in anything you create using this app, such as Socialnotes or MyPaths, although we may use that content' (ABOUT>CO-CREATED CONTENT).

Both sites, then, locate the text at the center of digital representation of Shakespeare: the text provides a template around which other activities can be mounted, and which can be represented in different ways: as speech, as character, as object of note taking and sharing, as the moment for instructional or experimental activity. In one sense, the impact of the apps is largely disintegrative, perhaps developing a tendency already evident in most scholarly editions: rather than looking across or down the page for a gloss, here the text signals a number of alternative items to read, concepts to engage, relationships to map. Yet while the relationship circles in the Cambridge app may seem to recall Franco Moretti's distanced reading, the apps only suggest modest ways of critically deforming the text, and nothing really approaching the kind of revision and reordering often demanded by performance (Moretti 2011). The thematic graphs of the Cambridge text (in which colored lines representing death, love, light and dark, and conflict bounce up and down across the horizontal axis of the play's temporal development) seem to set different themes running autonomously and inevitably through the action of the play (see EXPLORE>THEMES). The Cambridge app also provides Wordles for scenes and characters (EXPLORE>LANGUAGE). Unlike the imagery-hunting of New Criticism, the Wordles paint an instantaneous visual impression of a character's or a scene's most frequent words (larger, bolder) against a background cloud of less-frequent words, all shorn of their local grammatical, syntactic, or signifying logic.

Yet while both apps retain the text as the center of a user's activities, using the app tends to diversify the ways of using Shakespeare. The apps are hardly limited to 'reading' as the principal means of engagement with the Shakespearean text. In the Cambridge app, for instance, it's possible to interrogate 'The Story' of the play (EXAMINE>THE STORY), recognizing that 'There is no limit to the number of ways you can tell the story of Romeo and Juliet'. Each narrator can decide 'how much detail you wish to include (Rosaline? the musicians?)', 'the audience for your retelling (young children? examiners?)', 'the style in which you tell it (factual? nursery tale? Melodrama?)', 'the reasons why you tell it (to inform? entertain? teach a moral?)', and 'how much imagination you use (to add extra scenes, or characters' secret thoughts, to Shakespeare's version)', since 'Every story is a retelling, a different way of recounting what happens. Shakespeare used his imagination to create his own dramatic version of the story he had read'. Cambridge seems to recall one of Bertolt Brecht's insights as a director: begin by defining what story the production will tell, its *fable*. Here, the app characterizes the Shakespearean narrative as a site of work, creation, remaking, whose purposes are not reducible to the text itself. In this way and in others, the app models an encounter with the text that runs aslant the traditional text-to-performance paradigm. Recalling Tiffany Stern and Simon Palfrey's discussion of early modern sides, the apps seem to promote an encounter with Shakespeare that is – perhaps like the first encounter of some actors with their parts – not necessarily with the entire play, and not necessarily through reading, or at least not through reading alone. Users can listen to the play, and both apps have a wide range of alternate forms of exploration – through games, activities, commentaries, blogs, networking, 'authoring', and visual designs like the Wordles. The apps also illustrate – as, given the investment required, perhaps they must – a somewhat divided attitude toward Shakespeare, or Shakespearean writing. Shakespeare remains Shakespeare: what you make by using the app belongs (mostly) to you. The apps represent a Shakespearean text that is at once an object of interrogation and facilitates a process of dislocation; the apps represent Shakespearean knowledge as the outcome of reading, of listening, of engagement with a variety of traditional modes of instruction (lectures, commentaries) and also as the outcome of relatively structured play. What the apps don't quite permit is a direct intervention in the text, the kind of intervention typically undertaken by the agents of *theatre*, cutting, rearranging, modernizing, sampling, deforming and reforming the words on the page toward another mode of production: *dramatic performance*. The apps represent Shakespeare knowledge as the consequence of both reading and doing, but not of the kinds of doing that actors, or spectators, undertake.

And yet books have long had another use: making play. In an emerging era in which actors can audition online through sites like LET IT CAST (https://letitcast.com/en/), and most rehearsal rooms and performance spaces are driven by digital technologies, the notion that live acting exists in opposition either to digital means or to device culture more specifically seems passé.[5] Rather, apps like *Actsophia, Scene Partner*, and *Rehearsal* highlight the ways new instruments clarify the assumptions with which complex cultural practices are understood. Since these apps are not author- nor medium-specific, the 'text' tends not to provide the organizing structure or workspace as it does in the Shakespeare teaching apps. *Actsophia*, for instance, has six main menu areas: TRAIN, SUBMIT, AUDITION, PERFORM, TRACK, NETWORK, more or less neatly dividing the business of the actor's career from artistic training. TRAIN, for example, leads to a set of TIPS, to BEST BOOKS (Stanislavski, Meisner, Adler, Strasberg, Michael Chekhov, Uta Hagen, but also Suzuki, Mamet, Patrick Tucker, etc.), to a CLASS FINDER for New York or Los Angeles; to MONOS/SCRIPTS; to a GLOSSARY of TERMS, TECHNIQUE, ACTIONS, and OBJECTIVES; and to TRAIN NOW!, composed of a set of examples of different tonalities (Alerting: Tom Hanks, 'Houston, we have a problem'; Pity-partying: Humphrey Bogart, 'Of all the gin-joints in all the towns in all the world, she walks into mine') to model the actor's 'Playing', as well as several differently, rather seductively intoned, recorded phrases ('You have soft eyes') to which the actor can practice responding in different ways. Among other features for organizing headshots, sending résumés, and finding auditions, for a wide range of work (Episodics, Pilots, Features, Miniseries, Commercials, Plays), AUDITION>PRACTICE LINES opens a microphone, to record 'Other Lines' spoken by others, and 'My Lines', muting the actor's lines on playback to help memorization.

Like most, but not all, acting apps, *Actsophia* features a way to record and run lines, but *Actsophia* models acting less as content management than career management, as a craft that involves locating the body within a densely networked – both analog and digitally networked – commercial

---

[5] Brian Kulick, Artistic Director of the Classic Stage Company in New York, notes that in his rehearsals iPads and apps are frequently used to show research, or to pull up an image under discussion with the cast; he remarks that stage managers now typically make notes through digital instruments, and that Skype has greatly facilitated the participation of designers in design meetings (email to author 8 April 2012).

structure of commodified performance. Most of the other apps feature learning lines more prominently. *Scene Partner*, 'a powerful actor's app designed and built by actors' (ABOUT), is more strictly focused on preparing for performance: it allows downloading of some free (Shakespeare) and a wide range of purchased scripts through its direct link to Samuel French. Once the script is downloaded, an actor uses the device to 'GET OFFBOOK': here, by 'casting' him/herself – recording lines into the app. While this feature – recording one's own and/or others' lines – largely duplicates the recording feature already available on most smartphones, *Scene Partner* also provides a set of computer-generated voices, which can be assigned to the other parts in the play, providing a full cue script. The App comes with two free voices, '**Ryan** Male, English (U.S.)' and '**Heather** Female, English (U.S.)'; other voices – including (alongside a set of adult UK voices), '**Tyler**', a 'Male, English Australian' voice, and '**Deepa**', a 'Female, English (IN)' voice, **Micah**, 'a male voice with a Southern [African American?] twang', according to the website (https://www.scenepartnerapp.com/), a US Spanish-speaking voice, and voices speaking French, Spanish, German, Italian, and Mandarin Chinese – can be downloaded for $1.99 apiece. The downloaded voices clearly save time – actors need not record others' lines into the device – and also (increasingly, as more voices are added) model acting at the intersection of a globalizing practice.

While *Scene Partner* is clearly addressed to rehearsal, it is also intended to provide an interface between amateur and professional theatre organizations and casts, enabling a theatre to purchase a script and make it available through its 'Library'; the script can be cut and edited before being distributed to the cast, who can then both reconstruct it (as sides, with audio) in order to run lines, or simply to annotate it. Actors can also cut the script into various whole-play (Full Scene, Full Script, Original Script) or role-script (Just Me, Just My Cues, Me and My Cues, My Scenes) versions, which can be recorded, annotated, and edited. *Scene Partner* is not, apparently, intended to archive the rehearsal process, keeping a running multi-text of the evolution of a production; and, since the theatre sites are password protected, they would not be accessible to researchers outside the company. Habima seems to be a fan.

Scene Partner models the Shakespeare text as an object of work, as material to be refashioned to suit the actor's condition and practice of labor. In *Rehearsal 2*, the actor emails a PDF of the script to a username connected with the site, and then downloads it into *Rehearsal* for use. The *Rehearsal* app has a PDF reader/editor, enabling the user to emulate the by-hand inscription typically performed now on a paper copy of the play text. Scripts can be annotated as well as highlighted; it is also possible to highlight parts and temporarily black them out, making a virtual side (which can also be connected to the audio recording dimension of the app, as it can in *Scene Partner*). Recording is integrated into the menu – a red button at the bottom of the script PDF page – and so can be used at any moment; annotated scenes are preserved automatically, and the STORE area fittingly sells not only books (Patrick Tucker, *Secrets of Screen Acting*), scanners, microphones, and other apps, but a stylus as well. If *Actsophia* buries the rehearsal function within a dizzying menu of career-building and networking menus, *Rehearsal* performs an inverse model of acting. Enabling the actor to work with a paper-emulating onscreen script, the app provides only one page on which the actor can list pertinent information: email (used to upload texts to the app), stage name, address, casting age range, gender.

These apps generate digital texts resembling individual rehearsal scripts more than prompt copy, an avenue apparently being explored in a rehearsal app – *MyShx* – that Katherine Rowe and Bruce Smith are developing (see Rowe 2012). Although this app uses the New Cambridge edition (most of the apps that contain Shakespeare scripts, as *Scene Partner* does, have unidentified public domain texts), it seems to have many of the annotation and memorization elements of its predecessors. But Rowe notes that, by working with the American Shakespeare Center on a production of *Cymbeline* as a way to develop and test the app, she hoped 'to establish whether tablet devices are at a robust enough stage of development to support the complex recording, mnemonic, communication, and performance tasks of a play in production', especially determining 'what are the essential features of a mobile script and what downstream challenges of archiving, distribution and intellectual property might they spark' (525). This project is focused, in part, on developing 'a robust electronic promptbook', a central script sustaining and recording the production, a rehearsal instrument and a way of recording the changing textual dimension of performance-in-the-making. Rowe recognizes the challenges that such an endeavor poses both to the willingness of individuals and companies to have their intermediate thoughts, guesses, mistakes, and misdirections recorded as part of the process of the production, and, more broadly, about questions of intellectual property – does the actor own the markups to his/her script on the third day of rehearsal, which were replaced on the fourth day? At the same time, Rowe notes that the rehearsal features of *MyShx* replicate the ways actors are already using digital technologies to prepare and rehearse, whether via specific apps or otherwise. Rowe observes a 'surprisingly wide variation from actors concerning the degree to which they used the whole play text in role development and line learning'; indeed, some of the *Cymbeline* actors 'used the "voice memo" feature on their smartphones to record their scenes and then play them back, a procedure that turned out to be a highly effective self-cuing strategy. Those who had learned their lines in this way showed fuller command of the play as a whole (including the lines of other players) and required less prompting than those who did not' (530).

Like the postcard plays, Shakespeare apps demonstrate the multidirectionality and multitemporality of technological change, illustrating the principle that 'the tendency to elicit what is "new" about new media by contrasting its radical mutability with the supposed material stolidity of older textual forms is a misplaced gesture' (Kirschenbaum 2008: 166). So what does the design of instruments like this tell us about the contemporary intersection of dramatic writing, dramatic performance, and digital media, the ways in which knowledge representation is being developed in the digital sphere, and what reflexive pressure on the digital might arise from performance applications? How do these instruments model text/performance, what kind of knowledge do they represent about the conditions of contemporary Shakespearean performance? In the pedagogical apps, the function of the whole text remains central, though reading is only one way to engage with or contemplate it: the apps enable users to listen to the text, annotate it, switch to lectures, play games and activities. *Romeo and Juliet* or *The Tempest* are the workspace, both the object and the process of instruction and learning. *The* text, it might be fair to say, operates within a performance environment in which some activities are directed inward – activating glosses – and many are directed outward.

Perhaps not surprisingly, since the acting apps are directed to working actors, the theatre that emerges from them values a specific professional competence: learning lines, being ready with a solid command of the role and a fluid approach to rehearsal, and understanding some of the basic contours of the business. On the acting apps, performance is often modeled in terms of medium and genre (theatre, television, film; episodics, pilots, features, miniseries, commercials, plays); location (New York, Los Angeles, elsewhere); specific regimes of employment (connect to unions, casting directors, etc.). It demands rapid and precise line-learning through traditional means, underlining, so to speak, the fact that acting as a contemporary mode of production is both multimedial and intermedial.

And, while it continues to occupy the intersection of orality and literacy, that intersection is now the meeting point for a range of inscriptional (manuscript, print, digital) technologies and performance practices. Some apps notably restore a residual theatre practice – learning lines by ear rather than by eye, with a virtual 'partner' – and the whole-play organicism assumed in performance commentary and in the pedagogical apps is not always directly involved in how the language of plays is internalized toward enactment. Since all of the apps enable actors to construct both visual and audio sides easily, it seems as though the print-culture notion that actors should engage their role, their work as actors, through an encounter with the book continues to mark an important distinction between 'literary' notions of theatre still central to pedagogical apps and the practices of making play.

What's most visible in the acting apps' modeling of dramatic performance is that the text is clearly designed for use. Cut it, make it into sides, create audio cues, and record one's own speeches: the app works not to reproduce writing but gradually to eliminate it, to transform its status from digital design to analog memory, action. While the app is proprietary – on most of the apps, the advanced features (e.g., Deepa's voice) cost an additional fee, as do any scripts ordered from the 'store' – authorship remains surprisingly fungible: the script may have an author, but what the app enables is its de-authorization, or perhaps its transformation into a different kind of substrate, one workable by a different kind of author, the *auteur* of the stage. The *Explore Shakespeare* and *Tempest for iPad* apps also invite a wide range of activities, *doing* that is modeled as supplementary to *reading*. While they are in one sense very much in the tradition of Shakespeare by the book, in another sense these apps bypass the stage-and-page dialectic. The script is a different thing in motion, talking and walking itself down the screen; yet, the text itself remains inviolable. Readers can cut, highlight, annotate the text, but it is also possible – as it is not in a book – simply to 'hide' or delete all changes, restoring a pristine, apparently unused 'original'.

Much as 'Remediation makes the medium as such *visible*', the apps surprisingly intervene in the algorithmic dimension sometimes attributed to dramatic performance (Guillory 2010: 324).

> A digital text is like a music score or theater script: its written inscription is meant to be executed, either by the underlying code alone, or through a feedback loop that leads from the user to the underlying code to the display, and back to the user. Digital texts thus present the same contrast as the classic performing arts between the invariability of the script and the variability of its execution. (Ryan 2004: 416)

Execution, feedback, and *display*: as the *score* metaphor for dramatic performance implies, theatrical performance is modeled as an 'Algorithm-driven operation'. But this metaphor fails to account for the practical and ideological independence of performance practices from textual determination, their incommensurability with 'textual interpretation', the principal professional activity of literary scholarship. The acting apps interrupt the model of *execution, feedback,* and *display* as a representation of performance: they witness the extent to which the text, far from directing the performance, is directed – dissected might be a better word here – by it, subjected to a range of inscription and enactment designs for doing something other than *executing* textual commands. Acting apps present a structure for finding, discovering, or creating a means for conceiving the text as *capable of execution*; the means of this execution, as the career-building dimension of *Actsophia* and other apps suggests, is heavily over-determined and conventional. To this degree, though, acting apps perhaps also underline what the remediation of the book to the tablet computer also reveals. Although the pedagogical apps instrumentalize Shakespeare's plays – and 'Shakespeare' – for different purposes and performances, 'reading' is also displaced as the central activity they sustain; the tablet is not for reading but for interacting, through a variety of other performances, through other ways of reading, and – using the social media functions – through ways of knowing that are engaged in live and mediated social dialogue. As N. Katherine Hayles observes, 'it would be more accurate to call an electronic text a *process* than an object', a notion of the dramatic text visibly modeled by these apps (2005: 101).

The disciplinary discourse of digital humanities makes a powerful argument for the ongoing, interminable transformation of both the objects and the practices of the humanities by new technologies. This body of work should evoke a shrewd skepticism toward simplistic narratives of succession and obsolescence; the screen has yet to displace the book, and the acting apps subject digital means to analog work to enable a process that – with all necessary qualifications – gains much of its power from the analog interaction between embodied performers. Acting apps are a delivery system to be sure; but, as a system of 'knowledge representation', what they model is analog work – relaxation, networking, editing, cutting, memorizing – that transforms the digital text toward the making of a complex event, an event in which the analog and the digital are in various ways indivisible. Despite its analog character, theatre today cannot escape both the instruments and ideology of digital culture. Hayles takes as salutary the 'combination of analog and digital', a combination that may well 'prove far more powerful than either by itself [...] for each has properties that complement the other':

> digital representations allow for precise error control, extreme fragmentation and recombination, whereas analog processes have the advantages of the continuum, including the ability to transmit informational patterns between differently embodied entities. (2005: 29)

Wish you were here: The pedagogical and the acting apps occupy cultural temporality somewhere between the hand-inscribed printed postcard and the print-emulating Facebook post. While *Play Viewed from a Distance* exploits and ironizes the conventional notion of theatre as a page-to-stage process, *Explore Shakespeare* and *The Tempest for iPad* are, for all their emulation of print, postprint in a way that the postcard plays are not. Turn the features on, distort the text, play games around it, listen to its voices and commentators, share commentaries and discussions online, and then turn the features off: the text returns unblemished, unbent, unspindled, unfolded, unmutilated. These apps invite interaction with the text, but model something approaching the textual transcendentalism of the New Criticism, a text that can finally be freed from our corrupting use of it. The acting apps appear to enable considerably more intervention, an apparent subordination of the digital to the analog uncommon in device culture: annotation, highlighting, cutting, as well as the replication of a residual, oral-culture rehearsal process, learning one's lines from a partner, even if that partner speaks back not from a body but from a tiny screen, speaking sometimes in one's own voice, and sometimes as Tyler or Micah or Deepa. If the pedagogical apps model the permanence of the text, the acting apps model its supplementarity: rather than requiring what was once conceptualized as the 'completion' of performance, the text requires the actor's work in order to disappear into that other thing, the event of performance. Both the acting and the pedagogical apps dramatize the condition of dramatic performance today, a post print sense of performance beyond the fatigued oppositions of page and stage, the digital and the analog, the recorded and the live, a theatre in which writing continuously evanesces into acting, and acting repurposes writing toward the event of performance.

PART IV
Editorial legacies

CHAPTER 14

Theatre editions

Peter Holland

Two editions of *Hamlet*, 1676 and 2009

Consider for a while the paratexts of two editions of *Hamlet*. The first announces on its title page, among other details, that the published text represents the play 'As it is now Acted at his Highness the Duke of *York*'s Theatre', that the play is written by William Shakespeare and that it is published in 1676. On the following recto comes a message 'To the Reader':

> This Play being too long to be conveniently Acted, such places as might be least prejudicial to the Plot or Sense, are left out upon the Stage: but that we may no way wrong the incomparable Author, are here inserted according to the Original Copy with this Mark" ([A]2)

On the verso is a list of 'The Persons Represented', with actors' names attached. And then the play text begins.

The second has on its cover a photograph of Jude Law, the play's title and author, and the theatre company logo 'Donmar West End'. The bibliographical details show one conspicuous absence: there is no ISBN. There is confusion about the book's date: it was 'first published in 2008' but also states 'First edition 2009'. Its publisher is Donmar Warehouse, the theatre company rather than a trade publisher, and it carries the conventional stern warning about who owns the rights 'in this version of Hamlet' – again, the theatre company – to whom 'application for performance etc. should be made before commencement of rehearsal' (Shakespeare 2009a: [ii]). It also identifies the state of the text: 'This script is correct at the time of going to press.' We can assume that 'correct' means, in this context, that this is an accurate representation of the performance text for the production, then in rehearsal, at that point.

Its brief foreword, placed on page [iii], is by the Donmar's Artistic Director, Michael Grandage, who directed the production. The edition 'was published to accompany the production of *Hamlet* that was presented by the Donmar Warehouse at the Wyndham's Theatre'; David Hunt 'helped me cut the script'; the 'great Shakespearian scholar, Professor Russell Jackson played an important role throughout the rehearsal period as our text consultant'. The whole company of twenty actors 'played a part in contributing to the text that is published here'.

> We wanted a version with a strong, clear narrative and a playing time of around three hours including an interval. It is what felt right for the Donmar's production at the Wyndham's and in no way represents a definitive version for future productions ... I feel confident [Shakespeare's] genius remains intact with the cuts proposed here. ([iii])

Then there follow three pages listing, for the production which opened in May 2009, the cast (with all the doubling indicated), the crew and the Donmar's staff. And then this play text begins.

The 1676 version makes clear that its text will represent two layers of potentiality and realization. The first is, it seems, that version currently being performed at the Duke of York's Theatre. Unlike certain Restoration play texts, especially libretti for operas, this book is not announced as being sold at the theatre but through two booksellers at their usual places of business. It is aimed at a reader but one who is posited to be interested in differentiating between the performance-text and the text Shakespeare wrote. There is, unsurprisingly, no awareness here of the different early modern states of the text. No one yet cared or perhaps even knew about the instabilities of the 'Shakespeare' *Hamlet* text as it moves between and around its sequence of early publication, especially Q1, Q2 and F1. But there is a tension between the extensive writing of 'an incomparable Author' and the more limited quantity of text that can be performed 'conveniently' where the crucial criterion for deciding which passages need to be cut to fit the performance's time-span is to ensure that the plot and sense are clearly communicated. We could start to worry what exactly the author of this explanation thought that 'sense' might mean but we find it easier to understand that the theatre would not choose to omit passages whose absence would make the narrative unclear. Telling the story remains a dominant concern in most conventional forms of theatre performance now, just as much as in 1676. The script, therefore, appears with its two strata apparent: the lines spoken on stage and the passages omitted, the latter marked with the sign (") often used earlier for *sententiae* but here recoded to define the cuts. The reader is buying all of *Hamlet*: the full-length text Shakespeare wrote and the play as performed.

Except that that isn't what the reader turns out to have bought. The last line of dialogue on the first page of the play has Francisco say 'Good night', but early texts have him say 'Giue you good night', and, where those textual witnesses showed Marcellus asking him who 'hath' relieved him, the actor performing the 1676 text appears to have asked who 'has'. Since, by 1676, 'hath' would have sounded archaic, the theatre has modernized it. In case you might be starting to assume that the changes affect only the Restoration performance text at the Duke of York's and that, surely, the cut passages are accurately representing the pre-Restoration textual tradition, the very first passage marked as cut records Horatio saying, "Twill not appear' but not 'Tush, tush' before it. Later, much later, this Hamlet will not argue that 'the native hue of resolution / Is sicklied o'er with the pale cast of thought' but that 'the healthful face of resolution / Shews sick and pale with thought' (39), leaving the second line short of four syllables. Perhaps a careful reader might worry about that defective line and find another, earlier printing of *Hamlet* and realize what has happened. Checking the speech further, that reader might learn that earlier Hamlets questioned whether one would want to 'grunt and sweat' rather than 'groan and sweat under a weary life' and so on.

Though nothing in the edition tells the purchaser, this is a thoroughly revised version, its language recast in small ways hundreds of times. It probably started as that adapted, as we now think we know but the edition is silent about, by Sir William Davenant to the taste of the new times. Since Davenant died in 1668, this edition represents *Hamlet* as it had perhaps been played some years earlier than publication, possibly as early as when Samuel Pepys saw it on 24 August 1661. The identification of the reviser of the 1676 text as Davenant was proposed by Hazelton Spencer in 1923 and has not been substantially reinvestigated since (see Spencer 1923 and Spencer 1927: 178–87).

The 1676 edition makes it easy for us to see exactly what Davenant has done in shortening the text and we can start to analyse why. The cutting of the first scene, for instance, is often strikingly similar to the cut version that the company Grandage assembled around Jude Law played: in both, for instance, Horatio loses his fourteen lines about the prodigies seen before Caesar's death (115–28). Sometimes one version leaves in more text (e.g., in Grandage's, about eight lines more of Horatio's narrative about the wager between Old Hamlet and Old Fortinbras are spoken than in Davenant's version) but the effect overall in both is to speed up the scene considerably.

The edited texts – 'edited' in that sense, common for most, rare for Shakespeare scholars, of 'shortened' (cf. *Oxford English Dictionary*, 'edit', v., 2d) – are concerned to create a pacier opening, shortening back-story or historical narratives; neither wants to leave out any part of the ghost's startling appearances. The shortened scene increases excitement and cuts the time till the star's (Hamlet's) first appearance.

We would, I suspect, have been a little shocked if the Grandage/Hunt text proved to modernize extensively in the way that the 1676 text reveals it had, but their edition, reworking the play for twenty-first-century production, does record another common part of the process of the theatrical remaking of Shakespeare's text: the redistribution of lines. Here, for instance, it is Horatio who asks about the reasons for the war preparations that 'Doth make the night joint-labourer with the day', and the answer to his question, 'Who is't that can inform me?', turns out to be spoken by Marcellus, who speaks this version's abbreviated 'whisper' about 'the main motive of our preparations'. So the scholar who has been away from Denmark until recently asks the guards who turn out to have heard rumours that explain their orders. It is, in some respects, an easier explanation for the questioner and answerer to work with and communicate to the audience. It loses something of Marcellus' wondering quite why he and the rest of the armed forces are doing what they do and it misses out something of Horatio's greater knowledge of what is being talked about in the higher places of the court, the place where presumably he has picked up the rumours. This swapping of lines between Marcellus and Horatio continues at the end of the scene: here Marcellus talks about the effect of the cock crowing on ghosts while Horatio has heard the story about the beneficent effect of all-night cock-crowing near Christmas. Though Horatio keeps the image of 'the dawn in russet mantle clad', intriguingly it is now Marcellus who proposes that they should tell what they have seen to 'young Hamlet'. As so often in modern rewriting, some of the redistribution produces metrical awkwardnesses. Marcellus' scene-closing lines

> Let's do't, I pray, and I this morning know
> Where we shall find him most convenient.

become

BARNARDO. I this morning know
    Where we shall find him most convenient.
HORATIO. Let's do't, I pray. (Shakespeare 2009a: 5)

which includes all the words but not in a form which results in two iambic pentameters, leaving two awkward half-lines. Nothing in this version tells us that such redistribution has been happening. Only by collating with a conventional edition would a reader discover it.

Performance texts are not, of course, some kind of unspoken contract with their audiences or readers. Nothing obliges Grandage to have his actors speak only – let alone all of – the lines that early editions ascribe to them. Speech prefixes are not sacrosanct in the theatre. Equally, the text is not a fixed entity. That note on page [ii] of the edition pointedly mentions that 'This script is correct at the time of going to press.' Since the edition was sold at the Wyndham's Theatre as a kind of souvenir of the performance (and it was probably not widely distributed through normal bookselling channels), the edition needed to be in print close to, if not before, the first performance on 29 May 2009 which it mentions as part of the cast list. Rehearsals and runs change scripts right up to – indeed, well beyond – the last minute. The script available to buy in the theatre foyer thus may have significant differences from that which the playgoer then hears and sees.

I suggested earlier that the 1676 text might represent the text Davenant prepared for his company's hugely successful production of the play in 1661. John Downes, later a prompter but then an actor in the company, recorded in *Roscius Anglicanus* (1708) that 'No succeeding Tragedy for several Years got more Reputation, or Money to the Company than this' (21). But there is no reason to assume that Davenant's revision stayed stable from 1661 to 1676. It is much more likely that, though the 1676 text was derived from that prepared by Davenant, it had continued to change over the years as actors made their own changes to a stock repertory play.

The edition's title page emphasized its currency: 'As it is now Acted'. Certainly the cast list it included was not that noted by Downes for the first performances, even though some of the actors were the same: Thomas Betterton as Hamlet, Cave Underhill as 1st 'Grave-maker', Mary Betterton, *née* Saunderson, as Ophelia. But it is not the cast list for performances in 1676 either. It lists Guildenstern as played by Mr Cademan, but Philip Cademan had been forced to stop acting in 1673, after a stage accident during a duel in Davenant's play *The Man's the Master*. Cademan was, as his court testimony in 1696 explained, injured

> under his right eye, wch touch'd his Brain by means whereof he lost his memory his speech and the use of his right side, wch made him incapable of acting any more. (Highfill, et al. 1973–93: 3.5)

It is reasonable to think that such a terrible injury to a young actor would have been well-known to play-goers and perhaps to book-buyers too. The cast list is neither the original one for 1661 nor the current one for this version of *Hamlet*. Readers might well have realized that this edition is not consistently quite as immediately contemporary as the title page claims. The cast list has none of the precise accuracy of the Grandage/Hunt one, which is the cast for a limited West End run rather than the cast for a stock repertory play. What kind of moment of performance the two editions represent varies widely.

Theatres and the text: the critic's work

I have spent so long on these two texts because they can stand as examples for so much in the complex and messy world of the theatre and the versions of Shakespeare in print that theatre generates. There is the transformation of the text for reasons that have nothing to do with the labours of Shakespeare's scholarly editors and much to do with the practicalities of attracting audiences into the theatres: in 1676 and 2009 audiences cannot cope with more than three hours of Shakespeare on the West End stage (if the Duke of York's Theatre be allowed to stand as a proto-West End theatre). There is the shifting, unstable and usually unmarked morphing of the text, for, while the Royal Shakespeare Company used regularly to announce in its theatre programmes how many lines had been cut from the text, even it noted neither which lines were cut nor what redistributions had taken place and the 1676 *Hamlet* is strikingly unusual in its representation of the text's strata, even if inaccurate in what it claims to be stratifying. There is the ambiguity of precisely what a theatre edition might represent and what moments of production history it might purport to represent. There is the uneasy relationship between the performance and the distribution of the edition, whether through the normal book trade or by sale in the foyer alongside programmes, coffee mugs and other souvenirs. There is the potential for the text's re-production, becoming a potential for other performances but its editing being owned as intellectual property by the theatre workers (Grandage and Hunt). There is the theatre company as itself a publisher, its ownership of the records of performance matching some of the kinds of narratives that have been constructed for the movement of a Shakespeare play from the Lord Chamberlain's Men to the printer. There is the temporary, ephemeral status of the performance(s) to which the text bears witness. And there is, finally, in this list of just a few of the problems and tensions and indications of theatrical and textual cultures that such editions can generate, the question of what on earth the theatre edition is for, for I have to admit that my copy of the 2009 edition lay unopened from my buying it at the theatre to my starting to prepare to write this chapter. Scholarly editors must collate them but time is often too short for other scholars to attend to their significant alterations.

I should emphasize that my concerns so far have been entirely with printed and published texts. Theatres of course generate myriad other forms of texts. Actors and crew involved in, for example, the National Theatre production of *Timon of Athens* in 2012 were given copies of scripts that had been typed up in-house. Where many contemporary productions start from a published text, often using one that is convenient to hold while working on-book in the rehearsal room, such as, for example, the Penguin series which provides a clean page with a text not threatened by the upward imperialist expansionist movement of scholarly commentary from the foot of the page, this one needed a particular version because of the radical rewritings, cuttings and rearrangements of the text, as well as the importation of some lines from *Coriolanus*, undertaken by the director, Nicholas Hytner. But such texts are rarely published. They are working resources, means of ensuring that, quite literally, all the company can be on the same page. The audience sees the consequence of the company's reading and working with the text as script but it is not permitted to read that script. And, here too, the script-text proves to be a shifting target: copies carried a date prominently on the cover to separate out different stages of the distribution of the frequently changing script.

In addition, there are the annotated texts, many thousands of them from the history of Shakespeare in performance, some much prized and held by libraries, others used and discarded once the production is over. Often wrongly all labelled prompt-books, they can also include working copies for individual actors, heavily annotated as the actor thinks through the role in the process of rehearsal, a field which Barbara Hodgdon is currently brilliantly researching, as well as working copies for directors and designers, as preparatory thinking for performance. All represent the material practices of theatre, even when there is no eventuating performance to which they relate. What each one represents needs careful analysis if its status in relation to an actual or putative production is to be defined. Here too the cutting and adjustment of the text may often appear most visible: pages blocked for deletion, lines moved, speeches reassigned.

In the study of the history of Shakespeare in print, theatre-linked editions of Shakespeare tend to get remarkably short shrift. Andrew

Murphy acknowledges at the start of his superb exploration of *Shakespeare in Print*:

> I should also make clear that the focus of this book is on the printed text of Shakespeare's own plays. For this reason, theatrical adaptations are very largely ignored and theatrical issues more generally are not much attended to either. (Murphy 2003: 2–13)

Murphy's book is large enough in any case but the exclusion crucially limits the scope of what 'print' here means.

John Bell's Shakespeare

One major theatre-linked edition that Murphy briefly discusses is John Bell's (Murphy 2003: 116–18). Its bibliographical history is complex but Bell began publishing the plays in 1773, completing an eight-volume edition in 1774 and adding a ninth volume with the poems. One of Bell's achievements in later editions was the inclusion of illustrations of actors in particular roles (see Burnim and Highfill 1998 for an outstanding study of these images). But it is less the visual aids that defined the nature of this edition than the source of the initial volumes' texts, for these are the plays 'As they are now performed at the Theatres Royal in London; Regulated from the Prompt Books of each House By permission' (Shakespeare 1773–74: 1, title page). For the first time, the texts as currently being performed were brought together.

One of the strangenesses about the edition is the order in which the plays are presented: the first volume, for instance, contains *As You Like It, Macbeth, Othello* and *All's Well that Ends Well; Hamlet* is in volume three, placed with *Richard III, The Tempest, Measure for Measure* and *The Merry Wives of Windsor*. It is a random sequence probably based on the availability of the prompt-books. In the later volumes, Bell included the plays which were not part of the current theatre repertory, without changing the overall statement of the volume's title page. But the individual play texts of this latter group are no longer defined as deriving from the prompt-book, 'Regulated ... with permission of the Managers, by Mr. Hopkins, Prompter', as, for example, his performance version of *As You Like It* had stated (1.73). Bell or his editor had got his performance texts from William Hopkins, prompter at Drury Lane, and Joseph Younger, prompter at Covent Garden (see, on their careers, Highfill, et al. 1973–93: 7.407–10 and 16.364–8). The texts for the unperformed plays were probably constructed by publisher or editor.

Each of the plays, whether in the repertory or not, is accompanied by 'Notes critical and Illustrative; by the Authors of the *Dramatic Censor*'. The plural is untrue: there was only a single author, Francis Gentleman (1728–84), whose *The Dramatic Censor* in parts had been published by Bell in 1770 and then collected into two volumes in 1771. *The Dramatic Censor* analysed contemporary performances of a range of plays, not only Shakespeare, especially performances by David Garrick whose art Gentleman frequently idolized, even if at other times he squabbled with him as manager. Gentleman, who will become the hero of this chapter, dedicated his Shakespeare edition for Bell to Garrick, opposite a portrait engraving of the actor to match the one of Shakespeare that served as frontispiece, pronouncing Garrick as 'the best illustrator of, and the best *living comment* on, Shakespeare, that ever has appeared, or possibly ever will grace the British stage' and offering the edition 'as a grateful, tho' small, return, for the infinite pleasure, and extensive information, derived from your exquisite performance, and judicious remarks' (Shakespeare 1773–74: 1.3–4). Whatever the glosses that Gentleman might offer as commentary and whatever the illustrations that Bell included in this and later editions, it is Garrick who is effectively both commentator and illustrator. The great actor is, for Gentleman, critic and artist. But Gentleman's commentary is not designed to represent Garrick's performance; his aims are not a matter of descriptive reporting.

In the 'Advertisement' to the Shakespeare edition, Gentleman makes clear that his intention is to spell out all those ways in which Shakespeare fails, even if his faults, especially the indecent passages, 'may justly be attributed to the loose, quibbling, licentious taste of his time' (1.5). So, for Gentleman, the solution is to recognize that the theatres, 'especially of late, have been generally right in their omissions' and he has therefore 'printed our *text* after their regulations' with the advantage that:

> those who take books to the Theatre, will not be so puzzled themselves to accompany the speaker; nor so apt to condemn the performers of being imperfect, when they pass over what is designedly omitted. (1.6–7)

At the same time, Gentleman recognizes that the performance text is unstable since:

> the difference of power, of voice and execution, may make one erase more than another; nevertheless we come so near the mark of all, that scarce any perplexity can arise, in tracing them. (1.7)

That Gentleman is describing a cultural practice of reading while listening to the performance is interesting in itself, but he is also concerned to identify and include 'some passages, of great merit for the closet' even though 'never spoken': 'such, though omitted in the text, we have carefully preserved in the notes' (1.8). There is no intention here of including all those passages that the publishers of Davenant's *Hamlet* marked as omitted in performance, only those which seemed to Gentleman important. He could go further than this, though: Polonius' advice to Laertes, not spoken in contemporary performances, is included in the notes as a passage which, 'usually omitted, should certainly be retained' because '[t]here is a compact richness of instruction set forth in these lines, which well deserves attention in public, and perusal in private' (3.16–17). Though the edition has often been used as evidence of contemporary practice (see, e.g., Cunningham 2008 and Oya 2007), the specific contribution of performance analysis that Gentleman's work adds has largely been ignored, except for a fine article by Lois Potter (see Potter 1999).

In the layering of the functions of this text – for performance, for private reading or for a mixture of the two – Gentleman is concerned to act as an aggressively stern moral policeman, rooting out all obscenities. So, for instance, *Titus Andronicus*, a play which was not being performed, 'must be horrid in representation, and is disgustful in perusal' (Shakespeare 1773–74: 8.3). This is Gentleman the critic. He is also concerned to praise Shakespeare's dramaturgy: the opening scene of *Hamlet* 'is happily preparative to the future incidents and subject' (3.5). But he is equally ready to approve theatrical improvements: of Claudius' opening speech in 1.2, he comments, 'Four and twenty lines ... with a brace of useless ambassadors, are omitted, commendably' (3.9). This is Gentleman the dramatist who, among other work, had adapted Shakespeare's *Richard II* in 1755, Jonson's *Sejanus* in 1752 and *The Alchemist* in 1771. And his notes are also concerned to define the right kind of performer for each role: 'The requisites for *Horatio* are an easy deportment, genteel figure, and smooth level delivery' (3.5), while:

> the character of *Hamlet* should be a good, if not a striking figure; with very flexible, spirited, marking features; a sonorous voice, capable of rapid climaxes, and solemn gradations; if not so soft as the upper notes of expression, nor so deep as the lower ones, if otherwise sufficient in articulation and compass, it may do the part justice. (3.9)

This is Gentleman the erstwhile actor who writes with a fair sensitivity to the practices of casting. Such comments are prescriptive and there is little in the commentary drawn from contemporary performance. Pointing out that 'it is not strictly within our design to speak of Performers', Gentleman does introduce *Macbeth* by praising Garrick's 'unparalleled merit' which 'sustains the importance, marks the strong feelings, and illustrates the author's powerful ideas, with such natural, animated, forcible propriety' (1.61), while also finding space to complain that 'Theatrical managers are highly culpable when they do not dress this play in the martial, striking habits of the time and country' (1.64).

Though Dr Johnson, for instance, had commented on Hamlet's 'Now might I do it pat' that 'this speech ... is too horrible to be read or to be uttered' (Johnson 1916: 193), that is almost the only mention of even hypothetical performance that Johnson makes on the play in his notes. Limited though it is as performance commentary, Gentleman's is the first ever such project for Shakespeare. Indeed, it is easily the most important performance commentary since Aelius Donatus' massive commentary on Terence in the fourth century, with its remarkable analysis of look, gesture, movement, intonation, pace and volume (see, for the text and French translation, Donatus n.d.).

It was Garrick who mentioned to Gentleman 'a delicate fear' about the project:

> This fear was, lest the prunings, transpositions, or other alterations, which, in his province as a manager he had often found necessary to make, or adopt, with regard to the text, for the convenience of representation, or accommodation to the powers and capacities of his performers, might be misconstrued into a critical presumption of offering to the literati a reformed and more correct edition of our author's works ... In justification of ourselves also, we take the opportunity of declaring, that to expect any thing more of this work, than as *a companion to the theatre*, is to mistake the purpose of the editors. (Shakespeare 1773–74: 1.8)

As Laurie Osborne comments,

> Although Gentleman has suggested the greater purity of his text and its usefulness as a fixed standard for theatrical representation, he proves unexpectedly self-effacing in his retreat from competition with scholarly 'correct' editions. (Osborne 1996: 29)

There is, then, a tension, even a sense of inferiority that the theatre texts carry when set against the scholarly and cultural authority that accrues to the main line of eighteenth-century editing from Rowe to Malone. The edited texts offered to 'literati' are seen as unquestionably weightier than this 'compact' edition (Shakespeare 1773–74: 1.4); the intellectual effort behind the scholarship affords that achievement aimed for the reader more cultural power than something for playgoers. Bell's edition sold many more copies than rival scholarly editions, a sign of the theatre's strong position in creating the cultural meaning of Shakespeare (Sillars 2008: 115). But it is also the case that most Shakespeare editions in the period were theatre editions. The great line of scholarly editing, the major concern of our responses to eighteenth-century Shakespeare publishing, was a small minority of Shakespeare play-publishing, alongside the more frequent issuing of single-play theatre editions.

The progeny of Bell and Gentleman

Bell's edition of 1773–74 inaugurates a long line of theatre-centred editions of the plays, from Kemble's to Mrs Inchbald's, Oxberry's, Lacy's, Kean's and others that spread through the nineteenth century (Murphy 2003: 35). But, even at the point at which Richard Knowles, in a 1989 note that forms an appendix to the *Shakespeare Variorum Handbook*, is acknowledging theatre editions and trying to sort out their complex bibliographical history, he is disparaging their importance for textual scholarship: 'These editions are useless for textual purposes, occasionally interesting for stray comments, and very useful for stage history, especially the history of the text on the stage' (Knowles 2003: 182). It is, of course, the case that theatre editions may, without any pretensions to textual scholarship, hit upon important emendations not yet in the scholarly tradition. Actors cannot speak lines that make no sense to them – or, at least, we might reasonably credit them with a desire not to speak gibberish. But what theatre editions may offer is much more than textual evidence. Brief comments on four currently available series, rather than single-play editions like the Donmar *Hamlet*, may point effectively to the ways in which the negotiations with performances, past, present and putative, are currently being conducted.

Shakespeare in production

The most familiar of the four theatre series currently available is Cambridge University Press's *Shakespeare in Production* series, edited by Julie Hankey and J. S. Bratton, 14 volumes to date, where the introduction charts the play's performance history and the commentary steadfastly resists conventional glossing and sets out the evidence, moment by moment, for theatre workers' explorations of a scene, a line, a move across the centuries of production. Based on excellent archival work, the volumes are rich with theatrical materials. Directors and actors might turn to this for preparatory work but it is plainly directed at scholars.

The Applause Shakespeare Library

John Russell Brown's series, 11 volumes to date, intended always to offer 'a continuous commentary on the text by a professional director or a leading actor that considers the stage life of the play as its action unfolds' (Shakespeare 2001a: vi). Though it may use moments from past productions, its aim is to refuse to 'provide a single theatrical reading' in favour of offering 'a range of possibilities, a number of suggestions of what an actor might do'. The potentialities of the text are thereby to be 'open[ed] up to individual readers' so that they 'can "feel" what the play would be like in action' and 'the play can be produced in the theatre of the mind'. Commentary thus becomes dominantly a set of hypotheticals which sometimes serve to mask assumptions and a refusal of possibility. The primary syntactical form sometimes reveals a possibility: in *Measure for Measure* 1.1, the Duke's emphasis on haste means that, at 52–75, he 'may have stage business to complete, picking up suitcases or putting on a hat or coat' (7). But some comments become certainty: Escalus, asked by the Duke about Angelo, 'must feel put on the spot as the Duke looks him hard in the eye and suddenly asks his opinion' (5), though the moment might be played in many other ways.

In the event, most commentaries were not by theatre professionals: John Hirsch collaborated with Leslie Thomson on *A Midsummer Night's Dream*, Leon Rubin wrote the one for *Measure for Measure*, Peter Lichtenfels for *The Merchant of Venice* and Janet Suzman for *Antony and Cleopatra* (all published in 2000 and 2001). But six were written by John Russell Brown himself, which, without disparaging his incisive theatre intelligence, means the series loses the edge intended.

The [Cut] Shakespeare

The third example moves from the scholarly audience for the first and the imagined reader's imaginings of the second to the audience in the classroom or at a full production. In an unknowing throwback to the 1676 *Hamlet*, Steve Gooch, successful playwright and translator, literary manager and teacher of playwriting, created a series of editions offering a carefully and thoughtfully cut text with the main text in bold and the excised still present in a smaller, fainter font, thereby leaving to the reader/class/theatre company the option of restoring passages and of working on the cut text with an awareness of exactly what has been omitted. Presented with no commentary, the text is simply a presentation of skillful script-editing. Gooch's introduction is the only example I know of a rationale for cutting the text, of the choices he seeks to make, what constitutes the 'material' that needs to be removed in order to make 'the author's own intentions clearer and more vivid' (Shakespeare 2006a: 2), which, albeit couched in language scholars avoid at all costs, is at least frank. Using a cut text saves directors and actors 'energy often spent wrestling with the text ... and find a delivery more vivid to modern consciousness', encouraging them 'to focus on the qualities of characterization and storytelling which are the joys of Shakespeare in performance' (2), echoing the 1676 *Hamlet*'s concern with cutting 'least prejudicial to the Plot'. The final arbiter is 'the acid test of whether there is "something to play", a clear action, response or intention behind the line as opposed to just words' (6).

The result can be brutal. The opening of *Hamlet* now reads:

BERNARDO. Who's there?
MARCELLUS. Holla, Bernardo!

and poor, cold, 'sick at heart' Francisco has completely vanished. But the result can also be neat, clever and effective. Plot and sense are to the fore.

Samuel French's Acting Editions

It is my last example which most fascinates me. George Skillan (1893–1975) had a significant acting career at the Shakespeare Memorial Theatre in the 1920s and 1940s, playing roles such as Theseus, Henry V, Coriolanus, Othello, Orsino and Claudius for directors such as Ben Iden Payne, Bridges-Adams and Robert Atkins, as well as a film and television career that stretched from Antonio in a silent *Merchant of Venice* in 1916 to a role in the UK television soap *Crossroads* in 1964. In 1964, potent date, he also published his edition of *Hamlet* for Samuel French, the latest in a long line of editions he had created for them that had begun in the 1930s with five plays (*Henry IV, Part 1, The Merchant of Venice, Othello, Julius Caesar* and *Henry V*) and had covered eight further plays in the following decades, with two more (*Antony and Cleopatra* and *King Lear*) yet to come after *Hamlet*. For *Hamlet* there are sixty double-column pages of commentary, scene-by-scene, with a brief glossary too. It is an extraordinarily detailed analysis of dramatic pace and rhythm, of emotion and thought, of effect and character, of power and plotting, but not meaning and not really interpretation, since it assumes from the start a right way of performing the play, never a range of possibilities. In many ways it anticipates what Michael Pennington has offered in *Hamlet: A User's Guide* (1964).

French's Acting Editions are always a strange phenomenon and this one is no exception. There are plots for props, furniture and lighting and a plan for scenery that, with its backcloth of a castle (sketched at the start of the first scene), its proscenium arch, false proscenium, and act drop, seems to come from another age – as indeed it does, for Skillan's sense of how to stage *Hamlet* comes from his experiences in the 1920s, not the 1960s. Every move is precisely defined – 'The KING, who has leant forward, leans back in his seat' (75) – with sketches to show the blocking and movement. Everything is minutely prescribed, a theatre of the mind that can be translated confidently to any amateur performance in the world without the slightest need to investigate anything in rehearsal other than replication of the instructions, more IKEA self-assembly than do-it-yourself, or, to take the most complete example of such restagings now, the way in which every production of a Lloyd Webber musical anywhere in the world is exactly the same, Shakespeare now as global product of a multinational corporation, Samuel French, rather than Shakespeare, Inc.

Yet what is most remarkable about this edition, still in print, is the nature of the text, for, like the 1676 quarto, this both is and is not *Hamlet*:

> The excisions in the text of this edition of Hamlet have been made after careful reference to many authorities. They closely follow the version prepared by Sir Johnston Forbes-Robertson for his revival at the Lyceum Theatre. ([iii])

We speak readily of theatre as an ephemeral art but the publication of performance editions can confer a surprising longevity. Forbes-Robertson's production opened in 1897 and Samuel French continue to make available for performance now a version of *Hamlet* that is well over a century old, locked into the conventions of George Skillan's early professional career and sedulously refusing all traces of contemporary production. Publication as a potential for re-creation becomes rehearsal as a process of replication. Instead of 'as it hath beene diverse times acted', as in the first quarto of *Hamlet*, or 'as it is acted', as in the 1676 quarto, or, in effect, as it has just been acted, as in the Donmar text, this is the permanent prescriptive version, as it was in 1897, is in 1964 and evermore shall be. Perilously close to creating a theatre text that is anti-theatrical in its denial of immediacy, Skillan's and Samuel French's version of performance is like a bizarre transformation of Ben Jonson's words, making theatre, rather than Shakespeare, *both* of an age *and* for all time.

CHAPTER 15

Editing Shakespeare by pictures: illustrated editions
Keir Elam

First cuts

Until recently the illustrated editions of Shakespeare's plays have not received a great deal of critical attention, being generally considered unscholarly epiphenomena of editorial history, while the illustrations themselves have been largely ignored as superfluous extra-textual decorations. 'Serious' editions of Shakespeare are the ones not with pictures but with copious scholarly notes. Illustrated editions are often without notes and were long relegated to the lower echelons of the Shakespearian publishing trade, those associated with the popularizing, or at best the pedagogy, of the plays. The work of scholars such as Edward Hodnett, Claudia Corti, Jonathan Bate, Stephen Orgel and, especially, Stuart Sillars, has done much to restore dignity to pictorial editions as potentially valid contributions to the history of the published drama. In the light of such work, but also in the endeavour to extend its scope, I aim in this chapter to consider the ways in which illustrations – with particular reference to *The Tempest* – can be regarded as an integral part of the textual and paratextual apparatus of a Shakespeare edition alongside, or sometimes in place of, scholarly notes and critical commentary. I will argue that it is possible and legitimate, as the history of the plays in print goes to show, to edit Shakespeare by pictures.

The publisher of Rowe's pioneering 1709 *Works of Mr. William Shakespear*, Jacob Tonson, can be considered the father of the critical edition of Shakespeare, since he and his sons were responsible for publishing most of the major editions of the plays between 1709 and 1768, from Rowe to Theobald to Pope to Johnson to Capell. At the same time, and more specifically, he was the founder of the illustrated edition (having already published, among other engraved classics, the first illustrated *Paradise Lost* in 1688). In the beginning was the image: 'modern' editions of Shakespeare begin with pictures. Tonson, and presumably Rowe, considered the full-page engraved frontispiece an appropriate mode of presentation of the plays in their ambitious and unprecedented publishing enterprise. Tonson commissioned the drawings from François Boitard – nearly all the early illustrators of Shakespeare were French – and the line engravings from the Englishman Elisha Kirkall. This was doubtless in part a commercial move, designed to attract discerning subscribers to what were quite expensive quarto volumes. It was also favoured by Tonson's choice of typographical style. The engraving is, as it were, a function of the uncluttered text, the full-page picture corresponding to and mirroring the full page of play text. Rowe's edition is innocent of accompanying notes, so much so that Samuel Johnson praises the simplicity of Rowe's 1709 *Works*, which is 'without the pomp of notes or boasts of criticism' (Johnson 1790: 3.88): a somewhat ironical and perhaps backhanded compliment coming from Johnson, father of the scholarly editorial note.

In Rowe the copperplate engraving, while not of high artistic quality, plays a number of 'editorial' and paratextual roles. Immediately preceding the play, it introduces it to the reader, in lieu of other modes of introduction. The choice of a pictorial presentation of the play has important cultural implications. First, it establishes the visual as the primary domain of expression of the play script that follows, and is in this sense a semiotic genre marker, advising the reader that the dramatic text can be read not only as a linguistic artefact but also and above all as the verbal blueprint for action designed to register on the ocular plane. The legitimacy, not to say appropriateness, of this iconographic mode of introduction has not been generally recognized. Indeed, even scholars sympathetic to illustrated Shakespeare have found the picture of a play to be a somewhat self-contradictory if not perverse phenomenon. 'An illustration of a dramatic text is a peculiar thing', affirms Bate, 'It makes meaning by freezing a single moment, whereas the unstoppable motion of time ... is the very essence of drama' (2000: 33), while Sillars begins his exhaustive study of the illustrations with the consideration that pictures of plays are 'innately paradoxical', and that 'The very process of authenticating a performative entity in a finite material form is a logical contradiction' (2008: 1). One might argue the opposite case: the pictorial representation of a play is altogether congruous to a mode of performativity that unfolds in space as well as time. The spectator perceives the theatrical performance not as a staged text but as a complex continuum of images and sounds. If anything, it is the reduction of the intermodal complexity of performance to a purely verbal text – and especially to a purely verbal textual or editorial apparatus – that runs the risk of contradiction, phenomenal rather than logical.

The illustrations in Rowe, as in many later illustrated editions, do not 'freeze' a given performative moment, moreover, since they do not endeavour to represent one. The Boitard–Kirkall frontispiece to *The Tempest* in Rowe's 1709 *Works* (the first illustration of a Shakespeare play to appear in print), while it may partly recall the 1674 staging of Shadwell's operatic version of Dryden and Davenant's adaptation, which had 'Several Spirits in horrid shapes flying down amongst the Sailers' (Dryden and Davenant 1676: B1^r; see Merchant 1959: 49), does not aim to portray it or any specific performance. What many of the engravings do attempt to underline, instead, is the sheer theatricality of the represented scene. Other illustrations abound, for example, in stagey draperies, or heavy shadows projected by bodies in action, or – as in the case of the frontispiece to *Cymbeline* – characters blatantly meeting the eye of the spectator while going about their dramatic business. One engraving, the illustration to *Troilus and Cressida*, portrays a stage – but again not an actual staging – in part, perhaps, in order to underline the histrionic artificiality of much of the play's action. The object of representation here and elsewhere is not a given stage performance but theatrical performativity at large, reminding the reader of the text's primary allegiance, namely to the actor on stage, a primacy that later critical editions often tend to forget.

In keeping with this performative emphasis, Boitard and Kirkall's engravings endeavour to depict action, movement and gesture rather than characters statically posing. There is a certain family resemblance among several of the illustrations – due in part to Kirkall's limitations in the intaglio design of the human form as well as his heavy mix of engraving and etching (see Hodnett 1982: 47–8) – involving dark domestic interiors (prisons cells or gloomy rooms) in which more or less violent action takes place. The standard scene illustrated is, as it were, a great reckoning in a little room. These dark deeds may adumbrate, in all senses, an overall Shakespearean poetics consisting in primarily cruel and spectacular indoor action fitting to domestic tragedy, and possibly reflecting the taste for interior stage sets in contemporary productions (not to mention Rowe's own plays such as the pseudo-Shakespearean domestic tragedy *Jane Shore*). The illustrations also betray a neoclassical aesthetics, not only in the choice of classical architectural backgrounds for the Roman plays and for *Pericles* and *Locrine*, but also in the recurrent emphasis on action and setting rather than on single character.

The mixed costumes — a triangular meeting of classical, Elizabethan and modern, with an abundance of early eighteenth-century garb and wigs — may likewise reflect contemporary theatrical practice but at the same time act as an ideal graphic bridge between the world of the reader and the world of the play. The movement from frontispiece to text guides us from the pictorial to the lectorial, leading readers from a relatively habitual perceptual experience, looking at pictures, to the probably less familiar effort of deciphering a dramatic text.

The illustrations, here as in later editions, also fulfil a powerfully hermeneutic function, singling out a key scene by way of an interpretative frame for the reading of the text as a whole. The choice of scene orients the reader's reception of the play by emphasizing, for example, comic or tragic mode of action, as in the case of *Henry IV, Part 2* where the selected scene is not state politics but comic business between Falstaff and Doll Tearsheet, a choice that doubtless reflects the popularity of the fat knight, but also strongly tilts the play towards comedy. The choice may instead be thematic or interpretative: the opening storm in *The Tempest* (Figure 15.1) is taken as governing dramatic trope for the whole conflict-ridden play, from the title on; the scene of Iacomo's spying on Imogen in her chamber (*Cymbeline*), analogously, underlines the central role of deception and subterfuge in the play. Such illustrations are in some ways synecdoches for the overall action, and at the same time suggest a particular interpretative take on it.

In Boitard–Kirkall's frontispiece to Rowe's *Tempest* (another dark and violent scene, albeit outdoors), the first thing that strikes the eye is the vertical economy of the pictorial space, inviting us to read from below — the effects of the storm — to above, its causes, in a movement from the natural and human domain to the supernatural. The realism of the lower foreground, in which the sailors, as in the incipit of the play, go frantically about their task of crisis management while the waves assault the vessel, is in stark contrast with the events and style of the upper celestial regions with their somewhat caricatural diabolical creatures bringing about the storm (inspired by Medina's devils for *Paradise Lost* (Sillars 2008: 59)), and the stylized zig-zag of the lightning, which have a proto-cartoon quality and indeed anticipate recent cartoon versions of the play (see below, p. 268). Still on the vertical axis can be discerned Ferdinand vacating the vessel ('the first man that leaped', 1.2.214). On the perspective axis, on a diminutive rock in the distance beyond the ship, is the almost hidden *dominus* of the events, Prospero, seen actively wielding his wand, a point of conjunction between the human and the supernatural spheres. Miranda is not present;

Illustrated editions

Figure 15.1 Frontispiece to *The Tempest*, drawing by François Boitard, copperplate engraving by Elisha Kirkall (Nicholas Rowe, 'Some Account of the Life of Mr. William Shakespear', *The Works of Mr. William Shakespear*, 1709)

there is, however, a hint that the lightning above Prospero may be describing a calligraphic sign, the letter M, standing perhaps for his Magic, perhaps for Miranda.

The success of the Tonson–Rowe enterprise was such that the 1714 second edition was printed in an agile duodecimo format, as opposed to the original quarto, and grew to eight volumes, adding new illustrations and revisions of the Boitard–Kirkall frontispieces by another French designer and line engraver, Louis du Guernier. This makes it the first relatively cheap edition of the plays, a kind of paperback Shakespeare ante litteram, that sets up an association between illustration and accessibility (economic and cultural) destined to endure over time. The second edition replaces the original *Tempest* frontispiece with du Guernier's far less spectacular and altogether more reassuring copperplate tableau in the sentimental mode, which shows Prospero pointing out to his interlocutors (Gonzalo, Antonio and company) Miranda and Ferdinand as they play chess in the background (Shakespeare 1714: 5.1), a scene that suggests placid domesticity rather than violent natural and supernatural power. The choice of the final scene reverses the frontispiece's hermeneutic relationship with the play, projecting the reader ahead towards the conclusion rather than inviting her or him into the incipit, thus placing the emphasis on resolution and harmony rather than on danger and confusion. The du Guernier engraving also modifies the paratextual function of the illustration in relation to the text itself: while in Rowe's 1709 *Works* the frontispiece depicts an overall scene (1.1., with a proleptic glance towards 1.2), the 1714 version enters into a more direct relationship with the texture of the play, portraying a specific and identifiable moment in the action, namely the stage direction 'Here Prospero *discovers* Ferdinand and Miranda playing at Chess', deriving from the First Folio (TLN 2141). The illustration translates the stage direction in the guise of Prospero's pointing gesture, as he speaks to Alonso (the text does not attribute lines to him at this point), while Miranda and Ferdinand converse ('MIRANDA Sweet lord, you play me false', 5.1.172). It is in this sense a speaking picture, representing a double conversation in progress, and as such proposes a direct engagement with the play's dialogue as well as its action.

Illustration: from the iconographic to the verbal

The two successive editions of Shakespeare's plays published by Tonson, edited respectively by Alexander Pope (1725) and Lewis Theobald (1733), have no illustrations. In 1740, however, Tonson commissioned a highly successful illustrated edition of Theobald's Shakespeare, again in eight relatively inexpensive duodecimo volumes, with designs by yet another French artist, Hubert Gravelot, engraved by Gerard van der Gucht. The chosen iconographic mode is still the introductory frontispiece. Gravelot's thirty-five line engravings display a distinctly French rococo elegance and gentility, evoking a light and airy world of civilized intercourse rather than the dark and cruel spaces of Boitard–Kirkall. They also have none of the theatricality of the plates in Rowe's 1709 *Works*: Shakespeare has become 'a book to be embellished' (Orgel 2007: 72). Individual characters are foregrounded and enlarged, and tend to dominate their settings, suggesting a more subjective and intimate reading of the plays, with an emphasis on character rather than action. The scene chosen as frontispiece to *The Tempest* is no longer the storm but the more sentimental episode at the beginning of Act 3, depicting Ferdinand with his logs assisted by the doting Miranda, with Prospero looking shadily on ('PROSPERO, *[following at a distance]*'). It is again a readily identifiable and relatively static 'conversational' moment, as Miranda implores Ferdinand ('Alas, now pray you / Work not so hard', 3.1.16–17). All three figures are seen standing, the only movement involved being the micro-gesture of Miranda's left arm indicating the log.

Equally genteel are the thirty-six frontispieces to the first edition of Shakespeare to be published out of London, and not by Tonson, namely Sir Thomas Hanmer's elegantly bound six-volume edition which appeared in 1744 at Oxford ('Printed at the Theatre'). The title page announces that the volumes are '*adorned with sculptures*', thereby advertising the ornamental and statuesque immobility of the illustrations, drawn mainly by Francis Hayman and engraved – in a change of roles not unusual at the time – by Hubert Gravelot, who also drew the designs for his own copperplate engravings in volume 4. In Hanmer the relationship between engraving and text changes again. As his correspondence with Hayman shows (Allentuck 1976), Hanmer exercised strict editorial control over the contents and even the style of the illustrations. For the frontispiece to *The Tempest*, supposedly representing '1.6' (i.e. 1.2: Figure 15.2), he instructed the artist to provide a spatial and temporal synthesis of the play showing the main characters in various standing poses: 'Prospero and Miranda are to stand as in conference together'; Prospero sporting 'a cap lined with Ermyn' and 'pointing towards [Ferdinand] with his wand', as Miranda, dressed 'after the Italian or Spanish manner', looks on in wonder, while '[t]he Grotesque figure of Caliban' simultaneously bears his burden of

Figure 15.2 Frontispiece to *The Tempest*, designed by Francis Hayman, engraved by Hubert Gravelot (*The Works of Shakespear*, ed. Thomas Hanmer and Francis Hayman, 1744)

wood (294–5). All of this is to be set in '[a] Landskip the most pleasing that can be design'd' (294): Hayman responds with a dominant picturesque setting, marked by delicate landscape-garden contours, complete with grotto-like cave, making the island look reassuringly English and in any case well under Prospero's horticultural control.

The differences in style and content among the engravings certainly reflect changes in taste as well as in the target audience over a thirty-year time span. They also suggest an evolution in the role of the illustration, which becomes at once more decorative and more closely linked to the discursive and gestural texture of the drama. Hanmer's, however, is the last significant illustrated edition for several decades, as engraved plays evidently went out of fashion. What is arguably the decisive change in the editing of Shakespeare takes place with Samuel Johnson's celebrated eight-volume edition, published again by Tonson in 1765, the first to provide abundant notes. The title page advertises this novelty in the phrase 'with the corrections and illustrations of various commentators, to which are added notes by Sam Johnson'. It is significant that the term 'illustration' here has not iconographic but critical or meta-critical connotations (in the etymological sense of 'illumination' or 'elucidation': *Oxford English Dictionary* (n., 3a)): the plays are 'illustrated' or elucidated not by engravers but by the comments of editors and scholars. This semantic and representational shift marks a strategic move towards a non-pictorial critical edition, a move that is given immediate graphic expression on the first page of the text, in which four lines of dialogue are 'illustrated' by half a page of notes. In his Preface, Johnson famously expresses his ambivalence towards such verbal illustrations: 'Notes are often necessary, but they are necessary evils. . . . Notes clear particular passages, but the general effect of the work is weakened. The mind is refrigerated by interruption; the thoughts are diverted from the principal subject' (1765: lxix–lxx). Nonetheless, and influentially, he includes large numbers of them, and no pictures. This new conception of the 'illustrated' critical edition is consolidated in George Steevens's ten-volume 1773 edition, which adds further notes: the opening page of *The Tempest*, preceded by 346 pages of prefaces and commentary, has half a page of notes illustrating only two lines of text.

Historically, therefore, the illustration precedes the editorial note, and is in many ways its forerunner, especially within the series of the Tonson editions. The engraving is replaced by 'illustrative' commentary, or in a sense is transformed into it within Tonson's in-house style: a semiotic and typographic metamorphosis of the iconic into the verbal. That the illustration has a significant and indeed inaugural role in the history of the editing of Shakespeare is demonstrated precisely in the moment of its (temporary) exit from the editorial scene.

Variations on the pictorial

When the pictorial illustration reappears in Shakespeare editions late in the eighteenth century, it is in an altogether new guise. John Bell's 'acting' edition based on theatrical prompt-books, published in nine volumes between 1773 and 1778, was the first to include illustrations of actual performances on the contemporary London stage ('*as they are now performed at the Theatres Royal in London*'), and was followed by an illustrated 'literary' edition in twenty volumes, 1785–88. Bell's editions mark another radical change in paradigm, replacing imaginary scenes with theatrical portraiture, which to a large extent his edition inaugurates as a popular iconographic genre. Bell's 1785 *Tempest* has, inter alia, a frontispiece designed by J. H. Ramberg and engraved by C. Sherwin and C. Grignion, showing the actress and soprano Anna Maria Phillips (later Crouch) as Miranda in the 1781 Drury Lane production, discovered uttering the lines 'O the cry did knock/ Against my very heart', 1.2.8–9 (Burnim and Highfill 1998: 47–8). Phillips's Miranda, in fashionable sashed silk gown and long veil, a wind-driven ribbon in her hair, is perched precariously on a narrow cliff ledge gesticulating towards the angry waves: presumably a 'literary' re-elaboration of her stage performance. Bell's use of portraiture has an immediate fallout in the 'domesticating' of the bard through the reproduction of Shakespearean characters and actors on household objects – the engraving of 'Miss Phillips in [*sic*] Miranda', for example, is reproduced on a porcelain mug from the same period on display at the British Museum – and in the longer term it influenced later editors, including those of recent scholarly editions that often include photographs of actors in performance.

In the same period another hugely ambitious, if ill-fated, iconographic Shakespeare project got under way. In 1786, the engraver and publisher John Boydell launched his Shakespeare Gallery, commissioning paintings of the plays from many of the leading British and European artists of the day. Following the publication of a catalogue of pictures from the Gallery in 1789, Boydell went on to commission new plates for an illustrated nine-volume edition, overseen by George Steevens, which appeared in 1803. The engraved illustrations inevitably lack the full-colour splendour of the Gallery exhibits, but nonetheless involve important artists (including Joshua Reynolds, Henry Fuseli, William Hamilton and Robert Smirke) in an aesthetically ambitious pictorial programme. *The Tempest* has two plates from paintings in neoclassical mode by the Royal Academician Hamilton. The plate to 1.2, engraved on copper by James Parker, shows an erect Prospero peremptorily sending off a highly feminine and lyre-bearing Ariel in classical gown, as Miranda sleeps the while. The illustration to 3.1, engraved by Anker Smith, has Miranda, again in flowing classical dress and wind-blown veil, imploring a muscular Ferdinand in mock Elizabethan garb as he dallies with his log. Robert Smirke's more dynamic and somewhat caricatural design for 2.2, engraved by W. C. Wilson, shows the mask-like face of Stephano – with a hint of the Commedia dell'arte (appropriately for a Neapolitan character) – turning away aghast at his encounter with Caliban, whose even more grotesquely masked features peer up from under the tarpaulin. Smirke's powerful theatrical grouping, set against a picturesque maritime backdrop, has the rare virtue of directing the reader's apprehension towards the sheer corporeal energy of the comic subplot, often overlooked in other pictorial (and non-pictorial) editions.

What is in many ways the most innovative and wide-reaching transformation of the editorial role of pictures, however, takes place some four decades later, as part of the phenomenon of early Victorian mass literature. The transformation was made possible by technical innovations, notably the introduction of the stereotype plate and of the end-block wood engraving – in place of eighteenth-century copperplate engraving – which among other things facilitated rapid mass production and allowed the woodblock image to be integrated into the typeset page at low cost. The first popular edition of the plays, Charles Knight's *Pictorial Shakespeare*, which was issued in fifty-five parts between 1838 and 1843 and then collected in eight octavo volumes, was the product of both stereotyping and wood engraving. Knight commissioned close to a thousand illustrations by various artists and engravers. *Pictorial Shakespeare* is an unlikely candidate for ground-breaking novelty, since it appears to be above all an episode in the early Victorian domestication and moralization of the Bard. Knight's project was to provide an economically and culturally accessible edition in which pictures play a directly and declaredly editorial role. In his autobiographical essay *Passages of a Working Life During Half a Century* (1864), Knight explains and motivates his strategic use of illustration: 'it became necessary for me to look carefully at the plays, to see whether the aid of art might not be called in to add both to the information and enjoyment of the reader of Shakspere, by representing the Realities upon which the imagination of the poet must have rested' (1864: 284). 'Realities' here has a double meaning: on the one hand, the historiographical data on which the dramatist drew; on the other, the *realia* of material culture, the everyday objects and customs that fired his 'imagination'. It is especially the latter that constitute a barrier to the ready understanding of the plays and their language unless adequately illustrated. In his preface to the revised edition, Knight polemically contrasts his 'editorial' use of pictures to the standard practice of scholarly verbal commentary: 'Shakespere demands a rational edition of his wonderful performances, that should address itself to the popular understanding in a spirit of enthusiastic love, and not of captious and presumptuous cavilling; – with a sincere zeal for the illustration of the text, rather than a desire to parade the stores of useless learning' (Shakespeare 1867: 1.v). Knight explicitly offers his pictures as an accessible and 'popular' alternative to pedantic annotation, thereby reversing the Johnsonian gesture of de-visualizing the 'illustration'. His editorial policy takes on highly political implications as a means of bringing Shakespeare's dramatic 'performances' out of the study and into the Victorian home, and, as Sillars observes, of promoting 'Knight's concern with Christian education, coupled with self-advancement' (2008: 254).

In keeping with this policy, Knight deploys a twofold typology of illustrations, some of them narrative, others explicative. Knight's *Tempest* opens with three undistinguished wood engravings making up a sort of maritime narrative sequence: the opening shipwreck dominating the title page; the agitated waters of 'the still vexed Bermoothes' where Ariel hides the ship after the storm, inserted into the Introductory notice; and a kind of pictorial prequel on the first page of text, the visual picture of a verbal picture, namely Prospero's vivid ekphrastic evocation of the castaway episode in his narration to Miranda in 1.2: 'A rotten carcass of a butt, not rigged, / Nor tackle, sail, nor mast ... [T]here they hoist us / To cry to th' sea, that roared to us; to sigh / To th' winds, whose pity sighing back again / Did us but loving wrong' (1.2.146–51). The sequence draws attention to the interplay of natural, supernatural and political power in the drama through the crucial agency of the sea. The three wood engravings, recalling traditional English popular woodcuts, have little of the artistic refinement of earlier copperplate engravings à la Gravelot, not to mention Boydell's pictorial plates. What are particularly interesting and original in Knight's edition, however, are not so much the often rough-hewn narrative cuts as his visual explicative notes, or what we might term iconic glosses. Knight exploits the new technical possibility of integrating the engraving in the typeset text by inventing the hybrid note, a verbal-visual text-image[1] by way of semantic explication, in which alongside verbal footnotes the reader finds explanatory and interpretative illustrations, or, as it were, foot-pictures. For example, Prospero's threat to Ferdinand in 1.2, 'I'll manacle thy neck and feet together', is given a note that reads 'we subjoin an engraving which explains this threat better than any description' (see Figure 15.3).

This is among other things a kind of manifesto for Knight's iconic editorial policy (pictures explain more immediately than words). More intriguingly, Trinculo's cryptic allusion in 3.2 to 'the picture of Nobody' (3.2.120) is glossed precisely with the citation of an early modern picture from the comedy *No-body and Some-body* (1606), historicizing as well as visualizing the reference (see Figure 15.4).

These notes set up an internal paratextual dialogue between image and verbal gloss that re-enacts – or such appears to be Knight's intention – the dialectic beween the discursive and the visual in the play itself. Knight has been accused of historical literalism. It is true, as Jonathan Bate observes (2000: 46), that he expresses and in turn influences the unrelenting search for historical accuracy in realistic early Victorian productions. It is equally true, however, that his iconic glosses provide the reader with an immediate sense of early modern material culture, rendering accessible what would otherwise be lost in the sea-change of cultural history. Knight presents the reader with a semiotically mixed language that induces a particular sensibility to the visual. Underlying this enterprise is a conviction that drama itself is the expression of a kind of visual thinking and writing that cannot be adequately commented through words alone. Ironically, Knight's example has been followed in the very annotated scholarly editions to which he opposed his own endeavours, in which the use of early modern iconographic material is now fairly common.[2] He was the first editor, for example, to adopt (as in his introduction to *Othello*) engravings from Cesare Vecellio's *Degli habiti antichi e moderni* (1590) in order to illustrate early modern costume, a procedure that has become standard practice in recent annotated editions of the plays.

Another popular Victorian illustrated Shakespeare, edited by Howard Staunton and originally published by Routledge in monthly parts between 1857 and 1860, boasts 831 illustrations drawn by the woodblock designer

---

[1] This term varies W. J. T. Mitchell's 'image-text' (1994: 9).
[2] In my Arden 3 edition of *Twelfth Night*, I include Knight's iconic elucidations of some of the comedy's allusions to obscure items of early seventeenth-century material culture, such as the buttery-bar, the great bed of Ware, the parish top and sheriff's posts.

ILLUSTRATIONS OF ACT I.

¹ SCENE I.—"*Boatswain*," &c.

Upon this scene Dr. Johnson has the following remark:—" In this naval dialogue, perhaps the first example of sailors' language exhibited on the stage, there are, as I have been told by a skilful navigator, some inaccuracies and contradictory orders." Malone, in reply to this, very properly pointed out that the orders should be considered as given not at once, but successively, as the emergency required. In Boswell's edition we have a highly valuable communication from the second Lord Mulgrave, showing most conclusively that Shakspere's technical knowledge of seamanship must have been the result of the most accurate personal observation, or, what is perhaps more difficult, of the power of combining and applying the information derived from others. Lord Mulgrave supposes Shakspere must have acquired this technical knowledge "by conversation with some of the most skilful seamen of that time." He adds, "no books had then been published on the subject." Lord Mulgrave then exhibits the ship in five positions, showing how strictly the words of the dialogue represent these. We transcribe the general observations by which these technical illustrations are introduced:—

"The succession of events is strictly observed in the natural progress of the distress described; the expedients adopted are the most proper that could have been devised for a chance of safety; and it is neither to the want of skill of the seamen nor the bad qualities of the ship, but solely to the power of Prospero, that the shipwreck is to be attributed.

"The words of command are not only strictly proper, but are only such as point the object to be attained, and no superfluous ones of detail. Shakspeare's ship was too well manned to make it necessary to tell the seamen how they were to do it, as well as what they were to do.

"He has shown a knowledge of the new improvements, as well as the doubtful points of seamanship: one of the latter he has introduced under the only circumstances in which it was indisputable."

Mr. Campbell gives the testimony of Captain Glascock, R.N., to the correctness of Shakspere in nautical matters:—"The Boatswain in The Tempest delivers himself in the true vernacular style of the forecastle."

² SCENE I.—"*Down with the topmast.*"

Lord Mulgrave has the following note on this direction:—" The striking the topmasts was a new invention in Shakspeare's time, which he here very properly introduces. Sir Henry Manwaring says, 'It is not yet agreed amongst all seamen whether it is better for a ship to hull with her topmast up or down.' In the Postscript to the Dictionary he afterwards gives his own opinion:—' If you have sea-room it is never good to strike the topmast.' Shakspeare has placed his ship in the situation in which it was indisputably right to strike the topmast—where he had not sea-room."

³ SCENE II.—"*I'll manacle thy neck and feet together.*"

We subjoin an engraving which explains this threat better than any description.

417

Figure 15.3 Note to Charles Knight's *Pictorial Shakespeare*

ILLUSTRATIONS OF ACT III.

¹ Scene II.—" *The picture of Nobody.*"

Nobody was a gentleman who figured on ancient signs; and, in the anonymous comedy of 'Nobody and Somebody,' printed before 1600, he is represented as above.

² Scene III.— " *Here's a maze trod, indeed, Through forth-rights and meanders!*"

Mr. Hunter says that *forth-rights* here evidently means no more than *straight lines*. The passage is explained by the fact of the allusion being to an artificial maze, sometimes constructed of straight lines (forth-rights), sometimes of circles (meanders). The engraving exhibits a maze of forth-rights.

Figure 15.4 Note to *The Tempest* 3.2 from Charles Knight's *Pictorial Shakespeare* (1838–43)

John Gilbert and engraved by the Dalziel brothers. Staunton and Gilbert introduce another innovative pictorial paradigm, departing from earlier models – both the engraved frontispiece and the illustrated note – by incorporating the pictures directly into the text, thanks again to the co-presence of woodblock and moveable type. Figures interrupt and punctuate the dialogue, offering visual representations of the scene in progress. The illustrations in Staunton have a mainly narrative role, making the action immediately and continuously perceptible to the reader/beholder, thanks partly to '[Gilbert's] control of bodies as expressive, interacting elements in the whole concept' (Hodnett 1982: 77). They are a compromise between imaginary 'performance' (showing props, plausible costume, movement) and pictorial paraphrase, similar to Victorian illustrations of novels: see Figure 15.5, showing Caliban in 2.2, before and after his meeting with Trinculo ('Lo, now lo! / Here comes a spirit of his, and to torment me / For bringing wood in slowly. I'll fall flat', 2.2.14–16).

The sheer number of Gilbert's designs (twenty-six for *The Tempest* alone) and the amount of space they occupy on the page – often more or less equivalent to the notes in Johnson and Steevens, leaving room for only a few lines of text (Staunton also has some relatively brief footnotes and final 'illustrative comments') – make this Shakespeare by far the most densely iconographic of all editions. The pictures are so central to the reading experience as to anticipate, in some respects, the text-images of the graphic novels that would flourish a century later. Staunton invents, as it were, the graphic play.

Only slightly less intense in its graphic mode is Cassell's *Illustrated Shakespeare*, edited and annotated by Charles and Mary Cowden Clarke with designs by Henry Courtenay Selous, which appeared in parts between 1864 and 1868 and was intended as a cheap but iconographically rich family edition. Cassell's *Tempest* has a sequence of twelve narrative wood engravings, some of them full-page, some half-page above the text, which is further illustrated by the Cowden Clarkes' footnotes. The somewhat crowded pages that result from the co-habitation of the pictorial with the textual and the annotational bestow an extraordinary informational density on the edition. On the hermeneutic plane, while the title page of each volume cites Charles Cowden Clarke's *Shakespeare-characters; Chiefly those Subordinate* (1863) – which in its chapter on *The Tempest* (193–212) devotes far more attention to Ariel–Caliban and Miranda–Ferdinand than to Prospero – Selous's iconographic reading, on the contrary, decrees that it is very much the play of the paternalistic magus Prospero. The latter first

Illustrated editions 265

Their pricks at my footfall; sometime am I
All wound^a with adders, who, with cloven tongues,
Do hiss me into madness.—Lo, now! lo!

Here comes a spirit of his; and to torment me,
For bringing wood in slowly: I'll fall flat;
Perchance, he will not mind me.

Enter Trinculo.

Trin. Here's neither bush nor shrub, to bear
off any weather at all, and another storm brewing;

I hear it sing i' the wind: yond same black cloud,
yond huge one, looks like a foul bombard that

^a All wound with—] *All encircled by.*

Figure 15.5 Illustration to *The Tempest*, 2.2, designed by John Gilbert and engraved by the Dalziel brothers, from *Plays*, ed. Howard Staunton (1858–62)

appears on the title page in reclining pose commanding the storm, wand in his right hand and books under his left, while his Victorian sage-like beard is uplifted by the very wind he creates, as if to announce his absolute control of all that follows. A full-page engraving then shows him comforting Miranda in 1.2 ('No harm'), still clutching his wand the while; later in the same scene we find him berating Caliban ('What ho! Slave! Caliban!'), towards whom he gesticulates with his left hand as Miranda turns coyly away; in 3.3 he uses his inseparable wand to conjure up spirits for the benefit of Miranda and Ferdinand; he employs it again in 4.1 to set dogs, snakes and other fauna onto the plotting Caliban and his cohorts ('Fury! Fury!'). In the final half-page illustration to 5.1, the newly re-crowned Duke, embracing his magic wand with his left arm, uses his right to point out Caliban to the assembled company ('He is as disproportioned ... '). Selous's somewhat dictatorial colonial potentate goes out still in graphic command: no renunciation of magic for him, whatever the text may say.

Rowe goes manga: comic-book *Tempest*s

If the graphic Shakespeare play enjoyed a brief and precocious Victorian career with Staunton and Cassell, it has been fully realized only in the last two decades. The contemporary heirs to the pictorial editorial tradition are the various and numerous forms of graphic comic-book Shakespeare, which can be legitimately considered a mode of illustrated edition, albeit of often adapted or simplified texts. The official target audience of comic-book Shakespeare is made up of children and adolescents, but the actual readership of such books is probably far broader. Recent and commercially successful comic-book *Tempest*s include Saddleback's Illustrated Classics version (2006c), Comic Book Shakespeare's Cartoon Illustrated edition, edited and illustrated by Simon Greaves (2006d) and Classical Comics' *The Tempest: The Graphic Novel* illustrated by John McDonald, Jon Haward, Gary Erskine and Nigel Dobbyn (Shakespeare 2009b).[3]

The Japanese manga comic mode has also been applied to Shakespeare, both in Japan and in the West, for example by the British publisher SelfMadeHero, which in 2007 issued fourteen single-play manga editions based on abridged versions of the original texts in new settings, mainly

---

[3] On comic-book Shakespeare, see Jensen 2011.

Illustrated editions 267

Figure 15.6 The Cartoon illustrated *Tempest*, 1.1, designed by Simon Greaves (2006d)

Japan in the past and future.[4] The SelfMadeHero manga *Tempest*, illustrated by Paul Duffield, is 'set in the future after a global energy crisis has plunged mankind into a second dark age' (Hayley 2010: 275). Duffield's opening image shows the wand-wielding Prospero, 'wizard and real Duke of Milan', dominating stylized waves perfect for surfing, in what may be a visual echo of Rowe.

Likewise, in the recent *Cartoon Illustrated* edition of *The Tempest*, the two-colour graphic text-image of the opening page recalls, or indeed quotes, Boitard's frontispiece for Rowe, taking up and emphasizing both the violent waves battering the ship and the stylized ziz-zag of the lightning (Figure 15.6). By implicitly citing Rowe–Boitard, the editor-illustrator Greaves seems to be making a claim for his own comic book edition, locating it within an ancient – indeed the most ancient – tradition of Shakespeare editorship. At the same time, our own growing familiarity with graphic plays, graphic novels and similar intermedial forms may make us more receptive to once suspect pictorial editions, from Rowe on. Be that as it may, the comic-book/Rowe connection brings the history of illustrated Shakespeare full circle; this history suggests that although a picture may not be worth a thousand words, it is surely unjust to decree that a thousand words, especially Shakespeare's words, do not deserve a single picture.

---

[4] On manga Shakespeare see Hayley 2010, Minami 2010 and Pellis 2013.

CHAPTER 16

Format and readerships

Andrew Murphy

It is difficult to say what the smallest text of Shakespeare – in terms of physical dimensions – has been. One possible candidate is the 'Ellen Terry' edition, compiled by J. Talfourd Blair, and issued originally by David Bryce and Son in Glasgow in 1904. The individual volumes are in sexagesimoquarto format – 64° for short – and they measure approximately 50 mm by 35 mm (see Figure 16.1). Bryce was a specialist in miniature book publishing: his other titles included diminutive editions of the Bible, the *Bhagavad Ghita* and the *Koran* (Bondy 1981: 103–16). His Shakespeare appears to have been a reformatted version of an earlier edition, which he had published in the first instance in 1886, in eight volumes, boxed. While larger than the Ellen Terry, this too was a small-sized edition, 24°, measuring 90 mm by 60 mm.

What was the purpose of such miniature editions and what use were they put to? The volumes were clearly very popular: the Ellen Terry was issued in several different bindings and the series crossed the Atlantic, with Frederick A. Stokes of New York being added to the imprint of the volumes in the USA. Undoubtedly, they would have been viewed by many as novelty items and there is certainly evidence that some of them were given to children effectively as toys (one presumes in the hope that they might also have been read): one British auction house has offered for sale in recent times a 'Good Child's Cabinet' – a miniature book case complete with fifteen 'toy books', including a Bryce *Tempest* (Bolden Auction Galleries. n.d.). That the books were not wholly conceived as disposable ephemera is evidenced by the fact that Bryce worked in conjunction with two university presses: Oxford (through Henry Frowde) – credited on the Ellen Terry title pages as co-publisher – and Glasgow (credited as printers on the verso of the title pages). Production values for the diminutive volumes were very high and the books are comfortably readable, even without the aid of the magnifying glass that

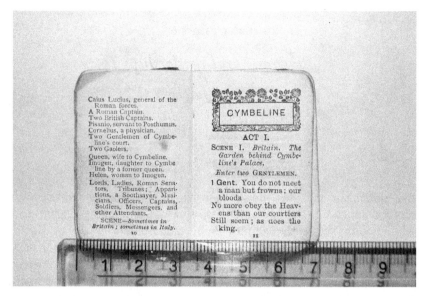

Figure 16.1 Bryce 64mo edition of *Cymbeline* (1904)

Bryce supplied as standard with some of his other publications (such as the miniature Bibles).

Being genuinely usable, the books reached serious adult readers as well as children: the library of the Dublin playwright Sean O'Casey (1880–1964), now held at the National Library of Ireland, includes a copy of volume 2 of the 1886 Bryce Shakespeare (call number LO 11953). Despite suffering from congenital eye problems, O'Casey was a voracious reader. Growing up in extreme poverty he is known to have stolen books when he could not afford to pay for them (see Murray 2004: 51). Might this have been the attraction of the Bryce volume for him? A small book would surely have been easier to purloin than a larger one after all.[1]

If O'Casey did employ a light-fingered touch in acquiring his Shakespeare he was not alone in his methods. The *Argus* newspaper for 29 June 1878 reports the case of a certain Richard Field who appeared before a Bow Street magistrate charged with a double theft: 'a pot of jam from one shop and "Dick's [*sic*] Shilling Shakspeare" from another'. Like O'Casey, Field was from humble origins. He had worked in the leather

---

[1] He also had access to a large format three-volume edition won as a college prize by his sister (see O'Casey 1942: 22).

trade, but 'took to literature' and his bibliophilic crime was, like O'Casey's thefts, driven by a desire for literary knowledge rather than for pecuniary gain. The theft of a copy of John Dicks's shilling edition is perhaps an indication of the extent of Field's poverty, since it was, at the time, the cheapest edition of Shakespeare that had ever been issued and it circulated widely among readers of restricted means, reaching sales in the region of 1 million copies (see 'The Shilling Shakspeares' 1868). Field must have been poor indeed if he could not afford simply to buy it (but, then, the humble pot of jam is perhaps a telltale sign in this regard also). Dicks published the plays individually in paper wrappers, then in a clothbound collected edition, following this with a further edition in what we would now call paperback format. It was by experimenting with different ways of packaging the text that he was able to achieve his unprecedented level of sales (on Dicks's Shakespeares, see Young 2012).

The Bryce and Dicks editions and their histories help to bring home to us the intimate relationship between formats and readerships – taking 'format' in both its narrow sense (the physical size of the book, traceable back to the way in which the large sheets of paper on which it is printed are folded to produce sets of pages) and also in its broader sense (the way in which a text is packaged and presented more generally). Though the examples considered here relate to the Victorian period, in fact, the relationship between format and readerships extends back to Shakespeare's own time. The unfortunate jam-and-book thief mentioned above by an odd coincidence bore the same name as Shakespeare's first publisher, a fellow Stratfordian, also called Richard Field. The latter Field published the first (surviving) text of Shakespeare's to appear in print: the 1593 edition of *Venus and Adonis*. He issued it in quarto (4°) size, one of the most common formats at that time (the large sheets of paper the book was printed on were folded twice to produce quartos – for a complete account of the way in which different formats were printed and assembled, see Gaskell 1995: 80–105). In the following year, Field also served as printer for the first edition of Shakespeare's *Lucrece* – again issued as a quarto. The subsequent history of these texts is noteworthy, in that they were very quickly reduced in size to the smaller octavo (8°) format.[2] This happens from the third edition of *Venus and Adonis* (probably 1595) and from the second edition with *Lucrece* (1598). In the case of *Venus and Adonis* most of the octavo reprints followed the original quartos page for page, with the result that only half the amount of paper was required in producing them

---

[2] What follows here draws in part on my 'Configuring the Book' (Murphy 2013).

(the full sheet of paper accommodated eight pages of text per side in octavo format by contrast with four pages in quarto). Press time was also reduced by fifty per cent, since only half the number of sheets were passing through the press. One major consequence of the change in format was therefore that the cost of producing the books would have been significantly reduced, given the savings on raw materials and labour. The Stationers' Company (the body which governed printing and publishing in this period) laid down, in 1598, a maximum price per sheet that could be charged for books.[3] The effect of this linkage between sheet count and price per copy would likely have been that a work issued in a new edition with a significantly reduced sheet count would have been sold to readers at a price lower than that of the original edition. In the case of *Venus and Adonis*, the number of sheets would, as we have seen, have been reduced by half – providing significant savings, at least some of which would likely have been passed on to purchasers.

The popularity of *Venus and Adonis*, which had been reprinted fifteen times by 1675 (giving an average reprint rate of a new edition about every five years) bears out the success of the 'downsizing' strategy: producing a smaller, cheaper text seems to have connected with a demand in the market, making *Venus and Adonis* a strikingly successful publishing venture. The instance of *Lucrece* is not quite so clear cut. The octavos were not page-for-page reprints of the quarto, but there was still a reduction in the sheet count, again effecting savings in paper and press time which may well have been passed on to the purchaser. By 1655 *Lucrece* had been reprinted seven times.

The publishing history of Shakespeare's plays offers a striking contrast. With just one exception – the 1595 *True Tragedie of Richard Duke of Yorke* (a variant version of *Henry VI, Part 3*), issued in octavo – publishers resolutely stuck to the quarto as the standard format for play texts. No play of Shakespeare's enjoyed the same degree of success as *Venus and Adonis*, at least as measured by reprint rates. As we have seen, the poem reached its sixteenth edition in 1675. This was the same as the combined total for Shakespeare's two most popular plays – *Richard III* and *Henry IV, Part 1* – each of which had been issued in eight editions by that year.

---

[3] '[N]ewe copies w^che hereafter shalbe printed w^thout pictures, in the pica[,] the Romane, the Italica, the Englishe letter & the Romane & Italica to the same and the breviere and longe pr[y]mers letters shall not be sold aboue these rat[es] following vi[z] Those of the pica, Romane[,] Italica, the Inglise[,] and the Romane & Italica to the same, to be sold, not aboue a penny for twoo sheet[s] Those of the brevier and the longe prymer letters not to be sold for aboue a penny for one sheete & a half.' (Greg and Boswell 1930: 58–9)

In total, seventy-three quarto editions of twenty-three plays (including *Edward III*, but excluding the apocrypha) had been published by 1675, giving an average reprint rate of 3.17 editions per title.[4] One (rough and ready) way of looking at these figures would be to say that *Venus and Adonis* outperformed the play text quartos' average by a factor of just over 5 to 1.

Of course, there may well be other factors involved here beyond format and cost. The potential readership for poetry may have been greater than (or at least differently constituted than) that for drama; certainly a readership for poetry had been well established early in the period through manuscript circulation and the practice of keeping commonplace books. Performance (and non-performance) history doubtless also had an impact on play text publication and sales: the closing of the theatres between 1642 and 1660 must, for example, be borne in mind (and see also below for the impact of the first collected edition on individual play publishing rates). Nonetheless, we might wonder whether Shakespearean textual history would have taken a different track had an enterprising play text publisher been willing to follow his poetry-publishing colleagues in exploring the possibility of broadening the market for plays by issuing them in a smaller, cheaper format. It is striking, for example, that only about half of Shakespeare's plays appeared in print during his own lifetime. If a downsizing of editions to octavo had served to create a more extensive market for play texts might we have seen more titles being brought to print at the time? And, if so, what *kinds* of texts would we have seen? Scholars have focused a great deal of attention on a relatively small number of plays that appeared in variant versions during Shakespeare's lifetime: the so-called 'good' and 'bad' quartos (see Maguire 1996). What other variant texts might have come to light had more of the canon been published during this period? Might scholars now, for example, be discussing normative variant octavos, rather than focusing so intently on aberrant bad quartos?

One enterprising publisher who did attempt something new shortly after Shakespeare's death was Thomas Pavier, who published quarto versions of ten plays (including the apocryphal *Sir John Oldcastle*) in 1619. What distinguishes Pavier's editions is that their make-up signals a clear intention that the plays might be aggregated into a larger unit – essentially something

---

[4] On the question of the comparative popularity of Shakespeare's printed plays relative to those of his fellow playwrights, see Erne 2013.

like a 'selected Shakespeare'. Ultimately, Pavier abandoned the project as originally conceived, apparently selling off the plays individually, in some cases providing them with falsely dated title pages, seemingly to disguise their actual year of issue.[5] A great deal of attention has been given to the question of what Pavier did 'after the fact', so to speak: to the whys and wherefores of his abandoning the selected works scheme. But it is worth noting here that his original plan was both innovative and very much ahead of its time (see also Zachary Lesser and Peter Stallybrass's chapter in this present volume). Pavier's model of individual texts which could be accumulated into a single collection had never before been tried by any publisher of Shakespeare. Indeed, it would be more than a century before another publisher returned to the idea of offering individual texts which could be collected into a greater whole: Robert Walker's edition of 1734–35 offered all of the texts piecemeal, with volume title pages also being provided along the way so that those who had collected a full set could, if they wished, combine them into a seven volume 'complete works'. This became quite a common practice in editions issued throughout the eighteenth and nineteenth centuries.

When the first collected edition of Shakespeare's plays appeared in 1623, it worked from a very different model from that attempted by Pavier. The plays were presented together in a single volume. To accommodate the full set of texts the publishers printed in double columns and upscaled to folio, the largest book size of the time (the volume is thus referred to as the First Folio, or F1). A bound copy of the First Folio cost about £1 to buy (see Blayney 1991). In fact, this is roughly what it would have cost to purchase an equivalent number of quarto play texts on an individual basis. I have, however, made the point elsewhere (Murphy 2013) that, since the issuing of individual text editions of the plays tailed off significantly after the appearance of F1, the 1623 edition created what almost amounted to a single, expensive 'access point' for the plays. Additionally, as already noted, F1 (and its successor folios – F2, F3 and F4 – issued in 1632, 1663/4 and 1685) provided the *only* text of those plays that had not been issued in individual editions. So, for most of the period up to the early eighteenth century, almost half of Shakespeare's plays could only be read if one had access to one of the expensive folios. We can say, then, that, whereas a shift in format in the case of *Venus and Adonis* and *Lucrece* probably had the effect of expanding Shakespeare's readership, a shift of format in the case of the

---

[5] For a compelling analysis of the project see Massai 2007: ch. 4; for Pavier's career more generally, see Johnson 1992.

plays had exactly the opposite effect, serving to narrow that readership – and probably quite considerably too.

F1, in fact, set a trend of Shakespeare publishers producing large-scale expensive collected editions, targeting a narrow readership. This was certainly the central tendency of the eighteenth century. The Tonson cartel, which dominated Shakespeare publishing in this era, did break with the single-volume model, issuing their editions as multi-volume sets, but their wares remained very expensive (for example, the 1725 edition, edited by Alexander Pope, cost about £7 7s. bound – see the review in *Weekly Journal or Saturday's Post*, 20 March 1725). Rather like modern software developers, the cartel also repeatedly refreshed their core product (and sought repeat sales) by providing constant 'upgrades' in the form of new (and cumulative) editorial commentary and annotation, with the result that editions swelled to an ever-greater number of volumes decade by decade. There was, however, a lively counter-tendency, with various publishers challenging the cartel's dominance (and their claims to exclusive ownership of the plays) by offering cheap texts. It was precisely the smaller formats of octavo and duodecimo (12°) to which these publishers turned, sometimes – as noted above in the case of Robert Walker – offering a full set of plays which could be collected individually and then bound into volumes.

The case of the Irish publishers who offered alternatives to the cartel's wares is particularly interesting. In broad, general terms, these publishers tended to release small-format editions to coincide with Dublin theatrical performances (though it is important to be careful here and to allow for the possibility that the performance record may be incomplete – and one would also have to allow for the fact that there are, in all likelihood, further eighteenth-century Irish editions that have not survived). The first surviving Irish Shakespeare text is an octavo edition of *Hamlet* issued by George Grierson in 1721. In April of this same year *Hamlet* was performed at the Smock Alley Theatre in Dublin.[6] A number of subsequent editions by Grierson or by his fellow publisher (and collaborator), George Ewing, also coincided with performances at Smock Alley: Grierson issued a *Henry IV, Part 1* in 1723 and records indicate a performance of the play in November of that year; Ewing issued a duodecimo *Macbeth* in the same year and, again, it coincided with a Smock Alley production. It is

---

[6] All information on performances is derived from the *Shakespearean Performance in Ireland* database. Smock Alley opened in October 1662 and was 'the first Restoration theatre to have been built and designed as a performance space from the ground up, starting with an empty cobbled yard' (Morash 2002: 13).

noteworthy, however, that there does not appear to be a perfect match-up between performance and publication. Grierson, for instance, issued a *Julius Caesar* in 1721, but the first eighteenth-century Irish production of the play seems not to have taken place until January 1723. Likewise, his *Othello*, also published in 1721, appears to have anticipated a Dublin production by a year – the previous performance having taken place in 1696. Print and performance history in Ireland continue to be intertwined in this way for much of the remainder of the century. Thus, for example, an Abraham Bradley edition of *As You Like It* in 1741 coincided with productions of the play at both Smock Alley and at the Theatre Royal in Aungier Street (indeed, the title page flagged up the Theatre Royal performance). By contrast, an edition of *Hamlet* published in the same year by Philip Crampton appeared in a gap between performances staged in 1740 and 1742. Dublin theatricals may also have prompted publishing ventures outside the metropolis: a duodecimo *Macbeth* published in Cork by Eugene Swiney in 1761 coincided with performances of the play at both Dublin theatres; two years later Phineas and George Bagnell issued an *Othello* in Cork which also coincided with a Dublin production.

What we appear to get in Ireland in this period, then, is a dynamic relationship between theatrical performance and small-format publication. In some instances the former seems clearly to be driving the latter, but, at times, the relationship appears possibly to be reversed, with popular editions at least anticipating, if not perhaps even prompting, theatrical productions. Theatre audiences and play text readerships are thus interlinked in a symbiotic fashion, with a likely high degree of overlap. This might be contrasted with the central publishing tendency in London in the same period which, as we have seen, privileged the expensive, monumentalized collected works edition: the text of the upmarket closet, we might say, rather than the socialized text of the theatre.

While Irish editions clearly found their primary market locally, particularly among theatregoers, some Irish texts were almost certainly also exported to the English market, where they would have offered exceptionally good value for money. When Grierson and Ewing published a complete works edition in Dublin in 1726, for example, it was priced at £1. As we have seen, the London edition issued in the previous year would likely have run to £7 7s. (bound) – thus the price of the Irish edition was just 14 per cent of that of its London equivalent (on which it was, in fact, textually based). The London cartel spent much of the century seeking to exclude cut-price editions from their own market, relying on threatened and actual legal action which exploited ambiguities in contemporary copyright legislation. In 1774, however, a House of Lords judgment clarified the legal situation and confirmed that copyright was of limited duration only (and not perpetual, as the Londoners had always claimed), with out of copyright texts – such as Shakespeare's works – falling into a 'public domain', and thus being freely available to be issued by any publisher.

The effects of the 1774 decision were far-reaching and, over time, they served radically to reshape British publishing.[7] The commercial mindset of the book trade changed very considerably from the late eighteenth century to the nineteenth century. This shift is neatly anticipated in the career of the bookseller James Lackington. The son of an alcoholic journeyman shoemaker, Lackington grew up 'in the extremest poverty' (Lackington 1794: 27). He received minimal education, being withdrawn from school when his 'mother became so poor that she could not afford the mighty sum of two-pence per week for my schooling' (30). After some years spent working as a shoemaker himself, Lackington managed to raise enough capital to open up a small bookshop and he quickly registered the fact that the demand for books was greater than the number of *affordable* books that were available to readers. 'Thousands', he noted, 'have been effectually prevented from purchasing [books,] whose circumstances in life would not permit them to pay the full price, and thus were totally excluded from the advantage of improving their understandings, and enjoying a rational entertainment' (217). Lackington set about remedying this situation, in the first instance by purchasing remaindered stock and making the books available at knock-down prices. His motto, emblazoned on the doors of his carriage, was 'SMALL PROFITS DO GREAT THINGS' (227). He took particular pride in the fact that, as a result of his business model, 'prodigious numbers in inferior or *reduced* situations of life, have been essentially benefitted in consequence of being thus enabled to indulge their natural propensity for the acquisition of knowledge, on easy terms' (217).

The commercial lesson that Lackington learned so quickly – that a sound and prosperous business can be built on small profits and high volume sales – was learned more slowly by the publishing trade over the course of the nineteenth century. In the wake of the 1774 judgment, the edition price of out of copyright authors such as Shakespeare did come down, with the cartel monopolies now broken. But publishers' own fixed costs – primarily labour and materials – remained relatively high and it was

---

[7] For the most thorough account, see St. Clair 2007.

not until technological developments helped to reduce these costs that book prices finally shifted significantly downward (see Eliot 1994). In his own time, Lackington could see that literacy rates were rising: that there were many who, like himself, were making a very small amount of education go a very long way, a little bit of schooling turning them into lifelong committed readers. This process intensified over the course of the nineteenth century as a national school system was slowly established and illiteracy was gradually reduced almost to zero. In time publishers came to see what Lackington had realized very early: that money could be made by meeting the demands of these new readers.

It is indicative of these developments that the nineteenth century was a period of restless innovation in the field of Shakespeare publishing. How, exactly, was one to reach these new readers – and how might one do so in a way that met their financial as well as their intellectual needs? We have seen that, in the eighteenth century, publishers such as Robert Walker offered complete editions piecemeal, selling the plays one at a time, with collected volume title pages being issued along the way. Some nineteenth-century publishers broke their editions down still further, offering parts of plays on a regular cycle – Shakespeare 'on the instalment plan', in effect. The first to do so was Robert Tyas, who launched a 'SHAKSPERE FOR THE PEOPLE' in 1839, issuing weekly numbers at two (pre-decimal) pence each, with each play running to four to six numbers (see Murphy 2008: 78–9). Next into the field was J. S. Moore, who offered customers a variety of different ways of acquiring and configuring their text. Adverts in the *Publishers' Circular* indicated that the edition was to be issued in penny weekly numbers, beginning on 28 June 1845. Alternatively, purchasers could receive the edition in monthly parts at 4½ pence, in a wrapper (Advertisement for 'The Penny Shakespeare' 1845: 181). The first thirty-six numbers constituted volume 1 of the edition, which included all of the comedies. Purchasers were notified that 'Cases for binding the First Volume may be had of the Publishers, One Shilling each; or Subscribers may have their copies bound by the Publisher, for One Shilling and Sixpence.' Alternatively, the volume was available for purchase by non-subscribers for 4 shillings and 6 pence, cloth, gilt. The complete edition ran to three volumes in total.[8] As an additional incentive for buying the edition, Moore indicated that 'With Part 1 (and also to every purchaser of the first four numbers) will be given an engraving of all the known portraits of

---

[8] For all these details, see the prospectus and other materials included with the British Library copy of Moore (call number 11762g4).

Shakspere' (181) – this is in keeping with a general trend over the course of the nineteenth century to offer 'added value' in the form of illustrations, which grew increasingly cheaper to produce with the emergence of new graphic technologies (see Sillars 2008: chs. 8–10).

Like most things offered for sale by instalments, Moore's text was, cumulatively, quite expensive and it is difficult to know how many would have bought the whole edition (though, doubtless, individual parts might be likely to have been attractive, given their price). As the century progressed, publishers sought new ways of reducing the cost of their wares. Cassell's 'National Library' series, edited by Henry Morley – which included Shakespeare's plays – incorporated advertisements in their end papers and, indeed, on their back covers, where the virtues of the 'Harness Electropathic Belt' were frequently heralded: 'invaluable in all Rheumatic or Nervous Affections, Liver and Kidney Diseases, Ladies Ailments, etc.' (Morley 1888: back cover). Beside the final page of Morley's *King Lear* sits an advert for 'Neave's Food for infants, invalids, growing children, and the aged' (193). One might wonder whether this is a coincidence or an early example of targeted advertising. In his biography of Morley, Henry Solley observed that 'Letters, which Professor Morley greatly prized, came from the far West in America, and from other lands on the borders of civilization, expressing gratitude for these cheap and handy volumes, which seemed almost as ubiquitous as Palmer's biscuits' (1898: 357). By the end of the century, edition prices had been reduced to extraordinarily low levels. Dicks's 'Shilling Shakespeare' has already been mentioned; by 1890, Ward and Lock were undercutting Dicks by 50 per cent with their 'Sixpenny Shakespeare', offering the entire canon for the same price – without adjusting for inflation – that a single play had cost in the playwright's own day.

The twentieth century witnessed a great proliferation of edition types, and Shakespeare texts were issued in all kinds of sizes and configurations. The Scottish publisher Blackie offered selected plays under the banner 'The Plain Text Shakespeare'. Their card-covered booklets had no introductory or ancillary materials and no annotation, effectively providing purchasers with the play, the whole play and nothing but the play. As Shakespeare increasingly became incorporated into university curricula, a range of editions appeared which were produced by university-based scholars for use by advanced students and academics (on the general topic of supplementary materials, with specific reference to *The Tempest*, see Leah Marcus's chapter in the present volume). By contrast with Blackie's 'Plain Text' editions, in these volumes Shakespeare's words fought a losing battle against a rising tide of annotation which crept ever higher up the page. Advanced study of the plays also prompted an interest in the texts as they were published in Shakespeare's own time and this led to various facsimile projects, including a series of reproductions of the early quarto texts issued by Sidgwick and Jackson, and then by Oxford University Press, between 1939 and 1975. In the closing decades of the twentieth century, interest specifically in the variations among the earliest texts encouraged projects which sought to facilitate a kind of 'simultaneous' reading of two or more versions of the same play. In 1989, for instance, Michael Warren edited *The Complete King Lear*, which offered unbound facsimiles of the first quarto, second quarto and first Folio texts of *Lear*, together with a bound parallel text of Q1 and F1. All of the materials were presented in a portfolio, tied together by a ribbon. Warren's *Lear* pushed the boundaries of what could be achieved in the medium of print, the unbound pages of some of its texts representing a breaking open of the conventional edition and a fracturing of closed, linear textual authority.

Though Warren's portfolio of texts was extraordinarily useful to scholars of the history of the play's evolution, it would not have had much appeal for a general reader who simply wanted *a* (single) text of *Lear* to read and who did not wish to engage in an exercise of cross-reading among the variant early versions of the play. Such a general reader was, however, well catered for in the twentieth century (and beyond) by a range of popular commercial editions. Penguin had, for instance, picked up where nineteenth-century mass-production publishers had left off and the firm can also be said to have followed James Lackington in believing that small profits could do great things. In the early years of the company, Penguin's margins were so low that titles typically needed to sell more than 17,000 copies before they became profitable (Banham 2007: 289). Shakespeare was quickly added to the Penguin list, with G. B. Harrison producing editions which, as a result of their competitive pricing, made inroads into several different markets at once, attracting general readers and school sales, while also competing with more heavyweight scholarly editions in the university market.[9]

---

[9] When Penguin launched their second edition in 1967 (under the general editorship of T. J. B. Spencer), Cambridge University Press felt pressured into accelerating their plans for revamping one of their own Shakespeare lines. Peter Burbidge at the Press wrote to John Dover Wilson: 'Dick has already explained to you and your fellow editors that the appearance of the paperback turned what we intended to be a very deliberately planned operation into a crash programme' (letter dated 26 January 1968, John Dover Wilson papers, National Library of Scotland, MS 14325).

For those who found even mass market editions challenging, a new phenomenon emerged in the twentieth century: comic book and graphic novel versions of the plays. These texts connected with a tradition extending back to Nicholas Rowe's edition of 1709, which indicated on its title page that it was 'Adorn'd with cuts' ('cuts' being woodcut illustrations). But where traditional illustrated editions provided images that *supplemented* the text, the new twentieth-century tradition offered texts where the visual and the textual were fully integrated – and, indeed, where the graphic aspect of the page often carried meaning beyond the text. Some of the clearest examples of this can be found in the various manga versions of Shakespeare that gained popularity from the end of the twentieth century. In SelfMadeHero's manga *Tempest* (Appignanesi 2007), illustrated by Paul Duffield, for instance, the final page of text is graphically rendered as a series of ribbons 'lifting' away from the book to 'reveal' the recto of the back cover beneath (see Figure 16.2). Prospero's final words – 'set me free' – are represented as a ribbon segment separated from the rest of the page image and located at the very edge of the book, as if indicating a point of exit (see Myklebost forthcoming). The image is a clever analogy both for the moment of liberation that Prospero seeks at the end of the play and for the disintegration of the theatrical fiction embodied in Prospero's metatheatrical epilogue.

Duffield's visual conception of *The Tempest* in his populist text can be said to have a certain amount in common with Warren's scholarly vision of *Lear* in his partly unbound edition of the variant versions of the play. In both cases, we find a straining against the limits of the conventional printed text. Warren 'unstitches' (some of) his pages so that they can be brought into comparison and dialogue with other sections of bound and unbound text; Duffield visually effects a cutting up of the text, so that it can – metaphorically at least – rise away from the confining enclosure of the physical book. Such strainings against the limits of the book-as-object can be said in a sense to have been very much of their time, since, with the rise of the digital text, the 'death of the book' was a much discussed topic in the closing years of the twentieth century (see, for example, Nunberg 1996).

Shakespeare's works were, in fact, rendered into digital format early in the era of mass computing. The 'Moby Shakespeare', based on the 1864 *Globe Shakespeare*, was made available through various websites, most notably those established by Matty Farrow in Australia and Jeremy Hylton at the Massachusetts Institute of Technology. The earliest online Shakespeare resources provided little in the way of 'added value': rather like Blackie's 'Plain Text' Shakespeare

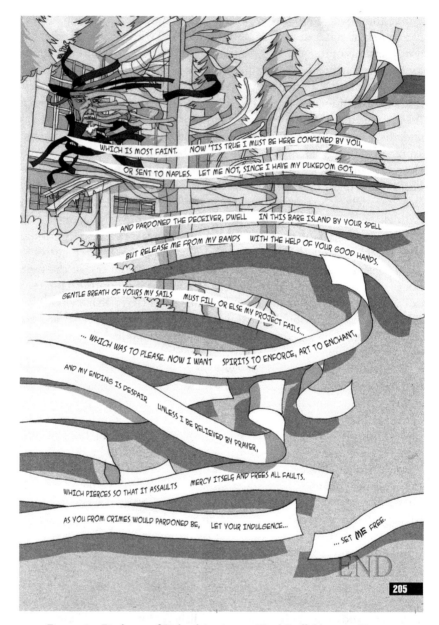

Figure 16.2 Final page of Richard Appignanesi/Paul Duffield manga *Tempest*

they tended to offer the text and nothing else. Over time, this began to change, with many digital editions providing significant additional resources. As electronic publishing moved from free-to-access websites, so – as in the case of print editions – the question of the cost of access became a significant issue. The price of the earliest resource-rich digital packages was set at an extraordinarily high level. Thus, for example, the CD-ROM version of the Arden Shakespeare – which included facsimiles of the earliest editions and various other resources in addition to a modern text – was offered for sale initially at £2,500/$3,995. Only libraries at research-intensive institutions could afford to buy the package, with the result that, just as we have seen with the case of the seventeenth-century folios, the audience for the text in this new format was very limited indeed. In more recent times – again, as in the case of printed texts – the entry price for digital Shakespeare products has come down very considerably. Notable innovative editions have included the Touch Press *Sonnets by William Shakespeare* app, which includes the text of the poems; video of all of the texts being read to camera by a range of leading actors; commentary on the poems by the poet Don Paterson; and interviews with a broad range of scholars (on apps more generally, see W. B. Worthen's chapter in the present volume). All of this content is available for £9.99 in the UK – or just 0.4 per cent of the cost of the Arden CD. Granted the Arden included the entire canon but, even so, the contrast is stark.

Packages such as the Touch Press *Sonnets* allow a certain amount of direct input from the reader: users can add their own notes or share the text of one of the poems on platforms such as Twitter and Facebook. Higher levels of input and interactivity are being developed within other Shakespeare digital text resources, with the result that, as W. B. Worthen observes elsewhere in this volume: 'the use of texts is not limited to reading them but is more akin to "processing" them, using them as one input in a multiplex armature of creation'. The *Shakespeare Quartos Archive* (www.quartos.org/), for instance, has been designed as a 'Web 2.0-enabled' project, providing an interactive interface and toolset enabling users to overlay pages of the early editions for comparison purposes; mark and tag images with annotations; and create public or private workspaces with illustrations, annotations and other materials. This raises the prospect of a wholly new edition format: one where the text is open to its readership, allowing the business of reading to be highly active and constructive.

That is, of course, if one *wishes* to interact with the text in these ways; many readers do not: they simply want to read the plays. But, for them, the digital format potentially has its own particular liberations. It is now possible to download the complete works to mobile devices at very little cost (or, indeed, even for no cost at all if one is not terribly choosy about what edition one reads); one can thus easily carry a complete Shakespeare in one's pocket, effectively as incidental content on a multipurpose device. Were they living in our time and in possession of a smartphone, then, the light-fingered Sean O'Casey and Richard Field would not need to risk a prison sentence in order to acquire a copy of Shakespeare's works – and they could, at the click of an app store button, take possession of a copy in a format even more portable than that of Bryce's miniature editions.

CHAPTER 17

A man who needs no introduction

Leah S. Marcus

In *Mansfield Park*, Jane Austen has Mr. Crawford comment on the Englishman's inborn kinship for Shakespeare:

> But Shakespeare one gets acquainted with without knowing how. It is a part of an Englishman's constitution. His thoughts and beauties are so spread abroad that one touches them everywhere, one is intimate with him by instinct. – No man of any brain can open at a good part of one of his plays, without falling into the flow of his meaning immediately. (Austen 1816: 3.60)

If Crawford is right, and the enthusiastic frequency with which his statement is recited on the World Wide Web suggests that for many readers the platitude still resonates, then Shakespeare is indeed a man who needs no introduction: his plays speak for themselves. Thomas Dibdin's account of early Shakespeare folios notes that they are frequently marred with pie stains and other evidence of avid readership, even though the early folios offer readers no introductions beyond Heming and Condell's prefatory epistles (Dibdin 1824: 792 n.). Editions of Shakespeare without introductions to individual plays were standard in the eighteenth century and continued to appear throughout the nineteenth and twentieth, though some of them offered introductory images to entice readers into the text. In the affordable Dicks's 'People's Edition', for example, *The Tempest* is introduced by an engraved scene from 3.1, complete with a quotation from a Prospero who is suspiciously Christ-like in appearance (Figure 17.1; see also Murphy 2008: 80–5).

Today it is still possible, of course, to buy the plays in cheap Globe reprints or to encounter them online without the intervening presence of an introduction. Even when modern readers use full-dress editions, they

---

The author would like to give special thanks to Georgianna Ziegler and Alan Katz of the Folger Shakespeare Library, who offered help and encouragement far beyond the call of duty when this chapter was being researched.

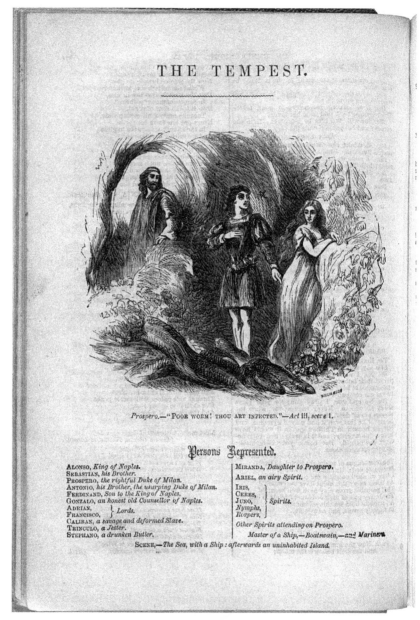

Figure 17.1 Introductory Image in Dicks's 'People's Edition' of *The Tempest*

frequently go straight to the plays themselves and read the introductions only later, if at all. In an informal survey of colleagues in the field I discovered that among those of us who profess literature, those who are native speakers of English are still likely to read the play before they read the material intended by the editor to introduce it; my non-native speaker colleagues, by contrast, make a habit of reading every word of the introduction before they tackle the play. Whether or not we are willing to acknowledge the fact, it would appear that many of us whose mother tongue is English still secretly subscribe to Crawford's fantasy of a special intimacy with Shakespeare, whether achieved by birth alone or by birth supplemented by education.

In the context of Austen's novel, Crawford's claim of mystical attunement to Shakespeare is decisively undercut: he turns out to be extremely unreliable and his protestations of intimacy with Shakespeare testify more to his gifts as an actor and prevaricator than to his moral elevation. Even as Austen was writing in the early nineteenth century, Shakespeare was beginning to appear in a few editions that included introductions preceding each play and sometimes also explanatory notes. This chapter will examine the phenomenon of the introduction in the history of editions of Shakespeare. In particular we will consider introductions to *The Tempest* from the earliest I have seen – in a John Bell theatre edition of 1773, which proudly proclaims on its title page that it offers 'An INTRODUCTION, and NOTES critical and illustrative', through two centuries to the Arden 3 *Tempest* edited by Virginia Mason Vaughan and Alden T. Vaughan (Shakespeare 1999b; rev. edn.: Shakespeare 2011). The voluminous introduction we expect to find intervening between us and the play in modern full-dress editions of *The Tempest* is a time-limited custom that had a beginning and that may now be reaching its end. I will argue here that there have been important correlations between the way editors of *The Tempest* envision their task of introducing the play and the vicissitudes of the British Empire that so many recent critics have seen as forecast, celebrated in its infancy and/or critiqued within the play itself. Moreover, those who edited this play and others for colonial audiences have made important, if unrecognized, contributions to the shape of the modern introduction.

Our history begins with the deep irony that the earliest introductions to *The Tempest* were introducing not Shakespeare's play but William Davenant and John Dryden's adaptation of it, which preserved only about a third of Shakespeare's lines. The eighteenth-century theatre editions I have seen often include appreciative introductions of less than a page, but a later example from the Theatres Royal published in 1823 has eighteen pages signed by 'P. P.' that hail Shakespeare as 'the admiration and glory of his countrymen' and offer homage to the 'grandest genius the world ever saw' across the empire: 'On the banks of the Nile, the Ganges, the torrid and the temperate zones, in regions which when he wrote were scarcely known to exist, in all climates and among all nations, are the works of Shakespeare read and admired' (Theatres Royal 1823: iv).

In a paradox that Michael Dobson has noted as characteristic of the age of Bardolatry more generally, the author of this 1823 introduction has no difficulty squaring his worship of Shakespeare with his neglect of Shakespeare's actual text. Typically, the theatre editions assure readers that despite the composite nature of what is being staged they are getting every word of the play as it was actually produced, and that Shakespeare, despite his diluted presence, is responsible for its success: 'once touched with the magic wand of the divine Shakespeare, the whole becomes a scene of enchantment' (Dolby 1824: sig. A2). These editions are designed as mementos of the purchaser's experience in the theatre, but some of them also acknowledge that they include 'baser metal incorporated with' Shakespeare's 'gold' because the Dryden additions are necessary to make Shakespeare 'palatable to the mob' (Theatres Royal n.d.). Shakespeare is repeatedly invoked as a spokesperson for empire, dramatizing 'wonders' of the New World, the Near East and South Asia. One of the added songs in the adapted version even has Ariel sing 'O, bid thy faithful Ariel fly / To the furthest India's sky' (Theatres Royal 1823: 8).

By contrast, editions of Shakespeare's complete works in the eighteenth and early nineteenth centuries did not typically offer introductions to individual plays, though they often included excerpted critical appreciations as the first note to the play. In Isaac Reed's edition (Reed 1803) and in Boswell's Malone edition (Boswell and Malone 1821), these appreciations are for the first time placed *before* the text of *The Tempest*, thus constituting an introduction. However, as a series of long quotations of previous critics they are multivocal rather than conveying a single editorial perspective, as do the theatrical texts. Ironically, then, in editions where the text of *The Tempest* is acknowledged to be a Restoration hybrid, the introduction is presented, as though in compensation, by means of a single authoritative voice; where the text is Shakespeare's, the introduction until quite late consists of a series of sometimes mutually contradictory critical remarks, among which are scattered comments on the play's proto-colonial setting. Malone was the first to note the wreck of the Sea Adventure in the Bermudas as a Shakespearean source; he also cites Magellan's Patagonian voyage for the origin of Caliban's god, Setebos, along with Pliny's *Natural History*, Montaigne's Cannibals and Spenser's Wild Man as possible sources for Caliban himself (15.11–15). The earliest examples I have found of Shakespeare's 'complete works' that contain introductions to each play in our modern understanding of the term – multiple topics discussed at some length in a single, authoritative voice – date from the 1850s (Halliwell-Phillipps 1853; Singer 1856; Collier 1858 (2nd edn.)).

In the Arden 3 *Tempest* the Vaughans claim that it is rare to find comments on the American sources of *The Tempest* before 1898, when Sidney Lee published an extended discussion of New World echoes in the play in his *Life of William Shakespeare*, later supplemented by further evidence such as the fact that Caliban's ability to make 'dams for fish' parallels a skill of New World natives that was never duplicated by their European 'masters' (Lee 1898: 297–9). Clearly, the Vaughans had not been reading nineteenth-century editors' introductions, in which New World parallels are common. Beginning in the 1850s we encounter a steady stream, and by the 1890s a plethora, of separate editions of *The Tempest*, most of which were intended for use in schools. We tend now to regard school editions as derivative, but some of the nineteenth-century *Tempest* editors, like the writers of introductions to the theatre editions that continued to be produced, were ahead of more mainstream critics in that they regularly interpreted the play in terms of colonial America and other colonial settings. In the Preface to a theatre edition of 1857 'to be had' in the Princess's Theatre, Charles Kean notes that the play symbolizes 'almost as much as a historical play, a definite period in the world's annals', namely, 'the century that followed the first revelation of a new hemisphere to the eyes of astonished Europe', a time during which the 'mind of man was repeatedly excited by the announcement of fresh wonders'. Kean links the age of discovery with the expansion of human intellect and foundation of modern science and discusses the play in terms of Sir George Somers and the wreck of his ship off the Bermudas and Sir Walter Ralegh's *Discovery of Guiana* (Kean 1857: v–vi).

Similarly, in 'Collins' School and College Classics' edition (1875), the editor D. Morris says that Shakespeare 'as if activated by the spirit of the times' gave us his own travel adventure, culminating in a specifically American monster:

> At a time when colonization was taking hold of the public mind in England, the contrast of the savage and the civilized man would do much to justify the formation of colonies in lands inhabited by rude races, and this probably may have been one of Shakespeare's objects in the delineation of Caliban. (Morris 1875: 10)

The American editor Henry N. Hudson rehearsed the usual parallels with 'recent marvels of Transatlantic discovery' in his 1881 school *Tempest* and took pride that 'America may justly claim to have borne a considerable part in suggesting and shaping [the play's] delicate workmanship', inspired by the wonders and enchantment of the Bermudas (Hudson 1883: 4). Other editors suggested a relationship between Caliban and black Africa or an Arabic origin for his name (Phillpotts 1876: xviii and n.).

G. G. Gervinus's *Shakespeare Commentaries*, originally published in German but available in English translation as early as 1863, offered a case for *The Tempest* as a critique of colonialism: 'It is not impossible that Shakespeare in this play, and especially in regard to this Caliban' intended to 'answer the great question of the day concerning the justifiableness of European usurpation over the wild aborigines of the new world; he felt a warm interest in English colonization, in the creation of new nations, that marked the reign of James'. Gervinus notes that Shakespeare's patron Southampton was a 'prominent character in the Virginia Company' and a proponent of political freedom for the colonists; but he also suggests that for Shakespeare colonization was problematic but inevitable: 'He perceived that what happened in the new world at that time was necessary, that with the extension of mankind superiority of spiritual and moral power would ever inundate the realms of rudeness and barbarism, streaming, as it were, into an empty space' (Gervinus 1883: 799–800). Gervinus's views – particularly his critique of Prospero as a usurper over Caliban – made their way into several nineteenth-century introductions to *The Tempest*, especially in those intended for colonial as opposed to English or American readers.

In an 1896 Madras edition of the play, for example, its editor E. E. Kellett offers a long introduction intended both for university students at his institution, Madras Christian College, and for 'students of English in general' in which he discusses the question, particularly fraught in his context as an educator under the Raj, of colonial usurpation and the 'governance of the world'. He acknowledges Prospero's usurpation but considers it just: 'Where usurpation is right, he is as thorough a usurper as Antonio himself' but his authority 'is always that of the superior intellect, not that of force'. The editor even goes so far as to suggest that in relation to Caliban, 'the poet endeavored to teach certain views about the lawfulness of colonization. The question was certainly a crying one at the time.' When it comes actually to defining Shakespeare's views, however, Kellett retreats into inscrutability, declining to judge whether the poet had 'any special purpose of this kind' (Kellett 1896: lxxxvii–xc). Similarly, in an 1889 edition of *The Tempest* specifically designed for Indian schools, Kenneth Deighton notes Gervinus's suggestion that Shakespeare meant the play to interrogate the morality of colonization, but dodges the question by claiming that Shakespeare's prime goal in the play was to demonstrate the need for responsibility for one's actions by showing the consequences of Prospero's neglect of his dukedom (Deighton 1890: vii–xix). On the island, Prospero finally gains the self-mastery required for successful discharge of his duties towards his various subalterns there – he learns, in other words, to be a good colonial administrator. Interestingly enough, editors of the play for colonial students are more likely to be critical of Prospero, their alter-ego in the role of educating young natives, than are editors in Britain or America. They are awkwardly, painfully aware of their duty both to model and to impart British civilization, and defensively dwell on the grave responsibilities of colonial rule rather than on the play's potential to interrogate it.

The colonial editions of *The Tempest* are of particular interest to our project here because they display a format that is very close to that of the first modern full-dress scholarly edition of the play, the first Arden *Tempest* (1901). Even in England, editors frequently expressed dissatisfaction with the pedagogical potential of existing school texts. J. Surtees Phillpotts, who edited *The Tempest* for the Rugby edition of the *Select Plays of Shakespeare*, complained that there would have been no need for his edition 'had the Clarendon Press edition of the play [1874] been as adequate on the aesthetic side as it is on the philological; but in all the one hundred closely printed pages of prefaces and notes in that edition there is not a word on the plot or the characters' (Phillpotts 1876: v). Deighton's Indian *Tempest* appeared as part of a new undertaking, Macmillan's 'English Classics for Indian University Students', which began publishing in 1888 and eventually included twenty-four of Shakespeare's plays along with other canonical literary authors from Chaucer to Tennyson and colonial mainstays like Macaulay's essays on Warren Hastings and Lord Clive. Deighton, who edited all but one of the Shakespeare plays for Macmillan's series, described the specific needs of Indian students in the preface to the first volume he published:

> For English-speaking schoolboys the select plays in the Clarendon Press and Rugby Series, and the complete edition by Mr. Rolfe, are so thoroughly what is wanted, that it would be presumptuous to try to improve upon them. It is different in the case of those for whom this Series is specially intended, the students of our Indian Universities. In their case, over and

above the ordinary difficulties that have to do with archaic language, classical and historical allusions, obsolete customs, etymology, and the numerous other points upon which a commentator must touch – over and above these is the difficulty of interpreting ideas to those cast in a mould of thought and living in an atmosphere of life so remote from anything English. To them the explanation of things that to an English boy would be plain enough, of things that no one who had not had experience of teaching Indian students would suppose possible to be misunderstood, is vitally necessary. (Deighton 1891)

Deighton's editions offered strong, clear introductions with emphasis on plot and character, but his more important innovation was in his notes, which exceed anything earlier in amplitude and clarity and leave out most of the dry philological speculations that were standard at the time. Typically, nineteenth-century school texts offered longer introductions and more copious notes than did other editions: even if a well-educated English gentleman could pride himself on not needing an introduction to Shakespeare, by the mid-nineteenth century younger English readers were regularly offered more help, and Indian students were assumed to be needier still. Without question, Deighton's Macmillan series offered ampler and more precise notes than had previous editions: in Act 1 Scene 1 of *The Tempest*, for example, most previous editors had postponed the first note to 'good' in line 3, but Deighton's edition begins its 1.1 notes with 'Boatswain' from line 1: 'an officer in a ship who has charge of the sails, rigging, etc., and who summons the crew to their duties with a whistle' (71 n.). Somewhat surprisingly, Deighton's Macmillan edition turned out to be highly successful in England as well as India: the series title was changed to 'Macmillan's English Classics' and it was marketed on both continents. Later school texts quickly picked up Deighton's formula of substantial introductions combined with more and clearer notes, and also on Macmillan's marketing strategy of aiming its editions at general as well as school audiences. The Folger Library copy of the Oxford and Cambridge *Tempest* of 1906, for example, has 'WITH INTRODUCTION, NOTES, ETC., FOR STUDENTS' PREPARATION' stamped rather than printed on its title page, which suggests that the edition was also marketed to a more general audience without the stamp (Wood and Wood 1906). Perhaps native British consumers of Shakespeare were not as far in advance of their Indian counterparts in terms of innate kinship with Shakespeare as had been thought.

As Andrew Murphy has pointed out, there is a direct continuity between elements of the arrangement of English schooltexts of

Shakespeare and the mainstream, full-dress editions that followed (Murphy 2003: 207 ff.). In the case of Deighton, the tie is even closer: after editing twenty-three plays for the Macmillan series in India, he went on to edit three plays for the first Arden Shakespeare, which, except for the addition of textual notes, had a format very similar to Deighton's and a similar emphasis on copious explanatory notes. It is hard to avoid the feeling that part of Deighton's need for detailed annotation had to do with editorial control over the terms in which the text could be read. The editor is a quasi-director: one of the functions of a long and generous introduction, we can speculate, was to create a reliable bond with readers so that they would accept the editor's take on the play as conveyed by his 'performance' of it through the shaping of the text and notes. Deighton complained of colonial students left to their own devices in reading passages of Shakespeare and that 'nothing is so disappointing as the ingenuity with which their words are tortured into nonsense. Even if the student goes away with something like the real gist of the passage, he will very rarely retain for any time an accurate idea of what he has been told, unless in a written note' (Deighton 1891: viii).

Were Deighton's Indian students torturing Shakespeare's words into nonsense, or were they simply reading them differently from how their professor wished? Were some of them, perhaps, unconvinced by Deighton's attempts to deflect issues such as Prospero's treatment of Caliban from its possible application to the colonial situation in India? Did they perceive Deighton's full notes as controlling as well as helpful? Other British teachers of Shakespeare under the Raj sometimes contended that the reason Indian students needed more notes than did English students was not because of their deficient cultural knowledge but because Indian students were interested in determining precise meanings, while the English were content with the general gist of a passage.[1] The intricate web of notes that characterized Deighton's Macmillan Shakespeare texts went on to become a hallmark of the new Arden Shakespeare as well. The Arden Shakespeare, with its quintessentially English and Shakespearean name, was born in part out of the experience of editing Shakespeare for the Raj, and its texts bear the imprint of colonial experience.

---

[1] For more details, see 'Editing Shakespeare for the Raj' in my forthcoming book (presently entitled, *How Shakespeare Became Colonial*).

A publisher's blurb included in many volumes of the first series Arden Shakespeare (Arden 1) states that the series aims 'to meet in some degree the requirements of three classes of readers': those 'who care only to enjoy the play without the disturbance of notes', who are supplied with a highly readable text; those 'who recognize the fact that many difficulties exist in what Shakespeare has written' and desire explanatory notes 'to make clear what was obscure, and to render easy what was difficult', who are provided with relatively copious notes; and those who have a scholarly interest in checking the editor's text against the quarto and Folio readings, who are offered textual notes (Hart 1905). None of these categories specifically mentions the Arden introductions, but it comes as no surprise that they were substantial: the Arden volumes would offer readers a reliable editorial voice before their encounter with the play itself, and that companion would follow them via the notes through their experience of the play. Shakespeare and his readers deserved no less. By the beginning of the series' publication in 1899, it could no longer be said, at least for a majority of its projected readers, that Shakespeare was a man who needs no introduction.

The first Arden *Tempest*, edited by Morton Luce, appeared in 1901. Its introduction begins in a language of discovery and desire that will not surprise us, given the patterns we have seen operating in earlier editions. As no adventurer had yet climbed Mount Everest or reached the South Pole, so 'No explorer in the regions of Shakespearean investigation has yet traced *The Tempest* to its sources; and with the exception of *Love's Labour's Lost*, in this respect of undiscovered origins the play stands alone' (Luce 1901: ix). The early parts of the introduction are structured as a careful, methodical exploration of various terrains with the editor as our guide. He discusses one strand of the play's origins as 'colonization, and the disaster of the Virginia fleet, 1609' (xii) and charts the maze of pamphlet material relating to the wreck of the Sea Adventure and the crew's sojourn in the Bermudas with a detail and authority unprecedented in any previous edition. He offers a similarly ample diagnosis of Caliban through three 'dissolving views' of the monster, each of which in fading helps form one of the others: an embodiment of the supernatural as the child of a witch and a demon; a strange being from the books of travel, perhaps a dispossessed Indian; or 'a (negro) slave' – a 'thing of darkness' that Prospero as his master must 'acknowledge mine' (xxxvi). For Luce, Caliban's slavery follows 'as a consequence on the failure of all attempts at conversion'. Prospero assumes that he was intended by Providence to be 'owner and master of the new discovered land' but Shakespeare was fully aware that

European civilization can be a curse for the savage: even Caliban 'puts to shame the rapacity which was too common among colonists' as we see this operating in the behavior of Stephano and Trinculo, not to mention Antonio and his retinue. Luce agrees with Deighton and others that Prospero had earlier neglected his duties, but now he bears a 'wiser power that seeks ever to disclaim itself, is exercised only for the general good, and will even be laid aside if it can subserve that good no longer' (lxviii). Luce's edition, like Deighton's, was produced during the heyday and from within a mindset of British imperialism. It is fairly complex, yet finally unapologetic about the 'white man's burden' to bring the Calibans of the world to enlightenment.

Luce's introduction imitates the structure of a voyage of discovery, moving from a careful, methodical navigation of facts and theories that 'locate' the play in terms of early colonization, into a highly poetic, even rhapsodic, conclusion that mimetically 'discovers' Shakespeare's island and celebrates his creative genius and the wonders of the play as though it was itself a marvel of the New World. The notes and appendices carry forward the overriding idea of colonial voyaging through ample references to the early modern literature of travel and exploration. Even in its critique of potential injuries to the natives, the first Arden *Tempest* is thoroughly immersed in the desire and romance of colonization. Luce's invitation to voyaging in the introduction was an enticing 'hook' that was repeated by later editors. The 'Teaching of English' *Tempest* edited by John Hampden in 1926, for example, has, instead of an 'Introduction' a 'Prologue to Adventure' promising students a vicarious voyage of exploration, now that 'the whole world is charted and measured', through the act of reading the play (Hampden 1926: 9). It is possible that something resembling this strategy was deployed in the First Folio itself (1623). It was common for Shakespeare's contemporaries to think of the theatre as a vicarious form of travel and exploration; William Sherman has pointed out that *The Tempest*, given strategic first place in the First Folio, bears an ornamental border at the top that is more elaborate than those heading later plays in the volume and that depicts a 'feathered fowler' recalling contemporary depictions of New World natives. The same image appeared in other volumes about travel and exploration, most significantly Hakluyt's *Principal Navigations*, which included the source text for Caliban's god, Setebos.[2]

---

[2] Personal communication from William H. Sherman to Marina Warner. See her essay in Hulme and Sherman 2000: 112 and n. The same ornamental border appears three more times in the 1623 folio (Hinman 1996): at the head of the prefatory letter to the brothers Pembroke (sig. A2r), at the head of the 'Catalogve' of plays (sig. A6r) and heading the epilogue to *Henry IV, Part 2* (sig. gg8r).

In the first Arden *Tempest* Luce has relatively little to say about the text of the play as opposed to its contexts. Indeed, with the odd exception of Hudson, the editors who preceded him had uniformly praised the first folio *Tempest* (1623) as well printed by the standards of its time, perhaps especially carefully printed because it came first in the volume. Horace Howard Furness called it 'almost the very best in the way of Text that has come down to us' (Furness 1892: v) and declined to include the most recent editions, including Phillpotts and Deighton, in his textual notes on grounds that the text of the play had become so settled in the previous quarter century that further collation would be 'supererogation' (452). This textual complacency was shattered with the publication of the New Cambridge *Tempest* (1921), which appeared first in a new series described as undertaken in a spirit of 'high adventure tempered by a consciousness of grave responsibility' and dedicated to cutting Shakespeare free 'from the accretions of a long line of editors' by bringing the 'new scientific method' of what is now termed the New Bibliography to bear on the text of the play (Quiller-Couch and Wilson 1921: vii). For John Dover Wilson, the textual editor for the series, there was nothing straightforward about the text of *The Tempest*. He detected many perturbations in it that he identified as signs of abridgement of an earlier, longer lost play, possibly also by Shakespeare. The primary purpose of the notes was to bring the new textual facts to light: Dover Wilson went line by line through the play, charting spots where he identified traces of the lost original and locating only three scenes that did not show such signs.

There is surprisingly little about the play's relation to travel literature in the New Cambridge Introduction, by Arthur Quiller-Couch. Rather, in high modernist fashion, Quiller-Couch discusses the play at length in terms of its relation to elite culture – its setting at James I's Banqueting House, where it was performed in 1612–13 as part of the festivities surrounding the wedding of James's daughter Elizabeth to the 'Winter King' of Bohemia. Rhetorically speaking, the New Cambridge Shakespeare relocates the excitement and 'high adventure' of exploration from the thematic content of the play to the realm of textual scholarship – the discovery of signposts to a still-mysterious original play looming in the mists behind the First Folio text. The romance of early colonization is reborn, but its object is not the world charted on maps but the multi-layered and still unknown world of Shakespeare's lost originals, their genesis and transmission. As the New Bibliographers tended to Orientalize Shakespeare's manuscripts of the plays, imagining them as existing behind a veil that needed to be pierced or rent in order to reveal their full beauty (Egan 2010: 47, citing Bowers), so Dover Wilson – reviving colonial desire but displacing it into a different register – imagines the *ur*-text of *The Tempest* as on the tantalizing frontiers of discovery. In the New Cambridge Shakespeare, the editorial continuity between introduction and notes is fragmented, as is the text of the play itself by Dover Wilson's 'scientific' findings. Instead of constructing a single editorial voice, the edition is dialogic, sometimes even contestatory, as Quiller-Couch pursues one agenda in the introduction and Dover Wilson pursues another in the notes. In the New Cambridge Shakespeare, the introduction and the textual scholarship behind the edition are beginning to diverge; in later twentieth-century editions, they will separate decisively.

The Arden second series (Arden 2) *Tempest* appeared in 1954, edited by the formidable Frank Kermode. In Arden 2 editions the topics to be covered by the introduction were loosely standardized, and first among these came matters relating to the text: thanks to the New Bibliography, the textual scholarship that had been peripheral to editors before the twentieth century now received top billing. Kermode dismisses Dover Wilson's 'Disintegrationist' theories, pronouncing the First Folio text 'exceptionally clean' and condemning the 'multiplication of shadow *Tempests*' as 'a barren occupation': readers should feel free to interpret the play as it stands because 'no one has even half succeeded in disintegrating it' (Kermode 1954: xxix). So much for Dover Wilson.

Kermode notes that despite his debts to the previous Arden editor, his edition will also not remain 'on the path beaten out by Luce': he discusses the travel literature briefly but finds nothing fundamental to the play's 'structure of ideas' that needs New World discovery (viii). Against a backdrop of the dismantling of the British Empire after the Second World War, Kermode dismantles a long tradition of colonially inflected interpretation. His overriding approach to the play is via the 'New Criticism' and his *Tempest* is, above all, a 'pastoral drama', like Milton's *Comus* or Book VI of the *Faerie Queene*. His introduction pulls the play's proto-colonial references back into a matrix of pre-existing classical ideas: Caliban recalls the medieval Wild Man and Old World monsters and is the 'natural' ground against which the civilized is measured; the idea of Europeans corrupting other civilizations is an 'ancient theme', and so is the art/nature controversy that the play pursues in accordance with its classical models (xxxvii–xlii).

For Kermode, the classics and the New World are distinct and unmixable spaces. He does not note, as a recent critic might, that many of the play's blatant echoes of *The Aeneid*, for example, are steeped in an ethos of Roman empire-building that in many ways paralleled the incipient imperialism of Elizabethan England (Mowat 2000). Like many other scholars of the 'New Criticism', Kermode is nervous about intentionalist interpretation and intent on protecting the integrity of the play as a work of art against the potentially damaging methodologies of historicism and the New Bibliography. With the Arden 2 Shakespeare, literary criticism and textual scholarship part ways, not to be reunited until the late twentieth century, as discussed elsewhere in the present volume.

There are many fine editions of *The Tempest* that must be omitted here for lack of space: Northrop Frye's Pelican edition, with its helpful discussion of the play's structure as a series of parallel pursuits of illusions, ordeals and symbolic visions; Anne Righter [Barton]'s Penguin edition (1968; rev. edn. 1988), which interprets the play from the perspective of the twentieth-century stage and analyses the theatre audience's response to the play's many gaps and riddles; Stephen Orgel's Oxford *Tempest* (1987), with its detailed treatment of the play's early modern visual and theatrical contexts; David Lindley's New[er] Cambridge edition (2002), which carries Barton's story of staging and reception back into seventeenth-century experiments with magic, illusionism and spectacle. We end with the Arden 3 *Tempest* because it closes a circle: if the Arden 1 edition was written from within a colonial perspective that correlated with the heyday of British imperialism and represented the culmination of the previous century's attention to the play's colonial contexts, the Arden 3 *Tempest* (1999b; rev. edn. 2011) brings the play back into conversation with issues of colonialism through its engagement with global postcolonial culture and theory. The Vaughans' introduction is, by comparison with Kermode's, extremely far-flung and expansive, discussing the play in relation to 'imperialism and its demise' not only in terms of the New World explorations of the 1590s and after, but also in terms of England's colonization of Ireland, the slave trade and colonial ties to Africa, always with an emphasis on 'appropriation and resistance' as well as the wonder attendant upon discovery and conquest.

This *Tempest* is the first of the three Arden editions to give sustained attention in its introduction to the play's life in the theatre; it is also offers a detailed account of its afterlives in literary adaptations and colonial and postcolonial appropriations: in the political struggles of post-Second World War Central and South America, which saw themselves as Calibans vis-à-vis the USA's intimidating Prospero, in Anglophone Caribbean literature and in film. The Vaughans' *Tempest* is a wellspring of multiple interpretations, endlessly fecund in its influence on subsequent culture and politics. In their second edition, they brought the introduction up to date with an additional twenty-one pages of 'Additions and Reconsiderations' (139–60). This introduction is turbulent and in process – never finished, forever in need of supplementation. It is worth noting, however, that even in its amplitude and open-endedness, their introduction also controls the text by harnessing its energies to an array of postcolonial encounters. Kermode would no doubt cringe: from a New Critical perspective, they have dissolved Shakespeare's play in a sea of global currents and cross-currents.

Perhaps one way of looking at the Vaughans' Arden 3 introduction is as a tradition in process of disintegration. Ann Thompson, one of the General Editors of the Arden 3 Shakespeare, informs me that when the series' editorial parameters were first discussed, she argued that the long, formal introduction with its single authoritative voice be dispensed with altogether in favour of more dispersed information for readers in the notes and appendices. She was not successful then, but she may well have been prescient. Given the direction of publishing today, the Arden 4 Shakespeare now in its early stages may exist only or primarily in Web format. Online, where we read in info-bytes that are training us away from elaborate critical syntheses stretched out over a hundred pages, the traditional introduction, with its imperial underpinnings and its magisterial air of editorial infallibility, may well have no place. Then Shakespeare will, yet once more, be a man who needs, or at least gets, no introduction.

CHAPTER 18

Emendation and the editorial reconfiguration of Shakespeare

Lukas Erne

The editing of Shakespeare has been characterized by two opposed trends in recent times, represented by the respective belief that what we need is more extensive or less extensive editorial intervention. Advocates for more editing ('interventionist editors') have called for and practised more thorough modernization of spelling and punctuation, added more and more detailed stage directions, and emended more readily and more daringly than most previous editors. Those who have called for less editing ('uneditors') hold, on the contrary, that the editorial tradition has increasingly distanced us from the Shakespearean text we should be reading today, and recommend that long-practised editorial interventions be removed. Asked how we need to reconfigure Shakespeare today, one group of scholars thus answers that we need to dress him up, the other that we need to strip him down.

My chapter focuses on a form of editorial intervention in which these opposed trends can be shown to crystallize: emendation. It shows that textual scholarship since the 1980s has followed two very different orientations in its thinking about emendation: we need more, better, more ingenious emendation to solve the cruces, thus leading us to a fuller understanding of the text; or we need to un-emend readings which the editorial tradition has unjustifiably imposed upon us in order to recover the text's true meaning. In the last part of this chapter, I ask what is ultimately at stake in the diametrical opposition between the two proposals to reconfigure Shakespeare. I argue that they reveal fundamentally different attitudes towards textual mediation, authority, and the value of tradition, which go back at least as far as the century in which Shakespeare was born.

***

Editorial emendation has attracted relatively little attention in recent times. It is true that editors carefully think about textual cruces and routinely practice emendation, and there is no shortage of proposed solutions published in *Notes & Queries* and elsewhere. Nonetheless, there has been little systematic work interested less in individual emendations than in emendation more generally. While circumstances of transmission and their impact on editing or the editorial mediation of stage action have been hotly debated in recent times, the editorial practice of emendation has not. This seems unremarkable until we remember that in the eighteenth century emendation was essentially what Shakespeare editing was about. Although John Heminge and Henry Condell had implied that emendation was unnecessary given that the 'maimed, and deformed' quarto texts had been 'cur'd' by the Folio (sig. A3r), eighteenth-century editors found that this was far from being the case. Early in the eighteenth century, Lewis Theobald and Alexander Pope were confident about their ability to improve the Shakespearean text and liberally emended. Disagreements between them resulted in the first book-length study of Shakespeare's texts, which is, significantly, about emendation: Theobald's *Shakespeare Restor'd: or, A Specimen of the Many Errors as well Committed, or Unamended, by Mr. Pope in his Late Edition of this Poet* (1726). Theobald's basic argument – to which Pope famously responded by satirizing Theobald in *The Dunciad* – is that Pope was an incompetent editor who did not emend when he should and did when 'there was no Occasion to depart from the Poet's Text' (quoted in Murphy 2007: 96). Later in the century, Samuel Johnson came to practise emendation much more cautiously, writing that 'my first labour is, always to turn the old text on every side, and try if there be any interstice, through which light can find its way ... In this modest industry I have not been unsuccessful. I have rescued many lines from the violations of temerity, and secured many scenes from the inroads of correction' (Murphy 2007: 98–9). Similar tendencies towards more or less emendation can also be observed later in history and beyond Shakespeare studies. For instance, the nineteenth-century German philologist Karl Lachmann 'encouraged editors to try to make sense of their copy-text rather than depart from it', a method to which A. E. Housman objected, preferring to come up with 'inspired emendations' (Egan 2010: 11, 7). Although it might be tempting to tell a diachronic story about the practice of emendation, from the adventurous follies of eighteenth-century editors to the sobriety and restraint of modern editors, the opposing tendencies for more and less emendation can in fact be observed at various points in the editorial history. They reflect not only shifting thinking about the ontology of the

(Shakespearean) text and the object of the editorial quest, but also the temperament of editors, who have usefully been divided into those who are 'conjecture-happy' and those who are 'conjecture-shy' (Taylor 1997: 59).

***

While there have been advocates for more or less thorough editing across the centuries, calls against editing in its traditional form have taken on new proportions in recent decades. What Margreta de Grazia and Peter Stallybrass in 1993 diagnosed as a 'mounting resentment toward the editorial tradition' can now be identified as a distinct movement in the history of Shakespearean textual studies (de Grazia and Stallybrass 1993: 255). What is central to this movement is the contention that the traditional editorial reproduction is harmful, that it oppresses and obscures, and that it therefore needs to be radically reformed. Several factors can partly account for its recent rise. One of them is the ground-breaking Oxford Shakespeare *Complete Works* of 1986 and its massive *Textual Companion*, both spear-headed by Stanley Wells and Gary Taylor. The most important editorial achievement in Shakespeare studies since the Cambridge Shakespeare *Works* of the 1860s, it fully embraces editorial intervention, takes numerous controversial decisions and has stirred debates in which many feel that less would have been more. Another factor is that the traditional object of editorial pursuit has been coming under attack: while the aim of the New Bibliography was to 'strip the veil of print', in Fredson Bowers's famous phrase (1955: 87), and thereby to recover the authorial text *behind* the printed text, de Grazia and Stallybrass hold that the early texts need to be 'looked at, not seen through', asking us to focus on the 'materiality of the text' (1993: 256–7). Related to this is the fact that, thanks to the electronic revolution, eschewing modern editorial mediations in favour of (electronic facsimiles of) the early printed texts has become easier than ever before.

The resentment against the editorial tradition has resulted in arguments that traditional emendations must be unemended. These arguments are advanced on different grounds, which can be summed up as ideological, epistemological and material. According to the *ideological* case, what is perilous about traditional emendation is, to put it in a nutshell, its politics. The editor, according to Leah Marcus, colludes with the conservative, indeed, oppressive forces within the fiction of the plays. Traditional emendation in *The Tempest*, for instance, reflects 'a set of strict cultural delimitations by which the witch [Sycorax] has been kept under control';

unemending traditional emendation, by contrast, 'is to open the play once more to an unsettling, polysemous menace that Prospero and modern editors have worked very hard to contain' (Marcus 1996: 17). The same logic applies, *mutatis mutandis*, to other plays: traditional editors of *The Taming of the Shrew* can be shown 'to mime the activity of *The Shrew*'s indefatigable and autocratic tamer, Petruchio', and editors of *Hamlet* reflect the Prince's cultural elitism, constructing the play 'along the lines of Hamlet's own taste', preferring 'the highly literate over the low and suspiciously oral ... Alas, poor Yorick!' (129, 176).

Whereas the ideological approach to unemending traditional emendations takes issue with earlier editors' politics, the *epistemological* approach questions the certainty with which editors claim to have identified textual error and thus justified the need to emend. When can we be sure that a passage is corrupt? On what grounds can an editor diagnose textual error with sufficient certainty to justify emendation? As one scholar has put it, 'On what basis should we assume that "corruption is everywhere", since the only possible measure of such corruption, the authorial manuscript, is not there to be consulted?' (Holderness 2003: 83). All too often, Michael Warren maintains, the reason why editors endorse and perpetuate emendations is the weight of tradition, which, however, constitutes no valid reason to endorse an emendation where its necessity cannot be established with a sufficient degree of certainty: 'much of the Shakespeare text' is 'difficult yet intelligible and interpretable', so 'another difficulty should not immediately be discerned and dismissed as an error' (2004: 139). Moreover, 'experience of performance often reveals that what presents problems in reading may present few upon the stage' (139). Stephen Orgel has advanced a similar argument, but in his view emendation of textual obscurity should be resisted not because obscurity may turn out to be intelligible but because obscurity may be the point: 'Of course, we assume that we are, by elucidating, recovering meaning, not imposing it; but is this assumption really defensible? How do we know that the obscurity of the text was not in fact precisely what it expressed to the Renaissance audience?' (1991: 434, 436). What makes editorial emendation problematic, it has been argued, is that too many emendations are based on assumptions rather than certainty: 'Error is a risky concept; the idea of others' error is a temptation' (Warren 2004: 137–8). Therefore, 'What if, denying the editorial impulse to detect and manage error, one were to assume that the text is correct?' (130).

Related to the epistemological approach is the *materialist* approach to unediting. Its basic tenet is that all features of an early printed text (such as a Shakespeare playbook) carry meaning, which modern editing threatens to efface. In the essay in which de Grazia and Stallybrass diagnose a 'mounting resentment toward the editorial tradition', they describe 'the focus of [their] essay' as follows:

> old typefaces and spellings, irregular line and scene divisions, title pages and other paratextual matter, and textual cruxes. They constitute what we term the 'materiality of the text'. Discarded or transformed beyond recognition in standard editions, they remain obstinately on the pages of the early texts, insisting upon being looked at, not seen through. (de Grazia and Stallybrass 1993: 256–7)

Far from stripping the veil of print to recover a 'privileged "original"' behind it, this 'return to the early texts ... bars access' for the modern reader: 'The features that modernization and emendation smooth away remain stubbornly in place to block the illusion of transparency' (256).

As far as editorial practice is concerned, the materialist approach to unediting can take two forms: the one is to edit in such fashion as to preserve certain features of the early texts (such as textual cruxes which editors traditionally emend); the other is to refuse to edit at all. The latter approach is associated with Randall McLeod, who has argued that 'In the present state of Shakespearean criticism ... we must sidestep the editors' (1981: 96), and 'proposes that we use only facsimiles, and thereby force ourselves and our students to confront the material reality of Renaissance literature, the Renaissance text in its genuine cultural context' (Orgel 2002: 18).[1] Some have agreed, arguing that 'the facsimile makes these historical features available to criticism in ways that the standard modern edition occludes' (Holderness 2003: 46).

Others have continued to edit for a mass market despite their sympathy for the materialist approach to unediting. Editor of *The Tempest* and *The Winter's Tale* in the Oxford Shakespeare series, Orgel writes: 'my basic feeling as an editor is that texts aren't ideas, they are artifacts, and I want to preserve as much as I can of their archeology'. He explains that one of the ways in which this belief has affected his editorial practice is his 'stubborn refusal to emend if I can get any sense at all out of the folio' (2002: 16), which means he has refused to endorse a number of traditional editorial emendations. Marcus has similarly advocated an editorial practice that

---

[1] See also McLeod 1982.

preserves original textual features which modern editions usually efface. Arguing that in modern editions, 'inconsistencies [in the early modern text] have been normalized out of existence in the editions we use', and that modern editors thus impose 'artificial clarity', she calls for 'editions that stimulate readers to experience elements of undecidability in their reading of Shakespeare' (2007: 135, 136, 142).

***

Recent arguments in favour of more thorough editing and, more specifically, emendation start from the observation that 'there is no avoiding edited Shakespeare, the question is only what kind of editing' (Gibbons 1999: v). Shakespeare's texts had an existence before they reached print: his plays existed in manuscript as well as in staged performances, but none of his manuscripts survives (with the likely exception of a small portion of *Sir Thomas More*), nor do we have any reliable records of his plays in performance. In other words, the earliest extant form of Shakespeare's plays, namely that of printed playbooks, has already undergone editorial mediation: 'All texts of Shakespeare are editions; all have been edited; all have been mediated by agents other than the author. This complicating limitation applies as much to the earliest extant editions as to the most recent' (Taylor 1997: 1). Given the unattainability of unmediated, unedited Shakespeare, 'we can only choose which mediator(s) to accept' (3). To the charge that modern editorial intervention modifies and falsifies the document on which it is based, the response is that any editorial intervention does so, including that which led to the earliest extant printed playbooks: 'We can only read Shakespeare's discourse through the filter of earlier readers, who have "translated" – handed over, transmitted, transmuted – his texts to us' (Taylor 1997: 1). As Taylor puts it, 'To translate is, notoriously, to betray; to communicate is to corrupt. Shakespeare's texts have thus inevitably been betrayed by the very process of their transmission' (1). The refusal to edit today would thus not lead to the avoidance of textual betrayal but to the unquestioned acceptance of one instance of it, namely that of the earliest editors. In short, the uneditors' impulse is to refrain from emendation on the grounds that such intervention misrepresents textual features; those who embrace emendation hold instead that textual misrepresentation has always already been an inevitable part of editorial mediation.

That Shakespeare's early printed playbooks already contain editorial misrepresentation can be easily demonstrated by reference to typographic nonsense they sometimes contain. Andrew Murphy has commented on a useful example: 'an editor encountering the word "aud" in the text may feel reasonably confident that it should be corrected to "and," arguing that no word "aud" appears to exist in the English language, that the context requires a conjunction, and that the likely explanation for the error is that the "u" is simply a turned "n"' (2007: 103). With a word like 'aud', emendation to 'and' proceeds by reference to a textual object which included the word 'and' – the manuscript – that is no longer extant. Yet the fact that the material object to which emendation conjecturally refers no longer exists does not make it doubtful, Murphy implies, that 'aud' is a simple misprint, occasioned by an instance of 'foul case'. In a case like this, an uneditor who advocates the use of facsimiles or who refuses to emend 'aud' to 'and' on the grounds that 'texts aren't ideas, they are artifacts' thus accepts that modern readers encounter editorial misrepresentation.

Many cases are less straightforward than 'aud': 'An editor, in emending, decides that a text is diseased; such decisions may be mistaken' (Taylor 1997: 60). Even though the presence of textual corruption in early printed Shakespeare playbooks can be taken for granted, the absence of documentary evidence in which to anchor emendations means they involve conjecture. As John Jowett puts it, 'The editor's base text ... will always be flawed. The emended text, however, will always be insecurely grounded.' He recognizes that 'This unresolvable dilemma leads editors often to declare their reluctance to emend', especially when there are no 'collateral texts' (such as another early quarto edition) with which to justify an emendation (2007a: 118). Yet once it has been accepted that textual misrepresentation is always already part of a printed Shakespeare text, such reluctance may in fact be misplaced: 'the editor can make a virtue of inaction and so avoid exercising choice and judgement' (122). In other words, even in the absence of independent textual evidence, editors who embrace their task do not shrink from emending.

By evoking the authority of a document (e.g., 'Shakespeare's manuscript') that is no longer extant or intentions (e.g., 'Shakespeare's intentions') that cannot be recovered in order to justify emendation, editors expose themselves to the charge – levelled at them by uneditors – that their editorial pursuit is governed by unwarranted idealism. Yet 'the more pernicious idealism', it has been replied, is an editorial policy which aims to produce of a document no more 'than an ideal version of itself', resulting in the wilful preservation of errors whose emendation could, and should, be attempted (116).

The editors' perceived responsibility towards their readers is an important argument for interventionist editors. One of them – having quoted a passage from *All's Well That Ends Well* which appears to make little sense as it appears in the Folio – asks: 'Should we leave the passage as it stands, and let the layman or the actor flounder? Should we expect our readers to come up with something better?' (Taylor 1986: 36). Another one quotes a passage from *Coriolanus* in which 'the conjunction of metrical irregularity and defect of sense gives' a clear 'indication of error', and states: 'In these circumstances an editor would be relinquishing his or her function if the text were not emended' (Jowett 2007a: 123). A third scholar, having referred to an editorial problem in *King Lear*, states that the use of a photofacsimile has been advocated by an uneditor, adding that 'rather than solving the problem this passes it on to the reader who must decide for herself which peculiarities are error and which art' (Egan 2010: 204). De Grazia and Stallybrass lament that the materiality of the text is lost in most modern editions and advocate 'a return to the early texts' that 'bars access' for the modern reader (de Grazia and Stallybrass 1993: 256). Yet interventionist editors argue that most modern readers do not want to have textual access barred: 'Editors and readers are interested, and rightly so, in having a text that can provide a suitable initial reading experience of a work, uninterrupted by textual problems or external considerations' (Shillingsburg 1996: 37). Indeed, facilitating access to the complexities of Shakespeare's text has been argued to legitimize the labour that goes into modern editions: editors 'spend prodigious stretches of time and effort trying to determine exactly what an author wrote, so that other people, with less time to spend, can read those words, and enjoy or interpret them as they wish' (Taylor 1997: 6).

As we have seen above, one objection to emendation in the editorial tradition is that its politics are wrong and elitist. Yet the refusal to edit and a policy that 'bars access' to the modern reader have similarly been accused of elitism: 'Although [de Grazia and Stallybrass] identify themselves as inclusive and egalitarian, conferring value upon the honest labour of printshop workers, the consequence of pursuing their project is to restrict Shakespeare to a privileged group, exclusively academic and exclusionary even within the precincts of the academy' (Pechter 1997: 61–2). Those who advocate a return to the early printed texts tend to be interested in, and experts of, textual and bibliographic scholarship, but they have been criticized for their assumption that students should share that interest or acquire some of that expertise before reading Shakespeare: 'the view that editions should be abandoned in the classroom and replaced with photofacsimiles [is] an impractical suggestion for most purposes' (Jowett 2006: 17). In other words, it is legitimate for readers to want to read Shakespeare without foregrounding questions of textual or bibliographic scholarship, and uneditors fail to cater to that large part of the readership by failing to produce what Wells calls 'a workable text' (1991: 34).

While uneditors argue that we have gone too far in the removal of perceived corruption and should now unemend in order to recover the original text, there are interventionist editors at the other end of the spectrum who claim that we have not yet emended enough, that the Shakespearean text can be further improved by means of additional and better emendations. Bowers has claimed that 'just about every emendation has been proposed that is likely to be adopted', and that 'editing has largely resolved itself to the exercise of personal choice among the known alternatives' (1955: 167). Taylor has responded that Bowers's prophecy is self-fulfilling: 'If editors believe that no future emendation is likely to gain currency, they will indeed see their task as "the exercise of personal choice among the known alternatives"' (1986: 27). Instead of choosing among the known alternatives, he argues, they should try to come up with new and better readings: 'The more editors who play the game, the more competing entries posterity and the public will have to choose from, and the more likely that their eventual choice will do credit to the author' (44).

Taylor advocates 'mimetic editing', that is, the attempt 'to emend in a manner entirely characteristic of his author' (30). Here is one of his examples, from the Chorus to Act Two in *Henry V*: 'Linger your patience on, and wee'l digest / Th'abuse of distance; force a play:' (TLN 493–4). The second line is a foot short, and its end is emended by Taylor to 'force (perforce) a play', the omission of the word being explicable through simple eyeskip. The collocation 'force perforce' occurs four times in other texts by Shakespeare, and in the present line it constitutes, as Taylor has it, 'a markedly Shakespearearian emendation' which 'exactly fits the aesthetic requirements of the context, rectifies the metrical deficiency, and explains how the error occurred in the first place' (32). The dominant principle in modern practice has been that an emendation 'should be as colourless as possible', 'a false principle', according to Taylor: 'if you must insert something, it is of course better to insert something neutral than something uncharacteristic; but if you *can* find something unmistakably characteristic to fill the gap, that is even better' (29, 30, 32).

Wells has similarly argued for more liberal emendation than prevailed for much of the twentieth century. For instance, he advocates emendation of the second 'my' in 'My father dead, my fortune liues for me', to 'his' (*The Taming of the Shrew*, TLN 757), even though the line in the Folio 'conveys a kind of sense'. Yet given that 'his fortune' makes 'much better sense', Wells adds, 'I do not think we should be inhibited from adopting a superior reading by a fear that we might be improving on Shakespeare rather than on the agents of transmission' (1984: 42). Other instances where an editor may legitimately improve on Shakespeare through emendation, according to Wells, are points at which Shakespeare seems to have committed inconsistencies of plotting which are easily ironed out and where an editor may reasonably feel justified in making the correction' (48). Similarly, Wells advocates more liberal emendation when the text is metrically deficient: modern editors have become suspicious of the inclination – prominent in the eighteenth century – to regularize Shakespeare's verse, yet 'the policy of refusing to mend metre', Wells writes, 'can be, and I think has been, taken too far. We should pay our poet the compliment of assuming that he cares for metrical values, and be willing to emend when the surviving text is demonstrably deficient' (50).

In the debate over whether editors should emend less or more, either side is blaming the New Bibliography for the alleged editorial excess or deficiency in emendation. For uneditors, the New Bibliography's focus on the manuscripts from which the printed texts were set up encouraged wrong-headed emendation by speculative reference to lost documents. Conversely, it has been argued that the New Bibliography, with 'its preference for mechanical explanations', has 'undermined editorial confidence in the validity of critical judgements' of the kind required for thorough emendation (Taylor 1986: 33). As Jowett has pointed out, 'The relative claims of bibliography (founded on scholarship) and aesthetics (founded on criticism) upon the practice of emendation came into focus in A. E. Housman's attack on what he saw as the mechanical approach to textual emendation brought in by the early New Bibliography' (2007a: 124). Housman's strictures live on long after his death: 'Insofar as modern textual criticism is defensively obsessed with its own seriousness, and increasingly ambitious to raise itself to the dignity of a science, to that very degree it inhibits its own imaginative capacity to solve the problems whose existence first brought it into being' (Taylor 1986: 43). Only once we will have accepted that emendation needs to be 'creative and critical' and not simply 'bibliographical' – the argument goes – will we produce editions with sufficient, and sufficiently ingenious, emendations (34).

***

My aim in presenting what I see as two opposed orientations in the editorial reconfiguration of Shakespeare, in particular as it relates to emendation, has not been to adjudicate between them but to anatomize them. What opposes them most essentially, I have argued, is that they ask for more or less editing – and emending – respectively, and I have tried to expose the grounds on which they do so. What then is at stake in the disagreement between uneditors and interventionist editors? One way of answering this question is that the opposed answers they give to the question of how much editing we need are complementary. Those who have been calling for less editing, or unediting, advocate what Peter Shillingsburg calls 'documentary', 'sociological' and 'bibliographic' editing: 'documentary' in that the imperative is to preserve a surviving document (or at least its essential features); 'sociological' insofar as that document is not the result of singular, authorial, but of multiple, socialized, agency; and 'bibliographic' in that the makeup of the physical object matters. Those who call for more extensive editing, on the other hand, practise what Shillingsburg calls 'authorial' or 'aesthetic' editing insofar as their imperative is to produce a better text by emending corrupt, inferior readings to readings which are perceived to be in keeping with the author's intentions and style. As Shillingsburg has written:

> Adherents of documentary, sociological, and bibliographic orientations frown on the authorial and aesthetic editors for violating historical documents, or failing to accept 'actual' social phenomena. Authorial and aesthetic editors do not find the significance or integrity of historical or social texts compelling enough reasons to maintain texts that are corrupt or impure. These editorial positions are all internally coherent and viable, but no single text will satisfy the needs of all five (1996: 26).

According to Shillingsburg, there is room for more and less editing, modernized and regularized texts which fully embrace editorial intervention and facsimiles which minimize it. The resulting editions need not be better or worse; they answer different needs.

Yet there is a different and, I believe, ultimately more compelling way of framing the differences in editorial theory and practice advocated by uneditors and interventionist editors respectively. The two orientations reflect attitudes towards canonical texts and mediatory authority which go

The editorial reconfiguration of Shakespeare 311

to the heart of Catholic and Protestant beliefs during the Reformation. How the Scriptural text is best mediated to, and accessed by, readers is an issue on which people disagreed in the early modern period in terms similar to those of modern uneditors and interventionist editors of the Shakespearean text. The Protestant insistence on direct exposure to the Bible and on the recovery of Scripture in its original purity contrasted with the Catholic insistence on the need for scriptural mediation by the Church. As Elizabeth Eisenstein sums up the issue, 'Was [Scripture] meant to be made directly available to all men in accordance with the mission to spread glad tidings? Or was it rather to be expounded to the laity only after passing through the hands of priests, as had become customary over the course of centuries?' (1980: 320). What editors are for canonical literary texts, priests are for canonical Scriptural texts, both being textual mediators. 'The office proper to a priest', as Thomas Aquinas put it, 'is to be a mediator between God and the people' (1913: 299). Luther rejected the idea of priests as a group with distinct mediatory authority and believed instead in a 'priesthood of all believers' (Mullett 2004: 105), just as Shakespeare's uneditors argue we are better off by not exposing ourselves to the mediation of the clergy of textual scholarship, the editors. In his disputations with Luther, the Catholic theologian Johann Eck insisted that the true understanding of Scripture was informed by and had to be mediated through the Church (Tavard 1959: 151) – just as interventionist editors believe readers are best served by modern editorial mediation. Protestants contended 'that some Catholic beliefs and practices were based on corruptions of Scripture' (Harrison 2007: 244) – just as uneditors claim the Shakespearean text is infected with errors introduced through editorial intervention. Catholics (not unlike Shakespeare's interventionist editors) held that there was no unmediated access to the text, and that the understanding of the text had grown and improved over the centuries.

Uneditors and interventionist editors also disagree on the value of tradition (as did Protestants and Catholics): according to one view, the original texts give us the best access to Shakespeare's plays and poems, whereas the editorial tradition exposes us to the dangers of accretions which obscure and falsify the original texts instead of clarifying them. Editorial tradition, for uneditors, is thus a source of corruption, which we are called to bypass by returning to the early material text. According to the other view, what allows us to arrive at the fullest understanding of Shakespeare's plays and poems is the early quartos, octavos and folios (the original texts), combined with and enriched by that which generations of editors have done to clarify them (the editorial tradition). Here is an account by an interventionist editor of how the editorial tradition has enriched our understanding of the Shakespearean text:

> Rowe ... did successfully eliminate most of the problems of mislineation in the Folio, and he did restore sense to many passages by means of obvious emendations ... Pope ... further corrected the lineation of the seventeenth-century texts: Rowe and Pope between them are responsible for most of the relineation accepted by all modern editors ... Warburton had contributed many conjectures to Theobald's edition, and Theobald had adopted the best of them ... Dr Johnson's edition ... contains many judicious notes, which draw upon the linguistic knowledge Johnson accumulated in compiling his *Dictionary*, and upon his own considerable common sense ... In the nineteenth century ... editions made minor contributions to the text, by conjectural emendations accepted and recorded by subsequent editors, or by explications of obscure passages accepted silently by subsequent editors. (Taylor 1997: 54–5)

The parallels to Catholic and Protestant views of the transmission of divine revelation should be clear: whereas Catholic theologians recognized two distinct modes of transmission, Sacred Scripture and Sacred Tradition, Protestants argued for one mode of transmission: sola scriptura (Sykes 1963: 175).

I have argued that the contrasting attitudes to the transmission of the Shakespearean text in our own time can be understood in terms familiar from early modern theological disagreements, so much so that it is useful to think of the opposed editorial trends as 'Catholic' and 'Protestant' editing. 'Catholic' editing believes that editorial tradition leads us to a fuller understanding of the text, whereas 'Protestant' editing holds that we need to revert to the text in its original purity, without the accretions of century-old tradition. In 'Catholic' editing, editors form a scholarly clergy, and the editor is a textual priest, a figure of authority to whose care the mediation of the text to the community of faithful readers is entrusted. In 'Protestant' editing, by contrast, the textual clergy has all too often led the community of readers into error. The wisdom they preach must therefore be questioned, their accretions removed, the editorial tradition reformed.

Significantly, early modern Protestant theology and modern 'Protestant' editing are accompanied and aided by the media revolutions of their respective time: 'The advent of printing', as Eisenstein has pointed out, 'was an important precondition for the Protestant Reformation taken as a whole; for without it one could not implement a "priesthood of all believers"' (1980: 310). Similarly, unediting as advocated by McLeod and others has become possible on a large scale thanks to the wide availability of digital facsimiles. For better or for worse, the digital revolution 'is helping to increase the authority of the early quarto and folio texts' (Marcus 1996: 130). Some will welcome that this 'enables the literary form to be transmitted intact, whilst liberating its possibilities of interpretation', thus 'permitting the formulation of independent interpretation' (Holderness and Banks 1995: 336). Others will consider that editorial interventions help interpretation and that readers will be better served by fully edited texts. The question of how to reconfigure the Shakespearean text – of whether we chiefly need to emend the earliest printed texts or the modern editions – is not about to go away. The answer we give to it, individually and collectively, not only impacts on the Shakespeare texts we choose to read but also reflects our attitude towards textual mediation, authority and the value of tradition.

PART V
Editorial practices

CHAPTER 19

Full pricks and great p's: spellings, punctuation, accidentals

John Jowett

Æsops fable's / in tru Ortŏ'graphy with Gram=/mar-nóts. / He'r-vntoo ar al'so iooined the short sentenc'es / of the wýz Cato im-printed with lýk / form and order: bóth of which / Autorź ar transláted / out-of Latin in=/too E'nglish

(William Bullokar, *Aesop's Fables*, title page)

LACTANTIO
    'Most fair Duchess!' Here's an admiration point.
DUCHESS
    'The rèport of your vow shall not fear me —
LACTANTIO 'Fear me:' — two stops at 'fear me'.
DUCHESS
    'I know you're but a woman — '
LACTANTIO   'But a woman,' —
    A comma at 'woman'.
DUCHESS
    'And what a woman is a wise man knows.'
LACTANTIO 'Wise man knows.' — A full prick there.
DUCHESS
    'Perhaps my condition may seem blunt to you — '
LACTANTIO 'Blunt to you,' — a comma here again.
DUCHESS
    'But no man's love can be more sharp set — '
LACTANTIO   'Sharp set:'
    There a colon, for colon is sharp set oftentimes.
DUCHESS 'And I know
    Desires in both sexes have skill at that weapon.'
LACTANTIO
    'Skill at that weapon.' — A full prick here, at 'weapon'.
DUCHESS So, that will be enough.
    (Thomas Middleton, *More Dissemblers Besides Women*, 3.2.94–108)

The book title and the passage of play dialogue that are quoted above testify to an early modern culture that was highly conscious of the uses, misuses, and vagaries of what in this chapter are called textual ephemera and are otherwise most commonly known as accidentals. William Bullokar's 1585 title page, transcribed above with some but not all of its typographical peculiarities, demonstrates his novel system for a reformed orthography. It is a bewildering response to the variable and arbitrary nature of English spelling. The second quotation, presented in modern spelling and punctuation, shows a woman of rank dictating a love-letter to a man acting, at this moment, as her secretary. The dramatist, Thomas Middleton, exploits to the full the possibilities for innuendo offered by the terms for punctuation marks. Comedy arises from a tactical confusion of the means (the letter) and the end in view (sex). The scene suggests an almost magical potency in the skill of correct pointing. These samples of printed text suggest that spelling and punctuation are efficacious, whether towards clear meaning, or social refinement, or achieving a desired end. Both passages are rich with a sense of innovation, as individuals achieve their particular ends through their active manipulation of textual ephemera.

These ephemera include punctuation, capitalization, and spelling. As will be seen, the bracketing term, no matter whether it is 'accidentals', 'incidentals', or 'ephemera', performs a misleading act whereby different elements are subsumed under a single heading. Their common feature is that they are particularly variable, and particularly malleable in the way they are treated by authors, scribes, and compositors. But this essentially negative criterion masks key differences in the way that the different species of textual emphemera operate. The later part of this chapter will argue that, for this and other reasons, one of the most fundamental binaries in the editing of Shakespeare and other early modern texts is not sustainable.

Punctuation is, as the historian of language Vivien Salmon puts it, 'a method (albeit a very crude one) of conveying meaning which is not expressed lexically' (1962: 348). Punctuation describes the structure of utterances, identifying phrases, clauses, and sentences; it restricts the possibilities for syntactic relationships; it is suggestive of mood (interrogative, exclamatory) and of emotional tone. These small marks are therefore critical to the reader's determination and interpretation of the larger semantic units. Punctuation, which will be the main focus of the present account, has its own history. In Shakespeare's time the range of usage in formal writing was far broader than it is today, and was in transition from its earlier function of reflecting the contours of spoken language to its additional new function of defining the components of grammar (Smith 1996). George Puttenham, in his *Arte of English Poesie* of 1589, noted that punctuation was 'diuersly vsed, by diuers good writers' (sig. L2r). Some scripts were only minimally punctuated, and this was not necessarily a sign that the writing was bad. Others, more sensitive to the traditions of rhetoric, were subject to pointing whose formal significance can now be hard to understand (Graham-White 1994). In such texts, for example, colons were more widely used to establish rhetorical or structural equivalence between the separated halves. As Simpson (1911: 8) pointed out in his seminal work on the topic, the pointing in John Donne's *Poems*, as published in 1633, is both extraordinarily sensitive and, to us, unfamiliar:

> For love, all love of other sights controules,
> And makes one little roome, an every where.

Texts of the early modern period might use a comma to indicate an interrupted utterance, or simply omit any mark (Maguire). Manuscripts also contained marks that are now unfamiliar. One example is the virgule or forward slash, in medieval texts and still in some early modern texts used as an equivalent of a comma, or as a mark of a caesura in verse.

A new awareness of punctuation is expressed in the letter-writing scene in *More Dissemblers Besides Women* with which we began. Scenes such as this, or its model in George Chapman's *Monsieur d'Olive* (1606) 4.2, or Malvolio's scrutiny of Olivia's supposed 'c's, her u's, and her t's' and 'her great P's' in *Twelfth Night* 2.5.85–6, reflect an emerging awareness of the formalities of script. Members of the gentry and their secretaries were writing letters in increasing numbers to regulate their financial and family affairs. Letters needed to be clear, and they needed to communicate the originator's social standing as an important adjunct to the letter's semantic content (Daybell). Middleton in particular suggests comic correspondences based on this development: between the material sign of the written ink-marks and the imagined material referent, between the letter as vehicle for a message and the desired person to whom it is addressed, between the marking of suggestively named or suggestively shaped punctuation and sexual access. Middleton's eroticization of the *punctus* as a sexual pun depends on some sense that the presentation of the script can enrich it with a new sub-stratum of implied meaning that will enable something to happen that would not otherwise have been possible.

As such over-investment might suggest, much of the terminology was itself new. The first attempt in England to describe punctuation came in Puttenham's *Art of English Poetry*, which notes the distinction in reformed classical practice between the comma, which separated 'pieces' of speech, the colon, which separated 'members', and the period, which separated complete utterances. Puttenham understands that signification involves more than the words that constitute these larger units. Though he dedicates himself to establishing a new English practice, his recommendations derive from the classical past; the emerging terms are Anglicizations of the rhetoricians' Latin words *comma, colon, periodos*. The first fully English use of the word *comma* to refer to the punctuation mark as identified in the *Oxford English Dictionary* (n., 2a) is dated ten years later than Puttenham's *Art*, in 1599. Shakespeare uses the word only twice, in neither instance to signify the punctuation.

Though the example from *More Dissemblers* involves the agency of the writing hand, the technology of print was generating its own protocols for navigating both punctuation and spelling. Print had the effect of producing more rigorously standardized forms of knowledge (Eisenstein 1979; Johns 1998). As an inevitable consequence, print generated texts that staked their claim for authority in part by achieving greater formality of presentation. Spelling and punctuation were both caught up in this drive towards reform and standardization (Bradbrook 1964; Howard-Hill 2006). In this climate, the irregular vagaries of English spelling became a topic for widespread comment. Bullokar's reformist idea of a 'true orthography' as applied to his edition of Aesop's *Fables* is a case in point. More conventional was Peter Bales's appeal to established practice in *The Writing Schoolmaster* (1590), the second and largest part of which was named on the general title page as 'THE ORDER OF ORTHOGRAPHIE: shewing / the perfect Method to write true Orthographie in our / *English tongue, as it is now generally printed, vsed,* / and allowed of the best & most learned Writers'. Bales addresses the composer of letters, but he appeals to standards that he says are now fully established in print. His manual provides an alphabetical listing of correct forms, advising his reader:

> when you shall haue occasion to write either to your friend or otherwise, or if you will voluntairlie make triall how you haue profited therein; whe[n] a word seemeth doubtfull vnto you, (as I would aduise you to doubt verie often, till you be somewhat perfect) then search the Table of *Orthographie* by the same letter, and set downe the word as you shall finde it there written. (sig. E1v)

He attempts to impose on his inexperienced reader a degree of consistency that is not always achieved by writers or print compositors:

Aier [*sic*] and *heire*, thus: *The aire is cleere. Sonne and heire. Raine, reigne, and reines*, thus: *The raine falleth. The Queenes reigne. The reines of the back.* *To, too,* and *two*, thus: *Glorie to God. Not too little. These two rings.* (sig. E1v)

The 'Hand D' passage of *Sir Thomas More*, which is thought to be Shakespeare's hand (Jowett 2011: 437–53) comparably spells *herring* as 'hearing' and *here* as 'heare'; its ambiguous 'on on' might indicate either *on one* or *one on*, both of which make sense in the context. Shakespeare printed texts offer many examples of alternate spellings that can confuse the reader, for example, *the* and *thee*, *wright* and *write*, and indeed he echoes Bales's examples of *air* and *heir*, and *to, too,* and *two*.

Bales is instructive because he identifies an aspiration towards standardization that was widespread in a period where actual practice often failed to match that aspiration. The most immediate and literal impact of print can be seen in the surviving examples of manuscripts used directly as printers' copy and the page proofs made from them. These have valuably been catalogued and illustrated by J. K. Moore. One example may be quoted. (The transcriptions of copy followed by print are themselves standardized as regards layout.)

> **Irelande** lieth a loofe in the weast Ocean, and is demed by the later Survay, to be in lengthe welnye thre hundred myles north and South: brod from est to west one hundred and twentie. In proportion it resemblith an egg blont and playne on the sydes not reaching forthe to Sea nooke and elbows of land, as Brytan doth. (Bodleian Library, MS Jones 6, f. 7r. Moore 1992: Plate 8)

> IRELAND lieth a-loofe in the West Ocean, and is deemed by the later Survey, to be in length well-nigh three hundred miles north & south: broad from East to West one hundred and twentie. In proportion it resembleth an egge, blunt and plaine on the sides, not reaching forth to Sea, in nookes and elbowes of Land, as Britaine doth. (James Ware, *Two Histories of Ireland* (1633). Moore 1992: Plate 9)

The example is chosen to illustrate differences introduced in typesetting. It serves this purpose richly because the manuscript in question, though prepared with print in view, nevertheless happens to follow conventions that lie at some remove from those of printed texts. Yet each text proceeds according to its own logic, albeit, in the case of the quoted manuscript, without regard to what Bales called a single 'perfect Method'. Apart from one substantive variant (nooke / in nookes), both texts are free from error. Such is the everyday malleability of textual ephemera in the early modern period. The print in the quoted example is more regular, more interpretative in its punctuation, and (on the whole) more modern in both spelling and punctuation. In all these respects it lies at a further remove from the author's practices. The changes introduced by the printers fall under the heading of house style, regularization, and clarification for the reader.

A standard orthography remained a goal rather than an achievement. Printers and even individual compositors varied in their preferences, and worked under the residual spell of their copy. On the whole, however, the house style prevailed. This was the case also with punctuation. D. F. McKenzie identified persistent changes to spelling and 715 changes of punctuation between Q1 (1600) and Q2 (1619) of *The Merchant of Venice*, some of the latter haphazard, but many constituting 'deliberate normalisation' (1959: 83). Charlton Hinman (1963) demonstrated in detail the insistently compositorial punctuation of the First Folio. The compositors increased the weight of punctuation, and increased the extent of capitalization. Moreover, they would sometimes alter the spellings, not to produce standardization, but to facilitate the justification of a prose line: if a compositor needed to stretch or squeeze the type to fit the set measure of the prose column, spelling could be lengthened or shortened, punctuation could be added or subtracted (Craven 1965).

The printed text of a play therefore usually tells us little about the preferences in an underlying manuscript. This seems to be even more emphatically the case if that manuscript had first been prepared for the theatre. In theatre playbooks, relatively new ideas about syntactical logic had as yet made little impact: a dramatist such as Shakespeare would have been more concerned with the older pointing based on speech patterns and 'the sound-producing capabilities of the human body' (Smith 1996: 27). Even in this respect, however, theatre-oriented manuscripts demonstrate little need to provide a stable, formalized presentation displaying the author's command of rhetorical sophistication and subtlety (Poole 2003). It is an ironic fact that Shakespeare's actors would have encountered fewer and less consistent rhetorical markings than the later reader of the Folio. In the passage of *Sir Thomas More* thought to be in Shakespeare's hand the punctuation is strikingly light. Shakespeare writes, for example, in prose:

> nay yt has infected yt w^t the palsey, for theise basterd*es* of dung as you knowe they growe in Dvng haue infected vs, and yt is our infeccion will make the Cytty shake which p*ar*tly Coms through the eating of parsnyps
>
> (Jowett 2011: 404)

Or in verse:

> Submyt yo^u to theise noble gentlemen
> entreate their mediation to the kinge
> gyve vp yor sealf to forme obay the maiestrate
> and thers no doubt, but mercy may be found yf yo^u so seek y^t
>
> (Jowett 2011: 412)

The punctuation identifies only a selection of the syntactic breaks, on an apparently almost random basis. For instance, in the first passage no pointing marks off the parenthesis 'as you knowe they growe in Dvng', and syntactic logic or even speech-rhythm might have precipitated a comma after 'shake', where there is both a break in syntax and a shift in tone. As in some other play manuscripts (the practice is highly variable), the ends of speeches are consistently unstopped; thus the end of a speech is itself a grammatical end-mark. The second passage shows that the ends of verse lines were also usually given no punctuation. The line-break itself implies at least the possibility of a pause. Spellings too can be highly idiosyncratic: searches of the database *Early English Books Online* indicate that 'parsnyp[s]' is without known parallel in the printed literature of the period, 'basterde' and 'sealf' are extremely rare. 'Cytty' is also rather unusual. If Shakespeare himself elsewhere wrote this form, it nowhere survives in a printed text. Hand D used capitals relatively sparsely. As is common in play manuscripts, the beginnings of verse lines are in lower case. The choice of words for capitals lacks consistency: the first instance of 'dung' is without capital, the second with, and it looks as though the capitalization of 'Cytty' might have prompted Shakespeare to make the next 'c' at the beginning of a word likewise a capital – though in Hand D and other scripts 'c' is more commonly capitalized than other letters.

Sir Thomas More was not printed in the period, so we are denied the opportunity to make the kind of comparison in relation to this text we have already undertaken with James Ware. However, examination of the printed texts of other Shakespeare plays shows that capitalization at the beginning of a verse line was normal in print, that the majority of verse lines attracted some form of punctuation at the end, and that the overall complexion of spellings and punctuation was far more regular than it is in *Sir Thomas More*. But this broad description covers a wide range of practice. Occasionally a printed text preserves an authorial lightness and irregularity of punctuation reminiscent of Hand D:

> Much deseru'd on his part and equally remembred
> by don Pedro he hath borne himselfe beyond the promise of

> his age, doing in the figure of a lamb, the feats of a lion, he hath
> indeed better bettred expectation then you must expect of me
> to tell you how.
>
> (*Much Ado About Nothing* 1.1.12–17; Q1 1600, sig. A2)

Thus the 1600 First Quarto of *Much Ado About Nothing*. The comma after 'lamb', one of only three in the passage, tellingly demarcates the two elements in a euphuistic oxymoron 'the figure of a lamb, the feats of a lion'. When the play was reprinted in the 1623 First Folio the speech appeared with this comma intact:

> Much deseru'd on his part, and equally remem-
> bred by Don *Pedro*, he hath borne himselfe beyond the
> promise of his age, doing in the figure of a Lambe, the
> feats of a Lion, he hath indeede better bettred expecta-
> tion, then you must expect of me to tell you how.
>
> (Hinman 1968: TLN 16–20)

But three further commas are carefully added to clarify the structure of the speech. One of them, after 'expectation', would not be expected in modern pointing but is normal within the practices of the early seventeenth century. The capital in 'Don', italics in '*Pedro*', and capitalized 'Lion' and 'Lambe' are other tokens of a more formal, regular, and reader-conscious style of presentation. Clearly, there is no truth in the common assumption (as argued, for example, by Don Weingust) that the Folio is a useful guide to Shakespeare's own pointing.

To generalize, the interventions of print would be more strongly marked when, as is often the case with Shakespeare, the manuscript was prepared without specific aim to provide printer's copy. In print, as has been shown, punctuation was likely to regularize, and to consolidate the syntactic form of a speech or sentence. But the pointing of manuscripts was highly variable, and if there were distinctive literary forms of punctuation in a printer's manuscript copy they might well survive into print. Demonstrably influenced by the preferences of compositors though it is (Jackson 1975), the 1609 First Quarto Shakespeare's Sonnets nevertheless exemplifies a recurrent Renaissance aspiration to express complex syntactical and rhetorical relationships through intensely careful pointing (Sherman 2013). In this case, clean and carefully presented copy might have been respected by the compositors, as was evidently the case with Donne's *Poems* as mentioned above. Despite the overwhelming influence of the compositors' preferences in the Shakespeare First Folio, the influence of the copy sometimes shows through. In *Loves Labour's Lost*, where the quarto of 1598 has:

> I do affect the verie ground (which is base) where her
> shoo (which is baser) guided by her foote (which is basest)
> doth tread. I shall be forsworne (which is a great argument
> of falsehood) if I loue. (sig. B3v)

– the Folio sets:

> I doe affect the very ground (which is base)
> where her shooe (which is baser) guided by her foote
> (which is basest) doth tread. I shall be forsworn (which
> is a great argument of falshood) if I loue.
> (Hinman 1968: TLN 470–73)

The compositor's fidelity to the distinctive use of parentheses is here absolute. By inference, such is the case also when the printer's copy is a lost manuscript. Unusually abundant and sometimes idiosyncratically positioned parentheses in a particular Folio text indicate a feature of the manuscript behind it. They are one of a number of characteristics seen in some plays indicating that the printer's copies were transcripts prepared in the distinctive hand of Ralph Crane, a scribe who worked for the King's Men in the years around 1619–23 (Howard-Hill 2006; Werstine). *The Tempest* is an example of a play set directly from manuscript that was almost certainly in Crane's hand:

> Me (poore man) my Librarie
> Was Dukedome large enough: of temporall roalties
> He thinks me now incapable. Confederates
> (so drie he was for Sway) with King of *Naples*
> To giue him Annuall tribute, doe him homage
> Subiect his Coronet, to his Crowne and bend
> The Dukedom yet vnbow'd (alas poore *Millaine*)
> To most ignoble stooping.
> (Hinman 1968: TLN 207–14)

These parentheses can be dissociated from both the Folio compositors and Shakespeare as author; they reflect Crane's practice. Here, as often in Crane, the words in brackets are not parenthetic in the sense of being incidental to the main text. They are important phrases. In grammatical terms they form subordinate elements within a complex sentence structure. In rhetorical terms they delineate complex and shifting thought.

Copies of Crane's workmanship survive in his manuscripts of plays such as Thomas Middleton's *The Witch* and *A Game at Chess*, and John Fletcher's *Barnauelt*. These provide a firm basis on which to assess his characteristics. His style of orthography was influenced by the classicizing example of Ben

Jonson. Crane evidently prepared highly literary transcripts – that is to say, manuscripts prepared with elegant formality for the reader rather than for theatrical use. *The Witch*'s dedication to a patron called Thomas Holmes confirms its status as a literary manuscript. In the case of the Folio plays it is more likely that Crane was preparing copy specifically for the setting of the plays in print, as Jonson had done for the 1616 Folio of his works. He nevertheless followed his usual habit in adopting the characteristics of a 'literary' manuscript. The compositors responded to the elaborate style manifest in Crane's manuscripts by preserving some of its key features.

We may therefore advance two propositions. First, the general complexion of punctuation and spellings in early Shakespeare printed texts simply does not reflect that of the authorial manuscripts. Second, the texts in which the punctuation and spellings of the copy show through in the printed text most clearly and persistently are precisely those in which the immediate printer's copy has conspicuously departed from the practices of Shakespeare as author and the usages observed in manuscripts of the theatre, as characteristics more typical of a 'literary' manuscript are imposed by a copying scribe such as Crane.

With these propositions in mind, we may now turn from early modern practice to the issues confronting modern editors who determine the form in which the text is presented to the reader. The most common editorial convention is to alter Shakespeare's spelling and punctuation to their modern equivalents. There is a major trade-off here between texture and clarity, between the typographical actuality of the copy-text and the meanings it represents. The authenticity of the original is surrendered in order to make the text more intelligible to its readers. Original spelling and punctuation are deemed distancing, difficult, and potentially misleading. As was demonstrated in the passage quoted from the quarto and Folio *Much Ado*, this has always been the case: the history of editing from the earliest printings onwards shows an incremental evolution in an attempt to keep pace with the standards that apply at the time. Centuries of editors behaved in much the same way as the original compositors. Mostly, this was taken as a self-evident procedure, and, as with any practice grounded in common sense, it was not applied systematically. Archaisms of spelling remained. Even today, reputable editions can be purchased that will have early modern *murther, wrack, alablaster*, and *porpentine* where the current equivalents are *murder, wreck, alabaster*, and *porcupine*.

In preparing the 1986 Oxford Shakespeare *Complete Works*, Stanley Wells pointedly objected to the inconsistencies in this editorial tradition (Taylor and Wells 1979; Wells 1984). Drawing carefully but critically on the documentation of the *Oxford English Dictionary*, he sought to discriminate more rigorously between words as lexical items and the variety of forms in which words existed historically. The procedure can be justified on theoretical grounds by recognizing that any editorial practice needs to take account not only of the original materials and any intent that may lie behind them, but also the interests of the reader as recipient of the editorial outcome. Absolute consistency is a challenge that is unlikely to be met in full. Jürgen Schäfer argued for consistent modernization of names, typically those in a foreign language; but, as will be recognized by anyone unfamiliar with Rosenkranz and Gyldenstierne, characters in a play set in what is today called Helsingør, any such project remains incomplete. It may well never be fully accomplished, not least because the modern form of a Shakespearian name is often actually *less* familiar than its early modern equivalent. In other situations too, modernization is often not a straightforward process. Shakespeare's own spellings were so variable that within a few lines of the Hand D section of *Sir Thomas More* the recurring word *sheriff* is given a different spelling at each occurrence: 'Shreiff', 'shreef', 'shreeve', 'Shrieue', and 'Shreue'. There is, moreover, a question as to the modern word equivalent to these forms; it might be monosyllabic *shrieve*, as all these forms suggest, rather than disyllabic but more familiar *sheriff* (Jowett 2011: 470–2).

Language is in a state of constant change. Word boundaries shift, divide, merge. The modern edition, benefiting from dictionaries that had no equivalent in Shakespeare's day, imposes a fixity of meaning that did not then pertain. The form 'inhumane' could represent the meanings that are now dispersed between the two words *inhuman* and *inhumane*, 'ere' could be realized today as either *e'er* (ever) or *ere* (before), 'reverent' could be equivalent to *reverent* or *reverend*, 'perillous' has in certain contexts evolved into *parlous*, and 'carnall' might be, in modern terms, *charnel* – or, rather, carry suggestions of both this word and *carnal*. An ambiguous form such as 'sonne', which could stand for *son* or *sun*, could operate as a kind of pre-loaded pun, as, famously, in the opening lines of *Richard III*.

A hostile critique of modernization would argue from such evidence that the early modern forms have a fluidity of signification that is belied by the standardized, modernized text. The difficulty for the reader, however, is that the range of signification that applies in a given case is not indicated by the form printed on the page or viewed on the screen. In modern Shakespeare editing, spelling and punctuation are things that are regarded as superficial and transitory. They are formations and ink marks that are suppressed, on the assumption that they bear trivial information that, if presented as in the early printed texts, would obstruct the present-day reader's understanding of the text. They are therefore replaced with modern normalized forms, with what should be a careful regard to the balance between loss and gain (Bevington 2004). Such an editorial process demands some way of differentiating between those features that are to be preserved and those features that are to be normalized to present-day usage.

Paradoxically, modernizing editors draw on a distinction that was first articulated as part of a rationale for establishing old-spelling editions. In the most influential statement on the subject, W. W. Greg urges a:

> distinction between the significant, or as I shall call them 'substantive', readings of the text, those namely that affect the author's meaning or the essence of his expression, and others, such in general as spelling, punctuation, word-division, and the like, affecting mainly its formal presentation, which may be regarded as the accidents, or as I shall call them 'accidentals', of the text. (1950–51: 21)

He refers to the accidentals as constituting no more than the 'general texture' of a text (25). There is a pragmatic pessimism in this: an editor of an old-spelling edition needed a copy text; the copy text should logically reflect the author's preferences as far as possible; but in reality a specific printing would retain little of the authorial texture. Greg saw the grounding of the edited text in the original edition that was closest to the author's manuscript as a necessity. An overall adherence to the copy created the risk that corrections and revisions introduced in later editions would be rejected. The 'Rationale' was designed to afford an escape from this potential 'tyranny of the copy-text' (26) so that the editor could be as receptive to later 'substantive' readings as the circumstances allowed. His overall aim was to enable the editor's text to draw eclectically on collateral texts, on the assumption that any substantive text was an imperfect witness to a single underlying version.

Greg's distinction between 'substantives' and 'accidentals' depends on two assumptions. The first is that words, as 'substantives' and bearers of significance, are fixed, stable, and determinate entities that can effectively be contrasted with the alternative term 'accidentals'. The second is that signification itself can be decomposed into the sequential operation of these words as a self-sustaining string of verbal signs. Neither assumption is properly valid. Especially when viewed, as is presupposed, in their historical dimension, words are not fixed, stable, and determinate entities. And textual ephemera are far from empty of semiotic significance. For reasons that will be explained, the *formal* character of accidentals as an aggregate of 'spelling, punctuation, word-division, and the [unspecified] like' does not match up with their supposed *functional* character as a casual background of 'general texture' that is separable from signification.

Shakespeare editors usually aim to alter the 'accidentals' to modern form whilst preserving the 'substantives'. The terminology is Greg's, but the practice is much older. Modern Shakespeare editors who proceed in this way are following in a traditional distinction that goes back to Joseph Moxon's *Mechanick Exercises* of 1683–84:

> *For by the Laws of* Printing, *a* Compositor *is strictly to follow his* Copy, *viz. to observe and do just so much and no more than his* Copy *will bear him out for; so that his* Copy *is to be his Rule and Authority: But the carelesness of some good Authors, and the ignorance of other Authors, has forc'd* Printers *to introduce a Custom, which among them is look'd upon as a task and duty incumbent on the* Compositor, *viz. to discern and amend the bad* Spelling *and* Pointing *of his* Copy, *if it be English*. (Moxon 1962: 192)

Moxon's formulation needs to be understood in the context of the late seventeenth-century professionalization of trades whereby they staked their claim as the 'mechanick' arm of the new science. A member of the Royal Society from 1678 to 1682, Moxon was a publisher of popular scientific treatises and technical handbooks designed to raise the skills of craftsmen. In the Preface to *Mechanick Exercises* he defined himself as a 'typographer' in the specific sense of one who *'can direct others to perform from the beginning to the end, all the Handy-works and Physical Operations relating to* Typographie'. He compares his elevated notion of the trade, in contrast to the humble carpenter or mason, with the new profession of architect (11–12). He accordingly needs to make strong distinctions in order to enable a consistent practice. One crucial distinction is that between the elements of the text that are to be faithfully transmitted and those that are to be subjected to systematic alteration. His formulation can be understood, in terms of the Gregian New Bibliography, to mean that the compositors are responsible for preserving the substantives as the realm of authorial intention, whereas they standardize the accidentals as the realm in which the book presents the text to the reader.

Moxon maintains a tactically idealized viewpoint. He assumes that there existed an accepted standard to which spelling and pointing could be amended. As Moxon's editors Herbert Davis and Harry Carter point out, it was only after about 1650 that spellings were sufficiently standardized for particular instances to be judged 'right' or 'wrong' (Moxon 1962: 381; cf. Dobson 1968: 2.1011 ff.). The word *spelling* made its symptomatic leap to its usual modern sense at this time (the *Oxford English Dictionary*'s first instance of it is dated *c*.1661). Nevertheless, in the decades before Samuel Johnson's 1755 *Dictionary of the English Language* the identification of the right spelling often remained an intuitive matter. Moxon offers guidance on punctuation only by referring vaguely to the 'many School-books' that teach the rules (1962: 215).

Greg appropriated Moxon's formalization of the early modern typographer's craft in order to apply it to his own formalization of the twentieth-century quasi-scientific craft of eclectic editing. Greg's is a kind of faux-conservatism as regards accidentals, for he recognizes that before about 1650 scribes and compositors would 'normally follow their own habits or inclination' (1950–51: 22). Although the first printing will, inevitably, be closer to the manuscript than are the subsequent reprints from that printing, the degree of proximity is nevertheless quite small. Greg, as if pondering on the discrepancy between Moxon's formulation and the practice he has observed in earlier printed texts, wonders passingly whether it might be justifiable to establish some kind of early modern standard of spellings (21). He quickly moves away from this idea, but it offers a telling glimpse into his frustration with the printers' failure either to reflect copy or to impose a consistency on it of the kind urged by Moxon.

The equivalence between Moxon's and Greg's treatment of textual ephemera is far from exact. Indeed, Moxon provides a better guide to editors of modern-spelling editions than he does to old-spelling editors seeking to follow Greg in treating accidentals and substantives differently. Standardization as recommended by Moxon and 'modernization' as described by Wells amount to very much the same thing: both bring the text up to date in terms of current notions of consistency. For Moxon, textual ephemera are a sphere of authorial variability and inexactness in the copy. For Greg, however, they represent a sphere of compositorial overlay in the print. An editor of an original-spelling text is not in the same position as Moxon. Where Greg was arguing for the preservation of 'accidentals' in order to facilitate the potential emendation of 'substantives', Moxon demanded that it was the substantives that should be preserved, and the accidentals that should be altered.

Moxon, however, does not refer to 'accidentals' but to 'Spelling *and* Pointing'. As already noted, Greg's 'accidentals' do not make up a coherent category of correlatable elements. Any affinity between punctuation, spellings, and other forms of accidentals is based on no more than a convenient negation: a negation that may be expressed as 'not "meaning" but mere "formal presentation" or "background to meaning"'. This negation identifies features whose only commonality lies in what the gathered items supposedly *do not* do: they *are not* words, and so in their original form *are removed from* or *are routinely altered in* modern-spelling editions. It is this, and only this, that they have in common. Yet the field of punctuation is so saturated with the responsibility of meaning and the consequent problematic of error that Fredson Bowers introduced the intermediate term 'semi-substantives' to negotiate it (1990: 85). Inevitably, punctuation supplements words in the determination of meaning; that is why it is there. In contrast, the concept of spellings entails at least an assumption that meaning is unaffected. If, as has been demonstrated, this assumption needs to be viewed and qualified historically, it remains the case that the term 'spellings' implies a suite of variable forms that a single lexical item might assume without fundamentally altering its function.

Record-worthy matters of accidence are not 'merely' matters of 'dress'. Some of them at least are so far implicated in signification that Greg's distinction, when pressed, cannot hold up. Yet that distinction is unnecessary – except, that is to say, to the specific Gregian project of eclectic editing. The alternative is to speak only of 'emendations', and therefore to record alike the source of every altered reading, whether traditionally regarded as 'accidental' or 'substantive'. This would eliminate the most vulnerable of the category boundaries that editors usually observe. To be clear, this more inclusive category of 'emendations' would apply only to such changes as are necessary to establish a text in original spelling and punctuation. Spellings cannot be emended; but 'substantive' words can, and so can 'accidental' (or 'semi-substantive') punctuation. The extent to which punctuation *should* be emended in the context of that real or imaginary old-spelling edition is another matter. Editors are not modern Moxons; a single standard of early modern correctness cannot apply. The case for an original-spelling edition depends on it being sensitive to the features that modernization routinely standardized, and that means reducing the scope for error of punctuation to the exceptional cases where the text fails to maintain its own standards of consistency. The most significant borderline in editing Shakespeare lies not between accidentals and substantives. That borderline lies between the changes made (whether in reality or merely in principle) to establish an original-spelling text, and the further changes that fall under the heading of modernization.

CHAPTER 20

Divided Shakespeare: configuring acts and scenes

Alan C. Dessen

Although taken for granted by most readers, the division of Shakespeare's plays into acts and scenes has a tangled history. In his massive study T. W. Baldwin has charted the history of five-act structure from Roman times to the Elizabethans and has argued for the presence of such organizational thinking in the Shakespeare canon. However, act divisions are not to be found in any of the eighteen quartos published during Shakespeare's lifetime (the only exception before the 1623 First Folio is the 1622 Quarto of *Othello* that signals formal breaks for Acts 2, 4, and 5). Such pauses in the onstage action were standard practice in private theaters like the Blackfriars and, according to Gary Taylor, this procedure migrated to public theaters after 1610, but, if printed texts are to be the evidence, plays at the Globe and comparable outdoor venues before that date were designed to be played from start to finish with no such breaks. By 1623, the fashion had changed so that readers might have expected five-act division in printed play texts and would have encountered twenty-eight of the thirty-six Folio plays divided into five acts and two others partly divided.

Editors since 1623, following the precedent of Renaissance editions of Roman comedy, have therefore supplied act divisions for many plays not composed with such breaks in mind (exceptions include editions of non-Shakespeare plays such as *Friar Bacon and Friar Bungay*, *The Shoemakers' Holiday*, and *A Woman Killed with Kindness*). The poster child for the pitfalls of arbitrary act division is *Pericles*, where such breaks first appeared in the Third Folio (1664) and were codified a century later by Edmond Malone, who (following the example of Folio *Henry V*) argued that 'the poet seems to have intended that each act should begin with a chorus' (1790: 92). However, as pointed out by Suzanne Gossett: 'The act divisions are not an editorial improvement' (2004: 82), for Gower's eight appearances actually divide the script into seven, not five, sections. Although such editorial intervention may elsewhere be less visible, James Hirsh has argued that the Folio act divisions 'were not based on the actual dramatic structure of each play' and therefore 'have profoundly misled readers' and that subsequent editorial divisions have furthered such confusion by suggesting 'that the end of an act marks the culmination of a large-scale and particularly significant dramatic movement or development' or 'that the scenes grouped together within an act form a distinct, unified, and particularly meaningful structural unit' (1981: 255–6).

Dividing a play into scenes can be even more problematic, for, although scholars agree that a clearing of the stage initiates a new scene, such divisions can generate problems and anomalies. The most rigorous analysis of scenic division is provided by James Hirsh, who argues: 'The continuity of a play is not broken, and hence a scene division does not occur, unless the stage is cleared of all living characters'; similarly, 'even if the stage is technically cleared for a moment', a new scene does not occur 'if either the exiting or the entering characters express awareness of the presence of the other group'; however, 'a break between scenes occurs even if the location of the second of two consecutive episodes is the same as the first and no discernible fictive time has elapsed between the episodes'. Moreover, in his formulation: 'If two sets of characters occupy the stage at the same time they belong to the same *dramatic scene* even if they are unaware of one another's presence and, furthermore, even if they are in separate fictive locations' (211). By these yardsticks, Prologues and Epilogues constitute individual scenes, as do groups that pass over the stage without any accompanying dialogue, and the battle sequence in what is traditionally *Cymbeline* 5.2 becomes five scenes, with the opening stage direction (in which the two armies appear and *exeunt*, then Iachimo and Posthumus enter and fight) counting as two.

Elsewhere, scholars such as Mark Rose and Emrys Jones have dealt tellingly with what has been termed *scenic design*, while in their 'unit analysis' Charles and Elaine Hallett argue that 'the designated scenes are not *always* units of action' and therefore invoke the term *sequence*, which 'is always an action, propelled in a discernible direction by the desires, goals, and objectives of its characters' (1991: 3, 5). In this formulation, a complex scene (e.g., the famous tavern scene in *Henry IV, Part 1*) may consist of several sequences, whereas a sequence (e.g., the build up to the death of Macbeth) may consist of several scenes.

As with act division, few plays linked to the public theaters and published during Shakespeare's life provide signals for scene division other than an *exit-exeunt* that clears the stage, though Jonson, who prefers to signal a new scene at the entrance of a new character, is a notable exception. The term *scene* can have a range of meanings and need not be linked to a clearing of the stage, whereas the few extant 'plots', backstage documents for use during a performance, divide the play into boxes rather than scenes. As Tiffany Stern notes, 'a box is not so much a dramatic unit as a unit of stage occupancy' that defines 'when the stage is empty and when it is full'. Information within the box signals only 'what is happening onstage, not off it', though 'the line along the bottom of the box' can represent 'any moment, scenic or not, at which everyone leaves the stage' (2009a: 211).

Also to be factored in is the practice found in pre-1580s plays, an alternative to the classical five acts or even the clearing of the stage to denote a distinct scene break. Here the key often was not scenic logic but theatrical exigency linked to performances by troupes of four to eight actors. Some of these plays do follow the familiar pattern. The best known of these items, Thomas Preston's *Cambyses* (1561), is scripted for eight actors so that, with no severe limits on personnel, the playwright clears the stage seven times to generate eight scenes.[1] Another play with recognizable scenes is Thomas Lupton's *All for Money* (1577), perhaps performed by only four actors, where the playgoer encounters not the typical through-line narrative dominated by a Vice but five discrete units, each of which demonstrates the primacy of money in contemporary society. For example, in a lengthy trial sequence in which corrupt petitioners get what they want from All for Money, he and Sin the Vice remain onstage while single litigants repeatedly exit and enter, thereby enabling two quick-changing actors to play many parts.

However, most of the play texts in this category display a more pragmatic approach to divisions to the extent that the *scene* category is no longer useful. In Ulpian Fulwell's *Like Will to Like* (1568), scripted for five actors, the roughly 1,275 lines contain three clearings of the stage to produce four scenes, but two of those scenes, dominated by the Vice Nichol Newfangle, add up to almost 1,100 lines. Of the roughly 1,450 lines in William Wager's *Enough is as Good as a Feast* (1560), scripted for seven actors, two key scenes with much coming and going contain 1,130 lines. In George Wapull's *The Tide Tarrieth No Man* (1576), scripted for four actors, Courage the Vice starts the play solus and stays there for roughly 750 of the play's 1,800 lines. Here a rationale linked to exigency is particularly clear when Wapull calls for onstage violence '*to prolong the time*' (1214) while an actor offstage is

---

[1] I am omitting the Prologues (some of them of considerable length) from these calculations.

making a difficult costume change. In such plays, with their small casts and an abundance of dramatis personae, a clearing of the stage has little to do with dramatic structure. Rather, practical theatrical demands trump rigid scenic logic.

The widely used scenic breakdowns found in most of today's editions do not rigorously follow the cleared-stage yardstick. Most obvious are several moments in *Romeo and Juliet*: the Capulet ball, regularly denoted as 1.5, is a continuation of 1.4 in that Romeo and his fellow masquers have not left the stage; and the Balcony Scene in most editions remains 2.2 but Romeo is on stage during 2.1 and stays there to begin the next scene (and his first line forms a couplet with Benvolio's final line in 2.1).[2] A less familiar example is found in *Henry VI, Part 1*, 4.3–4.4 as presented in most modern editions. With York '*and many Soldiers*' on stage (4.3.0), a figure later identified as Sir William Lucy enters to urge the rescue of Talbot beleaguered at Bordeaux. After York rejects the plea and exits, Lucy stays on stage to deliver a seven-line speech on 'the vulture of sedition' (47–53), at which point most editors indicate a new scene at the entrance of '*Somerset with his Army*' (4.4.0 in the Riverside). Somerset also quickly rejects the pleas on behalf of Talbot by a Captain and Lucy. The point behind the rejections of the parallel pleas is evident, for clearly Talbot is undone (unhistorically) by the internal divisions within the English forces, not by the prowess of the French. To establish this point emphatically, the playwright plays fast and loose with a neoclassic sense of place or scene division by having one figure (Lucy) provide two parallel pleas and a soliloquy in between without leaving the stage, while the York-army and Somerset-army are moved on and off. Concern for what I term *geographical realism* has been superseded not just by dramatic economy but also by a kind of symmetry of action, a parallel construction that makes the central point unmistakable. The thesis ('the vulture of sedition') trumps both verisimilitude and traditional scenic logic.[3]

---

[2] Also of interest (but perhaps the result of omitted mid-scene exits and entrances), is the situation in the First Quarto *Romeo and Juliet* (1597), where there is no signal for Romeo to exit at the end of the balcony scene, so that in this text (described on its title page as 'often (with great applause) plaid publiquely') he stays on stage from the beginning of Act 2 to the end of his scene with the Friar (2.3).

[3] In his Arden 2 edition Andrew Cairncross provides a scene break but argues in his note to 4.4.0 that 'Lucy does not leave the stage and return' but rather 'remains on stage, aside' (96). The Arden 3 editor Edward Burns breaks with editorial tradition by treating the sequence as a single scene (4.3) though retaining '[4.4]' in the right margin at Somerset's entrance. In his note to line 53 (239) he observes that by sidestepping 'the customary two [scenes], I may violate geographical probability, but this would be unlikely to trouble the original audience of the play, and it does produce a more cogent and emblematically telling shape to the scene, an option taken in the 1977 RSC production'.

A good test case is provided by Act 4 of *Henry IV, Part 2*. A survey of ten editions published between 1965 and 2007 reveals that editors have divided this act in two, three, or five scenes (the latter choice is the traditional one, an approach that does not observe the cleared-stage criterion).[4] Clearly, at the end of what is regularly designated 4.1, the rebel forces do not leave the stage but are joined by Prince John so that there is no reason, other than tradition, for a scenic break on the page to indicate a new scene, 4.2. At London's Bankside Globe in 2010, director Dominic Dromgoole chose not to clear the stage; rather, as in *Romeo and Juliet*, 1.4–1.5, the rebel group marched around a stage post while Prince John and his troops entered on the other side. Of my ten editions, two (New Cambridge, RSC Shakespeare) present the traditional 4.3 (Falstaff's encounter with Coleville) as part of an extended 4.1 so as to have only two scenes in Act 4; three (Folger, Oxford Wells–Taylor, Oxford World's Classics) treat Falstaff–Coleville as a separate scene and have three scenes in the act; the remaining five editions have the traditional five scenes.

Especially problematic is the final appearance of the dying Henry IV, a sequence traditionally divided into two scenes, 4.4 and 4.5, but presented without a break in both quarto and Folio. First, the ailing king enters to get reports (about Prince Hal and victories over the rebel forces) and then swoons. When he recovers, Henry instructs: 'I pray you take me up, and bear me hence / Into some other chamber' (4.4.131–2), at which point most editors, in keeping with long-standing practice, have indicated a new scene (4.5) and inserted a stage direction to indicate some movement of the ailing figure. What follows is the placing of the crown upon the pillow; Prince Hal's taking of that crown; the king's chastising of his son; and the reconciliation and final advice. At the end of the sequence, the king asks Warwick: 'Doth any name particular belong / Unto the lodging where I first did swound?' and gets the reply: ''Tis called Jerusalem, my noble lord.' Henry IV's final words then close the scene:

> Laud be to God! Even there my life must end.
> It hath been prophesied to me many years,
> I should not die but in Jerusalem,
> Which vainly I suppos'd the Holy Land.
> But bear me to that chamber, there I'll lie.
> In that Jerusalem shall Harry die.   (4.5.232–40)

---

[4] My list includes the Signet (1965); Arden 2 (1966); Oxford *Complete Works* (1986); New Cambridge (1989); revised Riverside (1997); Oxford World's Classics (1997); Folger (1999); revised Pelican (2002); Bevington (2004); and RSC Shakespeare (2007).

The group of figures then *exeunt* and Shallow, Falstaff, and others enter to begin 5.1.

Of interest here are (1) how editors treat the putative 4.4–4.5 break on the page; (2) what stage directions they insert; and (3) what if any adjustments are made to the final *exeunt*. Five of my editions indicate a new scene; of these, two do not supply a note or gloss (Riverside, revised Pelican), whereas three (Bevington, Signet, Arden 2) do provide some explanation. For example, in an appendix, the Arden 2 editor notes that the action is unbroken in both 4.4–4.5 as in 4.1–4.2 'even though it envisages a change of place from the Jerusalem chamber (where the King swoons), to some other, and back again. To convey the King out and in again, interrupting his speech, is wrong' (Arden 2: 240).

Three of the five editions that have no scenic break provide notes: 'Many editions begin a new scene at this point' (Folger: 186–7); 'Q and F clearly envisage the action to be continuous. There are no stage directions in QF to signal exits, and no new scene is signalled, but the King is clearly intended to be in a notionally different location when he speaks at l. 137' (Oxford World's Classics: 238); 'most editors since 1864 introduce exit and entrance directions and begin here a new scene, though the continuity is obvious in spite of the change of locale' (New Cambridge: 157).

As to stage directions, nine of the editors (the exception is the RSC Shakespeare) provide their version of the wording in the Riverside at line 132: '*The king is carried to one side of the stage and placed on a bed*' (the presence of a bed is keyed to the king's 'Come hither, Harry, sit thou by my bed' at 4.5.181). The staging of this 4.4–4.5 sequence has varied in recent productions. At the Swan in 2000, Royal Shakespeare Company director Michael Attenborough took the Gordian knot approach and cut 'I pray you take me up, and bear me hence / Into some other chamber', so that all the action took place around the same bed (the later reference to the Jerusalem chamber remained). At the London Globe in 2010, director Dominic Dromgoole cleared the stage for 4.4–4.5 so that the king was taken off, a huge bed was thrust on, and Henry re-entered from the center in a coughing fit. At the 2011 Oregon Shakespeare Festival, director Lisa Peterson kept her actors on stage but had a bed emerge from a trapdoor; similarly, in the 2007 Royal Shakespeare Company production at the Courtyard, director Michael Boyd started 4.4 with Henry IV in a wheelchair, then signaled a change of room by having a bed brought in with the wheelchair placed next to it. At the National Theatre in 2005 director Nicholas Hytner initially placed Henry IV in a wheelchair, but then with difficulty he was moved to a bed that was brought in, with some movement about the stage to establish a sense of a second room.

What is at stake here is a potential collision between the fluid staging of the original performances and the rigor of subsequent assumptions about scene division, clearing of the stage, and changes in locale. In an appendix (241), the Arden 2 editor notes: 'How the scene was arranged originally is not clear. The essential movements are (a) entrance (or disclosure) of the King at IV.iv.1; (b) transport without break of action at IV.iv.132 (from one part of the stage to another); and (c) re-transport at IV.v.239–40 to the spot where the King swooned' (none of the other editors posits a 're-transport'). My question is: what happens if (1) Henry IV, if not already seated, around line 110 would collapse into a sick-chair (a portable property regularly found in the Shakespeare canon);[5] (2) at his command ('take me up, and bear me hence / Into some other chamber') he is helped from that chair across the large platform stage to a bed that is thrust on so that in this 'other chamber' as defined by this physical displacement he would have his interview with Prince Hal; (3) the chair stays in its original position (later identified as the Jerusalem Chamber); and (4) the king's eventual exit is not towards the chair but in another direction.

Given such a staging, consider the added effect for a playgoer in the 1590s of the scene's closing lines devoted to Jerusalem. The king's query about 'the lodging where I first did swoon' makes good literal sense to the reader but can have a greater impact upon a playgoer, especially if a gesture from either the king or Warwick ("Tis called Jerusalem') to that part of the stage (perhaps defined by a visible sick-chair) vacated when Henry was carried to 'some other chamber' reminds that playgoer of the close proximity of 'Jerusalem'. In my reconstruction, however, the spectator would see a king who orders 'bear me to that chamber' so as to die 'in Jerusalem' but is then carried not to the place where he 'first did swoon' but rather to an adjacent stage door and off the stage. The playgoer is not shown or told whether or not Henry IV achieves his 'Jerusalem' before his death. Rather, the king is seen taken off in a direction away from the area now, *ex post facto*, defined as 'Jerusalem'; as a result, we recognize that, moments earlier, he had been where he most wanted to be but did not know it. My suggested ironic staging may be conjectural, but the question remains: to what extent do post-Elizabethan notions of scene division and 'place' blur or eliminate potentially meaningful images available to the original playgoers?

---

[5] See my 'Sick Chairs and Sick Thrones', in *Recovering Shakespeare's Theatrical Vocabulary* (Dessen 1995: ch. 6).

Configuring acts and scenes   339

This suggested juxtaposition of bed and sick-chair corresponds to two other sequences in the Shakespeare canon that cause problems for editors and directors. In Act 2 of *As You Like It* the banquet prepared for Duke Senior in 2.5 and eaten in 2.7 stays on stage during 2.6 (Orlando and Adam's arrival in Arden); and in Act 2 of *King Lear* Kent asleep in the stocks, presumably in the courtyard of Gloucester's castle, and found there by Lear in 2.4, is juxtaposed with Edgar in flight who, in what is traditionally designated as 2.3, speaks of having hid in the hollow of a tree. In both instances a significant property (a banquet table, the stocks) stays in view when the action switches to another place. To configure either sequence in terms of the traditional divisions is to enforce a sense of change of locale at the expense of meaningful juxtapositions. Whether to enhance the narrative pace or to italicize some point (as with the links between the plights of Kent and Edgar), Shakespeare and his colleagues were capable of dispensing with a form of verisimilitude prized highly today. The 'placing' of scenes is not irrelevant to Elizabethan theatrical practice, at least in their terms, but upon occasion something else – a concern for imagery or patterning or economy – could supersede what some readers today consider of primary importance.[6]

What then are the implications of divided Shakespeare for today's editors and users of editions? Here, like many readers of this chapter, I wear several hats. As a long-time teacher of the plays I welcome the convenience found in the standard scene breakdowns for quick reference in the classroom (and, I confess, in my head the Balcony Scene remains 2.2, even though I know better). Moreover, scholarly tools such as the Spivack concordance are keyed to the traditional divisions found in the Riverside edition, while any teacher who has even a single student using atypical scene breaks (as in the Oxford Wells–Taylor edition) will encounter problems in class discussions. The Arden 3 editor of *Romeo and Juliet* (René Weis) notes in his gloss on the 1.4–1.5 sequence: 'The action in Q2 is continuous here (as at 2.2 below), but most editors mark a new scene;

---

[6] In addition to changes of locale without clearing the stage in *Henry IV, Part 2* and *Romeo and Juliet*, the lengthy 2.3 of Marlowe's *The Jew of Malta* starts in a public slave market and, as clearly indicated in the dialogue, moves to Barabas's house. In John Day's *Law Tricks* the long final scene starts with a figure revealed in his study, continues as an inside-the-house scene, but ends with the sudden revelation of a supposedly dead figure in her tomb, the site of a previous scene clearly set in a graveyard. Perhaps closest to the situation in *Romeo and Juliet* 1.4–1.5 is Marlowe's *The Massacre at Paris* where the king announces hypocritically 'I will go visit the Admiral' who has been wounded and is 'sick in his bed'. Rather than using an *exit* and *re-enter* to move the king to the Admiral's chambers, Marlowe instead keeps the royal group on stage and has '*Enter the Admiral in his bed*' (4.48, 43, 49.s.d.).

this edition follows that pattern for convenience of reference' (Shakespeare 2012: 166). To call for a total break with long-standing on-the-page divisions strikes me as impractical.

On another front, as a theater historian who devotes much time to wrestling with various problems and anomalies, the how-to-divide choices in today's editions make little difference for my work, where I regularly ignore what today's editors present in terms of act–scene divisions, stage directions, or place–locale signals in favor of the evidence found in the early printed texts or the occasional manuscript play. What I find most troubling about the practices of editors (whose texts form the basis for interpretations in the study, in the classroom, and on the stage) is not that they are wrong-headed, unlearned, or imprecise (some of my best friends are editors) but that at times they can (often unwittingly) close down options that might seem negligible to them but could be of considerable interest to another interpreter, whether in the theater or on the page.

The question about divided Shakespeare remains: what approach is best for editions targeted at students or other first-time readers? Anomalies, as in *Henry IV, Part 2*, can be acknowledged in a gloss, textual note, or appendix, but many readers ignore such material or, in the case of textual notes, find them baffling. Some editors have experimented with various on-the-page solutions. For example, in her Arden 3 *Pericles* Suzanne Gossett keeps the standard divisions but places them in the left margin in square brackets and bold type. For the Act 2 sequence in *King Lear*, the Arden 3 editor, R. A. Foakes, presents 2.2–2.3–2.4 as one scene (2.2) but includes in the right margin in square brackets the traditional divisions for 2.3 and 2.4 along with line numbers for those scenes; similarly, in the New Cambridge edition of *Henry IV, Part 2* Giorgio Melchiori presents only two scenes in Act 4 but signals the traditional scenes and line numbers in the right margin. Such multiple numbering systems provide a solution to the historical versus traditional problem but at the risk of cluttering the page and perhaps adding to the obfuscation rather than providing clarity. How to navigate among (1) convenience in the classroom; (2) fidelity to the original theatrical practice; and (3) clarity for a first-time reader remains a puzzle for which I have no easy answer. As with other ahistorical features that remain part of the editorial landscape (e.g., place–locale indicators – '*Another part of the forest*'), the application of neoclassical act division and scenic precision to plays that may be operating by an alternative strategy can be misleading in various ways, but such may be the price tag for convenience of reference in our texts – at least in the short term.

In the future, when both students and general readers will be viewing a play on their Kindle or other digital format, this and related problems may be resolved. To set up an on-the-page text today with multiple approaches to scene divisions and line numbers may be daunting, but perhaps, not long from now, even a first-time reader of *Henry IV, Part 2* will be able to compare three different versions of Act 4 with the swipe of a finger or click of a mouse. An editor will then not have to make divisions that have the potential to screen out meaningful alternatives, and a savvy teacher will be able to ask students: what difference does a division into acts and scenes make to our understanding of this play? Perhaps the time is not far off when clarity, convenience of reference, and theater history will no longer be quarrelsome companions.

CHAPTER 21

Shakespeare's strange tongues: editors and the 'foreign' voice in Shakespearean drama

Matthew Dimmock

Editors are troubled by strangeness: we are trained, as Paul Hammond has noted, to 'normalize' and 'domesticate' (Hammond 2009: 11). This is as true of the linguistic strangeness of tragedy – Hammond's subject – as it is of the strangeness embodied in a nationally, theologically or ethnically different voice. What is now termed the 'foreign' had a number of early modern English synonyms, the most prominent of which was 'strange'. Although he is conventionally celebrated as a 'quiet countryman', lacking an engagement with the wider world characteristic of some of his contemporaries, Shakespeare's plays teem with strange voices and different tongues (Rowse 1955: 177). That the overwhelming majority are delivered in English, albeit sometimes in conspicuously 'broken' English (*Henry V*, 5.2.241), does not necessarily alleviate, and in some cases enhances, this strangeness. This chapter examines the fate of such voices at the hands of editors, arguing that their rich complexity might be better appreciated, but it also offers a sense of how Shakespeare signals strangeness on the early modern stage, and what it means when he does so.

To speak in a strange tongue had a range of associations in late sixteenth century English. In biblical terms it conjures God's punishment for the hubris of Babel, when language was confounded and mankind scattered (Genesis 11:8–9): the foundational Christian myth of difference. Babel was thus associated by polemicists of different stripes with Roman Catholicism or the London playhouses, or both (Goodwin 1624: 52). Yet speaking in strange tongues might conversely reference Pentecost and the xenoglossy of the apostles as they began 'to speak with other tongues' (Acts 2:4), a moment some theologians depicted as an inversion of Babel in order to assert the reconstitution of purity in the resurrection of Christ, and thus assert Christian universality. Strange tongues might also refer to a different kind of revelation, one more familiar from contemporary American evangelism: glossolalia, or speaking with no obvious meaning. This kind of talk was thought akin to the gabbling of animals (as Miranda characterizes Caliban's speech when remembering their first encounter – *The Tempest* 1.2.356), another potential connotation of a strange tongue. It was that animal-like repetitious senseless noise that was thought to provide an etymological root for 'Barbarian' – 'one that is not vnderstood' in Gervase Babington's words, and the figure of the Barbarian became the epitome of the uncivilized or pre-civilized: to be without understanding and not understood (1588: 31). Most often, however, to speak in a strange tongue was to adopt another language, a meaning that did not necessarily prelude these other associations: to speak another language could indicate prowess, experience and education, but it might also generate suspicion and the threat of pollution or instability. The native tongue, as Michael Neill has recognized, had gained an 'exceptional capacity for mobilizing the sense of extended community on which the new nation-state would come to depend' (1994: 14). Negative associations are evident in the use of the phrase itself, because 'strange tongue' carried a very specific religious and political charge. The only example of its use in Shakespeare's drama comes from the mouth of Queen Katherine in *Henry VIII*, as Cardinal Wolsey begins to address her with a Latin flourish. She responds:

> O, good my lord, no Latin.
> I am not such a truant since my coming
> As not to know the language I have lived in.
> A strange tongue makes my cause more strange suspicious –
> Pray, speak in English. (3.1.41–5)

On the surface, Katherine's meaning is straightforward and requires little or no editorial intervention. She presents her immersion in the English language as equivalent to an assumption of English national identity, positioning herself as deserving of the people's sympathy. Her willingness to discuss her case in English is shown to correspond with her determination to speak in public, for 'there's nothing I have done yet, o'my conscience, / Deserves a corner' (3.1.30–1), and her foreignness is here mitigated by 'living in' the language of her adopted nation. The choice of words in this scene seems deliberately to engage in a contemporary debate that had raged from the 1540s (and was still underway in the early seventeenth century when this play was written) over the use of Latin in church services, with the Mass a particular focus for contention. The Reformation had championed the vernacular as the primary vehicle for doctrine and ritual, yet the late sixteenth century saw ongoing skirmishes between those who argued that there was scriptural justification for the use of the vernacular (usually citing St Paul) and those who argued for the sole efficacy of Latin. The former repeatedly insisted on the 'great folly of many in ye world that delight to pray in a strange tongue', making a minister into 'a Barbarian to his people in the house of God' and the individual into a Barbarian to themselves, without understanding, for a 'strange tongue' prevents them praying 'openly' and in 'publique' (Babington 1588: 31, 33). The latter – those supporters of Latin – argued that there was no scriptural precedent and, moreover, that 'the Latine tongue is not in Englande a strange tongue' unlike, for example, delivering 'Masse at Rome in the English tongue' (Bristow 1580: 314).

This was a crucial distinction: the Latin tongue was rightfully and by tradition 'the Common tongue' whereas English, one of 'seuerall vulgare tongues' was a 'Priuate tongue'. Furthermore, those that 'speaketh in a tongue [not their own], speaketh not to man, but (yet) to God' (314, 313). The prominence given by the Protestants to mutual understanding in the formation of a legitimate community of believers has far-reaching implications for thinking about 'strange tongues': and by giving Wolsey (popularly represented as an Ipswich butcher's son) the Latin lines, and the Spanish Queen Katherine their denial, strangeness is used to challenge preconceptions and assert a more fluid model of national identity, distinct from the emphasis on 'native home' that dominated popular polemic. The difference between the two also suggests that class and gender have roles to play when speaking strange tongues: Katherine's elite royal status seems to diminish her strangeness, making her an amphibious subject; Wolsey's lower-class origins, when coupled with his strange tongue, seem to render him and his loyalty suspect. This exchange is also an intervention into the wider debate, a provocative one given the events that the play stages, and asserts that Latin *is* a strange tongue in England.

Katherine's calculated rejection of Latin in this English context reveals the intense self-consciousness that accompanied its use, something which appears elsewhere in Shakespeare's work. When, in the quarto of *The First Part of the Contention*, Lord Saye says of Kent, '*bona terra*' (a good land) to Jack Cade and his followers, their response is utter confusion:

CADE *Bonnum terrum*? Zounds, what's that?
DICK He speaks French.
WILL No, 'tis Dutch.
NICK No, 'tis Out-talian; I know it well enough. (4.7.39–42)

Their lack of education means they cannot recognize Saye's quotation from Caesar's *Commentaries*, nor that he is complimenting their Kentishness, and a prevalent xenophobia amongst Cade's crew leads them to mistake Latin for a range of other, equally strange and suspect tongues, and even to mangle them. Here the cosmopolitanism of Saye's elite status condemns him, manifested in the rich cloth covering his horse and his extensive experience in foreign courts, where he lost English territories without any display of masculine martial vigour. In the Folio *Henry VI, Part 2* this scene is extended but the mistaken languages are removed. Instead the exchange reads as follows:

BUTCHER. What say you of Kent?
SAYE. Nothing but this: 'tis *bona terra, mala gens*.
CADE. Away with him, away with him! He speaks Latin. (4.7.42–4)

Saye's Latin still defines him apart (here it is much more equivocal and translates as 'a good land, a bad people') but Cade's ability immediately to recognize this strange tongue marks him quite differently from the incomprehension evident in the quarto. Saye is still murdered for the same reasons, but there is more emphasis on his having 'parlayed unto foreign kings' (4.7.63), with Cade claiming that he has 'a familiar under his tongue' (4.7.89). The suggestion that the quarto is more oriented towards performance might make sense of these differences – the exaggeratedly ignorant perspective of the mob is certainly more comedic. Yet the Folio version of this scene hints at Cade's elevation above his followers, and more successfully highlights his pretentions and his hypocrisy, particularly when he casually introduces the Latin legal term *in capite* into a speech later in the same scene (4.7.101). The nuanced differences in the use of strange tongues between the quarto and the Folio thus have implications for an understanding of Cade's role and relation to his fellows, and they are lost when these scenes are conflated, as in the Oxford edition of the play (which includes the longer Latin phrase of the Folio, but the knockabout farce of the quarto).

The lessons in Latin offered by Sir Hugh Evans in *The Merry Wives of Windsor* are more benign (4.1.14–69), but again the scene uses comedy to articulate the particular strangeness associated with that language in England, particularly when mangled by the Welsh of Evans and the lewdness of Mistress Quickly's imagination; the more conventional comedy of love play is wrung from the extensive Latin teaching in *The Taming of the Shrew* (3.1.26–79). In these examples Latin is a means of asserting the neutral primacy of English, but also of playfully unpicking assumptions about language and the stability of meaning, for which the master/student dynamic used in both plays is particularly well-suited. The self-consciousness with which Shakespeare stages Latin in his plays is less about personal experience – he was famously supposed to have 'small Latin, and less Greek' – and more to do with the opportunities it offers for dramatizing class and gender divisions, for puncturing the grandiose, and above all for misunderstanding.

To argue that something of the charge of Latin on the stage is lost when translated across four centuries is an obvious point to make, and yet it has implications for editorial practice. The *Henry VI, Part 2* example is a useful one: when Lord Saye utters the line '*bona terra*' or '*bona terra, mala gens*', it seems clear that an audience is not expected to recognize the quotation, as Saye immediately notes the source when he next speaks. But, since the humour of this exchange does not depend on it, would they have been expected to understand the Latin, or even to recognize it as Latin? Its use on the stage – particularly in the context of the learned and learning – establishes a clear and exclusive linguistic community, as Katherine is only too aware in *Henry VIII*. Some in the playhouse were included in the joke; others, to whom Latin was as strange as any other alien tongue – stranger, perhaps, due to its association with papistry and the Catholic mass, were corralled together with Cade's rioters, uncomfortably laughing at their own ignorance. This is the oddness of Latin on the stage in this period and it is an oddness that is hard to reproduce on the page or on the stage: Latin has little or none of this *frisson* in the twenty-first century, and to most is simply strange. Standard editorial procedure is to supply translation in margins or notes, and some recent productions have chosen to follow suit and replace the Latin with English or introduce parallel translation with the understandable aim of ensuring comprehension. The danger is that such interventions flatten or 'domesticate' a contentious and carefully crafted engagement with a tongue becoming strange in early modern England.

The one celebrated example in which Shakespeare goes further, and seems to make a strange tongue absolutely incomprehensible to his audience, is when the rebels Mortimer and Hotspur visit Glendower's Welsh court in *Henry IV, Part 1* and Glendower's daughter (also Mortimer's wife) is introduced. Although his daughter can speak only Welsh, a fact much lamented by Mortimer, Glendower acts as translator, unnervingly assuring his visitors that he can speak English 'as well as you, / For I was train'd up in the English court' (3.1.119–20). Yet Shakespeare may have intended his voice to have a subtle Welsh inflection, one later ironed out by the determined – and English – metrical uniformity imposed on the text by Pope and many subsequent editors. There are hints of this in the early editions of the play in the protraction implied in his use of 'Ile' rather than the later emendation to 'I will' (3.1.112); 'sheele' rather than 'she will' (3.1.188); 'weele' rather than 'we will' (3.1.259); and 'nay' (3.1.205), the dissyllabic equivalence of which caught Coleridge's attention (quoted in Humphreys 1960: 97). This lingering over syllables may well have marked what A. R. Humphreys recognized as 'Glendower's Welsh tune' in his 1960 edition of the play (92). There can be no equivalent ironing out of Lady Mortimer's voice: on the page she is rendered voiceless, the directions indicating only that 'the Lady speaks in Welsh' or later that 'the Lady sings a Welsh song' (3.1.199s.d. and 245s.d.). Megan Lloyd (2002) has noted that she, 'like Kate in *Henry V*, requires translation [by her father] and is excluded from linguistic community' (Lloyd quoting Rackin 1994: 85). The decision to render Lady Mortimer's voice opaque, in stark contrast to the convention that 'the speech of foreigners (even when comically "broken") be transparent to English ears' (Neill 1994: 21), is no doubt deliberate.

There are at least two other Shakespearean characters whose ludic voices are composed of a carefully inflected Welsh English. Both are men and in some sort of English service. That it is a Welsh woman whose voice is unrecorded – unrecordable? – suggests that she is intended to embody the degenerative and seductive dangers that lay beyond what Edmund Spenser termed 'the kingdom of our own language' (letter to Gabriel Harvey, quoted in Helgerson 1983: 1 and in Neill 1994: 15): English is an easy surrogate for England. In this respect she is again connected to the French princess Katherine in *Henry V*, but in that case French gives way to English in a forced assimilation. For Mortimer and his unnamed Welsh wife there is only blank inaccessibility. This could only bode ill: as Sir John Hayward noted, the joining of 'strange tongues' had biblical and classical precedents:

> [God did] threaten as a plague to those that obey not his commandements: *The Lord shall bring a nation vpon thee, whose tongue thou shalt not vnderstand*. And againe, by the Prophet *Ieremie* hee menaced the Iewes, that hee would bring a nation vppon them, whose *language they knew not, neither vnderstood what they did say* ... To these I will adioyne the oracle of Philosophie, Plato, who doth truly determine those to be Barbarians, who in the manner both of their language and life hold no communitie or resemblance together. (1604: 30–1)

This strange and ill-fated union of English and Welsh thus prefigures the failure of the rebel cause, mired in self-interest, broken promises and incomprehension. Lady Mortimer's strange tongue is likened by Hotspur to his dog howling 'in Irish' (3.1.236), a barbarous animalistic noise that is 'understood not'. Although there has been critical debate over the extent to which audiences, company and Shakespeare himself would have been familiar with spoken Welsh (and whether the directions in this scene are some sort of prompt for Welsh-speaking actors), editors have in the main left this episode as it is found in the early print versions. Not so directors: forced to respond, most introduce Welsh language and song, as in the Royal Shakespeare Company's production of 1964, which has been influentially examined by Terence Hawkes (discussed in Hodgdon 1997: 272). For Shakespeare, in contrast, authenticity was unlikely to be a major concern – the point is incomprehension and untranslatability, for Hotspur, who repeatedly jokes about it as for an audience. To disregard this and Glendower's elusive inflections is once again to wrestle the strange tongue into normality: in both *Henry IV, Part 1* and *Henry V* the strange tongue, particularly the strange female tongue, throws difference into sharp relief and makes English the *sine qua non* of the rational, civilized masculine energies that justified and informed imperial expansion.

Queen Katherine cannily draws on such associations with English when she refuses Wolsey's Latin in *Henry VIII* 3.1, but the example of Glendower raises a different issue regarding this scene. Would Katherine's words mean differently if she spoke them with the heavy Spanish accent she often labours with in contemporary depictions? Although she acknowledges that she is a 'stranger, / Born out of your dominions' (2.4.15–16) her speech betrays no trace of inflection: to 'break' her English in the same way that Kate's is broken in *Henry V* would risk making her strange (even comic) in a way that would undermine her portrayal and make her insistence on English a self-serving and manipulative gesture. Shakespeare chooses on this occasion not to accentuate the strangeness of a strange character with a strange tongue. As we saw with the example of Glendower, this was not always the case. Whether subtle or exaggeratedly absurd, accents were a well-established way of signaling a strange tongue, and the early modern stage abounds with them, from the Italian English of the merchant Mercadorus in Robert Wilson's *Three Ladies of London* (1581), the French English of *The Wounds of Civil War* (1589) and *James IV* (1590) to the Dutch English of Hans in Thomas Dekker's *The Shoemaker's Holiday* (1599). As these examples again demonstrate, comedy is almost always a concomitant of this type of strange tongue, but the recreation of accent or dialect also serves an obvious dramatic need for comprehension between characters and cultures – in stark contrast to the exchanges between Lord and Lady Mortimer – and it is flexible enough to allow a dramatist to luxuriate in the difficult business of translation, or to present it as transparent.

Transparency is certainly not in evidence when Henry V's captains meet before the walls of Harfleur, but neither is incomprehension. As key players in the procession to Anglicizing unification that reaches its apotheosis at Agincourt and the events that follow, these captains and the nations they embody must find some common ground. The moulding of their strange tongues to English – albeit not in its 'native garb' (5.1.76) – makes it the ameliorating force that unifies and defines Henry's otherwise disparate army. John Hayward's reading of Augustine persuaded him that what made Rome 'imperious' was the confounding of diverse languages, for '*Diuersitie of tongues maketh one man a stranger to another*' (Hayward 1604: 31): in the same manner Henry builds an imperium of Englishes, making it the 'common tongue' equivalent of Roman Latin in his incorporation of Welsh, Irish, Scots and French. It is nevertheless a fragile unity: the conflict between Fluellen and Macmorris at the heart of the scene at Harfleur stems from a clash of temperaments comically manifest in the convolutions of their strange tongues. Together this combination of submission and belligerence, stereotyped national difference (the Folio's speech prefixes quickly give way to 'Welch', Scot and Irish – but not for the English Gower) and the difficult entwining of dialect and comedy have made this a celebrated and a controversial scene, and a challenge for editors.

There is little subtlety here – Shakespeare utilizes simple linguistic devices to break Fluellen, Jamy and Macmorris's English. Fluellen's Welsh English is the more complex of the three (perhaps indicating Shakespeare's confidence and familiarity with this particular strange tongue): it is marked by the substitution of letters, for instance ch for j and s for sh, and the repetition of the resulting word (one example is 'Cheshu' – 3.2.70 and elsewhere), but also the pluralizing of nouns, syntactical inversions and the general scrambling of standard grammar. Most distinctive is the stereotypical discourse tag – 'Look you' – which is a constant refrain. In contrast, the Scottish English of Jamy and the Irish English of Macmorris are more basic in conception and, although distinct in terms of spellings, they are similar to one another. Both voices are marked by the substitution of sh for s (as in 'Chrish' for Christ) and variation in vowels and consonants, hence Jamy's 'feith' for 'faith' 'gud' for 'good' (3.2.103) or 'lig' for 'lie' (3.2.111) and corresponding shifts in emphasis (see Crystal and Crystal for an elaboration of some of these effects). Where variation does occur, immediate repetition again gives it a characteristic emphasis, making each voice distinctively strange. The English captain Gower offers an ostensibly neutral contrast to all three, as does the king who, despite the appealingly inclusive acknowledgement of his own Welsh origins (4.1.52), is the point from which all linguistic divergence is implicitly measured.

For editors the issue is not dissonance itself, but rather how to accommodate it into modern editorial practice. Jamy's repetition of 'gud' is a useful example. Modernization is necessarily uniform, so for his recent Arden edition of *Henry V*, T. W. Craik resolved that the French and the dialect passages would be modernized along the same principle 'as that of the passages in standard sixteenth-century English'. He writes:

> in the dialect passages accepted modern dialect forms are substituted where they exist (thus, in 3.2, Jamy's 'gud' becomes 'guid', his 'bath' becomes 'baith' and his 'de' becomes 'dae', but his 'ay' has been normalized as 'I'); eccentricities of pronunciation have been retained but have not been uniformly imposed. (1995: 110)

Although it puts him at odds with the Oxford editors – who retain 'gud' and make relatively minor changes to the language of this scene – Craik's rationale makes sense. If modernization is to be applied to the standard English and French of this diverse play, then it needs to be extended to the dialect scenes. In his 1992 Cambridge edition of the play Andrew Gurr fretted over the same issue, and chose to modernize in broadly the same fashion, taking the further step of substituting the established 'Fluellen' for the more authentic 'Llewellyn'. Gurr gave one main caveat: that his modernization of the French and the dialect scenes 'may misrepresent the pronunciations which Shakespeare heard' since language (like Shakespearean editing) does not stay still for long (2005: 62).

My reservations with this practice go deeper, however, and relate to the underlying assumption that in writing these scenes Shakespeare was attempting a 'reasonably phonetic transcription of each mode of speech' (61). There can be no doubt that a certain degree of verisimilitude was necessary and would not have been difficult for a metropolitan playwright who is recorded living with French-speaking migrants. But these scenes are not 'standard': Shakespeare's deliberate exaggeration and repetition of national phonetic traits to create absurdity and caricature is, as Gurr acknowledges elsewhere, in the service of comedy (37). To treat these strange tongues in the same way as any other voice in the play is to naturalize and normalize them. Once again the danger in uniformly applying contemporary editorial techniques to an early modern play text is that the quirks of such voices are flattened out and at least part of their distinctive strangeness is defused.

Curiously for a play set largely in France, the 'Frenchness' of the French nobility is signaled only through their occasional use of exclamatory French phrases (*'le cheval volant'* 3.8.13). French English (or, for that matter, English French) is only used in the wooing scenes. This is a necessary dramatic tactic for an English play written for an English audience, but it does raise questions about the ways in which this stage could accommodate even stranger tongues with anything other than silence. There are not many non-Christian voices in Shakespeare's drama, but given the belligerent broken English associated with Wales, Scotland and Ireland, it is striking that each of these stranger voices that he does create is a peculiar combination of unusual eloquence and self-consciousness. Caliban in *The Tempest* is, admittedly, not often associated with eloquence but, as David Lindley has recognized, his voice is characterized 'by an Adamic pleasure in naming physical objects with a verbal caress' which troubles readings that focus solely on the ways in which language was imposed upon him (Lindley 2002: 41). The now common practice of lineating his voice in verse rather than the prose of the Folio, following Pope (Shakespeare 1725), makes his voice all the more lyrical. Othello, in contrast, has long been celebrated for his lyricism – A. C. Bradley remarked that he was 'the greatest poet' amongst Shakespeare's heroes (quoted in Pechter 2004: 239). The self-deprecating claim that he is 'rude' in speech, and 'little blessed with the soft phrase of peace' (1.3.82–3) is shown to be a rhetorical device by the eloquence of what follows: speeches 'larded with choice terms' and unfamiliar motifs (Neill 2006: 220). His non-native status in Venice is marked variously by sexualized somatic references and in the ways his 'sooty bosom' (1.2.70) is visually depicted on stage, but it is also manifest for early modern audiences in what Étienne Balibar calls 'linguistic ethnicity' rather than a 'racial (or hereditary) ethnicity' (quoted in Drakakis 2010: 85). It is the grandiose excess of Othello's language, and its extravagant breakdown later in the play, which show him to be different from those around him. The strange tongues of both these characters have seen considerable critical and editorial attention: far less notice has been taken of the earlier figure of the Prince of Morocco – 'Morochus' or 'Morrocho' in the quarto – who appears briefly to take the casket test for Portia's hand in *The Merchant of Venice*.

There is critical consensus that Morocco's distinctive voice owes something to Marlowe and to the *Tamburlaine* phenomenon, and he is often treated as a preparatory sketch for Othello, written five or six years later. There is disagreement over the nature of the portrayal: James Shapiro argues that through Morocco Shakespeare burlesques Marlowe's 'aggressive over-reachers' by placing one of them in a comedy 'where their heroic visions are misplaced' (Shapiro 1988: 273, also quoted in Drakakis 2010: 265), and Robert Logan agrees: for him Morocco is a 'comic characterization' of a 'Tamburlainian warrior hero' (2007: 156). Jonathan Burton has conversely argued that in Morocco Shakespeare presents a noble and dignified alternative to 'the stereotype of the lascivious, blustering' figure of the 'Turk' so popular on the early modern stage (2005: 208). I have argued elsewhere that this depiction of a Prince of Morocco who is not defined by his adherence to 'Mahomet' shows Shakespeare moving away from the now hackneyed bravado of the 'Turk play' (a genre largely initiated by *Tamburlaine*) in new directions (Dimmock 2015).

Morocco's voice is again the primary differential between him and the Italian world of the play, including Shylock, whose stage Jewishness is manifested less in the style of his voice than in the content (repeated references to his 'tribe' and to scripture, for instance) – although for both characters costume, which Shakespeare neglects to detail, inevitably plays an important role. Like each of the earlier strange tongues, Morocco's voice poses a challenge for the twenty-first-century editor. The echoes of *Tamburlaine* and the bombast associated with the 'Turk play' have long been recognized in his two main speeches. Having requested that Portia 'Mislike me not for my complexion' (2.1.1), and following assurances from her that he stands 'as fair as any comer I have look'd on yet / For my affection' (2.1.20–2), Morocco performs his valiance:

> By this Symitare
> That slew the Sophy, and a Persian Prince
> That wone three fields of Sultan Solyman,
> I would ore-stare the sternest eyes that looke:
> Out-braue the hart most daring on the earth:
> Pluck the young sucking Cubs from the she Beare,
> Yea, mock the Lyon when a roars for pray
> To win the Lady.   (Q1, sig. C.1r)

The sonorous dynamic of these lines, their distinctive configuration of blank verse, their superlatives and incorporation of exotic, polysyllabic nouns – 'Symitare', 'Sophy', 'Soliman' – make them clearly Marlovian. Even swearing by a sword was a Marlovian preoccupation. These lines also conspicuously echo the 'Turk play' *Soliman and Perseda* (1591, commonly attributed to Thomas Kyd), and Brusor's lines:

> Against the Sophy in three pitched fields,
> Vnder the conduct of great *Soliman*,
> Haue I bene chiefe commaunder of an hoast,
> And put the flint heart Perseans to the sword.
>
> (sig. B.1r; 1.3.51–4)

There are nevertheless clear differences: Brusor goes on to boast of how he made 'some Christians kneele to *Mahomet*' and concludes with a distinctively 'Mahometan' oath – '*Mahomet* for me and *Solyman*' (B.1r; 1.3.61, 63) – something Morocco never does.

Morocco's strange tongue therefore relates directly to an early modern stage culture that in the 1590s was preoccupied with post-Tamburlainian extrinsic bellicosity. Why Shakespeare enlists this particular voice in a play preoccupied with solving and effacing the problems posed by the stage Jew is more difficult to discern. I reproduce Morocco's speech from Q1 (1600 – the standard copytext since the early twentieth century) rather than from a recent edition to show its original form and punctuation. The most recent, John Drakakis's 2010 Arden edition, sets this speech thus:

> By this scimitar,
> That slew the Sophy and a Persian prince,
> That won three fields of Sultan Solyman,
> I would o'erstare the sternest eyes that look,
> Outbrave the heart most daring on the earth,
> Pluck the young sucking cubs from the she-bear,
> Yea, mock the lion when 'a roars for prey,
> To win the lady.
>
> (2.1.24–31)

Aside from the modernization of spelling, the addition of a comma at the end of l. 25 is the most obvious intervention: Drakakis's predecessor, John Russell Brown, in his 1955 Arden edition, followed the punctuation of Q1. Here Drakakis diverges from his copytext and adopts the punctuation of Q2 (1619), one of numerous commas added by the later compositor. He argues for this change on the basis of sense and clarity – that it makes Morocco (or rather his scimitar) the antecedent of the relative pronoun

'That' at the start of l.26 and thus 'that Morocco is enumerating his own military exploits' (2010: 225). The shift in punctuation between Q1 and Q2 has implications for the way an audience appraises Morocco: is he a mercenary, prepared to fight for both Persians and Turks (as Q2 implies); or is he an Ottoman client, and fought only for them against the Persians (as in Q1)?

The conflict between the Ottoman 'Turk' and the Safavid 'Persian' was so prominent that it became proverbial in early modern England: Samuel Purchas wrote that they hated each other 'more than they hate the Christians: like as the Traditionarie Iew doth the Textuarie, and the Papist the Protestant' (1613: 294). Although the Kingdom of Morocco was not part of the Ottoman Empire (and was often at odds with it), the two were connected in the English imagination, and the character of Morocco has an obvious precursor in Abdelmelec, the King of Morocco in George Peele's *The Battle of Alcazar* (1589?), who has similarly done service to 'Sultan Solimon' (1.ind.45). The renown of the conflict, also indicated in Brusor's words in *Soliman and Perseda*, and this dramatic precedent make it very unlikely Morocco fought on both sides: the addition of the comma seems misplaced.

Because they have less obvious implications for meaning, the other alterations the recent Arden introduces to the punctuation of Morocco's strange tongue are not as immediately apparent. For this opening speech the decision to remove the colons that conclude lines 27 and 28 and replace them with commas (liberally applied here and elsewhere) are a departure from Q1, Q2 and the Folio. Such changes are in keeping with those made to the speech that follows Morocco's second entrance, a speech Arthur Quiller-Couch and J. Dover Wilson observed was unusual in the intensity of its punctuation (in their 1926 New Cambridge edition). The mid-part as it appears in Q1 is set as follows:

> As much as he deserues, pause there *Morocho*,
> and weigh thy valew with an euen hand,
> If thou beest rated by thy estimation
> thou doost deserue enough, and yet enough
> May not extend so farre as to the Ladie:
> And yet to be afeared of my deseruing
> were but a weake disabling of my selfe.
> As much as *I* deserue, why thats the Ladie.
> *I* doe in birth deserue her, and in fortunes,
> in graces, and in qualities of breeding:
> but more than these, in loue *I* doe deserue,

> what if *I* straid no farther, but chose heere?
> Lets see once more this saying grau'd in gold:
> Who chooseth me shall gaine what many men desire:
> Why thats the Ladie, all the world desires her. (Q1, sig. D3r)

Here the punctuation accentuates how Morocco's previously swaggering and expansive speech has become halting in its uncertainty and self-doubt; a cascade of clauses run into and over commas and colons as his strange tongue 'lunges forward' (Brown 1955: 58). This is a conspicuous departure from the Marlovian affirmation of his opening lines. The 2010 Arden edition presents the same section thus:

> 'As much as he deserves.' Pause there Morocco,
> And weigh thy value with an even hand.
> If thou be'st rated by thy estimation
> Thou dost deserve enough; and yet, enough
> May not extend so far as to the lady.
> And yet, to be afeared of my deserving
> Were but a weak disabling of myself.
> As much as I deserve: why, that's the lady.
> I do in birth deserve her, and in fortunes,
> In graces and in qualities of breeding.
> But more than these, in love I do deserve.
> What if I strayed no farther, but chose here?
> Let's see once more this saying graved in gold:
> 'Who chooseth me shall gain what many men desire.'
> Why, that's the lady; all the world desires her. (2.7.24–38)

As one would expect from any of the major editions of Shakespeare, the spelling has been modernized, initial words capitalized, and text fixed in accordance with convention – each constituent elements of a well-established process to clarify the text for contemporary readers. Yet the repunctuation of Morocco's utterances goes much further and erases the impact of the hesitant linguistic lurches into which his earlier bombast has dissolved. This apparently slight difference would have seemed all the more stark on a stage so accustomed to the stalking arrogance and furious vociferation associated with such characters in the 'Turk play'. Instead Morocco's speech becomes more considered, more formal: more neutrally English. Drakakis's decision to use a sequence of full stops to break up this speech has the result – once again – of normalizing the strange tongue.

Punctuation is a contentious issue amongst editors of Shakespeare, and recent years have seen an emerging trend for a more interventionist approach predicated on the now well-founded presumption that printing houses were often at least as responsible (if not more so) for punctuation as the playwright. Such an approach can productively scour out the accretions of the printing process, but when applied without discrimination it can deaden the idiosyncratic nature of the strange tongue. Drakakis is not alone in this: his version of this section splits it into nine sentences in comparison with Q1's four, but the Oxford text similarly breaks it into eight. This process of punctuating Morocco's distinctive voice to 'domesticate' may even have begun soon after the publication of Q1: Q2 adds commas at the end of lines 26 and 29, and the Folio adds a comma (l. 29) and two full stops (ll. 34 and 36). Those who argue that a considerable degree of emendation is a necessary part of any modern edition might consider the earlier Arden edition. In that text John Russell Brown stayed close to the punctuation of Q1, keeping the original four sentences, and chose to add a series of em dashes (at lines 24, 25, 31 and 34) which usefully communicate the interrupted motion of the original; Shakespeare's creative riposte to the bombast associated with the strange tongues of the 'Turk play'.

* * *

Morocco's example shows how the search for the unorthodox, non-English, strange voice in Shakespeare is invariably caught up in the ways editors mediate the strangeness of Shakespeare's early modern voice for twenty-first-century readers, performers and audiences. If we are to retain the distinctiveness of such voices as we make Shakespeare contemporary, we need to resist the editorial impulse to 'normalize' and 'domesticate' and be more sensitive to their strangeness; more attuned to early modern ways of hearing them. Certainly Othello and Morocco – two of Shakespeare's most prominent non-Christians – are highly conscious of how they are heard and appraised and this gives their voices a distinctively epideictic quality. Unlike the bellicose rhetoric associated with Marlowe's strange tongues (and lampooned in the character of Pistol in the *Henriad*), these voices seem halting and self-referential, aware of the ways in which their difference is displayed. As is the case with Shakespeare's use of Latin, Welsh and French, and Welsh, Scottish and Irish dialects of English, the strange tongue is carefully crafted to draw attention to itself and its strangeness. In opposition, English is made natural and neutral, a 'common tongue' for a 'common faith', fit for imposition and exportation. There is dark irony in the way a modern English that was in part forged in early modern fictional encounters with strangeness now, in its twenty-first-century form, threatens through modernization to efface the difference on which such encounters were based. If we cannot recover Shakespeare's strange tongues we lose this history, embedded as it is in the unique characteristics of an extraordinary cast of strangers trapped in epideixis – trapped in an oratory of self-display.

CHAPTER 22

Before the beginning; after the end: when did plays start and stop?

Tiffany Stern

In 1993, Gary Taylor and John Jowett published an important chapter on act intervals in plays. They asked why editors and critics paid attention to pauses and silences in dialogue, yet neglected to think about the longer and weightier silences dividing one act from another. Pointing out that plays written for the major theatrical companies between 1616 and 1642, and many dating from earlier, will have had act-breaks – including Shakespeare's late plays – they proposed that 'act-intervals', which divide one act from another as separate units of thought, be recognized as significant 'elements of dramatic meaning, which we ignore to our cost' (1993b: 50).

That chapter reflected an editorial decision already made by Stanley Wells and Gary Taylor in their *Oxford Shakespeare* (Wells and Taylor 1986). They had chosen to present plays not as first written but as first 'acted in the London playhouses' (xxxix); as part of that aim, they acknowledged act-break pauses with a special symbol invented for the purpose, a geometrical 'Tudor' rose. By so doing, they drew particular attention to act-breaks, which they felt had the effect of placing 'more emphasis on the act as a unit' (xxx) – though they also risked closing down other act-scene options, as Alan Dessen discusses elsewhere in this volume.

Recently, Suzanne Gossett, John Jowett and Gordon McMullan have set up a series, Arden Early Modern Drama (AEMD), that likewise aims to produce texts in the form in which they were 'first performed in the theatre' ('General Editors' Preface', quoted, here, from Massinger 2010: x). The AEMD editors also employ act-break markers; they, however, represent the breaks on the page with a treble clef, reminding readers of the fact that music filled pauses between acts in the early modern playhouse (Holland 2001: 127–55). For the Arden editors, the fact of music, with its ability to change or intensify mood, is as crucial an aspect of the act-break as the pause itself.

But if some performative moments not generally recorded in early modern play texts, like act-breaks, are to be added to editions, then why are other aspects ignored? In particular, why do editions not draw attention to the rich and complex playhouse procedures that signified the start and end of plays, and that can, like act-breaks, make a claim to be interpretatively significant? The answer is partly that editors do not know about pre- and post-play events; partly that editors are more comfortable interspersing theatrical events within dialogue than before or afterwards into otherwise empty spaces.

This chapter will ask whether paratextual elements not usually materially appended to the text (what Gerard Genette (1997: 344) calls 'epitexts') are important to play, text, edition and/or meaning. It will investigate the blasts of a trumpet that heralded a play's 'beginning', and the prayer, music, clowning and announcement that followed a play's 'end', questioning when a play actually started and stopped. By so doing, it will complicate questions about how plays should be edited, while also asking what, ultimately, a 'play' is.

***

These days it is primarily visual clues that tell an audience when a play is due to start. Depending on the theatre, some of the following will occur: the lights in the auditorium will be lowered; the lights on the stage will be raised; a stage curtain, if there is one, will part. In the early modern period, however, the signal that told spectators to stop talking and look to the stage was primarily aural. A trumpeter, or sometimes several trumpeters, 'heralded' the start of a play with two or three sharp blasts – or even, sometimes, an entire 'flourish' (fanfare) – on his, or their, instrument(s).

That plays should start with trumpets is no surprise. With their bright tones and carrying resonance, trumpets were ideal for announcements of all kinds; they 'sounded' (were caused to make a sound; were blown upon – *Oxford English Dictionary*, 'sound', v.^{1} 7) before the publishing of a royal proclamation, for instance, in order 'to make way for it, to call people to the hearing of it, and to command attention to it' (Brinsley A6^r). A host of other important entertainments were announced with trumpets too, including betrothals, challenges, coronations, greetings, parleys, proclamations, processions and reconciliations. So a trumpet-blast at the opening of a play will have served the dual purpose of demanding audience attention, while conveying that something momentous and authoritative was about to happen.

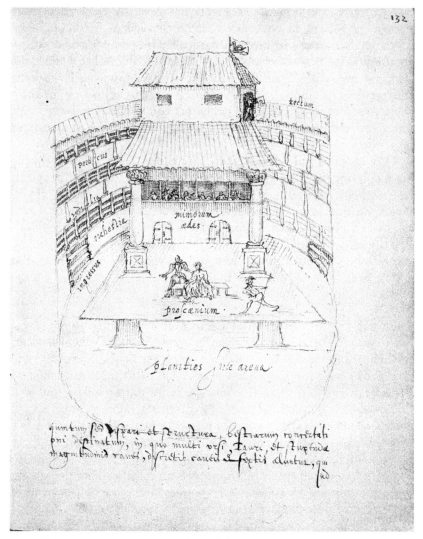

Figure 22.1 Aernout van Buchel after Johannes de Witt, *The Swan Playhouse*, c.1596

The trumpeter's importance to the theatre is illustrated by his depiction in the famous Swan Playhouse drawing, copied by Aernout van Buchel from a lost picture by Johannes de Witt (Figure 22.1). That picture includes, elevated high above the stage, a hut out of which a trumpeter leans (Figure 22.2). If this is a mid-play trumpeter, then the picture shows how

Figure 22.2 Aernout van Buchel after Johannes de Witt, close-up of trumpeter from *The Swan Playhouse*, c.1596

memorable a part of the performance was the trumpet-player and his instrument. But the drawing appears to show not a particular moment of performance but the general use of different bits of the playhouse: the galleries and yard are empty, but there are people in the lords' (or musicians') room; the doors of entrance are closed, but a play is in progress on the stage. As the trumpeter's instrument is angled away from the theatre out into Southwark, and as trumpeters did not usually perform during dialogue – as their strident sound drowned out words – this is probably a representation of the trumpeter in the very act of announcing the beginning of the play.

Hanging from the trumpet of the Swan Playhouse instrumentalist is a flag or 'banner'. It bears the same image as that on the theatre's main flag: the 'sign' of the theatre, a swan. Given that flags and trumpet banners regularly conveyed the same information – in *Henry V*, the French Constable, in need of a flag to illustrate his allegiance, decides 'I will the Banner from a Trumpet take, / And use it for my haste' (TLN 2234–5) – theatrical trumpets are likely to have been 'branded' with the sign of the theatre. This would have had the added advantage, when the players went into London to 'cry' that day's play, of reminding potential audiences which company's repertory was being announced: William Rankins despised the 'Drummes and Trumpets to cal menne to Plaies' (Ci^v), but Philip Henslowe, in 1599/1600, lent money to the Admiral's Men for '2 trumpettes' and 'a drome' for announcements when his company was going 'into the contry' (2002: 130).[1]

Yet if trumpets proclaiming performances were decorated with the sign of their playhouse, they will always have been metatheatrical, visually restating the theatre's symbol against whatever fiction was being played. For instance, if a 'Globe' trumpeter bore the banner depicting his theatre's sign – Atlas / Hercules carrying the globe / world on his back (Stern 1997) – then *Timon of Athens*, admittedly a play notoriously difficult to date or give a theatre to, may have been particularly loaded metatheatrically:

> *Enter Poet, Painter, Jeweller, Merchant, and Mercer, at severall doores.*
>
> POET. Good day Sir.
> PAIN. I am glad y'are well.
> POET. I have not seene you long, how goes the World?
> PAIN. It weares sir, as it growes. (TLN 2–9)

With its disdain for the aging and worn 'world', this dialogue at the Globe would have drawn attention both to the creaking space and to the sign just, in two senses, flourished: the image of a man weighed down by an intolerable burden.

More often attested to is the aural effect of the opening trumpet. *The Merrie Conceited Jests of George Peele* relates how George Peele, preparing to enter on stage to speak a prologue, waited until a single 'trumpet had

---

[1] Though it is sometimes said that plays were only cried until around 1600, they certainly continued to be cried in the country, and perhaps sometimes the town, for the next two centuries; see Stern 2009b: 37, 265.

sounded thrise' (D1ʳ). A version of this was clearly normal: Thomas Dekker in *Guls horne-booke* details the backstage activity that preceded the start of a play as an exchange between trumpets and prologue – 'the quaking prologue ... is ready to give the trumpets their Cue that hees upon point to enter' (E4ᵛ). Indeed, so connected was the sound of the trumpet with the prologue that John Earle, writing a definition of 'A Trumpeter' in *Micro-cosmographie*, describes him as 'alwaies the Prologues Prologue' (I5ᵛ). And, though the actual trumpet call before a prologue is only haphazardly recorded in playbooks, trumpets are generally assumed before prologues in plays-in-plays: the prologue to *Pyramus and Thisbe* in Shakespeare's *Midsummer Night's Dream* walks on stage preceded by a trumpeter, as will be addressed; the internal play in Munday et al.'s *Booke of Sir Thomas More* starts with '*The Trompet soundes, enter the Prologue*' (1911: 35).

Only when a variety of paratextual material is appended to a play, and the trumpet calls need to be interspersed between them, do early modern playbooks specifically refer to the sounds with which a play begins. For instance, after the induction to *Lady Alimony* there is a stage direction for '*the third Sound*'; then the '*Prologue*' speaks (clearly, then, two earlier 'sounds', not recorded, preceded the induction) (B2ᵛ). In the 1616 version of Ben Jonson's *Cynthias Revels*, likewise, the induction is said explicitly to begin after '*the second sounding*' and the prologue is then spoken after '*the third sounding*' (181, 185).[2] The same is the case in Jonson's *Every Man Out*, in which a series of characters enter onto the stage for an induction '*After the second sounding*' (G5ᵛ). In that induction, however, Asper has a passage in which he compares humours to 'the air (forc'd through a horn, or trumpet)' which 'Flows instantly away, and leaves behind / A kind of dew'; he, it seems, picks up on the transient sound just rendered into moisture as part of the play's larger exploration of the changeable nature of emotion; his words anticipate, too, the trumpet's reprise as sound before the prologue at the '*third sounding*' (H2ᵛ). In all these exchanges, the trumpet's preliminary calls are interspersed between the play's opening matter, resembling, perhaps, a modern 'five minute bell', a 'two minute bell' and a performance bell. That trumpets are sometimes said to have sounded twice before plays, and sometimes three times, may relate to this habit of scattering their calls between various different kinds of preliminary materials.

---

[2] Not recorded in the play's earlier iteration, *The Fountaine of Selfe-Love* (1601).

Only in a few rare instances, however, does the prologue's opening trumpet sound make it directly into a stage direction. William Percy's *The Cuck-Queanes and Cuckolds Errants* gives a direction for 'Tarltons Ghost' to speak the prologue '*after Second Sounding*', but that is partly because he is more sure about the fact of the sounding than the prologue, which may be '*omitted . . . and another prologue . . . be brought in Place*' (6). John Fletcher and Shakespeare's *Two Noble Kinsmen* has the direction 'Flourish' flanking the word 'Prologue'; here the sound may be recorded to match the play's conclusion, which is also a flourish – this is a tragedy that is to occur sandwiched, even on paper, between two aural displays of ceremony and royal assurance (A2^v).

Early modern plays do sometimes, however, assume the trumpet's sound has been heard though they do not record it. There is, for instance, no stage direction for a trumpet in front of the prologue to Thomas Heywood's *Foure Prentises*, though the speaker in that play asks 'Doe you not know that I am the Prologue? . . . Have you not sounded thrice?' (A4^r). Likewise, the prologue to *Henry V*, with its references to 'A Kingdome for a Stage, Princes to Act, / And Monarchs to behold the swelling Scene' (TLN 4–5) seems to follow on from a royal 'flourish' (choruses elsewhere in the play are flanked by the word 'flourish'); its later references to conjuring up 'The vastie fields of France' and the 'Caskes / That did affright the Ayre at Agincourt' (TLN 13–15) gesture to the military signals that the trumpet will use as a substitute for action; they seem, too, to pick up and reposition sounds just heard.

Plays spoken without prologues – after their second performance, when prologues habitually dropped away (Stern 2009c) – still began with trumpet blasts. Those sounds, likewise, are only intermittently recorded, and are easier to learn about from texts written on the subject of the theatre than actual playbooks. When, in Christopher Brooke's poem *The Ghost of Richard III*, Richard III prepares to enter the stage of the world, he commands that the 'Canker'd Trumpets of the Deepe; / Proclaime my Entrance, to this stagie Round' (B2^r). Likewise, *Lord Have Mercy Upon Us*, a pamphlet describing happenings in Oxford as though they were a play, relates: 'The scene is Oxford, and now sound Trumpets, my Lord enters' (3). Shakespeare, depicting plays-in-plays that do not begin with prologues, still assumes a trumpeter will proclaim them. The actors' entertainment for Christopher Sly in *The Taming of the Shrew*, for instance, begins '*Flourish. Enter Lucentio, and his man*

Triano' (TLN 299); *The Murder of Gonzago* in *Hamlet*, begins '*The Trumpets sounds. Dumbe show followes*' (Q2 H1ᵛ).³

It is only plays of the 1580s and 1590s that sometimes articulate in stage directions the fact that the action will begin after a trumpet blast: '*After you have sounded thrise, let Venus be let downe from the top of the Stage*' (Greene A3ʳ). But, as many plays of this period and later begin with a fictional trumpet call, the sound can be said to be often hidden in plain view. Robert Wilson begins *Three Ladies* (1584) with a stage direction for 'Fame' who is to '*Enter ... sounding before Love and Conscience*' – the trumpet takes to the stage as a character (A2ᵛ); Shakespeare's *Henry VI, Part 2* opens with the stage direction for a '*Flourish of Trumpets: Then Hoboyes. Enter King, Duke Humfrey, Salisbury, Warwicke, and Beauford on the one side*' (TLN 2–3), where it appears that a pre-play flourish turns into a flourish for a king. In these instances, the fictional trumpet is negotiating with the pre-play trumpet or, indeed, melding the two, so that what seemed to be an announcement of the imminent start of the play is in fact the actual start of the play.

Even in private theatres, the trumpet appears to have been the sound with which plays began. When, in November 1596, theatrical entrepreneur James Burbage declared his intention to build a playhouse in the Blackfriars precinct, the locals put together a petition to stop him because, amongst other objections, 'the ... playhouse is so neere the Church that the noyse of the drummes and trumpets will greatly disturbe and hinder ... the ministers and parishioners' (Chambers 1923: 4.319–20).⁴ Though that fear is anticipatory, the later Blackfriars Playhouse does appear to have used the instruments, for in Henry Fitzgeffrey's *Satyres and Satyricall Epigrams ... Intituled Notes from Black-Fryers* one audience member at Blackfriars is depicted asking another 'what may be found / To deceive Time with, till the second sound?' (E7ᵛ).⁵ While it is possible that 'indoor' instruments like cornets were, in this instance, being 'sounded', the term 'sound' was most often used of the trumpet, and the trumpet (and its banner) would have provided constancy between the Globe and Blackfriars, ensuring that all company plays began with equal urgency and royal sanction.

---

³ Interestingly, the trumpets are replaced by '*hoboyes play*' in folio (TLN 1990), perhaps because the play is reconceived for a different place of performance; perhaps because the company had acquired the use of the hoboy-playing London Waits.

⁴ It is possible that this document is a forgery, though Arthur Freeman, who has not located the document, agrees with Chambers that it is 'probably genuine' (Freeman and Freeman 2004: 2.1094).

⁵ Entire pre-performance concerts, which sometimes also heralded Blackfriars plays, will have been different. They might have substituted for the trumpet or have included it.

As few scholars have considered the play's opening trumpet calls, however, fewer still are conscious of the very particular standing that the trumpeter had in early modern England. Uniquely amongst instrumentalists, trumpeters were obliged to attain a special licence before they could play publicly. An officer chosen by the king, the 'Sergeant Trumpeter', had sole authority to license the playing of trumpets (and beating of drums) outside the royal household; anyone using trumpets without his authority was liable to prosecution. This was as true for theatrical as for military trumpets: 'All trumpet players had to apply for a license to perform in theatrical presentations and all military and naval trumpeters were appointed and licensed by the Sargeant-Trumpeter who accumulated ... a huge salary from his commissions' (Crispian Steele-Perkins, quoted in Brownlow 1996: 161). That meant, then, that trumpet players always had courtly (and costly) associations, which explains their belief in their own grandeur and superiority. 'No man,' punned John Earle in *Micro-cosmographie*, is 'so puft up' as a trumpeter (I5^r). The start of plays, heralded by a man of status, licensed by the king, will have sounded noble, portentous and regally 'allowed'.

As a little-known decree from the time of James I makes evident, the cost to playhouses of keeping one, or several, daily trumpeters in order to announce plays was significant. Issued by the king, perhaps because some theatrical companies had been remiss in payments, the decree reminds companies that:

> no Drum, Trumpett, nor fife, shall sounde at any plaies, Dumb-shewes or Modells, without the Lycence of our ... Serjant. And our Sargeant or his deputies, shall have out of every Playhouse to his or their owne use, twelve pence the daie on every daie in which they shall play ... (our owne Players excepted). ('Fees paid', Bodleian Library, MS Ashmole 857, 344. Contractions have been expanded.)

That arrangement, that sum of money, and even that boon for the king's players of free trumpeters was to remain a fixture well into the latter half of the century: on 18 June 1669, a group of trumpeters were apprehended 'for keeping playhouses and sounding trumpets ... without paying the fee due to his Majesty's serjeant trumpeter ... whereby the said serjeant ought to receive twelve pence from every playhouse for every day they act, his Majesty's players excepted' (quoted De Lafontaine 1909: 217).

Because trumpeters were central and expensive non-actor members of theatrical troupes that most plays for most companies abound in trumpet signals: tuckets, sennets, flourishes, alarums, charges, parleys and retreats are predominant non-verbal sounds of early modern drama. True, the trumpet was relished because it could, given its real-life use, musically create on stage most public ceremonies and most military events – but whenever it did so it will also have recalled its earlier use as herald of the play. A trumpet, then, was quintessentially metatheatrical.

The importance of the trumpet to Shakespeare's company is made obvious by the play-in-the-play in the folio (1623) version of *A Midsummer Night's Dream*. There, the prologue to *Pyramus and Thisby* is introduced by a stage direction for Pyramus, Thisby, Wall, Moonshine and Lion to enter preceded by '*Tawyer with a Trumpet before them*' (TLN 1924–5). 'Tawyer', a stranded 'real' name, is a reference to William Tawyer (or Toyer), a trumpeter also found on a list of musicians working for the King's Men in 1624 (Cutts 1967: 101–7).[6] His name is also to be found in the burial record of St Saviour's Southwark for June 1625, where he is described as 'Mr. Heminges man', that is, an employee of the actor, financial manager and Shakespeare editor, John Heminges (Halliwell-Phillipps 1887: 260). The reference, as well as suggesting that the folio version of *A Midsummer Night's Dream* is for a revival (particularly as 'Tawyer' is not in the 1600 or 1619 quartos), illustrates that one of the major decisions to make when (re)mounting a play was which trumpeter to use. Was Tawyer, who announced the prologue to the internal play, also the trumpeter who announced *A Midsummer Night's Dream*?

Collectively, the sound of the trumpet before a performance raises questions about when a play in the theatre began, and the related question about when an edition should begin. Is the trumpet the last sound heard *before* the play starts, or is it actually the play's start? Early modern playbooks, as shown, often do not directly record the trumpet's sound, but do assume it, imagining a readership conscious of a play's method of starting – aurally and perhaps also visually. As Simon Smith so thoughtfully illustrates, Shakespeare made careful use of trumpet calls within plays to highlight or destabilize stage action (2013: 101–19); might the instrument's first use, too, make a statement about the play to come, as well as creating a metatheatrical link between the play's 'factual' opening, and its subsequent 'fictional' music? The logic that governs editing plays in their 'first performance' form – and that leads to

---

[6] On that same list are other trumpeters whose names feature in plays as bit-parts – Samuel Underhill, who is found in *Barnauelt* (1619) and *Believe as you list* (1631), and George Rickner, who is in *The Honest Man's Fortune* (1625).

geometrical roses and treble clefs – might suggest adding to texts a trumpet call that was sometimes pre-play, but sometimes actual play. Shakespeare, at least, often uses trumpets to supply the first music heard after a drama's start, and asks for trumpets by name more than any other musical instrument. For plays by Shakespeare and his company – whose free trumpeter may have intensified their use of that instrument – might it be worth recording the sound that brought them into being?

***

When did early modern plays end? Not, it seems, when early modern playbooks do. Though texts of the period typically conclude on the Latin 'Finis', that final word seldom marks the completion of a play's actions. So the folio text for *Much Ado* reads:

> strike up Pipers. *Dance.*
> FINIS (TLN 2684–5)

As actors have to leave the stage after a dance for a play to end, an editor, confronted with this, will at least add a final stage direction to the text, 'exeunt'. Fletcher and Shakespeare's playbook of *Two Noble Kinsmen* (N1^r) ends:

> Gentlemen, good night.
> *Flourish.*
> FINIS.

Here, both the epilogue and the trumpeter(s) are left on stage. Again, exits (and perhaps an entrance, too, for the trumpeter) are, at the very least, required.

Hamlet, which survives in two variant 'good' forms, shows how 'finis' might be placed when words end, but before action does. The 1604 quarto reads:

> Goe bid the souldiers shoote.
> *Exeunt.*
> FINIS (G2^r)

Here, though an exeunt is supplied, the sound of the shooting is not. The folio text for that same moment ends on the same words but extends the action that follows them:

> Go, bid the Souldiers shoote.
> *Exeunt Marching: after the which, a Peale of*
> *Ordenance are shot off.*
> FINIS (TLN 3904–6)

Before the beginning; after the end 369

The comparison indicates how easy it was for 'finis' to be placed at the end of the dialogue (always recorded), rather than the theatrical event (not always recorded).

But perhaps it is wrong, anyway, to associate 'finis' with play endings. Shakespeare's *Pericles*, for example, has two different statements of 'finis' on its final page (I3^v). One demarcates the end of the play's dialogue, and the other, separately, the end of the epilogue:

> Lord *Cerimon* wee doe our longing stay,
> To heare the rest untolde, Sir lead's the way.
> *FINIS.*
>
> *Gower.*
> In *Antiochus* and his daughter you have heard
> Of monstrous lust ...
> So on your Patience evermore attending,
> New joy wayte on you, heere our play has ending.
> FINIS.

Here, the printers may have been given two documents: the play's dialogue and the play's epilogue, both of which were marked with 'finis', because both were separately written and separately concluded. Alternatively, given that printers characteristically concluded all books with 'finis', one or both of these instances may mark the end of the material given to the compositor at a particular moment. As William H. Sherman observes more generally of books of the period, 'Finis ... speaks in what we might call the voice of the book, which may or may not be that of the author or printer' (2011: 73).

As 'finis', then, is seldom the conclusion of the staged play, let alone the performance, it is worth considering how the theatrical occasion itself may actually have ended. Here, the confusing epilogue to *Henry IV, Part 2* is instructive. It anticipates at least two events about to occur that are not then specifically recorded. 'My Tongue is wearie', says the speaker, probably the clown Will Kempe, 'when my Legs are too, I will bid you good night' (TLN 3348–9), a gesture towards a post-epilogue dance that he will perform; and 'I will ... kneele downe before you: But (indeed) to pray for the Queene' (TLN 3349–50), a gesture towards a post-epilogue prayer he will say for the monarch. Both dance and prayer appear to have been usual ways of concluding theatrical events.

The terminal prayer to the monarch was, in the 1580s and 1590s, included in epilogues themselves. During that period, it is therefore regularly recorded: 'Preserve our noble Queene Elizabeth, and her councell all, / With thy heavenly grace, sent from thy seate supernall' (*New Custome* D4^v);

'Her counsel wise, and Nobles of this land / Blesse, and preserve O lord with thy right hand' (Wilson 1590: I4ʳ); 'As duty binds us, for our noble queene let us pray, / And for her honourable councel' (Preston 1570: F3ʳ). Yet, as *Henry IV, Part 2* suggests, when the prayer was no longer in the epilogue, it was still spoken: it simply was not written afresh for each play – presumably because it had become formulaic. So Thomas Freeman in *Rubbe and a great cast* (A3ʳ) writes a poem to James I pouring scorn on the kind of player who

> prophanes his lips
> With scurrile jeasts of some lewd ribald Play;
> And after all, upon the Scaffold skips,
> And for his Sov'raigne then begins to pray.

Writing in 1631 in the time of Charles I, Richard Brathwait in *Whimzies* likewise refers to the 'Actor after the end of a Play', who zealously 'prayes for his Majestie, the Lords of his most honourable privie Councell, and all that love the King' (1631: 56).[7] Yet the prayer itself, by that period, is only recorded in a single interlude, *Two Wise Men and All the Rest Fooles*. Obsessed with preserving 'aunciente and laudable custome' (A1ᵛ), that interlude probably records its words for the monarchical prayer because plays of old had done so: 'all our hearts pray for the King, and his families enduring happinesse, and our countries perpetuall welfare'. Concluding 'Si placet plaudite', *Two Wise Men* is also the only text that, using a formula taken from Plautus as a stage direction, assumes the audience's response to the completion of the drama, applause, is a further aspect of the play's end (O2ᵛ) (should applause, too, be recorded as part of a play?).

Yet though, with these rare exceptions, the words of the prayer are not recorded in seventeenth-century playbooks, the fact that it was spoken will have had a significant effect on plays. Declared by a supplicating player on his knees, it will visually have illustrated the humility of the theatrical company. With its recipient as God and monarch both, it will simultaneously have functioned, like 'vivat regina' and 'vivat rex' at the end of playbills, as a reminder to spectators that public theatre was regally approved. It will also, by extension, have ensured that every drama ended on a round statement of establishment values. Perhaps it therefore 'allowed' subversive or politically knotty plays, for monarchical prayers will have blunted (or, depending on interpretation, ironized) the preceding

---

[7] For more on terminal prayers in epilogues, see Hattaway 2009: 154–67 and Stern 2010: 122–9.

drama. There is, then, a logic for placing the fact that terminal prayers were spoken in modern editions: prayers may seem to alter subtly the meaning of the play just performed.

Other post-play events were, like the opening trumpet call, sometimes part of the fiction of the story, and sometimes not. For instance, in public and private theatre alike, some kind of music followed every drama. This often took the form of a dance involving several actors – presumably showcasing them for their final applause. Thomas Platter, a Swiss visitor to London in 1599, saw a production of *Julius Caesar*, probably Shakespeare's play, and records how 'when the play was over they danced very marvellously and gracefully together as is their wont, two dressed as men and two as women' (1937 [1599]: 166); a year earlier, Paul Hentzner, a German visitor, recorded that 'English Actors represent almost every day Tragedies and Comedies ... these are concluded with music, variety of dances, and the excessive applause of those that are present' (1757: 41). As plays, particularly comedies, regularly included dances in the conclusion to their stories, the dance sometimes merged the fictional celebration, often of a wedding, with the factual celebration of the end of the event. *All's Well*, quoted above, provides just one such instance, but other Shakespeare plays too conclude on dances, including *A Midsummer Night's Dream*, *Much Ado* and *As You Like It*. Should post-play dances, when not part of the play itself, be mentioned in editions? In all instances, factual and fictional alike, such dances will have altered the audience's mood.

The question is complicated by the fact that the music does not seem always to have taken dance form. Sometimes what was performed after the play was a song, which was even more likely to be seen as a comment on the preceding play. '*When that I was and a little tine boy*', with its burden of '*the raine it raineth every day*', which is sung as a conclusion to *Twelfth Night* when '*our Play is done*' (TLN 2560–79) is one such song; its world-weary attitude to life, love and marriage is often thought to mock or at least trouble the subject of its play. Other plays, too, ended on similarly resigned – and similarly weather-conscious songs – as the introduction of a drinking song 'to be sung at the latter end' of Dekker's *Shoemakers Holiday*, 'Cold's the wind, and wet's the raine', suggests (A4^r). Nor, however, did song necessarily substitute for dance: John Davies considers the moment in the theatre 'When ended is the play, the daunce, and song' (2^v). Should the potential for both events be recorded at the end of play texts?

Conflicting with this aim is the fact that jigs – comic song-and-dance combinations – are regularly described as being performed after plays: Lupton in 1632 records how 'most commonly when the play is done, you shal have a Jigge or dance of al trades' (1632: 81), and Knolles in 1606 relates that 'now adayes they put at the end of everie Tragedie (as poison into meat) a comedie or jigge' (1606: 645). Though jigs are sometimes said to have fallen out of fashion, repeated references to them suggest that they had a habit of re-emerging, or that activities designated 'dance' or 'song' might substitute for or have become them (Gurr 2004b: 69–77). With their frankness and bawdiness, jigs in their boldest form will have altered the entire feel of the theatrical occasion.

A different event, perhaps an alternative to dance/song/jig, or perhaps following on from it, was the clown's improvisation on a 'theme' provided by the audience. For this, spectators shouted out themes or questions to which the company clown improvised a song in response. 'The play being done', the great clown of the 1580s, Richard Tarlton, would request that, as *Tarltons Jeasts* records, 'every one so pleased to throw up his theame'; various jests of the time relate to the fact that 'it was his custome for to sing extempore of Theames given him' (C3^r). A book that may preserve some surviving themes from a later clown is Robert Armin's *Quips upon Questions*. It contains queries like 'Why barkes that Dogge?' to which it provides rhyming responses, generally poking fun at the questioners: 'wanting wit, better be Dogges, and barke' (A4^{r-v}). As 'themes' were often described as songs – 'I would ende in a song, yea an Extempore song on this Theame, Nequid nemis necessarium' (Chettle 1593: G4^v) – the words 'song', 'dance' and maybe even 'jig' might on occasion be interchangeable with 'theme'. It is therefore difficult to say how many separate events might follow on from a play, though the fact that post-play events were generally farcical and musical seems a given. Is it worth recording, perhaps even important to record, in serious play texts, that the event's ultimate conclusion probably involved music consisting of or enhanced by a clown's indecorums?

One more event took place before the occasion reached its end. As play runs had yet to come into being, and different plays were performed on a daily basis, generally 'after th'Epilogue there comes some one / To tell Spectators what shall next be shown' (Beaumont and Fletcher 1647: F6^r). Audiences, perhaps already involved in the stage action through 'themes', seem to have felt ready to take part in this particular announcement. When Antonio Foscarini, an Italian ambassador to England, was given the opportunity to '[invite] the public to the play for the next day', he found that 'the people, who wanted a different one, began to call out ... because they wanted one that they called "Friars"' (Orrell 1977–78). Did this moment mark the ultimate end of the play in every public (but obviously not court) performance – or did it mark the first clear moment after the play's end, as attention turned to what would be staged the next day?

The question, then, is the same as that for the trumpeter: are these events that follow on from a play, or are they part of the play – or are some the former and some the latter? In all instances, the answer partly depends on what 'the play' is thought to be. Modern editions that aim to produce the first day of performance (the second day of performance would make better sense, as first performances contained unique and unrepeated events – see Stern 2000: 113–21) should presumably embrace the performative actions addressed here.

Yet traditionally editors have been attempting to reproduce a play in the state in which it left the author's hand. That means that they have been resistant to the idea of inserting events that are part of the performance but not part of the author's script. Nevertheless, such editions – of which Arden 2 offers various examples – have always corrected missed entrances/exits and added necessary props for the sake of the logical coherence of the play. So whilst maintaining that they are returning to an earlier, page-focused, occasion, they are nevertheless edited in fact with an eye to the concerns of the stage. This is true even of the editions that privilege fictional story over performance or writer. 'Location' directions, once regularly added to texts to explain where the play's story rather than its staged event occurs – '*an apartment of the* PRINCE's', '*Another part of the field*' (Norton edition of *Henry IV, Part 1*, lightly updated by McMullan (Shakespeare 2003): 8, 88) – are still flanked by missing or instructive 'theatrical' stage directions, fusing 'story' with 'performance'.[8] Even the *RSC Shakespeare*, which prides itself on being based on the folio, 'a real book', rather than a notional performance, adds thoughtful performative stage directions to its text because it is simultaneously aiming to be the chosen edition of one of Britain's premiere acting companies (Bate and Rasmussen 2007: 56). As all 'book-based' editions for 'readers', then, remain frankly theatrical in many of their editorial insertions, there is still a rationale for sandwiching around them pre- and post-performance activities – particularly if the creating author believed these activities to be (unwritten) presences in his script.

***

---

[8] The text for this 2003 edition is that by James L. Sanderson, first published in 1962 and revised in 1968.

This chapter has not set out to solve the problem of how to edit the beginning and end of texts, but to show that there is a problem. It has shown greater problems, however, bedevilling what editors choose to acknowledge and what to leave out. As no editors have an entirely clear sense of what 'the play' as opposed to 'the occasion' is – because, of course, neither do early modern playbooks – so no edited text clearly represents either.

That returns us, then, to the question of whether or not it is useful or helpful or even permissible to include theatre-only activities in modern editions. Such happenings as this chapter has detailed are, after all, non-authorial, do not seem (often) to have been included in early modern printed versions of plays and belong more to the event than to the text. On the other hand, these happenings have also been shown to be, sometimes directly and sometimes indirectly, interpretatively relevant.

Countering that is the fact that it is impossible to be sure that each pre- and post-play event was part of *every* performance of *every* play. Additionally, each pre- and post-play event has a certain vagueness in number and nature that makes it hard to articulate as stage-directions: how many trumpet calls were there, and how often did a flourish substitute for them (i.e., what should an editor write for the 'trumpet' moment)? What was the nature of the post-play music and clowning, and did it alter from play to play, or day to day, or playhouse to playhouse (i.e., what should an editor write for the 'music' moment)? Should a slew of symbols be created to add to 'Tudor' roses and treble clefs, so that our texts are filled with stylized pictures of trumpets and/or banners, praying hands, gambolling clowns, speech bubbles? That, surely, is ridiculous. But so too is ignoring events around which playwrights seem (often) to have written – and companies (always?) to have performed – their plays.

PART VI

Apparatus and the fashioning of knowledge

CHAPTER 23

Framing Shakespeare: introductions and commentary in critical editions of the plays

Jill L. Levenson

> Reade him, therefore; and againe, and againe: And if then you doe not like him, surely you are in some manifest danger, not to vnderstand him. And so we leaue you to other of his Friends, whom if you need, can bee your guides: if you neede them not, you can leade your selues, and others.
> 'To the great Variety of Readers', The First Folio of Shakespeare (1623) (A3)

With these instructions John Heminge and Henry Condell (or their ghost writers) refer those readers who need help understanding Shakespeare's plays to guides more capable of explication than the actor-friends who assembled this Folio. 'Other of his Friends' remain unidentified in the address, but within a century named editors of Shakespeare's dramatic texts would provide instructions and notes in volumes which argued their individual views of both the works and their author. From then until now introductions and notes have become standard components in critical editions of Shakespeare's plays, although they differ in content, purpose, format, length, and eloquence.

Over more than four centuries the presentation of Shakespeare's drama in print has gone through several major phases. Inevitably, changes in standards for editing the texts themselves have influenced standards for composing introductions and commentary. The chapter which follows will consider four of these phases, with particular attention to introductions and notes: the earliest publications of Shakespeare's plays, which had preliminaries but lacked notes; the well-known eighteenth-century editions, which struggled to define the editor's task in prefaces and voluminous commentary; the twentieth-century editions, influenced by the New

---

Special thanks to the generous editors who provided information for this chapter: Michael Best, David Bevington, Brett Hirsch, David McInnis, and the general editors of the Revels Plays. David Bevington has made major contributions to several of the critical editions cited in the chapter.

Bibliography, which reduced the scope of the apparatus by concentrating on textual issues; and editions since the end of the twentieth century, which continue to extend ancillary materials in print and on line. Through these modulations each phase has shed new light, more or less, on Shakespeare's texts. During the eighteenth and twentieth centuries that light frequently illuminated the editors as much as it did the plays. Yet it has always revealed something new and valuable about the texts, adding dimensions by tracing the etymology of words or speculating about the process by which a manuscript had been printed. The most successful introductions and notes are probably still to come, heralded by recent experiments that give readers a wealth of information with which to understand and interpret each play. Like other intellectual endeavours, the best in this kind are inclusive, thoughtful, and accurate.

Preliminaries

Whereas commentary about Shakespeare's plays did not become formalized in editions before the eighteenth century, details of theatrical and printing history accompanied the earliest publications of his texts. As Thomas L. Berger writes in a survey of the quartos, 'title-pages of early modern English plays provide a wealth of information and, quite probably, a wealth of misinformation about English drama in print' (2007: 58–9). 'The title-pages of the eight early editions of *Richard III* . . . provide such a bounty', he adds, 'some of which may indeed be factual' (59).

The five quartos of *Romeo and Juliet* illustrate Berger's observations. For instance, the title page of Quarto 1 (1597) situates the text in more than one way. It calls *Romeo and Juliet* '*AN* EXCELLENT conceited Tragedie', the word 'conceited' emphasizing the play's wittiness in a formula used at the time primarily to advertise comedies. In another bid to attract purchasers, the title page refers to performances 'with great applause' by Lord Hunsdon's company. Here it identifies the Lord Chamberlain's Men by the title they held for a brief period in 1596 and 1597. Finally, it names the printer John Danter, reproduces one of his ornaments, and specifies the date 1597. By comparison, the title page of Quarto 2 (1599) presents the play with significant differences. While the tragedy remains excellent, it is no longer conceited, and it has been '*Newly corrected, augmented, and amended*'. This title page identifies the performers as the Lord Chamberlain's Men, who have now acted the play publicly 'sundry times'. It names the printer Thomas Creede, reproduces one of his ornaments, and specifies the date 1599 (Levenson 2000: 107, 111). When Berger reaches Quarto 5 (1637), he finds its title page the most thorough and accurate of the group:

> At last, a title-page behaving itself with all the necessary information: a title, a playing company, a theater, an author, a state of the text, a printing location, a printer, a bookseller, the location of the bookseller's shop, and a date. (2007: 61)

The prefatory material in the first Folio is far more extensive. It consists of nine separate components, four of them in verse, and its title page includes Martin Droeshout's engraving. On that page, and in 'A CATALOGVE' or table of contents ([A6]), this first collected edition of the plays spells out one reason why it had a formative influence on the reception of Shakespeare's dramatic canon. It divides the works by genre, into Comedies, Histories, and Tragedies, an arrangement still familiar today. By various means, it has also determined the reception of Shakespeare himself as a multifaceted iconic figure. The newly invented non-classical denomination 'Histories', focusing on a grand sequence of English kings, implies Shakespeare's status as a national poet. With other parts of the preliminaries, the implications become wider and deeper. Ben Jonson's famous poem, 'To the memory of my beloued, The AVTHOR MR. VVILLIAM SHAKESPEARE: And what he hath left vs', places Shakespeare pre-eminently in the history of English literature, in his immediate theatrical context, and in the long view of drama since antiquity ([A4–A4v]). The dedication to William, Earl of Pembroke, and Philip, Earl of Montgomery, expresses the compilers' aspirations to keep the memory of Shakespeare alive with this almost-perfect volume, the title page promising texts 'Published according to the True Originall Copies'. In its immortal longings and powerful influence, the first Folio may have distorted understanding of Shakespeare's works for generations of readers. John Jowett's discussion of 'The Folio as Representation and Misrepresentation' analyses five deficiencies, all of them appearing in the preliminaries (2007a: 84–92). Whatever the book's strengths and weaknesses, the prefatory matter encapsulates them, and this serves as an introduction to the complexities that follow.

Platforms

For almost a century the earliest editors of Shakespeare's plays remained anonymous and the practices in which they engaged lacked definition. The terms now associated with those practices – 'edit', 'edition', 'editor' – would fluctuate through the eighteenth century until they began to settle into the modern sense of 'prepar[ing] the literary work of another person, or number of persons for publication, by selecting, revising, and arranging the material' (*Oxford English Dictionary*, 'editor', sb. 2). During the eighteenth century no less was at stake than articulation of the editor's task, especially with regard to the commentary. Beginning with Nicholas Rowe's *Works* (1709), named editors of Shakespeare's plays attempted to explain their intentions in the apparatus of their books. Rowe included a biography of Shakespeare with his short preface (the preferred term in this period for an introduction), the first to identify the editor's task (Murphy 2007: 94); and Alexander Pope supplied a preface and commentary. With the publication of Pope's first edition (1723–25), a debate about the editor's duties extended beyond editorial apparatus to other kinds of publications such as pamphlets, monographs, and satirical verse. Opinions and data about the editor's responsibilities accumulated in the apparatus, other publications, and unpublished correspondence, each document absorbing material from the rest. Reviewing the debate, which continued more or less heatedly over four decades, Samuel Johnson observed in his own preface 'how much paper is wasted in confutation ... Thus the human mind is kept in motion without progress' (1968: 7.99). He hoped to avoid the 'spontaneous strain of invective and contempt' which he found in the commentaries of his predecessors (7.102).

If Johnson's *Plays* (1765) kept a distance from invective and contempt, his edition could not avoid the contradictions between theory and practice characteristic of its antecedents. In effect, eighteenth-century editors of Shakespeare worked out their functions as they fulfilled them, in the prefaces and commentaries which established their texts. As Simon Jarvis has demonstrated, their ambivalent concepts of editing – sometimes veering in a single edition between Pope's 'dull duty of an Editor' (Pope 1986: 2.24) and Johnson's 'art' (Johnson 1968: 7.108, 109) – led them to express ambitions which they could not achieve. Although they wanted to rescue Shakespeare's texts from obscurities and various agents of corruption, they lacked the means (or perhaps the inclination) to identify copy closest to the original. Even the most scrupulous eighteenth-century editions based their texts on printed versions of the plays far removed from the early quartos and the first Folio:

> Theobald's *Shakespeare* is based on Pope's second edition (1728), which was based on Rowe's third edition (1714), which in turn was based on the fourth

folio (1685). That is to say, instead of basing his edition on the printed texts closest to Shakespeare's manuscripts, he based it on a text eight printings removed from the first folio, which itself, in the case of a number of plays, was printed from quarto copy. (Seary 1990: 132–3)

Emending a text under these circumstances presented considerable difficulty, although Theobald rose to the challenge more than once, as with his now-accepted emendation of 'a table of green fields' as 'a babbled of green fields' (for discussion of this emendation, see: *King Henry V*, 2.3.14 n. (Gurr 2005)).

The ambivalence of eighteenth-century editors about their work affected their attitudes towards commentary as well: they disagreed about standards for annotation. When Theobald adapted methods from editing classical writers to his explication of Shakespeare, introducing parallel passages to elucidate the text, other editors resisted or mocked the minutescholarship that generated his commentary. Yet even Pope would incorporate some of Theobald's notes in the apparatus of his second edition; and Johnson assembled the commentary of his predecessors, including Theobald, into what would be the first variorum edition. In their prefaces, if not their practices, Theobald and Johnson shared a methodology summed up by Johnson: 'Not a single passage in the whole work has appeared to me corrupt, which I have not attempted to restore; or obscure, which I have not endeavoured to illustrate' (1968: 7.110). Neither these two editors nor their colleagues seem to lay out similar guidelines for the content of the prefaces themselves.

As eighteenth-century editors tried to define their task in the prefaces and commentary of their editions, they also argued with their critics, either in the apparatus or in ancillary publications. The best-known part of this exchange occurred at its launch, when Theobald responded to Pope's edition with *Shakespeare Restor'd: or, A Specimen of the Many Errors as well Committed, or Unamended, by Mr. Pope in his Late Edition of this Poet* (1726). Theobald prepared for his own edition of 1733 in this 194-page study, setting out his principles for editing and providing extensive commentary. He devoted the first 132 pages to *Hamlet*, at one point offering eighteen parallel readings for 1.2.36–7 in support of the Q/F reading 'To business with the King' over Pope's emended version 'Of treaty with the King', then acknowledging: 'I am afraid of growing too luxuriant in Examples of this Sort, or I could stretch out the Catalogue of them to a greater Extent' (quoted in Seary 1990: 69). Responding to Theobald's critique and his method, Pope made him the hero of *The Dunciad* in its first edition (1728):

> This Tibbald, or Theobald, published an edition of Shakespeare, of which he was so proud himself as to say, in one of Mist's Journals, June 8, 'That to expose any Errors in it was impracticable'. And in another, April 27, 'That whatever care might for the future be taken by any other Editor, he would still give about five hundred Emendations, that *shall* escape them all.'
> (Note to Book the First, l. 133 (p. 279))

Theobald supplied 1,356 notes in his edition (Seary 1990: 171), which increased from seven volumes in 1733 to eight volumes in 1740. Later eighteenth-century editions grew by accretion, following Johnson's example and recording the notes of previous commentators and editors. By 1821, two twenty-one-volume collections – James Boswell's completion of Edmond Malone's edition and the last of the series by Johnson, George Steevens, and Isaac Reed – monopolized Shakespeare in print. They brought to a culmination the first stage in what G. K. Hunter has called the 'history of Shakespearean annotation', or 'a history of the means by which the multiform indeterminacy of the original can be accommodated within the cultural expectations of one age after another' (2003: 177–8). In sheer magnitude these editions represent the great effort made to align Shakespeare's reputation with neoclassical standards over the course of a century. The weighty apparatus of the eighteenth- and early nineteenth-century collections supports a vernacular classic that must have seemed unable to stand on its own. Often the notes reveal at least as much about the editor's temperament and scholarly aspirations as they do about Shakespeare's text.

Periphery

Within four decades, a new phase in the history of Shakespearean annotation began with the Cambridge edition (1863–66), which focused on establishing texts and in the process narrowed the purview of explanatory comments. Collation notes accompanied the plays, while discursive commentary received a few pages at the backs of volumes. Horace Howard Furness revived the variorum format with *Romeo and Juliet* (1871); but the shift of focus to text overtook him with the New Bibliography, which started to declare itself at the turn of the twentieth century. In an essay published in 2004, Ernst Honigmann calls the New Bibliography 'a journey of discovery undertaken by a group of colleagues' who re-edited important Elizabethan documents and challenged the conclusions of their predecessors. Honigmann names three leaders (A. W. Pollard, R. B. McKerrow, and W. W. Greg); and he distinguishes four periods or generations in an evolutionary process: 1900–20, 1920–50, 1950–70, and the years following 1970 (Honigmann 2004: 77). In a book-length study six years later, Gabriel Egan has room to expand a definition of the New Bibliography. The timing of his stages differs somewhat from Honigmann's, because he deals with the period after 1970 by individual decades. In contrast, his second period covers 1939–68, a span which allows him to emphasize the technical means for analysing early books that became prominent with the contributions of Fredson Bowers and the 'Virginian School'. Bibliographers could produce detailed evidence from presswork, assessing running titles, broken type and type shortages; they could try to identify compositors by spelling habits, an approach Egan calls 'dauntingly technical' (2010: 57). However its evolution is calculated, the New Bibliography became authoritative during the 1960s. It influenced the format of critical editions, drawing attention to textual issues which occupied more and more of the introductions and commentary.

Signs of the new dispensation appeared in classrooms and publications as editing became professionalized. For example, Alfred Harbage had established a graduate half-course at Harvard by the autumn of 1964, when I enrolled in it. My notes from that course, unearthed while moving offices in 2012, have confirmed my recollections of the seminar. Specifically, they show that most of the time our small group concentrated on establishing text: we spent many sessions learning about the printing process, types of copy, collation and emendation. Our bibliography included McKerrow and a great deal of Greg. At our first meeting, Professor Harbage explained 'glossing' (identifying allusions, using the *Oxford English Dictionary*) and what an introduction should cover (authorship, date, sources, genre, brief critical comment, meaningful context). A few weeks later, he referred again to the introduction, adding that it should incorporate information about the play's theatre company and history. Each of us was assigned an unedited early modern play of which the Rare Book Library had an original copy; and at the end of the course we submitted an edition of the first gathering. If Professor Harbage approved our work, he would offer to supervise a full edition as our PhD thesis.

By late 1964, members of this seminar could consult such full editions in the university's archives, dissertations by notable scholars like Daniel Seltzer and Martin Wine. These projects had a particular format: facing pages contained the facsimile of a passage with emendations underneath on the left and a modernized version of the passage with gloss underneath on the right. When some of the theses were eventually published, their authors had to convert them to more streamlined formats, eliminating the facsimiles. Clearly, these exercises in editing constituted training to prepare a distinct kind of publication. If most graduate students knew little or nothing about editing when they enrolled in the course – I signed up only because I wanted to study English Renaissance drama with Alfred Harbage – we ended with confidence that we had acquired a useful academic skill-set. Literary criticism, staging and theatre history remained secondary to our editorial presentations of text.

While editing became an established discipline at Harvard, Clifford Leech gave it a different kind of presence at the University of Toronto. Leech had been the founding General Editor of the Revels Plays since 1958; and within a dozen years he had overseen fifteen published volumes, two more at press, and many additional commissions. In 1970, his seminal article 'On Editing One's First Play' surveyed the many series in which an editor's skill-set could be applied. These series, all centred on English Renaissance drama, included not only the Shakespearean editions but also the Revels, the Regents, the New Mermaids and the Fountainwell (Leech 1970: 63). Like Harbage's seminar, Leech's article spends more time on establishing a text than on composing the introduction and commentary. In order to present the text, a first-time editor must do serious homework, reading 'the main contributions to bibliographical and textual study of the last thirty years' (64). Then this editor needs to choose a copy-text, ready a provisional text, and collate extant versions of the copy-text as well as later editions of the play (64–7).

Although Leech expected a newly commissioned editor to have a comprehensive background in the drama of the period and in major non-dramatic works (64), his article fails to connect this education with the content of the introduction or commentary. The paragraph on preliminaries is more subjective than exact:

> And then there is the introduction, on which you will have been given a directive as to content and word-length. This may be the editor's most rewarding task and is certainly the most arduous ... The play that is being edited is one that has, in many instances, given rise to more than one interpretation. If it is by a major dramatist, the differences may be considerable. Part of the task is to give the reader an idea of previous views ... at the same time the general editor must be prepared to let the editor say what he himself thinks: that is one of the inalienable rights when one is editing a play. (68–9)

In his advice for compiling annotations, Leech proposes a method in two phases, before and after preparing the text for the general editor: underlining in a reprint words and phrases appearing to need annotation;

and refining the commentary by annotating 'as freely as your series allows' (68). He supplements this advice with a few suggestions about using the *Oxford English Dictionary* and parallel passages (64).

Shifting paradigms

Over the next two decades editors of Shakespeare's texts adjusted their priorities by fits and starts. In the course of these changes, the apparatus of critical editions became more inclusive and enlightening. Nevertheless, the most recent guidelines for the Revels Plays cite Leech's article on the first page. Until its cancellation a few years ago, the introductory course in bibliography for graduate students at the University of Toronto contained a unit on editing influenced by his views. When I offered my first section of Bibliography I in the 1970s, the New Bibliography loomed large in the sessions we devoted to the mechanics of printing and the establishment of text. It marginalized consideration of introductions and commentary. By the 1980s, however, I could broaden the scope of editing assignments, giving students more flexible guidelines to edit not only Shakespearean lines but also Romantic and postmodern texts. Each member of the class chose a short passage from three on offer and determined its audience and purpose. Among the components of their brief editions, introductions and commentary took a variety of forms.

By now editors and other textual scholars have charted the course of change which affected my pedagogy. Serious challenges to the New Bibliography during the 1980s – especially studies of multiple-text plays and publication of the Oxford Shakespeare *Complete Works* (1986) – loosened its grip on editions of early modern plays. Single editions in mainstream series such as Arden 3, the New Cambridge Shakespeare, and the Oxford Shakespeare, began to offer newly edited texts, individually shaped introductions, and freshly considered notes. Staging and theatre history became essential to the apparatus, as stated in the Editorial Procedures for the Oxford Shakespeare: 'In particular, we hope to find better ways of presenting to the reader works designed for performance' ([1978]: 5). The guidelines for the Revels Plays, which have undergone revision since Leech composed them, currently include detailed instructions for apparatus with a new emphasis on theatrical production.

When Stanley Wells invited me to edit *Romeo and Juliet* for the Oxford Shakespeare in the mid-1980s, I was completing research for a theatre history of the play. I had already explored the inventive use of sources, verse and genres in *Romeo and Juliet*; and I could see from the Editorial

Procedures that the edition might bring together all of this material to illuminate the text in new ways. Studying the guidelines I could hear Wells's voice, sensible and inflected with wit. On the scope of individual editions the guidelines explained: 'We hope to provide ... volumes which will be economically within the reach of students and scholars, and which will be encompassable by the mind' ([1978]: 4). They sounded reasonably permissive about the Introduction: 'Editors should shape their material as they think fit ... Guide-lines to content are given below. They should not be regarded as sacrosanct' (6). The discussion of Commentary begins: 'Notes should be succinct but not cryptic' (83).

Ultimately, the guidelines proved true to their words. They allowed editors to engage in original thinking not only about the control-text, but also about its apparatus. Consequently, I was free to assemble a database for the productions of *Romeo and Juliet* (still available at http://itergateway.org/romeo_juliet/), which collected profiles of 170 or so prompt-books, starting with those listed by Charles H. Shattuck, recording their cuts and stage directions. Before the advent of electronic editions, this database allowed anyone interested to explore the text of *Romeo and Juliet* – speech and actions – through its permutations from the seventeenth century to the late twentieth century. With Wells's help, I shaped the Introduction as I thought fit, with myth, literary influences and performance history at the front and more technical subjects, date and text, at the end. After I submitted my succinct notes, Wells came to the rescue in a demonstration of brilliant editing. He showed me how to reduce the Commentary by 15 percent through eliminating verbiage, not information, bringing the size of the volume below 500 pages, so that it would not far exceed G. R. Hibbard's edition of *Hamlet* (1987).

Critical editions of Shakespeare's plays soon began to share the openness and expectations written into Oxford's Editorial Procedures by 1978. Among them, Arden 3 has become the most explicit about its intentions, 'presenting the play as it has been shaped in history' (Holland 2013: xii). The general editors offer a substantial preface in recent editions: four pages or so spelling out the functions of commentary, textual notes and introductions meant to record insights collected from 'editors, critics and performers (on stage and screen)' (xii). On the last point they elaborate: 'Both the introduction and the commentary are designed to present the plays as texts for performance, and make appropriate reference to stage, film and television versions, as well as introducing the reader to the range of critical approaches to the plays. They discuss the history of the reception of the texts within the theatre and scholarship and beyond' (xv–xvi).

Apparently, the Arden 3 guidelines allow experienced editors to reconstruct familiar apparatus. Peter Holland explains that his introduction to *Coriolanus* substitutes an original arrangement for the conventional one. Replacing the usual disposition of topics, its table of contents begins with '*Coriolanus* in the 1930s' and ends with 'Filming *Coriolanus* (2011)', moving through a sequence of topics related in unpredictable ways (vii–viii). Moreover, 'the entire Introduction has deliberately been written without a single footnote' (xxviii), altogether an unorthodox and engaging interpretation of editorial preliminaries.

Holland's rethinking of the typical introduction reflects an important trend in recent and ongoing editions of early modern drama: experiments in presenting apparatus permit readers to see old texts with additional clarity in new frames of reference. Representing various approaches to apparatus, three types of projects stand at different points on a spectrum of possibilities: *The Cambridge Edition of the Works of Ben Jonson* (Jonson 2012); *Thomas Middleton: The Collected Works* (Taylor and Lavagnino 2007b); and two electronic versions, *Internet Shakespeare Editions* and *Digital Renaissance Editions* (in progress).

The Cambridge Edition of the Works of Ben Jonson, a magisterial seven volumes in print with an Electronic Edition in first release, begins with 229 pages of introductory material. Before the title page, a note identifies the distinguishing features of this edition; between 'Acknowledgements' and a 'Life of Ben Jonson' by Ian Donaldson, a 'General Introduction' by the general editors fills out what the note summarizes (lx–lxxxvi). Both the note and the 'General Introduction' state that each Jonson text has its own introduction. Further, they promise an elaboration of the print commentary and other ancillary material in the Electronic Edition. Launched early in 2014, the Electronic or Online Edition enhances the Print Edition in more than one way. It offers a fully searchable version of the Print Edition; and it contains an extensive collection of essays and archives essential to a full study of Jonson's life and works. According to promotional materials on the publisher's website, this is the first edition employing digital technology to reveal not only Jonson's writing practices but also the modern scholar's editorial procedures. The Online Edition remains a work in progress, as additional archival materials are prepared for inclusion.

Even without a supplement, this print edition invigorates Jonson's canon by presenting all of his writings in chronological order – including fragments, correspondence, and notes on lost plays – to follow the trajectory of his prolific creative life. The concentrated introductions to each text shed light on the background of its composition; and the commentary, arranged on the page with glosses above the textual notes, gives thorough explanations in economical prose. Wherever a reader looks, this commentary is uniformly current, clear, necessary and aware of drama in performance. In this instance, the electronic extension enriches a collected *Works* that makes the most of its traditional print format.

While *The Cambridge Edition of the Works of Ben Jonson* flexes its ancillaries by electronic means, *Thomas Middleton: The Collected Works* presents an unusually dynamic printed text supplemented by an expanding website with more information and perhaps, eventually, a concordance. A *Companion to the Collected Works* contains most bibliographical data, as well as Works Cited, 'minimizing the distraction caused to ordinary readers by the courtesy rituals of academic culture' (22). Contributing to the preliminaries of this one-volume printed edition – essays on Middleton's life, London and theatre – Gary Taylor instructs the reader on 'How to Use This Book' (18–22), sounding the multivocal keynote of the project. When he discusses commentary, he explains that the edition offers a variety of notes which provide distinctive annotations for individual works. He illustrates with a dozen or so examples, from *Your Five Gallants*, in which the notes focus on theatrical issues; to four plays which attract feminist commentary; to Middleton's adaptation of *Macbeth*, which is printed here without a gloss. Juxtaposing all these approaches in one volume will 'call attention to the ways in which annotation itself shapes our experience of a text' (18). Consequently, Taylor stresses that 'contributors come from different disciplines (literature, history, theatre, and theology); the ANNOTATIONS focus upon different aspects of the texts; ... and the critical introductions adopt different critical perspectives ... This diversity is deliberate ... a "federal" edition celebrates the play of difference and acknowledges the foreclosure of possibilities entailed in every act of choice' (19).

This print edition also renews a writer's canon, presenting all of Middleton's works in chronological order of composition from 1602 to 1627 (juvenilia appear separately at the end). In its arrangement *The Collected Works* sets familiar and unfamiliar texts side by side, and in the process 'shows the range of genres Middleton could juggle at one time' (19). Whereas its organization has an effect similar to that of the Cambridge *Ben Jonson*, the voices of individual editors differ in pronounced ways, especially in their concise introductions. The diversity advocated by Taylor, which allows each set of preliminaries its own vocality, at times becomes apparent as well in the treatment of text and annotations. A case in point, Valerie Wayne's edition of *A Trick to Catch the Old One* (1605–06) focuses on the character of Jane in performance. Wayne has adjusted speech prefixes in the text, using the proper name consistently and enabling readers to experience the character's roles as an audience would. 'Jane assumes three different subject positions in the play', Wayne states; 'I have altered the speech headings in this edition to "Jane" so that the subject positions of the character are associated with a name rather than a misleading occupational or sexual category' (375, 376). Her first note to the text announces: 'This commentary foregrounds issues relating to women, marriage, social class, and sexual commerce' (377).

Despite Taylor's convictions, the different voices of his contributors testify that even this 'federal' edition has had to foreclose on many possibilities. Digital technology alone effectively reduces the demand for acts of choice in editing. 'The possibilities are endless', states John Jowett in discussing electronic editions (2007a: 164), the most animated media for publishing early modern play texts with introductions and commentary. As Brett Hirsch has written:

> Electronic editions can present multiple and interlinked versions of the same texts and textual witnesses, alongside relevant sources, analogues, and adaptations, in both old and modern spelling, all with multiple levels of editorial annotation and commentary ... Unlike print editions, in which the contents are bound and static, electronic editions are able to facilitate dynamic interactions with [their] contents by and between users through customization, annotation, discussion, and play. (2011: 573–4)

Internet Shakespeare Editions illustrates this interaction, making its software platform available to a pair of projects that are putting early English drama online: *Digital Renaissance Editions* and *Queen's Men Editions*. At the same time, it has allowed the *Map of Early Modern London* to link with plays on its site and editors of plays for *Internet Shakespeare Editions* to integrate locations on the map with their editions.[1] Coordinating with the *Internet Shakespeare Editions*, Broadview Press will issue print versions of the plays. But the real innovation is happening online, with three levels of annotation (short glosses, longer notes and extended discussions); a series of interlinked essays rather than traditional introductions; and, for *Digital Renaissance Editions*, discursive collation notes.

Entry to the *Internet Shakespeare Editions* website gives access to many paths worth investigating. For example, it is possible to explore a

---

[1] This information comes from email correspondence with Michael Best, coordinating editor of the *Internet Shakespeare Editions*, 27 June 2013.

completed edition, such as John D. Cox's *Julius Caesar*, in whatever order the reader prefers. The table of contents lists eight subjects from the editor's introduction to performance materials; it covers a variety of media. At the time of writing, I could also look at a not-quite-complete edition of *King John* by Michael Best, already accompanied by a fully multimedia performance essay. Alerted by the author, I jumped ahead to see the section on Beerbohm Tree's spectacular production. In addition, databases of Shakespeare in performance and a performance chronicle are available for all plays, as is a substantial collection of facsimiles. Clearly, the online editions of early modern plays share high scholarly standards and a virtual wealth of resources. With their vision and energy, they should be able to overcome obstacles to their production, specifically copyright issues and sustainability (Hirsch 2011: 577–80). If '[t]he mind is refrigerated by interruption', as Dr Johnson worried, especially by the 'necessary evils' of notes compiled by other people (1968: 7.111), electronic editions and extensions of printed books may help to cool what can seem a hot medium. They invite the reader to participate in creating an early modern play text, customizing an edition through a search for information that will bring printed words to life.

CHAPTER 24

Editorial memory: the origin and evolution of collation notes

Eric Rasmussen

Complaints about textual notes have an illustrious history. It began as early as 1712, when Joseph Addison observed in an issue of the *Spectator* that editions of classic authors were too often 'taken up with various Readings' including 'various Blunders and Mistakes ... that only take up the Time of the learned Reader, and puzzle the Minds of the Ignorant' (Addison 1721: 578). Modern discussions of textual collations are almost invariably couched in negative modifiers and metaphors – 'mind-numbing', 'unintelligible', 'impenetrable', 'incomprehensible', 'a thin strip of hieroglyphics', 'a bristling hedge', 'a forbidding barrier', 'barbed wire', and, most famously, 'the band of terror' (McLeod 1982: 40, Kastan 2001: 124, Erne 2008: 48, Smith 2007: 50, Marcus 1996: 72) – and, like Addison's, rarely have anything good to say about their effect on the reading experience. Lukas Erne is no doubt correct in suspecting that most readers 'consistently ignore' the collations (48). Those who do attend to the critical apparatus may, like Samuel Johnson, find it distracting, 'the mind is refrigerated by interruption: the thoughts are diverted from the principal subject' (E4r), or, like Noël Coward, regard it as inimical to pleasure: 'Having to read footnotes resembles having to go downstairs to answer the door while in the midst of making love' (Grafton 1999: 31).

And yet, this much maligned feature of critical editions is seen as absolutely 'vital' for serious students of Shakespeare's text (Bowers 1982: 247). Even beginners are advised by the *Cambridge Introduction to Shakespeare* to select editions with copious textual notes: 'a good rule of thumb is that the more collation there is, the more work the editor has done' (Smith 2007: 50). Providing a complete listing of textual variants and editorial conjectures, along with access to discussions of the merits and demerits of those readings, has long been recognized as a means of empowering the user. As Johnson observes, 'if the reader is not satisfied with the editor's determination, he may have the means of choosing better for himself' – a sentiment echoed by Margreta de Grazia: 'the coveted privilege of "perfecting" the Shakespearean text' is thus 'taken from the "dictatorial editor" and invested in the general readership' (1991b: 69). Some recent editions have attempted to make the textual notes less intrusive (putting them at the foot of the page below the commentary, or relegating them to the back of the volume) and more palatable (by scaling them back to a simple listing of departures from the copy-text), but doing so might be said to privilege the comfort of the general reader over the needs of the scholar.

Having previously argued that rather than cutting back on collations perhaps we should be encouraging editors to assemble and analyse them more thoroughly (Rasmussen 2003), I now wish to explore the development of (and rationale for) the convention of attributing variant readings to named sources and to discuss innovations in the digital humanities that offer new solutions to the age-old problem of how best to present these repositories of editorial memory.

The historical moment at which the correction of error in Shakespearean texts became intellectual property can be dated with some precision. In 1744, the press at Oxford University published an elegant edition of Shakespeare's plays edited by Thomas Hanmer. Jacob Tonson and his associates, who considered themselves the owners of the rights to Shakespeare's works (see Dawson 1947: 26–33), responded in the following year by publishing a cheap edition of the Oxford text in which they flagged emendations and identified those that Hanmer had silently appropriated from Tonson's previous editions:

> This Edition is exactly copied from that lately printed in Quarto at Oxford; but the Editor of that not having thought proper to point out the Alterations he has made from the former Copies, we were advised to mark those Passages in the Text thus, / \ ... as also to point out the Emendations made by Mr. Theobald, Mr. Warburton, and Dr. Thirlby, in Mr. Theobald's Edition, which are used by this editor (A2)

Bernice W. Kliman suggested that the arduous task of assigning ownership to every emendation in the six-volume edition may have been undertaken by the young Samuel Johnson (Kliman 1997: 299–317).

Although seventeenth-century reprints had silently made corrections in Shakespeare's text (the Second Folio made over 1,600 seemingly deliberate changes in the text of the First; F3 introduced over 900 corrections; F4 made over 700; the reprinting of some sheets of F4, known as 'F5', made dozens of further corrections; see Black and Shaaber 1937 and Rasmussen 1997), the attribution of textual modifications in the eighteenth century was novel. De Grazia observes that the variorum apparatus evolved in order to satisfy this 'new preoccupation with identifying and acknowledging the words of others' by providing 'a format for attribution, registering critical as opposed to literary property' (1991b: 210, 213). As each new edition reproduced the notes of its immediate predecessor and added some of its own, editions of Shakespeare began to grow like Falstaff's men in buckram, with the number of volumes required for editions of the complete works more than doubling within less than two decades: the ten-volume Johnson and Steevens edition of 1785 was succeeded by the fifteen-volume Steevens and Reed edition in 1793, which was then succeeded by the twenty-one-volume Reed edition in 1803.

But what was the rationale behind the systematic recording of the original sources of emended readings? William Warburton's assertion that the emendations in his 1747 edition are 'carefully assigned to their respective authors', coupled with his aside that doing so represents 'A piece of justice which the *Oxford Editor* never did', implies a restoration of intellectual property rights (Warburton 1747: xiii), as does Johnson's complaint, in his 1765 edition, that Hanmer 'appropriated the labour of his predecessors' (Johnson 1765: D3v).

In the preface to his 1767 edition, Edward Capell explained why he had chosen not to attribute emendations:

> In the [printer's] manuscripts from which these plays are printed, the emendations are given their proper owners by initials and other marks that are in the margin of those manuscripts but they are suppressed in the print for two reasons: First their number, in some pages, makes them a little unsightly; and the editor professes himself weak enough to like a well-printed book; in the next place, he does declare, that his only object has been to do service to his Author; which provided it be done, he thinks it of small importance by what hand the service was administer'd. (Capell 1767–68: 23 n. 10)

Capell's extant holograph printer's copy does indeed feature marginal initials identifying the ownership of emendations throughout his edited text: 'R' for Rowe, 'P' for Pope, and 'T' for Theobald. Marcus Walsh sees Capell's decision to suppress these attributions in the published work as 'a privileging of text over gloss, the restored scripture of the author over the intrusions of the editor's secondary responsibility' and notes a similar 'act of self-effacement' in the fact that 'the name of Capell as editor appears nowhere on the title page' (Walsh 2001: 228, 231). However, Capell's tabular listing of variant readings from the early quartos and folios, published several years after his edition under the title *Notes and various readings*, included the initials 'r', 'p' and 'o' – one wonders if they are lower-case because they are of 'small importance'? – to inform the reader 'what followers the several readings have had among the moderns' (Capell 1774: A4).[1]

By the end of the eighteenth century, the requirement for assigning credit had become so absolute that editors who failed to provide the source of a reading were subjected to stinging indictments of 'literary theft' and 'plagiarism' from critics such as George Hardinge, who pointed out that George Steevens's edition of 1793 had incorporated without acknowledgement a conjectural emendation that had been previously suggested by Richard Simpson: 'Mr. Editor Steevens makes it his own ... appropriates to A the literary goods and chattels of B ... without a hint that he had been thus anticipated, and pre-occupied' (Hardinge 1801: 162–3). Similar complaints persisted for centuries. Suzanne Gossett, the only previous scholar to have examined the subject of the attribution of textual emendations, has pointed out that Alexander Dyce's 1857 edition objected to *two* different failures of attribution regarding the 'we are strong in easterne' crux at 3.1.52 in *Pericles*:

> Mr. Knight prints 'strong in, *astern*' – in his long note on which egregious lection he forgets to mention that it is a jewel picked out of Jackson's *Shakespeare's Genius Justified*. I have not the slightest doubt that Boswell proposed the true reading here: his note (*to which Mr. Collier does not even allude*) is as follows: 'I would read – "strong in custom"'. (cited in Gossett 2005: 39)

Even the twentieth-century editors of the New Arden Shakespeare have been accused, by Arthur Sherbo, of doing 'scant justice' to their eighteenth-century predecessors; Gossett rightly characterizes Sherbo's tone as that of one 'offended by an ethical failure to acknowledge earlier work' (2005: 39).

The first Cambridge editors, William George Clark and William Aldis Wright, followed in the tradition of providing notes crediting the origin of each emended reading in their edition of 1863–66. But, in the eyes of H. H. Furness, they did not go far enough:

> The respect wherein the Cambridge edition is open to improvement – and I say it with deference – is that, while it gives the readings of the old editions, it omits to note the adoption or rejection of them by the various editors, whereby an important element in estimating these readings is wanting ... In

---

[1] De Grazia mistakenly asserts that Capell continued to suppress the identities of the originators of emendations in his *Notes and various readings* (De Grazia 1991b: 211).

disputed passages it is of great interest to see at a glance on which side lies the weight of authority. (Furness 1871: vi–vii)

As we have seen, Furness's argument for full historical collation has its roots in Capell's notion that readers deserve to know the 'followers' who have supported individual emendations. Furness maintained that 'it was this omission in the textual notes of the Cambridge Editors' that occasioned his undertaking the New Variorum Shakespeare series (vii).

Of course, even variorum editions have never claimed to record *every* previously suggested reading. Furness himself imposed a 'no nonsense' clause: 'I do not bind myself to give all the conjectural emendations, with which conceit and ignorance have so thickly strewn the paths of the Shakespeare student. I shall never cumber my pages with the nonsense of Zachary Jackson' (Furness 1870: 388). A similar clause appears in the Modern Language Association's *Shakespeare Variorum Handbook: A Manual of Editorial Practice* (2003): 'In an attempt to keep relatively useless information from swelling the textual notes … variants of accidental details that do not affect meaning will be ignored … mere nonsense of course to be excluded' (Knowles 2003: 35, 106). So, too, in offering advice 'On Editing One's First Play', Clifford Leech warns that if one provides too many entries in collations, the user 'will not read any of them: do not bury the important things under a monument of trifles' (1970: 67).

The advent of electronic texts has, to a great extent, freed editors from concerns about encumbering printed pages. For instance, the editors of the New Variorum *Hamlet* (of which I am one, along with Hardin Aasand, Nick Clary and the late Bernice W. Kliman), have assembled an electronic database (available at *HamletWorks.org*) that records every textual variant, both substantive and accidental, from the early quartos to the most recent critical edition. In this spirit of inclusivity, the editors have also included all known conjectures, no matter how seemingly nonsensical. Thus, readers pondering the famous 'dram of eale' crux can access the full range of alternative readings, with a complete chronological listing of the editors who subsequently adopted each conjecture, and a listing of the editors who retained the Q2 reading 'eale':

> eale v1821, DYCE1, STAU, WHI, GLO, HAL, CAM1, RUG1, CLN1, RUG2, v1877, MULL, BRY, IRV2, OXF1, NLSN, VAND, RIDI, CAM2, ALEX, CHAL, CAM4, OXF4, ARD3 = Q2

> ease Q3, Q4, Q5, Q6, Q7, Q8, Q9, Q10, WILK1, WILK2, BECKET; **base** TJOH1, TJOH2, THEOBALD (1726, pp. 35–6) *conj.*, THEO1, THEO2, WARB, THEO3, JOHN, CAP, v1773, v1778, v1785, MAL, RANN, v1793, v1803, v1813, VERP,

HUDI, SING2, FIEB, C&MC; **ill** JEN, CAPN, CALDI, CALD2, KNTI, COLI, COL2, CHAM, ELZEI, COL3, COL4, RUG2 *conj.* BRY; **ale** JACKSON (1819) *conj.*; **bale** SINGI, DEL2, TSCH, DEL4; **evil** KEIGHTLEY (1855, pp. 305–6) *conj.*, KTLY, DYCE2, WH2, ARDI, CAM3, SIS, ARD2, BEV4; **lead** STAU *conj.*, FURNIVALL *conj.* (*apud* INGLEBY, -1866); **leaven** CARTWRIGHT (1866) *conj.*, HUD3; **e'il** WETHERELL *conj.* (1869, p. 672), KITI, KIT2; [ev'l] EVNSI; **vile** LEO (1862, p. 502) *conj.*, HUD2; **ail** MACL; **lees** HILL; **evil** CLN2, PEN2

The traditional variorum formatting of this *HamletWorks* note may soon become more user-friendly, thanks to the visualization prototype being developed by Alan Galey for the Electronic New Variorum Shakespeare. In Galey's prototype, designed in response to the 'thicket of notes' in print editions 'that fail to do justice to the histories of textual change and contestation they represent', at any given line a user can request that a block of colour-coded variant readings of that line appear in the text of the play, accompanied by a table of chronologically listed editions, similarly colour-coded to show agreement and disagreement among them in a visually appealing format (Galey n.d., Galey 2012).

Given that the presentation of detailed textual data in close proximity to the literary text has long posed a challenge in print variorums, designers of electronic editions have experimented with ways to separate the two. Both *HamletWorks* and Galey's prototype offer users the option of turning the collation data on or off as they read through the text of a play. Users of the Internet Shakespeare Editions (ISE) (http://internet shakespeare.uvic.ca/) are even more empowered. A toolbox gives ISE readers the ability to select individual editions – e.g., Rowe 1709, Pope 1723 or Theobald 1733 – and, once they do so, all variant readings from those particular editions will appear, color-coded, in the text throughout the play. Moreover, Michael Best, the prime mover behind the ISE, has suggested that 'a creative editor of an electronic edition might take advantage of the capacity of the medium for animation by recreating a semantic field where the text dances between variant readings . . . The text becomes visibly variant, teasingly slippery, as it makes manifest its actual instability, hidden by our meticulously edited print texts' (Best 2009: 34; see also Galey's discussion of 'animated variants' on his 'Visualizing Variation' website (n.d.)).

But a fundamental question remains unanswered: how many readers really care to know who first conjectured an emendation? It is virtually impossible to imagine a student reader who would actually accord greater value to a variant reading because of the stature of the editor who suggested it, or that of the editors who subsequently adopted it. But one can certainly imagine an editor-user who would be deeply interested in the details of the editorial tradition. As Gossett has finely observed, 'one of the hardest things an editor of Shakespeare has to do is to deal with her predecessors' (2005: 35). In the instance of the 'dram of eale' crux, given that the recent critical editions from Oxford, Cambridge and Arden all retain Q2's 'eale', surely an editor of a new edition might think thrice about adopting Jackson's 1819 conjecture 'ale', especially given that no other editor has seen fit to incorporate it into the text? Similarly, though it seems unlikely that an average student reader would be overly concerned about the intellectual property rights of an emendation, editors contemplating staking a claim that an emendation is unique to their edition would certainly find a database of all previous conjectures of enormous value. Their appreciation would be all the greater if they were aware that, 'as Eric Rasmussen has repeatedly shown in his reviews of editions for *Shakespeare Survey*, such claims for editorial originality are not always to be trusted' (Giddens 2011: 161). Indeed, when Jonathan Bate and I emended 'sledded pollax' to 'steelèd pole-axe' in our 2007 Royal Shakespeare Company edition of *Hamlet*, we were happy to discover in *HamletWorks* that we had been anticipated in this conjecture by F. A. Leo in 1885.

It may be time to acknowledge that students of Shakespeare (even 'serious students') do not need genealogies of emended readings to be present before them at every turn of the page. On the other hand, the glorious renaissance that textual notes are enjoying in the electronic environment tells us that readers do want the ability to explore the textual history at will. By allowing users to choose the amount of collation they view, electronic editions are providing today's editors with access to an extraordinarily complete record of the textual tradition, while granting more general users the freedom to read Shakespeare uninterrupted and unafraid.

CHAPTER 25

Shakespeare as network

David Weinberger

Our understanding of the role and nature of Shakespeare scholarship made perfect sense in the Age of Paper. But in the Age of the Internet, Shakespeare and scholarship are becoming networks. We may not like this, but we should understand it. And then we should like it.

We should also be adjusting how we do scholarship and how we convey the fruits of that scholarship to take advantage of this radically new medium.

In the traditional paper-based model, modern scholarship and Shakespeare's own work shared an essential property: they were conceived as forms of publishing. Shakespeare worked on his manuscripts privately until they were ready to be shown to the small public of his acting troupe, and then finally to the broad public in performances. Likewise for traditional scholarship. The scholar works in private, whether that is the privacy of a personal study or the slightly larger circle of trusted early readers and auditors. Once the scholar judges her article to be ready, she submits it to a journal where it is reviewed and winnowed. The scholarly paper is done, settled, and close to irrevocable ... as unchangeable as the ink that has settled into paper.

That is not a casual simile. As many have observed, albeit none as pithily as Marshall McLuhan(1964), a medium shapes its content. We need not afford the medium any mystical powers to explain this. Rather, media come with certain things they do better or more easily than other things. Drop that set of affordances into a culture, and the content takes on a particular topology, which in turn affects the culture's understanding of the field the content inhabits. The medium is far from being the sole determinant of the content and the discipline, but it is highly influential. The mechanics of this are as complex as any topic in history, especially since the process is far from mechanical. It is better understood as an emergent phenomenon, that is, as a determined result that is nevertheless unpredictable because of the complexity of the mix of factors, which in this case include the physical properties of paper, the economics of publishing, the requirements for building a career as an academic, the self-understanding of significant institutions, the personalities and strivings of individual scholars, and the occasional fluttering of butterfly wings. (And, if I were writing this for a hyperlinked medium, I would link that last phrase to a source about chaos theory's 'butterfly effect'.)

Scholarship and even knowledge itself have fit themselves to the affordances of paper. Topics have miraculously turned out to be the size of books. One becomes accredited as an expert using the same techniques by which manuscripts are selected for print, with having been published counting as a powerful credit toward that accreditation. The system of knowledge overall gained its efficiency from being a set of stopping points – backed by authority and credentials – that allow us to get answers and move on. Knowledge thereby reflects one of paper's most irksome limitations: each book is physically disconnected from every other.

Now, as the Internet becomes the medium of knowledge, it should come as no surprise that knowledge, knowing, and knowers are also changing. What we construed along the lines of publishing we now are beginning to understand within the frame of networks. Indeed, there is some literal sense in saying that whereas Shakespeare used to look like a writer and his works used to look like publications, now Shakespeare and his works are showing themselves to us as networks.

This presents a tremendous opportunity for advancing our scholarly understanding of Shakespeare. This in turn should change not only how we read Shakespeare, but how we prepare materials about Shakespeare. The network view is also, I will argue, closer to the truth about Shakespeare, his works, and what it means to understand them.

Networked scholarship

If you are trying to understand the vexingly amorphous FRBR standard – Functional Requirements for Bibliographic Records – there is a good chance the example you will come across is *Hamlet*. FRBR provides a conceptual model for understanding the relationships among the different versions and editions of what we usually think of as a single work. At the bottom are items: the thumb-worn copies on a library shelf. Each one of these is a manifestation of something like an edition. Above these is the expression, which ideally would be Shakespeare's original handwritten manuscript. And at the top of the FRBR heap is the work itself, of which that manuscript is itself an expression. With *Hamlet*, there are folios, annotated editions, large print versions of the annotated editions, versions in Braille, and graphic novels, each of which is some type of manifestation of the play that Shakespeare created and wrote down.

Hamlet is used as an example so often in explanations of FRBR not only because it is such a famous work, but because *Hamlet* makes apparent just how complex a problem it is simply to figure out what a work is. With Shakespeare we have not only the various editions, but also performances, recordings, films, and early quartos and folios. The one thing we don't have is a single manuscript recorded in the author's hand from which all other versions and variations can be seen to flow. Instead we have a ragbag of manifestations that each claim to be *Hamlet* in one form or another.

Except, as Shakespeare scholars understand better than anyone, a ragbag is a terrible metaphor, and not just because of the difference in cultural value between Shakespeare's works and scraps of cloth. Each item in a ragbag is independent of every other, whereas much of the work of Shakespeare scholarship is to discern the relationships among the manifestations of *Hamlet*. The differences among the early quartos and folios are noted and used to explain one another, and to hypothesize about the author's intention. The annotated versions refer to spots within, across, and beyond the Shakespearean corpus. The variorums bring the commentaries into conversation with one another across centuries.

So, suppose we were to drop the ragbag metaphor and try to come up with a better one. We would want it to give us a much richer model than the four-level structure that FRBR proposes. We would want to be able to show the relationships among the rest of Shakespeare's works, and its historical precedents, from Kyd backwards and forwards. It would be useful to note the centuries of critical responses. And since we are drawing connections, we would likely want to include not only canonical and responsible manifestations of *Hamlet*, but also derivatives that include Disney's *The Lion King* and the 1983 movie *Strange Brew*. This is not to accord Shakespearean status to either movie, but it would be useful to at least have those tenuous links noted, not necessarily because they shed light on *Hamlet* but because they may help us understand how cultures have taken up that work. For the same reason, someone somewhere will find value in following the links to all of the daily comic strips that have riffed on 'To be or not to be'. Again, this may be of no use to any serious scholar of the play itself, but it may reveal insights into how art is debased or how art shapes culture.

Now, if we were to take a bird's-eye view of the relationships we have mapped, it would not look like a ragbag. Nor would it look much like an

index or an outline, for those forms are too neat and constraining. Instead, it would look like a network: many pieces messily joined. This particular type of topography has a few prominent characteristics.
- It is without practical limits on how much it can contain and connect.
- It is composed by its participants over the centuries without a centralized or coordinated plan.
- There is no center. Or, more exactly, the center is whatever you happen to be interested in.
- There are no edges. Or, more exactly, the edges are where your curiosity ends.
- It is inclusive; every connection is by definition part of the network.
- The links may express any type of relationship. Those relationships are almost always explained in the text, explicitly or implicitly.
- The instantiated links are one-way.
- The objects linked to did not give permission to be linked to.
- It is extremely messy.
- Because no authority maintains or archives the objects and their links, it is not highly reliable.
- Anyone can add content or links.

These are, of course, properties of one particular type of network: The Internet's World Wide Web. They are distinctly not properties of paper-based objects of knowledge. Books and journals are limited vessels: relatively few manuscripts are accepted for publication, and the size of their contents is constrained by economics and engineering. Paper media divide knowledge up into topics, although they include footnotes and other forms of broken links. They limit the extent and timeliness of discourse. The difficulty, limitations, and expense of publishing also mean that most of the actual discourse is done in various types of private environments – letters, classrooms, discussion halls, pubs – that are lost to the public sphere.

The loss of that which fails to make it through the paper media's filters does not seem like much of a loss within the traditional domain of scholarship. What gets filtered out is exactly that which has little or negative value. But it only looks that way because we have so confused scholarship with publishing. And that has occurred not because the processes and institutions of scholarship are ideally like those of publishing, but because publishing – print publishing – has been its medium. For example, what gets filtered out may not have little value but just too little to justify the expense of printing it. Further, it may have no value to the vast majority of scholars, but would have tremendous value to one or two. Worse, what is relevant changes over time, as we have seen as issues of gender equity, racism, and animal rights have emerged historically. We have fitted our measure of 'little value' around the economic barriers print imposes.

Another important consequence of adapting scholarship to the strictures and structures of publishing has been that we think of scholars as authors, and have assumed (more so over time) that authors work primarily as individuals. So, we have traditionally thought of scholars as individual experts, working on the issues that have seized them, almost always in a competitive (yet, we hope, collegial) war of all against all. If two scholars are addressing the same question, they will be in contention, for they have chosen a question that has not been resolved, and they only succeed professionally as scholars if they stake out a claim that is different from the claim of others. So, although of course scholars work within a milieu and ride on the shoulders of history, it is still primarily an individual's game. We have not only assumed this, we have institutionalized that assumption into a system of credit and responsibility.

Networked scholarship does not negate the individual in favor of the network. The movement is more Hegelian than that: the network of scholars lets individual experts flourish, but creates a synthesis of individual and community that is other than a mere combination of the two. It locates knowledge not in the heads of individual experts but in the network itself. The individual experts remain in contention, but it is a linked contention. If two scholars are posting learned but opposing arguments about, say, the order of the plays' composition, even if they don't know about one another, the network does; if they are on the Web, they are perforce linked. Two experts might not know about each other, but a perspicacious reader or a clever search engine algorithm can bring them into juxtaposition, so what they have in common and where they disagree can be discussed – and that discussion itself becomes another node in the ever-expanding network. The result is not merely a series of position papers, some connected in tight clusters, but an open, shifting set of ideas that are in direct and indirect conversation. This is a network that is loose-edged, unsettled, and without filters that permanently exclude what they reject. In these ways and others, the scholarship has taken on the properties of its new medium.

This gives us a picture of scholarship that is by no means entirely new, yet is different. For example, we still need experts investigating the plays and the man. We need them to be using the traditional tools as well as the most modern tools. But, insofar as scholarship lives at the level of the network, it will be measured not simply as the practice of individuals but by how fully it develops a public web of experts in contention and in discussion. 'Fully' here means: many people, many levels and types of expertise, many topics, many conversations, many disagreements and differences, many many many links. If magnificent scholarship is being done but is not in direct conversation, then networked scholarship has failed. If there are ideas an interested person cannot get to, then the networked scholarship has failed. If there are bad ideas uncommented on and uncorrected, then networked scholarship has failed. If there are explanations but only for scholars, then networked scholarship has failed. It succeeds when it takes on the properties of the network: open, inclusive, linked, contentious and collaborative, unsettled and lively.

The networked knowledge that is the subject and fruit of networked scholarship has some important advantages. For one thing, it scales: it can get very big. It does not insist on drawing strict lines around topics or disciplines. It enables participation by people at their own levels of expertise and interest. But there are certainly dangers with networked knowledge as well. First, without the traditional filters in place, it is easy for the unsophisticated to go wrong. Second, you can not only go wrong, you can become more convinced of your erroneous views because you are hanging out online with people who all agree with one another; this is known as the 'echo chamber' effect (Sunstein 2001). Third, you can be distracted by trivialities and tangential ideas. Finally, there is some evidence – contested – that interaction with the Net affects our brains so that we find it harder to follow long chains of argument and to think deeply (Carr 2010).

Scholars are not powerless in the face of these dangers. They now have an opportunity to shape their practices to support the development of networked scholarship that both makes them better scholars and helps their culture learn from their work. Let us look at some of what we scholars can do to facilitate the development of networks of knowledge that make us all smarter.

Building smarter networks

We are still discovering how best to contribute to networks of knowledge. Here are some steps we can take with the confidence born of widespread experience.

Support open access. Knowledge networks only thrive when the relevant content is openly, freely available to all. Open access publishing achieves that. Note that this does not necessarily mean that scholars should publish in non-peer reviewed journals; most open-access journals are peer reviewed. There is, of course, still prestige in having one's work accepted by a for-pay journal, and that may matter a great deal, especially to younger scholars trying to make their name and to get tenure. But, it is quite likely that locking one's best work into journals that few can afford increasingly will be seen as a type of selfishness. (The same is true for writing a chapter for a closed access book.)

Post as well as publish. While the line between posting and publishing has always been fuzzy and is getting fuzzier, there is a different ethos to posting. Publishing implies a finality of the product, and some editorial filtering. Posting is just the sticking of some ideas into a public place, possibly before they have been fully thought through. Publishing is good, of course, but posting also has value. It gets ideas out faster, it gets them out before the author feels compelled to defend them as a matter of pride, and it provokes earlier discussion that can take ideas in new directions.

Be explicit with your metadata. The old paper world generally made clear the status of what we are reading, often implicitly. If it is a book or journal article, then we know it went through a careful editing process. If it is a paper presented at a conference, then it may be a bit more tentative in its findings. If it is a casual talk given at a weekly faculty get-together, the content may be exploratory. But as the Web makes it easier for us to post in a wide variety of forms – blogs, tweets, chats, hangouts, etc. – we will often find it advantageous to make public ideas that are more tentative. We may try on ideas in order to see how they look when worn. It is therefore incumbent upon us to make clear the status of our posts. If it is a draft, then that needs to be stated clearly, possibly in red font at the top. If it is a trifle, we need to let people know that. If it is as good as we can make it, it deserves to announce that.

Link everything. Of course you will link to the sources you use. That is your responsibility as a scholar. But in the networked environment your responsibility goes further. Ask yourself two questions. First, how can you help a reader who may come to your work not as well informed as you would like, because on an open Web there are no prerequisites for access? So, what can you link to that will explain concepts and terms that people need to understand your point? Be generous. What does it cost you to link your first mention of Ovid to the Public Broadcasting

System's page about him ('Ovid'). Wikipedia has an excellent article on iambic pentameter ('Iambic Pentameter'), so, even though – or because – readers ought to be familiar with the term you should throw in a link. You might even pander to your readers – that is, effectively stimulate the interest of your less-informed readers – by pointing them to Peter Sellers's 1965 reading of the lyrics of 'A Hard Day's Night' in the style of Sir Lawrence Olivier's Richard III.

Second, ask yourself how you can feed the curiosity of an intelligent reader. Since scholars are also teachers, what one-click access can you provide for your readers to stimulate their thinking beyond what you are saying? How can you get your readers out into the network of ideas in which your work resides? You might link to Jeremy McNamara's lively account of Ovid's influence on Shakespeare (McNamara n.d.), or Peter Hall's argument in favor of observing iambic pentameter in performance (Hall 2003). If someone doesn't know as much as you about a concept, a person, or a work, then do them the favor of linking to a source that will explain it to them. You do us all a special service if you link to works you disagree with, but that you think are worth our time. That is how we grow a web. Linking is not just a scholarly responsibility but a social duty.

Linking widely is especially important now that we are losing the natural filter paper imposed. In the past you could assume that the audience of your book primarily consisted of people who valued your work highly enough to have spent a fair bit of money to buy it, or were students or professors at a university that subscribed to the journal. As we begin posting and publishing on the open Web, we lose that filter. There is thus no way of controlling who sees what. This is a very good thing indeed. But it means that your work can have more effect – more people can learn from it – if you link to explanatory sources.

Try out ideas. As the network revolution continues, we will undoubtedly devise new techniques and norms to make networked scholarship and knowledge more useful. We should be experimenting, and paying attention to the experiments of others.

Supporting open access, posting, linking, adding contextualizing metadata, and experimenting are important even though they will not directly improve your scholarship. They will, however, make better the network in which your scholarship is developed, is encountered, and finds its meaning. These actions make the network better for its participants, whether as readers or contributors. These days, there is so little separating the two.

Networked readers

There is also work we need to do to improve the way students and other readers engage with scholarly networks. We will look at two areas: building better devices, and creating better sources.

Better devices

In one sense, we already have the ultimate device for reading online: the Web. But, we seem to be preferring either specialized devices such as the Kindle, or proprietary software on more open platforms, such as running Kindle software on a tablet or smart phone. While specialized devices and proprietary software can provide useful functionality and a pleasant experience, they often do so at steep social costs: they can limit the sources from which one can conveniently access books, they often lock the book's content into proprietary data formats that cannot be easily or legally shared, and they prevent others from adding functionality to the device or software. This last point is important because it means that, insofar as we give over our e-reading experience to these proprietary e-readers, the pace of innovation in this technology will be drastically slowed; think about the glacial pace of innovation in the telephone system versus the onrush of innovation on the open Web (see Zittrain 2008).

Worst of all, these proprietary devices and software applications are dead ends on the Web. They make it difficult or impossible for the human beings using them to link works together, or to discuss these works in real time with the rest of the world. They only marginally participate in the cumulative enrichment of the scholarly environment.

Apps, like the ones that run on the iPhone and Android devices, are a rising alternative. As W. B. Worthen's contribution to this volume makes clear, some of these apps are quite impressive. Shakespeare scholarship is especially appropriate to being accessed via apps because plays are inherently multimedia events and sonnets should be heard as well as read. We will undoubtedly see more and more apps that enhance our appreciation of Shakespeare.

But apps – at least the ones already developed – are too often self-contained environments. Apps tend to use network connectivity the way the Kindle does: simply to access materials. They generally do not provide links out to content and applications beyond their boundaries. They thus do not lead out into networked knowledge, and do not enrich the network of knowledge. Sometimes that's because the app makers have an economic reason to keep people within their boundaries, but at least as frequently they created an app because they could not deliver their desired functionality within the boundaries of a Web browser; the price of this high-value experience is that it occurs within the walls of the app. An app can illuminate, amaze, and delight. But apps in general do not directly enrich the networks of scholarship and education. For example, there are now tools that enable users to annotate pages, and to do so in the Open Annotation data format that is designed to make those annotations shareable and reusable; these annotation tools can be used with any HTML page, but not within apps. Annotations made using the Open Annotation standard contribute to the network of ideas and knowledge; annotations made in a proprietary format do not.

The trade-off between openness and specialized features will often be worth making. Still, we should recognize that it is a trade-off. Scholars can help encourage an open ecosystem by taking a few steps:

- Consider the trade-offs when developing an app or contributing to one.
- Avoid assigning works to students that are available only in proprietary formats.
- Post on the Web in HTML as opposed to PDF. PDF has the advantage of preserving the original page-based look of a work, but that can make it hard to read on devices with smaller screens. It is also harder to reuse the content of PDFs. It is also usually impossible for others to link to a particular portion of a PDF.

Unfortunately, the future direction of e-readers is likely to be far more influenced by economics than by the immense value openness brings to knowledge networks and to the Net overall.

Better sources

Fortunately, there is another approach we can also take to creating e-readers that work better for the networked understanding of Shakespeare. Scholars can create content that is better designed for maximal discovery, integration, and reuse.

Let us say that you are interested in producing a new variorum of *As You Like It*. You have four basic approaches.

The first is the traditional one. You gather your sources and interpolate them into the text of the play. For example, you will provide a footnote to line 178, bringing together the arguments among the scholars about whether Orlando's 'wherein I confess me' should in fact be 'herein I confess me' (Furness 1890: 38). You will make the decisions about how to arrange the play and the commentary on the page, and you will probably deliver it on paper or as a PDF file.

The second approach takes the path of the typical app. You gather your sources as before, but you make it interactive. The user can, perhaps, expose differing levels of detail. Perhaps the word 'wherein' is displayed in blue, indicating that a click will expose additional information, such as a translation into modern English. Perhaps that translation itself has a link to the next level of scholarship. Perhaps when the original commentaries are available online, your variorum app hyperlinks to them. This is, of course, just an example. The possibilities for interactivity with apps is as broad as our imagination.

With the third approach, in addition to publishing a traditional version or an interactive one, you could also make the data behind the variorum publicly available. That data consists of your extensive notes and clippings from the existing scholarship, and the logic you have used for putting them together. Before computers, you may have done this with index cards, or you may have availed yourself of some of the ingenious seventeenth-century scraps-assemblage apparatuses recorded by Ann Blair in *Too Much to Know* (2010). In the age of the computer, you almost certainly are using some application that lets you write notes, tag them with labels or other metadata, and then assemble them automatically on command. Let us refer to these notes as records, using database terminology that arose after computers but before the Web. (Current technology does not always require records and permits more ad hoc forms of 'scrap management'.) After years of research, you have thousands of these digital records. Each probably has a quote from a source, a pointer to bibliographic information about that source, a reference to the exact line in *As You Like It*, and perhaps some tags about the quotation's context such as 'grammar', 'misprints', or 'eighteenth century'. As you put together the draft of your new variorum, you will use the internal database functionality of whatever software you are using to pull together the pieces. In this third approach, you will choose to make these records publicly accessible, as well as your particular way of pulling these pieces together.

Why would you make your notes public? For two reasons. The first is that it provides the next level of scholarly footnotes. Someone who thinks, for example, that you got a source wrong will easily be able to find the original. Or someone who wants more information will be able to get it with a single click.

The second reason is ultimately more important. Your notes can become a public resource that makes the entire network smarter. Not only can any human user avail herself of your work, developers can create their own applications that wring more value from your work. For example, a developer might create software that plots commentary on a timeline, an educational application that lets classes select the commentary they find most helpful, or an analysis tool that finds unexpected relationships among sets of notes from multiple variorums. The New Variorum Shakespeare *Comedy of Errors* Digital Challenge is a good example of this ('The New Variorum Shakespeare Digital Challenge'). The Modern Language Association released that play's variorum under a Creative Commons license that permits reuse without permission for non-commercial purposes, and awarded prizes for applications that took advantage of this open data. The winner, Bill-Crit-O-Matic by Patrick Murray-John, lets users search for words in the commentaries and then click a link to see the relevant passage in the play, thus reversing the usual relationship between text and annotation.[1]

The fourth approach is an extension of this third approach. The MLA's contest worked because it made the text of the variorum available in a standard format designed for computer processing. This enabled innovators to download it and process it in interesting ways. The MLA could, however, choose to make the play and commentaries available to computers directly over the Internet in the form of a database without requiring a download. By providing an API (application programming interface), developers could write applications that could query that database directly. This approach is known as building an open platform: a set of resources that can be retrieved by computer applications written by anyone on the Net. For example, someone somewhere on the Net might write an application that lets users choose a time frame and then see all the commentaries within those dates. In a platform approach, when a user asks to see, say, the comments from 1850 to 1900, the application in real time requests that data from the MLA site. The MLA runs its database and returns the results to the application which then presents it to the user in a useful way.

An open platform has several important advantages when compared to the third approach.

First, in the third approach a developer downloads a file of information that a computer can process, and then writes software that makes that information useful to an end user. But then the developer has to host that

---

[1] Paul Werstine describes similar work done by Alan Galey that allows for very useful slicing and dicing of the *Winter's Tale* variorum.

data somewhere, which adds a level of expense and complexity. In the platform approach, the group providing the data hosts it.

Second, consider what happens when the original information provider – the MLA in our example – updates its data, perhaps correcting it or adding to it. In the third approach, the developer is using a copy of that data, which will become further out of date every time the MLA updates the original.

Third, open platforms encourage community and collaboration. The platform itself benefits by re-absorbing the work done by developers and even by the way users use that work. For example, if a developer creates an annotation tool that draws upon content from the MLA, those annotations could (with the permission of the users, of course) be made available to other developers. The platform has an incentive to let developers find one another, to discuss problems and possibilities, and to reuse code. Platforms provide a stable place where a community can continuously enhance the platform's offerings.

Finally, in a world of platforms, data can be 'mashed up' with other data. For example, an application could request commentaries from the MLA platform, but also request biographical information about the commentators from another platform, and about world historical events from yet another platform. Platforms dramatically improve the networking of what we know.

Whether a group takes the third or fourth approach, it is hugely helpful to make information available in a standard data format (as the MLA did). That way computers can access your data and make sense of it, recognizing one string of characters as a title, another as the author, another as the play to which the comment applies, another as the line number, and so forth. One particular standard is becoming quite important because it lets computers knit together differing sources of notes with great agility: Linked Data. Linked Data has a number of advantages, but one is crucial to the development of smarter networks.

Imagine two sets of scholars create Linked Data about Shakespeare. The first scholar refers to *Hamlet* as 'Hamlet' and the second refers to it by its First Folio name, 'Tragicall Historie of Hamlet, Prince of Denmarke'. Computers are too literal to recognize that these data sets refer to the same play. To get past this problem, Linked Data encourages using hyperlinks rather than text. So, rather than saying either 'Hamlet' or 'The Tragedy of Hamlet, Prince of Denmark', the Linked Data representation of this data would use a Web address of some public resource. For example, for the title of the play it might point to en.wikipedia.org/wiki/Hamlet, which is the address of the English-language Wikipedia page about *Hamlet*, or it might use shakespeare.mit.edu/hamlet/full.html, which is where the Massachusetts Institute of Technology has the text of *Hamlet* openly available. If a computer sees two data sets pointing to the same resource, it will correctly assume that they are talking about the same thing, getting past the problem that people refer to things in very different ways, and in different languages. Of course, it introduces a new problem because our two piles of Linked Data may be pointing at different sources. This, however, is relatively easily solved; over time public mappings will be developed that will tell the computer that those two Web addresses are in fact referring to the same thing. Once that connection is made and is made public, the two piles of data can become connected programmatically. This technique allows many different types of datasets to work together. For example, a Shakespeare dataset might contain a pointer to the town of Stratford-upon-Avon, but so might datasets about genealogies, local fauna and flora, and the historical spread of Catholicism. Linked Data lets all of these datasets be interrogated, yielding relationships that otherwise would have been extremely difficult to unearth. Linked Data makes the network smarter.

Even if Linked Data does not prevail as the dominant way of publishing information for computer access, making one's notes public in machine-readable form will still vastly increase their value. And not just notes toward a variorum. The data and research scholars use to write papers and books can also enrich scholarly networks if they are made publicly accessible in ways that make them findable and usable by computers. We will be able to connect many more dots within the Shakespeare universe now that information can be 'mashed up' with data from other fields. This will make Shakespeare an even more vital part of our culture.

Shakespeare as network

So far I have maintained that supporting research practices and technologies that enable the growth of scholarly networks has practical value. In this final section I want to take one further step: scholarly networks are a more appropriate and even more truthful representation of scholarship and of the content of scholarship, that is, of knowledge.

I advance this claim with trepidation in no small part because there is no clear path to verifying it. It is the same sort of a claim as maintaining that plays are more appropriate for depicting human existence than are, say, tweets or eulogies. To support this claim, one might show the ways in which the human personality can be understood as a type of performance, and the ways in which the liberty and constraints of a theatrical narrative well express the nature and limits of human agency. In the same way, we can argue that the form of networked knowledge is a better representation of human knowledge than was the prior print-based medium.

Shakespeare scholarship happens to provide us with a particularly apt example.

First, we know so little about Shakespeare the man that rather than using his biography to illuminate the works we often use the works to try to figure out who the man was, whether that means filling in our understanding of the personality and circumstances of the plays' author or even deciding on the identity of that author.

Second, there are few writers for whom we have less agreement about the authoritative versions of their works. Not only do we have multiple versions of many plays, scholars try to discern the plays' readings through the filter of the personal styles of the compositors who set the plays into print, analysis which is itself based upon minute differences. (On compositors' shaping of Shakespeare's plays, see John Jowett's chapter in this volume.)

Third, the unreliability of the printed copies, the evolution of English, and Shakespeare's constant inventiveness have resulted in centuries of academic dispute. Even what would seem to be relatively straightforward questions – 'sledded Pollacks' or 'sledded pole-axe', and what does the phrase mean anyway? – spawn cross-century arguments.

Fourth, these discussions matter because Shakespeare matters so much to our culture. Between sledded 'Pollacks' and 'pole-axe' there may not be a lot at stake, but between an intelligible Shakespeare and a Shakespeare who falls mute to our ears there is a tremendous difference.

So here we have scholarly questions – learned attempts to know Shakespeare and his work – that are hard to settle, have long histories, that have been much discussed, and that matter a great deal to our culture. The Internet is far better designed for this scholarly cacophony than print ever was, for the Internet is capacious, enables rapid as well as leisurely responses, is publicly accessible, and, most important, is linked.

Over the centuries of argument about every aspect of Shakespeare and his works, the vast majority of those disagreements were pursued in private, or in highly limited public spaces: a dinner table, the hallway of a theater, a classroom, the lobby of a public lecture. Of course, the vast majority of those disagreements were of little value except to those engaged in them;

history is none the poorer for not recording the conversation in our family car as we drove back from the 2005 Shakespeare & Co. performance of *The Taming of the Shrew* in Lenox, Massachusetts. But even discussions of such local interest might enable people to find others with similar interests and different viewpoints. And many discussions far more worth recording have been lost because to warrant their publication in the Age of Paper disagreements had to rise to levels of significance that excluded all but a tiny percentage of them.

The Internet's bar to publication is somewhere between most people's ankles and mid-shins, so much more makes it into the public sphere. But the new abundance of content and of disagreement is by far the lesser consequence of the Internet. Indeed, if that is all the Net did, then the claim of cacophony would be fully justified. But, the Net is composed not only of voices but of links. Responsible online scholarship provides clickable links not only to its sources but to the ideas with which it contends. Additional links are created among differing sources by those who respond, whether that is in another scholarly article, a blog post, an email to a mailing list, a Facebook entry, or any other of the Net's constantly extending conversational forms. Each of these links provides not just an easy way to go from one idea to a different idea but also builds a traversable map. This map is not an expression of our knowledge the way a library is. Rather, it is the knowledge. It is where knowledge is built and where it occurs. Knowledge itself is transformed by the linked structure it now inhabits. The network of scholarly articles shows knowledge to consist in their connections and disagreements. This is a territory of differences.

Of course scholarship has always been contentious, fractious. But now the primary objects of scholarship are not the individual works but the network that links them. The territory of perpetual disagreement is made richer by these linked disagreements, and the landscape those links form is a more accurate representation of scholarship than the old media enabled. In short, network knowledge contains difference. Disagreement is how you let knowledge get really really big.

As Neil Jeffries posted in the op-ed section of Wikipedia in 2012:

> Rather than always aiming for objective statements of truth we need to realize that a large amount of knowledge is derived via inference from a limited and imperfect evidence base, especially in the humanities. Thus we should aim to accurately represent the state of knowledge about a topic, including omissions, uncertainty and differences of opinion.

In this view, the 'state of knowledge' is better exemplified – or embodied – by a messy network of disagreements than by a neat shelf of vetted books.

But, surely including disagreement and argumentative uncertainty within the domain of knowledge is just a linguistic trick! Yes and no. Yes, in that we do not want to obliterate the difference between justified true belief and mere opinion, the distinction that gave birth to our concept of knowledge in Athens two and a half millennia ago. But, no, it is not a mere linguistic trick because there is value in remembering that even classic knowledge is less certain, more social, and more linked than the classic idea allows. That is, the state of knowledge is really no different from the state of scholarship.

Indeed, if I were a Shakespeare scholar, which I manifestly am not, I might suggest that this view of knowledge is far closer to Shakespeare's own. The hard nuggets of certainty in his plays often are known to the audience from the beginning to be false – Desdemona is unfaithful, Cordelia does not love Lear enough. And when the truth is stated starkly at the beginning – the witches' prediction to Macbeth, Hamlet's father's accusation – it does little to undo the swirling confusion and unknowing that is characteristic of the project of human knowing.

We have acted as if disagreement and argument were temporary phases as we work toward settled knowledge. That is an understandable assumption when the medium of knowledge was paper, for that assumption essentially repeats the publishing metaphor: ideas go through a period of development, and when they are ready and finalized they are committed to paper and put out into the public sphere. Knowledge exists in settled statements.

The Internet's metaphor for, and embodiment of, scholarship and knowledge seem to me to be closer to the truth about scholarship and knowledge. For example, Shakespeare's life and works have been a continuous subject of argument and disagreement not only because we have so little evidence but because a life is never fully understood, not by those who study it, and not even by the one who lived it. While we may someday come across a text that settles sufficiently whether it was a sledded pole-axe or Pollacks, we are not ever going to settle how exactly that phrase nudges the play into shape, much less settling 'the meaning' of the play so that now scholarship is done. Scholars will instead find new connections, new meanings, new links that cast reflected light in unpredicted hues. We will as audiences find new ways these plays simultaneously make sense of and alter our lives. We will continue to engage in the knowing of Shakespeare because Shakespeare – the person and the work – is itself a network of messy links, always in contention.

Works cited

Print and other media

Actsophia 2009. Actsophia LLC. App.
Addison, Joseph 1721. *Works of the Right Honourable Joseph Addison.*
Advertisement for 'The Penny Shakespeare'. 1845. *Publishers' Circular* 8:186 (16 June), advert number 670, p. 181.
Allentuck, Marcia 1976. 'Sir Thomas Hanmer Instructs Francis Hayman: An Editor's Notes to his Illustrator (1744)', *Shakespeare Quarterly* 27: 288–315.
Allott, Robert 1600. *Englands Parnassus: or The Choysest Flowers of our Moderne Poets.*
Andersen, Jennifer, and Elizabeth Sauer (eds.) 2002. *Books and Readers in Early Modern England: Material Studies.* Philadelphia: University of Pennsylvania Press.
Anderson, Dorothy 1980. 'Reflections on Librarianship: Observations Arising from Examination of the Garrick Collection of Old Plays in the British Library', *British Library Journal* 6: 1–6.
Anon. 1573. *New custome.*
    1591. *The troublesome raigne of Iohn King of England.*
    1592. *Present remedies against the plague.*
    1594a. *A pleasant conceited historie, called the taming of a shrew.*
    1594b. *Present remedies against the plague.*
    1594c. *The true tragedie of Richard the third.*
    1595. *The lamentable tragedie of Locrine, the eldest sonne of King Brutus.*
    1596a. *A pleasant conceited comedie, called, A knacke to know an honest man.*
    1596b. *The raigne of King Edward the third.*
    1605a. *Captain Thomas Stukeley.*
    1605b. *The London prodigall.*
    1607. *The Merrie Conceited Jests of George Peele Gentleman.*
    1609? *Pimlyco. Or, Runne Red-Cap.*
    1619. *Two Wise Men And All The Rest Fooles.*
    1648. *Lord have Mercy upon us, or the Visitation at Oxford.*
    1659. *Lady Alimony.*

Works cited

Appignanesi, Richard 2007. *The Tempest*, illustrated by Paul Duffield. London: SelfMadeHero.
Aquinas, Thomas 1913. *The 'Summa Theologica' of St. Thomas Aquinas*. Trans. fathers of the English Dominican province. London: Burns Oates and Washbourne.
Arber, Edward 1875–94. *A Transcript of the Registers of the Company of Stationers of London, 1554–1640 AD*.
Argus (newspaper), story concerning Richard Field, 29 June 1878: 586.
Ariosto, Lodovico 1591. *Orlando furioso in English heroical verse, by Iohn Haringto[n]*.
Armin, Robert 1600. *Quips upon Questions*.
Austen, Jane 1816. *Mansfield Park*. 3 vols.
Babington, Gervase 1588. *A profitable exposition of the Lords prayer, by way of questions and answers*.
Bald, R. C. 1931. '"Assembled" Texts', *The Library*. 4th ser. 12: 243–8.
  1938. *Bibliographical Studies in the Beaumont & Fletcher Folio of 1647*. London: Oxford University Press for the Bibliographical Society.
Baldwin, T. W. 1947. *Shakespeare's Five-Act Structure*. Urbana: University of Illinois Press.
Bales, Peter 1590. *The Writing Schoolmaster*.
Banham, Rob 2007. 'The Industrialization of the Book 1800–1900', in Simon Eliot and Jonathan Rose (eds.) *A Companion to the History of the Book*. Oxford: Blackwell, 273–90.
Barnes, Barnabe 1593. *Parthenophil and Parthenope*.
Barnfield, Richard 1595. *Cynthia. With certaine sonnets, and the legend of Cassandra*.
  1598. *The encomion of Lady Pecunia*.
Barroll, Leeds 1991. *Politics, Plague and Shakespeare's Theatre: The Stuart Years*. Ithaca, NY: Cornell University Press.
Barthes, Roland 1977. 'The Death of the Author', in *Image, Music Text*, trans. Stephen Heath. New York: Hill & Wang, 142–8.
Bate, Jonathan 2000. 'Pictorial Shakespeare: Text, Stage, Illustration', in Catherine J. Golden (ed.) *Book Illustrated: Text, Image, and Culture, 1770–1930*, New Castle, Del.: Oak Knoll Press, 31–59.
Bate, Jonathan, and Eric Rasmussen (eds.) 2007. *William Shakespeare: Complete Works*. New York: Random House.
Bawcutt, N. W. (ed.) 1991. *Measure for Measure*. By William Shakespeare. Oxford: Oxford University Press.
  1993. 'Ralph Crane's Transcript of *A Game at Chess*, Bodleian Manuscript Malone 25', *Collections XV*. London: Malone Society.
Beal, Peter 1980. *Catalogue of English Literary Manuscripts*. https://celm2.dighum.kcl.ac.uk (accessed 25 March 2015).
Beaumont, Francis, and John Fletcher 1647. *Comedies and Tragedies*.
Beckerman, Bernard 1980. 'The Persons Personated: Character Lists in English Renaissance Play Texts', *Poetry and Drama in the English Renaissance: in Honour of Professor Jiro Ozu*. Tokyo: Kinokuniya Company Ltd., 61–70.

Bednarz, James 2001. *Shakespeare and the Poets' War*. New York: Columbia University Press.
Bell, J. 1773. *The Tempest*.
Benedetti, Jean 2001. *David Garrick and the Birth of the Modern Theatre*. London: Methuen.
Bennett, Andrew 2005. *The Author*. New York: Routledge.
Bennett, Stuart 2004. *Trade Bookbinding in the British Isles 1660–1800*. New Castle, Del.: Oak Knoll Press.
Bentley, Gerald Eades 1941–68. *The Jacobean and Caroline Stage*. 7 vols. Oxford: Clarendon Press.
　1971. *The Profession of Dramatist in Shakespeare's Time, 1590–1642*. Princeton, NJ: Princeton University Press.
Berger, Thomas L. 2007. 'Shakespeare Writ Small: Early Single Editions of Shakespeare's Plays', in Andrew Murphy (ed.) *A Concise Companion to Shakespeare and the Text*. Oxford: Blackwell, 57–70.
Berger, Thomas L., and Sonia Massai (eds.) 2014. *The Paratexts in English Printed Drama to 1642*. Cambridge: Cambridge University Press.
Bergeron, David M. 2002. 'The King's Men's King's Men: Shakespeare and Folio Patronage', in Paul Whitfield White and Suzanne R. Westfall (eds.) *Shakespeare and Theatrical Patronage in Early Modern England*. Cambridge: Cambridge University Press, 45–63.
Bertram, Paul 1981. *White Spaces in Shakespeare: The Development of the Modern Text*. Cleveland, Ohio: Bellflower Press.
Best, Michael 2009. 'Standing in Rich Place: Electrifying the Multiple-Text Edition or, Every Text is Multiple'. *College Literature* 36.1: 26–39.
　(ed.). n.d. Internet Shakespeare Editions. www.internetshakespeare.uvic.ca (accessed 25 March 2015).
Bevington, David 2004. 'Modern Spelling: The Hard Choices', in Lukas Erne and Margaret Jane Kidnie (eds.) *Textual Performances: The Modern Reproduction of Shakespeare's Drama*. Cambridge: Cambridge University Press, 143–57.
Black, M. W., and M. A. Shaaber (eds.) 1937. *Shakespeare's Seventeenth-Century Editors, 1632–1685*. New York: Modern Language Association.
Blair, Ann 2010. *Too Much to Know: Managing Scholarly Information before the Modern Age*. Cambridge, Mass.: Yale University Press.
Blayney, Peter W. M. 1991. *The First Folio of Shakespeare*. Washington, DC: Folger Library Publications.
　1997. 'The Publication of Playbooks', in John Cox and David Scott Kastan (eds.) *A New History of Early English Drama*. New York: Columbia University Press, 383–422.
Blostein, David A. (ed.) 1978. *Parasitaster or The Fawn*. The Revels Plays. Manchester: Manchester University Press.
Blostein, James 1825. *Memoirs of the Life of John Philip Kemble, Esq.* 2 vols. London: Longman, Hurst, Rees, Orme, Brown and Green.

Boas, F. S. (ed.) 1968 [1929]. *Elizabethan and other Essays*. Freeport, NY: Books for Libraries Press.
Bodenham, John 1600. *Bel-vedére: or The Garden of the Muses*.
Bolden Auction Galleries. n.d. Lot 505. www.ukauctioneers.com/lots/1238417 (accessed June 2013). No longer available.
Bondy, Louis W. 1981. *Miniature Books: Their History from the Beginnings to the Present Day*. London: Sheppard.
Booth, Stephen (ed.). 1977. *Shakespeare's Sonnets*. New Haven, Conn: Yale University Press.
Boswell, J., and E. Malone (eds.) 1821. *Plays and Poems of William Shakespeare*. 21 vols. London: R. C. and J. Rivington.
Bowers, Fredson 1950–51. 'Some Relations of Bibliography to Editorial Problems', *Studies in Bibliography* 3: 37–62.
  1955. *On Editing Shakespeare and the Elizabethan Dramatists*. Philadelphia: University of Pennsylvania Library.
  1962. *Principles of Bibliographical Description*. New York: Russell & Russell.
  1974. 'Beggars Bush: A Reconstructed Prompt-Book and its Copy', *Studies in Bibliography* 27: 114–36.
  1982. 'Historical Collation in an Old-Spelling Shakespeare Edition: Another View', *Studies in Bibliography* 35: 234–58.
  1990. 'The Problem of Semi-Substantive Variants: An Example from the Shakespeare–Fletcher *Henry VIII*', *Studies in Bibliography* 43: 80–95.
Bradbrook, Muriel 1964. 'St. George for Spelling Reform! Social Implications of Orthography – Cheke to Whythorn; Mulcaster to Shakespeare's Holofernes', *Shakespeare Quarterly* 15: 129–41.
Brathwait, Richard 1631. *Whimzies*.
Brayman Hackel, Heidi 2005. *Reading Material in Early Modern England*. Cambridge: Cambridge University Press.
Briggs, Julia 1998. '"The Lady Vanishes": Problems of Authorship and Editing in the Middleton Canon', in W. Speed Hill (ed.) *New Ways of Looking at Old Texts, II: Papers of the Renaissance English Text Society, 1992–1996*. Tempe, Ariz.: Medieval & Renaissance Text & Studies in conjunction with Renaissance English Text Society, 109–20.
  (ed.) 2007. *The Lady's Tragedy*, in Gary Taylor and John Lavagnino (eds.) *Thomas Middleton: The Collected Works*. Oxford: Clarendon Press, 833–906.
Brinsley, John 1662. *The Christians cabala*.
Bristow, Richard 1580. *A reply to Fulke, In defense of M. D. Allens scroll of articles*.
Brooke, Christopher 1614. *Ghost of Richard the Third*.
Brooks, Douglas 1998. *From Playhouse to Printing House: Drama and Authorship in Early Modern England*. Cambridge: Cambridge University Press.
Brown, Arthur (ed.) 1953. *The Captives by Thomas Heywood*. Malone Society Reprints. London: Malone Society.
Brown, John Russell 1954. 'The Printing of John Webster's Plays (I)', *Studies in Bibliography* 6: 117–40.
  (ed.)1955. *The Merchant of Venice*. Arden 2. London: Methuen.

(ed.) 1964. *The Duchess of Malfi*. The Revels Plays. London: Methuen.
Brownlow, James Arthur 1996. *The Last Trumpet*. Stuyvesant, NY: Pendragon Press.
Bruster, Douglas 2000. 'The Structural Transformation of Print in Late Elizabethan England', in Arthur F. Marotti and Michael D. Bristol (eds.) *Print, Manuscript, & Performance: The Changing Relations of the Media in Early Modern England*. Columbus: Ohio State University Press, 49–89.
  2013a. 'Shakespeare the Stationer,' in Marta Straznicky (ed.) *Shakespeare's Stationers: Studies in Cultural Bibliography*. Philadelphia: University of Pennsylvania Press, 112–31.
  2013b. 'Shakespearean Spellings and Handwriting in the Additional Passages Printed in the 1602 *Spanish Tragedy*', *Notes and Queries* 60: 420–4.
Bullokar, William 1585. *Aesop's Fables in True Orthography*.
Bunbury, Sir Henry (ed.) 1838. *The Correspondence of Sir Thomas Hanmer*. London: Edward Moxon.
Burdick, Anne, Johanna Drucker, Peter Lunenfeld, et al. 2012. *Digital_Humanities*. Cambridge: Cambridge University Press.
Burgoyne, Frank J. 1904. *Collotype Facsimile & Type Transcript of an Elizabethan Manuscript Preserved at Alnwick Castle, Northumberland*. London: Longmans, Green, & Co.
Burnim, Kalman A., and Philip H. Highfill Jr. 1998. *John Bell Patron of British Theatrical Portraiture: A Catalog of the Theatrical Portraits in His Editions of Bell's Shakespeare and Bell's British Theatre*. Carbondale, Ill.: Southern Illinois University Press.
Burton, Jonathan 2005. *Traffic and Turning: Islam and English Drama, 1579–1624*. Newark: University of Delaware Press.
Butler, Martin (ed.) 2005. *Cymbeline*. New Cambridge Shakespeare. Cambridge: Cambridge University Press.
Cambridge Edition of the Works of Ben Jonson [2012]. 'Guidelines'. Unpublished.
Camp, Robert Quillen 2006. *The Secret Bear*. Brooklyn, NY: Paper Theatre.
Capell, Edward (ed.) 1767–68. *The Works of Shakespeare*. 10 vols. London.
  1774. *Notes and various readings to Shakespeare*. London: Printed for Edw. and Cha. Dilly, in the Poultry.
Carr, Nicholas 2010. *The Shallows: What the Internet is Doing to Our Brains*. London: Atlantic.
Carson, Christie 2008. 'eShakespeare and Performance', *Shakespeare* 4.3: 270–86.
Chambers, E. K. 1923. *The Elizabethan Stage*. 4 vols. Oxford: Clarendon Press.
Chambers, R. W. 1939. *Man's Unconquerable Mind: Studies of English Writers, from Bede to A. E. Housman and W. R. Ker*. London: Jonathan Cape.
Chapman, George 1605. *All Fools*.
  1613. *The Revenge of Bussy D'Ambois*.
Chartier, Roger, and Peter Stallybrass 2013. 'What is a Book?', in Neil Freistat and Julia Flanders (eds.) *The Cambridge Companion to Textual Scholarship*. Cambridge: Cambridge University Press, 188–204.

Cheney, Patrick 2008. *Shakespeare's Literary Authorship*. Cambridge: Cambridge University Press.
　2004. *Shakespeare, National Poet-Playwright*. Cambridge: Cambridge University Press.
Chettle, Henry 1593. *Kind-Harts Dreame*.
Child, Harold 1935. 'The Shakespearean Productions of John Philip Kemble', *Papers of the Shakespeare Association* 19: 6.
Chorney, Tatjana 2006. 'Book History and Reader-Response Theory: Teaching Shakespeare's *Romeo and Juliet* and *King Lear*', in Anne Hawkins (ed.) *Teaching Bibliography, Textual Criticism and Book History*. London: Pickering & Chatto, 167–73.
Cibber, Colley 1700. *The Tragical History of King Richard III*.
Citron, Marcia J. 1993. *Gender and the Musical Canon*. Cambridge: Cambridge University Press.
Collier, J. P. (ed.) 1858. *Shakespeare's Comedies, Histories, Tragedies and Poems*. 2nd edn. 6 vols. London: Whittaker.
Collinson, Patrick 2006. *From Cranmer to Sancroft*. London: Continuum.
Constable, Henry 1595? *Diana. Or, The excellent conceitful sonnets of H. C.*
Cook, Megan 2011. 'The Poet and the Antiquaries: Renaissance Readers and Chaucerian Scholarship'. PhD dissertation. University of Pennsylvania.
Coombs, James H., Allen H. Renear, and Steven J. DeRose. 1987. 'Markup Systems and the Future of Scholarly Text Processing'. *Communications of the Association for Computing Machinery* 30.11: 933–47.
Cormack, Bradin, and Carla Mazzio 2005. *Book Use, Book Theory, 1500–1700*. Chicago: University of Chicago Press.
Corti, Claudia 1996. *Shakespeare illustrato*. Rome: Bulzoni.
Covell, William 1595. *Polimanteia*.
Cowden Clarke, Charles 1863. *Shakespeare-characters; Chiefly those Subordinate*.
Craig, Hugh, and Arthur Kinney 2009. *Shakespeare, Computers, and the Mystery of Authorship*. Cambridge: Cambridge University Press.
Craik, T. W. (ed.) 1995. *King Henry V*. Arden 3. London: Routledge.
Crane, Mary Thomas 1997. *Framing Authority: Sayings, Self, and Society in Sixteenth-Century England*. Princeton, NJ: Princeton University Press.
Craven, Alan E. 1965. 'Justification of Prose and Jaggard Compositor B', *English Language Notes* 3: 15–17.
Crystal, David, and Ben Crystal 2004. *Shakespeare's Words: A Glossary & Language Companion*. London: Penguin.
Cunningham, Vanessa 2008. *Shakespeare and Garrick*. Cambridge: Cambridge University Press.
Cupper, William 1592. *Certaine sermons concerning Gods late visitation in the citie of London*.
Cutts, J. P. 1967. 'New Findings with Regard to the 1624 Protection List', *Shakespeare Survey* 19: 101–7.
Dane, Joseph A. 2012. *What is a Book? The Study of Early Printed Books*. South Bend, Ind.: University of Notre Dame Press.

Dane, Joseph A., and Alexandra Gillespie 2010. 'The Myth of the Cheap Quarto', in John N. King (ed.) *Tudor Books and Readers: Materiality and the Construction of Meaning.* Cambridge: Cambridge University Press, 24–45.
Daniel, Samuel 1595. *Delia and Rosamond augmented.*
Davies, John 1599. 'Cosmum', in *Epigrammes and elegies.*
Davies, Thomas 1780. *Memoirs of the Life of David Garrick, Esq.* vol. 1. Dublin: Joseph Hill.
Dawson, Giles E. 1946. 'The Copyright of Shakespeare's Dramatic Works', in Charles T. Prouty (ed.) *The University of Missouri Studies in Honor of A. H. R. Fairchild.* Columbia: University of Missouri Press, 2, 11–35.
Day, John 1950. *Law Tricks.* Ed. John Crow. Malone Society Reprints. London: Oxford University Press.
Day, John, George Wilkins, and William Rowley 1607. *The Travels of Three English Brothers.*
Daybell, James. 2012. *The Material Letter in Early Modern England: Manuscript Letters and the Culture and Practices of Letter-Writing, 1512–1635.* Basingstoke: Palgrave Macmillan.
de Grazia, Margreta 1991a. 'Shakespeare in Quotation Marks', in Jean I. Marsden (ed.) *The Appropriation of Shakespeare: Post-Renaissance Reconstructions of the Works and the Myth.* New York: St Martin's, 57–71.
  1991b. *Shakespeare Verbatim: The Reproduction of Authenticity and the 1790 Apparatus.* Oxford: Clarendon Press.
de Grazia, Margreta, and Peter Stallybrass 1993, 'The Materiality of the Shakespearean Text', *Shakespeare Quarterly* 44: 255–83.
De Lafontaine, Henry Cart (ed.) 1909. *The king's musick; a transcript of records relating to music and musicians, 1460–1700.* London: Novello.
De Ricci, Seymour 1930. *English Collectors of Books and Manuscripts, 1530–1930, and their Ownership.* Sandars Lectures, 1929–30. Cambridge: Cambridge University Press.
Deegan, Marilyn, and Kathryn Sutherland. 2009. *Transferred Illusions: Digital Technology and the Forms of Print.* Farnham: Ashgate.
DEEP: Database of Early English Playbooks 2007. Eds. Alan B. Farmer and Zachary Lesser. deep.sas.upenn.edu (accessed 25 March 2015).
Deighton, K. (ed.) 1890. *The Tempest.* London: Macmillan.
  (ed.) 1891. *Much Ado About Nothing.*
Dekker, Thomas 1600a. *Old Fortunatus.*
  1600b. *The Shomakers Holiday.*
  1607. *The Whore of Babylon.*
  1609. *The guls horne-booke.*
  1612. *If it be not Good the Devil is in it.*
Dekker, Thomas, and John Webster 1607. *Northward Ho!*
  1607. *Westward Ho!*
Dekker, Thomas, and Thomas Middleton 1611. *The Roaring Girl.*
Dent, R. W. 1981. *Shakespeare's Proverbial Language: An Index.* Berkeley and Los Angeles: University of California Press.

1984. *Proverbial Language in English Drama Exclusive of Shakespeare, 1495–1616: An Index*. Berkeley and Los Angeles: University of California Press.
Derrida, Jacques 1987. *The Post Card: From Socrates to Freud and Beyond*. Trans. Alan Bass. Chicago: University of Chicago Press.
Dessen, Alan 1995. 'Sick Chairs and Sick Thrones', in *Recovering Shakespeare's Theatrical Vocabulary*. Cambridge: Cambridge University Press, 109–26.
Devonshire, William Cavendish (Duke of) n.d. *Chatsworth Library: Kemble-Devonshire Collection of English Plays & Play-Bills*. London: Sotheby, Wilkinson & Hodge.
Dibdin, T. F. 1824. *The Library Companion*. London: Harding, Triphook and Lepard.
Dicks, J. (ed.) 1864. *Complete Works of Shakespeare*. London: John Dicks.
Dimmock, Matthew 2015. 'Shakespeare's Non-Christian Religions', in David Loewenstein and Michael Whitmore (eds.) *Shakespeare and Early Modern Religion*. Cambridge: Cambridge University Press.
Dobson, E. J. 1968. *English Pronunciation, 1500–1700*. 2 vols. Oxford: Clarendon Press.
Dobson, M. 1992. *The Making of the National Poet: Shakespeare, Adaptation and Authorship, 1660–1769*. Oxford: Clarendon Press.
Dolby, T. (ed.) 1824. *The Tempest*.
Donaldson, George 2008. 'The First Folio: "My Shakespeare"/ "Our Shakespeare": Whose Shakespeare?', in Richard Meek, Jane Rickard, and Richard Wilson (eds.) *Shakespeare's Book: Essays in Reading, Writing and Reception*. Manchester: Manchester University Press, 187–206.
Donatus, Aelius. n.d. 'Aeli Donati Quod Fertur Commentum Terenti'. Hyperdonat/ Hyperdonatus. http://hyperdonat.tge-adonis.fr/editions/index.html (accessed 4 October 2013).
Donker, Marjorie 1992. Shakespeare's *Proverbial Themes: A Rhetorical Context for the Sententia as Res*. Westport, Conn.: Greenwood Press.
Donnellan, Declan 2002. *The Actor and the Target*. [New York]: Theatre Communications Group.
Donno, E. S. (ed.) 1985. *Twelfth Night*. The New Cambridge Shakespeare. Cambridge: Cambridge University Press.
Downes, John 1708. *Roscius Anglicanus*.
Downes, Thomas 1620? *Bookes as they are sold bound*.
Drakakis, John (ed.) 2010. *The Merchant of Venice*. Arden 3. London: A & C Black.
Drayton, Michael 1593. *Idea the shepheards garland*.
  1598. *Englands Heroicall Epistles*. London.
  1599. *Englands Heroicall Epistles*. London.
Dryden, John, and William Davenant 1676. *The Tempest, or the Enchanted Island. A Comedy*.
Duncan-Jones, Katherine, and H. R. Woudhuysen (eds.) 2007. *Shakespeare's Poems*. Arden. London: Thomson Learning.
Dusinberre, Juliet (ed.) 2006. *As You Like It*. Arden 3. London: Thomson Learning.

Dutton, Richard 2011. 'A Jacobean *Merry Wives?*', *Ben Jonson Journal* 18: 1–26.
Earle, John 1628. *Micro-cosmographie.*
Early English Books Online (EEBO). Chadwyick Healy. http://eebo.chadwyck.com (accessed 25 March 2015).
Egan, Gabriel 2010. *The Struggle for Shakespeare's Text: Twentieth-Century Editorial Theory and Practice.* Cambridge: Cambridge University Press.
  2011. 'Precision, Consistency and Completeness in Early-Modern Playbook Manuscripts: The Evidence from *Thomas of Woodstock* and *John a Kent and John a Cumber*', *The Library* 7th ser. 12.4: 376–91.
Eisenstein, Elizabeth L. 1980 [1979]. *The Printing Press as an Agent of Change: Communication and Cultural Transformations in Early Modern Europe.* 2 vols.; repr as single vol. Cambridge: Cambridge University Press.
Eliot, John 1592. *The suruay or topographical description of France.*
Eliot, Simon 1994. *Some Patterns and Trends in British Publishing 1800–1919.* London: Bibliographical Society.
English Short Title Catalogue (ESTC). British Library. http://estc.bl.uk.
Erne, Lukas 2003. *Shakespeare as Literary Dramatist.* Cambridge: Cambridge University Press.
  2008. *Shakespeare's Modern Collaborators.* London: Continuum.
  2013. *Shakespeare and the Book Trade.* Cambridge: Cambridge University Press.
Erne, Lukas, and Margaret Jane Kidnie 2004. 'Introduction', *Textual Performances: The Modern Reproduction of Shakespeare's Drama.* Cambridge: Cambridge University Press, 1–20.
Estill, Laura 2015. *Dramatic Extracts in Seventeenth-Century English Manuscripts: Watching, Reading, Changing Plays.* Newark: University of Delaware Press.
Evans, G. Blakemore (ed.) 1960–96. *Shakespearean Prompt-books of the Seventeenth Century.* vol. 1 pts. 1–2 (1960); vol. 2, pts. 1–2 (1963); vol. 3, pts. 1–2 (1964); vol. 4 (1966); vol. 5 (1970); vol. 6 (1980); vol. 7 (1989); vol. 8 (1996) Charlottesville: University Press of Virginia and Bibliographical Society of the University of Virginia. Online edition. http://bsuva.org/bsuva/promptbook/ (accessed 29 April 2012).
  1962. 'The Douai Manuscript: Six Shakespearean Transcripts (1694–95)', *Philological Quarterly* 41.1: 158–72.
  (ed.) 1974a. *The Riverside Shakespeare.* Boston: Houghton Mifflin.
  (ed.) 1974b. 'Shakespeare's Text', in *The Riverside Shakespeare.* Boston: Houghton Mifflin, 27–41.
  1987. '*The Merry Wives of Windsor:* The Folger Manuscript', in Bernhard Fabian and Kurt Tetzeli von Rosador (eds.) *Shakespeare: Text, Language, Criticism: Essays in Honour of Martin Spevack.* Zurich and New York: Olms-Weidman, 57–79.
Evans, G. Blakemore, and George Walton Williams (eds.) 1974. *The History of King Henry IV, as revised by Sir Edward Dering, Bart.* Charlottesville: Published for the Folger Shakespeare Library by the University Press of Virginia.

Farmer, Alan B. n.d. 'Playbooks and the Question of Ephemerality'. Unpublished typescript.
Farmer, Alan B., and Zachary Lesser 2000. 'Vile Arts: The Marketing of English Printed Drama, 1512–1660', *Research Opportunities in Renaissance Drama* 39: 77–165.
  2005. 'The Popularity of Playbooks Revisited', *Shakespeare Quarterly* 56: 1–32.
  2006. 'Canons and Classics: Publishing Drama in Caroline England', in Adam Zucker and Alan B. Farmer (eds.) *Localizing Caroline Drama: Politics and Economics of the Early Modern English Stage, 1625–1642*. Basingstoke: Palgrave Macmillan, 17–41.
Fehrenbach, Robert and Elisabeth Leedham-Green 1992. *Private Libraries in Renaissance England*. Binghamton, NY: Medieval and Renaissance Texts & Studies.
Feuillerat, A. 1953. *The Composition of Shakespeare's Plays: Authorship, Chronology*. New Haven, Conn.: Yale University Press.
Fitzgeffrey, Henry 1617. *Satyres and Satyricall Epigrams: The Third Booke of Humours: Intituled Notes from Black-Fryers*.
Fleming, Juliet 2011. 'Changed Opinion as to Flowers', in Helen Smith and Louise Wilson (eds.) *Renaissance Paratexts*, 48–64.
Fletcher, Giles 1593. *Licia, or poemes of love*.
Fletcher, John 1610. *The Faithful Shepherdess*.
Fletcher, John, and William Shakespeare 1634. *The two noble kinsmen*.
Foakes, R. A. (ed.) 2002. *Henslowe's Diary*. Cambridge: Cambridge University Press.
Foot, Mirjam 2006. *Bookbinders at Work: Their Roles and Methods*. New Castle, Del.: Oak Knoll.
Foucault, Michel 1979. 'What Is an Author?', in Josué V. Harari (ed.) *Textual Strategies: Perspectives in Post-Structuralist Criticism*. Ithaca, NY: Cornell University Press, 141–60.
Foulface, Philip of Ale-foord, student in good fellowship (*pseud.*) 1593. *Baccus bountie, describing the debonaire dietie of his bountifull godhead*.
Foxon, David 1975. 'Stitched Books', *Book Collector* 24: 111–24.
Freeman, Arthur, and Janet Ing Freeman 2001. 'Did Halliwell Steal and Mutilate the First Quarto of *Hamlet?*', *The Library* 7th ser. 2: 349–63.
  2004. *John Payne Collier: Scholarship and Forgery in the Nineteenth Century*. 2 vols. New Haven, Conn.: Yale University Press.
Freeman, Thomas 1614. *Rubbe and a great cast*.
Frye, Northrop (ed.) 1970 [1959]. *The Tempest*. The Pelican Shakespeare. Baltimore, Md.: Penguin Books.
Fuller, Steve 2013. 'Deviant Interdisciplinarity as Philosophical Practice: Prolegomena to Deep Intellectual History'. *Synthese* 190: 1899–916.
Fuller, Thomas [1662]. *The History of the Worthies of England*.
Fulwell, Ulpian 1991. 'Like Will to Like', in Peter Happé (ed.) *Two Moral Interludes*. Malone Society Reprints. London: Malone Society.
Furness, H. H. 1870. 'The Cambridge Shakespeare', *Athenaeum* 2212: 388.

(ed.) 1871. *A New Variorum Edition of Romeo and Juliet.* Philadelphia: J. B. Lippincott & Co.
(ed.) 1890. *A New Variorum Edition of Shakespeare.* 8 vols. Philadelphia: J. B. Lippincott & Co.
(ed.) 1892. *A New Variorum Edition of Shakespeare, The Tempest.* Philadelphia: J. B. Lippincott.
Gabrieli, Vittorio, and Giorgio Melchiori (eds.) 1990. *Sir Thomas More.* The Revels Plays. Manchester: Manchester University Press.
Galbraith, Steven K. 2010. 'English Literary Folios 1593–1623: Studying Shifts in Format', in John N. King (ed.) *Tudor Books and Readers: Materiality and the Construction of Meaning.* Cambridge: Cambridge University Press, 46–67.
Galey, Alan. n.d. Visualizing Variation. http://individual.utoronto.ca/alangaley/visualizingvariation/.
  2012. 'Seeing the Spider: Visualizations of Textual Variation in Shakespearean Editing'. Unpublished paper presented at the Shakespeare Association of American meeting in Boston.
  2014. *The Shakespearean Archive: Experiments in New Media from the Renaissance to Postmodernity.* Cambridge: Cambridge University Press.
Garnier, Robert 1595. *The tragedie of Antonie. Doone into English by the Countesse of Pembroke.*
Gaskell, Philip 1995 [1972]. *A New Introduction to Bibliography.* New Castle, Del.: Oak Knoll.
Genette, Gerard 1997. *Paratexts: Thresholds of Interpretation.* Trans. Jane E. Lewin. Cambridge: Cambridge University Press.
Gentleman, Francis 1771. *The Dramatic Censor.* 2 vols.
[Sir Nicholas Nipclose] 1772. *The Theatres: A Poetical Dissection.*
  1773. *The Modish Wife.*
Gerritsen, J. (ed.) 1952. *The Honest Mans Fortune: A Critical Edition of MS Dyce 9 (1625).* Groningen: Wolters.
Gervinus, G. G. 1883 [1862]. *Shakespeare Commentaries.* Trans. F. E. Bunnett. London: Smith, Elder & Co.
Gibbons, Brian 1999. 'The New Cambridge Shakespeare: The Early Quartos', in Kathleen Irace (ed.) *The First Quarto of Hamlet.* Cambridge: Cambridge University Press.
Giddens, Eugene 2011. *How to Read a Shakespearean Play Text.* Cambridge: Cambridge University Press.
Gieskes, Edward 2006. *Representing the Professions: Administration, Law, and Theater in Early Modern England.* Newark: University of Delaware Press.
Gillespie, Alexandra 2004. 'Poets, Printers, and Early English Sammelbände', *Huntington Library Quarterly* 67.2: 189–214.
Goldberg, Jonathan 1991. *Writing Matter: From the Hands of the English Renaissance.* Stanford, Calif.: Stanford University Press.
Gondris, J. (ed.) 1998. *Reading Readings: Essays on Shakespeare Editing in the Eighteenth Century.* Madison, NJ: Fairleigh Dickenson University Press.
Goodwin, George 1624. *Babels balm: or The honey-combe of Romes religion.*

Gossett, Suzanne (ed.) 2004. 'Introduction', *Pericles*. Arden 3. London: Thomson Learning, 1–163.
  2005. 'Emendations, Reconstructions, and the Uses of the Past', *Text* 17: 35–54.
Grafton, Anthony 1997. 'Is the History of Reading a Marginal Enterprise? Guillaume Budé and his Books', *Papers of the Bibliographic Society of America* 91:2: 139–57.
  1999. *The Footnote: A Curious History*. Cambridge, Mass.: Harvard University Press.
  2011. *The Culture of Correction in Renaissance Europe*. London: British Library.
Grafton, Anthony, and Lisa Jardine 1990. 'Studied for Action: How Gabriel Harvey Read His Livy', *Past and Present* 129:1: 30–78.
Graham-White, Anthony 1994. *Punctuation and its Dramatic Value in Shakespearean Drama*. Newark: University of Delaware Press.
Graves, Thornton S. 1924. 'Ralph Crane and the King's Players', *Studies in Philology* 21: 362–6.
Greenblatt, Stephen 2004. *Will in the World: How Shakespeare Became Shakespeare*. New York: Norton.
Greene, Robert n.d. *The honorable historie of frier Bacon, and frier Bongay*.
  n.d. *Pandosto the triumph of time*.
  1592a. *The Repentance of Robert Greene*.
  1592b. *Greenes, groats-worth of witte, bought with a million of repentance* [ed. Henry Chettle].
  1599. *Alphonsus, King of Aragon*.
  1994. *Greene's Groatsworth of Wit*. Ed. D. Allen Carroll. Binghamton, NY: Medieval and Renaissance Texts & Studies.
Greg, W. W. 1908. 'On Certain False Dates in Shakespearian Quartos', *The Library* 9: 113–31.
  (ed.) 1909. *The Second Maiden's Tragedy 1611*. Malone Society Reprints. London: Malone Society.
  (ed.) 1910. *Shakespeare's Merry Wives of Windsor 1602*. Oxford: Clarendon Press.
  (ed.) 1911. *The Book of Sir Thomas More*. Malone Society Reprints. Oxford: Malone Society.
  1931. *Dramatic Documents from the Elizabethan Playhouses: Stage Plots, Actors' Parts, Prompt Books*. 2 vols. Oxford: Clarendon Press.
  1942. 'Some Notes on Crane's Manuscript of *The Witch*', *The Library*. 4th ser. 22: 208–22.
  1950–51. 'The Rationale of Copy-Text', *Studies in Bibliography* 3: 19–36.
  (ed.) 1951. *Bonduca*. Malone Society Reprints. London: Malone Society.
  1954 [1942]. *The Editorial Problem in Shakespeare: A Survey of the Foundations of the Text*. 3rd edn. Oxford: Clarendon Press.
  1955. *The Shakespeare First Folio: Its Bibliographical and Textual History*. Oxford: Clarendon Press.
Greg, W. W., and E. Boswell 1930. *Records of the Court of the Stationers' Company, 1576 to 1602: From Register B*. London: Bibliographical Society.

Greg, W. W., and F. P. Wilson (eds.) 1950. *The Witch, by Thomas Middleton.* Malone Society Reprints. Oxford: Malone Society.
Guillory, John 2010. 'Genesis of the Media Concept'. *Critical Inquiry* 36.2: 321–62.
Gurr, Andrew 2004a. *Playgoing in Shakespeare's London.* 3rd edn. Cambridge: Cambridge University Press.
  2004b. *The Shakespeare Company 1594–1642.* Cambridge: Cambridge University Press.
  (ed.) 2005. *King Henry V.* New Cambridge Shakespeare. Cambridge: Cambridge University Press.
  2006. 'Editing Stephano's Book', *Shakespeare Survey* 59: 91–107.
Hailey, R. Carter 2007. 'The Dating Game: New Evidence for the Dates of Q4 *Romeo and Juliet* and Q4 *Hamlet*', *Shakespeare Quarterly* 58: 367–87.
Halasz, Alexandra 2013. 'The Stationers' Shakespeare', in Marta Straznicky (ed.) *Shakespeare's Stationers: Studies in Cultural Bibliography*, Philadelphia: University of Pennsylvania Press, 17–27.
Hall, Peter 2003. *Shakespeare's Advice to the Players.* London: Oberon Books.
Hallett, Charles A. and Elaine S. Hallett 1991. *Analyzing Shakespeare's Action: Scene versus Sequence.* Cambridge: Cambridge University Press.
Halliwell-Phillipps, J. O. (ed.) 1853. *The Works of William Shakespeare.* 9 vols.
  1887. *Outlines of the Life of Shakespeare.* 2 vols.
Halpern, Richard 1991. *The Poetics of Primitive Accumulation: English Renaissance Culture and the Genealogy of Capital.* Ithaca, NY: Cornell University Press.
Hammond, Paul 2009. *The Strangeness of Tragedy.* Oxford. Oxford University Press.
Hampden, J. (ed.) 1926. *The Tempest.* Teaching of English Series. London: T. Nelson and Sons.
Hanna, Ralph 1996. *Pursuing History: Middle English Manuscripts and their Texts.* Palo Alto, Calif.: Stanford University Press.
Hardinge, George 1801. *Another Essence of Malone, Or, The 'Beauties' of Shakespeare's Editor.* London: T. Becket.
Harrison, Peter 2007. 'Philosophy and the Crisis of Religion', in James Hankins (ed.) *The Cambridge Companion to Renaissance Philosophy*, Cambridge: Cambridge University Press, 234–49.
Hart, H. C. (ed.) 1905. *Measure for Measure.* Arden 1. London: Methuen.
Hattaway, Michael 2009. 'Dating *As You Like It* and the Problems of "As the Dial Hand Tells O'er"', *Shakespeare Quarterly* 60: 154–167.
Hawkins, Anne (ed.) 2006 *Teaching Bibliography, Textual Criticism and Book History.* London: Pickering & Chatto.
Hayles, N. Katherine 2005. *My Mother was a Computer: Digital Subjects and Literary Texts.* Chicago: University of Chicago Press.
  2012. *How We Think: Digital Media and Contemporary Technogenesis.* Chicago: University of Chicago Press.
Hayley, Emma 2010. 'Manga Shakespeare', in Toni Johnson-Woods (ed.) *Manga: An Anthology of Global and Cultural Perspectives.* New York and London: Continuum, 267–80.

Hayward, John 1604. *A treatise of vnion of the two realms of England and Scotland*.
Hedbäck, Ann-Mari 1979. 'The Douai Manuscript Reexamined', *Papers of the Bibliographical Society of America* 73: 1–18.
Helgerson, Richard 1983. *Self-Crowned Laureates: Spenser, Jonson, Milton and the Literary System*. Palo Alto, Calif.: Stanford University Press.
  1992. *Forms of Nationhood: The Elizabethan Writing of England*. Chicago: University of Chicago Press.
Hentzner, Paul 1757. *A Journey into England in the year M.D.XC.VIII*. Trans. Horace Walpole.
Herford, C. H., Evelyn Simpson, and Percy Simpson (eds.) 1925–52. *Ben Jonson*. 11 vols. Oxford: Clarendon Press.
Heywood, Thomas 1611. *The Golden Age*.
  1615. *The foure prentises of London*.
Highfill, Philip A., Kalman A. Burnim, and Edward A. Langhans (eds.) 1973–93. *A Biographical Dictionary of Actors, Actresses, Musicians, Dancers, Managers & other Stage Personnel in London, 1660–1800*. 16 vols. Carbondale, Ill.: Southern Illinois University Press.
Hinman, Charlton 1963. *The Printing and Proof-Reading of the First Folio of Shakespeare*. Oxford: Clarendon Press.
  (ed.) 1968. *The Norton Facsimile: The First Folio of Shakespeare*. New York: W.W. Norton.
Hinman, Charlton, and Peter W. M. Blayney (eds.) 1996. *The First Folio of Shakespeare: The Norton Facsimile. Based on Folios in the Folger Shakespeare Library*. 2nd edn. New York and London: W.W. Norton & Company.
Hirsch, Brett (ed.) n.d. *Digital Renaissance Editions*. http://digitalrenaissance.uvic.ca (accesed 25 March 2015).
  2011. 'The Kingdom Has Been Digitized: Electronic Editions of Renaissance Drama and the Long Shadows of Shakespeare and Print', *Literature Compass* 8.9: 568–91.
Hirschfeld, Heather Anne 2004. *Joint Enterprises: Collaborative Drama and the Institutionalization of the English Renaissance Theater*. Amherst: University of Massachusetts Press.
Hirsh, James E. 1981. *The Structure of Shakespearean Scenes*. New Haven, Conn. and London: Yale University Press.
  2002. 'Act Divisions in the Shakespeare First Folio', *Papers of the Bibliographical Society of America* 96: 219–56.
Hodgdon, Barbara (ed.) 1997. *The First Part of King Henry the Fourth*. Boston, Mass.: Bedford.
Hodnett, Edward 1982. *Image and Text: Studies in the Illustration of English Literature*. London: Scolar Press.
Hoenselaars, Ton (ed.) 2012. 'Shakespeare: Colleagues, Collaborators, Co-authors', *The Cambridge Companion to Shakespeare and Contemporary Dramatists*. Cambridge: Cambridge University Press, 97–119.

Holderness, Graham 2003. *Textual Shakespeare: Writing and the Word*. Hatfield: University of Hertfordshire Press.
Holderness, Graham, and Carol Banks 1995. 'Mimesis: Text and Reproduction', *Critical Survey* 7: 332–8.
Holinshed, Raphael 1587. *The first and second volumes of Chronicles*.
Holland, Peter 2001. 'Beginning in the Middle', *Proceedings of the British Academy: Lectures and Memoirs*. Oxford: Oxford University Press, 127–55.
  (ed.) 2013. *Coriolanus*. Arden 3. London: Bloomsbury.
Hollyband, Claudius 1591. *The French Littelton*.
Honan, Park 1998. *Shakespeare: A Life*. Oxford: Oxford University Press.
Honigmann, E. A. J. 1965. *The Stability of Shakespeare's Text*. London: Edward Arnold.
  1996. *The Texts of 'Othello' and Shakespearian Revision*. London: Routledge.
  (ed.) 1997. *Othello*. Arden 3. Walton-on-Thames: Thomas Nelson.
  2004. 'The New Bibliography and its Critics', in Lukas Erne and Margaret Jane Kidnie (eds.) *Textual Performances: The Modern Reproduction of Shakespeare's Drama*. Cambridge: Cambridge University Press, 77–93.
Hooks, Adam 2008. 'Booksellers' Catalogues and the Classification of Printed Drama', *Papers of the Bibliographical Society of America* 102:4: 445–64.
  2011. 'Shakespeare at the White Greyhound', *Shakespeare Survey* 64, 260–75.
  2012, 'Book Trade', in Arthur F. Kinney (ed.) *The Oxford Handbook of Shakespeare*. Oxford: Oxford University Press, 126–42.
  2013. 'Wise Ventures: Shakespeare and Thomas Playfere at the Sign of the Angel,' in Marta Straznicky (ed.) *Shakespeare's Stationers: Studies in Cultural Bibliography*. Philadelphia: University of Pennsylvania Press, 47–62.
Howard-Hill, T. H. 1965. 'Ralph Crane's Parentheses', *Notes and Queries* 210: 334–40.
  1966. 'Knight, Crane and the Copy for the Folio *Winter's Tale*', *Notes and Queries* 211: 139–40.
  1974. *Ralph Crane and Some Shakespeare First Folio Comedies*. Charlottesville: University Press of Virginia.
  (ed.) 1979. *Sir John Van Olden Barnavelt by John Fletcher and Philip Massinger*. Malone Society Reprints. London: Malone Society.
  1991. 'Shakespeare's Earliest Editor, Ralph Crane', *Shakespeare Survey* 44: 113–30.
  1995. *Middleton's 'Vulgar Pasquin': Essays on A Game at Chess*. Newark: University of Delaware Press.
  2002. 'Ralph Crane: The Life and Works of a Jacobean Scribe in the Next Millennium', *Shakespearean International Yearbook* 2: 150–7.
  2004. 'Ralph Crane (*fl.* 1589–1632)' (q.v.) *Oxford Dictionary of National Biography*. Online edition. www.oxforddnb.com/view/article/6605.
  2006. 'Early Modern Printers and the Standardization of English Spelling', *Modern Language Review* 101: 16–29.
Hoy, Cyrus 1956. 'The Shares of Fletcher and his Collaborators in the Beaumont and Fletcher Canon', *Studies in Bibliography* 8:129–46.

1957. 'The Shares of Fletcher and his Collaborators in the Beaumont and Fletcher Canon', *Studies in Bibliography* 9:143–62 (II).

1958. 'The Shares of Fletcher and his Collaborators in the Beaumont and Fletcher Canon', *Studies in Bibliography* 11:85–106 (III).

1959. 'The Shares of Fletcher and his Collaborators in the Beaumont and Fletcher Canon', *Studies in Bibliography* 12:91–116 (IV).

1960. 'The Shares of Fletcher and his Collaborators in the Beaumont and Fletcher Canon', *Studies in Bibliography* 13:77–108 (V).

1961. 'The Shares of Fletcher and his Collaborators in the Beaumont and Fletcher Canon', *Studies in Bibliography* 14:45–67 (VI).

1962. 'The Shares of Fletcher and his Collaborators in the Beaumont and Fletcher Canon', *Studies in Bibliography* 15: 71–90 (VII).

Hudson, H. N. (ed.) 1883 [1879]. *The Tempest*. Boston: Ginn, Heath.

Hulme, P., and W. H. Sherman (eds.) 2000. *The Tempest and its Travels*. London: Reaktion Books.

Humphreys, A. R. (ed.) 1960. *King Henry IV Part 1*. Arden 2. London: Routledge.

Hunt, Maurice 1999. 'New Variorum Shakespeares in the Twenty-First Century'. *Yearbook of English Studies* 29: 57–68.

Hunter, G. K. 1951. 'The Marking of *Sententiae* in Elizabethan Printed Plays, Poems and Romances', *The Library* 6: 171–88.

2003. 'The Social Function of Annotation', in Ann Thompson and Gordon McMullan (eds.) *In Arden: Editing Shakespeare. Essays in Honour of Richard Proudfoot*. Arden Shakespeare. London: Thomson Learning, 177–93.

'Iambic Pentameter' (q.v.) Wikipedia. http://en.wikipedia.org/wiki/Iambic_pent ameter (accessed 25 March 2015).

Ioppolo, Grace 2006. *Dramatists and their Manuscripts in the Age of Shakespeare, Jonson, Middleton and Heywood: Authorship, Authority and the Playhouse*. New York: Routledge.

(ed.) 2012. *The Honest Man's Fortune*. Malone Society Reprints. London: Malone Society.

Iser, Wolfgang 1978. *The Implied Reader: Patterns of Communication in Prose Fiction from Bunyan to Beckett*. Baltimore, Md.: Johns Hopkins University Press.

Jackson, MacDonald P. 1975. 'Punctuation and the Compositors of *Shakespeare's Sonnets*, 1609', *The Library* 5th ser. 30: 2–23.

1979. *Studies in Attribution: Middleton and Shakespeare*. Salzburg: Institut für Anglistik und Amerikanistik.

1990. 'The Additions to "The Second Maiden's Tragedy": Shakespeare or Middleton?', *Shakespeare Quarterly* 41: 402–5.

Jarvis, Simon 1995. *Scholars and Gentlemen: Shakespearian Textual Criticism and Representations of Scholarly Labour, 1725–1765*. Oxford: Clarendon Press.

Jayne, Sears 1956. *Library Catalogues of the English Renaissance*. Berkeley: University of California Press.

Jeffries, Neil 2012. 'Representing Knowledge – Metadata, Data and Linked Data'. *The Signpost.* http://en.wikipedia.org/wiki/Wikipedia:Wikipedia_Signpost/ 2012-07-02/Op-ed (accessed 25 March 2015).

Jensen, M. P. 2011. 'Shakespeare and the Comic Book', in Mark Burnett, Adrian Streete, and Ramona Wray (eds.) *The Edinburgh Companion to Shakespeare and the Arts.* Edinburgh: Edinburgh University Press, 388–405.

Johns, Adrian 1998. *The Nature of the Book: Print and Knowledge in the Making.* Chicago: University of Chicago Press.

Johnson, Gerald D. 1992. 'Thomas Pavier, the Publisher, 1600–25', *The Library* 6th ser. 14: 12–50.

Johnson, Nora 2003. *The Actor as Playwright in Early Modern Drama.* Cambridge: Cambridge University Press.

Johnson, Samuel (ed.) 1765. *The Plays of William Shakespeare.*

  1790. 'Life of Rowe', *The Works of the English poets. With Prefaces, Biographical and Critical*, 3 vols. London: Printed by John Nichols, 88–99.

  1916. *Johnson on Shakespeare.* Ed. Walter Raleigh. London: Oxford University Press.

  1923 [1756]. *Johnson's Proposal for his Edition of Shakespeare, 1756.* Printed in Typefacsimile. Oxford and London: Oxford University Press and Humphrey Milford.

  1968. 'Preface to Shakespeare 1765', in Arthur Sherbo (ed.) *Johnson on Shakespeare.* The Yale Edition of the Works of Samuel Johnson. 7 vols. New Haven, Conn. and London: Yale University Press, 7. 59–113.

Jones, Emrys 1971. *Scenic Form in Shakespeare.* Oxford: Clarendon Press.

Jonson, Ben 1600. *Every Man out of his Humor.*

  1601a. *Cynthia's Revels.*

  1601b. *The Fountaine of Selfe-Love.*

  1607. *Volpone.*

  1616a. *Cynthias Revels.*

  1616b. *Every man out of his humor.*

  1631. '*The iust indignation the* Authour *tooke at the vulgar censure of his* Play, *by some malicious* spectators, *begat this following* Ode *to himselfe*', in *The Nevv Inne. Or, The Light Heart.* H1^v–H2^v.

  2012. *The Cambridge Edition of the Works of Ben Jonson.* Eds. David Bevington, Martin Butler, and Ian Donaldson. 7 vols. Cambridge: Cambridge University Press.

Jowett, John 1983. 'New Created Creatures: Ralph Crane and the Stage Directions in *The Tempest*', *Shakespeare Survey* 36: 107–20.

  2006. 'Editing Shakespeare in the Twentieth Century', *Shakespeare Survey* 59: 1–19.

  2007a. *Shakespeare and Text.* Oxford: Oxford University Press.

  2007b. '*Women, Beware Women*', in Gary Taylor and John Lavagnino (eds.) *Thomas Middleton and Early Modern Textual Culture.* Oxford: Clarendon Press, 1140–8.

  (ed.) 2011. *Sir Thomas More.* Arden 3. London: A. & C. Black.

2013. 'Private Iteration and Public Life: The Dering Manuscript of Henry IV'. Unpublished paper presented at the European Shakespeare Research Association congress (ESRA), Montpellier, France.

Kahrl, George M., and Dorothy Anderson 1982. *The Garrick Collection of Old English Plays: A Catalogue with an Historical Introduction.* London: British Library.

Kastan, David Scott (ed.) 1999. 'Shakespeare and the "Element" He Lived In', in *A Companion to Shakespeare.* Malden, Mass.: Blackwell, 3–8.

  2001. *Shakespeare and the Book.* Cambridge: Cambridge University Press.

  2002a. 'The Great Variety of Readers', *Critical Survey* 14:1: 111–15.

  (ed.) 2002b. *King Henry IV, Part One.* Arden. London: Thomson Learning.

Kean, C. (ed.) 1857. *The Tempest.* London. John K. Chapman.

Kelemen, Erick. 2006. '"Not to pick bad from bad, but by bad mend": What Undergraduates Learn from Bad Editions,' in Anne Hawkins (ed.) *Teaching Bibliography, Textual Criticism and Book History.* London: Pickering & Chatto, 161–6.

Kellett, E. E. (ed.) 1896. *The Tempest.* Madras: Srinivasa, Varadachari.

Kemble, J. P. 1817 *Macbeth and King Richard the Third: An Essay, in answer to Remarks on some of the Characters of Shakespeare.*

Kermode, F. (ed.) 1954. *The Tempest.* Arden 2. London: Methuen.

Kidnie, Margaret Jane 2009. *Shakespeare and the Problem of Adaptation.* London: Routledge.

  (ed.) forthcoming. *A Woman Killed with Kindness.* By Thomas Heywood. Arden Early Modern Drama. London: Bloomsbury.

Kirsch, Arthur C. 1969. 'A Caroline Commentary on the Drama', *Modern Philology* 66: 256–61.

Kirschenbaum, Matthew G. 2006. 'How Things Work: Teaching the Technologies of Literature,' in Anne Hawkins (ed.) *Teaching Bibliography, Textual Criticism and Book History.* London: Pickering & Chatto, 155–60.

  2008. *Mechanisms: New Media and the Forensic Imagination.* Cambridge, Mass.: MIT Press.

Kittler, Friedrich A. 2006. *Gramophone, Film, Typewriter.* Stanford, Calif.: Stanford University Press.

Kliman, Bernice W. 1997. 'Samuel Johnson and Tonson's 1745 Shakespeare: Warburton, Anonymity, and the Shakespeare Wars', in J. Gondris (ed.) *Reading Readings: Essays on Shakespeare Editing in the Eighteenth Century.* Madison, NJ: Fairleigh Dickenson University Press, 299–317.

Knapp, Jeffrey 2009. *Shakespeare Only.* Chicago: University of Chicago Press.

Knight, Charles 1864. *Passages of a Working Life During Half a Century: With a Prelude of Early Reminiscences.* London: Bradbury and Evans.

Knight, Jeffrey Todd 2009. 'Making Shakespeare's Books: Assembly and Intertextuality in the Archives', *Shakespeare Quarterly* 60: 304–40.

  2010. 'Invisible Ink: A Note on Ghost Images in Early Printed Books', *Textual Cultures* 5.2: 53–62.

  2013. *Bound to Read: Compilations, Collections, and the Making of Renaissance Literature.* Philadelphia: University of Pennsylvania Press.

Knolles, Richard 1606. *The Six Bookes of a Commonweale written by I. Bodin . . . out of the French and Latine Copies, done into English.*
Knowles, Richard 2003. *Shakespeare Variorum Handbook: A Manual of Editorial Practice.* 2nd edn. New York: Modern Language Association. www.mla.org/variorum_handbook/.
Knutson, Roslyn Lander 2001. *Playing Companies and Commerce in Shakespeare's Time.* Cambridge: Cambridge University Press.
Konkola, Kari 2000. '"People of the Book": The Production of Theological Texts in Early Modern England,' *Papers of the Bibliographical Society of America* 94: 5–31.
Kristeva, Julia 1980. 'Word, Dialogue, and Novel', *Desire in Language: A Semiotic Approach to Literature and Art*, New York: Columbia University Press, 64–91.
Krivatsy, Nati H., and Laetitia Yeandle 1992. 'Sir Edward Dering', in R. J. Fehrenbach and E. S. Leedham-Green (eds.) *Private Libraries in Renaissance England: A Collection and Catalogue of Tudor and Early Stuart Book-Lists.* 7 vols. Binghamton, NY: Medieval and Renaissance Texts and Studies, vol. 1, 137–269.
Kulick, Brian. 2012. Email to W. B. Worthen. 8 April. Unpublished.
Kyd, Thomas 1989. *The Spanish Tragedy.* Ed. J. R. Mulryne. New York: W.W. Norton.
  1592. *The Tragedie of Solyman and Perseda.*
L.S. 1593. *Resurgendum. A notable sermon concerning the resurrection.*
Lackington, James 1794. *Memoirs of the Forty-Five First Years in the Life of James Lackington.*
Lake, David J. 1975. *The Canon of Thomas Middleton's Plays: Internal Evidence for the Major Problems of Authorship.* London: Cambridge University Press.
Lancashire, Anne (ed.) 1978. *The Second Maiden's Tragedy.* The Revels Plays. Manchester: Manchester University Press.
Langbaine, Gerard 1691. *An Account of the English Dramatick Poets.*
Langhans, Edward A. 1981. *Restoration Promptbooks.* Carbondale and Edwardsville: Southern Illinois University Press.
Lee, Sidney 1898. *Life of William Shakespeare.*
Leech, Clifford 1970. 'On Editing One's First Play', *Studies in Bibliography* 23: 61–70.
Leedham-Green, Elisabeth 1986. *Books in Cambridge Inventories: Book-Lists from Vice-Chancellor's Court Probate Inventories in the Tudor and Stuart Periods.* Cambridge: Cambridge University Press.
Lehmann, Hans-Thies. 2006. *Postdramatic Theatre.* Trans. Karen Jürs-Munby. London and New York: Routledge.
Lennam, T. N. 1995. 'Sir Edward Dering's Collection of Playbooks, 1619–1624', *Shakespeare Quarterly* 16: 145–53.
Lerer, Seth 2003. 'Medieval English Literature and the Idea of the Anthology', *Publications of the Modern Language Association* 118: 1251–67.
Lesser, Zachary 2004. *Renaissance Drama and the Politics of Dramatic Publication: Readings in the English Book Trade.* Cambridge: Cambridge University Press.

Lesser, Zachary, and Peter Stallybrass 2008. 'The First Literary *Hamlet* and the Commonplacing of Professional Plays', *Shakespeare Quarterly* 59: 371–420.
Levenson, Jill L. (ed.) 2000. *Romeo and Juliet. The Oxford Shakespeare.* Oxford: Oxford University Press.
Levine, Nina 2007. 'Citizens' Games: Differentiating Collaboration and Sir Thomas More', *Shakespeare Quarterly* 58: 31–64.
Liebman, Dave. n.d. 'Summary of the Transcription Process'. www.daveliebman.com/Feature_Articles/.
Lindley, D. (ed.) 2002. *The Tempest.* Cambridge: New Cambridge Shakespeare.
Little, David M., and George M. Kahrl 1963. *The Letters of David Garrick.* 3 vols. Cambridge, Mass.: Belknap Press.
Liu, Alan 2013. 'The Meaning of the Digital Humanities', *PMLA* 128: 409–23.
Lloyd, Megan 2002. '"To Speak Welsh": Nonsense and Subversion in Shakespeare's *Henry IV, Part 1*', *North American Journal of Welsh Studies* 2:2: 7–14.
Lodge, Thomas 1593. *Phillis: honoured with Pastorall sonnets, elegies, and amorous delights.*
Lodge, Thomas, and Robert Greene 1594. *A looking glasse for London and England.*
Loewenstein, Joseph 2002. *Ben Jonson and Possessive Authorship.* Cambridge: Cambridge University Press.
Logan, Robert 2007. *Shakespeare's Marlowe: The Influence of Christopher Marlowe on Shakespeare's Artistry.* Aldershot: Ashgate.
London Chronicle, 31 August–2 September 1769. 'Some Strictures relative to Mr. Shakespeare and Mr. Garrick', 221–2.
Long, William B. 1989. '*John a Kent and John a Cumber*: An Elizabethan Playbook and its Implications,' in W. R. Elton and William B. Long (eds.) *Shakespeare and Dramatic Tradition: Essays in Honor of S. F. Johnson*, Newark: University of Delaware Press, 125–43.
  1999. '"Precious Few": English Manuscript Playbooks,' in David Scott Kastan (ed.) *A Companion to Shakespeare*, Oxford: Blackwell, 414–33.
Loomis, Catherine 2002. *William Shakespeare: A Documentary Volume, Dictionary of Literary Biography*, vol. 263, Detroit, Mich.: Thomson Gale.
Love, Harold 2002. *Attributing Authorship: An Introduction.* Cambridge: Cambridge University Press.
Luce, M. (ed.) 1901. *The Tempest.* Arden 1. London: Methuen.
Luminary Shakespeare iPad App. https://luminarydigitalmedia.com (accessed 10 June 2013).
Lupton, D. 1632. *London and the Countrey Carbonadoed.*
Lupton, Thomas 1904. 'All for Money'. Ed. Ernst Vogel. *Shakespeare Jahrbuch* 40: 129–86.
Lyons, Tara 2011. 'Pressing Issues: English Printed Drama in Collection before Jonson and Shakespeare'. Dissertation, University of Illinois Urbana-Champaign.
  2013. 'Serials, Spinoffs, and Histories: Making "Shakespeare" in Collection before the Folio'. *Philological Quarterly* 91.2: 185–220.
McCarty, Willard 2005. *Humanities Computing.* Basingstoke: Palgrave Macmillan.

McGann, Jerome 1991. *The Textual Condition*. Princeton, NJ: Princeton University Press.
  2001a. *Radiant Textuality: Literature after the World Wide Web*. Basingstoke: Palgrave Macmillan.
  2001b. 'Visible and Invisible Books: Hermetic Images in N-Dimensional Space'. *New Literary History* 32.2: 283–300.
  2002. 'Visible and Invisible Books: Hermetic Images in N-Dimensional Space'. *Literary and Linguistic Computing* 17.1: 61–75.
  2004. 'Visible and Invisible Books: Hermetic Images in N-Dimensional Space', in Peter Stoicheff and Andrew Taylor (eds.), *The Future of the Page*. Toronto: University of Toronto Press, 143–58.
McKenzie, D. F. 1959. 'Shakespearian Punctuation – A New Beginning', *Review of English Studies* 10: 361–70.
MacKenzie, Norman H. (ed.). 1991. *The Later Poetic Manuscripts of Gerard Manley Hopkins*. New York: Garland.
McLeod, Randall 1981. 'Unemending Shakespeare's Sonnet 111', *Studies in English Literature* 21: 75–96.
  1982. 'UnEditing Shak-speare', *Sub-stance* 33/34: 26–55.
  1991. 'Information on Information'. *TEXT* 5: 241–81.
McLunan, Marshall 1964. *Understanding Media: The Extensions of Man*. New York: Signet Books.
McManaway, James C. 1967. 'Excerpta Quaedam per A.W. Adolescentem', in Thomas P. Harrison, Archibald A. Hill, Ernest C. Mossner, and James Sledd (eds.) *Studies in Honor of DeWitt T. Starnes*. Austin: University of Texas Press, 117–29.
McMillin, Scott 1987. *The Elizabethan Theatre and The Book of Sir Thomas More*. Ithaca, NY: Cornell University Press.
McNamara, Jeremy n.d. '"Ovidius Naso Was the Man": Shakespeare's Debt to Ovid'. http://department.monm.edu/history/faculty_forum/ovid.htm (accessed 25 March 2015).
Maguire, Laurie E. 1996. *Shakespearean Suspect Texts: the "Bad" Quartos and their Contexts*. Cambridge: Cambridge University Press.
  (forthcoming). 'Textual Embodiment: The Case of Etcetera', in Valerie Traub (ed.) *The Oxford Handbook of Embodiment*. Oxford: Oxford University Press.
Malone, Edmond (ed.) 1790. *The Plays and Poems of William Shakespeare*. 10 vols. London: J. Rivington and Sons.
Marcus, Leah S. 1996. *Unediting the Renaissance: Shakespeare, Marlowe and Milton*. London: Routledge.
  1988. *Puzzling Shakespeare: Local Reading and its Discontents*. Berkeley and London: University of California Press.
  2007. 'Editing Shakespeare in a Postmodern Age', in Andrew Murphy (ed.) *A Concise Companion to Shakespeare and the Text*. Oxford: Blackwell, 128–44.
Marino, James J. 2011. *Owning William Shakespeare: The King's Men and their Intellectual Property*. Philadelphia: University of Pennsylvania Press.
Markham, Gervase 1593. *A discource of horsmanshippe*.

Marlowe, Christopher 1594? *The massacre at Paris*.
  1968. *Dido Queen of Carthage and The Massacre at Paris*. Ed. H. J. Oliver. The Revels Plays. London: Methuen.
  1978. *The Jew of Malta*. Ed. N. W. Bawcutt. The Revels Plays. Manchester: Manchester University Press.
Marotti, Arthur F. 1993. *Manuscript, Print and the English Renaissance Lyric*. Ithaca, NY: Cornell University Press.
Marotti, Arthur F., and Laura Estill 2012. 'Manuscript Circulation', in Arthur F. Kinney (ed.) *The Oxford Handbook of Shakespeare*. Oxford: Oxford University Press, 53–70.
Marston, John 1601. *Jack Drum's Entertainment*.
  1604. *The Malcontent*.
  1605. *The Dutch Courtesan*.
  1606. *Parasitaster, or The Fawne*.
Massai, Sonia 2007. *Shakespeare and the Rise of the Editor*. Cambridge: Cambridge University Press.
  2009. 'Shakespeare, Text, and Paratext', *Shakespeare Survey* 62: 1–11.
  2011. 'Editorial Pledges in Early Modern Dramatic Paratexts', in Helen Smith and Louise Wilson (eds.), *Renaissance Paratexts*, Cambridge: Cambridge University Press, 91–106.
  2012. 'Early Readers', in Arthur F. Kinney (ed.) *The Oxford Handbook of Shakespeare*. Oxford: Oxford University Press, 143–61.
  2013. 'Edward Blount, the Herberts, and the First Folio', in Marta Straznicky (ed.) *Shakespeare's Stationers: Studies in Cultural Bibliography*. Philadelphia: University of Pennsylvania Press: 132–46.
Massinger, Philip 2010. *The Renegado*. Ed. Michael Neill. London: Methuen.
Masten, Jeffrey 1997a. 'Playwriting: Collaboration and Authorship', *A New History of Early English Drama*. New York: Columbia University Press, 357–82.
  1997b. *Textual Intercourse: Collaboration, Authorship, and Sexuality in Renaissance Drama*. Cambridge: Cambridge University Press.
Maxwell, J. C. (ed.) 1960. *Cymbeline*. The New Shakespeare. Cambridge: Cambridge University Press.
May, Steven W., and Heather Wolfe 2010. 'Manuscripts in Tudor England', in Kent Cartwright (ed.) *A Companion to Tudor Literature*. Malden, Mass. and Oxford: Blackwell, 125–39.
Melchiori, Giorgio 1985. 'Hand D in "Sir Thomas More": An Essay in Misinterpretation', *Shakespeare Survey* 38: 101–14.
  1989. '*The Book of Sir Thomas More*: Dramatic Unity', in T. H. Howard-Hill (ed.) *Shakespeare and Sir Thomas More: Essays on the Play and its Shakespearian Interest*. Cambridge: Cambridge University Press, 77–100.
Merchant, William Moelwyn 1959. *Shakespeare and the Artist*. Oxford: Oxford University Press.
Meres, Francis 1598. *Palladis Tamia*.

Middleton, Thomas 2007a. *More Dissemblers Besides Women*. Ed. John Jowett. In Gary Taylor and John Lavagnino (Gen. Eds.) *Thomas Middleton: The Collected Works*. Oxford: Oxford University Press.

2007b. *Thomas Middleton: The Collected Works*. Eds. Gary Taylor and John Lavagnino. Oxford: Clarendon Press.

Minami, R. 2010. 'Shakespeare for Japanese Popular Culture: Shojo Manga, Takarazuka, and *Twelfth Night*', in Dennis Kennedy and Yong Li Lan (eds.) *Shakespeare in Asia: Contemporary Performance*, 109–31.

Mitchell, W. J. T. 1994. *Picture Theory: Essays on Verbal and Visual Representation*. Chicago: University of Chicago Press.

Moore, J. K. 1992. *Primary Materials Relating to Copy and Print in English Books of the Sixteenth and Seventeenth Centuries*. Oxford Bibliographical Society Occasional Publications 24. Oxford: Bodleian Library.

Moore, Joseph S. (ed.) 1856. *The Plays and Poems of William Shakespeare*.

Morash, Christopher 2002. *A History of Irish Theatre 1601–2000*. Cambridge: Cambridge University Press.

Moretti, Franco 2011. 'Networks, Plots', *New Left Review*, 2nd ser. 68 (March–April): 80–102.

Morley, Henry (ed.) 1888. *King Lear*.

Morris, D. (ed.) 1875. *The Tempest*. Collins School and College Classics. Glasgow: William Collins, Sons, and Co.

Moss, Gregory 2006. *Play Viewed from a Distance*. Brooklyn, NY: Paper Theatre.

Moulton, Ian Frederick 2000. *Before Pornography: Erotic Writing in Early Modern England*. Oxford: Oxford University Press.

Mowat, Barbara A. 2000. '"Knowing I loved my books": Reading *The Tempest* Intertextually', *The Tempest and its Travels*. London: Reaktion, 27–36.

2005. 'Q2 *Othello* and the 1606 "Acte to restraine Abuses of Players"', *Editio* 22: 91–106.

Mowat, Barbara A., and Paul Werstine (eds.) 1993. *King Lear. By William Shakespeare*. Folger Shakespeare Library. New York: Washington Square Press.

Moxon, Joseph 1962. *Mechanick Exercises on the Whole Art of Printing (1683–4)*. Eds. Herbert Davis and Harry Carter. Oxford: Oxford University Press.

Mullett, Michael A. 2004. *Martin Luther*. Abingdon: Routledge.

Mulryne, J. R. (ed.) 1975. *Women Beware Women. By Thomas Middleton*. The Revels Plays. London: Methuen.

Munday, Anthony, et al. 1911. *The Book of Sir Thomas More*. Ed. W. W. Greg. Oxford: Malone.

Munro, Lucy 2005. *Children of the Queen's Revels: A Jacobean Theatre Repertory*. Cambridge: Cambridge University Press.

Murphy, Andrew 2003. *Shakespeare in Print: A History and Chronology of Shakespeare Publishing*. Cambridge: Cambridge University Press.

(ed.) 2007. *A Concise Companion to Shakespeare and the Text*. Oxford: Blackwell.

2008. *Shakespeare for the People: Working-class Readers, 1800–1900*. Cambridge: Cambridge University Press.

2010. 'Shakespeare Goes Digital: Three Open Internet Editions', *Shakespeare Quarterly* 61.3: 401–14.

2013. 'Configuring the Book', *Early Modern Literary Studies*. Special Issue 21. http://extra.shu.ac.uk/emls/si-21/02-Murphy_ConfiguringTheBook.htm (accessed June 2013).

Murray, Christopher 2004. *Sean O'Casey: Writer at Work. A Biography*. Dublin: Gill & Macmillan.

Murray-John, Patrick. 'Bill-Crit-O-Matic'. http://billcritomatic.org/.

Myklebost, Svenn-Arve forthcoming 2016. 'Comic Books and Manga', in Bruce Smith (Gen. Ed.) *The Cambridge Guide to the Worlds of Shakespeare*. 2 vols. New York: Cambridge: Cambridge University Press.

Nashe, Thomas 1592. *Pierce Penilesse his supplication to the diuell*.

1593. *The apologie of Pierce Pennilesse. Or, strange newes, of the intercepting certaine letters*.

1594. *The vnfortunate traueller*.

1596. *Haue vvith you to Saffron-vvalden*.

Neidig, William J. 1910. 'The Shakespeare Quartos of 1619', *Modern Philology* 8: 145–63.

Neill, Michael 1994. 'Broken English and Broken Irish: Nation, Language, and the Optic Power in Shakespeare's Histories', *Shakespeare Quarterly* 45:1: 1–32.

(ed.) 2006. *Othello. The Oxford Shakespeare*. Oxford: Clarendon Press.

Nelson, Alan 2005. 'Shakespeare and the Bibliophiles: From the Earliest Years to 1616', in Robin Myers, Michael Harris, and Giles Mandelbrote (eds.) *Owners, Annotators, and the Signs of Reading*. London: British Museum, 49–74.

'The New Variorum Shakespeare Digital Challenge: The Second Round'. *Modern Language Association*. http://www.mla.org/nvs_challenge (accessed 25 March 2015).

Norton, David. 2005. *A Textual History of the King James Bible*. Cambridge: Cambridge University Press.

Norton, Thomas 1570. *The tragidie of Ferrex and Porrex [Gorboduc]*.

Nunberg, Geoffrey (ed.) 1996. *The Future of the Book*. Berkeley: University of California Press.

O'Casey, Sean 1942. *Pictures in the Hallway*. London: Macmillan.

O'Connor, Marion 2007. '*The Witch*', in Gary Taylor and John Lavagnino (eds.) *Thomas Middleton and Early Modern Textual Culture*. Oxford: Clarendon Press, 995–1009.

Oliver, H. J. (ed.) 1959. *Timon of Athens*. Arden 2. London: Methuen.

Orgel, Stephen 1981. 'What is a Text?', *Research Opportunities in Renaissance Drama* 24: 3–6.

(ed.) 1987. *The Tempest*. Oxford: Oxford University Press.

1988. 'The Authentic Shakespeare', *Representations* 21: 1–25.

1991. 'The Poetics of Incomprehensibility', *Shakespeare Quarterly* 42: 431–7.

1993. 'Acting Scripts, Performing Texts', in Randall McLeod (ed.) *Crisis in Editing*. New York: AMS, 251–94.
1995. 'What is a Character?,' *Text* 8: 101–8.
2000. 'Margins of Truth', in Andrew Murphy (ed.) *The Renaissance Text: Theory, Editing, Textuality*, Manchester: Manchester University Press, 91–107.
2002. *The Authentic Shakespeare and other Problems of the Early Modern Stage*. New York: Routledge.
2007. 'Shakespeare Illustrated', in Robert Shaughnessy (ed.) *The Cambridge Companion to Shakespeare and Popular Culture*. Cambridge: Cambridge University Press, 67–92.
Orrell, John 1977–78. 'The London Stage in the Florentine Correspondence 1604–18', *Theatre Research International* 3: 155–81.
Osborne, Laurie E. 1996. *The Trick of Singularity*. Iowa City: University of Iowa Press.
'Ovid', The Roman Empire in the First Century. PBS. www.pbs.org/empires/romans/empire/ovid.html (accessed 25 March 2015).
Ovid 1589. *P. Ouidii Nasonis Metamporphoseon libri XV*.
1594. *P. Ouidii Nasonis Heroidum epistolæ. Amorum, libri III De arte amandi, libri III De remedio amor*.
The Oxford Shakespeare [1978]. 'Editorial Procedures'. Unpublished.
Oxley, Philip 1987. *A Critical Edition of John Fletcher's 'The Humorous Lieutenant'*. New York: Garland.
Oya, Reiko 2007. *Representing Shakespearean Tragedy: Garrick the Kembles, and Kean*. Cambridge: Cambridge University Press.
Palfrey, Simon, and Tiffany Stern 2007. *Shakespeare in Parts*. Oxford: Oxford University Press.
Pechter, Edward 1997. 'Making Love to Our Employment; or, the Immateriality of Arguments about the Materiality of the Shakespearean Text', *Textual Practice* 11: 51–67.
(ed.) 2004. *Othello*. Norton Critical Editions. New York: W.W. Norton.
Pedicord, Harry William 1981. 'George Colman's Adaptation of Garrick's Promptbook for *Florizel and Perdita*', *Theatre Survey* 22:2: 185–90.
Peele, George 1961a. *The Battle of Alcazar*, in J. Yoklavich and Charles Tyler Prouty (eds.) *The Life and Works of George Peele*. 3 vols. New Haven, Conn. and London: Yale University Press.
1961b. *Edward I* in *The Life and Works of George Peele*, in Frank S. Hook and Charles Tyler Prouty (eds.) *The Life and Works of George Peele*, 3 vols. New Haven, Conn. and London: Yale University Press.
Pellis, Valeria 2013. 'Refashioning Drama in New Media and Hybrid Culture: The Anatomy of Shakespeare's Tragedies and Comedies in OEL Manga'. Unpublished paper presented at the Sixteenth AIA conference, Parma.
Pennington, Michael 1996. *Hamlet: A User's Guide*. London: Nick Hern Books.
Percy, William 1824. *The Cuck-Queanes and Cuckolds Errants*. Ed. Joseph Haslewood. London: from the Shakspeare Press by W. Nicol.
Phillpotts, J. S. (ed.) 1876. *The Tempest*. Rugby edition. London: Rivingtons.

Pickwoad, Nicholas 1995. 'The Interpretation of Bookbinding Structure: An Examination of Sixteenth-Century Bindings in the Ramey Collection in the Pierpont Morgan Library', *The Library* 6th ser. 17: 209–49.
  2005. Review of Bennett, *Trade Bookbinding in the British Isles 1660–1800*. *The Library* 7th ser. 6:4: 464–5.
Platter, Thomas 1937 [1599]. *Thomas Platter's Travels in England, 1599*. Trans. Clare Williams. London: J. Cape.
Plautus, Titus Maccius 1595. *Menaecmi*.
Playfere, Thomas 1596. *The Meane in Mourning*.
Plutarch 1595. *The liues of the noble Grecians and Romanes, tr. Thomas North*.
Pollard, Alfred W. 1906. 'A Literary Causerie: Shakespeare in the Remainder Market', *The Academy*, 528–9.
  1909. *Shakespeare Folios and Quartos: A Study in the Bibliography of Shakespeare's Plays, 1594–1685*. London: Methuen.
Pollard, Alfred W., and G. R. Redgrave (eds.) 1926 *A Short-Title Catalogue of Books Printed in England, Scotland, & Ireland and of English Books Printed Abroad, 1475-1640*. London: Bibliographical Society.
  (eds.) 1976–91. *A Short-Title Catalogue of Books Printed in England, Scotland, & Ireland and of English Books Printed Abroad, 1475–1640*. Revised by W. A. Jackson, F. S. Ferguson, and Katharine F. Pantzer. 2nd edn. 3 vols. London: Bibliographical Society.
Pollard, Alfred W., Gilbert R. Redgrave, R. W. Chapman, and W. W. Greg. 1926. '"Facsimile" Reprints of Old Books', *The Library* 4th ser. 6:4: 305–28.
Poole, William 2003. '"Unpointed Words": Shakespearean Syntax in Action', *Cambridge Quarterly* 32: 27–42.
Pope, Alexander 1963. 'The Dunciad', in *The Poems of Alexander Pope*. The Twickenham Edition of the Poems of Alexander Pope. Ed. James Sutherland. 3rd edn. 5 vols. London: Methuen, 247–409.
  1986. 'The Preface of the Editor to *The Works of Shakespear (1725)*', in Rosemary Cowler (ed.) *The Prose Works of Alexander Pope*. 2 vols. Hamden, Conn.: Archon Books, 2. 13–40.
Pope, Rob. 1995. *Textual Intervention: Critical and Creative Strategies for Literary Studies*. London: Routledge.
Potter, Lois 1999. 'Humor Out of Breath: Francis Gentleman and the *Henry IV* Plays', in Lois Potter and Arthur Kinney (eds.) *Shakespeare: Text and Theater*. Newark: University of Delaware Press, 285–97.
Pratt, Aaron T. In progress. 'Stab-Stitching and the Status of Playbooks as Literature', in 'Early Modern Print Culture and the Status of Playbooks as Literature'. PhD dissertation. Yale University.
Preston, Thomas 1570. *Cambises*.
  1910. *Cambyses King of Persia*. Ed. John Farmer. Amersham: Tudor Facsimile Texts.
Purchas, Samuel 1613. *Purchas his pilgrimage*.
Puttenham, George 1589. *The Arte of English Poesie: Continued into Three Bookes*.

Quiller-Couch, A., and J. Dover Wilson (eds.) 1921. *The Tempest*. New Cambridge Shakespeare. Cambridge: Cambridge University Press.

Quinn, James T. 1972. 'Antiquarianism as Moral Theory on the London Stage from 1794 to 1817: A Study of the Interrelationships between the Arts of Poetry and Painting in the Theatrical Productions of John Philip Kemble'. Unpublished dissertation, Ohio University.

Raber, Karen 2013. *Animal Bodies, Renaissance Culture*. Philadelphia: University of Pennsylvania Press.

Rackin, Phyllis 1994. 'Foreign Country: The Place of Women and Sexuality in Shakespeare's Historical World' in Richard Burt and John Michael Archer (eds.) *Enclosure Acts: Sexuality, Property, and Culture in Early Modern England*, Ithaca, NY: Cornell University Press, 68–95.

Ramsay, Stephen 2011. *Reading Machines: Toward an Algorithmic Criticism* (Urbana, Ill.: University of Illinois Press.

Rancière, Jacques 2009. *The Emancipated Spectator*. Trans. Gregory Elliott. London: Verso.

Randel, Don Michael 1992. 'The Canons in the Musicological Toolbox', in Katherine Bergeron and Philip V. Bohlman (eds.) *Disciplining Music: Musicology and its Canons*. Chicago: University of Chicago Press, 10–22.

Rankins, William 1587. *The Mirrour of Monsters*.

Rasmussen, Eric 1997. 'Anonymity and the Erasure of Shakespeare's First Eighteenth-Century Editor', in J. Gondris (ed.) *Reading Readings: Essays on Shakespeare Editing in the Eighteenth Century*. Madison, NJ: Fairleigh Dickenson University Press, 318–22.

  2003. 'Richly Noted: A Case for Collation Inflation', in Ann Thompson and Gordon McMullan (eds.) *In Arden: Editing Shakespeare*. London: Thomson Learning, 211–18.

Raymond, Joad 2003. *Pamphlets and Pamphleteering in Early Modern Britain*. Cambridge: Cambridge University Press.

Redding, David Coleman 1960. 'Robert Bishop's Commonplace Book: An Edition of a Seventeenth-Century Miscellany'. PhD dissertation. University of Pennsylvania.

Reed, I. (ed.) 1803. *Plays of William Shakespeare*. 21 vols.

Rehearsal 2 2103. Sotto FilmWorks LLC. App.

Reid, S. W. 2007. 'Compositor B's Speech-Prefixes in the First Folio of Shakespeare and the Question of Copy for *2 Henry IV*', *Studies in Bibliography* 58: 73–108.

The Revels Plays [2012]. 'Notes for the Use of Editors'. Unpublished.

Review of Alexander Pope's edition of Shakespeare, *Weekly Journal or Saturday's Post*, 20 March 1725: 2075–6.

Ridley, M. R. (ed.) 1958. *Othello*. Arden 2. London: Methuen.

Righter [Barton], Anne (ed.) 1988 [1968]. *The Tempest*. Harmondsworth: Penguin.

Roberts, Jeanne A. 1980. 'Ralph Crane and the Text of *The Tempest*', *Shakespeare Studies* 13: 213–33.

Roberts, Sasha 2003. *Reading Shakespeare's Poems in Early Modern England.* Basingstoke: Palgrave.
  2007. 'Women's Literary Capital in Early Modern England: Formal Composition and Rhetorical Display in Manuscript and Print', *Women's Writing* 14: 246–69.
Robinson, Benedict Scott 2002. 'Thomas Heywood and the Cultural Politics of Play Collections', *Studies in English Literature* 42:2: 361–80.
Robinson, P. R. 1980. '"The Booklet": A Self-Contained Unit in Composite Manuscripts', *Codicologica* 3: 46–69.
Romeo and Juliet: Explore Shakespeare 2012. Cambridge: Cambridge University Press. App.
Rooney, M. W 1856. *Hamlet First Edition (1603). The Last Leaf of the Lately Discovered Copy, Carefully Reprinted, With A Narrative of Its Discovery.*
Rose, Mark 1972. *Shakespearean Design.* Cambridge, Mass.: Harvard University Press.
Rowe, Katherine 2012. 'Sampling the Media Habits of a Shakespeare Company: Testing a Software Prototype in Rehearsal', *Shakespeare Bulletin* 30: 523–33.
Rowe, Nicholas 1709. 'Some Account of the Life of Mr. William Shakespear', *The Works of Mr. William Shakespear*, vol. 1: i–xl.
Rowse, A. L. 1955. *The Expansion of Elizabethan England.* London: Macmillan.
Ryan, Marie-Laure 2004. 'Multivariant Narratives', in Susan Schreibman, Ray Siemens, and John Unsworth (eds.) *A Companion to Digital Humanities*, Malden, Mass.: Blackwell, 415–30.
Salmon, Vivien 1962. 'Early Seventeenth-Century Punctuation as a Guide to Sentence Structure', *Review of English Studies* 13: 347–60.
Sanders, Julie 2011. *The Cultural Geography of Early Modern Drama.* Cambridge: Cambridge University Press.
Saunders, Robert 1823. *A Catalogue of the Library: Splendid Books of Prints, Poetical and Historical Tracts, of David Garrick, Esq.*
Scene Partner. LLC, 2102. https://www.scenepartnerapp.com/ (accessed 25 March 2015).
Schäfer, Jürgen 1970. 'The Orthography of Proper Names in Modern-Spelling Editions of Shakespeare', *Studies in Bibliography* 23: 1–19.
Schneider Jr., Ben Ross, 1974. *Travels in Computerland; or, Incompatibilities and Interfaces: A Full and True Account of the Implementation of the London Stage Information Bank.* Reading, Mass.: Addison–Wesley.
Schoenbaum, Samuel 1966. *Internal Evidence and Elizabethan Dramatic Authorship.* Evanston, Ill.: Northwestern University Press.
  1991. *Shakespeare's Lives.* New York: Barnes & Noble.
Schuessler, Jennifer 2013. 'Much Ado about Who: Is It Really Shakespeare?' *New York Times*, August 13, sect. A.
Schweidler, Max 2006. *The Restoration of Engravings, Drawings, Books, and other Works on Paper.* Trans. Roy Perkinson. Los Angeles, Calif.: Getty Conservation Institute.

Scragg, Leah 1997. 'Edward Blount and the Prefatory Material to the First Folio of Shakespeare', *Bulletin of the John Rylands University Library of Manchester* 79: 117–26.
Seary, Peter 1990. *Lewis Theobald and the Editing of Shakespeare*. Oxford: Clarendon Press.
Sellers, Peter 1965. 'A Hard Day's Night'. https://www.youtube.com/watch?v=zLEMncvI40s (accessed 25 March 2015).
Shaaber, M. A. (ed.) 1940. *The Second Part of Henry the Fourth*. A New Variorum Edition. New York: Modern Language Association.
Shakespeare, William 1594a. *The first part of the contention betwixt the two famous houses of Yorke and Lancaster with the death of the good Duke Humphrey.*
  1594b. *The Rape of Lucrece.*
  1594c. *Venus and Adonis.*
  1598a. *A Pleasant Conceited Comedie Called, Loues labors lost.*
  1598b. *The Rape of Lucrece.*
  1599a. *The History of Henrie the Fovrth.*
  1599b. *The most excellent and lamentable tragedie, of Romeo and Iuliet.*
  1600. *The Rape of Lucrece.*
  1602. *The Tragedie of King Richard the third.*
  1603 *Hamlet.*
  1604–05. *Hamlet.*
  1608. *The Tragedie of King Richard the Second.*
  1609a. *The Famous Historie of Troylus and Cresseid.*
  1609b. *Pericles.*
  1609c. *Troilus and Cressida.*
  1612. *The Passionate Pilgrime.*
  1616. *The Rape of Lucrece.*
  1619. *The Whole Contention betweene the two Famous Houses, Lancaster and Yorke.*
  1623. *Comedies, Histories, & Tragedies.*
  1630. *The Merry Wives of Windsor.*
  1676. *Hamlet.*
  1709. *The Works of Mr. William Shakespear; in Six volumes ... Revis'd and Corrected.* Ed. Nicholas Rowe.
  1714. *The Works of Mr. William Shakespear, in Nine Volumes: With his Life, by N. Rowe, Esq.* Ed. Nicholas Rowe. 2nd edn. 9 vols.
  1725. *The Works of Shakespear. In Six Volumes. Collated and Corrected by the Former Editions, by Mr. Pope.* Ed. Alexander Pope. 6 vols.
  1733. *The Works of Shakespeare: in Seven Volumes.* Ed. Lewis Theobald. 7 vols.
  1740. *The Works of Shakespeare in Seven Volumes. Collated with the Oldest Copies, and Corrected; With Notes, Explanatory, and Critical: by Mr. Theobald.* Ed. Lewis Theobald. 2nd edn. 12 vols.
  1744. *The Works of Shakespear. In Six Volumes. Carefully Revised and Corrected by the Former Editions, and Adorned with Sculptures, etc.* Eds. Thomas Hanmer and Francis Hayman.

1747. *The Works of Shakespeare*. Ed. William Warburton.
1765. *The Plays of William Shakespeare, in Eight Volumes, with the Corrections and Illustrations of Various Commentators, to Which are Added Notes by Sam. Johnson.* Ed. Samuel Johnson.
1773. *The Plays of William Shakespeare. In Ten Volumes. With the Corrections and Illustrations of Various Commentators; To which are Added Notes by Samuel Johnson and George Steevens.* Eds. Samuel Johnson and George Steevens.
1773–74. *Bell's Edition of Shakespeare's Plays, as they are now Performed at the Theatres Royal in London, Regulated from the Prompt books in Each House.* 8 vols.
1803a. *The Dramatic Works of Shakspeare Revised by George Steevens.* 9 vols.
1803b. *Plays of William Shakespeare.* Ed. Isaac Reed. 21 vols.
1821. *Plays and Poems of William Shakespeare.* Eds. J. Boswell and E. Malone. 21 vols. London: R. C. and J. Rivington.
1838–43. *The Pictorial Edition of the Works of Shakspeare.* Ed. Charles Knight.
1853. *The Works of William Shakespeare.* Ed. J. O. Halliwell-Phillipps. 9 vols.
1856. *Dramatic Works of William Shakespeare.* Ed. S. W. Singer. 10 vols. London: Bell and Daldy.
1858. *Shakespeare's Comedies, Histories, Tragedies and Poems.* Ed. J. P. Collier. 2nd edn. 6 vols. London: Whittaker.
1858–62. *The Plays of Shakespeare. Edited by Howard Staunton. The Illustrations by John Gilbert. Engraved by the Brothers Dalziel.* Ed. Howard Staunton.
1864–68. *The Plays of Shakespeare, Edited and Annotated by Charles and Mary Cowden Clarke ... Illustrated by H. C. Selous.* Eds. Charles Cowden Clarke and Mary Cowden Clarke.
1867. *The Pictorial Edition of Shakespeare.* Ed. Charles Knight. 2nd edn. Vol. 1. Comedies.
1885. *The Tempest.* Blackie's School Classics.
1926. The *Merchant* of Venice. Eds. Arthur Quiller-Couch and J. Dover Wilson. Cambridge Shakespeare. Cambridge: Cambridge University Press.
1955. *The Merchant of Venice.* Ed. John Russell Brown. Arden 2. London: Methuen.
1962. *Henry VI.* Ed. Andrew Cairncross. Arden 2. London: Methuen.
1964. *Hamlet.* Ed. George Skillan. London: Samuel French Ltd.
1965. *2 Henry IV.* Ed. Norman N. Holland. Signet Shakespeare. New York: Penguin.
1966. *2 Henry IV.* Ed. A. R. Humphries. Arden 2. London: Methuen.
1967. *King Lear.* London: Samuel French Ltd.
1981. *Shakespeare's Plays in Quarto.* Eds. Michael J. B. Allen and Kenneth Muir. Berkeley: University of California Press.
1986. *2 Henry IV.* Eds. Stanley Wells and Gary Taylor.
1989. *2 Henry IV.* Ed. Giorgio Melchiori. New Cambridge Shakespeare. Cambridge: Cambridge University Press.
1992. *King Henry V.* Ed. Andrew Gurr. New Cambridge Shakespeare. Cambridge: Cambridge University Press.

1995. *King Henry V*. Ed. T. W. Craik. Arden 3. London: Routledge.
1997a. *2 Henry IV*, in G. Blakemore Evans (ed.) *The Riverside Shakespeare*. Boston: Houghton Mifflin.
1997b. *2 Henry IV*. Ed. René Weis. Oxford World's Classics. Oxford: Oxford University Press.
1997c. *The First Part of King Henry the Fourth*. Ed. Barbara Hodgdon. Boston: Bedford.
1997d. 'Hamlet', in G. Blakemore Evans (ed.) *The Riverside Shakespeare*. Boston: Houghton Mifflin.
1997e. 'Henry V', in G. Blakemore Evans (ed.) *The Riverside Shakespeare*. Boston: Houghton Mifflin.
1997f. *King Lear*. Ed. R. A. Foakes. Arden 3 London: Thomson Learning.
1999a. *2 Henry IV*. Eds. Barbara A. Mowat and Paul Werstine. Folger Shakespeare. New York: Washington Square Press.
1999b. *The Tempest*. Eds. Virginia Mason Vaughan and Alden T. Vaughan. Arden 3. London: Nelson.
2000. *Henry VI*. Ed. Edward Burns. Arden 3. London: Thomson Learning.
2001a. *Measure for Measure*. Ed. Grace Ioppolo. Theatre commentary by Leon Rubin. New York: Applause Books.
2001b. *The Merchant of Venice*. Ed. Randall Martin. New York: Applause Books.
2002a. *2 Henry IV*, in Claire McEachern, A. R. Braunmuller, and Stephen Orgel (eds.) *The Complete Pelican Shakespeare*. New York and London: Penguin.
2002b. *The Tempest*. Ed. David Lindley. New Cambridge Shakespeare. Cambridge: Cambridge University Press.
2003. *1 Henry IV*. Ed. Gordon McMullan. New York: W.W. Norton.
2004a. *2 Henry IV*, in David Bevington (ed.) The Complete Works of Shakespeare. 5th edn. New York: Pearson Longman.
2004b. *Othello*. Ed. Edward Pechter. Norton Critical Editions. New York: W.W. Norton.
2006a. *The [Cut] Shakespeare, Tragedies I: Hamlet, Othello*. Ed. Steve Gooch. Robertsbridge: Steve Gooch Publications.
2006b. *Othello*. Ed. Michael Neill. Oxford Shakespeare. Oxford: Oxford University Press.
2006c. *The Tempest*. Irvine, Calif.: Saddleback's Illustrated Classics.
2006d. *The Tempest: The Cartoon Illustrated Edition*. Ed. Simon Greaves. Bronygarth: Shakespeare Comic Book Co.
2007a. *2 Henry IV*, in Jonathan Bate and Eric Rasmussen (eds.) *William Shakespeare: Complete Works*. New York: Random House.
2007b. *The Tempest*. London: SelfMadeHero.
2007c. *The Winter's Tale*. Eds. Susan Snyder and Deborah T. Curren-Aquino. Cambridge: Cambridge University Press.
2008. *Twelfth Night*. Ed. Keir Elam. Arden 3. London: Cengage.
2009a. *Hamlet*. London: Donmar Warehouse.

2009b. *The Tempest*. Illustrated by John McDonald, Jon Haward, Gary Erskine, and Nigel Dobbyn. Towcester: Classical Comics.

2010. *The Merchant of Venice*. Ed. John Drakakis. Arden 3. London: A & C Black.

2011. *The Tempest*. Eds. Virginia Mason Vaughan and Alden T. Vaughan. Rev. edn. Arden 3. London: Bloomsbury.

2012. *Romeo and Juliet*. Ed. René Weis. Arden 3. London: Bloomsbury.

Shakespearean Performance in Ireland 1660–1904. Database. http://web.archive.org/web/20130928090836/http://www.irishtheatricaldiaspora.net/shakespeare/index.html (accessed June 2013). No longer available.

Shapiro, James 1988. 'Which is the Merchant here, and which the Jew', *Shakespeare Studies* 20: 269–79.

1991. *Rival Playwrights: Marlowe, Jonson, Shakespeare*. New York: Columbia University Press.

2010. *Contested Will: Who Wrote Shakespeare?* New York: Simon & Schuster.

Sharpham, Edward 1607. *Cupid's Whirligig*.

Shattuck, Charles H. 1965a. *The Shakespeare Promptbooks: A Descriptive Catalogue*. Urbana: University of Illinois Press.

1965b. 'Romeo and Juliet', in *The Shakespeare Promptbooks: A Descriptive Catalogue*. Urbana: University of Illinois Press, 411–32.

Sherbo, Arthur 1986. *The Birth of Shakespeare Studies: Commentators from Rowe (1709) to Boswell–Malone (1821)*. East Lansing, Mich.: Colleagues Press.

Sherburn, George 1931. 'Huntington Library Collections', *Huntington Library Bulletin* 1: 33–106.

Sherman, William H. 2008. *Used Books: Marking Readers in Renaissance England*. Philadelphia: University of Pennsylvania Press.

2011. 'The Beginning of "The End": Terminal Paratext and the Birth of Print Culture', in Helen Smith and Louise Wilson (eds.) *Renaissance Paratexts*, Cambridge: Cambridge University Press, 65–88.

2013. 'Punctuation as Configuration; or, How Many Sentences are there in Sonnet 1?', *Early Modern Literary Studies* 21: http://extra.shu.ac.uk/emls/si-21/04-Sherman_Punctuation%20as%20Configuration.htm.

'The Shilling Shakspeares'. 1868. *The Bookseller*, 1 July: 451.

Shillingsburg, Peter L. 1996. *Scholarly Editing in the Computer Age: Theory and Practice*. Ann Arbor: University of Michigan Press.

Sidney, Philip 1590, 1593. *The countesse of Pembrokes Arcadia*.

Sillars, Stuart 2008. *The Illustrated Shakespeare, 1709–1875*. Cambridge: Cambridge University Press.

Simpson, James 2013. 'Cognition is Recognition: Literary Knowledge and the Textual "Face"', *New Literary History* 44: 25–44.

Simpson, Percy 1911. *Shakespearian Punctuation*. Oxford: Clarendon Press.

Sinfield, Alan 1992. *Faultlines: Cultural Materialism and the Politics of Dissident Reading*. Oxford: Clarendon Press.

Singer, S. W. (ed.) 1856. *Dramatic Works of William Shakespeare*. 10 vols. London: Bell and Daldy.

Sisson, Charles J. 1942. 'Shakespeare Quartos as Prompt-Copies: With Some Account of Cholmeley's Players and a New Shakespeare Allusion', *Review of English Studies* 18.70: 129–43.
Smith, Bruce R. 1996. 'Prickly Characters', in David M. Bergeron (ed.), *Reading and Writing in Shakespeare*. Newark and London: University of Delaware Press/Associated University Presses, 25–44.
Smith, Emma 2007. *Cambridge Introduction to Shakespeare*. Cambridge: Cambridge University Press.
Smith, Simon 2013. '"Flourish. Enter the King sicke": Exploring Kingship through Musical Spectacle in Richard III', in *Spectatorship at the Elizabethan Court*. Special issue of *Zeitsprünge: Forschungen zur Frühen Neuzeit* 17:101–19.
Solly, Henry S. 1898. *The Life of Henry Morley*. London: Arnold.
Spencer, Hazelton 1923. '*Hamlet* Under the Restoration', *PMLA* 38.4 770–91.
  1927. *Shakespeare Improved*. Cambridge, Mass.: Harvard University Press.
Spenser, Edmund 1595. *Amoretti and Epithalamion*.
Sperberg-McQueen, Michael. 1991. 'Text in the Electronic Age: Textual Study and Text Encoding, with Examples from Medieval Texts'. *Literary and Linguistic Computing* 6.1: 35–46.
St. Clair, William 2007. *The Reading Nation in the Romantic Period*. Cambridge: Cambridge University Press.
Stallybrass, Peter 2011. 'Visible and Invisible Letters: Text versus Image in Renaissance England and Europe', in Marija Dalbello and Mary Shaw (eds.) *Visible Writings: Cultures, Forms, Readings*. New Brunswick, NJ: Rutgers University Press, 77–98.
Stallybrass, Peter, and Roger Chartier 2007. 'Reading and Authorship: The Circulation of Shakespeare 1590-1619', in Andrew Murphy (ed.) *A Concise Companion to Shakespeare and the Text*. Malden, Mass.: Blackwell, 35–56.
Stern, Tiffany 1997. 'Was *Totus Mundus Agit Histrionem* ever the Motto of the Globe Theatre?', *Theatre Notebook* 51: 122–7.
  2000. *Rehearsal from Shakespeare to Sheridan*. Oxford: Clarendon Press.
  2004. *Making Shakespeare*. London: Routledge.
  2009a. 'Backstage-plots', *Documents of Performance in Early Modern England*. Cambridge: Cambridge University Press, 201–31.
  2009b. *Documents of Performance in Early Modern England*. Cambridge: Cambridge University Press.
  2009c. 'Prologues, Epilogues, Interim Entertainments', *Documents of Performance in Early Modern England*. Cambridge: Cambridge University Press, 81–119.
  2010. 'Epilogues, Prayers after Plays, and Shakespeare's *2 Henry IV*', *Theatre Notebook* 64: 122–9.
Stratford Shakespearean Festival. 2012. Stratford Festival, Stratford Ontario.
Straznicky, Marta (ed.) 2013. *Shakespeare's Stationers: Studies in Cultural Bibliography*. Philadelphia: University of Pennsylvania Press.

Sturgess, K. M. 1970. 'The Early Quartos of Heywood's *A Woman Killed with Kindness*', *The Library* 5th ser. 25.2: 93–104.
Summit, Jennifer 2008. *Memory's Library: Medieval Books in Early Modern England*. Chicago: University of Chicago Press.
Sunstein, Cass 2001. *Republic.com*. Princeton, NJ: Princeton University Press.
Sutton, Thomas 1616. *Englands First and Second Svmmons*.
Sykes, Norman 1963. 'The Religion of Protestants', in S. L. Greenslade (ed.) *The Cambridge History of the Bible*, vol. 3, *The West from the Reformation to the Present Day*. Cambridge: Cambridge University Press, 175–98.
Syme, Holger Schott 2013. 'Thomas Creede, William Barley, and the Venture of Printing Plays', in Marta Straznicky (ed.) *Shakespeare's Stationers: Studies in Cultural Bibliography*. Philadelphia: University of Pennsylvania Press, 28–46.
T.W. 1593. *The tears of fancie. Or loue disdained.*
Tarlton, Richard 1638. *Tarltons Jeasts.*
Tavard, George H. 1959. *Holy Writ or Holy Church: The Crisis of the Protestant Reformation*. London: Burns & Oates.
Taylor, Gary 1986. 'Inventing Shakespeare', *Shakespeare Jahrbuch* 122: 26–44.
  1997 [1987]. 'General Introduction', in Stanley Wells, Gary Taylor, John Jowett, and William Montgomery (eds.) *William Shakespeare: A Textual Companion*. New York: Norton, 1–68.
  1993. 'The Structure of Performance: Act-Intervals in the London Theatres, 1576–1642', in Gary Taylor and John Jowett, *Shakespeare Reshaped 1601–1623*. Oxford: Clarendon Press, 3–50.
  2004. 'Blount, Edward (*bap.* 1562, *d.* in or before 1632)' (q.v.) *Oxford Dictionary of National Biography*. Online edition. www.oxforddnb.com/view/article/2686?docPos=1.
  2006. 'Making Meaning Marketing Shakespeare 1623', in Peter Holland and Stephen Orgel (eds.) *From Performance to Print in Shakespeare's England*. Basingstoke: Palgrave Macmillan, 55–72.
Taylor, Gary, Celia R. Daileader, and Alexandra G. Bennett 2007. 'The Order of Persons', in Gary Taylor and John Lavagnino (eds.) *Thomas Middleton and Early Modern Textual Culture: A Companion to the Collected Works*. Oxford: Clarendon Press, 31–79, 62.
Taylor, Gary, and John Jowett 1993a. *Shakespeare Reshaped, 1601–1623*, Oxford: Clarendon Press.
  1993b. 'The Structure of Performance Act-Intervals in the London Theatres, 1576–1642', in *Shakespeare Reshaped, 1601–1623*. Oxford: Clarendon Press, 3–50.
Taylor, Gary, and John Lavagnino (eds.) 2007. *Thomas Middleton and Early Modern Textual Culture: A Companion to the Collected Works*. Oxford: Clarendon Press.
Taylor, Gary, and Stanley Wells 1979. *Modernizing Shakespeare Spelling: With Three Studies in the Text of 'Henry V'*. Oxford: Clarendon Press.
TEI (Text Encoding Initiative) Consortium. n.d. 'A Gentle Introduction to XML'. P5: Guidelines for Electronic Text Encoding and Interchange.

www.tei-c.org/release/doc/tei-p5-doc/en/html/SG.html (accessed 25 March 2015).

TEI By Example Project. http://teibyexample.org/.

Tempest for iPad 2012. Luminary LLC. App.

Theatres Royal n.d. [1823–24?]. *The Tempest*. London: John Cumberland.

1823. *The Tempest*. London: Oxberry.

Theobald, Lewis 1726. *Shakespeare Restor'd: or, A Specimen of the Many Errors as well Committed, or Unamended, by Mr. Pope in his Late Edition of this Poet*.

Thomson, Peter 2004. 'Kemble, John Philip (1757–1823)' (q.v.) *Oxford Dictionary of National Biography*. Online edition. www.oxforddnb.com/view/article/15322.

Thompson, Ann 2013. Personal communication, Toronto.

Thompson, Ann, and Gordon McMullan (eds.) 2003. *In Arden: Editing Shakespeare*. London: Thomson Learning.

Tomlin, E. W. F. 2006. 'Ferguson, Frederic Sutherland (1878–1967)' (q.v.) *Oxford Dictionary of National Biography*. Online edition. www.oxforddnb.com/view/article/33107.

Tompkins, Jane P. 1980. *Reader-Response Criticism: From Formalism to Poststructuralism*. Baltimore, Md.: Johns Hopkins University Press.

Turner, Robert Kean, Virginia Westling Haas, Robert A. Jones, et al. (eds.) 2005. *The Winter's Tale*. New York: Modern Language Association Press.

Van Lennep, William, Emmett L. Avery, Arthur H. Scouten, et al. (eds.). 1960–68. *The London Stage, 1660–1800*. 11 vols. Carbondale, Ill.: Southern Illinois University Press.

Vaughan, V. M., and A. T. Vaughan (eds.) 2001 [1999]. *The Tempest*. London: Arden Shakespeare.

Vickers, Brian 2004. *Shakespeare, Co-Author: A Historical Study of Five Collaborative Plays*. Oxford: Oxford University Press.

2011. 'Shakespeare and Authorship Studies in the Twenty-First Century', *Shakespeare Quarterly* 62: 106–42.

2012. 'Identifying Shakespeare's Additions to *The Spanish Tragedy* (1602): A New(er) Approach', *Shakespeare* 8: 13–43.

Wager, W. 1967. 'Enough is as Good as a Feast', in R. Mark Benbow (ed.) The Longer Thou Livest *and* Enough is as Good as a Feast, Regents Renaissance Drama. Lincoln: University of Nebraska Press.

Walsh, Marcus 2001. 'Form and Function in the English Eighteenth-Century Literary Edition: The Case of Edward Capell', *Studies in Bibliography* 54: 225–41.

Wapull, George 1907. *The Tide Tarrieth No Man*. Ed. Ernst Ruhl. *Shakespeare Jahrbuch* 43: 1–52.

Warburton, William (ed.) 1747. *The Works of Shakespeare*. London: Jacob Tonson et al.

Warner, Marina 2000. '"The foul witch" and Her "freckled whelp": Circean Mutations in the New World', in P. Hulme and W. H. Sherman (eds.) *The Tempest and its Travels*. London: Reaktion Books, 97–113.

Warren, Michael 2004. 'The Perception of Error: The Editing and the Performance of the Opening of *Coriolanus*', in Lukas Erne and Margaret Jane Kidnie (eds.) *Textual Performances: The Modern Reproduction of Shakespeare's Drama*, 127–42.

Warren, Roger (ed.) 1998. *Cymbeline*. The Oxford Shakespeare. Oxford: Clarendon Press.

Watson, Ben 1993. *Frank Zappa: The Negative Dialectics of Poodle Play*. New York: St Martin's Press.

Webster, John 1612. *The White Divel*.

Weimann, Robert 2000. *Author's Pen and Actor's Voice: Playing and Writing in Shakespeare's Theatre*. Cambridge: Cambridge University Press.

Weingust, Don 2006. *Acting from Shakespeare's First Folio: Theory, Text, and Performance*. New York and London: Routledge-Taylor and Francis.

Wells, Stanley 1984. *Re-Editing Shakespeare for the Modern Reader*. Oxford: Clarendon Press.

1991. 'To Read a Play: The Problem of Editorial Intervention', in Hanna Scolnicov and Peter Holland (eds.) *Reading Plays: Interpretation and Reception*. Cambridge: Cambridge University Press, 30–55.

1997 [1987] 'Love's Labor's Lost,' in Stanley Wells, Gary Taylor, John Jowett, and William Montgomery (eds.) *William Shakespeare: A Textual Companion*. New York: Norton, 270–8.

Wells, Stanley, and Gary Taylor 1986. *The Oxford Shakespeare*. Oxford: Oxford University Press.

Wells, Stanley, Gary Taylor, John Jowett, and William Montgomery (eds.) 1997. *William Shakespeare: A Textual Companion*. New York: Norton.

(eds.) 2005. *The Complete Works of William Shakespeare*, 2nd edn. Oxford: Clarendon Press.

Werstine, Paul 1984. 'Line Division in Shakespeare: An Editorial Problem', *Analytical and Enumerative Bibliography* 8: 73–125.

1985. 'Edward Capell and Metrically Linked Speeches in Shakespeare'. *The Library* 6th ser. 7.3: 259–61.

1989. 'On the Compositors of *The Two Noble Kinsmen*', in Charles H. Frey (ed.) *Shakespeare, Fletcher and The Two Noble Kinsmen*. Columbia: University of Missouri Press, 6–30.

1997. 'Plays in Manuscript', in John D. Cox and David Scott Kastan (eds.) *A New History of Early English Drama*, New York: Columbia University Press, 481–97.

1999, 'A Century of "Bad" Quartos', *Shakespeare Quarterly* 50: 310–33.

2008. 'Past is Prologue: Electronic New Variorum Shakespeares', *Shakespeare*, 4:3, 208–220.

2012. *Early Modern Playhouse Manuscripts and the Editing of Shakespeare*. Cambridge: Cambridge University Press.

Willet, Andrew 1608. *Hexapla in Genesis, That Is, a Sixfold Commentary Vpon Genesis*.

Wilson, F. P. 1926. 'Ralph Crane, Scrivener to the King's Players', *The Library* 4th ser. 7: 194–215.

(ed.) 1950. *The Witch*. Malone Society Reprint. London: Malone Society.
Wilson, J. Dover 1919. 'Shakespeare's Hand in the Play of "Sir Thomas More"', *Times Literary Supplement*, 8 May: 251.
  (ed.) 1922. *Measure for Measure*. Cambridge: Cambridge University Press.
  1923. 'Bibliographical Links between the Three Pages and the Good Quartos', in A. W. Pollard (ed.) *Shakespeare's Hand and in the Play of Sir Thomas More*. Cambridge: Cambridge University Press, 113–41.
  1931. 'The Copy for The Winter's Tale, 1623', in J. Dover Wilson and Arthur Quiller-Couch (eds.) *The Winter's Tale*. The New Shakespeare. Cambridge: Cambridge University Press, 109–27.
Wilson, Robert 1584. *The three ladies of London*.
  1590. *The Three Lordes and Three Ladies of London*.
Wood, Anthony 1691/2. *Athenae Oxoniensis*.
Wood, S., and A. S. Wood (eds.) 1906. *The Tempest*. Oxford and Cambridge Edition. London: George Gill and Sons.
Woudhuysen, H. R. (ed.) 1998. *Love's Labour's Lost*. Arden. London: Thomson Learning.
Wright, James 1694. *Country Conversations*.
Wynken de Worde. http://sarahwerner.net/blog/ (accessed 25 March 2015).
Yeandle, Laetitia 1986. 'The Dating of Sir Edward Dering's Copy of "The History of King Henry the Fourth"', *Shakespeare Quarterly* 37.2: 224–6.
Young, Alan 2012. 'John Dicks's Illustrated Edition of "Shakspere for the Millions"', *Papers of the Bibliographical Society of America* 106: 285–310.
Zittrain, Jonathan 2008. *The Future of the Internet and How to Stop It*. Yale University Press. Available free of charge under a Creative Commons licence. http://blogs.law.harvard.edu/futureoftheinternet/download/ (accessed 25 March 2015).
Zwicker, Steven 1998. 'Reading the Margins: Politics and the Habits of Appropriation', in Kevin Sharpe and Steven Zwicker (eds.) *Refiguring Revolutions: Aesthetics and Politics from the English Revolution to the Romantic Revolution*. Berkeley: University of California Press, 101–15.

Manuscripts

Alnwick Castle (Northumberland) 525.
Bodleian Library (Oxford) Sancroft 29. Bodleian Library (Oxford) Ashmole 857.
British Library (London) Additional 22608, Additional 30982, Additional 41063, Egerton 923, Royal 8 A.XXI.
Brotherton Collection, University of Leeds Lt 15, Lt 24, Lt 48, Lt 80.
Douai Municipal Library MS 787.
Folger Shakespeare Library (Washington, DC) V.a.262.
Meisei University Library (Tokyo) MR 0799.
Morgan Library and Museum (New York) MA 1057.
Rosenbach Library (Philadelphia) 1083/16.
William Salt Library (Staffordshire) 308-40.

Index

Aasand, Hardin, 395
absence of readerly paratexts, 60–1, 66, 89
accidentals, 2, 8, 207, 318–18, 322, 328–31, 395
act breaks, 8–9, 28, 29, 31, 32, 37, 137, 332–41, 358–9
adaptations, 7, 168–70, 171–6, 186–8, 233–9, 240, 248, 251, 287, 388, 389
Addison, Joseph, 391
Adler, Stella, 223
Admiral's Men, 61, 362
adult company playbooks, 61, 63, 64–8
Alexander, William
   Monarchick Tragedies, The, 141
Allde, Edward, 84
Allentuck, Marcia, 255–7
Alleyn, Edward, 36, 80
Allott, Robert
   Englands Parnassus: or The Choysest Flowers of our Moderne Poets, 150
American Shakespeare Center, 225
Andersen, Jennifer, 180
Anderson, Dorothy, 185–6
annotations, 5, 28, 95, 102–3, 144, 150–1, 180, 184, 224–5, 226, 227, 229, 260, 261, 264, 275, 279, 280, 283, 293, 381–3, 384–5, 388–9, 400, 407, 409, 410
annotations, theatrical, 6, 37, 163–76, 239
Appignanesi, Richard, 281
apps, 283–4, 406–7, 408
   acting, 223–9
   Actsophia, 6, 223–4, 225, 228
   Explore Shakespeare, 6, 218–20, 221–3, 229
   Luminary Shakespeare Romeo and Juliet, 85
   MyShx, 225–6
   pedagogical, 218–23, 226, 227–8, 229
   Rehearsal, 224–5
   Scene Partner, 224, 225
   Stratford Shakespearean Festival, 217
   Tempest for iPad, The, 6, 218, 220–3, 229

Touch Press *Sonnets by William Shakespeare*, 283
Aquinas. *See* Thomas Aquinas, Saint
Arber, Edward, 78, 80
Arden Shakespeare editions, 394, 397
   Arden 1, 291, 293–6, 298
   Arden 2, 41, 297–8, 335, 336, 337, 338, 353, 356, 373
   Arden 3, 1, 41, 95, 261, 287, 289, 298–9, 335, 339, 340, 350, 353–6, 385, 386–7
   Arden 4, 299
Arden Early Modern Drama, 9, 358
CD-ROM, 283
Argus, 270
Armin, Robert
   Quips upon Questions, 372
Atkins, Robert, 246
Attenborough, Michael, 337
Aubrey, John, 20
Augustine, Saint, 349
Austen, Jane
   Mansfield Park, 285, 287
authorial revision, 5, 25, 85, 90–104
authorial style, 3, 17–19, 22–5
authorship studies, 3, 13–26, 40, 51–2, 66, 88
authorship, marketing of, 5, 68, 78, 79, 84, 85, 87–104, 105–33, 142, 273–4

Babington, Gervase, 343, 344
Bacchus bountie, 76
'bad quartos', 58, 273
Bagnell, George, 276
Bagnell, Phineas, 276
Bald, R. C., 31–2, 37
Baldwin, T. W., 332
Bales, Peter
   Writing Schoolmaster, The, 320–1
Balibar, Étienne, 351
Banham, Rob, 280
Banks, Carol, 313
bardolatry, 288

452

Index

Barnes, Barnabe
  Parthenophil and Parthenope, 79
  The Devil's Charter, 96
Barnfield, Richard, 77–8, 85, 86
Barrenger, William, 111
Barroll, Leeds, 58
Barthes, Roland, 14, 20
Bate, Jonathan, 7, 43, 249, 250, 261, 373, 397
Bawcutt, N. W., 35, 138
Beal, Peter, 150, 152
Beaumont, Francis
  Knight of the Burning Pestle, The, 136
Beaumont, Francis and John Fletcher, 20, 21, 28
  1647 Folio, 20, 132, 372
  Custom of the Country, 37
  False One, The, 31
  Four Plays in One, 32
  Knight of Malta, The, 32
  Maid in the Mill, The, 31
  Philaster, 142
  Prophetesse, The, 31
  Rule a Wife, 37
  Spanish Curate, The, 31, 173, 174
  Wife for a Month, 37
  Womans Prize, The, 37
Beckerman, Bernard, 143
Bednarz, James, 19, 22
Beeston, Christopher, 144
beginnings of plays, 359–68
Believe as you list, 367
Bell, John. *See under* theatre editions
Benfield, Robert, 144
Bennett, Alexandra G., 142
Bennett, Andrew, 14
Bennett, Stuart, 127
Bentley, G. E., 15, 16, 20, 36–7, 88
Berger, Thomas L., 60, 378–9
Bergeron, David M., 134
Bertram, Paul, 203
Best, Michael, 201, 377, 389, 390, 396
Betterton, Mary. *See* Saunderson, Mary
Betterton, Thomas, 237
Bevington, David, 328, 336, 337, 377
Bhagavad Ghita, 269
Bible, 182, 269, 270, 311, 342, 347
  King James Bible (1611), 211
Bill-Crit-O-Matic, 409
Bishop, Robert, 151–2
Black, M. W., 392
Blackfriars playhouse, 59, 60, 332, 365
Blackie's 'The Plain Text Shakespeare' edition, 279, 281
Blackie's School Classics, 285
Blair, Ann, 408
Blair, J. Talfourd, 269

Blayney, Peter, 57, 58, 141, 164, 274
Blostein, David A., 102
Blount, Edward, 141, 142
Boaden, James, 193–4
Bodenham, John
  Bel-vedére: or The Garden of the Muses, 150
Bodiguel, Ashley, 196
Bodleian Library, 129
Bodley, Thomas, 145
Bogart, Humphrey, 223
Boitard, François, 250–4, 255, 268
Bolden Auction Galleries, 269
Bondy, Louis W., 269
Bonian, Richard, 66–7, 68, 112–13
Book of Martyrs, The, 182
Booth, Stephen, 208
Boswell, E., 272
Boswell, J., 288, 382, 394
Bowers, Fredson, 36, 37, 202, 297, 302, 308, 331, 383, 391
Boyd, Michael, 337
Boydell Shakespeare Gallery, 258–9, 260
Boydell, John, 258, 260
Bradbrook, Muriel, 320
Bradley, A. C., 351
Bradley, Abraham, 276
Brathwait, Richard
  Whimzies, 370
Bratton, J. S., 244
Brayman Hackel, Heidi, 63, 142, 180
Brecht, Bertolt, 222
Breton, Nicholas, 88, 90
Bridges-Adams, William, 246
Briggs, Julia, 48–9
Brinsley, John, 359
Bristow, Richard, 344
British Library, 115, 160, 177–8, 185–6, 189, 194
British Museum, 178, 185, 258
Broadview Press, 389
Brooke, Christopher
  Ghost of Richard III, The, 364
Brooks, Douglas, 88
Broughton, Hugh, 90
Brown, Arthur, 49
Brown, John Russell, 31, 245, 353, 355, 356
Brownlow, James Arthur, 366
Bruster, Douglas, 19, 24–5, 75, 90, 129
Bryce, David, 269–70, 271
Buc, George, 36, 48, 53
Bullokar, William
  Aesop's Fables, 317–18, 320
Bunbury, Henry, 178
Burbage, James, 365
Burbage, Richard, 144
Burbidge, Peter, 280

Burby, Cuthbert, 13–14, 16, 83–4, 85, 86, 89, 100–1, 103
Burdick, Anne, 218
Burgoyne, Frank J., 160
Burnim, Kalman A., 240, 258
Burns, Edward, 335
Burton, Jonathan, 352
Busby, John, 80
Butler, Martin, 34
Butter, Nathaniel, 68, 105, 111, 113–15, 131

Cademan, Philip, 237
Cairncross, Andrew, 335
Cambridge Shakespeare editions
  (1863–66), 302, 382, 394
  New Cambridge Shakespeare, 203, 225, 296–7, 298, 336, 337, 340, 350, 354–5, 385, 397
  Oxford and Cambridge, 292
  Shakespeare in Production, 244–5
Cambridge University Press, 218, 244, 280
Camp, Robert Quillen
  Secret Bear, The, 213–16
Capell, Edward, 125, 249, 393–4, 395
Captain Thomas Stukeley, 61
Carey, Henry, Lord Hunsdon, 122, 131, 378
'Caroline paradox', 68
Carr, Nicholas, 403
Carroll, D. Allen, 14
Carson, Christie, 217
Carson, Neil, 61
Carter, Harry, 329
Cassell's 'National Library' series, 279
cataloguing, 9, 116, 122–5, 176, 177–9, 183–4, 189, 195, 381
'Catholic' editing, 8, 312
Cavell, John
  Sodderd Cittizen, The, 37
Chambers, E. K., 365
Chambers, R. W., 44
Chapman, George, 33
  All Fools, 62
  Monsieur d'Olive, 319
  Revenge of Bussy D'Ambois, The, 63
character lists, 5, 134–46
Charles I, 370
Chartier, Roger, 19, 66, 130, 150, 182–3
Chaucer, Geoffrey, 182, 291
Chekhov, Michael, 223
Cheney, Patrick, 22, 66, 75
Chettle, Henry, 20, 372
Child, Harold, 194
Children of Paul's, The, 60, 62, 63, 65
Children of the Chapel, The, 62
Children of the Revels, The, 59, 60, 62–3, 65
children's company playbooks, 4, 59–68

Chorney, Tatjana, 204
chorus, 15, 61, 64, 66, 308, 332, 364
Cicero, 15
Citron, Marcia J., 206
Clarendon Press Shakespeare Series (eds. William George Clark and William Aldis Wright), 291
Clark, William George, 394
Clary, Nick, 395
Classic Stage Company, 223
classical models, 15, 18–19, 29, 64, 66–7, 76, 77, 86, 109, 113, 115, 141, 297, 320, 325, 332, 334, 335, 340, 379, 381, 382, *See also* Ovid
Cleaver, Robert, 100
Clergy of the Church of England Database, 153
closet drama, 77, 140–2, 242, 276
Coleridge, Samuel Taylor, 347
collaboration, 3, 4, 13, 20–4, 37, 40, 47, 48, 50, 53, 58, 81, 109, 115, 275, 403, 410
'collaborative edition', 204
collation, 9, 190, 296, 382, 383, 389, 391–7
collective binding, 6, 77, 178, *See also* Sammelbände
collectors, 5, 6, 125, 130, 172, 173, 177–95
  implied collectors / collections, 181–3, 184
Collier, J. P., 289, 394
Collins' School and College Classics, 289
Collinson, Patrick, 160
Colman, George, 190
  Sheep Shearing, 188–9
colonial editions, 290–3
commonplaces, 5, 17, 18, 75, 76–7, 101, 149–62, 166, 170–1, 234, 273
computational stylistics, 3, 23–5
Condell, Henry, 30, 143, 144, 145, 146, 285, 301, 377
Constable, Henry, 77–8
Cook, Megan, 113
Coombs, James H., 206
copyright, 221, 277, 390
Cormack, Bradin, 180
Cornwallis, William
  The Miraculous and happie union of England and Scotland, 141
Corti, Claudia, 249
court commonplace books, 160–1
Courtyard Theatre, 337
Covell, William
  Polimanteia, 78, 86
Covent Garden Theatre, 240
Coward, Noël, 391
Cowden Clarke, Charles, 264
Cowden Clarke, Mary, 264
Craig, Hugh, 23, 25
Craik, T. W., 350

Index

Crampton, Philip, 276
Crane, Mary Thomas, 149
Crane, Ralph, 3, 27–38, 50, 137–9, 325–6
Crashaw, William, 100
Craven, Alan E., 322
Creede, Thomas, 76, 80, 83, 85, 378
Crossroads, 246
Crouch, Anna Maria. *See* Phillips, Anna Maria
Crystal, Ben, 350
Crystal, David, 350
Cunningham, Vanessa, 242
Cupper, William
   Certaine sermons concerning Gods late visitation in the citie of London, 75
Curtain playhouse, 220
cuts, 6, 36, 43, 49–51, 163, 164–8, 171–2, 173–4, 227, 233–7, 238, 239, 241–2, 243, 245–6, 247, 337, 386
Cutts, J. P., 367

Daileader, Celia R., 142
Dalziel brothers, 264
Dane, Joseph A., 129, 130, 182
Daniel, Samuel, 33, 77–8, 140
   Certaine small poems lately printed with the tragedie of Philotas, 141
   Civil Wars, 100
   Panegyric Congratulatory, 100, 141
   Philotas, 141
   Queen's Arcadia, The, 183
   Works, 100
Danter, John, 75, 80–1, 83, 84, 378
Darnton, Robert, 127
Database of Early English Playbooks, 87, 141
Davenant, William, 7, 165, 171, 235, 237, 242, 251, 287
   The Man's the Master, 237
Davies, John, 371
Davies, Thomas, 186
Davis, Herbert, 329
Dawson, Giles E., 125, 392
Day, John
   Law Tricks, 339
Day, John, George Wilkins, and William Rowley
   Travels of Three English Brothers, The, 61
Daybell, James, 319
De Grazia, Margreta, 5, 57, 134, 150, 302, 304, 307, 391–3, 394
De Lafontaine, Henry Cart, 366
De Ricci, Seymour, 185
De Witt, Johannes, 360
dedications, 28, 61, 63, 64–5, 75, 78, 79, 89, 100, 115, 119, 134, 141, 145, 326, 379
Deegan, Marilyn, 198
Deighton, Kenneth, 291–3, 295, 296

Dekker, Thomas, 19, 20, 90
   Guls horne-booke, 363
   If it be not Good the Devil is in it, 65
   Old Fortunatus, 61
   Shoemakers' Holiday, The, 332, 348, 371
   Whore of Babylon, The, 65
Dekker, Thomas and John Webster
   Northward Ho!, 65
   Westward Ho!, 65, 131
Dent, Arthur, 84, 90, 100
Derby's Men, 79
Dering, Edward
   History of King Henry the Fourth, The, 172–6
DeRose, Steven J., 206
Derrida, Jacques, 212–13
Dessen, Alan, 200, 338
Devonshire, William Cavendish Duke of, 178, 189–90, 194
Dibdin, Thomas, 285
Dicks, John ('Shilling Shakespeare'), 270–1, 279, 285
Digby, Kenelm, 28
Digges, Leonard, 142
digital editions, 7, 9, 200, 217, 218–23, 229, 281–4, 299, 302, 341, 386, 387–8, 389–90, 395–6, 408–9, 411
digital humanities, 1, 30, 198–9, 209–10, 216–18, 220, 228, 392, *See also* apps
Digital Renaissance Editions, 9, 387, 389
digital scholarship, 1, 6, 9–10, 23–5, 30–1, 196–211, 386, 387–8, 389–90, 395–6, 398–414
Dimmock, Matthew, 352
disintegrationism, 20, 21, 53, 297
Dobbyn, Nigel, 266
Dobson, E. J., 329
Dobson, Michael, 288
Dod, John, 100
Dolby, T., 288
Donaldson, George, 134
Donaldson, Ian, 387
Donatus, Aelius, 243
Donker, Marjorie, 149
Donmar Warehouse, 7, 233–4
Donne, John, 319, 324
Donnellan, Declan, 208
Donno, Elizabeth Story, 33
Douai Municipal Library, 171
Dove, John, 84
Dover Wilson, John, 29–30, 40, 52, 138, 280, 296–7, 354
Downes, John, 237
Downes, Thomas, 127
Downham, John, 84
Drakakis, John, 351, 352, 353–4, 355–6
Drake, Francis, 83

'dramatist-as-pen', 17
Drayton, Michael, 18, 20, 88, 100, 101
　Englands Heroicall Epistles, 101
　Idea, 76
　Piers Gaveston, 79
Droeshout, Martin, 379
Dromgoole, Dominic, 336, 337
Drummond, William, 115
Drury Lane Theatre, 186, 240, 258
Dryden, John, 171, 251, 287, 288
Du Guernier, Louis, 254
Duffield, Paul, 268, 281
Duke of York's Theatre, 7, 233, 234–5, 238
Duke, John, 144
Duncan-Jones, Katherine, 77
Dusinberre, Juliet, 171
Dutton, Richard, 103
Dyce, Alexander, 394

Earle, John
　Micro-cosmographie, 363, 366
Early English Books Online, 1, 90, 96, 217, 323
Early Modern OCR Project, 203
Eck, Johann, 311
eclectic editing, 328, 330–1
editorial commentary, 9, 208, 218, 220, 222, 239, 241–3, 244–7, 249, 257, 260–1, 275, 377–8, 380–9, 392, 400, 408–10
editorial introductions, 7, 9, 41, 88, 166, 244, 246, 250, 261, 279, 285–99, 377–8, 380–1, 383–90
editorial pledges, 91–104
editorial representation of voice, 342–57
editorial training, 9, 383–5
Edward III, 69, 83, 84, 273
Egan, Gabriel, 297, 301, 307, 383
Eisenstein, Elizabeth L., 311, 312, 320
Elam, Keir, 261
Eliot, John
　Survey, 75
Eliot, Simon, 278
Elizabeth I, 369
Elizabeth, Princess, 296
'Ellen Terry' Shakespeare edition, 269–70
emendations, 8, 9, 41, 97, 155, 170–1, 209, 244, 300–13, 326–31, 347, 356, 381, 382, 383, 392–7
encoding, 6, 197–211, 227, 410
England's Parnassus, 142
English College of Douai, 171
English Short Title Catalogue, 1, 90, 96, 178
epilogues, 15, 136, 174, 281, 333, 368–70, 372
epitexts, 359
　and editing, 373–4
　announcements, 372–3

clowning, 372, 374
jigs, 371–2
opening trumpets, 359–68, 371, 373, 374
terminal dances, 369, 371–2, 374
terminal prayer, 369–71
terminal songs, 371–2, 374
Erasmus, Desiderius, 23
e-readers, 406, 407
Erne, Lukas, 4, 16, 17, 57, 58, 60, 66, 80, 81, 84, 85, 88–9, 90, 100, 101, 109, 112, 116, 122, 126, 130, 142, 179, 273, 391
Erskine, Gary, 266
Estill, Laura, 157
euphuism, 324
Evans, G. Blakemore, 88, 164–6, 167, 168, 169, 170, 171, 173
Ewing, George, 275, 276

Facebook, 220–1, 229, 283, 413
facsimiles, 151, 169, 173, 178, 202–3, 208, 280, 283, 302, 304, 306, 307–8, 310, 313, 383–4, 390
'fair copies', 3
Farmer, Alan B., 57, 58, 60, 67–8, 97, 112, 129
Farrow, Matty, 281
Fehrenbach, Robert, 179
Ferguson, Frederic Sutherland, 125
Feuillerat, Albert, 32, 34
Field, Nathan and Philip Massinger
　Fatall Dowry, 37
Field, Nathan, John Fletcher, and Philip Massinger
　Honest mans Fortune, The, 36–8, 367
Field, Richard, 75–7, 79, 83, 271
Field, Richard (1878), 270–1, 284
first editions, 3, 4, 57–68, 88, 96, 98, 101, 102, 113, 115, 131, 136, 233, 271
Fitzgeffrey, Henry, 365
Flanders, Julia, 196
Fleming, Juliet, 85
Fletcher, Giles
　Licia, 76
Fletcher, John, 142
　A King and No King, 141
　Beggars Bush, 37
　Bonduca, 27, 37–8
　Demetrius and Enanthe, 28, 31, 33, 35
　Faithful Shepherdess, 63
Fletcher, John and Philip Massinger
　Tragedy of Sr Iohn Van Olden Barnauelt, The, 28, 30–1, 36, 50, 52, 137, 325, 367
Fletcher, John and William Shakespeare
　Two Noble Kinsmen, The, 37, 364, 368
Foakes, R. A., 340
Folger Shakespeare edition, 336, 337

Index

Folger Shakespeare Library, 10, 122, 123–5, 126, 129, 196, 220, 285, 292
Folger *Union First Line Index*, 156
Folger, Henry Clay, 125
Foot, Mirjam, 181
Forbes-Robertson, Johnston, 247
Fornes, Maria Irene, 216
Foscarini, Antonio, 372
Foucault, Michel, 14, 20
'foul papers', 2, 3, 176
Fountainwell edition, 384
Foxon, David, 129
Frederick A. Stokes, 269
Frederick V, 296
Freeman, Arthur, 178, 365
Freeman, Janet Ing, 178
Freeman, Thomas
  Rubbe and a great cast, 370
frontispieces, 241, 250–7, 258, 264, 268
Frowde, Henry, 269
Frye, Northrop, 298
Fuller, Steve, 210
Fuller, Thomas, 157
Fulwell, Ulpian
  Like Will to Like, 334
Furness, Horace Howard, 296, 382, 394–5, 407
Fuseli, Henry, 259

Gabrieli, Vittorio, 45
Galbraith, Steven K., 144
Galey, Alan, 209, 396, 409
Garber, Marjorie, 220
Garnier, Robert, 77
Garrick, David, 185–94, 241, 243
  Florizel and Perdita, 186–9
Gaskell, Philip, 271
Genette, Gerard, 359
Gentleman, Francis, 7, 241–3
George III, 178, 185
Gerritsen, J., 36–7
Gervinus, G. G., 290–1
Gibbons, Brian, 305
Giddens, Eugene, 397
Gieskes, Edward, 19, 22
Gilbert, John, 261–4
Gillespie, Alexandra, 130, 182
Glasgow University Press, 269
Global Shakespeares, 217
Globe playhouse, 64–5, 66–7, 91, 113, 115, 332, 362, 365
Globe Shakespeare edition, 200, 281, 285
Globe Theatre (1997), 336, 337
glossolalia, 342
Goldberg, Jonathan, 18

Gooch, Steve, 245–6
'good quartos', 58, 273
Goodwin, George, 342
Gossett, Suzanne, 332, 340, 358, 394, 397
Gosson, Henry, 113, 115
Goughe, Mr., 48, 49, 51
Grafton, Anthony, 88, 180, 391
Graham-White, Anthony, 319
Grandage, Michael, 7, 234, 236, 237, 238
Gravelot, Hubert, 255, 260
Graves, Thornton S., 29
Greaves, Simon, 266–8
Green, James N., 127
Greenblatt, Stephen, 88
Greene, Robert, 83, 84
  Alphonsus, King of Aragon, 365
  Greene's Groatsworth of Wit, 13, 19
  Honorable historie of frier Bacon, and frier Bongay, The, 81, 332
  James IV, 348
  Pandosto, 76
  Repentance of Robert Greene, The, 13, 14
Greg, W. W., 3, 8, 27, 29–30, 35, 37, 39–40, 42–3, 51–2, 85, 91–5, 97, 119–22, 125–6, 132, 135–6, 138, 202–3, 272, 328–31, 382–3
Grierson, George, 275–6
Grignion, C., 258
Guillory, John, 227
Gurr, Andrew, 35, 60, 61, 64–5, 66, 144, 350–1, 372, 381
Gwinne, Matthew
  Nero Tragaedia Nova, 141
  Vertumnus siue Annus recurrens Oxonii, 141
Gwynne, Edward, 122, 123

Haas, Virginia Westling, 204
Hagen, Uta, 223
Hailey, R. Carter, 119
Hakluyt, Richard
  Principal Navigations, 295
Halasz, Alexandra, 85, 122
Hall, Joseph, 33, 90
Hall, Peter, 405
Hallett, Charles A., 333
Hallett, Elaine S., 333
Halliwell-Phillipps, J. O., 178, 289, 367
Halpern, Richard, 18
Hamilton, William, 259
HamletWorks, 395–6
Hammond, Paul, 342
Hampden, John, 295
Hankey, Julie, 244
Hanks, Tom, 223
Hanmer, Thomas, 170, 255–7, 392–3

Hanna, Ralph, 182
Harbage, Alfred, 383–4
Hardinge, George, 394
Harington, John
  Ariosto's *Orlando Furioso*, 76
Harrison, G. B., 280
Harrison, John, 76–7, 79, 83
Harrison, Peter, 311
Hart, H. C., 294
Harvard University, 383–4
Harvey, Gabriel, 75, 347
Hattaway, Michael, 370
Hatton Garden Nursery theatre, 164, 167, 168
Haward, Jon, 266
Hawkes, Terence, 348
Hawkins, Anne, 204
Hawkins, John, 83
Hayes, Lawrence, 132
Hayles, N. Katherine, 217, 228–9
Hayley, Emma, 268
Hayman, Francis, 255–6
Haymarket Theatre, 188
Hayward, John, 100, 347, 349
Hedbäck, Ann-Mari, 171
Helgerson, Richard, 15, 347
Heminge, John, 30, 143, 144, 145, 146, 285, 301, 367, 377
Henslowe, Philip, 20, 362
Hentzner, Paul, 371
Herbert, Henry, 36–7
Herbert, Mary (Sidney), 77–8
Herbert, Philip, fourth Earl of Pembroke and first Earl of Montgomery, 143, 145, 295, 379
Herbert, William, third Earl of Pembroke, 143, 145, 295, 379
Herford, C. H., 29
Heywood, Jasper, 140
Heywood, Thomas, 43, 66, 87
  Captives, The, 3, 49–50, 52
  Four Prentices of London, The, 99, 364
  Golden Age, The, 61
  Love's Mistress, 99
  Sir Thomas More, 49
  Woman Killed with Kindness, A, 123, 126–7, 129–33, 136, 332
Hibbard, G. R., 386
Highfill, Philip A., 237, 240
Highfill, Philip H., Jr., 240, 258
Hinman, Charlton, 135, 295, 322, 324, 325
Hirsch, Brett, 377, 389, 390
Hirsch, John, 245
Hirschfeld, Heather Anne, 22
Hirsh, James E., 333
historicism, 298

Hodgdon, Barbara, 239, 348
Hodgets, John, 131
Hodnett, Edward, 249, 251, 264
Hoenselaars, Ton, 24
Holderness, Graham, 303, 304, 313
Holinshed, Raphael
  First and second volumes of Chronicles, The, 76, 105, 109
Holland, Peter, 220, 358, 386–7
Holmes, Thomas, 326
Holyband, Claudius
  French Littelton, The, 76
Homer, 15, 216
Honan, Park, 88
Honigmann, E. A. J., 33, 34, 41–2, 47, 138, 382–3
Hooks, Adam, 57, 76, 100, 131, 183–4
Hopkins, Gerard Manley, 207–8
Hopkins, Samuel, 90
Hopkins, William, 240
Horace, 15, 76
House of Lords, 277
Housman, A. E., 301, 309
Howard-Hill, T. H., 28–36, 50, 137, 320, 325
Hoy, Cyrus, 20, 32, 37
Huculak, J. Matthew, 149
Hudson, Henry N., 290, 296
Humphreys, A. R., 347
Hunt, David, 234, 236
Hunt, Maurice, 204
Hunt, Peter, 238
Hunter, G. K., 150, 382
Huntington Library, 126, 129, 151, 177, 178, 185, 189–90, 194
Huntington, Henry E., 178, 189, 194
Hussey, E. W., 125
Hutton, Luke, 81
Hylton, Jeremy, 281
Hytner, Nicholas, 239, 337

'ideal reader', 63
illustrated editions, 7, 240, 249–68, 278–9, 285
  Boydell's *Dramatic Works of Shakspeare Revised by George Steevens, The* (1803), 258–9, 260
  Cassell's *Illustrated Shakespeare*, 264–6
  Charles Knight's *Pictorial Shakespeare*, 259–61
  comic-book Shakespeare, 266–8, 281
  manga, 266–8, 281
  Saddleback's Illustrated Classics, 266
  Staunton-Gilbert edition, 261–4
  Tempest, The (SelfMadeHero), 266–8, 281
  Tempest: The Cartoon Illustrated Edition, The, 266–8
  Tempest: The Graphic Novel, The, 266
  Works of Mr. William Shakespear, The (1709), 249–55

Works of Shakespear, The (1744), 255–7
Works of Shakespeare, The (1740), 255
'implied reader', 179
Inchbald, Elizabeth, 244
Inns of Court, 151, 152–3, 161, 172
interdisciplinarity, 210
Internet, 9, 398–9, 401, 403, 407, 409, 412–13, 414,
    See also World Wide Web
Internet Shakespeare Editions, 9, 200–1, 217, 387, 389–90, 396
'interventionist editors', 300, 307–8, 310–12, 355
Ioppolo, Grace, 22, 36–7, 38
Iser, Wolfgang, 179

Jackson, MacDonald P., 20, 23, 49, 324
Jackson, Russell, 234
Jackson, Zachary, 394, 395, 397
'Jacobean paradox', 68
Jaggard, Isaac, 126, 130–3
'Jaggard Quartos', 133
Jaggard, William, 130–3, 135, 136, 145
James I, 48, 90, 296, 366, 370
    Basilikon Doron, 90
    Trew Law of Free Monarchies, The, 90
Jardine, Lisa, 180
Jarvis, Simon, 380
Jayne, Sears, 179
Jeffes, Abel, 81
Jeffries, Neil, 413
Jensen, M. P., 266
Jerome, Saint, 23
Johns, Adrian, 320
Johnson, Arthur, 131, 132
Johnson, Gerald D., 122, 274
Johnson, Nora, 16
Johnson, Odai, 186
Johnson, Samuel, 58, 138, 243, 249–50, 257, 260, 264, 301, 312, 330, 380–2, 390, 391–3
Jones, Emrys, 333
Jonson, Ben, 19, 20, 35, 64, 66, 89, 113, 119, 137, 143, 157, 248, 333, 379
    1616 Folio, 29, 35, 58, 140, 144–5, 146, 325–6
    Alchemist, The, 58, 242
    Cambridge Edition of the Works of Ben Jonson, The, 9, 387–8
    Case is Altered, The, 109–11
    Cynthia's Revels, 62, 363
    Epicene, 58
    Every Man in his Humour, 144
    Every Man out of his Humour, 64, 96, 363
    Fountaine of Selfe-Love, The, 363
    Magnificent Entertainment, 141
    Pleasure reconcild to Vertue, 28, 31

Sejanus, 141, 242
Volpone, 64–5, 105–9, 161
Jonsonian elisions, 29, 31–2
Jowett, John, 32–5, 43, 45, 46, 51, 139, 174, 175, 306–8, 309, 321, 322, 358, 379, 389
JSTOR, 217

Kahrl, George M., 185, 186
Kastan, David Scott, 15, 16, 57, 95, 122, 180, 181, 391
Katz, Alan, 285
Kean, Charles, 244, 289
Keleman, Erick, 204–5
Kellett, E. E., 290–1
Kemble, John Philip, 189–94, 244
Kempe, Will, 144, 369
Kermode, Frank, 297–9
Kidnie, Margaret Jane, 17, 126, 176
King's Men / Lord Chamberlain's Men, 16, 27–8, 36–7, 38, 48, 50, 57, 58, 59–60, 61, 63, 67, 80, 91, 113, 115, 122, 131, 144, 145, 238, 325, 367, 378
Kinney, Arthur, 23, 25
Kirkall, Elisha, 250–4, 255
Kirsch, Arthur C., 157,
Kirschenbaum, Matthew G., 205, 226
Kittler, Friedrich A., 201
Kliman, Bernice W., 392, 395
Knacke to know an honest man, A, 84
Knapp, Jeffrey, 22
Knight, Charles. *See under* illustrated editions
Knight, Edward, 3, 27, 34–5, 36–8
Knight, Jeffrey Todd, 77, 122, 123, 125, 126, 127, 129, 132, 180, 182, 183
Knolles, Richard, 372
Knowles, Richard, 203, 244, 395
Knutson, Roslyn Lander, 60
Konkola, Kari, 90
Koran, 269
Kristeva, Julia, 181
Krivatsy, Nati H., 172
Kulick, Brian, 223
Kyd, Thomas, 80, 400
    Soliman and Perseda, 353, 354
    Spanish Tragedy, The, 81, 96
    representation of authorship in, 25–6
    Shakespearean additions to, 24–5

Lachmann, Karl, 301
Lackington, James, 277–8, 280
Lacy, Thomas Hailes, 244
Lady Alimony, 363
Lady Elizabeth's Men, 52, 59, 60
Lake, David J., 20
Lancashire, Anne, 49

Langbaine, Gerard, 20
Langhans, Edward A., 176
Latin, representation of, 343–6
Lavagnino, John, 142
Law, Jude, 233, 235
Law, Matthew, 89, 100, 103
Lawrence University, 196
Leare, Daniel, 152
Lee, Nathaniel
  Mithridates, 171
Lee, Sidney, 289
Leech, Clifford, 384–5, 395
Leedham-Green, Elisabeth, 179, 183
Lehmann, Hans-Thies, 213
Lennam, T. N., 172
Leo, F. A., 397
Lerer, Seth, 182
Lesser, Zachary, 57, 58, 60, 67–8, 77, 83, 85, 97, 112, 150, 184
letitcast.com, 223
Levenson, Jill L., 378
Levine, Nina, 44
Library of Alexandria, 23
Lichtenfels, Peter, 245
Liebman, Dave, 202, 207
Lindley, David, 298, 351
Ling, Nicholas, 80, 89, 100–1, 103
Linked Data, 410–11
Lion King, The, 400
Literature Online, 156
Little, David M., 186
Liu, Alan, 218
Lloyd Webber, Andrew, 247
Lloyd, Megan, 347
Locrine, 69, 83, 96, 251
Lodge, Thomas
  Phillis, 76
  Wounds of Civil War, The, 348
Lodge, Thomas and Robert Greene
  Looking glasse for London and England, A, 83
Loewenstein, Joseph, 88, 95
Logan, Robert, 352
London Chronicle, 193
London Prodigal, The, 68, 83, 87, 204
London Waits, 365
Long, William B., 39
Loomis, Catherine, 160
Lord Chamberlain's Men. *See* King's Men / Lord Chamberlain's Men
Lord have Mercy upon us, or the Visitation at Oxford, 364
Love, Harold, 23
Lowin, John, 143–4
Lownes, Humphrey, 77
Luce, Morton, 294–6, 297

Lupton, D., 371
Lupton, Thomas
  All for Money, 334
Luther, Martin, 311
Lydgate, John, 182
Lyly, John, 84
  Six Court Comedies, 129
Lyons, Tara, 183, 184

Mabbe, James, 142
McCarty, Willard, 198
McDonald, John, 266
McGann, Jerome, 175, 205, 207, 210–11, 216–17
McInnis, David, 377
McKenzie, D. F., 322
MacKenzie, Norman H., 208
McKerrow, R. B., 382–3
McLeod, Randall, 200, 208–9, 210, 304, 312, 391
McLuhan, Marshall, 398
McManaway, James C., 157
Macmillan's English Classics, 292
Macmillan's English Classics for Indian University Students, 291–3
McMillin, Scott, 51
McMullan, Gordon, 358, 373
McNamara, Jeremy, 405
Madden, Frederic, 178
Madras Christian College, 290
Madras Shakespeare edition, 290
Magellan, 288
Maguire, Laurie E., 58, 273, 319
Malone, E., 77, 243, 288, 332, 382
Mamet, David, 223
manuscript revision, 39–53
  and character, 39, 41–50, 53
Map of Early Modern London, 389
Marcus, Leah S., 5, 10, 134, 143, 144, 200, 293, 302–3, 304–5, 313, 391
Marino, James, 25, 83, 103
Markham, Gervase
  Discourse of horsmanshippe, A, 76
Marlowe, Christopher, 19, 356
  Jew of Malta, The, 339
  Massacre at Paris, The, 81, 339
  Tamburlaine, 174, 352–3
Marotti, Arthur F., 151
Marston, John, 19, 87
  Dutch Courtesan, The, 62, 153
  Jack Drum's Entertainment, 62, 140
  Malcontent, The, 63, 98
  Parasitaster, 62, 63, 98, 102–3
Massachusetts Institute of Technology, 281, 411
Massai, Sonia, 4, 57, 60, 66, 81, 85, 91, 97, 102–3, 113, 122, 130, 132, 142, 143, 168, 274
massed entries, 28–30, 31, 34, 137

Massinger, Philip, 132
  Beleeue as You List, 37
  Unnatural Combat, 37
Masten, Jeffrey, 20–3, 24, 52
Maxwell, J. C., 34
May, Steven W., 161
Mazzio, Carla, 180
Meade, Jacob, 36
Medina, John Baptiste de, 252
Meisner, Sanford, 223
Melchiori, Giorgio, 42–3, 44, 45–6, 340
Merchant, William Moelwyn, 251
Meres, Francis
  Palladis Tamia, 18–19, 85–6, 91
Merrie Conceited Jests of George Peele, The, 362
Middleton, Thomas, 20, 132, 139–40, 142, 183
  Game at Chesse, A, 28, 30–1, 34–5, 137, 325
  Macbeth, 388
  More Dissemblers Besides Women, 317–18, 319–20
  Nice Valour, 139
  Second Maiden's Tragedy, The, 3, 27, 47–9, 50–3
  Thomas Middleton and Early Modern Textual Culture: A Companion to the Collected Works, 142
  Thomas Middleton: The Collected Works, 1, 9, 23, 387, 388–9
  Measure for Measure, 139–40
  Timon of Athens, 23
  Trick to Catch the Old One, A, 389
  Witch, The, 28, 29, 30–1, 33, 35, 137–8, 325
  Women Beware Women, 32
  Your Five Gallants, 388
Middleton, Thomas and Thomas Dekker
  Roaring Girl, The, 63
Middleton, Thomas and William Rowley, 20
  Fair Quarrel, A, 96, 98
Millington, Thomas, 80–1
Milton, John, 206–7
  Comus, 297
  Paradise Lost, 249, 252
Minami, R., 268
miniature editions, 269–70
Mitchell, W. J. T., 261
Moby Shakespeare, 281
Modern Languages Association, The, 409–10
modernization, 8, 9, 168, 171, 180, 235–6, 300, 304, 310, 326–31, 350–1, 353, 355, 357, 383
Montaigne, Michel de, 289
Moore, J. K., 321
Moore, Joseph S., 278–9
Morash, Christopher, 275
Moretti, Franco, 221

Morley, Henry, 279
Morris, D., 289
Moss, Gregory
  Play Viewed from a Distance, 213, 229
Moulton, Ian Frederick, 151
Mowat, Barbara A., 33, 88, 298
Moxon, Joseph
  Mechanick Exercises, 329–31
Mullett, Michael A., 311
Mulryne, J. R., 32–3
Munday, Anthony, 20, 40, 43, 45–6, 47, 363
Munro, Lucy, 60
Murphy, Andrew, 10, 88, 90, 122, 239–40, 244, 271, 274, 278, 285, 292–3, 301, 305–6, 380
Murray, Christopher, 270
Murray-John, Patrick, 409
Myklebost, Svenn-Arve, 281

Nashe, Thomas, 74–5, 84
  Apologie of Pierce pennilesse, The, 76
  The unfortunate traveller, 79
National Library of Ireland, 270
National Theatre, 239, 337
Neidig, William J., 122
Neill, Michael, 41, 343, 347, 351, 358
Nelson, Alan, 179
networked scholarship, 9–10, 398–414
New Bibliography, 1, 2, 121, 123, 126, 176, 296, 297, 298, 302, 309, 329, 378, 382–3, 385
New Criticism, 14, 221, 229, 297, 298, 299
New Custome, 369
New Mermaids edition, 384
New Textualism, 1
New Variorum Shakespeare, 203–4, 382, 395–6, 409
  Electronic New Variorum Shakespeare, 396
  Shakespeare Variorum Handbook, 244, 395
New York Times, 25
Newes from Brest, 81
Niles, Rebecca, 196
No-body and Some-body, 261
North, Thomas
  Plutarch's *Lives*, 76
Norton Shakespeare edition, 373
Norton, David, 211
Norton, Thomas
  Tragidie of Ferrex and Porrex [Gorboduc], The, 77
Notes & Queries, 301
Nunberg, Geoffrey, 281

O'Casey, Sean, 270–1, 284
O'Connor, Marion, 28
Okes, Nicholas, 136, 143
Oliver, H. J., 32

Olivier, Lawrence, 405
Open Access, 10, 404, 405
open platforms, 409–10
Oregon Shakespeare Festival, 337
Orgel, Stephen, 17, 35, 47, 51–2, 170, 176, 180, 255, 298, 303, 304
Orrell, John, 372
Osborne, Laurie E., 243
Ovid, 76, 85, 119, 151, 404, 405
   Amores, 75–6
   Heroides, 76
   Metamorphoses, 76
Oxberry, William, 244
Oxford Shakespeare editions, 298, 304, 385–6, 397
   Complete Works, 52, 302, 326, 336, 339, 345, 350, 356, 358, 385
   editorial procedures, 385–6
   Hanmer (1744), 255, 392
   Oxford and Cambridge, 292
   Textual Companion, 302
   World's Classics, 336, 337
Oxford University Press, 269, 280, 392
Oxley, Philip, 35
Oya, Reiko, 242

Palfrey, Simon, 222
pamphlets, 81, 86, 127–30, 131, 133, 177, 179, 182–3, 294, 364, 380
Paper Theatre, 212
Parker, James, 259
Parsons, Marmaduke, 140
Passionate Pilgrim, The, 78, 88
Paterson, Don, 283
patronage, 15, 28, 65, 79–80, 86, 109, 134, 145, 290, 326
Paul, Saint, 344
Paul's playhouse, 59
'Pavier Quartos', 5, 119–33, 136, 273–4
Pavier, Thomas, 7, 109, 122, 131, 132, 273–4
Payne, Ben Iden, 246
Pechter, Edward, 307, 351
Pedicord, Harry William, 188
Peele, George, 23, 362
   Battle of Alcazar, The, 354
Pelican Shakespeare edition, 298, 336, 337
Pellis, Valeria, 268
Pembroke's Men, 79, 81, 83
Penguin Shakespeare edition, 239, 280, 298
Pennington, Michael, 247
Penny Shakespeare, The, 278
Pepys, Samuel, 235
Percy, Thomas, 123, 126, 132
Percy, William
   Cuck-Queanes and Cuckolds Errants, The, 364

performance commentary, 227, 243
Perkins, William, 90, 99–100
Peterson, Lisa, 337
Phillips, Anna Maria, 258
Phillips, Augustine, 144
Phillpotts, J. S., 290, 291, 296
Pickwood, Nicholas, 127
Pierson, Thomas, 100
Pimlyco. Or, Runne Red-Cap, 113
plague, the, 15, 58, 74–5, 86
Platter, Thomas, 371
Plautus, 18–19, 64, 67, 76, 113, 370
Playfere, Thomas
   Meane in Mourning, The, 100
Pliny
   Natural History, 289
Plutarch, 76
Poets' War, 19
pointing, early modern, 8, 150, 317–26
Politeuphuia, 101
Pollard, Alfred W., 58, 87, 125, 202, 382
Ponsonby, William, 77
Poole, William, 322
Pope, Alexander, 249, 254, 275, 301, 312, 347, 351, 380–2, 393, 396
Pope, Rob, 205
Pope, Thomas, 144
postcard plays, 6, 212–17, 226
postcards, 212
postcolonialism, 298–9
poststructuralism, 10, 181
Potter, Lois, 242
Pratt, Aaron T., 127, 129, 130
Present remedies against the plague, 75
Preston, Thomas
   Cambises, 334, 370
pricing of editions, 271, 272, 277–9, 280, 284
Primanis, Olivia, 129
Prince Henry's Men, 63, 65
Princess's Theatre, 289
printer's copy, 27–8, 30, 31, 32–4, 37, 85, 133, 321, 324–5, 326
printing in 1590s, 69–86
Private Libraries in Renaissance England, 179
prologues, 61–2, 64, 85, 113, 174, 219, 333, 362–4
'promptbooks', 2, 3, 39, 167, 176, 194, 225, 239, 240, 258, 386
Proot, Goran, 127
'Protestant' editing, 8, 312
Publishers' Circular, 278
publishing formats, 269–84
punctuation, 8, 28–34, 35, 37, 40, 95, 202–3, 207, 208–9, 300, 353–6, *See also* pointing, early modern

Purchas, Samuel, 354
Puritan, The, 87, 90
Puttenham, George
   Arte of English Poesie, 77, 318, 319–20

Quaritch (bookseller), 125
Queen Anne's Men, 61
Queen's Men, 61, 65, 66
Queen's Men Editions, 389
Quiller-Couch, Arthur, 296–7, 354
Quinn, James T., 193

Raber, Karen, 76
Rackin, Phyllis, 347
Ralegh, Walter
   Discovery of Guiana, 289
Ramberg, J. H., 258
Ramsay, Stephen, 201
Rancière, Jacques, 213
Randel, Don Michael, 206
Randolph, Thomas, 152
Rankins, William, 362
Rasmussen, Eric, 43, 373, 392, 397
Raymond, Joad, 129
reader-response criticism, 179–81
Redding, David Coleman, 152
Redgrave, G. R., 87, 125
Reed, Isaac, 288, 382, 393
Reformation, 310–12, 343–4
Regents Renaissance Drama, 384
Reid, S. W., 32
Renear, Allen H., 206
reprints, 2, 58, 67–8, 91–104, 112, 119, 142, 271–3, 324, 330, 392
Resurgendum. A notable sermon concerning the resurrection, 76
Revels Plays, 377, 384–5
Reynolds, Joshua, 259
Rickner, George, 367
Ridley, M. R., 41–2, 47
Righter (Barton), Anne, 298
Rigogne, Thierry, 127
Riverside Shakespeare edition, 88, 102, 335, 336, 337, 339
Roach, Joe, 220
Roberts, Jeanne A., 34–5
Roberts, Sasha, 151, 152, 154, 160
Robinson, Benedict Scott, 181
Robinson, P. R., 129
Rocket, Henry, 131
Rolfe, William James, 291
Romeo and Juliet: Searchable Database for Promptbooks, 386
Rooney, M. W., 177
Rose playhouse, 80

Rose, Mark, 333
Routledge, 261
Rowe, Katherine, 220, 225–6
Rowe, Nicholas, 140, 170, 243, 249–55, 268, 281, 312, 380, 393, 396
   Jane Shore, 251
Rowland, Richard, 80
Rowlands, Samuel, 88
Rowse, A. L., 342
Royal Shakespeare Company, 217, 238, 335, 337, 348
Royal Society, 329
RSC Shakespeare edition, 336, 337, 373, 397
Rubin, Leon, 245
Rugby Shakespeare edition, 291
Ryan, Marie-Laure, 227

Salmon, Vivien, 318
Sammelbände, 131, 132, 178–9, 180, 182–3, 185, 190, *See also* collective binding
Sancroft, William, 157, 159–60
Sanders, Julie, 69
Sanderson, James L., 373
Sauer, Elizabeth, 180
Saunders, Robert, 185
Saunderson, Mary, 237
Scarlet, Thomas, 83
scene breaks, 8, 28, 29, 31, 32, 137, 304, 332–41
Schäfer, Jürgen, 327
Schneider, Ben Ross, Jr., 196–7, 198–9, 203, 209–10
Schoenbaum, Samuel, 21, 88–9
school editions, 289–93
Schuessler, Jennifer, 25
Schweidler, Max, 190
Scragg, Leah, 134
scribal copy, 27–38, 47
Seary, Peter, 380–2
SelfMadeHero, 266, 268, 281–2
Sellers, Peter, 405
Selous, Henry Courtenay, 264–6
Seltzer, Daniel, 383
semi-substantives, 8, 331
Seneca, 15, 18, 141, 142
   Tenne Tragedies, 129, 140
Seymour, William, 48
Shaaber, M. A., 31, 33, 392
Shadwell, Thomas, 251
Shakespeare & Co., 413
Shakespeare Birthplace Trust, 170
Shakespeare Memorial Theatre, 246
Shakespeare Quartos Archive, 177, 283

Shakespeare, William
  First Folio, 3, 5, 23, 29–34, 38, 41, 50, 61, 85,
    111–12, 122, 130, 132, 133, 134–41, 142–6,
    150, 164, 166–7, 168, 170, 172, 180, 200–1,
    204, 254, 274–5, 280, 294, 295–7, 301, 304,
    307, 309, 312, 313, 322, 324–6, 332–3, 336,
    337, 345, 349, 351, 354, 356, 367, 368, 373,
    377, 379, 381, 392, 410
  Second Folio, 168, 171, 274, 392
  Third Folio, 164, 165, 166, 168–70, 274, 332, 392
  Fourth Folio, 168, 274, 381, 392
  Fifth Folio, 392
  All's Well That Ends Well, 30, 136, 240, 307, 371
  Antony and Cleopatra, 136, 141, 245, 247
  As You Like It, 159, 171–2, 240, 276, 339, 371, 407–8
  Comedy of Errors, The, 3, 18, 30, 34, 76, 85, 136, 145, 164–5, 167–8, 171, 409
  Coriolanus, 38, 239, 307, 387
  Cymbeline, 34, 225–6, 251, 252, 333
  First Part of the Contention, The (2 Henry VI), 80–1, 344–5
  Hamlet, 9, 15, 66, 91, 95, 98, 99, 100, 101,
    103, 136, 150, 157, 158, 159, 165–8, 170,
    177–9, 180, 182, 189–90, 193, 194, 233–8,
    240, 242–3, 244, 246–8, 275–6, 303,
    365, 368–9, 381, 386, 395–7, 399–400,
    410–11, 414
  Henry IV, Part 1, 18, 85, 91–5, 98, 99–100, 102, 104, 172–5, 272, 275, 333, 346–9, 356, 373
  Henry IV, Part 2, 3, 9, 18, 31–2, 33, 80, 85, 134–5, 137, 172–5, 252, 295, 336–8, 339, 340–1, 356, 369–70
  Henry V, 15, 61, 81, 119, 122, 125, 126, 133, 140, 175, 246, 308, 332, 342, 347–51, 356, 362, 364
    representation of characters' voices, 349–51
  Henriad, the, 175, 356
  Henry VI, Part 1, 80, 335
  Henry VI, Part 2, 44, 46, 80, 81, 83, 85, 122, 345, 346, 365
  Henry VI, Part 3, 80, 81, 83, 85, 122, 272
  Henry VIII, 166, 343–4, 346, 348
  Julius Caesar, 171, 246, 276, 371, 390
  King John, 18, 85, 390
  King Lear, 66, 68, 105–9, 112, 115, 122, 123, 125, 129, 131, 133, 170, 186, 204, 247, 279, 280, 281, 307, 339, 340, 414
  Love's Labour's Lost, 18, 30, 52, 76, 80, 83, 85, 87, 91–5, 96, 98, 99, 100, 101, 116, 294, 324–5
  Love's Labour's Won, 18, 69, 85
  Macbeth, 164–5, 166–8, 171, 240, 243, 275–6, 333, 388, 414
  Measure for Measure, 15, 30–1, 32, 134, 136, 138–40, 165, 166–7, 240, 245
  Merchant of Venice, The, 18, 85, 122, 125, 132, 140, 153, 156, 160, 245, 246, 322, 351–6
    representation of Prince of Morocco's voice, 352–6
  Merry Wives of Windsor, The, 30–2, 104, 122, 125, 131, 136–7, 170, 240, 345
  Midsummer Night's Dream, A, 18, 85, 122, 125, 164, 168–70, 200–1, 245, 363, 367, 371
  Much Ado About Nothing, 18, 30–1, 292, 293, 323–4, 326, 368, 371
  Othello, 3, 33, 41, 134–5, 137, 143, 157, 158–9, 166, 240, 246, 261, 276, 332, 351–2, 356, 414
    representation of Othello's voice, 351
  Pericles, 23, 61, 66, 99, 113–15, 122, 123–5, 131, 133, 183, 251, 332, 340, 369, 394
  Rape of Lucrece, The, 69–79, 85, 88, 104, 150–1, 160, 183, 274
  Richard II, 18, 32, 80, 84–5, 87, 91, 95, 97, 98, 99, 100, 104, 153–6, 159, 242
  Richard III, 18, 32, 84–5, 87, 91–5, 98, 99–100, 102, 104, 146, 161, 171, 240, 272, 327, 378, 405
  Romeo and Juliet, 18, 32, 41, 75, 83–5, 91, 95, 97, 100–1, 103, 115–16, 119, 152–3, 171–2, 204, 219–20, 222, 226, 335, 336, 339, 378–9, 382, 385–6
  Sir Thomas More, additions to, 40–3, 46–7, 51, 321, 322–3
  Sonnets, 86, 88, 118–19, 152, 208–9, 283, 324
  Taming of the Shrew, The, 30–1, 81, 159, 303, 309, 345, 364, 365, 413
  Tempest, The, 6, 15, 30, 34–5, 134–6, 137, 218, 220–1, 226, 227, 229, 240, 249, 251, 252–9, 260–3, 264–8, 269, 279, 281, 285–93, 294–9, 302–3, 304, 325, 343, 351
    representation of Caliban's voice, 351
  Timon of Athens, 23, 32, 134–7, 160, 239, 362
  Titus Andronicus, 18, 23, 76, 79, 80–1, 85, 119, 242
  Troilus and Cressida, 66–8, 112–15, 132, 136, 159–60, 251
  True Tragedie of Richard Duke of York, The, 81, 272
  Twelfth Night, 33, 77, 171, 261, 319, 371
  Two Gentlemen of Verona, The, 18, 30, 85, 134–5, 143
  Venus and Adonis, 69–79, 83, 85, 88, 119, 151–2, 160, 183, 271–3, 274
  Whole Contention, The (2 and 3 Henry VI), 122, 123–5, 129, 131
  Winter's Tale, The, 29–30, 134–5, 138, 160, 186–8, 203–4, 304, 409
Shakespearean Performance in Ireland, 275
Shapiro, James, 19, 88, 352

Sharpham, Edward
   Cupid's Whirligig, 62
Shattuck, Charles H., 176, 386
Sherbo, Arthur, 394
Sherburn, George, 190
Sheridan, Thomas, 186
Sherman, William H., 63, 180, 209, 295, 324, 369
Sherwin, C., 258
Shillingsburg, Peter L., 307, 310
Short, Peter, 85, 86
Sidgwick and Jackson, 280
Sidney, Philip
   Arcadia, 77, 153, 156
Signet Shakespeare edition, 336, 337
Sillars, Stuart, 7, 244, 249, 250, 252, 260, 279
Simmes, Valentine, 84–5
Simpson, Evelyn, 29
Simpson, James, 194
Simpson, Percy, 29, 319
Simpson, Richard, 394
Sinfield, Alan, 44
Singer, S. W., 289
Sir John Oldcastle, 122, 125, 133, 273
Sir Thomas More, 3, 25, 40–53, 305, 321, 322–3, 327, 363
Sisson, Charles J., 163
Skillan, George, 246–8
Sly, William, 144
Smethwick, John, 115
Smirke, Robert, 259
Smith, Anker, 259
Smith, Bruce R., 225, 318, 322
Smith, Emma, 391
Smith, Henry, 84, 90, 101
Smith, Richard, 77
Smith, Simon, 367
Smock Alley Theatre, 165–70, 275–6
Solley, Henry, 279
Somers, George, 289
Sophocles, 18
Spectator, The, 391
Spencer, Hazelton, 235
Spencer, T. J. B., 280
Spenser, Edmund, 77–8, 289, 297, 347
Sperberg-McQueen, Michael, 206–7
Spivack concordance, 339
St. Clair, William, 195, 277
stab-stich holes, 127–31
Stallybrass, Peter, 18–19, 57, 66, 77, 130, 150, 182–3, 211, 302, 304, 307
Stanbridge, Alan, 196
Stanislavski, Konstantin, 223

stationers, 3–4, 13, 57–8, 66–8, 69–86, 89, 95–6, 97, 100–1, 102, 103–4, 105–22, 127–33, 134, 135–6, 142, 183–4, 272, 321–2, 356, 378
Stationers' Company Registers, 69, 75, 78, 80
Stationers' Company, The, 272
Staunton, Howard, 261–4, 266
Steele-Perkins, Crispian, 366
Steevens, George, 203, 257, 258, 264, 382, 393, 394
Stern, Tiffany, 222, 334, 362, 364, 370, 373
Sternhold, Thomas and Samuel Hopkins
   Whole Book of Psalms, 90
Stonley, Richard, 69, 75
Stow, John, 100
Strange Brew, 400
Strasberg, Lee, 223
Straznicky, Marta, 57, 143
Stuart, Arbella, 48
Sturgess, K. M., 126
substantives, 2, 8, 35, 321, 328–31, 395
Summit, Jennifer, 184
Sunstein, Cass, 403
Sussex's Men, 79
Sutherland, Kathryn, 198
Sutton, Bartholomew, 109–11
Sutton, Christopher, 84
Sutton, Thomas, 100
Suzman, Janet, 245
Suzuki, Tadashi, 223
Swan Playhouse, 220, 360–2
Swan Theatre (Royal Shakespeare Company), 337
Swann, Joel, 149, 153
Swiney, Eugene, 276
Sydenham, Humphrey, 157
Sykes, Norman, 312
Syme, Holger Schott, 83

Tabor, Stephen, 178
Taming of A Shrew, The, 69, 81–3, 87
Tarlton, Richard, 364
   Tarlton's Jeasts, 372
Tavard, George H., 311
Tawyer (Toyer), Willam, 367
Taylor, Gary, 16, 28, 34, 36, 88, 134, 141, 142, 302, 305–10, 312, 326, 332, 336, 339, 358, 388–9
Taylor, Joseph, 144
Teaching of English Series, 295
Tears of fancie, The, 76
TEI (Text Initiative Encoding) Consortium, 208
TEI By Example, 198
Tennyson, Alfred, 291
Terence, 64, 67, 113, 243
Texas Christian University, 122, 125, 127

textual notes, 340, 391–7
theatre editions, 6–7, 244, 287–8, 289, *See also* annotations, theatrical
  Applause Shakespeare Library, The, 245
  Bell's Edition of Shakespeare's Plays, 7, 240–4, 258, 287
  [Cut] *Shakespeare, The*, 245–6
  Hamlet (1676), 7, 233, 234–6, 237–9, 242, 245–6, 248
  Hamlet (2009), 7, 233–4, 236–7, 238–9, 244, 248
  Samuel French's Acting Editions, 246–8
  Shakespeare in Production, 244–5
  unpublished theatrical texts, 239
Theatre playhouse, 220
Theatres Royal, 240, 258, 276, 287–8
Theobald, Lewis, 249, 254–5, 301, 312, 380–2, 392, 393, 396
Thirlby, Styan, 392
Thomas Aquinas, Saint, 311
Thomas Lord Cromwell, 68, 87, 90
Thompson, Ann, 299
Thomson, Leslie, 245
Thomson, Peter, 193
Thorpe, Thomas, 78, 105, 108–9, 111, 118–19
Tilney, Edmund, 44
title pages, 5, 20, 60, 64, 67, 68, 69, 75, 76–80, 81–4, 85, 87–102, 105–22, 123, 126, 130–1, 134, 140, 143, 179, 180, 188, 190, 202, 233, 237–8, 240, 255, 257, 260, 264–6, 269, 274, 276, 278, 281, 287, 292, 304, 318, 378–9
Tomlin, E. W. F., 125
Tompkins, Jane P., 179
Tonson, Jacob, 249–50, 254–5, 257, 275, 276–7, 392
Tree, Beerbohm, 390
Troublesome raigne of Iohn King of England, [The], 69
Troublesome raigne of King Iohn, The second part of the, 69
True Chronicle Historie of King Leir and his three daughters, The, 105
True tragedie of Richard the third, The, 83
Tucker, Patrick, 223, 225
Turner, Robert Kean, 204
Twitter, 283
Two Wise Men and All the Rest Fooles, 370
Tyas, Robert
  'SHAKSPERE FOR THE PEOPLE', 278

Underhill, Cave, 237
Underhill, Samuel, 367
unediting, 10, 200, 208, 304, 310, 312
uneditors, 300, 305–8, 309, 310–11

university commonplace books, 151–2
University of Cambridge, 78, 125, 151
University of Edinburgh, 116
University of Oxford, 145, 151, 153, 157, 364
University of Padua, 164
University of Texas, 129
University of Toronto, 205, 384, 385

Vai, Steve, 199–200, 201, 204
Valla, Lorenzo, 23
Van Buchel, Aernout, 360, 361
Van der Gucht, Gerard, 255
variorum, 381, 382, 393, 400, 407–8, 411, *See also* New Variorum Shakespeare
Vaughan, Alden T., 287, 289, 298–9
Vaughan, Virginia Mason, 287, 289, 298–9
Vecellio, Cesare
  Degli habiti antichi e moderni, 261
Vergil, 15
  Aeneid, The, 298
Vickers, Brian, 21, 23–5
Victoria and Albert Museum, 129
'Visualizing Variation', 201, 396

Wager, William
  Enough is as Good as a Feast, 334
Walker, Robert, 274, 275, 278
Walley, Henry, 66–7, 68, 112–13
Walsh, Marcus, 393
Wapull, George
  Tide Tarrieth No Man, The, 334–5
Warburton, William, 312, 392–3
Ward and Lock ('Sixpenny Shakespeare'), 279
Ward, John, 167
Ware, James, 323
  Two Histories of Ireland, 321
Warner, Marina, 295
Warner, William
  Menaecmi, 83
Warren, Michael, 280, 281, 303
Warren, Roger, 34
Waterson, John, 143
Waterson, Simon, 77
Watson, Ben, 199, 201
Watson, Thomas
  Amintæ Gaudia, 79
  First sett, of Italian madrigalls Englished, The, 79
  Hekatompathia or Passionate centurie of loue, The, 79
Wayne, Valerie, 389
Webster, John, 20, 65, 98, 157
  Duchess of Malfi, The, 31, 137, 143
Weimann, Robert, 17
Weingust, Don, 324

Weis, René, 339–40
Wells, Stanley, 34, 52, 89, 95, 302, 308–9, 326, 330, 336, 339, 358, 385–6
Welsh voices, representation of, 346–8
Werner, Sarah, 217
Werstine, Paul, 32, 34–6, 37–8, 39, 46, 49, 50, 58, 88, 163, 203, 325, 409
White, Edward, 80, 81
White, William, 85
Whitehall, James, 153–6, 158
Wikipedia, 405, 411, 413
Wilkins, George, 61, 113
  Painfull Aduentures of Pericles Prince of Tyre, The, 113–15
Willet, Andrew
  Hexapla in Genesis, That Is, a Sixfold Commentary Vpon Genesis, 97
Williams, George Walton, 173
Wilson, F. P., 29, 30, 137
Wilson, Robert
  Three Ladies of London, The, 348, 365
  Three Lordes and Three Ladies of London, The, 370
Wilson, W. C., 259
Wine, Martin, 383
Winship, Michael, 129
Wise, Andrew, 85, 89, 100, 103
Witmore, Michael, 220
Woffington, Margaret, 186
Wolfe, Heather, 161, 196
Wolfe, John, 75
Wood, Anthony, 157, 158
Wood, S., 292
Wooster Group, The, 217
World Wide Web, 7, 196, 221, 224, 281–3, 285, 299, 387–8, 389, 396, 401, 404–8, 411,
  See also Internet
Worthen, W. B., 200
Woudhuysen, H. R., 77, 91
Wright, Abraham, 157–9, 160
Wright, James, 157–8
Wright, Kailin, 149
Wright, William Aldis, 394
Wriothesley, Henry, third earl of Southampton, 75, 79, 88, 290
Wyndham's Theatre, 234, 237

Yale University, 129
Yeandle, Laetitia, 172, 173
Yorkshire Tragedy, The, 68, 87, 109, 122, 123, 125, 133
Young, Alan, 271
Younger, Joseph, 240
YouTube, 217

Zappa, Frank, 199, 201, 209
Zentralbibliothek, 115
Ziegler, Georgianna, 285
Zittrain, Jonathan, 406
Zwicker, Steven, 180